THE FILM YEARBOOK

In-house editor
JANE CHARTERIS

Editor's assistant and
picture researcher
MARY VOLK

Cover by
KEN ANSELL AND DAVE DRAGON, THE DESIGN CLINIC

Design by
URSULA SHAW
WITH SUE WALLIKER, FRASER McDERMOTT AND CHRIS McCOWAN

THE FILM YEARBOOK 1987.

Library of Congress Catalog Number 83-644931

ISBN 0-312-289367

Printed in Great Britain by The Thetford Press, Thetford

Bound by D R Skinner & Company, Cambridge

Typeset by Keyline Graphics, London

ACKNOWLEDGEMENTS

Thanks, as ever, to the production companies, distributors, publicity firms, publications and film archives which supplied pictures or information, or both, and especially to the individuals within them who provided such unswerving assistance.

Anglo American, Artificial Eye, Blue Dolphin, Brent Walker, BFI Production Board, The British Film Institute, Dennis Davidson Associates, Electric Pictures, Embassy, Enterprise, Entertainment, Gala, ICA Projects, Mike Laye, Mainline, Media Releasing, MGM-UA, Miracle, The National Film Archive, New Realm Entertainments, The Other Cinema, PIC Publicity, PSA, Palace, Paramount, Premier Releasing, Rank, RCA Columbia, Recorded Releasing, Room With A View Productions, Screen International, Society of Film Distributors, Thorn EMI, Time Out, Tri-Star, 20th Century-Fox, UIP, UKFD, Universal, Variety, Virgin, Walt Disney, Warner Bros, Warner Home Video, Zakiya & Associates.

An appreciative nod to Rachel Marks, Linda Wood and Tina McFarling, who assembled much of the book's data; and to Chris McGowan, Fraser McDermott and Dill Anstey, the in-house design/picture research supporting cast. Thanks also to Geoff, Jim, Jackie and Pete at Keyline.

Particular thanks to Ursula Shaw and Sue Walliker, who gave a new lustre to a limiting format; and to Jane Charteris and Mary Volk, without whose resilience and tenacity a devoted but distracted editor would probably have packed it in. AC

THE FILM YEARBOOK 1987

EDITED BY AL CLARK

St Martin's Press
New York

EDITOR

AL CLARK is the author of *Raymond Chandler in Hollywood*, the editor of three volumes of *The Rock Yearbook*, and the editor of *The Film Yearbook* since its inception in 1982. He is Head of Production at Virgin Films, executive producer of *Secret Places, Absolute Beginners, Captive* and *Gothic*, and co-producer of *Nineteen Eighty-Four.*

CONTRIBUTORS

GEOFF ANDREW is a film critic for *Time Out.* He has also contributed to the *Radio Times*, and has written a book on *Hollywood Gangster Movies.* Before becoming a journalist he was manager and co-programmer of London's Electric Cinema.

SIMON BANNER is a freelance writer contributing articles to *The Times*, the *Guardian*, the *Sunday Times, Observer* and *Sunday Telegraph.*

TONY CRAWLEY is the author of *The Films of Sophia Loren, Bébé: The Films of Brigitte Bardot, Screen Dreams: The Hollywood Pin-Up* and *The Steven Spielberg Story.* He has written on films for publications throughout the world and now lives in France. He is foreign editor of *Starburst.*

DAVID EHRENSTEIN is a freelance writer, contributing to the *Los Angeles Herald Examiner, Village Voice, Rolling Stone, Cahiers du Cinema, Film Culture, Film Comment, Film Quarterly* and the anthologies *Jean-Luc Godard* and *The New American Cinema.* He is also the co-author, with Bill Reed, of *Rock on Film* and is currently editor of *Laserworks* magazine and *On Film.* His book *Film: The Front Line – 1984* was published in December 1984.

QUENTIN FALK is the author of *Travels in Greeneland: The Cinema of Graham Greene* and *Last of a Kind: The Sinking of Lew Grade.* A contributor to *Anatomy of the Movies* and *British Cinema Now*, he is a past joint editor of *Screen International* and assistant entertainments editor of the *Daily Mail.* He regularly writes reviews and articles for publications like *Punch, Radio Times*, the *Guardian, Today* and *Sight & Sound.*

HARLAN KENNEDY is the European correspondent for *Film Comment.* He is a member of the Critics' Circle and of FIPRESCI, the international federation of film critics. For four years he was the London contributing editor of *American Film*, and now writes regularly for *Film Review, The Face* and *Emmy* magazine.

TODD McCARTHY was co-editor of *Kings of the Bs.* He has contributed to many film publications including *Film Comment, American Film* and *Cahiers du Cinema.* He is also a critic and reporter on *Variety.*

MYRON MEISEL is a writer-producer based in Los Angeles. His credits include *Final Exam, A Savage Hunger, I'm a Stranger Here Myself: A Portrait of Nicholas Ray* and the forthcoming French production, *Machete!* A member of the National Society of Film Critics, his reviews appear in *Movies on TV.* He also works as a lawyer and marketing consultant.

BART MILLS writes about films and television from Hollywood for such publications as the *Guardian*, the *Los Angeles Times* and *American Film.*

NANCY MILLS writes about film and television for the *Los Angeles Times* and numerous other newspapers in America, Canada and England.

NEIL NORMAN is the film critic for *The Face*, and contributes to a variety of publications including the *Guardian, Photoplay* and the *Sunday Times.* He has written three plays, the second of which, 'The Misfits', was about Montgomery Clift. He is also the author of *Insignificance*, the book of the film.

JAMES PARK has covered the film beat for *Variety* for the past three years. The author of *Learning to Dream: The New British Cinema*, he is currently working on other book ideas.

CHRIS PEACHMENT is the film editor of *Time Out* and also writes for *The Times.* He was once a pilot.

DILYS POWELL was the film critic of the *Sunday Times* from 1939 to 1976, and has since written for the same newspaper about films on television. She is also the film critic of *Punch*, a frequent broadcaster and the author of several books about Greece.

TIM PULLEINE is deputy film critic of the *Guardian.* He is the author of *Heart Throbs* and contributes reviews and articles to various publications, including *Sight & Sound, Stills, Films and Filming* and *Monthly Film Bulletin.*

PAUL TAYLOR currently works for the British Film Institute as a programme advisor to regional cinemas. While continuing to write on movies and television for various publications, he is also chairman of the Leicester City Supporters Club, London Branch.

JOHN WALKER is the author of *The Once and Future Film: British Cinema in the 70s and 80s* and has worked as a critic and as a showbusiness editor for several national magazines and newspapers. He is also the author of the *Which? Software Guide* and of a forthcoming book on desktop publishing.

CONTENTS

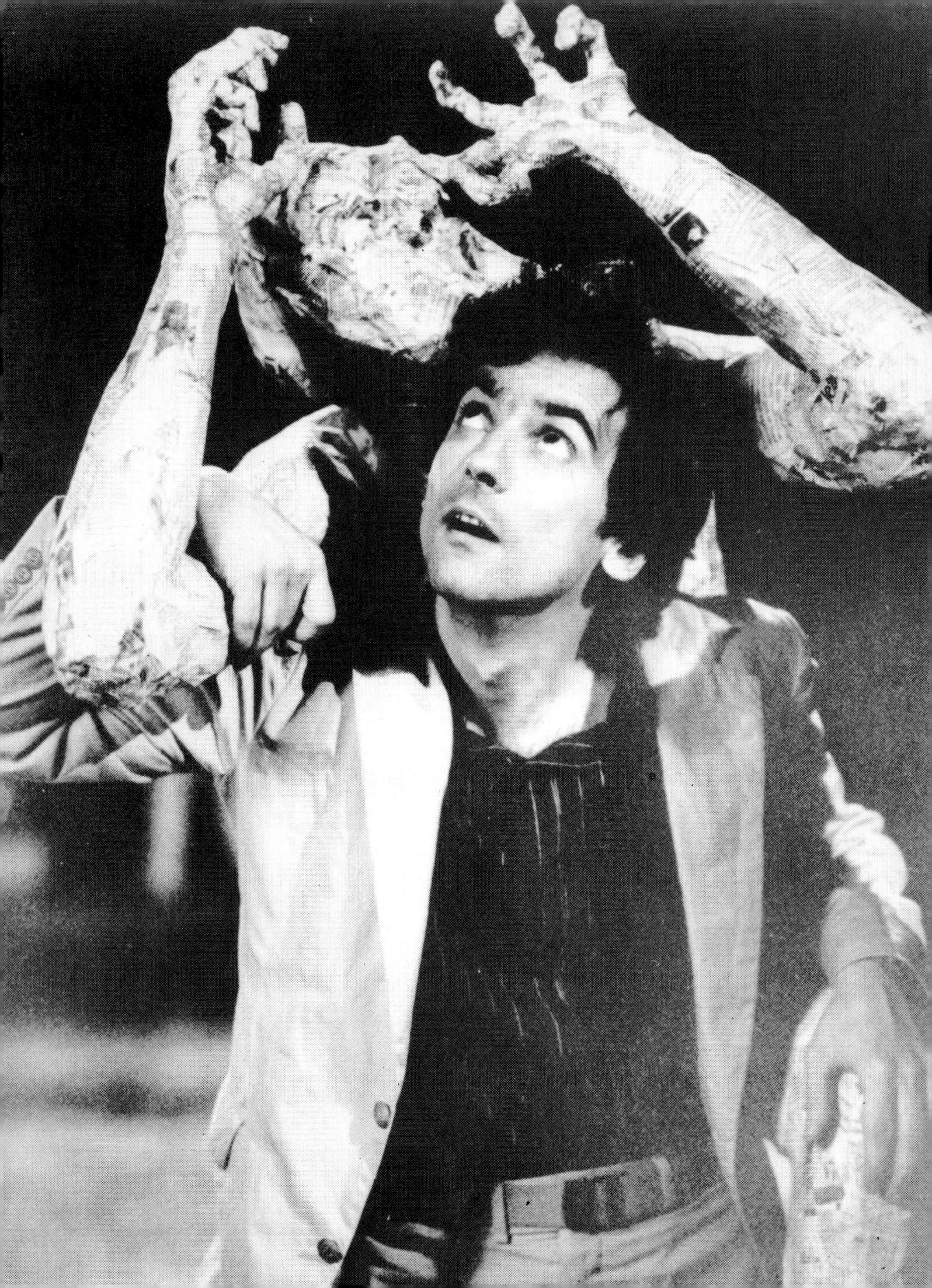

THE FILMS

Reviews by Tim Pulleine, Paul Taylor, Myron Meisel, Geoff Andrew, Anne Billson, John Walker and Al Clark.

1 JULY 1985–30 JUNE 1986

Like the book in general, this covers the year as indicated above. The first section includes all the feature films – excluding most documentaries, reissues and 16mm movies – released in both the US and UK during this time, plus those which opened only in the UK. Note is made if a film has appeared in the US prior to the books coverage period. A second section lists in further detail those films released only in the US between the dates in question. Wherever there is a descrepancy between British and American titles, the original is used, with the appropriate cross-reference. Foreign language films are listed under the title by which they are best known.

Abbreviations are as follows: *dir* director *pro* producer *exec pro* executive producer *scr* screenplay *ph* director of photography *ed* editor *pro des* production designer *art dir* director *mus* music.

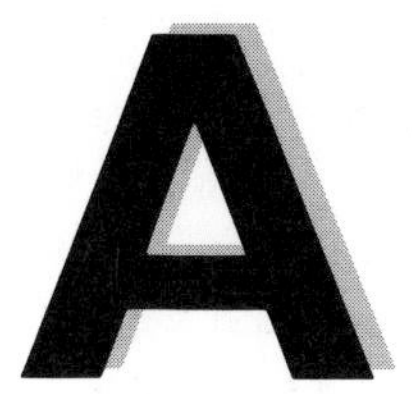

ABSOLUTE BEGINNERS
(Virgin-Goldcrest-Palace/Orion)
dir Julien Temple *pro* Stephen Wooley, Chris Brown *exec pro* Nik Powell, Al Clark, Robert Devereux *scr* Richard Burridge, Christopher Wicking, Don MacPherson, based on the novel by Colin MacInnes *ph* Oliver Stapleton, in Scope, System 35, colour *ed* Michael Bradsell, Gerry Hambling, Richard Bedford, Russell Lloyd *pro des* John Beard *mus* Gil Evans *r time* 108 mins *US opening* Apr 18 *UK opening* Apr 4.
cast Patsy Kensit, Eddie O'Connell, David Bowie, James Fox, Ray Davies, Mandy Rice-Davies, Eve Ferret, Tony Hippolyte, Graham Fletcher-Cook, Joe McKenna, Steven Berkoff, Sade, Tenpole Tudor, Bruce Payne, Alan Freeman, Anita Morris, Paul Rhys, Julian Firth, Chris Pitt.

A musical (in the proper Minnelli/Donen sense of the term) version of Colin MacInnes's contemporary novel of London life just prior to the dawn of the swinging sixties, 'Absolute Beginners' represents a triumph of ambition and instinctive skill over a residue of ideological axe-grinding about the denial of working-class culture and suchlike. What counts is the joie de vivre *of the realisation, thanks in no small way to the choreography of David Toguri and the brilliantly poised caricatures by David Bowie, James Fox and Lionel Blair, who easily compensate for the somewhat negative performances of*

the leads. Complaints that the music does not belong to the period seem about as far off the mark as suggesting that the score of 'Seven Brides for Seven Brothers' ought to have been in the idiom of the mid-nineteenth century. **TP**
(See Films of the Year.)

AFTER HOURS
(Double Play-Geffen Company/Warner)
dir Martin Scorsese *pro* Amy Robinson, Griffin Dunne, Robert F Colesberry *scr* Joseph Minion *ph* Michael Ballhaus, in DuArt Colour *ed* Thelma Schoonmaker *pro des* Jeffrey Townsend *mus* Howard Shore *r time* 97 mins *US opening* Sep 13 *UK opening* May 30.
cast Griffin Dunne, Rosanna Arquette, Verna Bloom, Thomas Chong, Cheech Marin, Linda Fiorentino, Teri Garr, John Heard, Catherine O'Hara, Dick Miller, Will Patton, Robert Plunket, Bronson Pinchot, Rocco Sisto, Larry Block, Victor Argo, Murray Moston, John P Codiglia, Clarence Felder.

There are directors who give pleasure by striving after the extraordinary, and there are those who give it simply by being in fluent and effortless command of their material. Scorsese, who has often been the former, becomes the latter with 'After Hours', his low(ish)-budget act of atonement for the expensive and commercially disastrous 'The King of Comedy', and it's a measure of his assurance that one views the whole thing not as a step down but as the work of a master showing off his box of tricks on a fizzy, knowing black comedy that glows and jokes and teases. Some wonderful cameos generally and a winning performance from Griffin Dunne as the computer operator trapped without money in a nightmarish, predatory downtown New York. **AC**
(See Films of the Year.)

AGNES OF GOD
(Columbia)
dir Norman Jewison *pro* Patrick Palmer, Norman Jewison *scr* John Pielmeier, based on his play *ph* Sven Mykvist, in Metrocolor *ed* Antony Gibbs *pro des* Ken Adam *mus* Georges Delerue *r time* 98 mins *US opening* Sep 13 *UK opening* Feb 21.
cast Anne Bancroft, Jane Fonda, Meg Tilly, Anne Pitoniak, Winston Rekert, Gratien Gelinas, Guy Hoffman, Gabriel Arcand, Françoise Faucher, Jacques Tourangeau, Janine Fluet, Deborah Grover, Michèle George, Samantha Langevin, Jacqueline Blais, Françoise Berd, Mimi D'Estee, Rita Tucket, Lillian Graham.

Chain-smoking shrink Fonda and Mother Superior Bancroft conduct a theatrical ding-dong debate over matters of the psyche and the soul after 'innocent' novice Tilly commits bloody infanticide in her convent cell. Jewison bats back and forth between cloisters and courtroom as the mysteries of spirituality and sanity get an all-too-schematic gloss, and settles for a problem-pic even-handedness over both the respective merits of Faith and Freud and the enigmatic place of miracles amid the mundane. For all its heavenward wailings and wide-eyed whisperings, a dullish sermon. **PT**

Opposite: After Hours Above: Agnes of God

AGONY
(Mosfilm/Thorn EMI Classics)
dir Elem Klimov *pro* Semion Kutikov *scr* Semion Lungin, Ilya Nusinov, from the author A Kalyagin *ph* Leonid Kalashnikov, in Sovcolor, black and white *ed* Valery Belovoi *art dir* Yu Liublin *mus* Alfred Schnitke *r time* 148 mins *UK opening* Nov 28.
cast Velta Linei, Alisa Freindlikh, Anatoly Romashin, Alexei Petrenko, A Romantsov, S Muchenikov, Y Katin-Yartsev, B Ivanov, A Pavlov, L Bronevoi, B Omarov, P Pankov, M Danilov, V Oseney, P Arzhanov, A Arkadev, V Raikov, B Romanov, A Trishkin, A Maikova, N Pshennaya.

A two-part account of the penultimate year of the Romanov Dynasty, focusing on the role of Rasputin and interspersed with historical newsreel material from the years 1904-1917. Completed in the mid-seventies but not premiered until the Moscow Film Festival in 1981. Unseen by the FYB team.

A.K.
(Greenwich Films-Herald Nippon-Herald Ace/Orion Classics/Virgin)
dir-scr-ed Chris Marker *pro* Serge Silberman *ph* Frans-Yves Marescot, in colour *mus* Toru Takemitsu *r time* 75 mins *US opening* Jan 29 *UK opening* Mar 21.

Marker's chapter-headed study of Kurosawa and associates at work on the Mount Fuji locations of 'Ran' has an attractive simplicity about it which matches that of its main subject, who treats the complicated business of shooting big-scale setpieces with patrician ease. The tone of the voice-over, however, has a reverential quality which often borders on the risible and sometimes lapses into full-scale mystical absurdity. **AC**

ALAMO BAY
(Tri-Star/Columbia)
dir Louis Malle *pro* Louis Malle, Vincent Mall *exec pro* Ross E Milloy *scr* Alice Arlen *ph* Curtis Clark, in Metrocolor *ed* James Bruce *pro des* Trevor Williams *mus* Ry Cooder *r time* 99 mins *US opening* prior to Jul 1985 *UK opening* Jan 31.
cast Amy Madigan, Ed Harris, Ho Nguyen, Donald Moffat, Truyen V Tran, Rudy Young, Cynthia Carle, Martino Lasalle, William Frankfather, Lucky Mosley, Bill Thurman, Michael Ballard, Gary Basaraba, Jerry Biggs, Mark Hanks, Khoa Van Le, Tony Frank, Caroline William, Max Evers, Buddy Killen, Doris Hargrave, Harvey Lewis, Ed Opstad, Christopher Blum, Xuan Thi Le, Lan Ti Do, Le Nguyen, Tuan Tran.

Given the wit and vitality of Malle's response to the American scene in 'Atlantic City', this heavygoing social tract is all the more of a disappointment. The subject is the racialist xenophobia with which Vietnamese refugees were apparently treated by the fishing communities on the Gulf coast of Texas, but the screenplay's response to it is one of cardboard melodrama. Some persuasive playing, notably by Ed Harris, and occasional shafts of documentary observation are overcome by a dispiriting combination of hysteria and downright dullness. **TP**

ALWAYS: See US section

Agony

American Ninja

Alamo Bay

AMERICAN ANTHEM: See US section

AMERICAN FLYERS: See US section

AMERICAN NINJA
[UK TITLE: AMERICAN WARRIOR]
(Cannon)
dir Sam Firstenberg *pro* Menahem Golan, Yoram Globus *scr* Paul De Mielche, based on a story by Avi Kleinberger, Gideon Amir *ph* Hanania Baer, in TVC colour *ed* Andrew Horvitch, Marcus Manton, Marcel Mindlin, Peter Lee-Thompson, Dan Wetherbee *pro des* Adrian H Gorton *mus* Michael Linn *r time* 95 mins *US opening* Aug 30 *UK opening* Oct 11.
cast Michael Dudikoff, Steve James, Judie Aronson, Guich Koock, John Fujioka, Don Stewart, John LaMotta, Tadashi Yamashita, Phil Brock, Tony Carreon, Roi Vinzov, Jerry Bailey, Willie Williams, Christopher Hoss, Joey Galvez, Nick Nicholson, Eric Hahn, Jacob Mendoza, Avi Charupe, Esher Zewko.

Dudikoff is a top-grade Ninja, zapping nasty foreign types and struggling with his own inexplicable amnesia in the Philippines. Such story as there is is not worth recounting. An endless series of ineptly choreographed martial arts battles, and clichéd, laconic lines of supposedly heroic dialogue, this flaccid fiasco's sole point of interest is Stewart's swarthy European gun-runner, played with an accent so atrociously thick that even the simplest sentences become totally incomprehensible. **GA**

ANGRY HARVEST See BITTER ERNTE

ANNE DEVLIN
(Aeon Films/Cinema of Women)
dir-scr Pat Murphy *pro* Pat Murphy, Tom Hayes *exec pro* Tom Hayes *ph* Thaddeus O'Sullivan, in Eastman Colour *ed* Arthur Keating *pro des* John Lucas *mus* Robert Boyle *r time* 121 mins *UK opening* Mar 14.
cast Brid Brennan, Bosco Hogan, Des McAleer, Gillian Hackett, David Kelly, Ian McElhinny, Chris O'Neill, Pat Leavy, Marie Conmee, John Cowley, Bernie Downes, Niall O'Brien, Eamonn Hunt, Martin Dempsey, Noel O'Donovan, Vinnie Murphy, Liam Halligan, Isobel Stephenson, Gabrielle Hyland.

The subject of Pat Murphy's second film (the first was 'Maeve') is an unsung Irish heroine of the early nineteenth century, who was involved in Robert Emmet's abortive attempt to overthrow British rule in 1803. The deliberately slow pace is sometimes taxing, but for much of the time the film imposes itself commandingly. The understated manner achieves a dialectical view of the past, and the ultimate effect is a dramatisation of the processes rather than the simple events of history in a fashion that sometimes brings Rossellini to mind. **TP**

THE ANNIHILATORS: See US section

APRIL FOOL'S DAY: See US section

THE ASSAM GARDEN
(Moving Picture Co/Contemporary)
dir Mary McMurray *pro* Nigel Stafford-Clark *scr* Elisabeth Bond *ph* Bryan Loftus, in colour *ed* Rodney Holland *art dir* Jane Martin *mus* Richard Harvey *r time* 90 mins *UK opening* Jul 5.
cast Deborah Kerr, Madhur Jaffrey, Alec McCowen, Zia Mohyeddin, Anton Lesser, Iain Cuthbertson, Tara Shaw, Dev Sagoo, Paul Brown, Simon Hedger, Maiser Aschan, Paula Jacobs.

A deceptively simple account of the relationship that develops between two ageing women, an English ex-colonial widow and her Indian immigrant neighbour who hankers to return home, as they tend the former's Gloucestershire garden. Mary McMurray's film is not only beautifully shot and played but achieves a sympathetic insight into character of a kind all too rare in the modern cinema. Despite its enclosed setting, it has a visual expansiveness and modulation which remove it entirely from the preserves of a TV play, and altogether represents as promising a directorial debut as the British cinema has seen for some time. **TP**

THE ASSISI UNDERGROUND: See US section

AT CLOSE RANGE: See US section

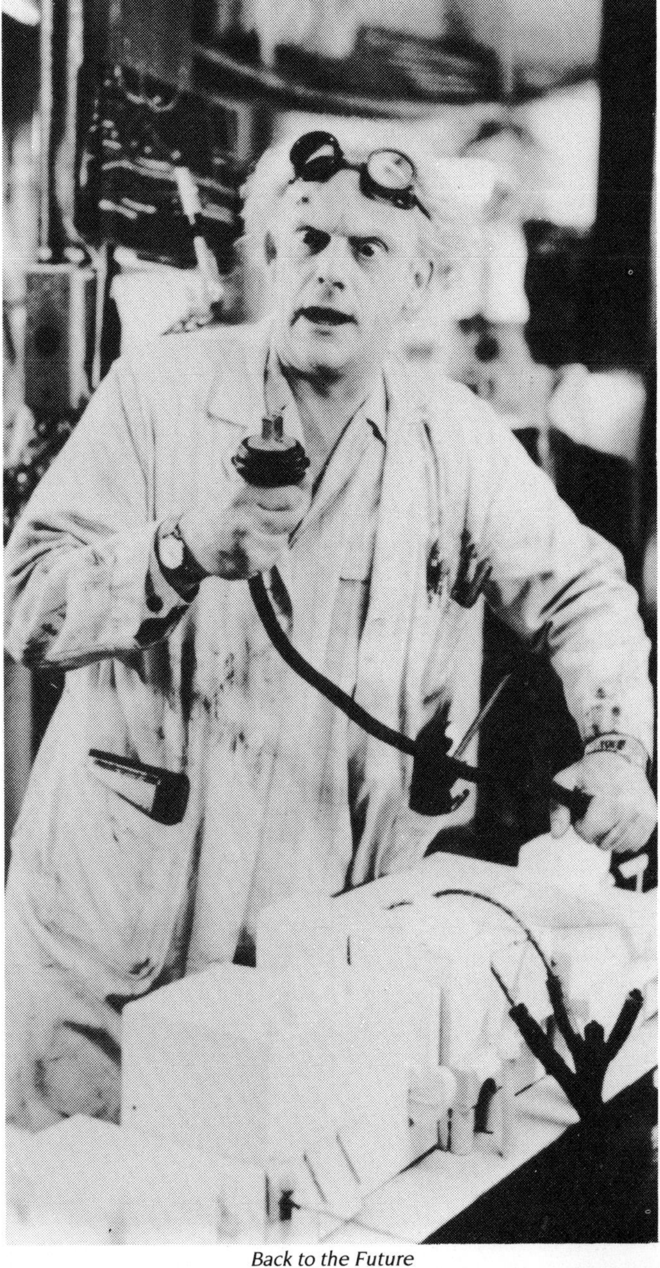
Back to the Future

B

BACK TO SCHOOL: See US section

BACK TO THE FUTURE
(Amblin/Universal)
pro Robert Zemeckis *pro* Bob Gale, Neil Canton *exec pro* Steven Spielberg, Frank Marshall, Kathleen Kennedy *scr* Robert Zemeckis, Bob Gale *ph* Dean Cundey, in Technicolor *ed* Arthur Schmidt, Harry Keramideas *pro des* Lawrence G Paull *mus* Alan Silvestri *r time* 116 mins *US opening* Jul 3
UK opening Dec 4.
cast Michael J Fox, Christopher Lloyd, Lea Thompson, Crispin Glover, Thomas F Wilson, Claudia Wells, Marc McClure, Wendie Jo Sperber, George DiCenzo, James Tolkan, Jeffrey Jay Cohen, Casey Siemaszko, Billy Zane, Harry Waters Jr, Donald Fullilove, Lisa Freeman, Cristen Kauffman.

Deservedly a great popular success, this Spielberg-backed comic fantasy, about a teenage boy unwittingly propelled backwards in time to 1955 and alarmed to find himself becoming amorously entangled with his own mother-to-be, strikes an exact balance between spectacle (impressive) and human interest (affectingly funny). Mixing an intoxicating cocktail of sci-fi, teen romance and small-town nostalgia, the film provides a heartening reminder that Hollywood expertise is still capable of carrying all before it. **TP**
(See Films of the Year and Michael J Fox, Faces of the Year.)

The Assam Garden

Best Defence

Beyond the Walls

BAD MEDICINE: See US section

BAND OF THE HAND: See US section

BEST DEFENCE

(Paramount)
dir Willard Huyck *pro* Gloria Katz *scr* Gloria Katz, Willard Huyck, based on the novel 'Easy and Hard Ways Out' by Robert Grossbach *ph* Don Peterman, in Movielab colour *ed* Sidney Wolinsky, Michael A Stevenson *pro des* Peter Jamison *mus* Patrick Williams *r time* 94 mins *US opening* prior to Jul 1985 *UK opening* Jan 3.
cast Dudley Moore, Eddie Murphy, Kate Capshaw, George Dzundza, Helen Shaver, Mark Arnott, Peter Michael Goetz, Tom Noonan, David Rasche, Paul Comi, Darryl Henriques, Joel Polis, John A Zee, Matthew Laurance, Christopher Mahar, Lorry Goldman, Stoney Richards, Tyler Tyhurst.

Arriving in Britain after a lengthy sojourn on the shelf, 'Best Defence' provides ample justification for its distributors' lack of faith. The direly witless proceedings are notable only for a construction so peculiar as to be positively perverse, with twin strands of action (Murphy testing a tank in Kuwait, Moore designing it in California two years previously) which bafflingly fail to achieve any convergence. Ingratiating displays of 'personality' by the stars may be understandable in the circumstances but only compound the overall embarrassment. **TP**

BEER: See US section

BELIZAIRE THE CAJUN: See US section

THE BEST OF TIMES: See US section

BETTER OFF DEAD: See US section

BEYOND THE WALLS

(April Films/Warner)
dir Uri Barbash *pro* Rudy Cohen *scr* Benny Barbash, Eran Preis *ph* Amnon Salomon, in colour *ed* Tova Asher *art dir* Eitan Levy *mus* Ilan Virtzberg *r time* 103 mins *UK opening* Oct 3.
cast Arnon Zadok, Muhamad Bakri, Hilel Ne'eman, Assi Dayan, Boaz Sharaabi, Roberto Polak, Adib Jahashan, Louteteof Noussir, Jacob Ayali, Issa Mugrabi, Salach Houssain, Iris Kanner, David Kedem, Micha Sharfstein, Dana Katz, Dina Ladani, Shura Greenhoise, Omri Marian, Dan Raviv.

Israeli prison melodrama which seeks, courageously enough, to examine such questions as Israeli-Arab relations and the ethics of terrorism and reprisal within the violent microcosm of a top-security jail. Despite the seemingly authentic setting, however, the stock characterisations and rambling structure mean that the relationship between the prison environment and the wider political realm is never satisfactorily established. The final effect is unfortunately more of vague good intentions than of realised analytical ones. **TP**

BIG TROUBLE: See US section

BIGGLES

(Compact Yellowbill/UIP)
dir John Hough *pro* Kent Walwin, Pom Oliver *exec pro* Adrian Scrope, Paul Barnes-Taylor *scr* John Grove, Kent Walwin, based on characters created by W E Johns *ph* Ernest Vincze, in Technicolor *ed* Richard Trevor *pro des* Terry Pritchard *mus* Stanislas *r time* 92 mins *UK opening* May 22.
cast Neil Dickson, Alex Hyde-White, Peter Cushing, Fiona Hutchison, Marcus Gilbert, William Hootkins, Alan Polonsky, Francesca Gonshaw, Michael Siberty, James Saxon, Daniel Flynn, Ron Boyd, Terry Mountain, Fanny Carby, Alibe Parsons, Patricia Ford, Pam St Clement, Christopher Robbie, Jonathan Steward, Frank Singuinean.

'Biggles' funks out as a movie by not having the courage of its stiff-upper-lipped convictions. Sopwith Camels are not enough, it would seem, for today's sophisticated audiences, so an absurd

Biggles

Billy the Kid and the Green Baize Vampire

The Black Cauldron

Black Moon Rising

time travel plot has been incorporated, and Captain W E Johns's hero is whisked between the trenches and present day tourist London in the company of an American fast-food entrepreneur. Dogfights set to disco music don't help either. **AB**

BILLY THE KID AND THE GREEN BAIZE VAMPIRE
(Zenith/ITC)
dir Alan Clarke *pro* Simon Mallin *scr* Trevor Preston *ph* Clive Tickner, in colour *ed* Stephen Singleton *pro des* Jamie Leonard *mus* George Fenton *r time* 93 mins *UK opening* May 9.
cast Phil Daniels, Alun Armstrong, Bruce Payne, Eve Ferret, Richard Ridings, Don Henderson, Neil McCaul, Zoot Money, David Foxxe, Johnny Denis, Trevor Laird, Daniel Webb, Louise Gold.

Considerably more weird, but unfortunately no more appealing, than last year's 'Number One', this would-be surrealist musical about the snooker circuit pits young Cockney twerp against lugubrious Yorkshire veteran (the latter inexplicably rigged out in Dracula guise), while the wretched audience is dragged through a succession of 'stylised' (ie virtually non-existent) sets and raucous, tuneless songs, each one more miserable than the last. Alun Armstrong's 'vampire' has his moments, but the movie is unredeemable. **TP**

BITTER ERNTE: See US section

THE BLACK CAULDRON
(Silver Screen Partners II/Buena Vista/ Disney)
dir Ted Berman, Richard Rich *pro* Joe Hale *exec pro* Ron Miller *scr* David Jonas, Vance Gerry, Ted Berman, Richard Rich, Al Wilson, Roy Morita, Peter Young, Art Stevens, Joe Hale, based on the series 'The Chronicles of Prydain' by Lloyd Alexander *anim ph* Jim Pickel, Ed Austin, John Aardal, Errol Aubry, Frank Tompkins, Brandy Whittington, James Catania, PaulWainess, Kieran Mulgrew, Roy Harris, Jere Kepenek, Niel Viker, Steve Hale, Brian Holechek, Rick Taylor, Dan Bunn, in Technicolor *mus* Elmer Bernstein *r time* 80 mins *US opening* Jul 26 *UK opening* Oct 11.
narrator John Huston *voices* Grant Bardsley, Susan Sheridan, John Hurt, Freddie Jones, Nigel Hawthorne, Arthur Maler, John Byner.

After years of promising that this was an animated movie to rival the best of the past, Disney produces a damp squib, spoiling one of the best of recent children's books in the process. Its central character, a magical pig, lacks any personality and deserves to be eaten by the Big Bad Wolf. Its animation, too, is inferior in quality to modern rivals such as Don Bluth's 'The Secret of Nimh'. Back to the drawing board. **JW**

BLACK MOON RISING
(New World Pictures/Thorn EMI)
dir Harley Cokliss *pro* Joel B Michaels, Douglas Curtis *scr* John Carpenter, Desmond Nakano, William Gray, based on a story by John Carpenter *ph* Mischa Suslov, in CFI colour *ed* Todd Ramsay *pro des* Bryan Ryman *mus* Lalo Schifrin *r time* 99 mins *US opening* Jan 10 *UK opening* Jun 13.
cast Tommy Lee Jones, Linda Hamilton, Robert Vaughn, Richard Jaeckel, Lee Ving, Bubba Smith, Dan Shor, William Sanderson, Keenan Wynn, Nick Cassavetes, Richard Angarola, Don Opper, William Marquez, David Pressman, Stanley De Santiis, Edward Parone, Al White, Bill Moody.

Wisely sitting in the pits while his latest supercar gets a full-blast test drive from Harley Cokliss, John Carpenter must have known he'd here blueprinted a mere gimmick rather than a true motorised glory like 'Christine'. The jet-propelled Black Moon itself remains sidelined for much of the time, awaiting its final spectacular stunt leap (between the top floors of two tower blocks), while federal freelance Jones shrugs off two sets of violent corporate criminals. Hardly a high-octane gripper, but a neat formulaic giggle. **PT**

BLUE CITY: See US section

BLUE MOUNTAINS
(Gruziafilm/The Other Cinema)
dir Eldar Shengelaya *scr* Revaz Cheyshvili, Eldar Shengelaya *ph* Levan Paatashvili, in Sovcolor *pro des* Boris Tskhakaya *mus* Giya Kancheli *r time* 97 mins *UK opening* Jun 27.
cast Ramaz Giorgobiani, Vasili Kakhnishvili, Teymuraz Chirgadze, Ivan Sakvarelidze, Daredzhan Sumbatashvili.

A delightfully funny Georgian comedy, following a year in the life of a rambling, inefficient publishing house, where everybody is too obsessed with their own problems to get anything done. Far more than a mere satire on the pitfalls of bureaucracy, it's a perfectly underplayed farce endowed with a sharp but generous eye for the petty absurdities of human behaviour. Beautifully detailed observation and a gradual, inexorable escalation into surreal fantasy bring to mind both Keaton and Buñuel, but with its strangely successful repetition of gags and formal devices, it's finally a film of engaging originality. Surely the most purely enjoyable film to emerge from Russia in decades. **GA**

Blue Mountains

BODY DOUBLE
(Columbia)
dir-pro Brian De Palma *exec pro* Howard Gottfried *scr* Robert J Avrech, Brian De Palma *ph* Stephen H Burum, in Metrocolor *ed* Jerry Greenberg, Bill Pankow *pro des* Ida Random *mus* Pino Donaggio *r time* 109 mins *US opening* prior to Jul 1985 *UK opening* Sep 20.
cast Craig Wasson, Gregg Henry, Melanie Griffith, Deborah Shelton, Guy Boyd, Dennis Franz, David Haskell.

Body Double

Brian De Palma's ransacking of Hitchcockian motifs gets more meaningless each time out. Vileness and voyeurism stamp this indelibly as a personal work, but the themes are shallow and the style superficial. Melanie Griffith's phlegmatic porn star makes for bright scenes, but even these are undermined by Craig Wasson's charmlessness as the hapless actor-protagonist. **MM**

THE BOY IN BLUE: See US section

THE BOYS NEXT DOOR
(New World-Republic/Cannon-Gala) *dir* Penelope Spheeris *pro* Keith Rubinstein, Sandy Howard *exec pro* Mel Pearl, Don Levin *scr* Glenn Morgan, James Wong *ph* Arthur Albert, in CFI Colour *ed* Andy Horvitch *art dir* Jo-Ann Chorney *mus* George S Clinton and others *r time* 91 mins *US opening* Nov 1 *UK opening* Nov 22.
cast Maxwell Caulfield, Charlie Sheen, Patti D'Arbanville, Christopher McDonald, Hank Garrett, Paul C Dancer, Richard Pachorek, Lesa Lee, Kenneth Cortland, Moon Zappa, Dawn Schneider, Kurt Christian, Don Draper, Blackie Dammett, Phil Rubenstein, James Carrington, Grant Heslov.

Two low-caste high school graduates, with only dead-end jobs ahead of them, take off for a weekend in Los Angeles and casually embark on an orgy of violence and murder. Under a guise of refusing liberal soft options, this crudely made piece of exploitation puts the spectator into the driving seat (literally so in a sequence in which a woman finds herself clinging for dear life on the bonnet of the killers' car) for its parade of mayhem, and in so doing seems liable to stir a defence of censorship in even the most dedicatedly liberal breast. **TP**

BRAZIL: See US section

BREWSTER'S MILLIONS
(Universal)
dir Walter Hill *pro* Lawrence Gordon *exec pro* Gene Levy *scr* Herschel Weingrod, Timothy Harris, based on the novel by George Barr McCutcheon *ph* Ric Waite, in Technicolor *ed* Freeman Davis, Michel Ripps *pro des* John Vallone *mus* Ry Cooder *r time* 92 mins *US opening* prior to Jul 1985 *UK opening* Aug 16.
cast Richard Pryor, John Candy, Lonette McKee, Stephen Collins, Jerry Orbach, Pat Hingle, Tovah Feldshuh, Joe Grifasi, Peter Jason, David White, Jerome Dempsey, Ji-Tu Cumbuka, Yakov Smirnoff, Hume Cronyn.

The classic farce has oft been remade, most memorably by Allan Dwan in 1945. This attempted modernisation lacks invention or wit, misfiring badly in its otherwise laudable attempt by star Richard Pryor and director Walter Hill to instil a certain wistful romance and deeper feelings in the clanging mechanism of having to squander a fortune to inherit a bigger one. Pryor once again fails to sustain a comic lead in a narrative context. As for Hill, though one can detect his operating intelligence derailing, this is his sole impersonal work to date. **MM**

THE BRIDE
(Columbia)
dir Franc Roddam *pro* Victor Drai *exec pro* Keith Addis *scr* Lloyd Fonvielle *ph* Stephen H Burum, in colour *ed* Michael Ellis *pro des* Michael Seymour *mus* Maurice Jarre *r time* 119 mins *US opening* Aug 16 *UK opening* Nov 1.
cast Sting, Jennifer Beals, Anthony Higgins, Clancy Brown, David Rappaport, Geraldine Page, Alexei Sayle, Phil Daniels, Veruschka, Quentin Crisp, Carey Elwes, Tim Spall, Ken Campbell, Guy Rolfe, Andrew De La Tour, Tony Haygarth, Matthew Guinness, Tony Brutus, Gary Shail, Carl Chase.

After the promising 'Quadrophenia', in the eighties Franc Roddam has become that most frustrating of figures: a good director in search of a decent script. 'The Bride' certainly doesn't provide it. A very distant relation to James Whale's distinctive original, it might've been more effective had it built on the exuberant gothic camp of its opening sequence. Instead, it aspires towards 'significance' when it isn't suffocating the viewer with sentimentality. It's the kind of film that needs to be a fireworks display if it's to work at all. The fact that it so rarely is characterises the whole misjudged affair. **AC** *(See Turkeys of the Year.)*

BRING ON THE NIGHT
(A&M Films/Goldwyn/Miracle)
dir Michael Apted *pro* David Mansion *exec pro* Gil Friesen, Andrew Meyer *ph* Ralph D Bode, in Metrocolor *ed* Robert K Lambert, Melvin Shapiro *art dir* Juan Carlos Conti *mus* Sting *r time* 97 mins *US opening* Nov 8 *UK opening* Jun 27.
cast Sting, Omar Hakim, Darryl Jones, Kenny Kirkland, Bradford Marsalis, Dolette McDonald, Janice Pendarvis, Trudie Styler, Miles Copeland, Kim Turner, Max Vadukul, Lou Salvatore, Jake Summer.

Michael Apted's portrait of Sting rehearsing a new group with jazz overtones for a try-out concert in Paris maintains a remarkable visual flow for film-making on the run. The individual musicians emerge as independent spirits, while Sting obviously relishes the parallel between the birth of his band and of his baby. Like the best so-called documentaries, this is really an incisively crafted film devised out of found materials but more real than any script could have been. **MM**

The Boys Next Door

The Bride

Brewster's Millions

CAME A HOT FRIDAY
(Shaker Run Productions/Orion Classics/ Miracle)
dir Ian Mune *pro* Larry Parr *scr* Dean Parker, Ian Mune, based on the novel by Ronald Hugh Morrieson *ph* Alun Bollinger, in colour *ed* Ken Zemke *pro des* Michael Seymour *mus* Stephen McCurdy *r time* 101 mins *US opening* Oct 4 *UK opening* Dec 13.
cast Peter Bland, Phillip Gordon, Billy T James, Michael Lawrence, Marshall Napier, Don Selwyn, Marise Wipani, Erna Larsen, Phillip Holder, Tricia Phillips, Bruce Allpress, Michael Morrissey, Roy Billing, Hemi Rapata, Bridgett Armstrong, Stephen Tozer, Ian Watkin, Norm Keesing.

This New Zealand comedy is a broad but mainly engaging variation on the old theme of city slickers running up against hick-town guile and greed. Directing his first feature, Ian Mune shows both pictorial skill and an instinct for building sequences up to, and not beyond, the point of maximum return. Things get a bit over-frantic in the latter part of the picture, but amends are made with a particularly deft and inventive finale. Local in the best sense, this is a modest movie but a distinctly likeable one, with a keen eye for period detail (the setting is 1949) as well as for human failing. **TP**

CAMILA
(GEA Cinematografica-Impala/ Enterprise/European Classics)
dir Maria Luisa Bemberg *pro* Angel Baldo, Hector Gallardo, Edecio Imbert *exec pro* Lita Stantic *scr* Maria Luisa Bemberg, Beda Docampo Feijoo, Juan Bautista Stagnaro *ph* Fernando Arribas, in colour *ed* Luis Cesar D'Angiolillo *art dir* Miguel Rodriguez *mus* Luis Maria Serra *r time* 97 mins *US opening* Mar 15 *UK opening* Sep 27.
cast Susu Pecoraro, Imanol Arias, Hector Alterio, Elena Tasisto, Carlos Munoz, Hector Pellegrini, Claudio Gallardou, Boris Rubaja, Mona Maris, Lelio Incrocci.

A costume melodrama, deriving from real events in mid-nineteenth century Argentina, this is a slow-moving but richly atmospheric movie. The story of an upper-class girl's infatuation with a priest, which ultimately places them both before a firing squad, communicates not just a romantic fatalism but a powerful critique of political repression. Hector Alterio's playing of the heroine's unyieldingly bigoted father is exceptional. **TP**

CAR TROUBLE
(Double Helix Films/Thorn EMI)
dir David Green *pro* Howard Malin, Gregory De Santis *exec pro* Howard Goldfarb, Laurence Myers *scr* James Whaley, A J Tipping *ph* Mike Garfath, in colour *ed* Barry Reynolds *pro des* Hugo Luczycwyhowski *r time* 93 mins *UK opening* Feb 28.
cast Julie Walters, Ian Charleson, Vincenzo Ricotta, Stratford Johns, Hazel O'Connor, Dave Hill, Anthony O'Donnell, Vanessa Knox-Mayer, Roger Hume, Veronica Clifford, Laurence Harrington, John Blundell, Jeff Hall, Roy Barraclough, Sheila Bernette, Sally Hughes, Haydn Gwynne, Charles Cork.

Appalling 'comedy' featuring the increasingly strident Julie Walters and Ian Charleson as a couple of suburban stereotypes who bicker over his new E-Type Jaguar. She borrows it for a spot of extra-marital nooky with a salesman, and an unfortunate vaginal spasm results in them being locked in the front seat in flagrante. *The plot might have passed muster as the basis for an excruciatingly embarrassing short film, but here it is padded out to feature length with lamentable jokes about women drivers and sexual frustration.* **AB**
(See Turkeys of the Year.)

Caravaggio

Came a Hot Friday

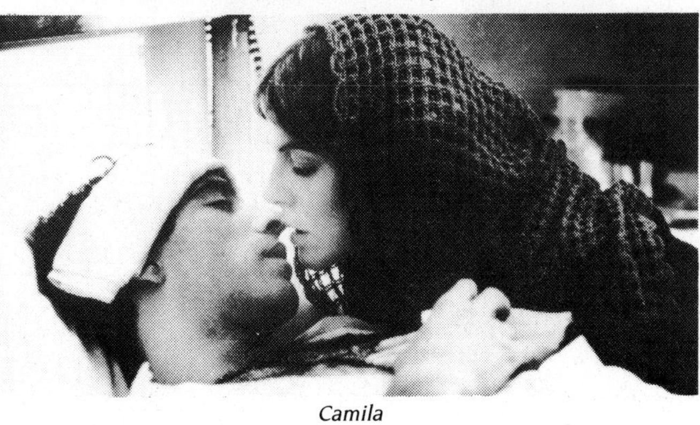

Camila

CARAVAGGIO
(BFI-Channel 4/BFI)
dir Derek Jarman *pro* Sarah Radclyffe *exec pro* Colin McCabe *ph* Gabriel Beristain, in colour *ed* George Akers *pro des* Christopher Hobbs *mus* Simon Fisher Turner *r time* 93 mins *UK opening* Apr 24.
cast Nigel Terry, Sean Bean, Garry Cooper, Dexter Fletcher, Spencer Leigh, Tilda Swinton, Nigel Davenport, Robbie Coltrane, Michael Gough, Noam Almaz, Dawn Archibald, Jack Birkett, Una Brandon-Jones, Imogen Claire, Sadie Corre, Lol Coxhill, Vernon Dobtcheff.

Derek Jarman, enfant terrible *of the British Film Industry, turns his hand to the* enfant terrible *of Italian late-Renaissance painting. The scandalous aspects of Caravaggio's career – his homosexuality, use of low-life characters as models for religious figures, and the fatal knifing of a youth which sent him into exile – are woven into an impressionistic series of flashbacks,* tableaux vivants *and scenes lit in a* chiaroscuro *manner. The effect is both low-key and hypnotic, and the exquisite look of the film belies its low budget. Despite Jarman's deliberate and playful use of anachronisms – typewriters, electronic calculators and motor-bikes – the painter's life is evoked with an authenticity which far exceeds that of the most elaborate and expensive biopic.* **AB**

THE CARE BEARS MOVIE
(Nelvana/Samuel Goldwyn/Miracle) *dir* Arna Selznick *pro* Michael Hirsch, Patrick Loubert, Clive Smith *exec pro* Carole MacGillvray, Robert Unkel, Jack Chojnacki, Lou Gioia *scr* Peter Sauder *mus* John Sebastian *r time* 75 mins *US opening* prior to Jul 1985 *UK opening* Jul 26.
voices Mickey Rooney, Georgia Engel, Harry Dean Stanton.

Composed of the sort of candy-floss visuals you fear will rot your teeth as you watch, and blessed with sentiments to match, this spins off the tender-hearted, cloud-borne cuddlies already notorious from greetings cards, toy counters and TV, and sets them once again to teaching evilly-tempted earthlings to emote correctly. The animation is predictably tacky (the eight technicians credited for 'quality control' were clearly somewhere else at the time), but marketing is all with this sort of product. **PT**

THE CARE BEARS II: THE NEW GENERATION: See US section

CAREFUL, HE MIGHT HEAR YOU
(Syme International – NSW Film Corp/ TLC Films/Cannon-Gala)
dir Carl Schultz *pro* Jill Robb *scr* Michael Jenkins, based on the novel by Summer Locke Elliott *ph* John Seale, in Panavision, Eastman Color *ed* Richard Francis Bruce *pro des* John Stoddart *mus* Ray Cook *r time* 116 mins *US opening* prior to Jul 1985 *UK opening* Jul 12.
cast Wendy Hughes, Robyn Nevin, Nicholas Gledhill, John Hargreaves, Geraldine Turner, Isabelle Anderson, Peter Whitford, Colleen Clifford.

The Care Bears Movie

A Chorus Line

Careful, He Might Hear You

Despite the Australian Academy Awards, this overwrought and underdramatised soap opera feints at Sirk territory and comes up with Tradition of Quality melodrama instead. A boy in care of a poor but loving aunt and uncle is stolen by a wealthy aunt from the city, in whose custody he suffers and rebels. All technique in the film is so crashingly obvious that no one can miss the clumsy stabs at artistry. One of the worst scores of recent memory. **MM**

CAT'S EYE
(MGM-US/Thorn EMI)
dir Lewis Teague *pro* Martha J Schumacher *scr* Stephen King *ph* Jack Cardiff, in JDC Widescreen, Technicolor *ed* Scott Conrad *pro des* Giorgio Postiglione *mus* Alan Silvestri *r time* 93 mins *US opening* prior to Jul 1985 *UK opening* Nov 8.
cast Drew Barrymore, James Woods, Alan King, Kenneth McMillan, Robert Hays, Candy Clark, James Naughton, Tony Munafo, Mary D'Arcy.

Three Stephen King short stories, linked omnibus-style by the eponymous animal and representing yet another attempt (after 'Creepshow', 'Cujo' and 'Firestarter') to make King source material a success at the box office. This one wasn't. **AC**

CATHOLIC BOYS: See HEAVEN HELP US

CEASE FIRE: See US section

THE CHECK IS IN THE MAIL: See US section

A CHORUS LINE
(Embassy-Polygram/Columbia/Rank)
dir Richard Attenborough *pro* Cy Feuer, Ernest H Martin *exec pro* Gordon Stulberg *scr* Arnold Schulman, based on the play by James Kirkwood, Nicholas Dante *ph* Ronnie Taylor, in Technicolor *ed* John Bloom *pro des* Patrizia von Brandenstein *mus* Marvin Hamlisch *r time* 118 mins *US opening* Dec 13 *UK opening* Jan 10.
cast Michael Douglas, Alyson Reed, Terrence Mann, Michael Blevins, Yamil Borges, Jan Gan Boyd, Gregg Burge, Cameron English, Tony Fields, Nicole Fosse, Vicki Frederick, Janet Jones, Michelle Johnston, Audrey Landers, Pam Klinger, Charles McGowan, Justin Ross, Blane Savage, Matt West.

Attenborough again demonstrates his talents for orchestrating crowds, and for coping with the logistics of musicals. It's a pity, though, that he doesn't seem interested in dance, preferring to photograph his cast from the waist up when what was needed was a foot fetishist of a director. The essentially theatrical nature of the original – it was a front-stage musical, not the backstage kind that movies have always done so well – translates uneasily to film. **JW**

CITY LIMITS: See US section

THE CLAN OF THE CAVE BEAR
(Jonesfilm/Warner/Rank)
dir Michael Chapman *pro* Gerald I Isenberg *exec pro* Mark Damon, John Hyde, Jon Peters, Peter Guber *scr* John Sayles, based on the novel by Jean M Auel *ph* Jan De Bont, in Technovision, Technicolor *ed* Wendy Greene Bricmont *pro des* Anthony Masters *mus* Alan Silvestri *r time* 98 mins *US opening* Jan 17 *UK opening* May 30.
cast Daryl Hannah, Pamela Reed, James Remar, Thomas G Waites, John Doolittle, Curtis Armstrong, Martin Doyle, Adel C Hammond, Tony Montanaro, Mike Muscat, John Wardlow, Keith Wardlow, Karen Austin, Barbara Duncan, Gloria Lee, Janne Mortil, Lycia Naff, Linda Quibell, Bernadette Sabath.

Despite obvious efforts all round – attested by credits for sign language and primitive skill training – this everyday story of cave-dwelling folk some 35,000 years ago resembles nothing so much as some Club Med holiday gone dreadfully wrong. Unfortunately, a few hints of proto-feminism (the heroine is a Cro-Magnon orphan adopted by the less advanced Neanderthals) don't add up to a storyline; and the gestures towards 'seriousness' – the actors converse in grunts and groans, with sub-titled translations – only serve to underline the comic-strip absurdity of the whole affair. **TP**

Above: Cat's Eye *Opposite: The Clan of the Cave Bear*

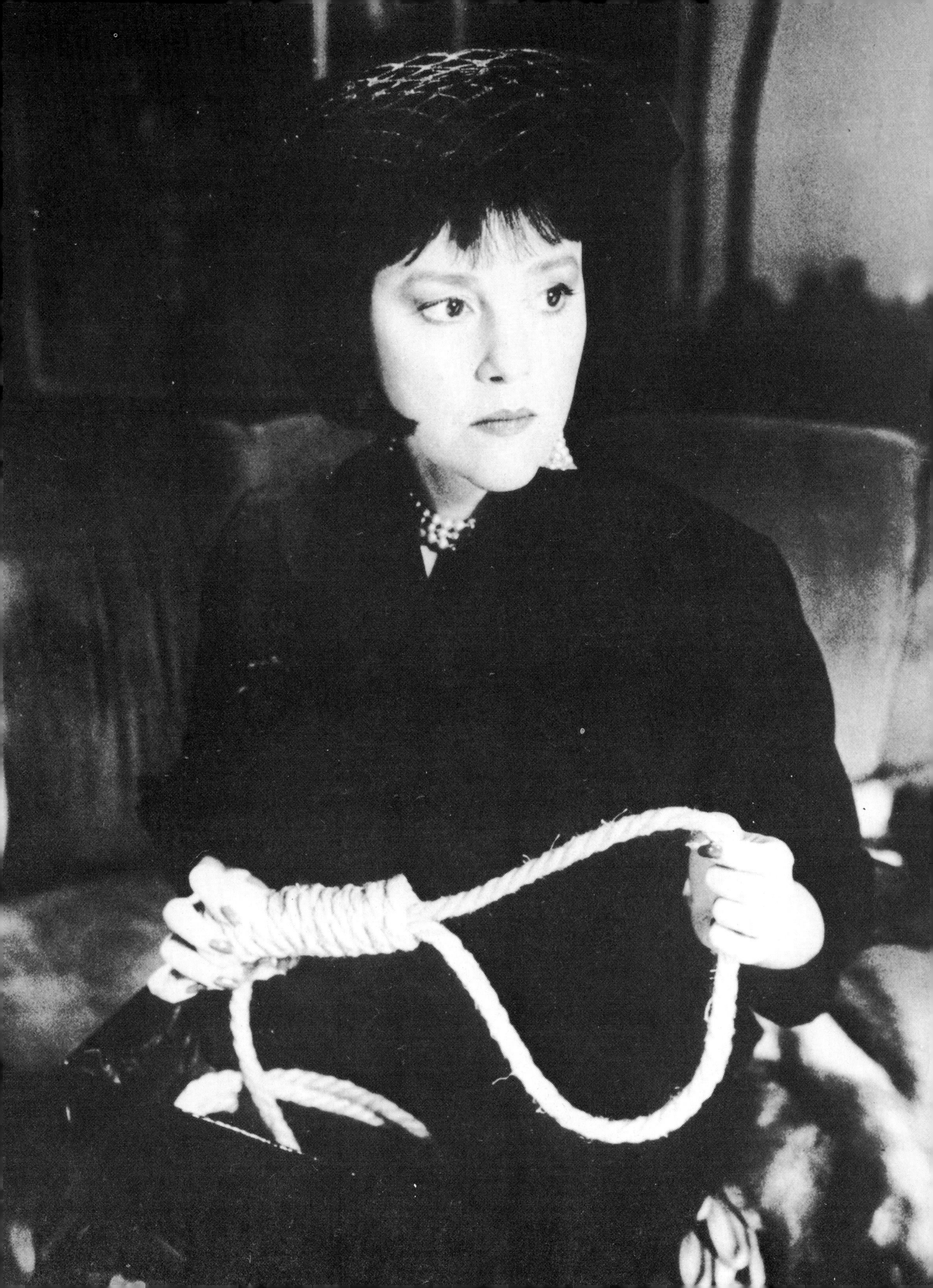

CLOCKWISE
(Thorn EMI)
dir Christopher Morahan *pro* Michael Codron *exec pro* Verity Lambert, Nat Cohen *scr* Michael Frayn *ph* John Coquillon, in Technicolor *ed* Peter Boyle *pro des* Roger Murray-Leach *mus* George Fenton *r time* 96 mins *UK opening* Mar 14.
cast John Cleese, Alison Steadman, Sharon Maiden, Stephen Moore, Penelope Wilton, Joan Hickson, Michael Aldridge, Benjamin Whitrow, Geoffrey Palmer, Nicholas LeProvost, Sidney Livingstone, John Bardon, Pat Keen, Geoffrey Hutchings, Charles Bartholomew, Sheila Keith, Chip Sweeney.

Michael Frayn's screenplay may be mere farce, but it is original, imaginative and often very funny. Detailing the disasters that befall Cleese's punctiliously punctual comprehensive headmaster as he drives hell for leather in a hijacked car across the Midlands countryside to an important conference, this furiously paced film is full of delightfully inventive plot twists, hysterical dialogue and absurd character collisions. Cleese's character, barely holding on to his sanity as the chaos escalates, may not stretch his acting talents, but it does provide him with ample opportunity to demonstrate his immaculate command of timing and enraged facial expressions. **GA**

The Coca Cola Kid

Opposite: Clue Above: Clockwise

CLUE
(Paramount)
dir-scr Jonathan Lynn, from a story by John Landis, based on the board game 'Clue/Cluedo' *pro* Debra Hill *exec pro* Jon Peters, Peter Guber, John Landis, George Folsey Jr *ph* Victor J Kemper, in Metrocolor *ed* David Bretherton, Richard Haines *pro des* John Lloyd *mus* John Morris *r time* 87 mins* *US opening* Dec 13 *UK opening* May 9.
cast Eileen Brennan, Tim Curry, Madeline Kahn, Christopher Lloyd, Michael McKean, Martin Mull, Lesley Ann Warren, Colleen Camp, Lee Ving, Bill Henderson, Jane Wiedlin, Jeffrey Kramer, Kellye Nakahara, Will Nye, Rick Goldman, Don Camp.
* This film has alternate endings.

'Clue' is the sort of idea that probably sounded irresistible over dinner, but which should never have got as far as celluloid. Inspired by the 'Cluedo' board game, it posits a number of cardboard (or should that be plastic?) characters known as Professor Plum, Miss Scarlet, Mrs White etc in a New England mansion circa 1954. Their blackmailing host, a Mr Boddy, duly becomes the body in the library, and everyone rushes from room to room in an unfunny frenzy. There were originally three final solutions to the mystery, none of them in any way satisfying. Jonathan Lynn, co-writer of TV's 'Yes, Minister', is capable of better things, but that's not saying much. **AB**

COBRA: See US section

THE COCA COLA KID
(Grand Bay Films-Cinema Enterprises/ Palace/Cinecom)
dir Dusan Makavejev *pro* David Roe *scr* Frank Moorhouse, based on his own short stories *ph* Deam Semler, in Eastman Colour *ed* Frans Vandenburg, Philippa Harvey *art dir* Anni Browning *mus* Bill Motzing *r time* 98 mins *US opening* Aug 9 *UK opening* Jul 19.
cast Eric Roberts, Greta Scacchi, Bill Kerr, Max Gillies, Kris McQuade, Tony Barry, Chris Haywood, Paul Chubb, David Slingsby, Tim Finn, Colleen Clifford, Rebecca Smart, Esben Storm, Angelo D'Angelo, Gia Carides, Steve Dodd, John Ewing, Annie Semmler, Jane Markey, Ian Gilmour, David Argue, Pola Negri.

A rare duffer from peripatetic Makavejev, here popping up Down Under with an international cast and a 'Local Hero'-ish satire on canny cobbers resisting the march of Coca-Colonisation. A customarily over-the-top Roberts is the company troubleshooter irked by the competition of some outback brew and distracted by the charms of free spirit Scacchi, but it's Makavejev's desperate ogling of the latter which finally confirms overall impressions of the project as a misfired Carry-On-with-knobs rather than some antipodean extension of its begetter's usual anarchic absurdism. **PT**

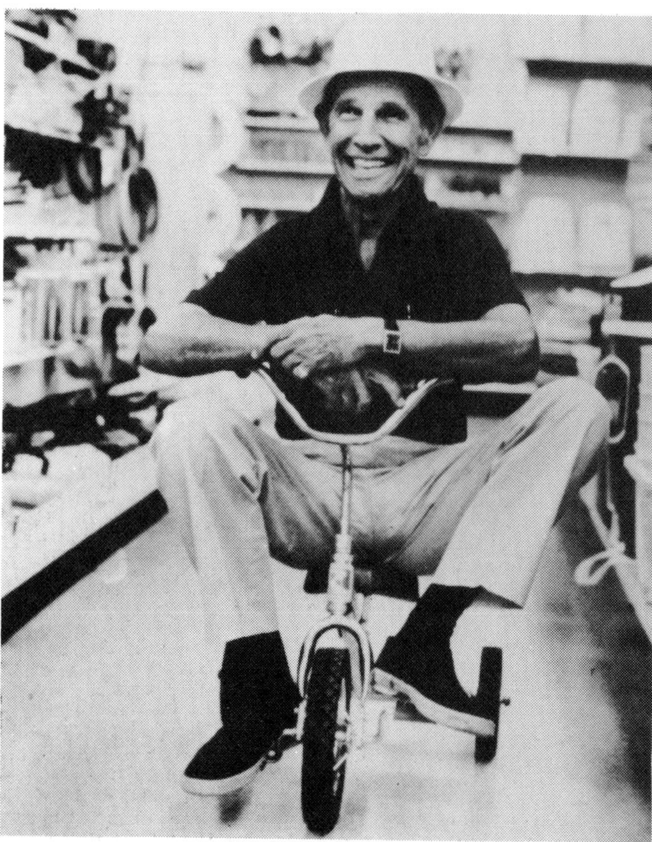
Cocoon

COCOON 
(Fox)
dir Ron Howard *pro* Richard D Zanuck, David Brown, Lili Fini Zanuck *scr* Tom Benedek, based on a novel by David Saperstein *ph* Don Peterman, in colour *ed* Daniel Hanley, Michael J Hill *pro des* Jack T Collis *mus* James Horner *r time* 117 mins *US opening* prior to Jul 1985 *UK opening* Sep 13.
cast Don Ameche, Wilford Brimley, Hume Cronyn, Brian Dennehy, Jack Gilford, Steve Guttenberg, Maureen Stapleton, Jessica Tandy, Gwen Verdon, Herta Ware, Tahnee Welch, Barret Oliver, Linda Harrison, Tyrone Power Jr, Clint Howard, Charles Lampkin, Mike Nomad, Rance Howard.

Aliens disguised as humans return to earth to rescue their comrades left behind in an earlier visit, but a by-product of their operations is a Fountain of Youth that changes the lives of three couples in a neighbouring retirement community. Director Ron Howard ('Splash') applies a deft touch to this suspect mix of old-fart comedy and Spielbergian benign visitations, aided particularly by a dashing group of elderly players who bring genuine humanity to their roles. The final reels, in particular, are contrived and phoney, fatal to a movie whose sole virtue is charm. Howard is undeniably talented: but has he anything at all to say artistically? **MM**

Code of Silence

Colonel Redl

CODE OF SILENCE
(Orion/Rank)
dir Andy Davis *pro* Raymond Wagner *scr* Michael Butler, Dennis Shryack, Mike Gray *ph* Frank Tidy, in colour *ed* Peter Parasheles, Christopher Holmes *pro des* Maher Ahmed *mus* David Frank *r time* 101 mins *US opening* prior to Jul 1985 *UK opening* Sep 20.
cast Chuck Norris, Henry Silva, Bert Remsen, Molly Hagan, Joseph Guzaldo, Mike Genovese, Nathan Davis, Ralph Foody, Allen Hamilton, Ron Henriquez, Ron Dean, Wilbert Bradley.

Director Andrew Davis ('Stony Island') accomplishes the challenging task of building an effective, dynamic action film around Chuck Norris. Basically, he keeps a lot of balls in the air around the phlegmatic hero while making no demands on him, adding a sense of complexity with acute sociological observation in the characterisations and use of Chicago locations. First rate in all departments, it might have been a major film with any iconographically potent star in the lead. **MM**

COLONEL REDL
(Mafilm Studio Objektiv-Mokep-Manfred Durniok-ZDF-ORF/Orion Classics/Cannon-Gala)
dir Istvan Szabo *scr* Istvan Szabo, Peter Dobai *ph* Lajos Koltai, in Eastman Colour *ed* Zsuzsa Csakany *art dir* Jozsef Romvari *mus* Zdenko Tamassy and others *r time* 149 mins *US opening* Oct 4 *UK opening* Nov 22.
cast Klaus Maria Brandauer, Hans-Christian Blech, Armin Müller-Stahl, Gudrun Landgrebe, Jan Niklas, Laszlo Mensaros, Gabor Svidrony, Eva Szabo, Tamas Major, Gyula Benko, Peter Gaal, Janos Ujlaki Toth, Gyula Gazdag.

A powerhouse performance by Brandauer, climaxing in a no-holds-barred prelude to suicide, provides the centre of a fictionalised account of the life and times of Alfred Redl, who became head of military intelligence in Vienna in the closing years of the Austro-Hungarian Empire. Long and episodic, the film, though intermittently shot through with telling observation, lacks the compression of Szabo's 'Mephisto', and there are times when the use of the Radetzky March over the opening titles comes to seem an all too apt harbinger of TV-style costume drama. **TP**

THE COLOR PURPLE: See US section

COMMANDO
(Fox)
dir Mark L Lester *pro* Joel Silver *scr* Steven E de Souza *ph* Matthew F Leonetti, in DeLuxe Colour *ed* Mark Goldblatt, John F Link, Glenn Farr *pro des* John Vallone *mus* James Horner *r time* 90 mins *US opening* Oct 4 *UK opening* Feb 21.
cast Arnold Schwarzenegger, Rae Dawn Chong, Dan Hedaya, Vernon Wells, James Olson, David Patrick Kelly, Alyssa Milano, Bill Duke, Drew Snyder, Sharon Wyatt, Michael deLano, Bob Minor, Mike Adams, Carlos Cervantes, Lenny Juliano, Charles Meshack, Hank Calia, Walter Scott.

'Boys Own' vehicle for Schwarzenegger and his impressive musculature. With his pecs kitted out in an array of combat gear and designer hardware, he is pitted against a team of renegades who have kidnapped his daughter as part of their plan to restore a Central American dictatorship. The mindless 'Rambo' action and constant gatta-gatta of automatic weaponry is mitigated somewhat by a mildly witty script, by Rae Dawn Chong as a wisecracking air hostess, and by Big Arnie himself, who

Commando

Compromising Positions

fortunately seems incapable of taking his macho image seriously. **AB**

COMPROMISING POSITIONS
(Paramount)
dir-pro Frank Perry *exec pro* Salah M Hassanein *scr* Susan Isaacs, based on her novel *ph* Barry Sonnenfeld, in colour *ed* Peter Frank *pro des* Peter Larkin *mus* Brad Fiedel *r time* 98 mins *US opening* Aug 30 *UK opening* Jun 13.
cast Susan Sarandon, Raul Julia, Edward Herrmann, Judith Ivey, Mary Beth Hurt, Joe Mantegna, Anne De Salvo, Josh Mostel, Deborah Rush, Joan Allen, Kaiulani Lee, Tanya Berezin, William Youmans, Amanda Lyons, Chris Cunningham, Jason Beghe, Timothy Jerome, Jack Gilpin, Bill Cobbs.

Suburban housewife turns detective when a local Lothario is murdered. Promising material is compromised by inappropriate casting and a reluctance to realise the sardonic sexual satire. Despite the timidity, there's some welcome bite and charm to an adult view of adultery and a host of superb female cameos (itself a rarity in an American film) by stage actresses mostly unfamiliar on film. **MM**

LE COP
(Films 7-Editions 23/Cannon)
dir-scr Claude Zidi, based on an original idea by Simon Mickael *ph* Jean-Jacques Tarbes, in Panavision, Eastman Colour *ed* Nicole Saunier *art dir* Françoise De Leu *mus* Francis Lai *r time* 107 mins *UK opening* Jan 31.
cast Philippe Noiret, Thierry Lhermitte, Régine, Grace De Capitani, Claude Brosset, Albert Simono, Julien Guiomar, Henri Attal, Abou Bakar, Pierre Baton, Bernard Bijaoui, Jean-Claude Bouillaud, Julien Bukouski, François Cadet, Jocelyn Canoen, Kamel Cherif, Jean Cherlian, Louise Chevalier, Salah Cheurfi.

A featherweight farce on corruption in the Parisian police force, inexplicably weighed down with both Cesars and controversy on home turf, and buoyed up only by a typically professional performance from Noiret, as a veteran cop cheerfully working both sides of the street until afflicted by enforced partnership with a green, straight-arrow recruit. Apparently authentic incidentals in the plotting (supplied to the script by a pseudonymous bean-spilling flic) do nothing to disturb the air of insouciant artificiality and comic cosiness with which Zidi inflates the affair. **PT**

COP AU VIN: See Poulet Au Vinaigre

THE CRAZY FAMILY
(Art Theatre Guild/New Yorker/ The Other Cinema)
dir Sogo Ishii *pro* Banmel Takahashi *exec pro* Kazuhiko Hasegawa, Yoyoji Yamane, Shiro Sasaki *scr* Yoshinori Kobayashi, Fumio Konami, Sogo Ishii, based on an idea by Yoshinori Kobayashi *ph* Masaki Tamura, in colour *ed* Junichi Kikuchi *art dir* Terumi Hosoishi *mus* 1984 *r time* 107 mins *US opening* Feb 11 *UK opening* Feb 21.
cast Katsuya Kobayashi, Mitsuko Baisho, Yoshiki Arizono, Yuki Kudo, Hitoshi Ueki.

Thoroughly rebarbative without ever becoming properly provocative, this peculiar movie offers a would-be black-comic fantasy in which the pressures of suburban living reduce a Japanese paterfamilias to a chainsaw-wielding maniac. The premise seems oddly old-fashioned, an Oriental equivalent to the sort of thing Ionesco was doing decades ago; the chief reaction aroused in the viewer is an impulse to flee the theatre. **TP**

CREATOR: See US section

Le Cop

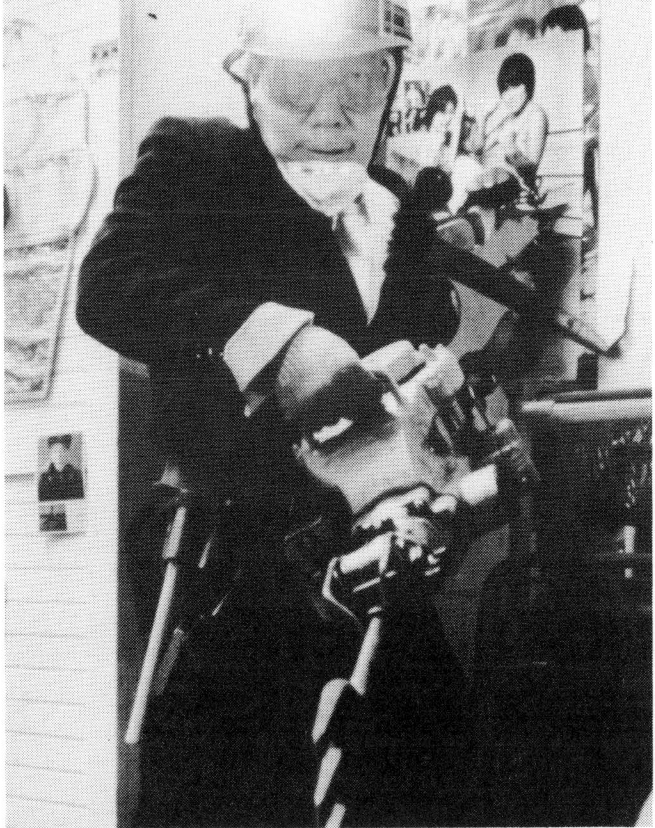
The Crazy Family

CREEPERS
(Dacfilm/New Line/Palace)
dir-pro Dario Argento *scr* Dario Argento, Franco Ferrini *ph* Romano Albani, in Technicolor *ed* Franco Fraticelli *pro des* Maurizio Garrone, Nello Giorgetti, Luciano Spadoni, Umberto Turco *mus* various *r time* 110 mins *US opening* Aug 30 *UK opening* Apr 18.
cast Jennifer Connelly, Daria Nicolodi, Dalila Di Lazzaro, Patrick Bauchau, Donald Pleasence, Fiore Argento, Federica Mastoianni, Davide Marotta, Fausta Avelli, Marta Biuso, Sophie Bourchier, Paola Gropper, Ninke Hielkema, Mitzy Orsini, Geraldine Thomas.

The trademarks of a Dario Argento film are as follows: gore galore, stylish stalk 'n' slash, scientific mumbo-jumbo, incomprehensible plot and a score consisting of loud, totally inappropriate rock music. 'Creepers' has all these, plus a teenaged heroine who is able to communicate with insects. Dotty entomologist Donald Pleasence fixes her up with a Great Sarcophagous Fly so she can track down the psychopath who is carving up her schoolmates in the Swiss Transylvania. There are enough maggots to please the director's hardcore addicts, but the film never reaches the inspired heights of lunacy attained in his earlier supernatural chillers. **AB**

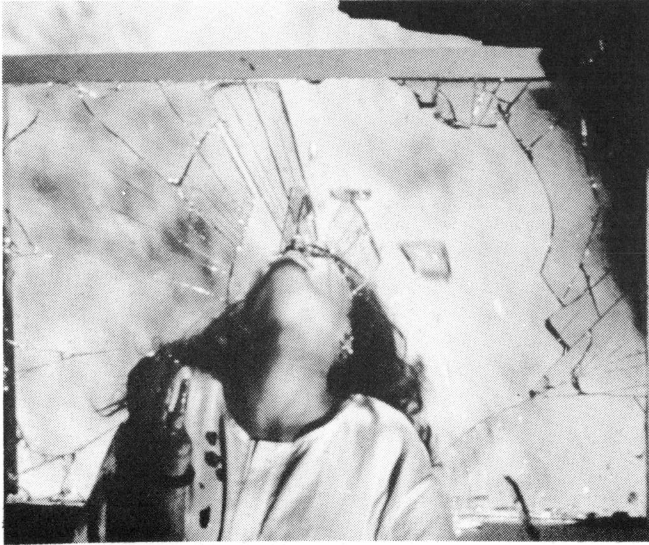
Creepers

CRIMES OF PASSION
(New World/Rank)
dir Ken Russell *pro* Barry Sandler, Donald P Borchers *exec pro* Larry Thompson *scr* Barry Sandler *ph* Dick Bush, in colour *ed* Brian Tagg *pro des* Richard Macdonald *mus* Rick Wakeman *r time* 101 mins *US opening* prior to Jul 1985 *UK opening* Sep 13.
cast Kathleen Turner, Anthony Perkins, John Laughlin, Annie Potts.

Ken Russell revels in sexual excess yet again, this time without any sense of cultural importance. The result is daft, witty and bracing, enhanced by courageous performances by Kathleen Turner, who as a top designer with a secret nightlife as a hooker takes more risks than Russell, and Anthony Perkins, who flirts with self-parody as a degenerate religious madman. Silly when serious, it conveys great conviction at its most apparently facetious. **MM**

CRIMEWAVE
(Embassy Pictures-Renaissance/Rank)
dir Sam Raimi *pro* Robert Tapert *exec pro* Robert R Pressman, Irvin Shapiro *scr* Ethan Coen, Joel Coen, Sam Raimi *ph* Robert Primes, in Technicolor *ed* Kathie Weaver, Louis Kleinman *art dir* Gary Papierski *mus* Arlon Ober *r time* 86 mins *UK opening* Apr 25.
cast Louise Lasser, Paul Smith, Brion James, Sheree J Wilson, Edward R Pressman, Bruce Campbell, Reed Birney, Richard Bright, Antonio Fargas, Hamid Dana, John Hardy, Emil Sitka, Hal Youngblood, Sean Farley, Richard DeManincor, Carrie Hall-Schalter, Wiley Harker, Julius Harris, Ralph Drischell.

After the DC-inspired demonology of 'The Evil Dead', director Sam Raimi has once more plundered comic strip conventions for a live-action loony-tune caper. It takes the form of a flashback, generated by a nerd who is protesting his innocence as he is led towards the electric chair to fry for a couple of murders which were actually committed by a pair of psychopathic exterminators. Despite some splendidly inventive chase sequences and enjoyably grotesque characterisation, the film is in sore need of a disciplined plot on which to hang its zaniness; surprising since Raimi's co-writers were the Coen Brothers, responsible for the perfectly structured 'Blood Simple'. **AB**

CRITTERS: See US section

CROSSROADS: See US section

DANGEROUS MOVES
(Spectrafilm/Enterprise)
dir-scr Richard Dembo *pro* Arthur Cohn *ph* Raoul Coutard, in colour *ed* Agnès Guillemot *art dir* Ivan Maussion *mus* Gabriel Yared, César Frank *r time* 110 mins *US opening* prior to Jul 1985 *UK opening* Feb 6.
cast Michel Piccoli, Alexandre Arbatt, Liv Ullmann, Leslie Caron, Daniel Olbrychski, Michel Aumont, Serge Avedikian, Pierre Michael, Pierre Vial, Wojtek Pszonia' 'ean-Hughes Anglade, Hubert Saint-Macary, Bernhard Wicki, Benoît Regent, Jacques Boudet, Jean-Paul Eydoux, Albert Simono, Sylvie Granotier.

Set against a world chess championship in Geneva, this modest, but altogether civilised and intelligent film is not so much about chess as such as about personality and obsession. Tracing the contest between the guarded old crocodile of a Soviet veteran and a Lithuanian dissident who has opted for the West, the film succeeds, wittily and in the end affectingly, in dramatising the labyrinthine ways in which an ideological system such as that operated by the Kremlin seeps into and distorts human experience. Thus, the 'system' of chess playing becomes a correlative of the process of coping with the pressures of political manipulation. Admirable performances by Piccoli (the champion) and Arbatt (the attitudinising contender): self-effacing direction by Dembo, here making his feature debut. **TP**

DANGEROUSLY CLOSE: See US section

D.A.R.Y.L.
(World Film Services/Columbia)
dir Simon Wincer *pro* John Heyman *scr* David Ambrose, Allan Scott, Jeffrey Ellis *ph* Frank Watts, in Panavision, TVC Colour *ed* Adrian Carr *pro des* Alan Cassie *mus* Marvin Hamlisch *r time* 100 mins *US opening* prior to Jul 1985 *UK opening* Mar 28.
cast Mary Beth Hurt, Michael McKean, Kathyryn Walker, Colleen Camp, Josef Sommer, Ron Frazier, Steve Ryan, David Wohl, Danny Corkill, Amy Linker, Barret Oliver, Ed L Grady, Tucker McGuire, Pat Fuleihan, Noreen Lange, Joseph Reed, Jessica Johnson, Ginny Light.

Starting off as a smalltown sitcom about a ten-year-old amnesiac whose behaviour is just too perfect for words, 'D.A.R.Y.L.' switches channels in midstream when the little brat is revealed to be a Data Analysing Robot Youth Lifeform. Government agencies want him scrapped, and the film turns into a high-tech thriller as kindly scientists attempt to restore him to the bosom of his all-American adoptive family. Lots of hideously heart-warming moments, accompanied by a syrupy soundtrack. **AB**

D.A.R.Y.L.

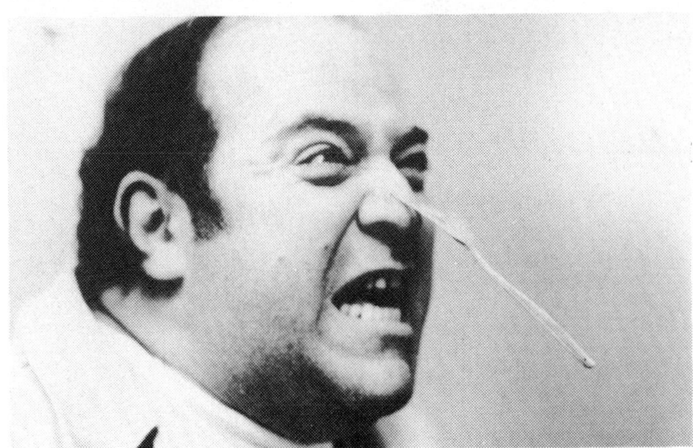

Opposite: Crimes of Passion Above: Crimewave

Dangerous Moves

DAY OF THE DEAD: See US section

DEATH IN A FRENCH GARDEN
[US TITLE: PERIL]
(Gaumont/Artificial Eye)
dir Michel Deville *pro* Emmanuel Schlumberger *exec pro* Rosalinde Damamme *scr* Michel Deville, Rosalinde Damamme, based on the novel 'Sur la terre comme au ciel' by Rene Belletto *ph* Martial Thury, in Eastman Colour *ed* Raymonde Guyot *art dir* Philippe Combastel *r time* 101 mins *UK opening* Jan 23.
cast Michel Piccoli, Nicole Garcia, Anemone, Christophe Malavoy, Richard Bohringer, Anaïs Jeanneret, Jean-Claude Jay, Hélène Roussel, Elisabeth Vitali, Frank Lapersonne, Danel Vérité.

Voyeurism, kidnapping, robbery, suicide, a bit of traditional murder, and more than a bit of sex, both traditional and otherwise . . . there is no shortage of narrative substance in this thriller about a down-at-heel musician involved with a rich woman and her maybe-not-so-complaisant husband, as well as with a cryptic character (beautifully played by Bohringer) who proves to be a hitman with a death wish. All the same, the plot – ultimately rather baffling – is not the important thing here; what really counts is the stylistic luxuriance and literary wit with which Michel Deville crosses the precepts of James Hadley Chase with those of Lewis Carroll. A divertissement de luxe. **TP**

DEATH WISH 3
(Cannon)
dir Michael Winner *pro* Menahem Golan, Yoram Globus *scr* Michael Edmonds, based on characters created by Brian Garfield *ph* John Stanier, in colour *ed* Arnold Crust *pro des* Peter Mullins *mus* Jimmy Page *r time* 90 mins *US opening* Nov 1 *UK opening* Jan 17.
cast Charles Bronson, Deborah Raffin, Ed Lauter, Martin Balsam, Gavan O'Herlihy, Kirk Tayor, Alex Winter, Tony Spiridakis, Joseph Gonzalez, Francis Drake, Leo Kharibian, Hana-Maria Pravda, John Gabriel, Manning Redwood, Lee Patterson, Joe Cirillo, Ricco Ross.

'The streets are full of degenerates – I want some bodies on slabs,' shouts Ed Lauter's hard-nosed police chief. And once he has conscripted vigilante Charles Bronson as a freelance assistant, it is no time before the corpses start to pile up. With an arsenal that eventually runs to a missile-launcher (seemingly available by mail order), Bronson comes to the aid of an apartment block where residents are at the mercy of a ferocious street gang, and the movie ends with a pitched battle in which the decent folk conspire, in the words of the script, to "blow the scum away". The situation is stylised in terms that deny any kind of realism, but the film is scripted with dark humour and realised with considerable gusto. Just because 'Death Wish 3' is frankly unserious and sensationalist, it manages to sound a note of genuine provocation. **TP**

Above: Death Wish 3   Opposite: Defence of the Realm

The Delta Force

Death in a French Garden

DEFENCE OF THE REALM 
(Enigma/Rank)
dir David Drury *pro* Robin Douet, Lynda Myles *exec pro* David Puttnam *scr* Martin Stellman *ph* Roger Deakins, in colour *ed* Michael Bradsell *pro des* Roger Murray-Leach *mus* Richard Harvey *r time* 96 mins *UK opening* Jan 3.
cast Gabriel Byrne, Greta Scacchi, Denholm Elliott, Ian Bannen, Fulton Mackay, Bill Paterson, David Calder, Frederick Treves, Robbie Coltrane, Annabel Leventon, Graham Fletcher-Cook, Steven Woodcock, Alexei Jawdokimov, Daniel Webb, Prentis Hancock, Michael Johnson, Mark Tandy.

An impressively mounted conspiracy thriller, in which hack journalist Byrne investigates a complex political scandal and uncovers a mystery concerning nuclear weapons. The final pay-off is both predictable and unsatisfactory, but en route to the explosive denouement we are led along a dark and devious path through the corridors of power. Drury directs with solid professionalism, coaxing strong performances from his excellent cast and building up an atmosphere of real menace in locations as diverse as the Fens and the Mall. Stylish, taut and intelligent, it's a glossy but incisive account of paranoia in Thatcher's Britain. **GA**

THE DELTA FORCE
(Cannon)
dir Menahem Golan *pro* Menahem Golan, Yoram Globus *scr* Menahem Golan, James Bruner *ph* David Gurfinkel, in colour *ed* Alain Jakubowicz *pro des* Luciano Spadoni *mus* Alan Silvestri *r time* 129 mins *US opening* Feb 14 *UK opening* May 30.
cast Chuck Norris, Lee Marvin, Martin Balsam, Joey Bishop, Robert Forster, Lainie Kazan, George Kennedy, Hanna Schygulla, Susan Strasberg, Bo Svenson, Robert Vaughn, Shelley Winters, William Wallace, Charles Floye, Steve James, Kim Delaney, Gerry Weinstock, Marvin Freedman.

A curious blend of actual incident – the abortive attempt to rescue the Iranian hostages, and the hi-jacking of a TWA jet – and gung-ho Ramboics, mostly involving Chuck Norris bombing around Beirut on a souped-up motorcycle. In between there is a slice of pure 'Airplane!'-style melodrama, with Shelley Winters and George Kennedy, among others, spilling out clichés in a fuselage full of hostages. Ridiculously enjoyable, provided you overlook the questionable morality and rabidly anti-Arab stance. **AB**

Desperately Seeking Susan

Diary for My Children

Detective

Dim Sum

DESERT BLOOM: See US section

DESERT HEARTS: See US section

DESPERATELY SEEKING SUSAN
(Orion/Rank)
dir Susan Seidelman *pro* Sarah Pillsbury, Midge Sanford *exec pro* Michael Peyser *scr* Leora Barish *ph* Edward Lachman, in colour *ed* Andrew Mondshein *pro des* Santo Loquasto *mus* Thomas Newman *r time* 104 mins *US opening* prior to Jul 1985 *UK opening* Sep 6.
cast Rosanna Arquette, Madonna, Aidan Quinn, Mark Blum, Robert Joy, Laurie Metcalf, Anna Levine, Will Patton, Peter Maloney, Steven Wright, John Turturro, Anne Carlisle, Shirley Stoler.

Stylish farce that plausibly revives the old chestnut of amnesia and exchanged identities, this time between a bored young housewife and an amoral drifter. Director Susan Seidelman ('Smithereens') has a keen command of textures and glances that helps bring out the humour from the able cast. The last reel smacks of too much studio-style advice, merely working out the plot instead of climaxing it, but otherwise a delightful and unusual contemporary wrinkle on screwball comedy. **MM**
(See Aidan Quinn, Faces of the Year.)

DETECTIVE
(Sara Films-JLG Films/Spectrafilm/Artificial Eye)
dir Jean-Luc Godard *pro* Alain Sarde *scr* Jean-Luc Godard, Anne-Marie Miéville, based on a story by Alain Sarde, Philippe Setbon *ph* Bruno Nuytten, in colour *ed* Marilyne Dubreuil *r time* 98 mins *US opening* Aug 23 *UK opening* Mar 7.
cast Nathalie Baye, Claude Brasseur, Johnny Hallyday, Eugène Berthier, Stéphane Ferrara, Laurent Terzieff, Jean-Pierre Léaud, Aurèle Doazan, Anne Gisèle Glass, Alain Cuny, Pierre Bertin, Emmanuelle Seigner, Cyril Autin, Julie Delpy, Alexandra Garijo, Xavier Saint Macary.

Godard at play in a Grand Hotel, apparently utilising the lobby register as his only script, as a selection of oddball guests find themselves unwitting suspects in an absurd murder mystery of the past which is obsessively raked over by the sacked house 'tec. The hotel might conceivably be Hollywood, with a different genre of fiction unreeling in every bedroom, but the whole ramshackle edifice of a non-sequitur narrative is merely the backdrop for more of Godard's puns on love and money, more of his rimshot gags on the strange convergences of literature and life, and more gems from his inventory of inspiredly irrelevant images. **PT**

DIARY FOR MY CHILDREN
(Mafilm Studio-Hungarofilm/New Yorker Films/Artificial Eye)
dir-scr Marta Meszaros *ph* Miklos Jancso *ed* Eva Karmento *pro des* Eva Martin *mus* Zsolt Domer *r time* 85 mins *US opening* prior to Jul 1985 *UK opening* Jul 18.
cast Zsuzsa Czinkoczi, Anna Polony, Jan Nowicki, Pal Zolnay, Mari Szemes, Tamas Toth.

Surprisingly underquoted and underrated by feminist critics, Marta Meszaros' cinema is also a surprisingly warm experience, given its tendency to feature everyday heroines searching longingly for shafts of sustaining independence amid the greyness of Hungarian life. Here that search is undertaken by a teenage girl at the time the greyness itself darkened significantly – the immediate post-war years under Stalinism's dulling and deathly shadow – and Meszaros' bravely analytical remembrance subtly details an individual flight from the ultimate patriarchal order. **PT**

DIM SUM
(Project A Partnership-CIM Productions/Orion Classics/Mainline)
dir Wayne Wang *pro* Tom Sternberg, Wayne Wang *exec pro* Vincent Tai *scr* Terrel Seltzer, based on an idea by Terrel Seltzer, Laureen Chew, Wayne Wang *ph* Michael Chin, in colour *pro* Ralph Wikke *art dir* Danny Yung *mus* Todd Boekelheide *r time* 87 mins *US opening* Aug 9 *UK opening* Sep 13.
cast Laureen Chew, Kim Chew, Victor Wong, Ida F O Chung, Cora Miao, John Nishio, Amy Hill, Keith Chow, Mary Chew, Nora Lee, Joan Chen, Rita Yee.

Quiet is the word for this small-scale, almost miniaturist, view of a Chinese-American family in San Francisco and the dilemma of an adult daughter staying at home to care for her elderly widowed mother. With a minimum of camera movement or musical accompaniment and a virtual absence of plot, the film (played by a real-life mother and daughter) has a touching simplicity; yet in the end its lack of drama becomes something of a liability. Sympathetic though the movie is, it leaves the impression more of a sketch than of a full-scale family portrait. **TP**

The Doctor and the Devils

Down and Out in Beverly Hills

Echo Park

Dreamchild

THE DOCTOR AND THE DEVILS
(Brooksfilms/Fox)
dir Freddie Francis *pro* Jonathan Sanger *exec pro* Mel Brooks *scr* Ronald Harwood, based on an original script by Dylan Thomas *ph* Gerry Turpin, Norman Warwick, in Scope, colour *ed* Laurence Mery-Clark *pro des* Robert Laing *mus* John Morris *r time* 92 mins *US opening* Oct 4 *UK opening* May 30.
cast Timothy Dalton, Jonathan Pryce, Twiggy, Julian Sands, Stephen Rea, Phyllis Logan, Lewis Fiander, Beryl Reid, T P McKenna, Patrick Stewart, Sian Phillips, Philip Davis, Philip Jackson, Danny Schiller, Bruce Green, Toni Palmer, David Bomber.

Well-worn Burke and Hare territory, adapted by Ronald Harwood from a script written in the late forties by Dylan Thomas. No major new insights are offered into its Bodysnatcher material, other than the notion that Jonathan Pryce and Stephen Rea can be atrocious hams when given the chance to cart corpses around, and that Twiggy does not make a supremely credible Cockney prostitute. The theme, that the ends will justify the iffy means, is further hammed home by Timothy Dalton's Dr Rock, whose anatomical experiments are fuelled by a supply of fresh low-life cadavers. The all-purpose period setting gives director Freddie Francis an excuse to indulge in stock scenes full of rhubarbing extras. **AB**

DOIN' TIME: See US section

DOWN AND OUT IN BEVERLY HILLS
(Touchstone/Buena Vista/Disney)
dir Paul Mazursky *scr* Paul Mazursky, Leon Capetanos, based on the play 'Boudu sauvé des eaux' by René Fauchois *ph* Donald McAlpine, in Technicolor *ed* Richard Halsey *pro des* Pato Guzman *mus* Andy Summers and others *r time* 103 mins *US opening* Jan 31 *UK opening* May 23.
cast Nick Nolte, Bette Midler, Richard Dreyfuss, Little Richard, Tracy Nelson, Elizabeth Pena, Evan Richards, Donald F Muhich, Paul Mazursky, Valerie Curtin, Jack Bruskoff, Geraldine Dreyfuss, Barry Primus, Irene Tsu, Michael Yama, Ranbir Bhai, Felton Perry, Eloy Casados, Michael Greene.

Mazursky has raided the classics before, but his misappropriation of Renoir's 'Boudu' results in a discomfortingly bourgeois comedy with some droll observations and funny gags, yet little bite. Nolte's vagrant lacks the spiritual force and stubbornness of Michel Simon's original creation, while Mazursky's satire is always comfortably directed away from the middle-class audience so it can relish its sense of social superiority, never a healthy thing. The incessant recourse to trained dog reaction shots emphasises Mazursky's fundamental lack of inspiration. Naturally, it has been his biggest hit to date. **MM**
(See Films of the Year.)

DOWN BY LAW: See US section

DREAM LOVER: See US section

DREAMCHILD
(Universal/Thorn EMI)
dir Gavin Millar *pro* Rick McCallum, Kenith Trodd *exec pro* Dennis Potter, Verity Lambert *scr* Dennis Potter *ph* Billy Williams, in Technicolor *ed* Angus Newton *pro des* Roger Hall *mus* Stanley Myers *r time* 94 mins *US opening* Oct 18 *UK opening* Jan 24.
cast Coral Browne, Ian Holm, Peter Gallagher, Caris Corfman, Nicola Cowper, Jane Asher, Ameilia Shankley, Imogen Boorman, Emma King, Rupert Wainwright, Roger Ashton-Griffiths, James Wilby, Shane Rimmer, Peter Whitman, Ken Campbell, William Hootkins, Jeffrey Chiswick, Pat Starr.

Centring less on Lewis Carroll than on Alice Hargreaves, née Liddell, who as a child was the model for the heroine of the Alice stories, 'Dreamchild' shows her arriving in New York, an unfeeling eighty-year-old, to attend the Carroll centenary celebrations of 1932, with flashbacks and fantasy inserts intruding to summon up Carroll and the figures of his imagination. This structure at times seems over-intricate and the paraphernalia of thirties scene-setting rather gets in the way of the real focus of interest, the old lady's reaching of an accommodation between the shrivelling reality of her adult experience and the lost world of imaginative freedom which Carroll opened up for her. Flawed though it is, however, this is a work at once ambitious and attractive; particularly, impressive are the fabled creatures of the Alice tales realised by Jim Henson and his team with beguiling originality, becoming in the process a good deal more mordant than mere nursery illustrations. **TP**

ECHO PARK
(Sascha-Wien Film/Miracle/Atlantic)
dir Robert Dornhelm *pro* Walter Shenson *exec pro* Ralph E Cotta *scr* Michael Ventura *ph* Karl Kofler, in colour *ed* Ingrid Koller *art-dir* Bernt Capra *mus* David Ricketts *r time* 89 mins *US opening* Mar 28 *UK opening* Mar 14.
cast Susan Dey, Tom Hulce, Michael Bowen, Christopher Walker, Shirley Jo Finney, Heinrich Schweiger, Richard Marin, John Paragon, Cassandra Peterson, Timothy Carey, Martin Suppan, Robert R Shafer, Dorothy Dells, Yana Nirvana, Dee Cooper, Douglas M Ford, Stephen Gaines.

Striving artists battle the twin threats of starvation and anonymity in this East Hollywood fringe community. Despite many clumsy passages, the charm and sweetness of the conception survives, primarily through the players, with Dey standing out as an aspiring actress whose first break is delivering striptease greeting cards. Dornhelm and Ventura have a nice feeling for the positive side of everyday delusion that's so essential to emotional survival for creative folk. **MM**

8 MILLION WAYS TO DIE: See US section

ELENI: See US section

ELIMINATORS: See US section

THE EMERALD FOREST
(Christel Films-Embassy Pictures/ Embassy/Rank)
dir-pro John Boorman *exec pro* Edgar F Gross *scr* Rospo Pallenberg *ph* Philippe Rousselot, in Panavision, Eastman Colour *ed* Ian Crafford *pro des* Simon Holland *art dir* Marcos Flacksman *mus* Junior Homrich, Brian Gascoigne *r time* 114 mins *US opening* Jul 3 *UK opening* Nov 1.
cast Powers Boothe, Meg Foster, William Rodriquez, Yara Vaneau, Estee Chandler, Charley Boorman, Dira Paes, Eduardo Conde, Ariel Coelho, Peter Marinker, Mario Borges, Atilia Iorio, Claudio Moreno, Gabriel Archanjo, Gracindo Junior, Arthur Muhlenberg, Rui Polonah, Maria Helena Velasco.

Intense, dense movie about a man's search for his lost son, captured by Indians, in the rain forests of the Amazon. Modern society is judged by the standards of tribal life and found wanting – although that summary does no justice to the power of Boorman's images to convey his meaning. There are times when the film falters and retreats into private mythology, but at least that's a fault on the right side, of trying to say too much. **JW**

THE EMPTY TABLE
(Marugen Building Group-Haiyu-za-Herald Ace/Electric Pictures)
dir-scr Masaki Kobayashi, based on a story by Fumiko Enji *pro* Ginichi Kishimoto, Kyoto Oshima *exec pro* Genjiro Kawamoto *ph* Kozo Okazaki, in colour *ed* Nobuo Ogawa *pro des* Shigemasa Toda *mus* Toru Takemitsu *r time* 142 mins *UK opening* Feb 13.
cast Tatsuya Nakadai, Mayumi Ogawa, Kie Nakaj, Miichi Nakai, Takeyuki Takemoto, Shima Iwashita, Mikijiro Hira, Azusa Mano, Shinobu Otake.

A deadly dull study of the emotional havoc wrought on a family by a student son's involvement in a terrorist siege, this centres on the unbending father's refusal either to resign from his job or to commit suicide (entire families take responsibility for an individual's actions in Japan). Limply liberal in its assertion of the value of personal needs over the demands of a conformist society, overlong and overschematic in its portrait of a communal crack-up, the film is archetypal art-house dross: glossily vacuous, 'significantly' slow and very vaguely politicised. **GA**

ENEMY MINE: See US section

EXPLORERS: See US section

UNE FEMME OU DEUX
[UK TITLE: A WOMAN OR TWO]
(Hachette Première-Philippe Dussart-FR3-DD Prods/Virgin)
dir Daniel Vigne *pro* Michel Choquet *exec pro* Philippe Dussart *scr* Daniel Vigne, Elisabeth Rappeneau, based on an idea by David Vigne *ed* Marie-Josèphe Yoyotte *art dir* Jean-Pierre Kohut Svelko *mus* Kevin Mulligan, Evert Verhees, Toots Thielemans *r time* 97 mins *UK opening* Jun 13
cast Gérard Depardieu, Sigourney Weaver, Ruth Westheimer, Michel Aumont, Zabou, Jean-Pierre Bisson, Yann Babilée, Maurice Barrier, Robert Blumenfeld, Michael Goldman, Adrian Howard, Tanis Vallely, Jean-Quentin Chatelain, Axel Bogousslavsky, André Julien, Jean-Paul Muel, Jean-François Perrier.

After 'The Return of Martin Guerre', Daniel Vigne here treats another unlikely romance, and comes somewhat unstuck in the process. The intension of his new film would seem to be an updating of screwball comedy in the 'Bringing Up Baby' mould, with Depardieu as a bashful archaeologist who loses his heart to Sigourney Weaver's machinating adwoman. After a tolerably diverting start, the picture succumbs to a severe lack of narrative nourishment; some chichi surface distraction only compounds the felony. **TP**

Empty Table

FERRIS BUELLER'S DAY OFF: See US section

FEVER PITCH: See US section

FIRE FESTIVAL
(Gunro Productions-Seibu Group-Cine Saison/Recorded Releasing)
dir Mitsuo Yanagimachi *exec pro* Kazuo Shimizu *scr* Kenji Nakagami *ph* Masaki Tamura, in Eastman Colour *ed* Sachiko Yamaji *art dir* Takeo Kimura *mus* Toru Takemitsu *r time* 118 mins *UK opening* Jan 3.
cast Kinya Kitaoji, Kiwako Taichi, Ryota Nakamoto, Noribei Miki, Rikiya Yasuoka, Seiji Kurasaki, Maido Kawakami, Junko Miyashita, Kin Sugai, Sachiko Matsushita, Masako Yagi, Aoi Nakajima, Kenzo Kaneko, Ban Kojika, Masato Ibu, Kosanji Yanagiya, Aiko Morishita.

Working back from the inspiration of a news story about a domestic mass murderer, Yanagimachi's anti-hero is a middle-aged lumberjack with a religiously macho relationship with the forests and the sea, while his ambiguous meditation on the value(s) of tradition involves a complex portrayal of a rural community painfully coming to terms with the loss of its isolation. Heavy, unleavened stuff; but its entry into British distribution says something about the growing confidence of the independent exhibition sector. **PT**

FIRE WITH FIRE: See US section

THE FLAMINGO KID
(ABC Motion Pics/Fox/Palace)
dir Garry Marshall *pro* Michael Phillips *scr* Neal Marshall, Garry Marshall *ph* James A Kontner, in DeLuxe colour *ed* Priscilla Nedd *pro des* Lawrence Miller *r time* 100 mins *US opening* prior to Jul 1985 *UK opening* Oct 18.
cast Matt Dillon, Richard Crenna, Hector Elizondo, Jessica Walter, Fisher Stevens, Brian McNamara, Carole R Davis, Martha Gehman, Molly McCarthy, Leon Robinson, Janet Jones, Bronson Pinchot.

Pleasingly old-fashioned comedy-drama of a teenager grappling with materialistic values during a summer job at a country club in the early sixties. The emphasis on recognisable value conflicts is refreshing, and the cast exudes feeling, especially Matt Dillon, Richard Crenna as a sharp operator and Hector Elizondo as Dillon's proud plumber father. **MM**

Opposite: The Emerald Forest *Above: Fire Festival*

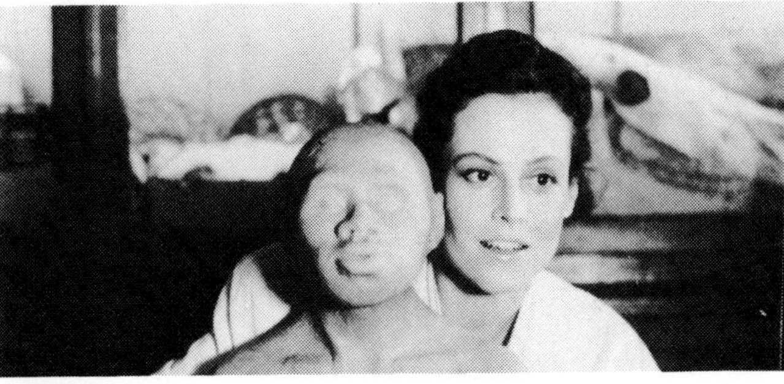

Une Femme ou Deux

The Flamingo Kid

Flesh and Blood

Fletch

FLESH AND BLOOD
(Orion/Rank)
dir Paul Verhoeven *pro* Gys Versluys *scr* Gerard Soeteman, Paul Verhoeven, based on a story by Gerard Soeteman *ph* Jan De Bont, Technovision, in colour *ed* Ine Schenkkan *art dir* Felix Murcia *mus* Basil Poledouris *r time* 127 mins *US opening* Aug 30 *UK opening* May 2. *cast* Rutger Hauer, Jennifer Jason Leigh, Tom Burlinson, Jack Thompson, Fernando Hillbeck, Susan Tyrrell, Ronald Lacey, Brion James, John Dennis Johnston, Simon Andrew, Bruno Kirby, Kitty Courbois, Marina Saura, Hans Veerman, Jake Wood, Hector Alterio, Blanca Marsillach, Nancy Cartwright.

Hobbesian medieval fable realised with unsentimental dash by Verhoeven, who combines visual talent with a penchant for eroticism and cruelty. Hauer makes a credible period anti-hero, a betrayed mercenary who kidnaps a betrothed heiress for ransom. She in turn deploys her sexual favours for survival. Against a backdrop of plague, superstitious piety and casual treachery, the movie builds suspensefully to a powerful climax. **MM**

FLETCH
(Universal)
dir Michael Ritchie *pro* Alan Greisman, Peter Douglas *scr* Andrew Bergman, based on the novel by Gregory McDonald *ph* Fred Schuler, in Technicolor *ed* Richard A Harris *pro des* Boris Leven *mus* Harold Faltermeyer *r time* 98 mins *US opening* prior to Jul 1985 *UK opening* Sep 27. *cast* Chevy Chase, Joe Don Baker, Dana Wheeler-Nicholson, Richard Libertini, Tim Matheson, M Emmet Walsh, George Wendt, Kenneth Mars, Geena Davis, Bill Henderson, William Traylor, George Wyner, Tony Longo, James Avery, Larry Flash Jenkins, Ralph Seymour, Reid Cruickshanks, Bruce French.

Chevy Chase's best solo vehicle to date features the comedian as a sarcastic investigative reporter tracking down corruption and drug rings while using an array of aliases, disguises and wisecracks. The character (and the movie itself) inconsistently adopts a superior, condescending tone to everyone else, and the humour is entirely grounded on the tonic effect of snide put-downs and put-ons, a dubious talent at which Chase excels. No one else in the film matters. Michael Ritchie directs efficiently without apparent personal engagement **MM**

FOOL FOR LOVE: See US section

FORBIDDEN
(Mark Forstater Prods-Clasart-Anthea-Stella/Enterprise)
dir Anthony Page *pro* Mark Forstater *exec pro* Gerland I Isenberg *scr* Leonard Gross, based on his novel 'The Last Jews in Berlin' *ph* Wolfgang Treu, in colour *ed* Thomas Schwalm *pro des* Tony Ludi *mus* Tangerine Dream *r time* 114 mins *UK opening* Feb 28. *cast* Jacqueline Bisset, Jürgen Prochnow, Irene Worth, Peter Vaughan, Robert Dietl, Avis Bunnage, Malcolm Kaye, Georg Tryphon, Annie Leon, Amanda Cannings, Osman Ragheb, Guntbert Warns, Herta Schwarz, Ulli Kinalzik, Gerhard Frey, Erich Will, Friedhelm Lehmann, Susanne Bonsewicz.

A dramatised account of real events during World War II when a German countess became active in the underground to save Jewish lives, and in addition kept her own Jewish lover hidden in her small Berlin flat for years on end: the subject compels admiration, but the treatment fails to do it justice. Decent and unsensational though the tone is, there is still a fancy-dress air about the proceedings; the protocols are those of soap opera, and a credit for 'teleplay' rather gives the game away. **TP**

FRENCH LESSON: See The Frog Prince

FRIDAY THE 13TH – A NEW BEGINNING
(Paramount)
dir Danny Steinmann *pro* Timothy Silver *exec pro* Frank Mancuso Jr *scr* Martin Kitrosser, David Cohen, Danny Steinmann *ph* Stephen L Posey, in Metrocolor *ed* Bruce Green *pro des* Robert Howland *mus* Harry Manfredini *r time* 92 mins *US opening* prior to Jul 1985 *UK opening* Sep 13. *cast* John Shepard, Melanie Kinnaman, Shavar Ross, Richard Young, Carol Lacatell, Vernon Washington, Dominic Brascia, Tiffany Helm, Debbisue Vorhees, John Robert Dixon, Ron Sloan.

Part V by any other name, this pathetically scrawled postscript to the original day-and-date exploiter series has masked bogeyman Jason stalking the nightmares of one of his traumatised near-victims, and a copy-cat killer stalking the woods around a halfway-house for disturbed adolescents. Long on closely censor-shaved goriness and lame-brained comic relief, short on anything approximating to a redeeming feature. **PT**

Forbidden

Friday the 13th – A New Beginning

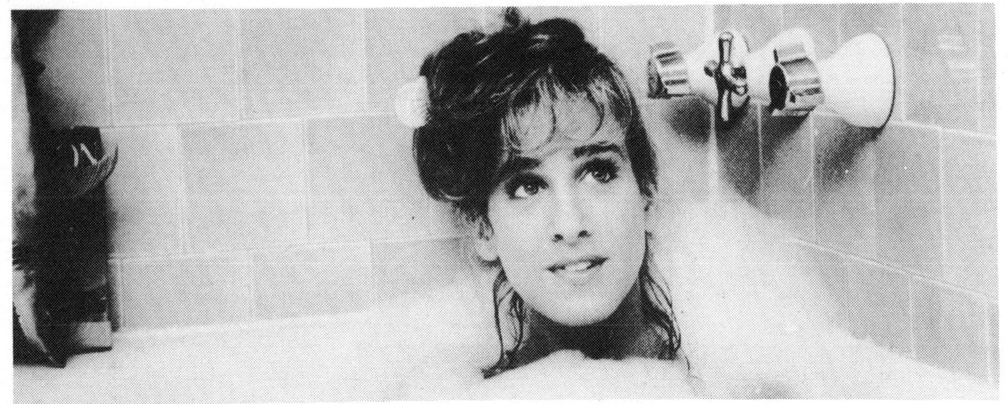

Girls Just Want to Have Fun

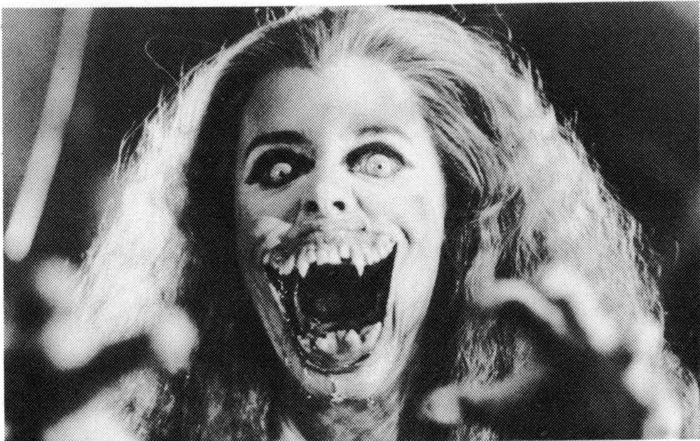

Fright Night

Girl in the Picture

The Frog Prince

FRIGHT NIGHT
(Vistar/Columbia)
dir-scr Tom Holland *pro* Herb Jaffe *ph* Jan Kiesser, in Metrocolor *ed* Kent Beyda *pro des* John De Cuir Jnr *mus* Brad Fiedel *r time* 106 mins *US opening* Aug 2 *UK opening* Apr 11.
cast Chris Sarandon, William Ragsdale, Amanda Bearse, Roddy McDowall, Stephen Geoffreys, Jonathan Stark, Dorothy Fielding, Art J Evans, Steward Stern, Heidi Sorenson, Irina Irvine, Robert Corff, Pamela Brown.

Mixing equal parts parody, homage and conviction, Holland's directing debut maintains the balancing act between originality and imitation that any contemporary vampire movie must sustain. Sarandon finds a fresh erotic component to the nocturnal swagger, lightly camping while making the menace credible. McDowall's vaudeville pathos as a washed-up horror star provides sweet counterpoint, and even the inevitable youth angle and special effects enhance the joy and horror. It's not easy to execute these genre pieces with honour anymore. **MM**

THE FROG PRINCE:
[US TITLE: FRENCH LESSON]

(Enigma-Goldcrest/Warner)
dir Brian Gilbert *pro* Iain Smith *exec pro* David Puttnam *scr* Posy Simmonds *ph* Clive Tickner, in Eastman Colour *ed* Jim Clark *pro des* Anton Furst *mus* Enya Ni Bhraonain *r time* 90 mins *UK opening* Sep 13 *US opening* Feb 21.
cast Jane Snowden, Alexandre Sterling, Jacqueline Doyen, Raoul Delfosse, Jeanne Herviale, Françoise Brion, Pierre Vernier, Diana Blackburn, Øystein Wiik, Fabienne Tricottet, Jean-Marc Barr, Arabella Weir, Lucy Durham-Matthews, Marc André Brunet, Brigitte Chamarande, Caterine Berraine.

First love, in Paris 1961, for a Surrey boarding-school girl, who is spending a year en famille in the French capital. The tone is affectionate and the manners and attitudes of the time are quite accurately reflected, but the narrative is stretched perilously thin. The script tends to rely for its humour on such assumptions as that a Frenchman's mention of Crawley, or anyone's mention of Chipping Sodbury, is enough to raise a laugh of its own accord and the overall effect, as with a good few other modestly budgeted British features, is of an only partly expanded TV production. **TP**

F/X: See US section

THE GIG: See US section

GINGER AND FRED: See US section

GIRL IN THE PICTURE
(Antonine/Rank)
dir-scr Cary Parker *pro* Paddy Higson *ph* Dick Pope, in Fuji-colour *ed* Bert Eels *pro des* Jemma Jackson *mus* Ron Geesin *r time* 91 mins *UK opening* Mar 28.
cast Joh Gordon-Sinclair, Irina Brook, David McKay, Gregor Fisher, Paul Young, Rikki Fulton, Caroline Guthrie, Joyce Deans, Katy Hale, Valerie Holloway, Wendy Holloway, Benny Young, Mairi Wallace, Helen Pike, Simone Lahbib, Walter Carr, William Elliott, Sarah Wishart.

Treading rather too evidently in the steps of Bill Forsyth, this comedy of love's young dream in Glasgow, centring round the 'Smile Please' photographic studio, wears its low-key romanticism on its sleeve to the extent of surrendering spontaneity. Attractively made and played, it passes ninety minutes disarmingly enough, but vanishes quickly from recollection. **TP**
(See Irina Brook, Faces of the Year.)

GIRLS JUST WANT TO HAVE FUN
(New World/Miracle)
dir Alan Metter *pro* Chuck Russell *exec pro* Stuart Cornfeld *scr* Amy Spies *ph* Thomas Ackerman, in CFI colour *ed* David Rawlins, Lorenzo DeStefano *pro des* Jeffrey Staggs *mus* Thomas Newman *r time* 89 mins *US opening* prior to Jul 1985 *UK opening* Aug 2.
cast Biff Yeager, Kristi Somers, Richard Blade, Jan Giatti, Shannen Doherty, Sarah Jessica Parker, Lee Montgomery, Helen Hunt, Morgan Woodward, Ed Lauter, Jonathan Silverman, Holly Gagnier, Margaret Howell.

Yet another variation on the bopsical theme. This time the protagonist is female, but her attempts to train for the big dance contest and a regular slot on the local TV show are thwarted in time-honoured style by the usual combination of strict parents and corrupt rich-kid rivals. The actual dance sequences seem to have been structured around the need to incorporate athletic stand-ins, resulting in routines which are full of flashy gymnastics, but the performances are zesty and the script is blessed with enough odd notions and snappy one-liners to make it all mildly diverting. **AB**

Goodbye New York

Gulag

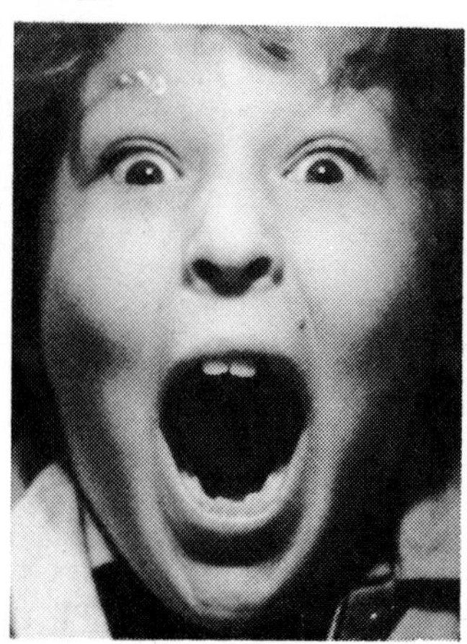

The Goonies

Hail Mary

GOODBYE NEW YORK
(Kolehill/Blue Dolphin)
dir-pro-scr Amos Kollek *ph* Amnon Salomon, in colour *ed* Alan Heim *mus* Michael Abene *r time* 90 mins *US opening* prior to Jul 1985
UK opening Jun 6.
cast Julie Hagerty, Amos Kollek, Shmuel Shiloh, Aviva Ger, David Topaz, Jennifer Babtist, Christopher Goutman, Hanan Goldblat, Mosku Alkalav, Yaacov Ben Sira, Chaim Banai, Irit Ben Zur, Chaim Girafi, Bella Ben David, Moshe Ishkassit, Lasha Rosenberg, Ali Reed, Danny Segev, Reuven Dayan.

A thoroughly unfunny romantic comedy built shamelessly around Hagerty's sub-Judy Holliday persona, recounting the disasters that befall her when, in flight from an unfaithful husband, she ends up in Israel without money or possessions. Seemingly intended as a moralistic satire extolling the virtues of kibbutz life, it trades in reactionary sexual stereotyping (the director-cum-romantic lead is only marginally less macho than the other men who pay suit to Hagerty), and glossy travelogue camerawork. Embarrassing. **GA**

THE GOONIES
(Amblin/Warner)
dir Richard Donner *pro* Richard Donner, Harvey Bernhard *exec pro* Steven Spielberg, Frank Marshall, Kathleen Kennedy *scr* Chris Columbus, based on a story by Steven Spielberg *ph* Nick McLean, in Panavision, Technicolor *ed* Michael Kahn *pro des* J Michael Riva *mus* Dave Grusin *r time* 111 mins *US opening* prior to Jul 1985
UK opening Nov 29.
cast Sean Astin, Josh Brolin, Jeff Cohen, Corey Feldman, Kerri Green, Martha Plimpton, Ke Huy Quan, John Matuszak, Robert Davi, Joe Pantoliano, Anne Ramsey.

Kiddie rendition of Tom Sawyer pluck and Indy Jones thrills, as a motley group of youngsters foils comic criminals and seeks out pirate treasure in an underground world bedecked with natural disasters and Rube Goldberg booby traps. The sentimentality and manipulation are laid on thickly in the patented Spielberg manner, but the film is so unabashedly aimed at its youthful audience that it would be churlish to expect any adult pleasures or restraint. Director Richard Donner turns in a splendid job, keeping the complicated action coherent and overlapping the babbling dialogue effectively. **MM**

THE GREAT WALL IS A GREAT WALL: See US section

GRUNT! THE WRESTLING MOVIE: See US section

GULAG
(Lorimar-HBO Premiere-MFI/Miracle)
dir Roger Young *pro* Andrew Adelson *exec pro* James Retter, Dan Gordon *scr* Dan Gordon, based on a story by Dan Gordon, Raphael Shauli, Yehoshua Ben-Porat *ph* Kelvin Pike, in colour *ed* John Jympson *pro des* Keith Wilson *mus* Elmer Bernstein *r time* 119 mins *UK opening* Oct 11.
cast David Keith, Malcolm McDowall, David Suchet, Warren Clarke, John McEnery, Nancy Paul, Brian Pettifer, George Pravda, Shane Rimmer, Bruce Boa, Eugene Lipinski, Ray Jewers, Bogdan Kominowski, Barrie Houghton, Alexei Jawdokimov, Ivan Lee, Forbes Collins, Stuart Milligan, Bibbs Ekkel, Dallas Adams.

Cobbled together with telemovie blandness as a crude, Red-baiting amalgam of 'Ivan Denisovich', 'Midnight Express' and the latest in missing-in-action mythologies, this abysmal Cold War II farrago dumps naively idealistic US athlete Keith into a Siberian prison-camp after a routine KGB frame-up, and sees how he runs. Resident cynic McDowall replays his 'Figures in a Landscape' escape, and sundry sadistic tormentors, sacrificial dissidents and State Dept worriers rhubarb away in equally familiar incarnations. Helping yoke together an Israeli script source, an American production team and British and Norwegian location shooting is a budgetary back-up from the MFI Furniture Group PLC, which says everything about discount merchandising. **PT**

HAIL MARY
(Sara Films-Pegase Films-H G Films/New Yorkers-Gaumont/Other Cinema)
dir-scr Jean-Luc Godard *pro* Jean-Bernard Menoud, Jacques Firmann, in colour *mus* Bach, Dvorak, John Coltrane *r time* 107 mins *US opening* Oct 11
UK opening Oct 11.
cast Myriem Roussel, Thierry Rode, Philippe Lacoste, Manon Andersen, Juliette Binoche, Malachi Jara Kohan, Dick, Johann Leysen, Ann Gauthier.

Not one of Godard's most immaculate conceptions – though far from the blasphemous vision that a few myopics claim to have witnessed – his quirky update on the Biblical birth story represents (after 'Passion' and 'Prénom Carmen') another episode in his series of provocative inspections of Romantic icons. The extremely intimate inspection of his contemporary Swiss Virgin does occasionally bring out the dirty-mac aesthete in him, but the wordplay jester and celluloid sensualist is here, too. **PT**

HAMBURGER ... THE MOTION PICTURE See US section

HANNAH AND HER SISTERS: See US section

HE DIED WITH HIS EYES OPEN
(Swaine Prods-TFI Films/Cannon)
dir Jacques Deray *pro* Norbert Saada *scr* Jacques Deray, Michel Audiard, based on the novel by Derek Raymond (Robin Cook) *ph* Jean Penzer, in Eastman Colour *ed* Henri Lanoë, Sylvia Pontoizeau *art dir* François De Lamothe

mus Claude Bolling *r time* 106 mins
UK opening May 16.
cast Michel Serrault, Charlotte Rampling, Xavier Deluc, Elizabeth Depardieu, Jean Leuvrais, Jean-Paul Roussillon, Maurice Barrier, Jean-Pierre Darroussin, Julie Jezequel, Albert Delpy, Riton Liebman, Gérard Darmon, Philippe Auge, Jean-Pierre Bacri.

After a cracklingly atmospheric start, with a fur-coated figure decanting a corpse from the boot of her car, this tale of a police detective increasingly mixed up with a duplicitous shady lady becomes rather protracted and mechanical. The film remains enjoyable after its fashion, however, thanks to some sharp dialogue, a nice jazz-tinged score, and especially Michel Serrault's brilliantly sardonic and nuanced performance as the individualistic cop. **TP**

He Died With His Eyes Open

HEAD OFFICE: See US section

HEARTBREAKERS
(Jethro Films/Orion/Rank)
dir-scr Bobby Roth *pro* Bob Weis, Bobby Roth *exec pro* Lee Muhl, Harry Cooper, Joseph Franck *ph* Michael Ballhaus, in DeLuxe colour *ed* John Carnochan *mus* Tangerine Dream *r time* 98 mins
US opening prior to Jul 1985
UK opening Apr 11.
cast Peter Coyote, Nick Mancuso, Carole Laure, Max Gail, James Laurenson, Carol Wayne, Jamie Rose, Kathryn Harrold, George Morfogen, Jerry Hardin.

Contemporary study of male bonding actually achieves original insights with good characterisations and provocative relationships. Exceptionally strong and individualised work by Peter Coyote and Nick Mancuso, a skilful evocation of the Los Angeles art scene and a fresh awareness of how sex is lived today create a bracing work that augurs much from writer-director Roth. **MM**

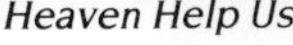

Heaven Help Us

Heartbreakers

HEAVEN HELP US
[UK TITLE: CATHOLIC BOYS]
(HBO Pictures/Tri-Star/Thorn EMI)
dir Michael Dinner *pro* Dan Wigutow, Mark Carliner *scr* Charles Purpura *ph* Miroslav Ondricek, in Technicolor *ed* Stephen A Rotter *pro des* Michael Molly *mus* James Horner *r time* 104 mins
US opening prior to Jul 1985
UK opening Oct 25.
cast Donald Sutherland, John Heard, Andrew McCarthy, Mary Stuart Masterson, Kevin Dillon, Malcolm Danare, Jennie Dundas, Kate Reid, Wallace Shawn, Jay Patterson, George Anders, Dana Barron, John Bentley, Imogene Bliss, Philip Bosco, Donahl Breitman, Nolan Carley.

Creditable debut film for Michael Dinner, a coming-of-age comedy-drama set in a Catholic boys' school in the early sixties. The able script creates sufficient fresh characters and situations to overcome the familiarity of the subject, and the youthful players make uniformly believable and individualised impressions. **MM**

THE HEAVENLY KID: See US section

THE HITCHER
(HBO/Tri-Star/Columbia)
dir Robert Harmon *pro* David Bombyk, Kip Ohman *exec pro* Edward S Feldman, Charles R Meeker *scr* Eric Red *ph* John Seale, in Panavision, Metrocolor *ed* Frank J Urioste *pro des* Dennis Gassner *mus* Mark Isham *r time* 97 mins
US opening Jan 17 *UK opening* May 16.
cast Rutger Hauer, C Thomas Howell, Jennifer Jason Leigh, Jeffrey DeMunn, John Jackson, Billy Greenbush, Jack Thibeau, Armin Shimerman, Eugene Davis, Jon Van Ness, Henry Darrow, Tony Epper, Tom Spratley, Colin Campbell.

'Halloween' meets the road movie in the Texas-set tale of a maniac killer determined to keep death on the roads as gorily as possible and whilst he's about it to push a fresh-faced youth into an ever tighter corner of apparent culpability. The narrative is on the artificial side, with the logic of nightmare sometimes conveniently used to paper over a degree of cheating in the plot. But individual sequences are strikingly staged, and John Seale's cinematography is frequently superb. **TP**

The Hitcher

THE HOLCROFT COVENANT
(Thorn EMI/Universal)
dir John Frankenheimer *pro* Edie Landau, Ely Landau *exec pro* Mort Abrahams *scr* George Axelrod, Edward Anhalt, John Hopkins, based on the novel by Robert Ludlum *ph* Gerry Fisher, in Technicolor *ed* Ralph Sheldon *pro des* Peter Mullins *mus* Stanislas *r time* 112 mins *US opening* Oct 18 *UK opening* Sep 20.
cast Michael Caine, Anthony Andrews, Victoria Tennant, Lilli Palmer, Mario Adorf, Michael Lonsdale, Bernard Hepton, Richard Munch, Carl Rigg, André Penvern, Andrew Bradford, Shane Rimmer, Alexander Kerst, Michael Wolf, Hugo Bower, Michael Balfour.

Two decades ago, with movies like 'Seven Days in May' Frankenheimer was the undisputed master of the paranoia thriller. The sad extent of his subsequent decline is made only too evident by his inability to render this hotch-potch of a plot about a neo-Nazi conspiracy into even watchable hokum. Despite George Axelrod's participation in the script, it is the supposedly straight-faced dialogue which provides laughter, with the later stages of the picture regressing from mere unwitting parody to scenes worthy of a Whitehall farce. **TP** *(See Turkeys of the Year.)*

HOME OF THE BRAVE: See US section

HOUSE
(New World/Entertainment)
dir Steve Miner *pro* Sean S Cunningham *scr* Ethan Wiley, from a story by Fred Dekker *ph* Mac Ahlberg, in colour *ed* Michael N Knue *pro des* Gregg Fonseca *mus* Harry Manfredini *r time* 93 mins *US opening* Feb 28 *UK opening* Jun 20.
cast William Katt, George Wendt, Richard Moll, Kay Lenz, Mary Stavin, Michael Ensign, Susan French, Alan Autry, Steven Williams, Jim Calvert, Mindy Sterling, Jayson Kane, Billy Beck, Erik Silver, Mark Silver, Bill McLean, Steve Susskind, John Young, Dwier Brown, Joey Green.

Fashioned by alumni of the 'Friday the 13th' school of grisly murder, 'House' is the harbinger of a new trend in horror, a film which borrows its conventions from the genre but which adds dollops of humour aimed at a post-'Ghostbuster' audience who prefer their fear laced with funnies. This is the one about the Old Dark House, exercising its malevolent influence over a horror writer who also happens to be a Vietnam veteran with plenty of war trauma to exorcise. Once this premise is established, however, there is little in the way of plot apart from disconnected episodes of spooky sitcom farce: the occupier is menaced by the animated contents of a toolshed and his dead buddy, plus stray bits of Vietnamese vegetation. **AB**

The Holcroft Covenant

Impulse

House

IMPULSE
(ABC Motion Pictures/Fox/Odyssey)
dir Graham Baker *pro* Tim Zinnemann *scr* Bart Davis, Don Carlos Dunaway *ph* Thomas Del Ruth, in DeLuxe colour *ed* David Holder *pro des* Jack T Collis *mus* Paul Chihara *r time* 91 mins *US opening* prior to Jul 1985 *UK opening* Mar 14.
cast Tim Matheson, Meg Tilly, Hume Cronyn, John Karlen, Bill Paxton, Amy Stryker, Claude Earl Jones, Robert Wightman, Lorinne Vozoff, Peter Jason, Abigail Booraem, Mary Celio, Jack T Collis, Christian Crane, Chuck Dorsett, Christian Giannini, Anne Haney, Bernard Kuby, Darren Muir, Svi Peters, Dawn Eisler Smith.

Eco-horror about a smalltown population driven to oddball, sometimes murderous, behaviour by something nasty in the milk supply. There are some amusing early scenes, mostly involving senior citizens behaving like delinquents, but the film is ultimately too low-key for its own good. The depiction of a community riven by paranoia and chemical threat was achieved far more effectively by Romero in 'The Crazies'. **AB**

INSIGNIFICANCE
(Zenith-Recorded Picture Company/ Island/Palace)
dir Nicolas Roeg *pro* Jeremy Thomas *exec pro* Alexander Stuart *scr* Terry Johnson, based on his play *ph* Peter Hannan, in colour *ed* Tony Lawson *pro des* David Brockhurst *mus* Stanley Myers, Hans Zimmer *r time* 109 mins *US opening* Aug 2 *UK opening* Aug 9. *cast* Michael Emil, Theresa Russell, Tony Curtis, Gary Busey, Will Sampson, Patrick Kilpatrick, Jan O'Connell, George Holmes, Richard Davidson, Mitchell Greenberg, Raynor Scheine, Jude Ciceolella, Lou Hirsch, Ray Charleson, Joel Cutrara, Raymond Barry, John Stamford, Desiree Erasmus.

Exploding Terry Johnson's stage play into myriad brilliant shards of 'what if?' wit, Roeg diverts nuclear-age icons Monroe, Einstein, McCarthy and DiMaggio from their respective stellar orbits and has them collide one out-of-time New York night in 1954. Punning provocatively on big-bang theories of the Beginning and the End and the possibilities of parallel universes, 'Insignificance' effectively sifts the fall-out debris of Hiroshima to explore the relatives of fact and fantasy. A dazzlingly cinematic juggling act with the sickest of cosmic jokes. **PT**

INVADERS FROM MARS: See US section

INVASION U.S.A.
(Cannon)
dir Joseph Zito *pro* Menahem Golan, Yoram Globus *scr* James Bruner, Chuck Norris, *ph* Joao Fernandes, in TVC colour *ed* Daniel Loewenthal, Scott Vickrey *pro des* Ladislav Wilheim *mus* Jay Chattaway *r time* 107 mins *US opening* Sep 27 *UK opening* Nov 15. *cast* Chuck Norris, Richard Lynch, Melissa Prophet, Alexander Zale, Alex Colon, Eddie Jones, John DeVries, James O'Sullivan, Billy Drago, Jaime Sanchez, Dehl Berti, Stephen Markle, Shane McCamey, Martin Shakar, James Pax, Nick Ramus, Bernie McInerney, Lorraine Morin, Marilyn Romero, Anthony Marciona.

Another red invasion film with Chuck Norris, whose expressive range increasingly resembles that of a kitchen table, as a retired American intelligence agent who holds back the beginnings of a Commie tide in Florida. **AC**

IRON EAGLE: See US section

Jagged Edge

Insignificance

J

JAGGED EDGE 
(Columbia)
dir Richard Marquand *pro* Martin Ransohoff *scr* Joe Eszterhas *ph* Matthew F Leonetti, in Metrocolor *ed* Sean Barton, Conrad Buff *pro des* Gene Callahan *mus* John Barry *r time* 109 mins *US opening* Oct 4 *UK opening* Mar 14. *cast* Jeff Bridges, Glenn Close, Maria Mayenzet, Peter Coyote, Dave Austin, Richard Partlow, Lance Henriksen, William Allen Young, Ben Hammer, James Karen, Sanford Jensen, Woody Eney, Al Ruscio, Sharon Hanian, Sarah Cunningham, Ann Walker, James Winker, Bruce French, Brandon Call.

An old-fashioned thriller in the Hitchcock tradition, hingeing on the simple question of 'did he or didn't he?' as Close's divorced, cautious lawyer agrees to defend Bridges, on trial for the murder of his wife. What lifts this above the level of conventional courtroom drama is its emphasis on the emotional importance of trust and betrayal, with Close fighting off doubts about her client's innocence at the same time as falling in love with him. Solid intelligent entertainment, superbly performed and scripted, with Marquand tightening the screws until the very last frame. **GA** *(See Films of the Year.)*

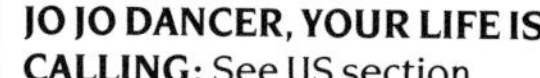

JAKE SPEED: See US section

JAMES JOYCE'S WOMEN: See US section

THE JEWEL OF THE NILE
(Stone/Fox)
dir Lewis Teague *pro* Michael Douglas *scr* Mark Rosenthal, Lawrence Konner, based on characters created by Diane Thomas *ph* Jan De Bont, in Technicolor *ed* Michael Ellis, Peter Boita *pro des* Richard Dawking, Terry Knight *mus* Jack Nitzsche and others *r time* 106 mins *US opening* Dec 13 *UK opening* May 2.
cast Michael Douglas, Kathleen Turner, Danny DeVito, Spiros Focas, Ayner Eisenberg, Paul David Magid, Howard Jay Patterson, Randall Edwin Nelson, Samuel Ross Williams, Timothy Daniel Furst, Hamid Fillali, Holland Taylor.

'Romancing the Stone' rides again, less effectively than the first time around and even more obviously an attempt to out-adventure Indiana Jones without spending too much money. Michael Douglas underplays the humour as he grits his teeth, Danny DeVito displays his usual lamentable lack of comic timing, and Kathleen Turner once again shows herself worthier of better things. **JW**

JO JO DANCER, YOUR LIFE IS CALLING: See US section

JOSHUA THEN AND NOW: See US section

THE JOURNEY OF NATTY GUNN
(Silver Screen Partners II/Buena Vista/Disney)
dir Jeremy Kagan *pro* Mike Lobell *scr* Jeanne Rosenberg *ph* Dick Bush, in Technicolor *ed* David Holden, Steven Rosenblum *pro des* Paul Sylbert *mus* James Horner *r time* 101 mins *US opening* Sep 27 *UK opening* Feb 7.
cast Meredith Salenger, John Cusack, Ray Wise, Lainie Kazan, Scatman Crothers, Barry Miller, Verna Bloom, Bruce M Fischer, John Finnegan, Jack Radar, Matthew Faison, Jordan Pratt, Zachary Ansley, Campbell Lane, Max Trumpower, Doug MacLeod, Peter Anderson, Corliss M Smith Jr.

A delightful little film which manages to avoid most of the pitfalls of winsome sentimentality while juggling with the elements of a typically Disney plot – a young girl, trekking across Depression America to join her beloved father, befriends a wild wolf on the way. The picaresque story, while romantically escapist, deals quite admirably with the hardships of hobo life. **AB**

The Jewel of the Nile

The Journey of Natty Gun

THE KARATE KID PART II: See US section

KEY EXCHANGE: See US section

KILLER PARTY: See US section

KING DAVID
(Paramount)
dir Bruce Beresford *pro* Martin Elfand *scr* Andrew Birkin, James Costigan, based on a story by James Costigan *ph* Donald McAlpine, in Panavision, Technicolor *ed* William Anderson *pro des* Ken Adam *mus* Carl Davis *r time* 114 mins *US opening* prior to Jul 1985 *UK opening* Jun 20.
cast Richard Gere, Edward Woodward, Alice Krige, Denis Quilley, Niall Buggy, Cherie Lunghi, Hurd Hatfield, Jack Klaff, John Castle, Tim Woodward, David De Keyser, Ian Sears, Simon Dutton, Jean-Marc Barr, Arthur Whybrow, Christopher Malcolm, Valentine Pelka, Ned Vukovic, Michael Mueller.

Not a great film by any means, but far from being the disaster which everyone (including, in interviews, Beresford himself) claims it to be. The main problem is that it tries to pack the narrative content of a sprawling mini-series into the running time of an average-length feature, which results in a scramble of information that's peripheral to the action. The other one is that an actor of Richard Gere's mannered 'contemporary' qualities is completely out of sync with the solid conviction of the supporting cast of British character actors, nowhere more so than in his Dervish dance which had American audiences in fits of derisive laughter. That apart, it's a rare attempt at an intelligent, literate entertainment that's relatively (though not completely) bereft of Bible-speak. **AC**

KING SOLOMON'S MINES
(Cannon)
dir J Lee Thompson *pro* Menahem Golan, Yoram Globus *scr* Gene Quintano, James R Silke, based on the novel by H Rider Haggard *ph* Alex Phillips, in colour *ed* John Shirley *pro des* Luciano Spadoni *mus* Jerry Goldsmith *r time* 100 mins *US opening* Nov 22 *UK opening* Dec 20.
cast Richard Chamberlain, Sharon Stone, Herbert Lom, Bernard Archard, John Rhys-Davies, Ken Gampu, June Buthelezi, Sam Williams, Shai K Ophir, Fidelis Che A, Mick Lesley, Vincent Van Der Byl, Bob Greer, Oliver Tengende, Neville Thomas, Bishop McThuzen, Isiah Murert, Anna Ditano, Andrew Whaley.

A world away from Rider Haggard, but a close neighbour of Indiana Jones, with the usual emphasis on action setpieces, cartoon villains and a bludgeoningly insistent score. **AC**

Above: King Solomon's Mines   Opposite: King David

KISS OF THE SPIDER WOMAN
(HB Films/Island/Palace)
dir Hector Babenco *pro* David Weisman *exec pro* Francisco Ramalho Jr *scr* Leonard Schrader, based on the novel by Manuel Puig *ph* Rodolfo Sanchez, in colour *ed* Mauro Alice *art dir* Clovis Bueno *mus* John Neschling *r time* 121 mins *US opening* Jul 26 *UK opening* Jan 16.
cast William Hurt, Raul Julia, Sonia Braga, José Lewgoy, Milton Goncalves, Miriam Pires, Nuno Leal Maia, Fernando Torres, Patricio Bisso, Herson Captri, Denise Dummont, Nildo Parente, Antonio Petrin, Wilson Grey, Miguel Falabella, Luis Serra, Ana Maria Braga, Joe Kantor.

Perhaps over-laurelled by the liberal establishment, Babenco's seductive diminution of Manuel Puig's novel is still quite an achievement. The man-to-man confrontations in a claustrophobic South American cell between political prisoner Julia and gay provocateur Hurt represents a neat enough critique of machismo. But in the larger shared space occupied by the pair's common commitment to celluloid-derived dreams (verbalised by Hurt, visualised by Julia) there are a few suspect, overly glib correspondences forged between posturing and politics, and almost a suggestion that even acts of revolution and resistance can only be played out as Hollywood melodrama, at one remove. Maybe unsurprisingly, there is eventually a stronger link on view here with Schrader's 'Mishima' than with Babenco's own previous foray into the exotic, 'Pixote'. **PT**
(See Films of the Year.)

KNIGHTS OF THE CITY: See US section

KRUSH GROOVE: See US section

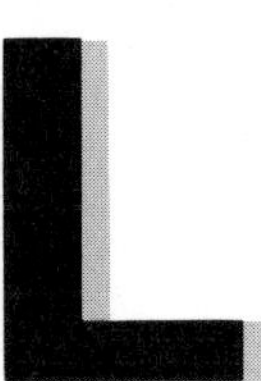

LABYRINTH: See US section

THE LADIES CLUB: See US section

LADY JANE
(Paramount)
dir Trevor Nunn *pro* Peter Snell *scr* David Edgar, based on a story by Chris Bryant *ph* Douglas Slocombe, in Technicolor *ed* Anne V Coates *pro des* Allan Cameron *mus* Stephen Oliver *r time* 142 mins *US opening* Feb 7 *UK opening* May 29.
cast Helena Bonham Carter, Cary Elwes, John Wood, Michael Hordern, Jill Bennett, Jane Lapotaire, Sara Kestelman, Patrick Stewart, Warren Saire, Joss Ackland, Ian Hogg, Lee Montague, Richard Vernon, David Waller, Richard Johnson, Pip Torrens, Matthew Guinness, Guy Henry.

Starchy, static, stately account of power and intrigue among the ruling classes in sixteenth-century England. Well acted and precisly designed and directed, it never really ignites and suggests more a short television series than a long film. **AC**

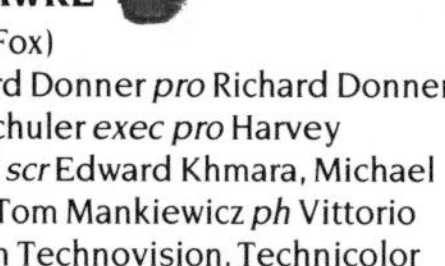

LADYHAWKE
(Warner/Fox)
dir Richard Donner *pro* Richard Donner, Lauren Schuler *exec pro* Harvey Bernhard *scr* Edward Khmara, Michael Thomas, Tom Mankiewicz *ph* Vittorio Storaro, in Technovision, Technicolor *ed* Stuart Baird *pro des* Wolf Kroeger *mus* Andrew Powell *r time* 124 mins *US opening* prior to Jul 1985 *UK opening* Aug 9.
cast Matthew Broderick, Rutger Hauer, Michelle Pfeiffer, Leo McKern, John Wood, Ken Hutchinson, Alfred Molina, Giancarlo Prete, Loris Loddi, Alessandro Serra.

Unseen by the FYB team, but from all accounts a handsomely mounted, rather unconvincing would-be medieval epic. The presence of the very contemporary-looking Matthew Broderick and Michelle Pfeiffer is a further reminder that Hollywood no longer seems to have any young actors who don't look silly in period costume. **AC**

LAMB
(Flickers Prod-Limehouse Pictures/Cannon)
dir Colin Gregg *pro* Neil Zeiger *exec pro* Al Burgess *scr* Bernard MacLaverty, based on his own novel *ph* Mike Garfath, in Eastman Colour *ed* Peter Delfgou *pro des* Austen Spriggs *mus* Van Morrison *r time* 110 mins *UK opening* Jun 6.
cast Liam Neeson, Harry Towb, Hugh O'Conor, Frances Tomelty, Ian Bannen, Ronan Wilmot, Denis Carey, Eileen Kennally, David Gorry, Andrew Pickering, Stuart O'Connor, Ian McElhinney, Bernadette McKenna, Jessica Saunders, Robert Hamilton, Roger Booth, Marjie Lawrence, Nicola Wright.

A young Christian Brother, unhappily working in a grim remand home on the Antrim coast, escapes to Dublin, then to London, with one of the most put-upon of his charges, a ten-year-old epileptic. The tone of 'Lamb' is decent and humane, but somehow the film is thrown back on to a literal, anecdotal level, and on that level the contrivance of the narrative is unduly exposed; nor is the melodramatically tragic conclusion made to seem an inevitable outcome. There are, though, two sterling character performances, by Ian Bannen as the jovially brutal headmaster of the remand home, and Dudley Foster as the pedantic drunkard who ambiguously invites the runaways to share his squat. **TP**

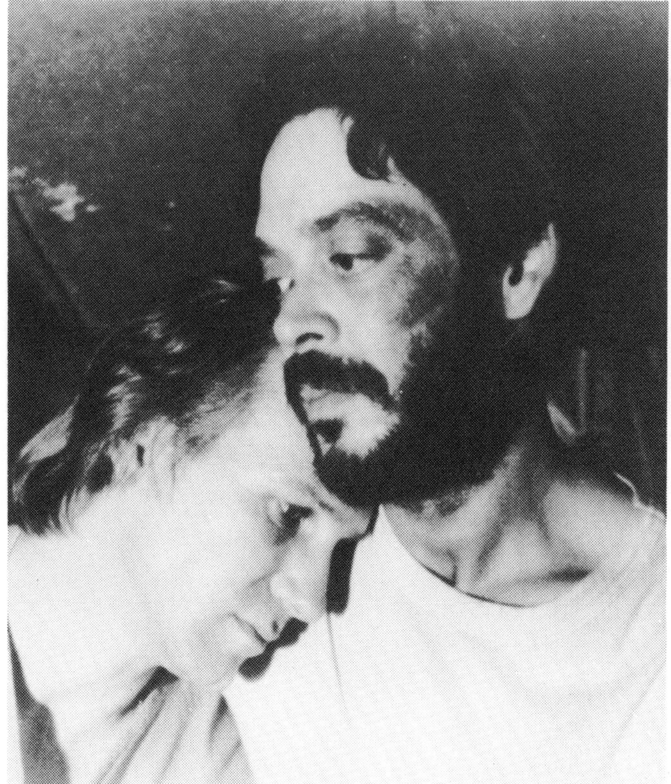

Opposite: Ladyhawke Above: Kiss of the Spider Woman

Lady Jane

Lamb

The Last Dragon

THE LAST DRAGON
(Motown Prods/Tri-Star/Columbia)
dir Michael Schultz *pro* Rupert Hitzig *exec pro* Berry Gordy *scr* Louis Venosta *ph* James A Contner, in Technicolor *ed* Christopher Holmes *pro des* Peter Larkin *art dir* William Barclay *mus* Misha Segal *r time* 109 mins *US opening* prior to Jul 1985 *UK opening* Jul 12.
cast Taimak, Vanity, Chris Murney, Julius J Carry III. Faith Prince, Leo O'Brien, Mike Starr, Jim Moody, Glen Eaton, Ernie Reyes Jnr, Roger Campbell, Esher Marrow, Keshia Knight, Jamal Mason, B J Barie, André Brown, David Claudio, Kirk Taylor, Henry Yuk, Michael G Chin.

A rather disarming dollop of teen musical miscegenation which combines elements from the recent wave of hip-hop movies (young black hero and a latterday Motown disco beat) with kung-fu rivalries and a touch of cod zen. The film's tiresome reliance on pop promo conventions, and an irrelevant rock video incorporated wholesale into the plot, are thankfully offset by the hero's charmingly naive aspirations to become the Bruce Lee of the Big Apple and by his equally charming insistence upon eating popcorn with chopsticks. **AB**

LAST NIGHT AT THE ALAMO
(Southwest Alternate Media Project-National Endowment for the Arts-Southwest Independent Production Fund/Cinecom/ICA)
dir Eagle Pennell *pro* Kim Henkel, Eagle Pennell *exec pro* Ed Hugetz *scr* Kim Henkel *ph* Brian Haberman, Eric A Edwards *ed* Eagle Pennell, Kim Henkel, Gary Seal *art dir* Fletcher Mackey *mus* Chuck Pinell, Wayne Bell, Richard Mercado *r time* 80 mins *US opening* prior to Jul 1985 *UK opening* Apr 4.
cast Sonny Carl Davis, Louis Perryman, Steven Mattilla, Tina-Bess Hubbard, Amanda Lamar, Peggy Pinnell, Doris Hargrave, J Michael Hammond, Henry Wideman, George Pheneger, Earnest Huerta Jr, David Schied, John Heaner, Sarah Louise Hudgins, Kim Henkel, Jeanette Wiggins, Judie Stephen, Hi Bice, Oscar James, Henry Kana, Pam Feight, Eagle Pennell, Eric A Edwards, Arnold Cavasos.

Legend

The Legend of Billie Jean

A Letter to Brezhnev

Another Texan script from 'Chainsaw Massacre' begetter Henkel, but the constant loud buzz this time is of emptily bragging male gab, as a bar-load of insecurely macho good ol' boys mourn the imminent demolition of their womb-like watering hole (The Alamo) and pin vain hopes of reprieve on the self-styled Cowboy in their midst. Perhaps over-ambitious in orchestrating its downbeat post-Western parody as a clash between motormouth crudity and devalued mythical currency, Pennell's low-budget effort nonetheless isn't wholly overwhelmed by recent forays into similar territory by a master like Altman. **PT**

LATINO See US section

LEGAL EAGLES: See US section

LEGEND
(Fox/Universal)
dir Ridley Scott *pro* Arnon Milchan *scr* William Hjortsberg *ph* Alex Thomson, in Scope, Fujicolor *ed* Terry Rawlings, Pam Bower *pro des* Assheton Gorton *mus* Jerry Goldsmith *r time* 94 mins *US opening* Apr 18 *UK opening* Dec 6.
cast Tom Cruise, Mia Sara, Tim Curry, David Bennent, Alice Playten, Billy Barty, Cork Hubbert, Peter O'Farrell, Kiran Shah, Annabelle Lanyon, Robert Picardo, Tina Martin, Ian Longmuir.

No-expense-spared expedition into sub-sub-Tolkien terrain, set in a studio forest that seems more suited to a toilet-paper commercial than a fairy story. A few striking effects of lighting and design offer no contest to a scenario weighed down by the worst sort of faux-naif whimsy, as well as being remarkably hard to follow. Only the unexpectedly brief running time affords any consolation. **TP**
(See Turkeys of the Year.)

THE LEGEND OF BILLIE JEAN
(Tri-Star/Columbia)
dir Matthew Robbins *pro* Rob Cohen *exec pro* Jon Peters, Peter Guber *scr* Mark Rosenthal, Lawrence Konner *ph* Jeffry L Kimball, in Metrocolor *ed* Cynthia Scheider *pro des* Ted Haworth *mus* Craig Safan *r time* 95 mins *US opening* Jul 19 *UK opening* May 2.
cast Helen Slater, Keith Gordon, Christian Slater, Richard Bradford, Peter Coyote, Martha Gehman, Yeardley Smith, Dean Stockwell, Barry Tubb, Mona Fultz, John M Jackson, Rodney Rincon, Caroline Williams, Rudy Young, Bobby Fite, Kim Valentine, Robby Jones.

A very mild-mannered account of teen rebellion down in the boondocks. Billie Jean, her brother and a couple of squeaky-voiced pals take off into the yonder after a shooting incident. Our heroine crops off her long blonde tresses after a dose of Preminger's 'Saint Joan' on TV, and inspires a whole generation of Texas teenyboppers to emulate her non-confrontational policies in the teeth of continuing adult antagonism. James Dean would have wept. **AB**

A LETTER TO BREZHNEV
(Yeardream-Film Four International/Palace/Circle Releasing)
dir Chris Bernard *pro* Janet Goddard *scr* Frank Clarke *ph* Bruce McGowan, in colour *ed* Lesley Walker *pro des* Lez Brotherston, Nick Englefield, Jonathan Swain *mus* Alan Gill *r time* 95 mins *UK opening* Nov 8 *US opening* Feb 14.
cast Alfred Molina, Peter Firth, Margi Clarke, Tracy Lea, Alexandra Pigg, Susan Dempsey, Ted Wood, Carl Chase, Robbie Dee, Sharon Power, Syd Newman, Eddie Ros, Mandy Walsh, Angela Clarke, Joey Kaye, Frank Clarke, Paul Beringer, Ken Campbell, Neil Cunningham, John Carr.

Two Liverpool girls, one unemployed and the other a factory worker, meet a couple of Russian sailors on shore leave. One of the girls falls in love and determines, despite the disapproval of family and officialdom, to follow the object of her passions back to the USSR. Although saddled with some cringe-making romantic dialogue, 'A Letter to Brezhnev' disarms criticism by the sheer spunk of its performers – Alexandra Pigg and Margi Clarke give an unforgettable portrait of girls out on the town, foulmouthed and witty and having a whale of a time. Shoestring film-making at its best, and an evocation of Liverpool in the midst of the eighties depression that says more about Thatcher's Britain than any amount of dour documentaries. **AB**
(See Alexandra Pigg/Margi Clarke, Faces of the Year.)

Lifeforce

The Lightship

The Little Drummer Girl

Lost in America

LIFEFORCE

(Tri-Star/Cannon)
dir Tobe Hooper *pro* Menahem Golan, Yoram Globus *scr* Dan O'Bannon, Don Jakoby, based on the novel 'The Space Vampires' by Colin Wilson *ph* Alan Hume, in colour *ed* John Grover *pro des* John Graysmark *mus* Henry Mancini *r time* 101 mins *US opening* prior to Jul 1985 *UK opening* Oct 4.
cast Steve Railsback, Peter Firth, Frank Finlay, Mathilda May, Patrick Stewart, Michael Gothard, Nicholas Ball, Aubrey Morris, Nancy Paul, John Hallam.

A paradigm of dumb, opportunistic producing with absolutely no sense of the marketplace: one can only hope that Cannon is fibbing about the megabudget on this tacky sci-fi vampire/zombie movie since it looks as cheapjack as its omnibus exploitation concept. Stupefyingly bad dialogue provides the only amusement, despite indications that Tobe Hooper ('Poltergeist', 'The Texas Chainsaw Massacre') wanted to connect with something deeper in the material. This one plays like the screenwriters pillaged the novel's notions, and tossed off a single-draft continuity for quick bucks, and the producers couldn't tell the difference. **MM**
(See Turkeys of the Year.)

THE LIGHTSHIP

(CBS/Warner/Rank)
dir Jerzy Skolimowski *pro* Moritz Borman, Bill Benenson *exec pro* Rainer Soehnlein *scr* William Mai, David Taylor, based on the novel 'Das Feuerschiff' by Siegfried Lenz *ph* Charly Steinberger, in colour *ed* Barry Vince, Scott Hancock *art dir* Holger Gross *mus* Stanley Myers *r time* 88 mins *US opening* Sep 6 *UK opening* May 2.
cast Robert Duvall, Klaus Maria Brandauer, Tom Bower, Robert Costanzo, Badja Djola, William Forsythe, Arliss Howard, Michael Lyndon, Tim Phillips.

Hardly a bright beacon in Skolimowski's increasingly erratic career, this little morality tale about fathers, sons and doubles (and chains and freedom) is unfortunately as tied to the predictable as is the eponymous vessel, anchored immobile off the Virginia coast with intellectual currents from Conrad and 'Key Largo' flowing around it. Brandauer's the stubborn captain with the guilty past, Lyndon his surly son, and Duvall the leader of the gangster triumvirate who commandeer the ship, and tauntingly lay down the 'no man is an island' theme as a challenge to its motley crew. Duvall, in fact, represents the one trump card the movie possesses – incarnating a lisping, leering, demonic narcissist with a performance that's a must for collectors of eccentric acting. **PT**

THE LITTLE DRUMMER GIRL

(Pan Arts/Warner)
dir George Roy Hill *pro* Robert L Crawford *exec pro* Patrick Kelly *scr* Loring Mandel, based on the novel by John Le Carré *ph* Wolfgang Treu, in Technicolor *ed* William Reynolds *pro des* Henry Bumstead *mus* Dave Grusin *r time* 130 mins *US opening* prior to Jul 1985 *UK opening* Jul 5.
cast Diane Keaton, Yorgo Voyagis, Klaus Kinski, Sami Frey, Michael Cristofer, David Suchet, Eli Danker, Thorley Walters, Kerstin De Ahna, Anna Massey, Dana Wheeler-Nicholson, Robert Pereno, Moti Shirin.

Keaton, as a provincial British rep actress with vaguely pro-Palestinian instincts, is assigned a new, dangerous double-role by Israeli agents to flush out an Arab terrorist psycho, gets her ideology and her emotions in a twist, and is soon consumed by the (all-too-carefully apolitical) miasma of moral murkiness about causes and commitments that shrouds all. A film both fraudulent and self-defeating in its determined fence-sitting, and almost inept in its indexing of international intrigues, 'Drummer Girl' might have been better off taking a less pretentious, B-pic tone from tormentor-in-chief Klaus Kinski's patented sneer'n'leer performance. **PT**

THE LONGSHOT: See US section

LOST IN AMERICA

(Geffen Company/Warner)
dir Albert Brooks *pro* Marty Katz *exec pro* Herb Nanas *scr* Albert Brooks, Monica Johnson *ph* Eric Saarinen, in Technicolor *ed* David Finfer *pro des* Richard Sawyer *mus* Arthur B Rubinstein *r time* 91 mins *US opening* prior to Jul 1985 *UK opening* Nov 22.
cast Albert Brooks, Julie Hagerty, Garry Marshall, Art Frankel, Michael Greene, Tom Tarpey, Ernie Brown.

Albert Brooks continues to be the most innovative comic actor-director in films, Woody Allen's post-'Manhattan' heir. Brooks isn't afraid to explore the obnoxious side of his characters, and here he delves deeply into the self-absorbed pseudo-idealism of the 'yuppie' class. His visual approach isn't nearly as uniquely inventive as it was in 'Real Life' or 'Modern Romance', and the film ends abruptly and unsatisfyingly, circumventing its third act, but what's there is choice, timely satire. **MM**

LOVE LETTERS
(Millennium/New Horizon/ICA)
dir-scr Amy Jones *pro* Roger Corman *exec pro* Mel Pearl, Don Levin *ph* Alex Hirschfeld, in DeLuxe Colour *ed* Gwendolyn Greene *art dir* Jeannine Oppewall *mus* Ralph Jones *r time* 89 mins *US opening* prior to Jul 1985 *UK opening* May 9.
cast Jamie Lee Curtis, Bonnie Bartlett, Matt Clark, James Keach, Bud Cort, Amy Madigan, Brian Wood, Phil Coccioletti, Larry Cedar, Michael Villella, Betsy Toll, Lyman Ward, Shelby Leverington, Emma Chapman, Scott Henderson, Robin Thomas, Michelle Cundey, Rance Howard, Jeff Doucette, Sally Kirkland.

Rather misleadingly sold as an instance of feminist exploitation cinema – on the strength of the Corman connection rather than on-screen evidence – 'Love Letters' actually marks Amy Jones' emphatic graduation from that realm, with an economically classical revision of the family romance from the point of view of a daughter and 'other woman'. Curtis is superb as the bewildered apex of two triangles, surrendering herself to ill-directed desire as she attempts to work through her own familial traumas in a doomed, intense affair with married man Keach; and Jones subtly and intelligently modulates the tender-tough perspective on her painful emotional growth. **PT**

LUCAS: See US section

LUST IN THE DUST
(Fox Run/New World/RCA Columbia)
dir Paul Bartel *pro* Allan Glaser, Tab Hunter *exec pro* James C Katz *scr* Philip John Taylor *ph* Paul Lohmann, in colour *ed* Alan Toomayan *pro des* Walter Pickette *mus* Peter Matz *r time* 85 mins *US opening* prior to Jul 1985 *UK opening* Nov 29.
cast Tab Hunter, Divine, Lainie Kazan, Geoffrey Lewis, Henry Silva, Cesar Romero, Gina Gallego, Nedra Volz, Courtney Gains, Pedro Gonzalez-Gonzalez, Woody Strode, Daniel Fishman, Al Cantu, Ernie Shinagawa, Clinton S Doran, Pit Ginsburg.

Lust in the Dust

Marie

Love Letters

Mad Max Beyond Thunderdome

Parody western, with divine as a mountainous saloon singer and Tab Hunter as a genially geriatric gunslinger, which gets off to a quite lively start but soon loses thrust and falls back into a fairly threadbare succession of grotesquerie and revue-style skits. A few nice moments ("Freeze, hombre, or I'll be wearing your asshole for a garter" cries a shotgun-toting lady), and a straight-faced piece of spoof villainy from Henry Silva; but on the whole the film suggests that in retreating from the future ('Death Race 2000') to the present ('Eating Raoul') and now to the past, Bartel is finding it increasingly difficult to harness satiric instinct to satisfactory comic form. Anyway, considering the virtual disappearance of the Western, is there really any popular audience for an enterprise like this? **TP**

MACARONI: See US section

MAD MAX BEYOND THUNDERDOME
(Warner)
dir George Miller, George Ogilvie *pro* George Miller *scr* Terry Hayes, George Miller *ph* Dean Semler, in Panavision colour *ed* Richard Francis-Bruce *pro des* Graham Walker *mus* Maurice Jarre *r time* 107 mins *US opening* Jul 12 *UK opening* Oct 18.
cast Mel Gibson, Tina Turner, Bruce Spence, Adam Cockburn, Frank Thring, Angelo Rossitto, Paul Larsson, Angry Anderson, Robert Grubb, Helen Buday, Mark Spain, Mark Kounnas, Rod Zuanic, Tom Jennings, Adam Willits, Justine Clarke, Shane Tickner, Toni Allaylis, George Spartels, Edwin Hodgeman.

Further evidence, if required, that a bigger budget does not lead to a better film. The third Mad Max Movie (and the first to look like a Hollywood studio product) makes the mistake of assuming that it does, piling on the extravagant setpieces and adding a rather pompous and redundant 'mythic' dimension completely at odds with what gave its predecessors their rancid, stripped-down, B-movie charm. The humour, too, has become leaden and self-parodying – always the first sign of a series that's run out of steam. **AC**

THE MAN WITH ONE RED SHOE: See US section

THE MANHATTAN PROJECT: See US section

MARIE
(Dino De Laurentiis/MGM-US/Columbia)
dir Roger Donaldson *pro* Frank Capra Jnr *exec pro* Elliot Schick *scr* John Briley, based on the book 'Marie: A True Story' by Peter Maas *ph* Chris Menges, in Technicolor *ed* Neil Travis *art dir* Ron Foreman *mus* Francis Lai *r time* 112 mins

US opening Sep 27 *UK opening* Apr 25.
cast Sissy Spacek, Jeff Daniels, Keith Szarabajka, Morgan Freeman, Fred Thompson, Lisa Banes, Trey Wilson, John Cullum, Don Hood, Graham Beckel, Macon McCalman, Collin Wilcox Paxton, Robert Green Benson III, Dawn Carmen, Shane Wexel, Vincent Irizarry, Michael P Moran, Clarence Felder, Lisa Foster.

The opening reels of this true story of a former abused housewife who ended up bringing down a corrupt state government represent expository cinema at its most incisive: director Donaldson communicates his facts through astute visual means. Unfortunately, the script follows real events so faithfully that the dramatic arc of the narrative builds poorly to a courtroom climax over a collateral issue. The parts are vallid, even admirable, but the movie fizzles. **MM**

MARLENE

(OKO Filmproduktion-Karel Dirka/ Blue Dolphin)
dir Maximilian Schell *pro* Peter Genée
scr Meir Dohnal, Maximilian Schell
ph Ivan Slapeta, Pavel Hispler, Henry Hauck, in colour *ed* Heidi Genée
art dir Heinz Eickmeier, Zbynek Hloch
mus Nicholas Economou *r time* 94 mins
UK opening Feb 7.
cast Annie Albers, Bernard Hall, Marta Rakosnik, Patricia Schell, Evana Spinell, William von Stranz, *voices* Marlene Dietrich, Maximilian Schell.

Entertainingly shambolic as a deconstructed documentary, Schell's attempted portrait of the artiste unravels into near-abstract doodling around the enigmatic Marlene mythology. The daunting Ms Dietrich not only doggedly refuses to appear on-camera, but her disembodied voice-over testimony is almost wholly a matter of truculent tetchiness and tantrums; an imperious dismissal of cinema and her iconic career within it; and an unwise dabbling in camped-up cruelty to her current director. Who, not unnaturally, retaliates by 'remaking' his absent subject according to his own, no-longer-neutral notions of grotesque 'grande dame-ry'. Scrappy film history but an intriguing slugging match. **PT**

MAXIE: See US section

MISHIMA

(Zoetrope-Lucasfilm-Filmlink International-M Film Company/Warner)
dir Paul Schrader *pro* Mata Yamamoto, Tom Luddy *exec pro* George Lucas, Francis Coppola *scr* Paul Schrader, Leonard Schrader, Chieko Schrader, based on works by Yukio Mishima *ph* John Bailey, in Panavision, Technicolor and b/w *ed* Michael Chandler, Tomoyo Oshima *pro des* Eiko Ishioka *mus* Philip Glass *r time* 120 mins *US opening* Oct 4
UK opening Oct 31.
cast Ken Ogata, Masayuki Shionoya, Junkichi Orimoto, Naoko Otani, Go Riju, Masato Aizawa, Yuki Nagahara, Kyuzo Kobayashi, Yasosuke Bando, Hisako Manda, Kenji Sawada, Sachiko Hidari, Toshiyuki Nagashima, Hiroshi Katsuno, Toshio Hosokawa, Hideo Fukuhara, Yosuke Mizuno, Eimei Ezumi.

The late Japanese iconoclast as both major novelist and militarist nut, with Schrader bravely picking up Yukio Mishima's legacy and himself trying to reconcile art and action in filmic terms. This modernist masterpiece failed to find its market after a misleading pre-sell made it look a likely gut-spilling gore-fest. Hara-kiri has its place, but it's the life and work and their contradictions and contrasts, rather than the spectacular suicide, which exercise the considerable combined talents of Schrader and his first-rate collaborators. For all the Oriental specificities, and the superb, rigorously worked-through structure of stylisations, there's nothing remotely inscrutable about this trans-Pacific meeting of obsessive minds. **PT**

Marlene

The Money Pit

Mixed Blood

Mishima

MIXED BLOOD

(Sara Films/Alain Sarde Prods/Mainline)
dir-scr Paul Morrissey *pro* Antoine Gannage, Steven Fierberg
exec pro Alain Sarde *ph* Stefan Zapasnik, in colour *ed* Scott Vickrey
art dir Stephen McCabe *mus* Andy Hernandez and others *r time* 99 mins
US opening Oct 18 *UK opening* Apr 18.
cast Marilla Pera, Richard Ulacia, Geraldine Smith, Rodney Harvey, Alvaro Rodriguez, Linda Kerridge, Ulrich Berr, Marcelino Rivera, William Rodriguez, Eduardo Gonzalez, Steven Garcia, Edwina Ebron, Andres Castillo, Angel David, Pedro Sanchez, Fabio Urena, Yukio Yamomoto.

A scabrous black comedy of drug-dealing gangs in the Manhattan slums that marks a resurgence in the vigorous talent that had been Paul Morrissey. Marilla Pera ('Pixote') creates an indelible impression as the matriarchal crime chieftain, and the entire cast reflects a grungy hipness that invigorates the sordid subject with daring and energy. The grotesqueries are direct descendants of the bizarre characters of 'Trash' with a visual style that has been liberated from Warholian stupor. **MM**

MONA LISA: See US section

THE MONEY PIT

(Amblin/Universal)
dir Richard Benjamin *pro* Frank Marshall, Kathleen Kennedy, Art Levinson
exec pro Steven Spielberg, David Giler
scr David Giler *ph* Gordon Willis, in Du Art colour *ed* Jacqueline Cambas
pro des Patrizia von Brandenstein
mus Michel Colombier and others
r time 91 mins *US opening* Mar 28
UK opening Jun 27.
cast Tom Hanks, Shelley Long, Alexander Godunov, Maureen Stapleton, Joe Mantegna, Philip Bosco, Josh Mostel, Yakov Smirnoff, Carmine Caridi, Brian Backer, Billy Lombardo, Mia Dillon, John Van Dreelan, Douglass Watson, Lucille Dobrin, Tetchie Agbayani, Lutz Rath.

Something like a latterday version of 'Mr Blandings Builds His Dream House', this is a rather uncertain mixture of intimately scaled romantic comedy and elaborately staged knockabout farce. Expert performances by Tom Hanks and especially Shelley Long, as the yuppies duped into buying a near-collapsing country mansion, go quite a long way toward holding the disparate elements together, and the movie benefits further from an unassumingly polished surface and a prevailing air of good humour. **TP**

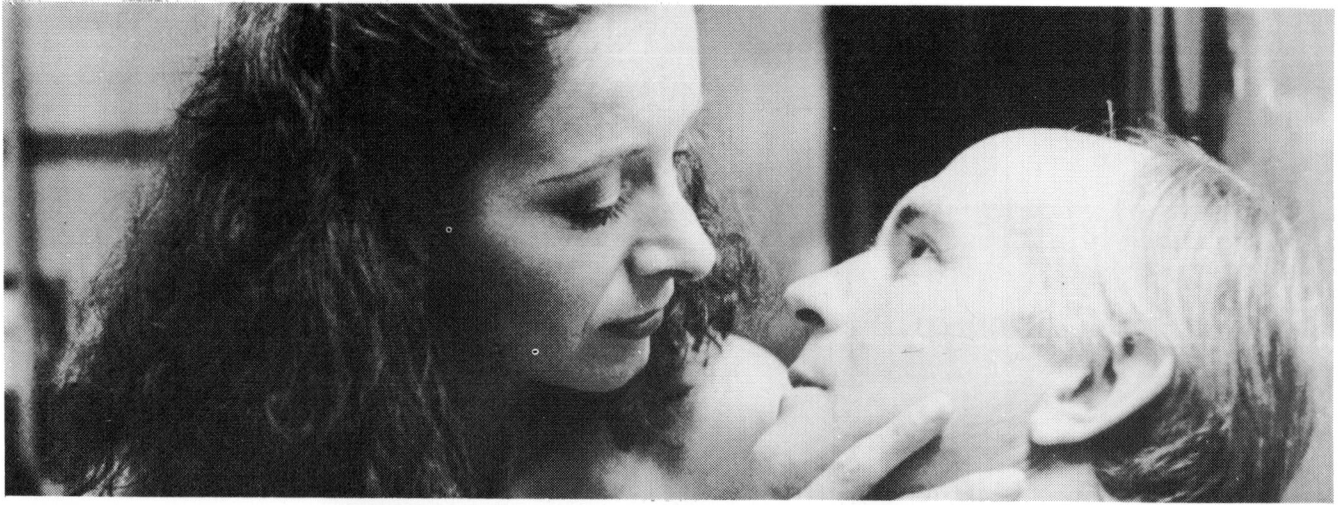
Mr Love

MR LOVE
(Enigma/Warner)
dir Roy Battersby *pro* Susan Richards, Robin Douet *exec pro* David Puttnam *scr* Kenneth Eastaugh *ph* Clive Tickner, in colour *ed* Alan J Cumner-Price *art dir* Adrienne Atkinson *mus* Willy Russell *r time* 91 mins *UK opening* Feb 21 *US opening* Mar 14.
cast Barry Jackson, Maurice Denham, Margaret Tyzack, Linda Marlowe, Christina Collier, Helen Cotterill, Julia Deakin, Donal McCann, Marcia Warren, Tony Melody, Kay Stonham, Patsy Byrne, Jeremy Swift, Janine Roberts, John Joyce, Dave Atkins, George Malpas, Chris Jury, James Benson, Jacki Piper.

Southport's answer to 'The Man Who Loved Women', in which the municipal gardener of the title carries on any number of (seemingly platonic) extra-marital relationships, and posthumously, as well as improbably, ends up a local hero. Odd moments of authentic feeling, and an appealing scene involving a cinema projectionist and usherette acting out the finale of 'Casablanca' after the screening has to be abandoned due to technical problems, lose out to an air of under-budgeted whimsicality. The final effect is parochial rather than authentically provincial. **TP**

My Beautiful Laundrette

The Muppets Take Manhattan

THE MUPPETS TAKE MANHATTAN
(Delphi II/Tri-Star/Columbia)
dir Frank Oz *pro* David Lazer *exec pro* Jim Henson *scr* Frank Oz, Jay Tarses *ph* Robert Paynter, in Technicolor *ed* Evan Lottman *pro des* Stephen Hendrickson *mus* Ralph Burns *r time* 94 mins *US opening* prior to Jul 1985 *UK opening* Feb 15.

The further adventures of the motley band, as they hit the pavement in the Big Apple trying to sell their college revue to Broadway. The Muppets haven't lost their unflagging pleasantness, but the novelty and bite are long gone. Nice songs and jokes aren't enough to sustain adult interest, and the attempted transformation of Kermit the Frog from a Bing Crosby to a Gene Kelly figure isn't credible. The concluding nuptials of Kermit and Miss Piggy bodes ill for the next sequel. **MM**

MURPHY'S ROMANCE See US section

MY BEAUTIFUL LAUNDRETTE
(Working Title-SAF Prods-Channel 4/Mainline/Orion Classics)
dir Stephen Frears *pro* Sarah Radclyffe, Tim Bevan *scr* Hanif Kureishi *ph* Oliver Stapleton, in colour *ed* Mick Audsley *pro des* Hugo Luczyc Wyhowski *mus* Ludus Tonalis *r time* 97 mins *UK opening* Nov 16 *US opening* Mar 7.
cast Saeed Jaffrey, Roshan Seth, Daniel Day Lewis, Gordon Warnecke, Derrick Branche, Shirley Anne Field, Rita Wolf, Souad Faress, Richard Graham, Winston Graham, Dudley Thomas, Garry Cooper, Charu Bala Choksi, Persis Maravala, Nisha Kapur, Neil Cunningham, Walter Donohue, Gurdial Sira.

Modestly mounted (on a TV budget), Kureishi and Frears' crossover success story empties the contents of three old kitchen sinks into one washing machine, amuses itself at the tangles of race, sex-pol and Thatcherism which appear through the distorting porthole, and proudly steps back to see what comes out in the rinse. An ex-National Front bootboy and a second generation Anglo-Asian prove strange bedfellows in both the entrepreneurial and erotic spheres, while the fortunes of their gaudy washeteria follow but one of the many crazy-paved paths of multi-cultural free

enterprise. The politics of pleasure, of opportunity and opportunism, all get an engagingly quizzical airing, but the movie is at its niftiest in neither whitewashing Britain's dirty linen nor ironing out the contradictions of its post-Imperial progress. **PT**
(See Daniel Day Lewis, Faces of the Year.)

MY CHAUFFEUR: See US section

MY FIRST WIFE
(Dofine Productions-Film Victoria/Spectrafilm/Artificial Eye)
dir Paul Cox *pro* Jane Ballantyne, Paul Cox *scr* Paul Cox *ph* Yuri Sokol *ed* Tim Lewis *pro des* Asher Bilu *mus* Christoph von Gluck, Carl Orff, Franz Joseph Haydn and others *r time* 98 mins
US opening prior to Jul 1985
UK opening Aug 1.
cast John Hargreaves, Wendy Hughes, Lucy Angwin, David Cameron, Anna Jemison, Charles Tingwell, Betty Lucas, Robin Lovejoy, Lucy Uralov, Xenia Groutas, Jon Finlayson, Julia Blake, Ron Falk, Reg Roddick, Renee Geyer, Sabrina Lorenz, Christopher Holligan.

It seems to be something of an open secret that 'My First Wife' is autobiographical in inspiration, deriving (though only in part) from the break-up of its maker's marriage. Certainly the result has a masochistic intensity which reflects an anything but distanced attitude to its subject; it does, however, achieve the perspective of an artist's sensibility. Despite its preoccupation with emotional pain, moreover, the film is frequently abrasively funny, and it is crafted by Cox and his regular team of collaborators with streamlined skill: the gloss and accessibility align it as much to popular as to art cinema, and confirm Cox's place in the forefront of Australian film-making. **TP**

MY LITTLE PONY: See US section

MY SCIENCE PROJECT: See US section

THE MYSTERY OF ALEXINA
(Les Cinéastes Associés-TFI/European Classics/Electric Pictures)
dir-scr René Féret *scr* Jean Gruault, René Féret *ph* Bernard Zitzermann, in colour *ed* Ariane Boeglin *set des* Georges Stoll, Isabelle Manescau *mus* Anne-Marie Deschamps *r time* 90 mins
UK opening May 23.
cast Philippe Vuillemin, Valérie Stroh, Véronique Silver, Bernard Freyd, Marianne Basler, Pierre Vial, Philippe Clévenot, Isabelle Gruault, Lucienne Hamon, Claude Bouchery, Olivier Sabran, Michel Amphoux, Anne Cornaly, Vincent Pinel, Paul Descombes.

A minor art-house contribution to the cinema's current interest in gender definition and sexual difference. Féret's film about a nineteenth-century hermaphrodite carries behind it the weight of French philosopher Foucault's historical researches, but can itself bring to bear on the subject little beyond a tentatively titillatory perspective. Vuillemin is the technically unsexed Alexina, convent-raised as a girl but discovering her maleness in the midst of a boarding-school passion, then falling prey to the love-denying systems of the religious, medical and legal establishments. **PT**

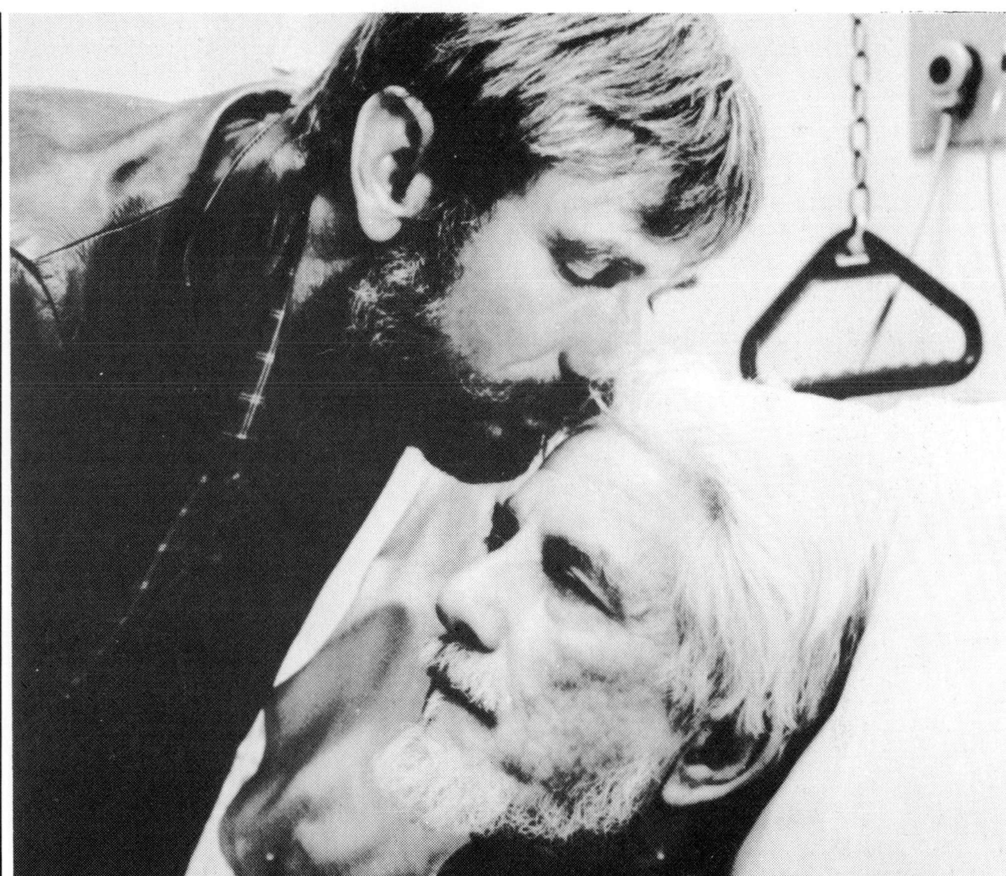
My First Wife

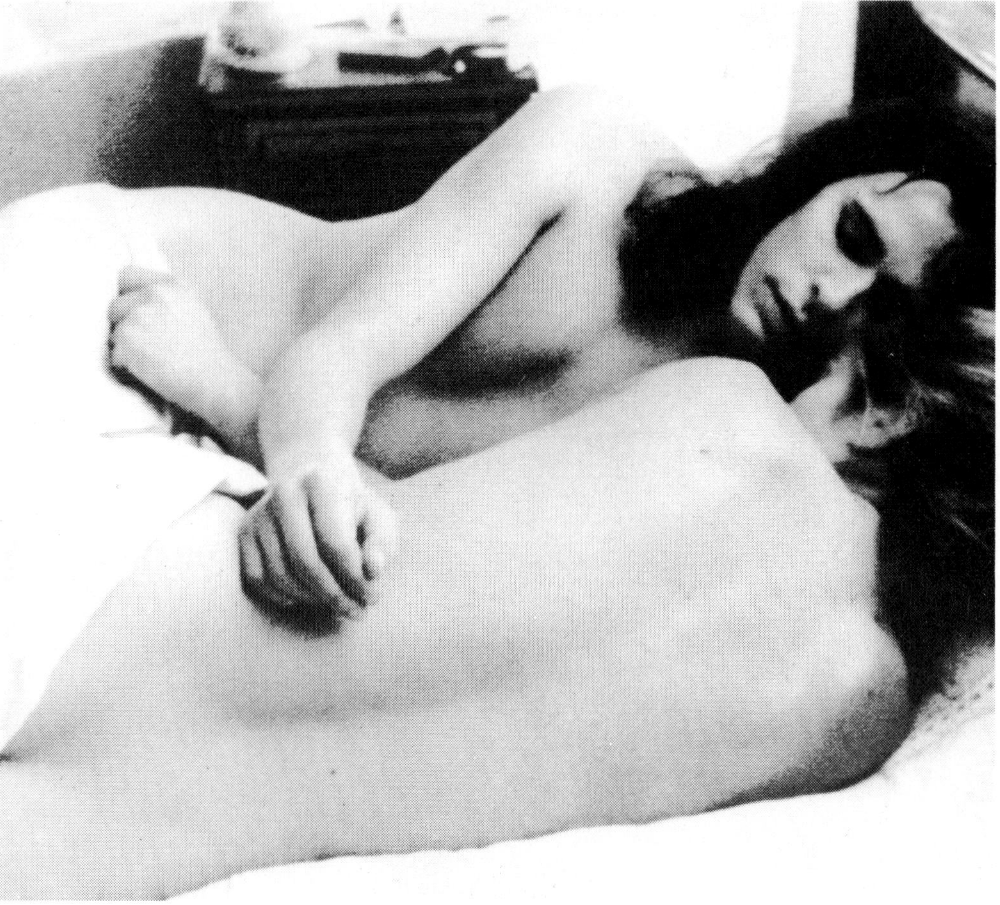
The Mystery of Alexina

NATIONAL LAMPOON'S EUROPEAN VACATION: See US section

NEVER TOO YOUNG TO DIE: See US section

A NIGHTMARE ON ELM STREET
(Media Home Ents-Smart Egg Pics/New Line/Palace)
dir-scr Wes Craven *pro* Robert Shaye *exec pro* Stanley Dudelson, Joseph Wolf *ph* Jacques Haitkin, in DeLuxe colour *ed* Rick Shaine *pro des* Greg Fonseca *mus* Charles Bernstein *r time* 91 mins *US opening* prior to Jul 1985 *UK opening* Aug 30
cast John Saxon, Ronee Blakeley, Heather Langenkamp, Amanda Wyss, Nick Corri, Johnny Depp, Robert Englund, Charles Fleischer, Joseph Whipp, Lin Saye.

Wes Craven's horror film surmounts its conventional boogey-man plot with an above average youth cast and a genuine appreciation for the persistence of dreams in our waking consciousness. Its virtues are matters merely of moments, but they are memorable. **MM**

A NIGHTMARE ON ELM STREET PART II: FREDDY'S REVENGE See US section

9½ WEEKS
(Jonesfilm/MGM-UA/Palace)
dir Adrian Lyne *pro* Antony Rufus Isaacs, Zalman King *exec pro* Keith Barish, Frank Konigsberg *scr* Patricia Knop, Zalman King, Sarah Kernochan, based on the novel by Elizabeth McNeill *ph* Peter Biziou, in Technicolor *ed* Caroline Biggerstaff, Tom Rolf *pro des* Ken Davis *mus* Jack Nitzsche *r time* 117 mins *US opening* Feb 7 *UK opening* May 16.
cast Mickey Rourke, Kim Basinger, Margaret Whitton, David Margulies, Christine Baranski, Karen Young, William De Acutis, Dwight Weist, Roderick Cook, Victor Truro, Justine Johnson, Cintia Cruz, Kim Chan, Lee Lai Sing, Rudolph Willrich, Helen Hanft, Michael P Moran.

Major studio films rarely tackle sexuality as a subject, let alone its nether reaches, so the idea behind this project could have been intriguing. Instead, it's so diluted and worried over that a movie about passionate abandon expresses itself almost entirely through a rhetoric of repression. It's more about dating, snacking and the plumage of the species than it is about sex or emotional enslavement. Rather as if 'Last Tango in Paris' were reduced, after the current fashion, to postures and attitude. **MM**
(See Turkeys of the Year and Kim Basinger, Faces of the Year.)

NINETEEN NINETEEN
(Channel 4/BFI)
dir Hugh Brody *pro* Nita Amy *exec pro* Peter Sainsbury *scr* Hugh Brody, Michael Ignatieff, based on an idea by Michael Ignatieff *ph* Ivan Strasburg, in colour *ed* David Gladwell *art dir* Caroline Amies *mus* Maurice Ravel, Brian Gascoigne *r time* 99 mins *UK opening* Dec 6.
cast Paul Scofield, Maria Schell, Frank Finlay, Diana Quick, Clare Higgins, Colin Firth, Sandra Berkin, Jacqueline Dankworth, Alan Tilvern, Christopher Lahr, Bridget Amies.

Anthropologist Brody and philosopher Ignatieff come together on an ill-invested BFI budget to produce an illustrated segment of Radio 4 think-piece drama about the analytical failings of Freud. Two ageing ex-patients of the old shrink reticently unite in Vienna in 1970, and reveal themselves as the respective repositories of every twentieth-century trauma that the collision of private psyches and public histories could produce. The intellectual arguments might be stimulating, but the camera is wholly redundant and the sense of cinema atrophied beyond belief. **PT**

NO RETREAT NO SURRENDER: See US section

NO SURRENDER
(Dumbarton/Palace)
dir Peter Smith *pro* Mamoun Hassan *exec pro* Michael Peacock *scr* Alan Bleasdale *ph* Mick Coulter, in colour *ed* Rodney Holland *pro des* Andrew Mollo *mus* Daryl Runswick *r time* 104 mins *UK opening* Mar 28.
cast Michael Angelis, Avis Bunnage, James Ellis, Tom Georgeson, Bernard Hill, Ray McAnally, Mark Mulholland, Joanne Whalley, J G Devlin, Vince Earl, Ken Jones, Michael Ripper, Marjorie Sudell, Joan Turner, Elvis Costello, Richard Alexander, Pamela Austin, Ina Clough, Paul Codman.

Alan Bleasdale's script, so sharp you could cut your wrists on it, is let down by the leaden direction, but there is still much to treasure in this deeply black comedy set in a dead end of Liverpool. Two rival parties of pensioners, one Catholic, and the other Protestant, descend on a rundown nightclub for New Year's Eve. There is an IRA terrorist hiding in the toilets, the club's former manager is being beaten up in one of the back rooms and the wildly inappropriate cabaret acts are going down like a lead balloon. Add a coachload of drooling lunatics and you've got what the film refers to as 'a normal night out, these days'. Nasty. **AB**

9½ Weeks

Nineteen Nineteen

Opposite: A Nightmare on Elm Street   Above: No Surrender

OFF BEAT: See US section

THE OFFICIAL VERSION
[US TITLE: THE OFFICIAL STORY]
(Historias Cinematograficas-Progress Communications/Virgin/Almi)
dir Luis Puenzo *pro* Marcelo Pineyro *scr* Aida Bortnik, Luis Puenzo *ph* Felix Monti, in Eastman Colour *ed* Juan Carlos Macias *art dir* Abel Facello *mus* Atilio Stampone *r time* 115 mins *US opening* Nov 8 *UK opening* Sep 20.
cast Hector Alterio, Norma Aleandro, Chela Ruiz, Chunchuna Villafane, Hugo Arana, Patricio Contreras, Guillermo Battaglia, Maria Luisa Robledo, Analia Castro, Jorge Petraglia, Augusto Larreta, Leal Rey.

Like 'Camila', this movie reflects Argentinian cinema's new-found freedom to scrutinise political issues; the difference is that the material of 'The Official Version' is contemporary. The subject is the 'desaparecidos', families who 'disappeared' during the decade prior to 1983, and the manner in which the children of such people were in some cases given away to childless couples sympathetic to the military regime. The central character, finely played by Norma Aleandro, is – with fitting but not overplayed irony – a history teacher, and her gradual realisation that her own 'adopted' daughter is one such child causes her radically to rethink her situation, and permits the audience a revised perspective on recent Argentinian history. The film's ostensible soap opera style cunningly accommodates a metaphorical treatment of the wider issues, although rather plodding direction sometimes blunts the movie's edge. **TP**

ONCE BITTEN: See US section

ON THE EDGE: See US section

ON VALENTINE'S DAY: See US section

ONE MAGIC CHRISTMAS: See US section

Above: Orion's Belt Opposite: Pale Rider

ORION'S BELT
(Filmeffekt/Enterprise)
dir Ola Solum *pro* Dag Alveberg, Petter Borgli *scr* Richard Harris, based on the novel by Jon Michelet *ph* Harald Paalgard, in Eastman Colour *ed* Bjørn Breigutu, Yngve Refseth *art dir* Harald Egede-Nissen *mus* Geir Bøhren, Bent Åserud *r time* 103 mins *UK opening* Jan 10.
cast Helge Jordal, Sverre Anker Ousdal, Hans Ola Sørlie, Kjersti Holmen, Vidar Sandem, Nils Johnson, Jon Eikemo, Johan Sverre, Jan Harstad, Holger Vistisen, Erik Øksnes, Bjørg Telsted, John Ousland, Jarl E Goli, Tor Stokke, Jarl Staernes, Knut Ørvig, Steve Plytas, Steinar Danielsen.

Norway has at least some justification in registering its Cold War shivers on screen. But the predictable progress of this ramshackle thriller from minor-league action-man jauntiness to out-of-its-depth paranoia didn't really justify its British release. A trio of roguish seamen operating minor scams out of Spitzbergen eventually stumble across a Soviet spy station, shots are exchanged, the survivors must be silenced . . . and diplomacy must be maintained. All QED in a second-hand mode, though the sight of a handy harpoon bringing down a helicopter gunship raises an odd cheer. **PT**

OUT OF AFRICA
(Mirage/Universal)
dir-pro Sydney Pollack, *exec pro* Kim Jorgensen *scr* Kurt Luedtke, based on 'Out of Africa', 'Shadows on the Grass', 'Letters from Africa' by Isak Dinesen (Karen Blixen); 'Isak Dinesen: The Life of a Storyteller' by Judith Thurman; 'Silence Will Speak' by Errol Trzebinski *ph* David Watkin, in Technovision, Technicolor *ed* Fredric Steinkamp, William Steinkamp, Pembroke Herring, Sheldon Kahn *ed* Claudio Cutty *pro des* Stephen Grimes *mus* John Barry and others *r time* 162 mins *US opening* Dec 20 *UK opening* Mar 5.
cast Meryl Streep, Robert Redford, Klaus Maria Brandauer, Michael Kitchen,

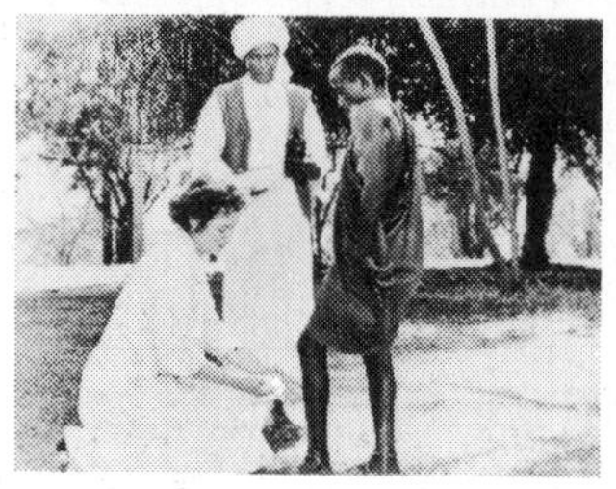

Malick Bowens, Joseph Thiaka, Stephen Kinyanjui, Michael Gough, Suzanna Hamilton, Rachel Kempson, Graham Crowden, Leslie Phillips, Shane Rimmer, Mike Bugara, Job Seda, Mohammed Umar, Donal McCann, Kenneth Mason.

Meryl's Streep's cool qualities, her distance from the characters she plays, work wonderfully for her here, in what is her best screen performance so far as the enigmatic, aristocratic Danish writer Karen Blixen. Redford, hopelessly miscast as her upper-class English lover (a part he doesn't even attempt to play) works his flip charm to less effect. Class and colonialism, the real matter of Blixen's book 'Out of Africa' are subjugated to glossily shot, effectively sentimental romance in the traditional Hollywood style. **JW**
(See Films of the Year.)

OUT OF ORDER
(Laura Film/Sandstar/Virgin)
dir-scr Carl Schenkel *pro* Thomas Schühly, Mathias Deyle, based on the novel by Wilhelm Heyne *ph* Jacques Steyn, in colour *ed* Norbert Herzner *art dir* Tony Lüdi *mus* Jacques Zwart *r time* 88 mins *US opening* Oct 25 *UK opening* Feb 28.
cast Götz George, Renee Soutendijk, Wolfgang Kieling, Hannes Jaenicke, Klaus Wennemann, Ralph Richter, Kurt Raab, Jan Groth, Ekmekyemez Firdevs, Hans Schwofker.

West German director Schenkel milks a stock thriller situation for all it's worth – four characters stuck in a broken-down elevator. Lots of high-rise tension, fraying cables and nerves snapping under stress. Quite a neat little nail-biter. **AB**

THE OUTCASTS
(Arts Council of Ireland-Channel 4/ Cinegate)
dir-scr Robert Wynne-Simmons *ph* Seamus Corcoran, in colour *ed* Arthur Keating *des* Bertram Tyrer *mus* Stephen Cooney *r time* 104 mins *UK opening* Oct 3
cast Mary Ryan, Mick Lally, Don Foley, Tom Jordan, Cyril Cusak, Brenda Scallon, Bairbre Ni Chaoimh, Mairtin O'Flathearta, Brendan Ellis, Gillian Hackett, Hilary Reynolds, Donal O'Kelly, James Shanahan, Paul Bennett.

A brave foray into Celtic magic. A young peasant girl, living in a poor, remote Irish village during the last century, escapes from hardship and cruelty by joining up with an outlawed musician possessed of unearthly powers. Managing to avoid whimsical-leprechaun lyricism, Wynne-Simmon's low-budget feature balances perilously but gracefully on a strange uncharted point between an unsentimental portrait of an ignorant, inward-turned society and a matter-of-fact evocation of supernatural legend. Not altogether convincing, perhaps, but with magnificent landscape photography and a quietly rapt performance from Mary Ryan. **GA**

PALE RIDER
(Warner)
dir-pro Clint Eastwood, *exec pro* Fritz Manes *scr* Michael Butler, Dennis Shryack *ph* Bruce Surtees, in Panavision, Technicolor *ed* Joel Cox *pro des* Edwart Carfagno *mus* Lennie Niehaus *r time* 115 mins *US opening* prior to Jul 1985 *UK opening* Oct 4.
cast Clint Eastwood, Michael Moriarty, Carrie Snodgress, Christopher Penn, Richard Dysart, Sydney Penny, Richard Kiel, Doug McGrath, John Russell.

Clint Eastwood makes a valiant attempt to resurrect the traditional Western on his mighty box-office shoulders, adapting the classic situation from 'Shane' to his satisfying persona. He's more persuasive than Alan Ladd, but the rest of the plot elements fare less well: the development of the civilised characters (here gold miners instead of farmers) is unconvincing and uncompelling. His direction of action remains solid, enhanced by fresh landscapes and Bruce Surtees' patented backlighting. Eastwood remains a fascinating talent open to challenges, and one wishes this endeavour had worked out better. **MM**

PARADE OF THE PLANETS
(Mosfilm/The Other Cinema)
dir Vadim Abdrashitov *scr* Alexander Mindadze *ph* Vladimir Sheytsik, in colour *ed* R Rogatkina *pro des* Alexander Tolkachev *mus* Vyacheslav Ganelin, and others *r time* 96 mins
UK opening Apr 24
cast Oleg Borisov, Sergei Nikonenko, Sergei Shakurov, Alexei Zharkov, Pyotr Zalcehnko, Aleksandr Pashutin, Boris Romanov, Lilis Gritsenko.

Clearly allegorical, this bizarre tale of a group of men embarking on a surreal spiritual odyssey after being declared 'dead' during territorial army manoeuvres has not travelled well to the West. Uneven in tone (alternating between austere moments of almost Tarkovskian mysticism and silly visions of 'liberation', oddly reminiscent of late sixties hippy Hollywood), it's virtually indecipherable, not only in terms of its meaning, but even as to whether it's intended as comedy or serious drama. It is also very tedious. **GA**

PARTING GLANCES: See US section

PEE-WEE'S BIG ADVENTURE: See US section

PEPPERMINT FREEDOM
(Nourfilm/The Other Cinema)
dir-scr Marianne S W Rosenbaum *exec pro* Monika Aubele *ph* Alfred Tichawsky, partly colour *ed* Gérard Samaan *art dir* Franz Tyroller, Eva Müschner, S W Deva Mani, Roland Sviboda, Inge Schumacher *mus* Konstantin Wecker *r time* 112 mins
UK opening Jan 10.
cast Peter Fonda, Saskia Tyroller, Hans Brenner, Hans Peter Korff, Cleo Kretschmer, Elisabeth Neumann-Viertel, Gesine Strempel, Konstantin Wecker, Sigi Zimmerschied, Robby Spitz, Ute Hofinger, Beate Rose, Ernst Klünner, Gideon Bachmann, Veronika von Quast, Cornelia Maué.

War, history and politics through the eyes of a child who moves from the city to a remote country village in the American Zone at the end of World War II. Not seen by an FYB correspondent.

PERFECT
(Columbia)
dir-pro James Bridges *exec pro* Kim Kurumanda *scr* Aaron Latham, James Bridges *ph* Gordon Willis, in Panavision, Technicolor *ed* Jeff Gourson *pro des* Michael Haller *mus* Ralph Burns *r time* 120 mins *US opening* prior to Jul 1985
UK opening Aug 23.
cast John Travolta, Jamie Lee Curtis, Anne De Salvo, Marilu Henner, Laraine Newman, Mathew Reed, Jann Wenner, Charlene Jones.

The ethics of journalism are given a thoroughly shallow going-over in a script by real-life 'Rolling Stone' writer Aaron Latham which posits his fictional counterpart, Travolta, in a situation where he must surrender the tapes of an interview or go to prison for contempt of court. More narrative mileage is extracted from a second-string plot about California health clubs and a romance with aerobics instructress Jamie Lee Curtis, whom Travolta is tempted to exploit for the sake of good

Parade of the Planets

Peppermint Freedom

Plenty

Perfect

copy. But the film itself seems to have sacrificed its own integrity somewhere along the line and to have replaced it with endless footage of groins grinding aerobically to the requisite thumping disco beat. **AB**
(See Turkeys of the Year.)

PERVOLA (US TITLE: TRACKS IN THE SNOW): See US Section

THE PLEASURE
(Filmirage/Elephant Entertainment)
dir Joe D'Amato (Aristide Massaccesi) *scr* Homerus S Zweitag, Clyde Anderson *ph* Aristide Massaccesi, in colour *ed* Franco Alessandri *art dir* Italo Focacci *mus* Cluster *r time* 90 mins *UK opening* May 2.
cast Steve Wyler, Laura Gemser, Isabelle Andrea Guzon, Marcò Mattioli, Lillie Carati, Dagmar Lassander.

Pseudonymous dubbed sexploiter from the cinematographer of numerous 'Emanuelle' films. Terrible from all accounts.

PLENTY 
(Edward R Pressman Productions-RKO/Fox/Thorn EMI)
dir Fred Schepisi *pro* Edward R Pressman, Joseph Papp *exec pro* Mark Seiler *scr* David Hare, based on his play *ph* Ian Baker, in Panavision, Technicolor *ed* Peter Honess *pro des* Richard MacDonald *mus* Bruce Smeaton *r time* 124 mins *US opening* Sep 20 *UK opening* Nov 22.
cast Meryl Streep, Sam Neill, Charles Dance, John Gielgud, Tracey Ullman, Sting, Ian McKellen, André Maranne, Tristram Jellinek, Peter Forbes-Robertson, Hugo De Vernier, James Taylor, Ian Wallace, Andy De La Tour.

Inept treatment, with no feeling for period, of David Hare's play about a woman who had been involved with the Resistance in France and was unable to come to terms with the shoddy compromises of postwar Britain. The film turns that political statement on its head in a movie about a restless, neurotic woman who marries a diplomat and ruins his career. Gielgud and Ian McKellen contribute amusing cameos, but Meryl Streep is no match for Kate Nelligan's original performance in the central role, demonstrating only the compromises the star system imposes upon film-makers. **JW**

Police

Police Academy 2: Their First Assignment

POLICE

(Gaumont-TFI Films/Artificial Eye) *dir* Maurice Pialat *pro* Emmanuel Schlumberger *scr* Catherine Breillat, Sylvie Danton, Jacques Fieschi, Maurice Pialat, based on an idea by Catherine Breillat *ph* Luciano Tovoli in Panavision, Eastman Colour *ed* Yann Dedet, Hélène Viard, Nathalie Letrosne *art dir* Constantin Mejinsky *mus* Henryk Mikolaj Gorecki *r time* 113 mins *UK opening* Jun 11.
cast Gérard Depardieu, Sophie Marceau, Richard Anconina, Pascale Rocard, Sandrine Bonnaire, Franck Karoui, Jonathan Leina, Jacques Mathou, Bernard Fuzellier, Meaachou Bentahar, Mohamed Ayari, Abdel Kader Touati, Jamil Bouarada, Bechir Idani, Sylvain Maupu, Taya Ouzrout, Jocelyn Persillet.

A gritty, acidic, semi-improvised attempt to inject an extra dose of realism into the contemporary flic formula, Pialat's portrait of the dog-eat-dog dirty work within and around a Parisian precinct eventually fails to break its chosen mould. Depardieu's casually racist, sexist and brutalist copy bustles through a murky plot about Tunisian dope-dealers, slowing moodily down only to ruefully romance the implicated Marceau, while Pialat shuffles his styles wilfully between verité eye-opening on rough justice and a more enigmatic encapsulation of street-level power struggles. **PT**

POLICE ACADEMY 2: THEIR FIRST ASSIGNMENT

(Ladd Co/Warner) *dir* Jerry Paris *pro* Paul Malansky *exec pro* John Goldwyn *scr* Barry Blaustein, David Sheffield, based on characters created by Neal Israel, Pat Proft *ed* James Crabe, in Technicolor *ed* Bob Wyman *pro des* Trevor Williams *mus* Robert Folk *r time* 87 mins *US opening* prior to Jul 1985 *UK opening* Jul 19.
cast Steve Guttenberg, Bubba Smith, David Graf, Michael Winslow, Bruce Mahler, Marion Ramsey, Colleen Camp, Howard Hesseman, Art Metrano, George Gaynes.

Nobody could ever accuse the 'Police Academy' films of peddling sophisticated humour, but, within its lowbrow limits, number two in the cycle is a worthy sequel in its espousal of slapstick, stereotypes and corny sight gags. The formula is much the same as before: inept rookies causing mischief and mayhem on and around the beat, with a superbly daffy romantic subplot thrown in. **AB**

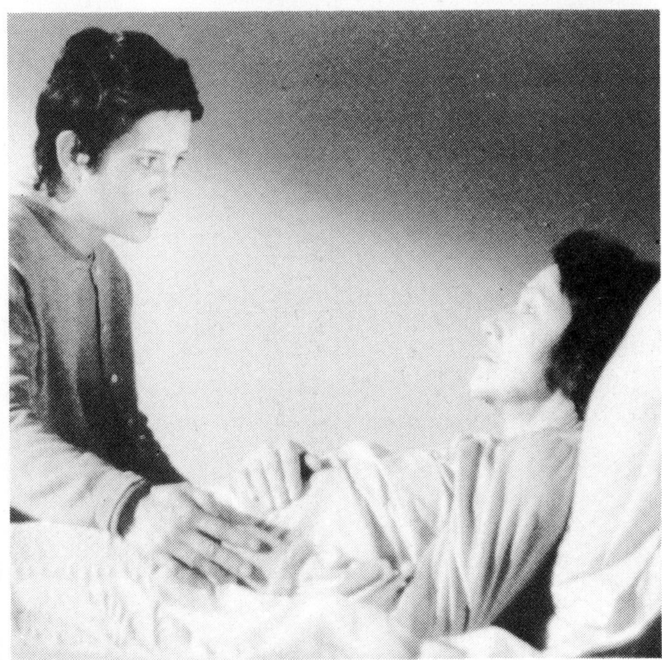

A Portuguese Goodbye

Porky's Revenge

POLICE ACADEMY 3: BACK IN TRAINING: See US section

POLTERGEIST II: THE OTHER SIDE: See US section

PORKY'S REVENGE

(Simon-Astral Bellevue Pathe/Fox) *dir* James Komack *pro* Robert L Rosen *exec pro* Melvin Simon, Milton Goldstein *scr* Ziggy Steinberg, based on characters created by Bob Clark *ph* Robert Jessup, in DeLuxe colour *ed* John W Wheeler *pro des* Peter Wooley *mus* Dave Edmunds *r time* 92 mins *US opening* prior to Jul 1985 *UK opening* Jul 5.
cast Dan Monahan, Wyatt Knight, Tony Ganios, Mark Herrier, Kaki Hunter, Scott Colomby, Nancy Parsons, Chuck Mitchell, Rose McVeigh, Fred Buch, Wendy Feign, Eric Christmas, Ilse Earl, Kimberley Evanson, Bill Hindman, Nancy Hassinger, Sandy Mielke, William Fuller, Tom Bishop, James Cassidy.

The mixture as before – unremittingly crude, gossamer-thin, wearily familiar. It really is time that somebody put this series out of its misery. **AC**

A PORTUGUESE GOODBYE

(Electric Pictures) *dir-pro* Joao Botelho *scr* Joao Botelho, Leonor Pinhao *ph* Acacio de Almeida, in colour and b/w *mus* Oliver Messaien *r time* 85 mins *UK opening* Jun 20.
cast Rui Fortado, Isabel de Castro, Maria Cabral, Fernando Heitor, Cristina Hauser, Antonio Sequeira Lopes, Luis Lucas, Diogo Doria.

Interweaving two stories – the first (in black and white) about a platoon of Portuguese soldiers lost and menaced by unseen guerillas in Portuguese Africa in 1973; the second (in colour) charting the visit of an elderly couple, still mourning the death of their son in Africa, to their Lisbon-based offspring in the mid-eighties – this bravely transposes Ozu's classic 'Tokyo Story' to an altogether different culture – and gets away with it. Shot in largely static, immaculately composed images, performed with a taciturn serenity, the film's melancholy portrait of loss, compromise, and communication breakdown gradually builds into an elegy of sweet, unsentimental sadness. **GA**

POULET AU VINAIGRE
[UK Title: Cop Au Vin]
(MK 2/Virgin)
dir Claude Chabrol *pro* Marin Karmitz *scr* Claude Chabrol, Dominique Roulet, based on the novel 'Une Mort en trop' by Dominique Roulet *ph* Jean-Marc Rabier, in Eastman Colour *ed* Monique Fardoulis *art dir* Françoise Benoit-Fresco *mus* Matthieu Chabrol *r time* 110 mins *UK opening* Oct 11
cast Jean Poiret, Stephane Audran, Michel Bouquet, Jean Topart, Lucas Belvaux, Pauline Lafont, Andrée Tainsy, Jean-Claude Bouillaud, Jacques Frantz, Caroline Cellier, Josephine Chaplin, Dominique Zardi, Henri Attal.

Given his gastronomic propensities, this is presumably Chabrol's idea of nouvelle cuisine; *a mere morsel of sardonic smalltown muck-raking and murder compared to the gourmet multi-course treats he's tabled in the past. For starters there's a rather cloudy soup of provincial conspiracy around money and mistresses, into which a teenage postman pours sugar, with unexpectedly disastrous results. The meat is only served belatedly, with Poiret's eccentric cop throwing both his wit and weight around to spice up proceedings somewhat. But there's still a distinct sense of appetite unfulfilled by the time the comedy-thriller menu has been completed.* **PT**

POWER: See US section

P.O.W. THE ESCAPE: See US section

PRETTY IN PINK: See US section

THE PRINCESS
(Tarsulas Studio-Mafilm/Cinegate)
dir Pál Erdöss *scr* Istvan Kardos *ph* Ferenc Pap, Lajos Koltai, Gabor Szabo *ed* Klara Majoros *pro des* Andras Gyurki *r time* 113 mins *UK opening* Jul 11.
cast Erika Ozsda, Andrea Szendrei, Denes Diczhazi, Arpad Toth, Juli Nyako, Lajos Soltis.

A grim account of growing up in Budapest, with a fifteen-year-old orphaned schoolgirl arriving fresh and hopeful from the country, only to have her dreams dashed by a harsh, adult world of compromise, betrayal and violence. Shot in grainy verité style, the film's endless catalogue of disasters might be depressing were it not for Erika Ozsda's glowing central performance, which suggests throughout an overwhelming ability to survive with dignity against all odds. The social and political factors affecting her life are never neglected; at heart, however, this is an intimate personal drama, intelligent and moving. **GA**

PRIZZI'S HONOR
(ABC Motion Pictures/Fox/Rank)
dir John Huston *pro* John Foreman *scr* Richard Condon, Janet Roach *ph* Andrzej Bartkowiak, in colour *ed* Rudi Fehr, Kaja Fehr *pro des* Dennis Washington *mus* Alex North *r time* 129 mins *US opening* prior to Jul 1985 *UK opening* Oct 25.
cast Jack Nicholson, Kathleen Turner, Robert Loggia, William Hickey, John Randolph, Lee Richardson, Anjelica Huston, Michael Lombard, Lawrence Tierney, Joseph Ruskin, Ann Selepegno.

John Huston's black comedy variation on 'Godfather' themes is frequently clever, boldly acted, and sports a rigorously applied visual approach. Like 'Beat the Devil', though, its wit is never quite amusing enough nor its focus on romantic entanglements persuasive enough, to accord it status as a major work. Jack Nicholson gives yet another courageous performance as a pro hit man who is heir apparent to the Mob, while Kathleen Turner as his wife and rival assassin continues to establish herself as the pre-eminent star of her generation, but their passion for one another is more postulated than communicated. The deliberately slow pace magnifies small flaws. Huston tackles another difficult assignment here, once again proving better on defence than offence. **MM**
(See Films of the Year.)

THE PROTECTOR: See US section

PUMPING IRON II: THE WOMEN
(Cinecom/Blue Dolphin)
dir-pro George Butler *exec pro* Bernard Heng, Lawrence Chong *scr* Charles Gaines, George Butler, based on their book 'Pumping Iron II: The Unprecedented Woman' *ph* Dyanna Taylor, in colour *ed* Paul Barnes, Susan Crutcher, Jane Kurson *mus* David McHugh, Michael Montes *r time* 107 mins *US opening* prior to Jul 1985 *UK opening* Nov 29.
cast Lori Bowen, Carla Dunlap, Bev Francis, Rachel McLish, Kris Alexander, Lydia Cheng, Steve Michalik, Steve Weinberger, Randy Rice, Tina Plakinger.

An elderly male czar of the international bodybuilding fraternity harangues his fellow judges into tentative agreement on 'a definition of femininity'. 'His' sport faces a crisis: should women who've entered the pump'n'pose arena of competitive muscle-culture look ideally more like Cher or Arnold Schwarzenegger's sister? George Butler's follow-up to his original documentary hit can hardly help pumping irony as it observes the ethics of flex-appeal feminism being debated in the incongruous surroundings of Caesar's Palace. Yet it also plays wittily with the double-edged competition satire of a fiction like Michael Ritchie's 'Smile', without ever merely demeaning its dedicated subjects. The balancing act – and the bodies – are phenomenal. **PT**

Above: Poulet au Vinaigre Opposite: The Purple Rose of Cairo

The Princess

Prizzi's Honor

Pumping Iron II: The Women

THE PURPLE ROSE OF CAIRO 
(Orion/Rank)
dir-scr Woody Allen *pro* Robert Greenhut *exec pro* Charles H Joffe *ph* Gordon Willis, in colour *ed* Susan E Morse *pro des* Stuart Wurtzel *mus* Dick Hyman *r time* 82 mins *US opening* prior to Jul 1985 *UK opening* Jul 26.
cast Mia Farrow, Jeff Daniels, Danny Aiello, Irving Metzman, Stephanie Farrow, David Kieserman, Elaine Grollman, Victoria Zussin, Mark Hammond, Wade Barnes, Joseph G Graham, Don Quigley, Maurice Brenner, Paul Herman, Rick Petrucelli, Peter Castellotti, Milton Seaman, Mimi Weddell, Tom Degidon, Mary Hedahl.

Woody Allen's selection of material and treatment is consistent only in its capacity to take us by surprise. Here the leading man (Daniels) of a film-within-the-film is translated from the 'imaginary' world of the screen to the 'real' one of the audience and the world outside the theatre. What brings this about is the cinephiliac devotion of Allen's heroine (Farrow), a housewife in Depression era New Jersey for whom movies are the one escape from her dreary surroundings and loutish husband (brilliantly played by Aiello). Her absorption in a particular film causes its hero to stroll off the screen and become her flesh-and-blood companion, with gratification for her but comic discomfiture for nearly everyone else. It is not only the semantic brilliance of the film which muffles some apprehension in the middle that a single joke is being stretched too far, but also the eventual audacity with which Allen refuses a conventional happy ending. As it is, Farrow is finally seen once again a spectator in the movie house, forlorn but enraptured: Allen has succeeded in juggling not just the real and the imaginary, but the tragic and the comic as well. **TP**

QUICKSILVER: See US section

THE QUIET EARTH
(Capricorn International/Skouras/Cannon)
dir Geoffrey Murphy *pro* Don Reynolds, Sam Pillsbury *scr* Bill Baer, Bruno Lawrence, Sam Pillsbury, based on the novel by Craig Harrison *ph* James Bartle, in colour *pro* Michael Horton *pro des* Josephine Ford *mus* John Charles *r time* 91 mins *US opening* Oct 18 *UK opening* Feb 7.
cast Bruno Lawrence, Alison Routledge, Peter Smith, Anzac Wallace, Norman Fletcher, Tom Hyde.

After the concentrated achievement of 'Utu', Murphy attempts a sci-fi allegory of post-apocalypse survival. His penchant for vital framing still creates effective imagery, but the plot mechanisms are swamped by almost every cliché of the form, leading to a mystical denouement of utter claptrap. Lawrence has some fine demented moments when he believes himself to be the last man alive. **MM**

The Quiet Earth

Rambo: First Blood, Part II

RAD: See US section

RAINBOW BRITE AND THE STAR STEALER: See US section

RAMBO: FIRST BLOOD, PART II
(Carolco/Tri-Star/Thorn EMI)
dir George Pan Cosmatos *pro* Buzz Feitshans *exec pro* Mario Kassar, Andrew Vajna *scr* Sylvester Stallone, James Cameron *ph* Jack Cardiff, in Panavision, Technicolor *ed* Mark Goldblatt, Mark Helfrich *pro des* Bill Kenney *mus* Jerry Goldsmith *r time* 96 mins *US opening* prior to Jul 1985 *UK opening* Aug 30.
cast Sylvester Stallone, Richard Crenna, Julie Nickson, Charles Napier, Steven Berkoff, Martin Kove, Andy Wood, George Kee Cheung, William Ghent, Steve Williams, Don Collins, Chris Grant, John Sterlini, Alain Hocquenghem, William Rothlein, Tonu Munafo, Tom Gehrke.

Ran

Where 'First Blood' was about bringing the Vietnam war back home, this blockbuster sequel seems to be seeking to re-export it. 'Do we get to win this time?' Stallone's discredited veteran asks his former CO in the pre-credit sequence. What ensues might be seen as an attempt to exorcise the Vietnam legacy through the stylised medium of a one-man army capable of sweeping all opposition before him. 'Rambo' touches on valid issues but blankets them in spectacular fantasy, with the eponymous hero able to withstand any amount of ferocity and firepower by all but miraculous means. But even on these terms, despite the asset of Jack Cardiff's wide-screen camerawork, there is no shortage of implausibility, and certainly no shortage of sickeningly hyped-up violence. **TP** *(See Films of the Year.)*

RAN
(Greenwich-Herald Ace-Nippon Herald/Orion Classics/Virgin)
dir Akira Kurosawa *pro* Serge Silberman, Masato Hara *exec pro* Katsumi Furukawa *scr* Akira Kurosawa, Hideo Oguni, Masato Ide *ph* Takao Saito, Masaharu Ueda, in colour *pro des* Yoshiro Muraki, Shinobu Muraki *mus* Toru Takemitsu *r time* 160 mins *US opening* Dec 20 *UK opening* Mar 7.
cast Tatsuya Nakadai, Akira Terao, Jinpachi Nezu, Daisuke Ryu, Mieko Harada, Yoshiko Miyazaki, Kazuo Kato, Peter (Shinnosuke Ikehata), Hitoshi Ueki, Jun Tazaki, Norio Matsui, Hisachi Igawa, Kenji Kodama, Toshiya Ito, Takeshi Kato, Takeshi Nomura, Mayayuki Yui, Heihachiro Suzuki.

Great epic treatment of Shakespeare's 'King Lear', fiercer and less forgiving than the original, in which Kurosawa rages against the dying of the light and creates the definitive samurai film. A masterly film by a master film-maker, and one that repays repeated watchings. **JW**
(See Films of the Year.)

RAPPIN'
(Cannon)
dir Joel Silberg *pro* Menahem Golan, Yoram Globus *scr* Robert Litz, Adam Friedman *ph* David Gurfinkel, in TVC

colour *ed* Andy Horvitch, Bert Glatstein *pro des* Steve Miller *mus* Larry Smith, Paul Erickson *r time* 92 mins *US opening* prior to Jul 1985 *US opening* Aug 23.
cast Mario Van Peebles, Tasia Valenza, Charles Flohe, Eriq La Salle, Kadeem Hardison, Richie Abanes, Leo O'Brien, Melvin Plowden, Harry Goz, Rony Clanton, Rutanya Alda, Edye Byrde, Ruth Jaroslow, Michael Esihos, Anthony Bishop, Frederic Mao, Brandi Freund, Debra Greenfield.

Silberg's companion piece to last year's 'Breakin' 'shares pretty much the same assets and liabilities: it's cheerful and energetic, but is suffocated by its cliché-ridden trivialisation of urban deprivation. In the fairy-tale finale, all problems are solved by rappin'. **AC**

RAW DEAL: See US section

REAL GENIUS: See US section

RE-ANIMATOR
(Empire/Entertainment)
dir Stuart Gordon *pro* Brian Yuzna *exec pro* Michael Avery, Bruce Curtis *scr* Dennis Paoli, William J Norris, Stuart Gordon, based on a story by H P Lovecraft *ph* Mac Ahlberg, in DeLuxe colour *ed* Lee Percy *art dir* Robert A Burns *mus* Richard Band *r time* 86 mins *US opening* Oct 18 *UK opening* Jan 17.
cast Jeffrey Combs, Bruce Abbott, Barbara Crampton, David Gale, Robert Sampson, Gerry Black, Carolyn Purdy-Gordon, Peter Kent, Barbara Pieters, Ian Patrick Williams, Bunny Summers, Al Berry, Derek Pendleton, Gene Scherer, James Ellis, James Earl Cathay.

Proof positive that the exploitation horror pic is alive, kicking and ready to rip your throat out, even as you chuckle. Stuart Gordon's first foray into film direction is based on a six-part story by H P Lovecraft, about a brilliant young medical student with a penchant for bringing corpses back to life. The result is a fun-filled gorefest packed with commendably deadpan performances and ultra-sick jokes, most notably the scene with the severed head which gets the hots for the heroine and sticks its tongue in her ear. **AB**

RED SONJA
(MGM-UA/Thorn EMI)
dir Richard Fleischer *pro* Christian Ferry *exec pro* A Michael Liberman *scr* Clive Exton, George MacDonald Fraser, based on stories by Robert E Howard *ph* Giuseppe Rotunno, in Metrocolor *ed* Frank J Urioste *pro des* Danilo Donati *mus* Ennio Morricone *r time* 89 mins *US opening* prior to Jul 1985 *UK opening* Oct 18.
cast Brigitte Nielsen, Arnold Schwarzenegger, Sandahl Bergman, Paul Smith, Ernie Reyes Jr Ronald Lacey, Pat Roach, Terry Richards, Janet Agren.

Pre-historic pap of the comic-strip kind, with Nielsen – who speaks very slowly, as if unable to remember her lines without a prompter – as the Hyborean warrior teaming up with Arnie's muscle-bound romantic interest to prevent an evil queen from destroying the world. Flatly directed by Fleischer without a hint of wit or irony, murkily shot and unimaginatively scripted. **GA**
(See Turkeys of the Year.)

Rappin'

Re-animator

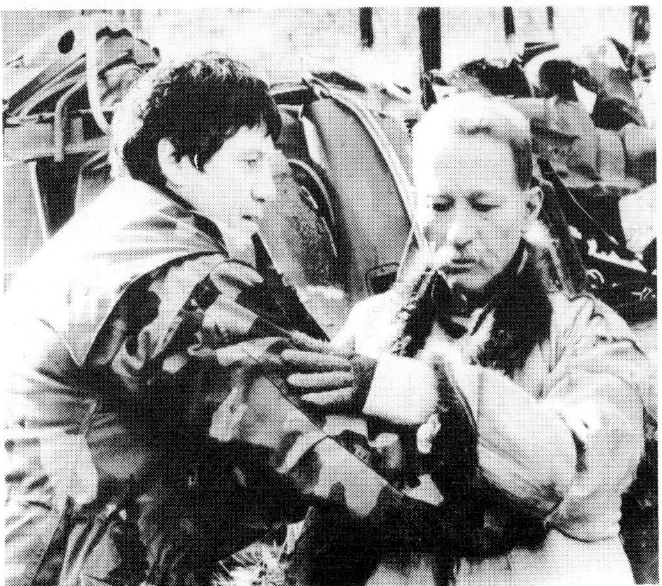
Remo Williams: The Adventure Begins

Red Sonja

REMO WILLIAMS: THE ADVENTURE BEGINS
[UK TITLE: REMO – UNARMED AND DANGEROUS]
(Orion/Rank)
dir Guy Hamilton *pro* Larry Spiegel *exec pro* Dick Clark, Mel Bergman *scr* Christopher Wood, based on the 'Destroyer' series by Richard Sapir, Warren Murphy *ph* Andrew Laszlo, in DeLuxe colour *ed* Mark Melnick *pro des* Jackson De Govia *mus* Craig Safan *r time* 121 mins *US opening* Oct 11 *UK opening* Apr 25.
cast Fred Ward, Joel Grey, Wilford Brimley, J A Preston, George Coe, Charles Cioffi, Kate Mulgrew, Patrick Kilpatrick, Michael Pataki, Davenia McFadden, Cosie Costa, J P Romano, Joel J Kramer, Frank Ferrara, Marv Albert, Ray Woodfork, Phil Neilson, Webster Whinery, Frank Simpson, Dodi Kenan.

A film which is even pulpier, and far less fun, than the pulp books – the 'Destroyer' series – from which it was adapted. Fred Ward is the New York cop who is given a face-job and a silly new name by a secret government agency. Joel Grey, unrecognisable under ten tons of make-up, is the elderly Korean who teaches him martial artistry in between uttering cod-Confucian homilies. The film rapidly degenerates into routine Action Man heroics, with Ward dangling from a lot of very high places. **AB**

THE RETURN OF THE LIVING DEAD

(Fox Films-Cinema '84/Orion/Tartan)
dir-scr Dan O'Bannon, based on a story by Rudy Ricci, John Russo, Russell Streiner *pro* Tom Fox *exec pro* John Daly, Derek Gibson *ph* Jules Brenner, in CFI Colour *ed* Robert Gordon *pro des* William Stout *mus* Matt Clifford *r time* 91 mins *US opening* Aug 16 *UK opening* Mar 21.
cast Clu Gulager, James Karen, Don Calfa, Thom Mathews, Beverly Randolph, John Philbin, Jewel Shepard, Miguel Nunez, Brian Peck, Linnea Quigley, Mark Venturini, Jonathan Terry, Cathleen Cordell, Drew Deighan, James Dalesandro, John Durbin, David Bond, Bob Libman, John Stuart West.

A crude but sporadically enjoyable zombie romp, the directorial debut of 'Alien' writer Dan O'Bannon, which purports, tongue-in-cheek, to be a sequel to 'Night of the Living Dead'. Remaining zombies from the earlier film are sealed in containers in the basement of a medical supply warehouse. One of the containers is accidentally breached, and the ensuing gas leak pollutes the nearby graveyard where a group of punks is partying down. Plenty of splatstick for aficionados of the genre, plus an excellent New Wave score. Particularly endearing is the zombies' habit of demanding 'Brains!' and 'More Brains!' as they lurch after potential victims. **AB**

RETURN TO OZ

(Buena Vista/Disney)
dir Walter Murch *pro* Paul Maslansky *exec pro* Gary Kurtz *scr* Walter Murch, Gill Dennis, based on 'The Land of Oz', 'Ozma of Oz' by L Frank Baum *ph* David Watkin, in Technicolor *ed* Leslie Hodgson *pro des* Norman Reynolds *mus* David Shire *r time* 110 mins *US opening* prior to Jul 1985 *UK opening* Jul 11.
cast Nicol Williamson, Jean Marsh, Fairuza Balk, Piper Laurie, Matt Clark, Michael Sundin, Tim Rose, Sean Barrett, Mak Wilson, Denise Bryer, Brian Henson, Stewart Larange, Lyle Conway, Steve Norrington, Justin Case, John Alexander, Deep Roy, Emma Ridley, Sophie Ward, Fiona Victory, Pons Maar.

A glum charmless sequel to 'The Wizard of Oz', more faithful to the spirit of the L Frank Baum originals perhaps, but lacking the enriching character relationships and magic of the musical classic. The first half hour plunges a depressed Dorothy into frightening electroshock therapy by a threatening quack, until she escapes to a devastated, lifeless Oz she must reanimate. Highly variable effects-work promoted by cost-cutting undermine the spell, which rarely aims at being bewitching anyway. The puppet characters and clay animated villains are not sufficiently imaginative to overcome their essential lifelessness. **MM**
(See Turkeys of the Year.)

Opposite: The Return of the Living Dead   Above: Rocky IV

Revolution

REVOLUTION

(Goldcrest-Viking/Warner)
dir Hugh Hudson *pro* Irwin Winkler *exec pro* Chris Burt *scr* Robert Dillon *ph* Bernard Lutic, in Scope, System 35, Technicolor *ed* Stuart Baird *pro des* Assheton Gorton *mus* John Corigliano *r time* 125 mins *US opening* Dec 25 *UK opening* Jan 31.
cast Al Pacino, Donald Sutherland, Nastassja Kinski, Joan Plowright, Dave King, Steven Berkoff, John Wells, Annie Lennox, Dexter Fletcher, Sid Owen, Richard O'Brien, Paul Brooke, Eric Milota, Felicity Dean, Jo Anna Lee, Cheryl Miller, Harry Ditson, Rebecca Calder, Theresa Boden.

An example of how not to make a big budget costume epic, 'Revolution' is a disaster from start to finish, although it now seems almost wilfully cruel to add to the chorus of critical disapproval which greeted its release. The screenplay, however, is woefully inadequate: the American War of Independence has been reduced to a couple of hours of milling extras, interspersed with confusing battle scenes and an excruciating half-hour chunk of Al Pacino in full method-acting flight. As a trapper drawn reluctantly into the conflict, he is presumably supposed to represent Everyman adrift in the inexorable march of history, but he merely comes across as a big name actor left stranded by the ebb tide of the British Film Industry. **AB.**
(See Turkeys of the Year.)

A Room With A View

ROCKY IV

(MGM-UA)
dir-scr Sylvester Stallone *pro* Irwin Winkler, Robert Chartoff *exec pro* James D Brubaker, Arthur Chobanian *ph* Bill Butler, in Metrocolor *ed* Don Zimmerman, John W Wheeler *pro des* Bill Kenney *mus* Vince DiCola, Bill Conti *r time* 91 mins *US opening* Nov 29 *UK opening* Jan 24.
cast Sylvester Stallone, Talia Shire, Burt Young, Carl Weathers, Brigitte Nielson, Tony Burton, Michael Pa taki, Dolph Lundgren, R J Adams, Al Bandiero, Dominic Barto, Danial Brown, James Brown, Rose Mary Campos, Jack Carpenter, Mark Dealessandro, Marty Denkin, Lou Filippo.

Early in the latest (dare one hope last?) in the series, one feels a momentary sympathy for the Soviet heavyweight who as he enters the ring in Las Vegas for a 'friendly' exhibition bout with an American opponent is met by a roof-raising cacophony of catcalls and boos. But really it is impossible to feel sympathetic to anybody connected with this farrago of mawkish implausibility, wherein the 'Italian stallion' goes to Moscow and avenges himself on the Russkie who has caused his buddy's death in the ring; he wins, of course, and receives a standing ovation from the Politburo when he delivers some mumbled platitudes about the universal capacity for change. **TP**
(See Films of the Year.)

THE ROOMMATES: See US section

A ROOM WITH A VIEW

(Merchant Ivory/Cinecom/Curzon)
dir James Ivory *pro* Ismail Merchant *scr* Ruth Prawer Jhabvala, based on the novel by E M Forster *ph* Tony Pierce-Roberts, in Technicolor *ed* Humphrey Dixon *pro des* Gianni Quaranta, Brian Ackland-Snow *mus* Richard Robbins and others *r time* 117 mins *US opening* Mar 7 *UK opening* Apr 11.
cast Maggie Smith, Helena Bonham Carter, Denholm Elliott, Julian Sands, Daniel Day Lewis, Simon Callow, Judi Dench, Rosemary Leach, Rupert Graves, Patrick Godfrey, Fabia Drake, Joan Henley, Maria Britneva, Amanda Walker, Peter Cellier, Mia Fothergill, Patricia Lawrence, Mirio Guidelli.

Delicate, leisurely literary treatment, complete with chapter headings, of Forster's story of love across Edwardian class barriers. What gives it a special quality is the acting, notably Maggie Smith's repressed chaperone, all nostrils and hauteur, and Daniel Day Lewis's fastidious lover. **JW**
(See Helena Bonham Carter and Daniel Day Lewis, Faces of the Year.)

RUNAWAY TRAIN
(Northbrook/Cannon)
dir Andrei Konchalovsky *pro* Menahem Golan, Yoram Globus *exec pro* Roger Whitmore, Henry Weinstein, Robert A Goldston *scr* Djordje Milicevic, Paul Zindel, Edward Bunker, based on a screenplay by Akira Kurosawa *ph* Alan Hume, in colour *ed* Henry Richardson *pro des* Stephen Marsh *mus* Trevor Jones *r time* 110 mins *US opening* Dec 6 *UK opening* Jun 27.
cast Jon Voight, Eric Roberts, Rebecca De Mornay, Kyle T Heffner, John P Ryan, T K Carter, Kenneth McMillan, Stacey Pickren, Walter Wyatt, Edward Bunker, Reid Cruikshanks, Michael Lee Gogin, John Bloom, Norton E (Hank) Warden, John Otrin, Norman Alexander Gibbs, Wally Rose, Daniel Trejo.

Konchalovsky's second American movie (after 'Maria's Lovers') is a powerhouse action picture (deriving, though apparently at considerable remove, from a Kurosawa scenario) in which two convicts break out of a top-security jail and stow away on an empty train whose driver proceeds to drop dead at the controls – the train is launched on a headlong rush to perdition with the helicopter bearing the vengeful warden hovering overhead like an angel of doom. At one level, the film is American to the core, with the desperate lifer (a brilliant anti-typecast performance by Jon Voight) in direct line of succession to the psychotic anti-heroes of Walsh and Siegel, and the violence orchestrated to create a vortex of nihilism. Yet the film is inescapably Russian too. The snowy wastes of Alaska could just as well be Siberia, and the escapers inevitably bring to mind victims of the Gulag archipelago; the crazed warden even looks somewhat like Stalin. The Dostoievskian ambition of the regenerative finale does not quite manage to be an inevitable outcome of what has preceded it; to some extent, in its final phase, the film as well as the train is out of control. Nonetheless, it remains a remarkable combination of popular form and personal expression. **TP**

RUNNING SCARED: See US section

RUTHLESS PEOPLE: See US section

Runaway Train

S

ST ELMO'S FIRE
(Columbia)
dir Joel Schumacher *pro* Lauren Shuler *exec pro* Ned Tanen, Bernard Schwartz *scr* Joel Schumacher, Carl Kurlander *ph* Stephen H Burum, in Panavision, Metrocolor *ed* Richard Marks *art dir* William Sandell *mus* David Foster *r time* 108 mins *US opening* prior to Jul 1985 *UK opening* Nov 1.
cast Rob Lowe, Demi Moore, Andrew McCarthy, Judd Nelson, Ally Sheedy, Emilio Estevez, Mare Winningham, Martin Balsam, Jon Cutler, Joyce Van Patten, Andie MacDowell, Jenny Wright, Blake Clarke.

At times this youth-audience knockoff on 'The Big Chill' verges into unintentionally funny parody, but it's meant to be deeply felt and might have been, too, if a well-designed outline promisingly setting up the characters and situations had been developed with any attention to truth instead of carelessly careening through sloppy plotting and maudlin interactions. Not really bad, it's still something of a monstrosity to behold. **MM**

SANS TOIT NI LOI: See VAGABONDE

SALVADOR: See US section

SANTA CLAUS – THE MOVIE
(Rank/Tri Star)
dir Jeannot Szwarc *pro* Ilya Salkind, Pierre Spengler *scr* David Newman, based on a story by David and Leslie Newman *ph* Arthur Ibbetson, in colour *ed* Peter Hollywood *pro des* Anthony Pratt *mus* Henry Mancini *r time* 108 mins *UK opening* Nov 26 *US opening* Nov 29
cast Dudley Moore, John Lithgow, David Huddleston, Burgess Meredith, Judy Cornwell, Jeffrey Kramer, Christian Fitzpatrick, Carrie Kei Heim, John Barrard, Anthony O'Donnell, Melvyn Hayes, Don Estelle, Tim Stern, Peter O'Farrell, Christopher Ryan, Dickie Arnold, Aimee Delamain, Dorothea Phillips.

The sub-title is not the only redundant thing about this ghastly gesture toward a comedy-spectacle for the family audience, which contrives to lend a whole new dimension to the commercialisation of Christmas. To say that Dudley Moore plays an elf (cue for 'jokes' about elf-confidence and elf-control) who seeks to introduce mass production techniques into toy making at the North Pole probably gives more than enough of an idea about an experience which rather resembles being locked for two hours in a Santa's grotto at the wrong end of the High Street with the Yuletide muzak amplified to Dolby stereo proportions. **TP**
(See Turkeys of the Year.)

St Elmo's Fire

Santa Claus – The Movie

The Scorpion

THE SCORPION
(Movies Filmproductions/Thorn EMI)
dir Ben Verbong *pro* Chris Brouwer, Haig Balian *scr* Ben Verbong, Pieter De Vos *ph* Theo Van D Sande, in Fujicolor *ed* Ton De Graaff *art dir* Dorus Van Der Linden *mus* Nicola Piovani *r time* 98 mins *UK opening* Feb 7.
cast Peter Tuinman, Monique Van De Ven, Rima Melati, Senne Rouffaer, Walter Kous, Adrian Brine, Huub Stapel, Henk Van Ulsen, Edwin De Vries, Teddy Schaank, Marijke Veugelers, Hans Holtkamp, Hans Kerckhoffs, Albert Abspoel, Loes Luca, Diane Lensink, Willem Van Rinsum, Ernst Zwaan, Frank Van Oortmerssen.

After the assurance of Verbong's 'The Girl With the Red Hair', this awkwardly constructed conspiracy thriller comes as a relative disappointment. About an ex-criminal who, after a deal with false passports, finds himself first reported dead and then threatened by murderous strangers, it examines the legacy of Holland's involvement in forties' Indonesia upon the colonising country's political, military and economic powers in the mid-fifties. While Verbong's abandoning of suspense in favour of theme, atmosphere and characterisation does no real harm, a major problem remains in that the question of where Sukarno's rebels obtained their arms is answered in unconvincing fashion. Noir-style photography and strong, surly performances may help, but the overall effect, especially during the flashbacks, is curiously lifeless. **GA**

SESAME STREET PRESENTS: FOLLOW THAT BIRD: See US section

SEVEN MINUTES IN HEAVEN: See US section

SEX MISSION
(Zespóly Filmowe, Kadr/Cinegate)
dir Juliusz Machulski *scr* Juliusz Machulski, Jolanta Hartwig, Pavel Hajny *ph* Jerzy Lukaszeeicz, in colour *ed* Miroslawa Garlicka *art dir* Janusz Sosnowski *mus* Henryk Kuzniak *r time* 121 mins *UK opening* Aug 22
cast Olgierd Lukaszewicz, Jerzy Stuhr, Bozena Stryjkowna, Boguslawa Pawelec, Hanna Stankowna, Beata Tyszkiewicz, Dorota Stalinska, Janusz Michalowski, Piotr Stefaniak, Julius Lisowski, Ryszarda Hanin, Barbara Ludwizanka, Zofia Pelwinska, Miroslawa Marcheluk, Hanna Mikuc.

'Sleeper' meets 'Nineteen Eighty-Four' with a smidgeon of Polish political allegory, as the two subjects of an experiment in hibernation wake up to find themselves in a subterranean world populated entirely by women – the men have apparently been wiped out in the aftermath of a nuclear war which has left the earth's surface uninhabitable. Unfortunately, the film is pitched on a level of low-tech sci-fi farce which rarely rises above crude 'Carry On'-style lipsmacking sexism: the women are portrayed as curvaceous cuties whose humourless feminist instincts need nothing more than a good stiff dose of violent virility for them to be awakened to all of life's rich possibilities. **AB**

SHADEY
(Larkspur-Film Four International/Mainline)
dir Philip Saville *pro* Otto Plaschkes *scr* Snoo Wilson *ph* Roger Deakins, in colour *ed* Chris Kelly *pro des* Norman Garwood *mus* Colin Towns *r time* 106 mins *UK opening* May 2.
cast Antony Sher, Billie Whitelaw, Patrick Macnee, Katherine Helmond, Leslie Ash, Bernard Hepton, Larry Lamb, Jesse Birdsall, Olivier Pierre, Jon Cartwright, Stephen Persaud, Basil Henson, Peter Kelly, Madhav Sharma, Susan Engel, Zohra Segal, Jenny Runacre, Jane Myerson, Gillian De Tourville.

In dealing with the exploits of the eponymous, wimpy hero – who sells his ability to translate his thoughts onto film in order to finance a sex-change operation – Snoo Wilson's screenplay toys around with topical themes like kidnapping, terrorism, industrial and military espionage, pop-promo production, incest and insanity, and juggles them with such persistently whimsical abandon that the final result makes no sense – in terms of narrative or emotional effect – whatsoever. Crammed full of silly, irrelevant surrealism, it's neither funny, touching nor illuminating. The abiding impression, indeed, is one of an almost obscene waste of money, time and talent. **GA**

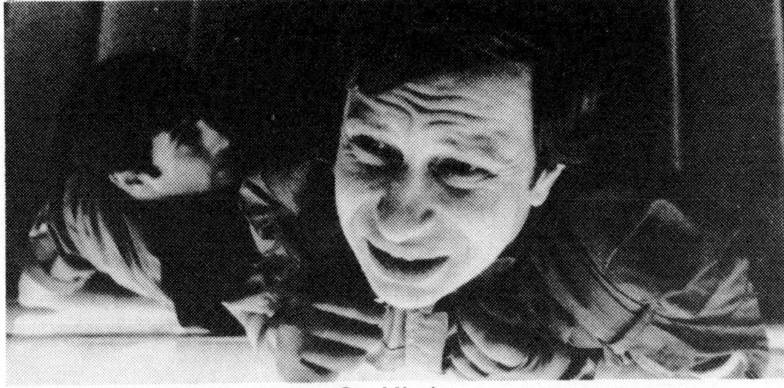
Sex Mission

Shadey

Silver Bullet

Silverado

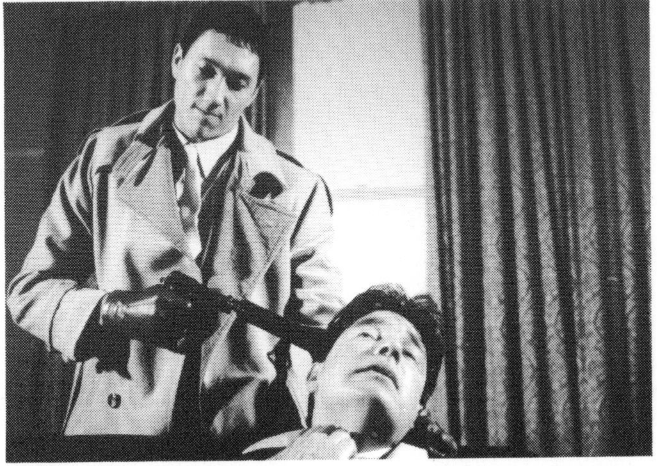
Shaker Run

SHAKER RUN
(Mirage-Aviscom/Miracle)
dir Bruce Morrison *pro* Larry Parr, Igo Kantor *exec pro* Henry Fownes *scr* James Kouf Jr, Henry Fownes, Bruce Morrison *ph* Kevin Hayward, in colour *ed* Ken Zemke, Bob Richardson *pro des* Ron Highfield *mus* Stephen McCurdy *r time* 90 mins *UK opening* Feb 28.
cast Cliff Robertson, Leif Garrett, Lisa Harrow, Shane Briant, Peter Hayden, Peter Rowell, Bruce Phillips, Ian Mune, Fiona Samuels, Deidre O'Connor, Mat Lees, Daniel Gillion, Geoffrey Heath, Dave Smith, Igo Kantor, Barry Dorking, John Bray.

With a stolen, suspiciously AIDS-like virus as its back-seat McGuffin, this numbskull car-chase movie is all stunts, slapstick and stupidity, as superannuated hell-driver Robertson speeds worried scientist Harrow towards the edge of New Zealand, pursued by government hit-men and blithely trusting to the tender mercies of the CIA. Truly witless. **PT**

SHORT CIRCUIT: See US section

SIGNAL SEVEN: See US section

SILVER BULLET
(Dino De Laurentiis/Paramount/Cannon)
dir Daniel Attias *pro* Martha Schumacher *scr* Stephen King, based on his novelette 'Cycle of the Werewolf' *ph* Armando Nannuzzi, in Technicolor *ed* Daniel Loewentha, *pro des* Giorgio Postiglione *mus* Jay Chattaway *r time* 95 mins *US opening* Oct 4 *UK opening* Jun 20.
cast Gary Busey, Everett McGill, Corey Haim, Megan Follows, Robin Groves, Leon Russom, Terry O'Quinn, Bill Smitrovich, Joe Wright, Kent Broadhurst, Heather Simmons, James A Baffico, Rebecca Fleming, Lawrence Tierney, William Newman, Sam Stoneburner, Lonnie Moore, Rick Pasotto.

Yet another screen adaptation of a Stephen King story, this is a distinctly unoriginal tale of lycanthropy decimating the redneck population of a small American town. The werewolf's chief opponents are a crippled boy and his alcoholic uncle. The characters do the usual stupid things like going off on their own into the woods at night; the adults are endlessly sceptical about the werewolf's existence, and the transformation sequences, though well done, are tiresomely déjà-vu. **AB**

SILVERADO
(Columbia)
dir-pro Lawrence Kasdan
exec pro Charles Okun, Michael Grillo *scr* Lawrence Kasdan, Mark Kasdan *ph* John Bailey, in Super Techniscope, Technicolor *ed* Carol Littleton *pro des* Ida Random *mus* Bruce Broughton *r time* 132 mins *US opening* Jul 12 *UK opening* Jan 3.
cast Kevin Kline, Scott Glenn, Kevin Costner, Danny Glover, Brian Dennehy, Linda Hunt, Jeff Goldblum, Rosanna Arquette, John Cleese, Marvin J McIntyre, Brad Williams, Todd Allen, Kenny Call Hartline, Rusty Meyers, Zeke Davidson, Lois Geary, James Gammon, Troy Ward, Pepe Serna, Ted White, Ray Baker.

High, wide, but only intermittently handsome, 'Silverado' seems too gripped by self-consciousness to amount to more than pastiche. The plot is so anthological and the style so studied – as if every time a horseman mounts up he must be seen silhouetted against the sky – that the narrative is left to ramble around all over the place. Enjoyable in parts nonetheless, with performances by Linda Hunt and Brian Dennehy that properly go with the territory, even if it is difficult to tell whether John Cleese's dour lawman is meant to be funny or not. **TP**
(See Kevin Costner, Faces of the Year.)

SIXTEEN DAYS OF GLORY: See US section

SMOOTH TALK: See US section

SOTTO ... SOTTO: See US section

SPACECAMP: See US section

SPIES LIKE US
(Warner)
dir John Landis *pro* Brian Grazer, George Folsey Jr *exec pro* Bernie Brillstein *scr* Dan Aykroyd, Lowell Ganz, Babaloo Mandel, based on a story by Dan Aykroyd, Dave Thomas *ph* Robert Paynter, in Technicolor *ed* Malcolm Campbell *pro des* Peter Murton *mus* Elmer Bernstein *r time* 102 mins *US opening* Dec 6 *UK opening* Feb 14. *cast* Dan Aykroyd, Chevy Chase, Steve Forrest, Charles McKeown, Donna Dixon, Derek Meddings, Ray Harryhausen, Robert Paynter, Terry Gilliam, Gusti Bogok, Stephen Hoye, Ronald Reagan, Tom Hatten, Bruce Davison, William Prince, Bernie Casey, Jim Staahl, James Daughton, Tony Cyrus.

In being a 'vehicle' for Aykroyd and Chase, 'Spies Like Us' lacks some of the subtle pleasures of Landis's engaging comedy-thriller 'Into the Night', but it's enjoyable enough. The beginning is very funny indeed as our incompetent heroes are selected as decoys for a dangerous mission. After that, it's largely a question of keeping the jokes coming, and they do, although with increasing hit-and-miss irregularity. **AC**

STAND ALONE: See US section

STARCHASER: THE LEGEND OF ORIN
(Atlantic Entertainment)
dir-pro Steven Hahn *exec pro* Thomas Coleman, Michael Rosenblatt *scr* Jeffrey Scott *ph* Charles Flekal, in DeLuxe colour *ed* Donald W Ernst *mus* Andrew Belling *r time* 100 mins *US opening* Nov 22 *UK opening* May 23. *cast (voices)* Joe Colligan, Carmen Argenziano, Noelle North, Anthony Delongis, Les Tremayne, Tyke Caravelli, Ken Sansom, John Moschitta Jr, Mickey Morton, Herb Virgan, Dennis Alwood, Mona Marshall, Tina Romanus.

An animated cartoon in 3-D, at any rate one which essays a representational style, might sound like a contradiction in terms, since animation should surely create its own perspectives. In the event, this interminable yarn of inter-galactic derring-do mostly resembles a succession of pop-up tableaux which look as if they had been cut from the back of a cereal packet. It would probably require a further dimension to make any sense of the plot. **TP**

STATIC
(Necessity Films/Blue Dolphin)
dir Mark Romanek *pro* Amy Ness *exec pro* Julio Caro *scr* Keith Gordon, Mark Romanek *ph* Jeff Jur, in colour *ed* Emily Paine *pro des* Cynthia Sowder *mus* various *r time* 93 mins *UK opening* Jun 13. *cast* Keith Gordon, Amanda Plummer, Bob Gunton, Lily Knight, Barton Heyman, Reathel Bean, Kitty Mei-Mei, Jane Hoffman, Eugene Lee, Joel K Rehbeil, Jack Murakami, Mike Murakami, Uma Ridenhour, Janice Abbott, Tamma Allgood, Dean B Winans, Mary Hunka, Paul Stucky, David Pape, Art Louisignau.

A dizzyingly idiosyncratic debut feature performs the unlikely feat of raising agnosticism to a deadpan art. A disturbing, distorted tragi-farce constructed around the figure of a young Arizonan video visionary, convinced of his discovery of a cathode-ray hotline to Heaven, it belies the threat of its title at every eccentric turn. Built upon credible, consistently bizarre observation and characterisation, the movie prods audaciously at the wafer-thin boundaries between faith, fantasy and fanaticism. **PT**
(See Keith Gordon, Faces of the Year.)

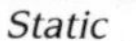

Static

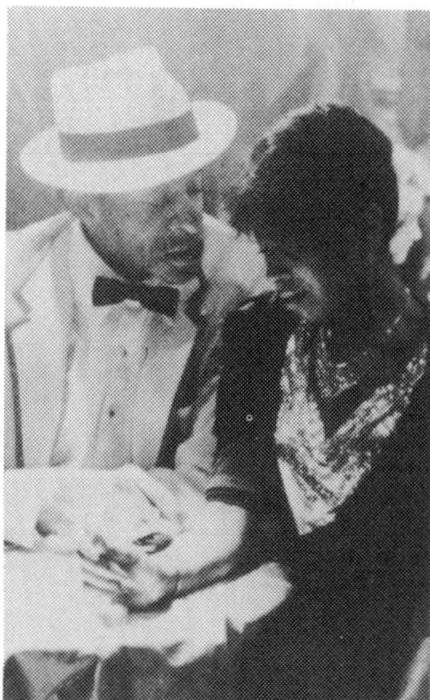

Streetwalkin'

Above: Streetwise Opposite: Subway

STREETWALKIN'
(Rodeo Prods/Concorde/ICA)
dir Joan Freeman, *pro* Rober Alden *exec pro* Roger Corman *scr* Joan Freeman, Robert Alden *ph* Steven Fierberg, in DeLuxe Colour *ed* John K Adams, Patrick Rand *art dir* Jeffery Robbins *mus* Matthew Ender, Doug Timm and others *r time* 85 mins *US opening* Aug 30 *UK opening* May 16. *cast* Melissa Leo, Randall Batinkoff, Dale Midkiff, Deborah Offner, Julie Newmar, Julie Cohen, Greg Germann, Kirk Taylor, Antonio Fargas, Khandi Alexander, Annie Golden, Leon Robinson, Jason Walker, Michael Torres, Bill Shuman, Jake Reno, Garth Gardner, Gary Klar, Samantha Fox.

During the course of one ever more frenzied New York night, a youthful hooker tries to change employers and only narrowly escapes (as sundry other members of the cast do not) ending up on a mortuary slab. The scenes of violence are assembled with undeniable skill, but though the director has a background in documentary, the effect remains specious, not to say pretty dubious. Dale Midkiff's performance as the psychotic pimp, a well-nigh indestructible figure on horror-movie lines, is a collector's item of Method-style mannerism. **TP**

STREETWISE
(Angelika Films-Bear Creek/Angelika/Mainline)
dir-ph Martin Bell, in Eastman Colour *pro-scr* Cheryl McCall, developed from her story 'Streets of the Lost' *ed* Nancy Baker *mus* Baby Gramps, Tom Waits *r time* 91 mins *US opening* prior to Jul 1985 *UK opening* Feb 14. *with* Alabama, Annie, Antoine, Biker Kim, Black Junior, Breezy, Buddha, Butch, Calyn, Chrissie, Dawn, DeWayne, Drugs, Eddie, Erica, Erin ('Tiny'), Floyd, JR, James, Jim, John, Juan, Justin, Kim, Michele, Mike, Patti, Munchkin, Patrice, Peehole, Rat, Red Dog, Roberta, Russ, Sam Shadow, Shellie, Smurf, Sparkles, Steve, Tracy, White Junior, William.

Documentary slice of low-life about a group of teenagers who forage for a meagre existence on the mean streets of Seattle by pimping, prostitution and petty theft. The 'fly-on-the-wall' nature of the film is troubling: while one cannot help but admire the resilience of the children, it is difficult to gauge how much they are playing to the camera, and even more difficult to condone the way in which they have fallen unquestioningly into the stereotyped roles of adults who regard bodies as commodities to be bought or sold. The suicide of a drug-pushing 14-year-old comes across as less of a poignant end to a wasted life and more of a convenient device with which to round off the cinema verité material. One is left with the impression of having been press-ganged into participating in someone's well-meaning but voyeuristic colour supplement project. **AB**

STRIPPER: See US section

THE STUFF: See THAT'S THE STUFF

SUBWAY
(Les Films du Loup-TSF-Gaumont/Artificial Eye/Island)
dir Luc Besson *pro* Luc Besson, François Ruggieri *exec pro* Louis Duchesne *scr* Luc Besson, Pierre Jolivet, Alain Le Henry, Marc Perrier, Sophie Schmit *ph* Carlo Varint, in CinemaScope, colour *ed* Sophie Schmit *art dir* Alexandre Tauner *mus* Eric Serra, Rickie Lee Jones, Corinne Marieneau *r time* 102 mins *UK opening* Sep 5 *UK opening* Nov 8 *cast* Isabelle Adjani, Christopher Lambert, Richard Bohringer, Michel Galabru, Jean-Hugues Anglade, Jean-Pierre Bacri, Jean-Claude Lecas, Jean Bouise, Pierre-Ange Le Pogam, Jean Reno, Arthur Simms, Constantin Alexandrov, Eric Serra, Benoît Regent, Isabelle Sadoyan, Jimmy Blanche, Michel d'Oz.

In every way an advance on Besson's 'The Last Battle', his second film shares its predecessor's originality in the use of Scope and Dolby but applies them to a subject of melodramatic density. Almost entirely set in the labyrinthine 'backstage' areas of the Paris Metro, the picture takes on overtones of 'The Phantom of the Opera' as the anti-hero (Lambert, sporting dinner jacket and punk-yellow hair) ventures forth from his secret lair to woo his enigmatic lady fair (Adjani). The conclusion is reached in a hail of bullets, but remains cloaked in neo-romantic ambiguity. This is modernist movie-making as exciting as the precursors of the nouvelle vague a generation ago. **TP**

SUMMER RENTAL: See US section

SUPERGRASS
(Recorded Releasing)
dir Peter Richardson *pro* Elaine Taylor *exec pro* Michael White *scr* Peter Richardson, Pete Richens *ph* John Metcalfe, in colour *ed* Geoff Hogg *art dir* Niki Wateridge *mus* Keith Tippett, Working Week Big Band and others *r time* 107 mins *UK opening* Nov 8. *cast* Adrian Edmondson, Jennifer Saunders, Peter Richardson, Dawn French, Keith Allen, Nigel Planer, Robbie Coltrane, Danny Peacock, Ronald Allen, Alexei Sayle, Michael Elphick, Patrick Durkin, Marika Rivera, Rita Treisman, Neil Cunningham, Michael White, David Beard.

A big screen outing by personnel from the 'Comic Strip' TV series, this is in outline a rather old-fashioned comedy-thriller of cops (undercover) v robbers (or drug-runners) in deepest Devon, on to which has been grafted a variety of absurdist and off-colour jokes (including an episode involving a corpse in a urinal of which Hitchcock himself might have been proud). Superior scenic and pictorial values unfortunately tend to obstruct the pace of a narrative which is none too sure of itself in the first place; all the same, a promising debut. **TP**

THE SURE THING
(Monument/Embassy/Rank)
dir Rob Reiner *pro* Roger Birnbaum *exec pro* Henry Winkler *scr* Steven L Bloom *ph* Robert Elswit, in colour *ed* Robert Leighton *pro des* Lilly Kilvert *mus* Tom Scott *r time* 94 mins *US opening* prior to Jul 1985 *UK opening* Jan 17. *cast* John Cusack, Daphne Zuniga, Anthony Edwards, Boyd Gaines, Tim Robbins, Lisa Jane Persky, Viveca Lindfors, Nicollete Sheridan, Larry Hankin.

Rob Reiner follows 'This Is Spinal Tap' with a more conventional variation on 'It Happened One Night', with two spatting college freshmen falling in love as they hitch across the country. The plot material is often suspect, but the humour is genuine and the players achieve a consistent behavioural charm that renders the spurious pandering elements inoffensive. This may be as close to a credible comedy as contemporary commercial requirements allow. **MM**

SWEET DREAMS
(HBO Pictures-Silver Screen Partners/Tri Star/EMI)
dir Karel Reisz *pro* Bernard Schwartz *scr* Robert Getchell *ph* Robbie Greenberg, in Technicolor *ed* Malcolm Cooke *pro des* Albert Brenner *mus* Charles Gross *r time* 115 mins *US opening* Oct 4 *UK opening* Jan 31. *cast* Jessica Lange, Ed Harris, Ann Wedgeworth, David Clennon, James Staley, Gary Basaraba, John Goodman P J Soles, Terri Gardner, Caitlin Kelch, Robert L Dasch, Courtney Parker, Colton Edwards, Holly Filler, Bruce Kirby, Jerry Haynes, Kenneth White, Stonewall Jackson.

Supergrass

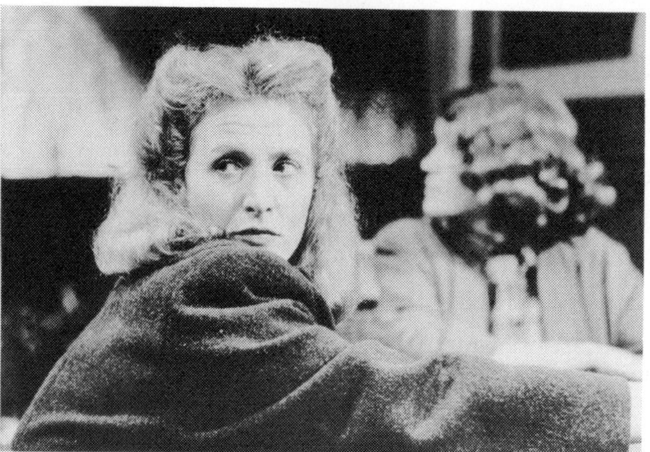

Above: Sylvia   Opposite: Sweet Dreams

A surprisingly intelligent biopic of Country and Western star Patsy Cline, which concentrates less on her career than on her stormy relationship with second husband, Charlie Dick. Cline fans would probably have preferred more emphasis on the Nashville side of things, but they can have no quibbles about the sublime performance of Jessica Lange in the central role, miming faultlessly to Cline's original recordings. **AB**

SWEET LIBERTY: See US section

SYLVIA
(Unitel-Southern Light Pictures-Cinepro/Enterprise)
dir Michael Firth *pro* Don Reynolds, Michael Firth *scr* Michael Quill, F Fairfax, Michael Firth, based on the books 'Teacher', 'I Passed This Way' by Sylvia Ashton-Warner *ph* Ian Paul, in colour *ed* Michael Horton *pro des* Gary Hansen *mus* Leonard Rosenman *r time* 98 mins *UK opening* Jul 26. *cast* Eleanor David, Nigel Terry, Tom Wilkinson, Mary Regan, Martyn Sanderson, Terence Cooper, David Letch, Sarah Pierce, James Cross, Peter Thorpe, Roy Pearse, Ian Harrop, Te Whatanui Skipwith, Norman Forsey, Margaret Murray.

An episode from the early life of the New Zealand writer Sylvia Ashton Warner, when circa 1950 she taught at a remote rural school and attempted in the face of official discouragement to pioneer more imaginative classroom methods. The background is persuasively sketched in, and there are sympathetic performances from Eleanor David (Sylvia) and Tom Wilkinson (her husband), yet the film lacks the heightening and compression which would have allowed it to rise above the level of a somewhat inconsequential anecdote. **TP**

TARGET: See US section

TEEN WOLF
(Atlantic/Entertainment)
dir Rod Daniel *pro* Mark Levinson, Scott Rosenfelt *exec pro* Thomas Coleman, Michael Rosenblatt *scr* Joseph Loeb III, Matthew Weisman *ph* Tim Suhrstedt, in colour *ed* Lois Freeman-Fox *mus* Miles Goodman *r time* 92 mins *US opening* Aug 23 *UK opening* Jan 24. *cast* Michael J Fox, James Hampton, Susan Ursitti, Jerry Levine, Matt Adler, Lorie Griffin, Jim MacKrell, Mark Arnold, Jay Tarses, Mark Holton, Scott Paulin, Elizabeth Gorcey, Melanie Manos, Doug Savant, Charles Zucker, Harvey Vernon, Clare Peck, Gregory Itzen, Doris Hess, Troy Evans, Linda Wiesmeier.

'Teen Wolf', made before 'Back to the Future', rests squarely on the slight shoulders of new teenybopper idol Michael J Fox. He is a personable enough juvenile lead, even if the material here – a mild sitcom affair about a high-school student whose unexpected lupine metamorphosis makes him the most popular jock in town – leaves something to be desired. The moral of the tale is crashingly obvious: be yourself and don't overlook the girl next door in favour of the class tart. And the special effects make-up is not so much lupine as monkeyish. **AB** *(See Michael J Fox, Faces of the Year.)*

Teen Wolf

THAT'S THE STUFF
[UK TITLE: THE STUFF]
(New World/Recorded Releasing)
dir-scr Larry Cohen *pro* Paul Kurta *exec pro* Larry Cohen, Peter Sabiston *ph* Paul Glickman, in colour *ed* Armond Lebowitz *art dir* Marlene Marta, George Stoll *mus* Anthony Guefen *r time* 87 mins *US opening* Sep 20 *UK opening* Apr 18.
cast Michael Moriarty, Andrea Marcovicci, Garrett Morris, Paul Sorvino, Scott Bloom, Danny Aiello, Patrick James Dixon, Alexander Scourby, Russell Nype, Gene O'Neal, James Dukas, Catherine Schulz, Peter Hock, Colette Blonigan, Frank Telfer, Brian Bloom.

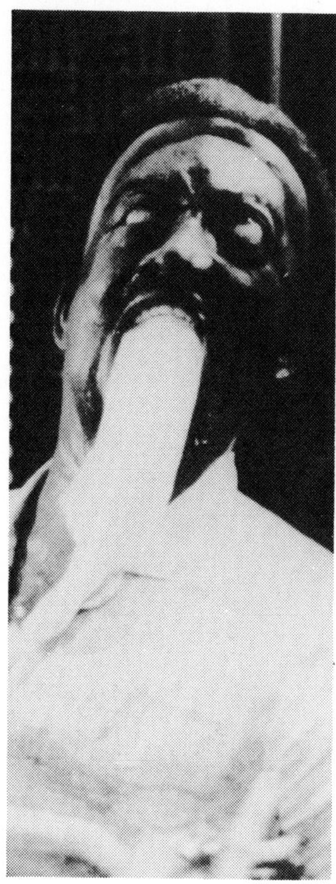

While most screen monsters spend their time battering down doors to get at their victims, 'The Stuff' employs more insidious methods – you take it home with you and stockpile it in your fridge. It's a delicious dessert which proves fatally addictive to its consumers, some of whom are seen indulging in the most disgusting sort of Technicolor yawn. Larry Cohen's humour is decidedly offbeat, his style verges on the tacky side of low-budget, but just when you think you've got his measure, he throws in yet another wacky element, such as a private army of right-wing fanatics whose leader decides the dessert is a commie plot to sap the country's moral fibre. Michael Moriarty delivers a delirious piece of overacting as the man assigned to discover The Stuff's secret ingredient. A dire warning to junk food addicts, and a true treat for fans of subversive, oddball film-making. **AB**

THAT WAS THEN ... THIS IS NOW: See US section

LE THÉ AU HAREM D'ARCHIMEDE: See US section

To Live and Die in L.A.

Trial Run

The Trip to Bountiful

TO LIVE AND DIE IN L.A.
(New Century-SLM/MGM-UA)
dir William Friedkin *pro* Irving H Levin *exec pro* Samuel Schulman *scr* William Friedkin, Gerald Petievich, based on the novel by Gerald Petievich *ph* Robby Muller, in Technicolor *ed* Scott Smith *pro des* Lilly Kilvert *mus* Wang Chung *r time* 116 mins *US opening* Nov 1 *UK opening* May 30.
cast William L Petersen, Willem Dafoe, John Pankow, Debra Feuer, John Turturro, Darlanne Fluegel, Dean Stockwell, Steve James, Robert Downey, Michael Greene, Christopher Allport, Jack Hoar, Val DeVargas, Dwier Brown, Michael Chong, Jackelyn Giroux, Michael Zand, Anne Betancourt, Katherine M Louie.

Ultra-slick thriller which is a mixture of flashy imagery, tour-de-force editing and driving rock soundtrack from Wang Chung, woven by Friedkin into a sort of update of 'The French Connection' crossed with a truly vicious episode of 'Miami Vice', in which a couple of cops set out to nab a master forger. A weirdly compelling film, despite its total lack of sympathetic characters. **AB**

TOP GUN: See US section

TORMENT: See US section

TRANSYLVANIA 6-5000: See US section

TRIAL RUN
(Double Feature Investments/Miracle)
dir-scr Melanie Read, based on an idea by Catarina Da Nave, Melanie Read *pro* Dona Reynolds *ph* Allen Guilford, in colour *ed* Finola Dwyer *pro des* Judith Crozier *mus* Jan Preston, Blair Greenberg *r time* 89 mins *UK opening* Jul 26.
cast Annie Whittle, Judith Gibson, Christoper Broun, Philippa Mayne, Stephen Tozer, Martyn Sanderson, Lee Grant, Frances Edmond, Teresa Woodham, Allison Roe, Karen Sims, Maggie Eyre, Margaret Blay.

Starting off with some crypto-feminist allusions which prove to be no more than red herrings, this New Zealand movie turns into a contemporary variant on the frightened lady theme, with Annie Whittle as a wildlife photographer who rents an isolated rural cottage for professional purposes and rapidly finds herself prey to enigmatic rustics and things that go bump (and worse) in the night. Smart cinematography and some atmospheric scene-setting compensate for a rather thin narrative, but the explanation for the rum goings-on vouchsafed by the twist ending is so contrived as to sabotage somewhat the effect of what has preceded it. **TP**

THE TRIP TO BOUNTIFUL
(Filmdallas-Bountiful/Island/Mainline)
dir Peter Masterson *pro* Sterling Van Wagenen, Horton Foote *exec pro* Sam Grogg, George Yaneff *scr* Horton Foote, based on his play *ph* Fred Murphy, in colour *ed* Jay Freund *pro des* Neil Spisak *mus* J A C Redford *r time* 107 mins *US opening* Dec 20 *UK opening* Jun 6.
cast Geraldine Page, John Heard, Carlin Glynn, Richard Bradford, Rebecca De Mornay, Kevin Cooney, Norman Bennett, Harvey Lewis, Kirk Sisco, Dave Tanner, Gil Glasgow, Mary Kay Mars,

Wezz Tildon, Peggy Ann Byers, David Romo, Alexandra Masterson, Don Wyse, Tony Torn, John Torn, James Drake.

Geraldine Page finally copped her Oscar for her portrayal of an elderly woman trekking off for a last look at the old homestead. By the standards of her particular school of acting, she is indeed nearly perfect; by other lights, perhaps highly technical and too consciously worked out. If anything, John Heard as her put-upon son does even purer work. Horton Foote's adaptation of his early fifties television play (which starred Lillian Gish) remains doggedly true to its original, and debut director Masterson brings nothing to the project beyond his work with the players. **MM**

TROLL: See US section

TROUBLE: See US section

TUFF TURF
(Blue Dolphin/New World Pictures)
dir Fritz Kiersch *pro* Donald P Borchers *scr* Jette Rinck, based on a story by Greg Collins O'Neill, Murray Michaels *ph* Willy Kurant, in CFI Colour *ed* Marc Grossman *art dir* Craig Stearns *mus* Jonathan Elias and others *r time* 111 mins *UK opening* Dec 6 *US opening* Jan 11.
cast James Spader, Kim Richards, Paul Mones, Matt Clark, Claudette Nevins, Olivia Barash, Robert Downey, Panchito Gomez, Michael Wyle, Catya Sassoon, Frank McCarthy, Art Evans, Herb Mitchell, Ceil Cabot, Donald Fullilove, Lou Fant, Vivian Brown, Bill Beyers, Jered Barclay.

Formula exploitation teenpic in which the hero, a new boy in town, takes on the dirty-fighting might of the local gang of louts and walks off with the gangleader's girlfriend. Token tuff-boy brooding and a modicum of violence fail to conceal the soft centre of a film in which even the bad guy proposes marriage. **AB**

TURK 182
(Fox)
dir Bob Clark *pro* Ted Field, Rene DuPont *exec pro* Peter Samuelson, Robert Cort *scr* James Gregory Kingston, Denis Hamill, John Hamill, based on a story by James Gregory Kingston *ph* Reginald H Morris, in colour *ed* Stan Cole *pro des* Harry Pottle *mus* Paul Zaza *r time* 98 mins *US opening* prior to Jul 1985 *UK opening* Sep 6.
cast Timothy Hutton, Robert Urich, Kim Cattrall, Robert Culp, Darren McGiven, Steve Keats, Peter Boyle, Paul Sorvino, Thomas Quinn, Norman Parker, Dick O'Neill.

Trumped up rabble-rouser that opens with some fair sketches of blue collar life but degenerates into terminal nonsense as Timothy Hutton becomes a New York Kilroy dogging a corrupt mayor with his graffiti to protest against the treatment of his older brother, a crippled former firefighter. The shamelessness of the Rocky-like attempt to orchestrate audience cheers guarantees all loss of sympathy for such transparent manipulation. Bob Clark ('Porky's') possesses an unerring instinct for exploiting the least compelling aspects of his material. **MM**

Turtle Diary

Tuff Turf

Turk 182

TURTLE DIARY
(United British Artists-Britannic/Rank/Samuel Goldwyn)
dir John Irvin *pro* Richard Johnson *exec pro* Peter Snell *scr* Harold Pinter, based on the novel by Russell Hoban *ph* Peter Hannan, in Technicolor *ed* Peter Tanner *pro des* Leo Austin *mus* Geoffrey Burgon *r time* 96 mins *UK opening* Dec 1 *US opening* Feb 4.
cast Glenda Jackson, Ben Kingsley, Richard Johnson, Michael Gambon, Rosemary Leach, Eleanor Bron, Harriet Walter, Jeroen Krabbe, Nigel Hawthorne, Michael Aldridge, Rom Anderson, Tony Melody, Gary Olsen, Peter Capaldi, Harold Pinter, Barbara Rosenblat, Chuck Julian.

A risibly 'sensitive' reduction of Russell Hoban's eccentric novel to the dimensions of a virtual nature-watch on a Hampstead sub-species – a static scrutiny of two lives of (almost) quiet desperation, with timid bedsit bookworms Jackson and Kingsley bringing each other out of their shells by conspiring to liberate a couple of zoo-reared turtles into the wide blue yonder. This needed the bold strokes of a Mike Leigh – not the dead hand of Pinter's patented pauses and two of the most sincerely furrowed brows in the business. **PT**

TWICE IN A LIFETIME: See US section

UFORIA: See US section

UP YOUR ANCHOR (LEMON POPSICLE 6)
(Cannon)
dir Dan Wolman *pro* Menahem Golan, Yoram Globus *scr* Dan Wolman, Eli Tavor, based on the characters created by Boaz Davidson, Eli Tavor *ph* Ilan Rosenberg, in colour *ed* Alan Yakobovitz *art dir* Yoram Barzilai *mus* various *r time* 87 mins *UK opening* Oct 18.
cast Zachi Nov, Yftach Katzur, Joseph Shiloah, Yehuda Efroni, Deborah Keidar, Petra Koglenik, Alexander Arelson, Biah Fidler.

This sixth instalment in the egregious Popsicle series achieves the not inconsiderable feat of demonstrating that the standard of witlessness and sheer ineptitude set by the preceding five can still be surpassed. In the circumstances about the only surprising thing is that one item of comic business, in which a cache of smuggled diamonds disappears among the shards of a fallen chandelier, actually manages to provoke a titter. **TP**

VAGABONDE (SANS TOIT NI LOI)
(Ciné-Tamaris-Films à 2/Electric Pictures)
dir-scr Agnès Varda *pro* Oury Milshtein *ph* Patrick Blossier, in colour *ed* Agnès Varda, Patricia Mazuy *set dec* Jean Bauer, Anne Violet *mus* Joanna Bruzdowicz and others *r time* 106 mins *UK opening* May 9.

Vagabonde

cast Sandrine Bonnaire, Macha Méril, Yolande Moreau, Stéphane Freiss, Marthe Jarnias, Joël Fosse, Patrick Lepcynski, Laurence Cortadellas, Yahiaoui Assouna, Setti Ramdane, Dominque Durand, Patrick Schmit, Daniel Bos, Katy Champaud, Raymond Roulle, Henri Fridani, Patrick Sokol, Pierre Imbert.

The corpse of a young female derelict is found in a wintry ditch in the South of France and, almost as if in a detective story, the last few weeks of her life are summoned up through the recollection of those whose path she crossed. 'Vagabonde' combines documentary elements – it was entirely shot on location and many of the performers are non-professionals recruited on the spot – with a highly formalised, even choreographed, visual style. And certainly the effect is not sociological, any more than it is sentimental: we are offered no explanation for the girl's rejection of convention and propriety, and there is no attempt to present her as other than the kind of person one would go a long way to avoid. But allowing for a degree of schematism in the construction, the effect is consistently gripping. **TP**

VARIETY: See US section

VIOLETS ARE BLUE: See US section

VOLUNTEERS
(HBO Pictures/Tri-Star/EMI)
dir Nicholas Meyer *pro* Richard Shepherd, Walter F Parkes *scr* Ken Levine, David Isaccs, based on a story by Keith Critchlow *ph* Ric Waite, in Metrocolor *ed* Ronald Roose, Steven Polivka *pro des* James Schoppe, Delia Castaneda Millan *mus* James Horner *r time* 107 mins *US opening* Aug 16 *UK opening* Apr 18.
cast Tom Hanks, John Candy, Rita Wilson, Tim Thomerson, Gedde Watanabe, George Plimpton, Ernest Harada, Allan Arbus, Xander Berkeley, Ji-Tu Cumbaka, Jacqueline Evans, Pamela Gual, Philip Guilmann, Chick Hearn, Virginia Kiser, Clyde Kusatsu, Jude Mussetter, Carlos Romano.

An amiable but uncertain movie, 'Volunteers' is a zany comedy about a Peace Corps mission to Thailand during the Kennedy era. Despite the period trappings, laid on with a trowel in the establishing sequences, the tone is entirely that of eighties style college capers, and a further discrepancy arises between the travelogue-inflected presentation and the artificial, pop-absurdist conception. Some snappy one-liners and a couple of tolerably energetic knockabout setpieces are somewhat offset by a string of obscurantist in-jokes about 'The Bridge on the River Kwai'. **TP**

WARNING SIGN: See US section

WEIRD SCIENCE
(Universal)
dir-scr John Hughes *pro* Joel Silver *ph* Matthew F Leonetti, Joseph Calloway, in Technicolor *ed* Mark Warner, Christopher Lebenzon, Scott Wallace *pro des* John W Corso *mus* Ira Newborn *r time* 94 mins *US opening* Aug 2 *UK opening* Nov 1.
cast Anthony Michael Hall, Kelly LeBrock, Ilan Mitchell-Smith, Bill Paxton, Suzanne Snyder, Judie Aronson, Robert Downey, Robert Rusler, Vernon Wells, Britt Leach, Barbara Lang, Michael Berryman, Ivor Barry, Anne Bernadette, Suzy J Kellems, John Kapelos, Jill Whitlow.

Weird Scene

John Hughes, here drawing on his 'National Lampoon' track record rather than the tasteful teen traumas of 'The Breakfast Club', has concocted a spectacularly vulgar example of male adolescent fantasy fulfilment. Two high-school nerds utilise their computer to create the Ideal Woman, a voluptuous sexpot whose magical powers transform their lives after a few rocky rites of passage. The film's total failure to explain or even delineate the extent of these powers results in a morass of anarchic special effects and non sequitur *sight-gags laced with unthinking sexism and film buff references. It is as though a load of twelve-year-old schoolboys had been let loose in a film studio.* **AB**

WHEN FATHER WAS AWAY ON BUSINESS
(Forum Sarajevo Film/Cannon/Cannon-Gala)
dir Emir Kusturica *pro* Mirza Pasic *exec pro* Vera Mihic-Jolic *scr* Abdulah Sidran *ph* Vilko Filac, in colour *ed* Andrija Zafranovic *art dir* Predrag Lukovac *mus* Zoran Simjanovic *r time* 136 mins *US opening* Oct 11 *UK opening* Nov 22.
cast Moreno de Bartoli, Miki Manojlovic, Mirjana Karanovic, Mustafa Nadarevic, Mira Furlan, Predrag Lakovic, Pavle Vujisic, Slobodan Aligrudic, Eva Ras, Aleksander Dorcev, Davor Dujmovic, Amer Kapetanovic.

This Yugoslav movie is set some thirty-five years ago, during the period of Tito's break with Moscow, when by a grim sort of irony it was those deemed to be pro-Stalinist who were singled out for the attention of the secret police. The central character here is the young son of one such victim, and the film charts an episodic, serio-comic course through the family's break-up to the father's eventual 'rehabilitation' and return home. But the effect seems to be neither to communicate a sense of events unfolding from his juvenile perspective, nor to make fruitful play of the discrepancy between his viewpoint and a more objective one. However, the 1985 Cannes jury thought differently enough to award the film their Palme d'Or. **PT**

When Father Was Away on Business

WHEN WE WERE YOUNG
(Dovzhenko Studio/The Other Cinema)
dir-scr Mikhail Belikov
pro A Vishnyevsky, N Fedyuk *ph* Vasily Trushkovsky, in Sovcolor *ed* N Akaemovoi *art dir* Alexei Levchenko *mus* Y Vinnik, Frederic Chopin, George Gershwin *r time* 92 mins
UK opening Mar 28.
cast Taras Denisenko, Elena Shkurpelo, N Sharolapova, A Pashtin, A Syiridovsky, A Lukyanenko, M Kokshenov.

Apparently trying to be a sort of 'Soviet Graffiti' (and seemingly a big success on home ground), this serio-comic account of young love in the Ukraine, circa 1959, gives a rather rigged impression, in terms of both the comic boisterousness in the background and the romantic idylls (complete with near-fatal illness) that are the main focus of attention. This impression is hardly alleviated by the concluding sequence showing students taking en masse to the streets in nationalistic celebration of Gagarin's space flight, for all the world as if there had been no official prompting of the display. **TP**

WHERE ARE THE CHILDREN?: See US section

WHITE NIGHTS
(Columbia)
dir Taylor Hackford *pro* Taylor Hackford, William S Gilmore *scr* James Goldman, Eric Hughes, based on a story by James Goldman *ph* David Watkin, in Metrocolor *ed* Frederic Steinkamp, William Steinkamp *pro des* Philip Harrison *mus* Michel Columbier and others *r time* 134 mins
US opening Nov 22 *UK opening* Mar 21.
cast Michael Baryshnikov, Gregory Hines, Jerzy Skolimowski, Helen Mirren, Geraldine Page, Isabella Rossellini, John Glover, Stefan Gryff, William Hootkins, Shane Rimmer, Florence Faure, David Savile, Ian Liston, Benny Young, Daniel Benzali, Maria Werlander, Galina Pomerantzerva, Maryam D'Abo.

A genuinely exhilarating affair whenever Hackford's mobile camera locks into his virtuoso dancing leads, this otherwise has to be the most leaden-footed trudge through the Cold War slush since détente died. A plane-crash lands long-time defector Baryshnikov back in the USSR, and smiling KGB-man Skolimowski applies the psychological thumbscrews to get him back to the Kirov. Tap-master Hines, who flew the other way at the time of Vietnam but naturally wishes he hadn't, is bullied into backing up the argument. It's not long, though before four feet itching for Freedom are tracing the choreography not of the Big Gig, but of the Great Escape. It's not surprising that the stellar toes are the only things to twinkle amid this tosh. **PT**

When We Were Young

WILDCATS: See US section

THE WIND (FINYÉ)
(Souleymane Cissé/BFI)
dir-scr Souleymane Cissé *ph* Etienne Corton de Grammont, in colour *ed* André Davanture *art dir* Malick Guisse *mus* Pierre Gorse, Mali Folklore, Radio Mogadishu *r time* 105 mins
UK opening Oct 25.
cast Fousseyni Sissoko, Goundo Guisse, Balla Moussa Keita, Ismaila Sarr, Oumou Diarra, Ismaila Cissé, Massitan Ballo, Dioncounda Kone, Yacouba Samabaly, Dunanba Dani Kulibali.
Not seen.

WISE GUYS: See US section

A WOMAN OR TWO: See Une Femme ou Deux

The Wind

White Nights

THE FILMS RELEASED ONLY IN THE US

1 JULY 1985–30 JUNE 1986

Reviews by Myron Meisel

ALWAYS

(Jagtown Film-International Rainbow Pictures/Goldwyn)
dir-pro-scr Henry Jaglom *ph* Hanania Baer, in DeLuxe colour *mus* Miles Kreuger *r time* 105 mins *US opening* Oct 4.
cast Patrice Townsend, Henry Jaglom, Joanna Frank, Alan Rachins, Melissa Leo, Jonathan Kaufer, Amnon Meskin, Bud Townsend, Bob Rafelson, Michael Emil, André Gregory.

Jaglom's psychodrama relishes its exhibitionism while maintaining a deceptively even tone. Based on the break-up of his own marriage (and starring himself and his ex-wife), the film achieves many small insights about relationships while coming to conclusions that are inherently shallow and suspect. Attempting an LA 'Rules of the Game' was a dangerous ambition for a movie of small virtues, but Jaglom's hubris and vanity have always obscured the more valuable aspects of his talents.

AMERICAN ANTHEM

(Lorimar/Columbia)
dir Albert Magnoli *pro* Robert Schaffel, Doug Chapin *exec pro* Freddie Fields *scr* Evan Archerd, Jeff Benjamin *ph* Donald E Thorin, in MGM Colour *ed* Jaems Oliver *pro des* Ward Preston *mus* Alan Silvestri *r time* 100 mins *US opening* Jun 25.
cast Mitch Gaylord, Janet Jones, Michelle Phillips, R J Williams, Michael Pataki, Patrice Donnelly, Stacey Maloney, Maria Anz, Andrew White.

AMERICAN FLYERS

(Warner)
dir John Badham *pro* Gareth Wigan, Paula Weinstein *scr* Steve Tesich *ph* Don Peterman, in Panavision, Technicolor *ed* Frank Morriss *pro des* Lawrence G Paull *mus* Lee Ritenour, Greg Mathieson *r time* 114 mins *US opening* Aug 16.
cast Kevin Costner, David Grant, Rae Dawn Chong, Alexandra Paul, Janice Rule, Luca Bercovici, Robert Townsend, John Amos.

THE ANNIHILATORS

(New World)
dir Charles E Sellier Jr *pro* Allan C Pedersen, Tom Chapman *scr* Brian Russell *ph* Henning Schellerup, in colour *ed* Dan Gross *art dir* Simon Gittins *mus* Bob Summers *r time* 84 mins *US opening* Nov 15.
cast Christopher Stone, Andy Wood, Lawrence Hilton-Jacobs, Gerrit Graham, Dennis Redfield, Paul Koslo, Cavanaugh Yelling, Bruce Evers, Tom Harper, Lonnie Smith, Josh Patton, Jim Antonio, Bruce Taylor.

APRIL FOOL'S DAY

(Paramount)
dir Fred Walton *pro* Frank Mancuso Jr *scr* Danilo Bach *ph* Charles Minsky, in Panavision, Metrocolor *ed* Bruce Green *art dir* Stewart Campbell *mus* Charles Bernstein *r time* 88 mins *US opening* Mar 28.
cast Jay Baker, Pat Barlow, Lloyd Berry, Deborah Foreman, Deborah Goodrich, Tom Heaton, Mike Nomad, Ken Olandt, Griffin O'Neal, Leah King Pinsent, Clayton Rohner, Amy Steel, Thomas F Wilson.

THE ASSISI UNDERGROUND

(Cannon)
dir-scr Alexander Ramati, based on his own novel *pro* Menahem Golan, Yoram Globus *ph* Guiseppe Rotunno, in colour *ed* Michael Duthie *pro des* Luciano Spadoni *mus* Dov Seltzer *r time* 178 mins *US opening* Aug 23.
cast Ben Cross, James Mason, Irene Papas, Maximilian Schell, Karl-Heinz Hackl, Riccardo Cucciolla, Angelo Infanti, Paolo Malco, Tom Felleghy, Della Boccardo, Roberto Bisacco, Did Ramati.

AT CLOSE RANGE

(Hemdale/Orion)
dir Jaes Foley *pro* Elliott Lewitt, Don Guest *exec pro* John Daly, Derek Gibson *scr* Nicholas Kazan *ph* Juan Ruiz-Anchia, in Panavision, CFI colour *ed* Howard Smith *pro des* Peter Jamison *mus* Patrick Leonard *r time* 111 mins *US opening* Apr 11.
cast Sean Penn, Christopher Walken, Mary Stuart Masterson, Christopher Penn, Millie Perkins, Eileen Ryan, Alan Autry, Candy Clark, R D Call, Tracey Walter, J C Quinn, David Strathairn, Jake Dengel, Crispin Glover, Kiefer Sutherland, Noelle Parker.

A criminal father enlists his estranged sons in his gang and proceeds to murder them and their friends to ensure their silence during an investigation. Powerful real-life material is muzzled under a surfeit of show-off visual style by James Foley ('Reckless') who seems to be aiming for a teen-tinged expressionism. Penn and Walken, with their intense narcissism, are both excellent in one-shot but fail to strike sparks off one another.

B

BACK TO SCHOOL

(Orion)
dir Alan Metter *pro* Chuck Russell *exec pro* Estelle Endler, Michael Endler, Harold Ramis *scr* Steven Kampmann, Will Porter, Peter Torokvel, Harold Ramis *ph* Thomas E Ackerman, in DeLuxe colour *ed* David Rawlins *pro des* David Snyder *mus* Danny Elfman *r time* 96 mins *US opening* Jun 13.
cast Rodney Dangerfield, Sally Kellerman, Burt Young, Keith Gordon, Robert Downey Jr, Paxton Whitehead, Terry Farrell, M Emmet Walsh, Adrienne Barbeau, William Zabka, Ned Beatty, Severn Darden, Sam Kinison, Robert Picardo, Kurt Vonnegut Jr, Edie McClure.

Rodney Dangerfield proves he's a genuine star in this messy vehicle that packs a substantial number of irresistible belly-laughs, along with sloppy stretches of story. A self-made millionaire enrolls as a college freshman to help out his son. However uneven the calibre of wit, the cast uniformly displays keen comic panache, especially Kellerman's Joyce specialist. Still, the show is Dangerfield's, who can't act but puts over every joke for maximum hilarity.

BAD MEDICINE

(Lantana/Fox)
dir-scr Harvey Miller, based on the novel 'Dr Horowitz' by Steven Horowitz, Neil Offen *pro* Alex Winitsky, Arlene Sellers *exec pro* Sam Manners *ph* Kelvin Pike, in DeLuxe Colour *ed* O Nicholas Brown, John Jympson *pro des* Les Dilley *mus* Lalo Schifrin *r time* 96 mins *US opening* Nov 22.
cast Steve Guttenberg, Alan Arkin, Julie Hagerty, Bill Macy, Curtis Armstrong, Julie Kavner, Joe Grafasi.

BAND OF THE HAND

(Tri-Star)
dir Paul Michael Glaser *pro* Michael Rauch *exec pro* Michael Mann *scr* Leo Garen, Jack Baran *ph* Reynaldo Villalobos, in Metrocolor *ed* Jack Hofstra *pro des* Gregory Bolton *mus* Michael Rubini *r time* 109 mins *US opening* Apr 11.
cast Stephen Lang, Michael Carmine, Lauren Holly, John Cameron Mitchell, Daniele Quinn, Leon Robinson, Al Shannon, Danton Stone, Paul Calderon, Larry Fishburne, James Remar.

BEER

(Orion)
dir Patrick Kelly *pro* Robert Chartoff *exec pro* James D Brubaker *scr* Allan Weisbecker *ph* Bill Butler, in Deluxe colour *ed* Alan Heim *pro des* Bill Bordie *mus* Bill Conti *r time* 82 mins *US opening* Aug 30.
cast Loretta Swift, Rip Torn, Kenneth Mars, David Alan Grier, William Russ, Saul Stein, Peter Michael Goetz, David Wohl, Dick Shawn, Alar Aedma.

BELIZAIRE THE CAJUN

(Côte Blanche/Skouras)
dir-scr Glen Pitre *pro* Allan L Durand, Glen Pitre *exec pro* James B Levert Jr *ph* Richard Bowen, in DuArt colour *ed* Paul Trejo *pro des* Randall LaBry *mus* Michael Doucet *r time* 101 mins *US opening* Jun 13.
cast Armand Assante, Gail Youngs, Michael Schoeffling, Stephen McHattie, Will Patton, Nancy Barrett, Loulan Pitre, Andrew Delaunay, Jim Levert, Ernie Vincent, Paul Landry, Robert Duvall.

Independent regional film-making can be earnestly sympathetic, as this examination of Cajun culture in 1859 Louisiana bayou country often is, with a sly, charismatic central performance, authentic costumes and music, production value beyond its meagre budget, and vats of local colour. It can also be woefully inept, the simplistic narrative amateurishly rambling and sputtering as supporting players chew the swamp roots. It might have been a good yarn, too, with even a little native story-telling prowess.

THE BEST OF TIMES

(Kings Road/Universal)
dir Roger Spottiswoode *pro* Gordon Carroll *scr* Ron Shelton *ph* Charles F Wheeler, in colour *ed* Garth Craven *art dir* Anthony Brockliss *mus* Arthur B Rubinstein *r time* 104 mins *US opening* Jan 30.
cast Robin Williams, Kurt Russell, Pamela Reed, Holly Palace, Donald Moffat, Margaret Whitton, M Emmet Walsh, Donovan Scott, R G Armstrong.

A refreshingly sharp and skillful comedy, one of the most assured and accomplished of recent years. A bank officer obsessed about the big football game he lost in high school hatches a demented scheme to rematch the teams and rewrite personal and community history. Williams and Russell with their opposing styles complement each another perfectly, and the movie is populated with supporting players who all reach Sturgesian heights of satiric fervour. The comedy, drama and sentiment all develop in synch, culminating in a truly suspenseful climax that cheats neither audience expectations nor a respect for reality.

BETTER OFF DEAD

(CBS-A&M/Warner)
dir-scr Savage Steve Holland *pro* Michael Jaffe *exec pro* Gil Friesen, Andrew Meyer *ph* Isidore Mankofsky, in Technicolor *ed* Alan Balsam *pro des* Herman Zimmerman *mus* Rupert Hine *r time* 98 mins *US opening* Oct 11.
cast John Cusack, David Ogden Stiers, Kim Darby, Demian Slade, Scooter Stevens, Diane Franklin, Laura Waterbury, Curtis Armstrong, Amanda Wyss, David Schneider, Aaron Dozier.

BIG TROUBLE

(Columbia)
dir John Cassavetes *pro* Michael Lobell *scr* 'Warren Bogle' (Andrew Bergman) *ph* Bill Butler, in Panavision, Metrocolor *ed* Donn Cambern, Ralph Winters *pro des* Joe J Tompkins *mus* Bill Conti *r time* 93 mins *US opening* Nov 15.
cast Peter Falk, Alan Arkin, Beverly D'Angelo, Charles Durning, Paul Dooley, Robert Stack, Valerie Curtin, Richard Libertini, Steve Alterman, Jerry Pavlon, Paul La Greca, John Finnegan, Karl Lukas, Gloria Gifford.

Bergman's grafting of a deadpan parody of 'Double Indemnity' on to the character dynamics of his hit comedy 'The In-Laws' degenerates into last-act incredulities, but the trio of lead players sustains brilliantly original characterisations under the tutelage of replacement director Cassavetes. Falk's benign sociopath, Arkin's terminally pressured average guy and D'Angelo's post-modernist femme fatale *create a web of offbeat verbal jousts delivered with unerring rhythm.*

BITTER ERNTE (ANGRY HARVEST)

(Filmkunst/European Classics)
dir Agnieszka Holland *pro* Artur Brauner *scr* Paul Hengge, Agnieszka Holland *ph* Josef Ort-Snep, in colour *ed* Barbara Kunze *mus* Jorg Strass Burger *r time* 102 mins *US opening* Mar 14.
cast Armin Müller-Stahl, Elisabeth Trissenaar, Käthe Jaenicke, Hans Beerhenke, Isa Haller, Margit Carstensen, Wojciech Pszioniak, Gerd Baltus, Anita Höfer, Kurt Raab, Gunter Berger, Wolf Donner.

A sexually repressed farmer shelters an escaped Jewess out of a mixture of charity and lust, but their doomed relationship leads to tragedy. Polish exile Holland's strident intelligence gives her film an admirable toughness of attitude, creating complex characters for her superlative lead players. But the movie is lumpy and graceless for all its novelistic density, and the emotions are more often indicated than expressed. Academy Award nominee, Best Foreign Language Film.

BLUE CITY

(Paramount)
dir Michelle Manning *pro* William Hayward, Walter Hill, based on the novel by Ross MacDonald *ph* Steven Poster, in Technicolor *ed* Ross Albert *art dir* Richard Lawrence *mus* Ry Cooder *r time* 83 mins *US opening* May 2.
cast Judd Nelson, Ally Sheedy, David Caruso, Paul Winfield, Scott Wilson, Anita Morris, Luis Contreras, Julie Carmen.

Blasphemously bad pillaging of the Ross MacDonald novel for purposes of making a contemporary teen-oriented hardboiled crime drama, which even in Hollywood is a contradiction in terms. Judd Nelson is laughably awful as a preppie wimp masquerading as a touch, and the movie accumulates ridicule with each turn of the plot. This could have been plausibly presented as a parody of the terminal confusion of the American film industry.

THE BOY IN BLUE

(ICC-Denis Heroux-John Kemeny/Fox)
dir Charles Jarrott *pro* John Kemeny *exec pro* Steve North *scr* Douglas Bowie *ph* Pierre Mignot, in colour *pro* Rit Wallis *pro des* William Beeton *mus* Roger Webb *r time* 93 mins *US opening* Jan 17.
cast Nicolas Cage, Cynthia Dale, Christopher Plummer, David Naughton, Sean Sullivan, Melody Anderson, James B Douglas, Walter Massey, Austin Willis, Philip Craig, Robert McCormick.

BRAZIL

(Universal)
dir Terry Gilliam *pro* Arnon Milchan *scr* Terry Gilliam, Tom Stoppard, Charles McKeown *ph* Roger Pratt, in colour *pro* Julian Doyle *pro des* Norman Garwood *mus* Michael Kamen *r time* 142 mins *US opening* Dec 18.*
cast Jonathan Pryce, Robert De Niro, Katherine Helmond, Ian Holm, Bob Hoskins, Michael Palin, Ian Richardson, Peter Vaughan, Kim Greist, Jim Broadbent, Barbara Hicks, Charles McKeown, Derrick O'Connor, Kathryn Pogson, Bryan Pringle, Sheila Reid, John Flanagan, Ray Cooper, Brian Miller, Simon Nash.
*(Released in UK prior to July 1985, but see Films of the Year.)

C

THE CARE BEARS II: A NEW GENERATION

(Columbia)
dir Dale Schott *pro* Michael Hirsh, Patrick Loubert, Clive A Smith *exec pro* John Bohach, Jack Chojnacki, Harvey Levin, Carle MacGillvray, Paul Pressler *scr* Peter Sauder *ed* Evan Landis, Keith Traver, Brian Feeley, Monica Falton, Peter Branton, Phillip Stillman, Jamie Whitney *art dir* Wayne Gilbert *mus* Patricia Cullen *r time* 76 mins *US opening* Mar 21.
voices Hadley Kay, Chris Wiggins, Cree Summer Francks, Alyson Court, Michael Fatini, Sunny Besen Thrasher, Maxine Miller, Pam Hyatt, Dan Hennessey, Brillie Mae Richards, Eva Amos, Bob Dormer, Patrice Black, Nonnie Griffin, Jim Hensahw, Melleny Brown, Janet-Laine Greene, Marla Kukofsky, Gloria Figura.

CEASE FIRE

(Double Helix/Cineworld Enterprises)
dir David Nutter *pro* William Grefe *exec pro* George Fernandez, Ed Fernandez *scr* George Fernandez, from his play 'Vietnam Triology' *ph* Henming Schellerup, in Continental Colour *ed* Julio Chaves *art dir* Alan Avchen *mus* Gary Fry *r time* 97 mins *US opening* Aug 30.
cast Don Johnson, Lisa Blount, Robert F Lyons, Richard Chaves, Rick Richards, Chris Noel, Jorge Gil, John Archie.

THE CHECK IS IN THE MAIL

(Joseph Wolf/Ascot Entertainment Group)
dir Joan Darling *pro* Robert Kaufman, Robert Krause *exec pro* Joseph Wolf, Simon Tse *scr* Robert Kaufman *ph* Jan Kiesser, in colour *mus* David Frank *r time* 91 mins *US opening* Mar 28.
cast Brian Dennehy, Anne Archer, Hallie Todd, Chris Hebert, Michael Bowen, Nita Talbot, Dick Shawn.

CITY LIMITS

(Sho Films-Videoform/Atlantic)
dir Aaron Lipstadt *pro* Rupert Harvey, Barry Opper *exec pro* Warren Goldberg *scr* Don Opper *ph* Timothy Suhrstedt, in colour *ed* Robert Kizer *art dir* Cyd Smilie *mus* John Lurie *r time* 85 mins *US opening* Sep 13.
cast Darrell Larson, John Stockwell, Kim Cattrall, Rae Dawn Chong, Robby Benson, James Earl Jones, John Diehl, Norbert Weisser.

Futuristic gangs fight turf wars in this uncertainly mounted drama. The script suggests a strong concept underdeveloped, and a generally impressive cast fails to deliver on incomplete characters. Lipstadt made an auspicious debut with the well-calibrated 'Android', but his command of action vocabulary here is limited. Sharp editing can't camouflage the lack of organising vision.

COBRA

(Cannon/Warner)
dir George Pan Cosmatos *pro* Menahem Golan, Yoram Globus *exec pro* James D Brubaker *scr* Sylvester Stallone, based on the novel 'Fair Game' by Paula Gosling *ph* Ric Waite, in Technicolor *ed* Don Zimmerman, James Symons *pro des* Bill Kenney *mus* Sylvester Levay *r time* 87 mins *US opening* May 23.
cast Sylvester Stallone, Brigitte Nielsen, Reni Santoni, Andrew Robinson, Lee Garlington, John Herzfeld, Art Le Fleur, Brian Thompson, David Rasche, Val Avery, Marco Rodriguez, Christine Craft, Bert Williams.

THE COLOR PURPLE

(Amblin/Warner)
dir Steven Spielberg *pro* Steven Spielberg, Kathleen Kennedy, Frank Marshall, Quincy Jones *exec pro* Jon Peters, Petr Guber *scr* Menno Meyjes, based on the novel by Alice Walker *ph* Allen Daviau, in DeLuxe colour *ed* Michael Kahn *pro des* J Michael Riva *mus* Quincy Jones *r time* 152 mins *US opening* Dec 20.
cast Danny Glover, Whoopi Goldberg, Margaret Avery, Oprah Winfrey, Willard Pugh, Akosua Busia, Desreta Jackson, Adolph Caesar, Rae Dawn Chong, Dana Ivey.
(See Films of the Year.)

CREATOR

(Kings Road/Universal)
dir Ivan Passer *pro* Stephen Friedman *scr* Jeremy Leven, based on his novel *ph* Robbie Greenberg, in color *ed* Richard Chew *art dir* Josan F Russo *mus* Sylvester Levay *r time* 107 mins *US opening* Sep 20.
cast Peter O'Toole, Mariel Hemingway, Vincent Spano, Virginia Madsen, David Ogden Stiers, John Dehner, Karen Kopins, Kenneth Tigar, Elsa Raven, Lee Kessler, Rance Howard, Ellen Geer, Jeff Corey.

Offbeat dramatic comedy that treats issues like medical research ethics and the meaning of life lightly yet with respect. O'Toole scores yet again as another dreamy eccentric, and Passer's direction manages to remain cogent even when embracing the romantic. The plot developments slip occasionally into the mechanical, and the entire enterprise skirts the clichés of nonconformist comedy established by 'A Thousand Clowns', but the sense of gravity makes a welcome tonic in a contemporary comedy.
(For a different view, see Turkeys of the Year.)

CRITTERS

(Sho Films/New Line)
dir Stephen Herek *pro* Rupert Harvey *exec pro* Robert Shaye *scr* Stephen Herek, Domonic Muir *ph* Tom Suhrstedt, in DeLuxe colour *ed* Larry Bock *pro des* Gregg Fonseca *mus* David Newman *r time* 86 mins *US opening* Apr 11.
cast Dee Wallace Stone, M Emmet Walsh, Billy Green Bush, Scott Grimes, Nadine Van Der Velde, Terrence Mann, Don Opper, Billy Zane, Ethan Phillips, Jeremy Lawrence, Lin Shaye, Michael Lee Gogin, Art Frankel.

CROSSROADS

(Columbia)
dir Walter Hill *pro* Mark Carliner *exec pro* Tim Zinneman *scr* John Fusco *ph* John Bailey, in Technicolor *ed* Freeman Davies *art dir* Albert Heschong *mus* Ry Cooder *r time* 96 mins *US opening* Mar 14.
cast Ralph Macchio, Joe Seneca, Jami Gertz, Joe Morton, Robert Judd, Steve Vai, Dennis Lipscomb, Harry Carey Jr, John Hancock, Allan Arbus, Gretchen Palmer, Tim Russ, Akosua Busia.

Walter Hill explores deep Mississipi delta blues country in this exuberant, if ultimately shallow, examination of a Julliard guitar student apprenticing himself to an elderly bluesman on the road back home. Excessive calculation towards the youth market compromises the credibility of the story, which builds up Macchio's role for 'The Karate Kid' audience at the expense of Seneca's cantankerous artist of soul. Despite flagrant lapses into self-conscious fabulism, the film does respect the blues idiom, and boasts some good character work from Seneca as well as several of Hill's rollicking club sequences.

DANGEROUSLY CLOSE

(Cannon)
dir Albert Pyun *pro* Harold Sobel *exec pro* Menahem Golan, Yoram Globus *scr* Scott Fields, John Stockwell, Marty Ross, based on a story by Marty Ross *ph* Walt Lloyd, in TVC Colour *ed* Dennis O'Connor *pro des* Marcia Hinds *mus* Michael McCarty *r time* 95 mins *US opening* May 9.
cast John Stockwell, J Eddie Peck, Carey Lowell, Bradford Bancroft, Don Michael Paul, Thom Mathews, Jerry Dinome, Madison Mason, Anthony DeLongis,

Carmen Argenziano, Miguel Nunez, Dedee Pfeiffer, Karen Witter, Greg Finley, Debra Berger, Angel Tompkins.

DAY OF THE DEAD

(Laurel/United Film Distribution)
dir-scr George A Romero *pro* Richard P Rubinstein *exec pro* Salah M Hassanein *ph* Michael Gornick, in colour *ed* Pasquale Buba *pro des* Cletus Anderson *mus* John Harrison *r time* 102 mins *US opening* Oct 4.
cast Lori Cardille, Terry Alexander, Joseph Pilato, Jarlath Conroy, Antone DiLeo Jr, Richard Liberty Howard Sherman, Gary Howard Klar, Ralph Marrero, John Amplas, Philip G Kellams, Taso N Stavrakis, Gregory Nicotero.

The concluding instalment of Romero's great trilogy is neither a masterpiece like Dawn of the Dead *or as terrifying as* Night of the Living Dead, *but it does endeavour to resolve the fundamental issues explored by the earlier works. Questions of survival finally focus on what it means to be human, and Romero borrows a subplot from the Frankenstein myth to illuminate the humanistic underpinnings to his apparent nihilistic vision. As always, the film-making is supple and expressive (with the best performances yet), the generic elements used to profound ends.*

DESERT BLOOM

(Carson Prods Group/Columbia)
dir-scr Eugene Corr, based on a story by Linda Remy and Eugene Corr *pro* Michael Hausman *exec pro* Richard Fischoff *ph* Raynaldo Villalobos, in Metrocolor *ed* David Garfield, John Currin, Cari Coughlin *art dir* Lawrence Miller *mus* Brad Fiedel *r time* 104 mins *US opening* Apr 18.
cast Jon Voight, JoBeth Williams, Ellen Barkin, Allen Garfield, Annabeth Gish, Jay D Underwood, Desiree Joseph, Dusty Balcerzak.

Developed by Redford's Sundance Institute, this consciously sensitive coming-of-age story of a teenage girl enduring physical abuse from her alcoholic stepfather, set against a backdrop of early Nevada nuclear tests, represents a particular school of film-making devoted to small character revelations, obvious sociological comment and worked-out portrayals. Aspiring to poetic realism, it's neither realistic nor poetic. Its values may be laudable, but its cinematic sense is stillborn. Whatever virtues it achieves are relentlessly minor.

DESERT HEARTS

(Samuel Goldwyn)
dir-pro Donna Deitch *scr* Natalie Cooper, based on the novel 'Desert of the Heart' by Jane Rule *ph* Robert Elswit, in colour *ed* Robert Estrin *pro des* Jeannine Oppewall *mus* various *r time* 93 mins *US opening* Apr 4.
cast Helen Shaver, Patricia Charbonneau, Audra Lindley, Andra Akers, Dean Butler, Katie La Bourdette, Jeffrey Tambor, Gwen Welles.

A lesbian romance between a divorcing professor and a casino worker set in fifties Reno that avoids the usual handwringing and tragic denouement. In fact, it's so romantic that it reclaims the classic prerequisites of Hollywood love affairs for homosexuals. It isn't a daring or innovative film, but it would make any reasonably open heart feel warm and caressed. While Charbonneau and Shaver render convincing characterisations, Lindley and Akers are especially memorable as satellites orbiting about the lovers.

DOIN' TIME

(Filmcorp-Ladd/Warner)
dir George Mendeluk *pro* Bruce Mallen, George Mendeluk *exec pro* Ken Sheppard, Carol Mallen *scr* Franelle Silver, Ron Zwang, Dee Caruso *ph* Ronald V Garcia, in DeLuxe colour *ed* Stanford C Allen *pro des* Jack McAdam *mus* Charles Fox *r time* 77 mins *US opening* Nov 29.
cast Jeff Altman, Dey Young, Richard Mulligan, John Vernon, Colleen Camp, Melanie Chartoff, Graham Jarvis, Pat McCormick, Eddie Velez, Jimmie Walker, Judy Landers, Nicholas Worth, Mike Mazurki, Muhammad Ali.

DOWN BY LAW

(Black Snake-Grokenberger/Island)
dir-pro-scr Jim Jarmusch *ph* Robby Müller, in black and white *ed* Franck Kern *pro des* Roger Knight *mus* John Lurie *r time* 106 mins *US opening* May 16.
cast Tom Waits, John Lurie, Roberto Benigni, Nicoletta Braschi, Ellen Barkin.

DREAM LOVER

(MGM-UA)
dir Alan J Pakula *pro* Alan J Pakula, Jon Boorstin *exec pro* William C Gerrity *scr* Jon Boorstin *ph* Sven Nykvist, in Technicolor *ed* Turdy Ship *pro des* George Jenkins *mus* Michael Small *r time* 104 mins *US opening* Feb 21.
cast Kiristy McNichol, Ben Masters, Paul Shenar, Justin Deas, John McMartin, Gayle Hunnicutt, Joseph Culp, Matthew Penn, Paul West, Matthew Long.

A sheltered young girl slays her attacker and is plagued by nightmares that could cause her to kill again. Some of the information on dream research is interesting, and Pakula manages to create an atmosphere of sexual repression that is peculiarly contemporary, but the story mechanism creaks so conventionally that the movie trails off into triviality.

8 MILLION WAYS TO DIE

(P.S.O./Tri-Star)
dir Hal Ashby *pro* Steve Roth *scr* Oliver Stone, David Lee Henry, based on the book by Lawrence Block *ph* Stephen H Burum, in colour *ed* Robert Lawrence, Stuart Pappe *pro des* Michael Haller *mus* James Newton Howard *r time* 115 mins *US opening* Apr 25.
cast Jeff Bridges, Rosanna Arquette, Alexandra Paul, Randy Brooks, Andy Garcia.

An alcoholic ex-cop loses everything and must save himself by avenging the murder of a hooker who had sought his protection. Ashby was fired after completion of principal photography, and the subsequent editing obviously reflects no particular vision beyond crass commercial miscalculation. Intended as a serious character study of addiction and redemption, the film ended up an incoherent mishmash of Florida crime-show riffs transplanted to LA. Sole standout: Andy Garcia as a scuzzy druglord finding new notes to play in that familiar role.

ELENI

(CBS/Warner)
dir Peter Yates *pro* Nick Vaoff, Mark Pick, Nicholas Gage *scr* Steve Tesich, based on the book by Nicholas Gage *ph* Billy Williams, in colour *ed* Ray Lovejoy *pro des* Roy Walker *r time* 117 mins *US opening* Nov 1.
cast Kate Nelligan, John Malkovich, Linda Hunt, Ronald Pickup, Oliver Cotton, Rosalie Crutchley, Peter Woodthorpe, John Runney, Alison King, Alfred Molina, Steve Plytas, Lisa Rose, Ianthi Vracas, Maria Alvarez Calvente, Claudia Gouch, Andrea Laskaris, Glenne Headly, Norman Chancer, Leo Kharibian, Leon Lisseck, Stefan Gryff, Anthony Stambouli, Christiana Fragou, Noam Almaz.

A thrilling, true-life premise: a New York journalist returns to his native Greece to track down the Communist killers of his mother, who sacrificed her life to get her children out of the country. Yet virtually nothing in the film credibly addresses that potential. Kate Nelligan is valiantly miscast as an earth mother, and the movie finds foreignness only in subtlety and substance. The weak screenplay receives equally poor direction, and the modern-day scenes lack the chill and suspense they must have had in real life.

ELIMINATORS

(Empire)
dir Peter Manoogian *pro* Charles Band *scr* Paul DeMeo, Danny Bilsen *ph* Mac Ahlberg, in Fotofilm colour *ed* Andy Horvitch *pro des* Philip Foreman *mus* Bob Summers *r time* 96 mins *US opening* Jan 31.
cast Andrew Prine, Denise Crosby, Patrick Reynolds, Conan Lee, Roy Dotrice, Peter Schrum, Peggy Mannix, Fausto Bara, Tad Horino, Luis Lorenzo.

ENEMY MINE

(Kings Road/Fox)
dir Wolfgang Petersen *pro* Stephen Friedman *exec pro* Stanley O'Toole *scr* Edward Khmara, based on a story by Barry Longyear *ph* Tony Imi, in Arriflex Widescreen, DeLuxe colour *ed* Hannes Nikel *pro des* Rolf Zehetbauer *mus* Maurice Jarre *r time* 108 mins *US opening* Dec 20.
cast Dennis Quaid, Louis Gossett Jr, Brion James, Richard Marcus, Carolyn McCormick, Bumper Robinson, Jim Mapp.

Megabudget sci-fi fable about brotherhood with Gossett delightful as an hermaphroditic alien replete with otherworldly speech pattern. Unfortunately, the movie lacks the gritty sauciness of 'Hell in the Pacific', which it resembles. Its best passages are sentimental, involving Quaid's fatherly love for Gossett's Drac offspring. Petersen's direction is overblown and uninspired. With daring and a much smaller budget, this could have been a lot more interesting.

EXPLORERS

(Paramount)
dir Joe Dante *pro* edward S Feldman, David Bombyk *exec pro* Michael Finnell *scr* Eric Luke *ph* John Hora, in Technicolor *ed* Tina Hirsch *pro des* Robert F Boyle *mus* Jerry Goldsmith *r time* 109 mins *US opening* Jul 12.
cast Ethan Hawke, River Phoenix, Jason Presson, Amanda Peterson, Dick Miller, Robert Picardo, Leslie Rickert, James Cromwell, Dana Ivey, Bobby Fite, Mary Kay Place.

Joe Dante specialises in debunking Spielbergian fantasies, so most of this juvenile space-travel adventure is disappointingly obeisant to the master's formula. Dante's visual style has grown smoother and slicker, but it isn't until the last twenty minutes, when his kids closely encounter an alien who studies mankind through television signals, that the movie breaks out into delirious verbal slapstick. Slavish imitation is redeemed by an extended sequence of inspired satire of civilisation as we know it.

F

FERRIS BUELLER'S DAY OFF

(Paramount)
dir-scr John Hughes *pro* John Hughes, Tom Jacobson *exec pro* Michael Chinich *ph* Tak Fujimoto, in Panavision, Metrocolor *ed* Paul Hirsch *pro des* John W Corso *mus* Ira Newborn *r time* 103 mins *US opening* Jun 13.
cast Matthew Broderick, Alan Ruck, Mia Sara, Jeffrey Jones, Jennifer Grey, Cindy Pickett, Lyman Ward, Edie McClurg, Charlie Sheen, Ben Stein, Del Close, Virginia Capers, Richard Edson, Larry Flash Jenkins.

FEVER PITCH

(MGM-UA)
dir-scr Richard Brooks *pro* Freddie Fields *ph* William A Fraker, in Metrocolor *ed* Jeff Jones *pro des* Raymond G Storey *mus* Thomas Dolby *r time* 96 mins *US opening* Nov 22.
cast Ryan O'Neal, Catherine Hicks, Giancarlo Giannini, Bridgette Andersen, Chad Everett, John Saxon, Hank Greenspun, William Smith, Keith Hefner.

Purportedly an exposé of the extent to which gambling has permeated American society, this endearingly silly movie disguises its anachronisms with energetic editing and pulsating music, never achieving the slightest credibility. Brooks cites statistics at breakneck speed but he hasn't the pulpy relish of a Sam Fuller. Its dogged earnestness tries so hard to please and be tough at the same time. It's hard not to enjoy, at least until the compromise upbeat ending that sells out any integrity the movie ever had. Chad Everett surprises as a memorably sadistic collector.

FIRE WITH FIRE

(Paramount)
dir Duncan Gibbins *pro* Gary Nardino *exec pro* Tova Laiter *scr* Bill Phillips, Warren Skaaren, Paul Boorstin, Sharon Boorstin *ph* Hiro Narita, in colour *ed* Peter Berger *pro des* Norman Newberry *mus* Howard Shore *r time* 105 mins *US opening* May 9.
cast Craig Sheffer, Virginia Madsen, Jon Polito, Jeffrey Jay Cohen, Kate Reid, Jean Smart, Tim Russ, David Harris, D B Sweeney, Dorrie Joiner, Evan Mirand, Ann Savage.

FOOL FOR LOVE
(Cannon)
dir Robert Altman *pro* Menahem Golan, Yoram Globus *scr* Sam Shepard, based on his play *ph* Pierre Mignot, in J D C Widescreen, Rank colour *ed* Luce Grunenwaldt, Steve Dunn *pro des* Stephen Altman *mus* George Burt, Sandy Rogers *r time* 106 mins *US opening* Dec 6.
cast Sam Shepard, Kim Basinger, Harry Dean Stanton, Randy Quaid, Martha Crawford, Louise Egolf, Sura Cox, Jonathan Skinner, April Russell, Deborah McNaughton, Lon Hill.

Shepard's play is not one of his strongest, and its transfer to film emphasises its weaknesses. Altman deploys visual stratagems from his earlier theatre adaptations, but they undercut the hothouse intensity that drives the drama. Shepard may embody the essence of his own character, but he is a fundamentally inexpressive actor here, while Basinger does no better than creditable work. An honourable misfire which never comes close to the target.

F/X
(Orion)
dir Robert Mandel *pro* Dodi Fayed, Jack Wiener *exec pro* Michael Peyser *scr* Robert I Megginson, Gregory Fleeman *ph* Miroslav Ondricek, in Technicolor *ed* Terry Rawlings *pro des* Mel Bourne *mus* Bill Conti *r time* 106 mins *US opening* Feb 7.
cast Bryan Brown, Brian Dennehy, Diane Venora, Cliff DeYoung, Mason Adams, Jerry Orbach, Joe Grifasi, Martha Gehman, Roscoe Orman, Trev Wilson, Tom Noonan.

The plot is full of holes, and so what, when the yarn is entertaining, the characterisations fresh, and novelty is integrated into the action. A movie special effects man is framed by rogue federal agents into an assassination ruse and becomes a hunted man. Brown as the resourceful but thick master of illusion makes a sympathetic hero, and Dennehy is an effective foil as a dogged cop. Mandel's direction isn't especially inventive, but it crackles and does the job.

G

THE GIG
(McLaughlin, Piven, Vogel Inc/ The Gig Co)
dir-scr Frank D Gillroy *pro* Norman I Cohen *ph* Jeri Sopanen, in DuArt colour *ed* Rick Shane *mus* Warren Vache *r time* 92 mins *US opening* Nov 26.
cast Wayne Rogers, Cleavon Little, Andrew Duncan, Jerry Matz, Daniel Nalbach, Warren Vache, Joe Silver, Jay Thomas, Stan Lachow, Celia Bressack, Georgia Harrell, Michael Fischetti, Susan Egbert, Karen Ashley, Virginia Downing, Chuck Wepner.

Agreeable comedy of middle-aged men who pursue a long-held dream of playing Dixieland jazz together professionally for just one gig. Independently produced film goes slack at critical moments, but the humour proceeds from keen character observations, and the actors make their types flesh and blood, not caricature. Standouts include Rogers as a used-car salesman, Little as the one true pro and Silver as the scoundrel-owner of the Catskills resort at which they play.

GINGER AND FRED
(Instituto Luce/Italnoleggio Cinematografico/MGM-UA)
dir Federico Fellini *pro* Alberto Grimaldi *scr* Federico Fellini, Tonino Guerra, Tullio Pinelli *ph* Tonino Delli Colli, Ennio Guarnieri, in colour *ed* Nino Baragli, Ugo De Rossi, Ruggero Mastroianni *art dir* Dante Ferretti *mus* Nicola Piovani *r time* 126 mins *US opening* Apr 11.
cast Giulietta Masina, Marcello Mastroianni, Franco Fabrizi, Frederick Von Ledenburg, Martin Blau, Toto Mignone, Augusto Poderosi, Francesco Casale, Frederick Von Thum, Henry Lartigue, Jean Michel Antoine, Antonio Iurio, Nando Pucci Negri, Laurentina Guidotti, Elena Cantarone.

THE GREAT WALL IS A GREAT WALL
(Orion Classics)
dir Peter Wang *pro* Shirley Sun *exec pro* Wu Yanchian, Zhu Youiun, E N Wen *scr* Wang Sun *ph* Peter Stein, Robert Primes, in colour *ed* Graham Weinbren *mus* David Liang, Ge Ganru *r time* 97 mins *US opening* Jan 31.
cast Peter Wang, Sharon Iwai, Kelvin Han Yee, Li Qinqin, Hu Xiaoguang, Shen Guanglan, Wang Xiao, Xio Jisn, Ran Zhijuan, Han Tan.

GRUNT! THE WRESTLING MOVIE
(New World)
dir Allan Holzman *pro* Non Normann, Anthony Randel *exec pro* James G Robinson *scr* Roger D Manning *ph* Eddie van der Enden, in colour *ed* Allan Holzman, Barry Zetlin *mus* Susan Justin *r time* 90 mins *US opening* Nov 22.
cast Jeff Dial, Robert Glaudini, Marilyn Dodds Farr, Greg Magic Schwartz, Bill Grant, Steve Cepello, Dick Murdoch, Exotic Adrian Street, John Tolos, Wally George, Victor Rivera, Count Billy Varga.

H

HAMBURGER . . . THE MOTION PICTURE
(F/M Entertainment)
dir Mike Marvin *pro* Edward S Feldman, Charles R Meeker *scr* Donald Ross *ph* Karen Grossman, in CFI colour *ed* Steven Schoenberg, Ann E Mills *pro des* George Costello *mus* Peter Bernstein *r time* 90 mins *US opening* Jan 31.
cast Leigh McCloskey, Dick Butkus, Randi Brooks, Chuck McCann, Jack Blessing, Charles Tyner, Debra Blee, Sandy Hackett, John Young, Chip McAllister, Barbara Whinnery, Maria Richwine, Karen May-Chandler.

HANNAH AND HER SISTERS
(Orion)
dir-scr Woody Allen *pro* Robert Greenhut *exec pro* Jack Rollins, Charles H Joffé *ph* Carlo Di Palma, in Technicolor *ed* Susan E Morse *pro des* Stuart Wurtzel *mus* Giacomo Puccini, Johann Sebastien Bach and others *r time* 106 mins *US opening* Feb 7.
cast Woody Allen, Michael Caine, Mia Farrow, Carrie Fisher, Barbara Hershey, Lloyd Nolan, Maureen O'Sullivan, Daniel Stern, Max Von Sydow, Dianne Wiest, Sam Waterston, Tony Roberts, Lewis Black, Julia Louis-Dreyfus, Christian Clemenson, Julie Kavner, J T Walsh, John Turturro, Rusty Magee.
(See Films of the Year and Dianne Wiest, Faces of the Year.)

HEAD OFFICE
(HBO-Silver Screen Partners/Tri-Star)
dir-scr Ken Finkleman *pro* Debra Hill *exec pro* Jon Peters, Peter Guber *ph* Gerald Hirschfeld, in colour *ed* Danford B Greene, Bob Lederman *pro des* Elayne Barbara Ceder *mus* James Newton Howard *r time* 90 mins *US opening* Jan 3.
cast Eddie Albert, Danny DeVito, Lori-Nan Engler, Don King, Judge Reinhold, Don Novello, Jane Seymour, Wallace Shawn, Rick Moranis.

THE HEAVENLY KID
(Orion)
dir Cary Medoway *pro* Mort Engelberg *exec pro* Gabe Sumner, Stephen G Cheikes *scr* Cary Medoway, Martin Copeland *ph* Steven Poster, in DeLuxe colour *ed* Christopher Greenburg *pro des* Ron Hobbs *mus* Kennard Ramsey *r time* 89 mins *US opening* Jul 26.
cast Lewis Smith, Jason Gedrick, Jane Kaczmarek, Richard Mulligan, Mark Metcalf, Beau Dremann, Stephen Gregory, Nancy Valen, Anne Sawyer.

HOME OF THE BRAVE
(Talk Normal-Warner Bros Records/ Cinecom International)
dir-scr-mus Laurie Anderson *pro* Paula Mazur *exec pro* Elliott Abbott *ph* John Lindley, in colour *ed* Lisa Day *pro des* David Gropman *r time* 90 mins *US opening* Apr 18.
cast Laurie Anderson, Joy Askew, Adrian Belew, Richard Landry, Dollette McDonald, Janice Pendarvis, Sand Won Park, David Van Tiegham, Jane Ira Bloom, Bill Obrecht, William S Burroughs.

I

INVADERS FROM MARS
(Cannon)
dir Tobe Hooper *pro* Menahem Golan, Yoram Globus *scr* Dan O'Bannon, Don Jakoby, based on the 1953 motion picture written by Richard Blake *ph* Daniel Pearl, in J D C Widescreen, TVC Colour *ed* Alain Jakubowicz *pro des* Leslie Dilley *mus* Christopher Young *r time* 100 mins *US opening* Jun 6.
cast Karen Black, Hunter Carson, Timothy Bottoms, Laraine Newman, James Karen, Louise Fletcher, Bud Cort, Jimmy Hunt.

IRON EAGLE
(Tri-Star)
dir Sidney J Furie *pro* Ron Samuels, Joe Wizan *exec pro* Kevin Elders *scr* Kevin Elders, Sidney J Furie *ph* Adam Greenberg, in colour *ed* George Grenville *pro des* Robb Wilson King *mus* Basil Poledouris *r time* 119 mins *US opening* Jan 17.
cast Louis Gossett Jr, Jason Gedrick, David Suchet, Tim Thomerson, Larry B Scott, Caroline Lagerfelt, Jerry Levine, Robbie Rist, Michael Bowen, Bobby Jacoby, Melora Hardin, David Greenlee.

J

JAKE SPEED
(New World)
dir Andrew Lane *pro* Andrew Lane, Wayne Crawford, William Ivey *exec pro* John Roach *scr* Wayne Crawford, Andrew Lane *ph* Bryan Loftus, in colour *ed* Fred Stafford *art dir* Norman Baron *mus* Mark Snow *r time* 100 mins *US opening* May 30.
cast Dennis Christopher, Karen Kopins, John Hurt, Leon Maes, Donna Pescow, Roy London, Barry Primus, Monte Markham, Alan Shearman, Rebecca Ashley.

Amiably derivative of 'Romancing the Stone' and 'Indiana Jones', this film from the producers of 'Valley Girl' and 'Night of the Comet' features first-rate technical work for its budget. It might have been fun, but producer-writer Crawford makes an insufficiently charismatic paperback hero, and the story meanders without ever focusing clearly enough to engross.

JAMES JOYCE'S WOMEN
(Rejoycing Company/Universal)
dir Michael Pearce *pro-scr* Fionnula Flanagan *exec pro* Garrett O'Connor *ph* John Metcalfe, in colour *ed* Arthur Keating, Dan Perry *mus* Vincent Kilduff, Arthur Keating, Garrett O'Connor *r time* 91 mins *US opening* Sep 13.
cast Fionnula Flanagan, Timothy E O'Grady, Chris O'Neill, Tony Lyons, Gerald Fitzmahony, Joseph Taylor, Martin Dempsey, Paddy Dawson.

Flanagan's adaptation of Joyce's works into a panorama of his depictions of women in fiction and his relationships with them in life becomes a tired pseudoliterary exercise in shallow, suspect criticism, viable only as a pretext for the actress's incarnation of the various female personages, which in this context comes off as a stunt. Exception: a brilliant, stirring rendition of Molly Bloom's soliloquy, which Flanagan was born to play.

JO JO DANCER, YOUR LIFE IS CALLING
(Columbia)
dir-pro Richard Pryor *scr* Rocco Urbisci, Paul Mooney, Richard Pryor *ph* John Alonzo, in DeLuxe colour *ed* Donn Cambern *pro des* John D Cuir *mus* Herbie Hancock *r time* 97 mins *US opening* May 2.
cast Richard Pryor, Debbie Allen, Art Evans, Fay Hauser, Barbara Williams, Carmen McRae, Paula Kelly, Diahnne Abbott, Scoey Mitchill, Billy Eckstein, E'lon Cox.

Richard Pryor's thinly disguised autobiography makes his life much less interesting than it must have been. The early sequences of his childhood in a brothel and his start in show business have a certain sweetness and sense of time and place, but all the more sensational stuff involving success and drugs is undramatised, strident and shallow. Pryor dealt with this same material with greater insight (and more laughs) in his last concert film.

JOSHUA THEN AND NOW

(Fox)
dir Ted Kotcheff *pro* Robert Lantos, Stephen J Roth *scr* Mordecai Richler, based on his novel *ph* Francois Protat, in colour *ed* Ron Wisman *pro des* Anne Pritchard *mus* Philippe Sarde *r time* 127 mins *US opening* Sept 27.
cast James Woods, Gabrielle Lazure, Alan Arkin, Michael Sarrazin, Linda Soresen, Alan Scarfe, Kate Trotter, Alexander Knox, Chuck Shamata, Paul Hecht, Henry Beckman, Eric Kimmel, Harvey Atkin, Ken Campbell, Robert Joy.

Kotcheff and Richler reunite in a Canadian variant on the life and loves of a working-class Jewish author. Woods devilishly incarnates the gentile nightmare of a Jew, but the show is stolen by Arkin's flamboyant portrayal of a petty thief and devoted father, capable of both Biblical disputation and burglary. The movie lurches through its episodes without achieving much depth of observation or feeling, but its ethnic boldness engenders much goodwill and interest.

THE KARATE KID PART II

(Columbia)
dir John G Avildsen *pro* Jerry Weintraub *exec pro* R J Louis *scr* Robert Mark Kamen *ph* James Crabe, in Deluxe colour *ed* David Garfield, Jane Kurson, John G Avildsen *pro des* William J Cassidy *mus* Bill Conti *r time* 113 mins *US opening* Jun 18.
cast Ralph Macchio, Noriyuki 'Pat' Morita, Nobu McCarthy, Danny Kamekona, Yuji Okumoto, Tamlyn Tomita.

KEY EXCHANGE

(Fox)
dir Barnet Kellman *pro* Mitchell Maxwell, Paul Kurta *exec pro* Michael Pochna, Ronald Winston *scr* Kevin Scott, Paul Kurta, based on Kevin Wade's play *ph* Fred Murphy, in Eastman Colour *ed* Jill Savitt *pro des* David Gropman *mus* Mason Daring *r time* 90 mins *US opening* Aug 16.
cast Ben Masters, Brooke Adams, Danny Aiello, Daniel Stern, Nancy Mette, Tony Roberts, Seth Allen.

Arch relationship comedy between Manhattan singles, an attempt to update the Doris Day-Rock Hudson comedies to the eighties. That it succeeds is censure enough. Bright lines and a misplaced maturity in Brooke Adams' performance are not enough to salvage the debased dramaturgy, distasteful sexual values and muddled TV direction.

KILLER PARTY

(Marquis Prods/MGM-UA)
dir William Fruet *pro* Michael Leipiner *exec pro* Kenneth Kaufman *scr* Barney Cohen *ph* John Lindley, in Technicolor *ed* Eric Albertson *pro des* Reuben Freed *mus* John Beal *r time* 91 mins *US opening* May 23.
cast Martin Hewitt, Ralph Seymour, Elaine Wilkes, Paul Bartel, Sherry Willis-Burch, Alicia Fleer, Woody Brown, Joanna Johnson, Terri Hawkes.

KNIGHTS OF THE CITY

(Grace Production/New World)
dir Dominic Orlando *pro* Leon Isaac Kennedy, John C Strong *exec pro* Michael Franzese, Robert E Schultz *scr* Leon Isaac Kennedy *ph* Rolf Kesterman, in CFI colour *ed* John O'Connor, Nicholas Smith *mus* Misha Segal *r time* 88 mins *US opening* Mar 14.
cast Leon Isaac Kennedy, John Mengati, Nicholas Campbell, Jeff Moldovan, Stoney Jackson, Janine Turner, Michael Ansara, Wendy Barry, Karin Smith, Smokey Robinson, Fat Boys, K C, Jeff Kutash, Deney Terrio, Cammy Garcia, T K & Jessie, Kurtis Blow.

KRUSH GROOVE

(Warner)
dir Michael Schultz *pro* Michael Schultz, Doug McHenry *exec pro* George A Jackson, Robert O Kaplan *scr* Ralph Farquhar *ph* Ernest Dickerson, in Technicolor *ed* Alan J Koslowski, Jerry Bixman, Conrad M Gonzalez *pro des* Mischa Petrow *r time* 97 mins *US opening* Oct 25.
cast Blair Underwood, Joseph Simmons, Sheila E, Mark Morales, Damon Wimbley, Darren (Buffy) Robinson, Daryll McDaniels, Jason Mizell, Kurtis Blow, Richard E Gant, Lisa Gay Hamilton, Daniel Simmons, Rick Rubin, Sal Abbatiello.

L

LABYRINTH

(Henson Associates-Lucasfilm/Tri-Star)
dir Jim Henson *pro* Eric Rattray *exec pro* George Lucas *scr* Terry Jones *ph* Alex Thomson, in J D C Widescreen, Fujicolor *ed* John Grover *pro des* Elliot Scott *mus* Trevor Jones, David Bowie *r time* 101 mins *US opening* Jun 25.
cast David Bowie, Jennifer Connelly, Toby Froud, Shelley Thompson, Christopher Malcolm, Natalie Finland, Shari Weiser, Brian Henson, Ron Mueck, Rob Mills, Dave Goetz, David Barclay, David Shaughnessy, Karen Prell, Timothy Bateson.

THE LADIES CLUB

(Media Home-Heron/New Line)
dir A K Allen *pro* Nick J Mileti, Paul Mason *scr* Paul Mason, Fran Lewis Ebeling, from the novel 'Sisterhood' by Betty Black, Casey Bishop *ph* Adam Greenberg, in colour *ed* Marion Segal, Randall Torno *pro des* Stephen Myles Berger *mus* Lalo Schifrin *r time* 90 mins *US opening* Apr 11.
cast Karen Austin, Diana Scarwid, Christine Belford, Bruce Davison, Shera Danese, Beverly Todd, Marilyn Kagan, Kit McDonough, Arliss Howard, Randee Heller, Paul Carafotes, Nicholas Worth, Scott Lincoln.

LATINO

(Lucasfilm/Cinecom)
dir-scr Haskell Wexler *pro* Benjamin Berg *ph* Tom Sigel, in colour *ed* Robert Dalva *mus* Diane Louie *r time* 108 mins *US opening* Nov 8.
cast Robert Beltran, Annette Cardona, Tony Plana, Ricardo Lopez, Luis Torrentes, Juan Carlos Ortiz, Marta Tenorio, Michael Goodwin, Walter Marin, James Karen.

Wexler's saga of the Sandinista resistance to American-sponsored Contra attacks doesn't mind bearing comparisons to Soviet agitprop epics. Its dramatic deck may be badly stacked, but the aggressive partisanship is also rousing. Since the Nicaraguan people are the collective hero, the villains have all the most individual parts: Robert Beltran ('Eating Raoul') as a Chicano CIA operative beset by doubts, and especially Tony Plana as his gung-ho buddy, disadvantaged Americans who have achieved upward mobility through sanctioned violence.

LEGAL EAGLES

(Universal)
dir-pro Ivan Reitman *exec pro* Joe Medjuck, Michael C Gross *scr* Jim Cash, Jack Epps Jr *ph* Laszlo Kovacs, in Panavision, Technicolor *ed* Sheldon Kahn, Pem Herring, William Gordean *pro des* John DeCuir *mus* Elmer Bernstein *r time* 114 mins *US opening* Jun 18.
cast Robert Redford, Debra Winger, Daryl Hannah, Brian Dennehy, Terence Stamp, Steven Hill, David Clennon, John McMartin, Jennie Dundas, Roscoe Lee Browne, Christine Baranski, Sara Botsford.

A straight-arrow DA joins forces with an eccentric woman lawyer to defend a gorgeous performance artist from a charge of murder. Outlandishly expensive comedy set against the New York art world with little wit, suspense, characterisation or style. Redford at least tries to give a performance for a change, but no one in the impressive cast is particularly effective. Far more symptomatic of Hollywood's waste of money and talent than 'Heaven's Gate', the movie reeks of corrupt taste and deal-making masquerading as creativity.

THE LONGSHOT

(Orion)
dir Paul Bartel *pro* Lang Elliott *exec pro* Mike Nichols *scr* Tim Conway *ph* Robby Muller, in DeLuxe colour *ed* Alan Toomayan *pro des* Joseph M Altadonna *mus* Charles Fox *r time* 89 mins *US opening* Jan 17.
cast Tim Conway, Jack Weston, Harvey Korman, Ted Wass, Anne Meara, Jorge Cervera, Stella Stevens, George DiCenzo, Joseph Ruskin, Jonathan Winters.

LUCAS

(Fox)
dir-scr David Seltzer *pro* David Nicksay *ph* Reynaldo Villalobos, in DeLuxe colour *ed* Priscilla Nedd *art dir* James Murakami *mus* Dave Grusin *r time* 100 mins *US opening* Mar 28.
cast Corey Haim, Kerri Green, Charlie Sheen, Courtney Thorne-Smith, Winona Ryder, Thomas E Hodges, Ciro Poppiti, Guy Boyd, Jeremy Piven, Kevin Gerard Wixted.

Modestly observant study of a thoughtful boy persecuted by his peers, and his unrequitable first love with an older girl. Seltzer carefully avoids compromising his characters and material, achieving a few blessed insights to what had become an almost hopeless genre. Some commercial concessions of credibility were perhaps inevitable, but the overall piece remains engaging, decent and at least fundamentally real.

MARCARONI

(Filmauro-Massfilm/Paramount)
dir Ettore Scola *pro* Luigi & Aurelio De Laurentiis, Franco Committeri *scr* Ruggero Maccari, Furio Scarpelli, Ettore Scola *ph* Claudio Ragona, in Eastman Colour *ed* Carla Simoncelli *pro des* Luciano Ricceri *mus* Armando Trovajoli *r time* 104 mins *US opening* Nov 1.
cast Jack Lemmon, Marcello Mastroianni, Daria Nicolodi, Isa Danieli, Maria Luisa Saniella, Patrizzie Sacchi, Bruno Esposito, Marc Berman, Jean-François Perriere, Fabio Tenore.

THE MAN WITH ONE RED SHOE

(Fox)
dir Stan Dragoti *pro* Victor Drai *scr* Robert Klane, based on the film 'The Tall Blond Man With One Black Shoe' by Francis Veber and Yves Robert *ph* Richard H Kline, in DeLuxe colour *ed* Bud Molin, O Nicholas Brown *pro des* Dean E Mitzner *mus* Thomas Newman *r time* 93 mins *US opening* Jul 19.
cast Tom Hanks, Dabney Coleman, Lori Singer, Charles Durning, Carrie Fisher, Edward Herrmann, Jim Belushi, Irving Metzman, Tom Noonan, Gerrit Graham, David L Lander, Ritch Brinkley, Frank Hamilton.

Tiresome adaptation of Pierre Richard slapstick spy comedy, with most of the gags slavishly duplicated without comic flair. One can see the intelligence operating behind the timing and structure, which isn't too funny and thus isn't too smart. Hanks and Singer deliver more poise than the script would seem to permit: they remain pleasantly watchable even as the farce crumbles about them.

THE MANHATTAN PROJECT

(Gladden Entertainment/Fox)
dir Marshall Brickman *pro* Jennifer Ogden, Marshall Brickman *scr* Marshall Brickman, Thomas Baum *ph* Billy Williams, in Technicolor *ed* Nina Feinborg *pro des* Philip Rosenberg *mus* Philippe Sarde *r time* 117 mins *US opening* Jun 13.
cast Joth Lithgow, Christopher Collet, Cynthia Nixon, Jill Eikenberry, John Mahoney, Sully Boyar.

A teenage boy, resentful of a scientist's attentions to his newly separated mother, steals plutonium from a secret laboratory and builds his own atomic bomb. A cautionary yarn for the youth market ith an appealing humanism and careful dramaturgy, in which believable characters face real dilemmas, Brickman's excellent script demands more passion and invention than his acceptably pedestrian direction provides. Less supercharged than 'WarGames', the movie showcases largely forgotten possibilities for responsible entertainment.

MAXIE

(Orion)
dir Paul Aaron *pro* Carter De Haven *exec pro* Rich Irvine, James L Stewart *scr* Patricia Resnick, based on the novel 'Marion's Wall' by Jack Finney *ph* Fred

Schuler, in DeLuxe colour *ed* Lynzee Klingman *pro des* John Lloyd *mus* Georges Delerue *r time* 90 mins *US opening* Sep 27.
cast Glenn Close, Mandy Patinkin, Ruth Gordon, Barnard Hughes, Valerie Curtin, Googy Gress, Michael Ensign, Michael Laskin, Harry Hamlin.

MONA LISA
(HandMade-Palace/Island)
dir Neil Jordan *pro* Stephen Woolley, Patrick Cassavetti *exec pro* George Harrison, Denis O'Brien *scr* Neil Jordan, David Leland *ph* Roger Pratt, in Technicolor *ed* Lesley Walker *pro des* Jamie Leonard *mus* Michael Kamen *r time* 104 mins *US opening* Jun 13.
cast Bob Hoskins, Cathy Tyson, Michael Caine, Robbie Coltrane, Clarke Peters, Kate Hardie, Zoe Nathenson, Sammi Davies, Rod Bedall, Joe Brown, Pauline Melville, David Hallwell.

MURPHY'S ROMANCE
(Columbia)
dir Martin Ritt *pro* Laura Ziskin *scr* Harriet Frank Jr, Irving Ravetch *ph* William A Fraker, in Panavision, colour *ed* Sidney Levin *pro des* Joel Schiller *mus* Carole King *r time* 107 mins *US opening* Dec 25.
cast Sally Field, James Garner, Brian Kerwin, Corey Haim, Dennis Burkley, Georgann Johnson.

Field flees a shiftless husband and tries to run a stable on her own, while Garner plays the local pharmacist and iconoclast who wins her over. They make an attractively mature couple in this amiable, innocuous comedy that coasts entirely on charm and a certain sense of adult responsibility that skirts shy of smugness.

MY CHAUFFEUR
(Crown)
dir-scr David Beaird *pro* Marilyn J Tenser *ph* Harry Mathias, in DeLuxe colour *ed* Richard E Westover *pro des* C J Strawn *mus* Paul Hertzog *mus* 97 mins *US opening* Jan 24.
cast Deborah Foreman, Sam J Jones, Sean McClory, Howard Hesseman, E G Marshall, Penn Jillette, Teller, Leland Crooke, John O'Leary, Julius B Harris, Laurie Main, Stanley Brock, Jack Stryker, Vance Colvig, Ben Slack.

MY LITTLE PONY
(Sunbow Prods-Hasbro/D.E.G.)
dir Michael Jones *pro* Joe Bacal, Tom Griffin *exec pro* Margaret Loesch, Lee Gunther *scr* George Arthur Bloom *ph* Jongsuk Kim, Jaebog Jung, Sanghoa Lee, Eunill Haw, Changbum Kim, Junho An, Johnhyn Lee, Hisao Shirai, in Technicolor *ed* Mike DePatie *mus* Rob Walsh, Spencer Michlin, Ford Kinder *r time* 100 mins *US opening* Jun 6.
voices Danny DeVito, Madeline Kahn, Cloris Leachman, Rhea Perlman, Tony Randall, Tammy Amerson, Jon Bauman, Alice Playton, Charlie Adler, Michael Bell, Sheryl Bernstein, Susan Blu, Cathy Cavadini, Nancy Cartwright, Peter Cullen, Laura Dean, Ellen Gerstell, Keri Houlihan, Katie Leigh, Scott Menville, Laurel Page, Sarah Partridge, Russie Taylor, Jill Wayne, Frank Welker.

MY SCIENCE PROJECT
(Touchstone/Buena Vista)
dir-scr Jonathan Betuel *pro* Jonathan Taplin *ph* David M Walk, in Technicolor *ed* C Timothy O'Meara *pro des* David L Snyder *mus* Peter Bernstein *r time* 94 mins *US opening* Aug 9.
cast John Stockwell, Danielle Von Zerneck, Fisher Stevens, Raphael Sbarge, Dennis Hopper, Barry Corbin, Ann Wedgeworth, Richard Masur.

N

NATIONAL LAMPOON'S EUROPEAN VACATION
(Warner)
dir Amy Heckerling *pro* Marty Simmons *scr* John Hughes, Robert Klane *ph* Bob Paynter, in Technicolor *ed* Pembroke Herring *pro des* Bob Cartwright *mus* Charles Fox *r time* 94 mins *US opening* Jul 26.
cast Chevy Chase, Beverly D'Angelo, Jason Lively, Dana Hill, Eric Idle, Victor Lanoux.

NEVER TOO YOUNG TO DIE
(Paul Entertainment)
dir Gil Bettman *pro* Steven Paul *exec pro* Hank Paul, Dorothy Koster-Paul *scr* Lorenzo Semple Jr, Steven Paul, Anton Fritz, Gil Bettman *ph* David Worth, in Metrocolor *ed* Bill Anderson, Paul Seydor, Ned Humphreys *pro des* Dale Allen Pelton *mus* Chip Taylor, Ralph Lane, Michael Kingsley, Irene Koster *r time* 92 mins *US opening* Jun 13.
cast John Stamos, Vanity, Gene Simmons, George Lazenby, Peter Kwong, Ed Brock, John Anderson, Robert Englund.

A NIGHTMARE ON ELM STREET, PART II: FREDDY'S REVENGE
(Heron Communications-Smart Egg/New Line)
dir Jack Sholder *pro* Robert Shaye *exec pro* Stephen Diener, Stanley Dudelson *scr* David Chaskin *ph* Jacques Haitkin, in DeLuxe Colour *ed* Bob Brady *mus* Christopher Young *r time* 84 mins *US opening* Nov 1.
cast Mark Patton, Kim Myers, Robert Rusler, Clu Gulager, Hope Lange, Marshall Bell, Robert Englund.

NO RETREAT NO SURRENDER
(Seasonal Films/Balcor/New World)
dir Corey Yuen *pro* Ng See Yuen *scr* Keith Strandberg, based on an original story by Ng See Yuen *ph* John Huneck, David Golia, in Technicolor *ed* Alan Poon, Mark Pierce, James Melkonian, Dane Davis *mus* Paul Gilreath *r time* 83 mins *US opening* May 2.
cast Kurt McKinney, Jean-Claude Van Damne, J W Fails, Kathie Sileno, Kim Tai Chong, Kent Lipham, Ron Pohnel, Dale Jacoby, Pete Cunningham, Tim Baker, Gloria Marziano, Joe Vance.

O

OFF BEAT
(Touchstone/Buena Vista)
dir Michael Dinner *pro* Joe Roth, Harry Ufland *scr* Mark Medoff, from story by Dezso Magyar *ph* Carlo di Palma, in Technicolor *ed* Dede Allen, Angelo Corrao *pro des* Woods MacKintosh *mus* James Horner *r time* 92 mins *US opening* Apr 11.
cast Judge Reinhold, Meg Tilly, Cleavant Derricks, Joe Mantegna, Jacques D'Amboise, Fred Gwynne, Harvey Keitel.

ON THE EDGE
(Alliance/Skowias)
dir-scr Rob Nilsson *pro* Jeffrey Hayes, Rob Nilsson *ph* Stefa Czapsky, in colour *ed* Richard Harkness *art dir* Steve Burns *mus* Herb Pilhofer *r time* 92 mins *US opening* Mar 21.
cast Bruce Dern, Pam Grier, Bill Bailey, Jim Haynie, John Marley.

Dogged drama of a marathon runner, unjustly disqualified from amateur competition, who returns twenty years later to prove his mettle against all odds. Wisely eschewing 'Rocky'-like heroics while recasting many of its clichés into the lexicon of rebellion, the movie satisfies on its limited, monomaniacal terms. It may lack texture, weight and a sense of proportion about its self-righteousness, but it makes one care about the race and experience some of its sensations without insulting the intelligence. Marley's trainer and Spanish Civil War vet Bill Bailey stand out amidst the sweat and flaring nostrils.

ON VALENTINE'S DAY
(American Playhouse/Angelika Films)
dir Ken Harrison *pro* Lillian V Foote, Calvin Skaggs *exec pro* Lewis Allen, Lindsay Law, Ross Milloy, Peter Newman *scr* Horton Foote, from his play 'Valentine's Day' *ph* George Tirl, in DuArt colour *ed* Nancy Baker *art dir* Howard Cummings *mus* Jonathan Sheffer *r time* 105 mins *US opening* Apr 11.
cast Hallie Foote, William Converse-Roberts, Michael Higgins, Steven Hill, Rochelle Oliver, Richard Jenkins, Carol Goodheart, Jeanne McCarthy, Horton Foote Jr, Matthew Broderick.

ONCE BITTEN
(Goldwyn)
dir Howard Storm *pro* Dimitri Villard, Robby Wald, Frank E Hilderbrand *exec pro* Samuel Goldwyn Jr *scr* David Hines, Jeffrey Hause, Jonathan Roberts, from a story by Dimitri Villard *ph* Adam Greenberg, in Metrocolor *ed* Marc Grossman *pro des* Gene Rudolf *mus* John Du Prez *r time* 93 mins *US opening* Nov 15.
cast Lauren Hutton, Jim Carrey, Karen Kopins, Cleavon Little, Thomas Ballatore, Skip Lackey.

ONE MAGIC CHRISTMAS
(Walt Disney/Buena Vista)
dir-exec pro Philip Borsos *pro* Peter O'Brian *scr* Thomas Meecham, based on a story by Thomas Meecham, Philip Borsos, Barry Healey *ph* Frank Tidy, in DeLuxe colour *ed* Sidney Wolinsky *pro des* Bill Brodie *mus* Michael Conway Baker *r time* 88 mins *US opening* Nov 22.
cast Mary Steenburgen, Gary Basaraba, Harry Dean Stanton, Arthur Hill, Elizabeth Harnois, Robbie Magwood, Michelle Meyrink, Elias Koteas, Wayne Robson, Jan Rubes.

PARTING GLANCES
(Rondo/Cinecom International)
dir-scr-ed Bill Sherwood *pro* Yoram Mandel, Arthur Silverman *exec pro* Paul A Kaplan *ph* Jacek Laskus, in colour *pro des* John Loggia *r time* 90 mins *US opening* Jan 24.
cast Richard Ganoung, John Bolger, Steve Buscemi.

Landmark independent film set in New York gay community, distinguished by its insider's lack of sentimentality and a welcome foray into contemporary comedy of manners. An aspiring writer is torn between his current lover, a dullish professional about to leave on a year abroad, and his former flame, a rock musician dying of AIDS. Despite limitations of resources and craft, the movie fulfills its most important ambition: to capture the brittle buoyancy of an alternative culture on its own terms.

PEE-WEE'S BIG ADVENTURE
(Warner)
dir Tim Burton *pro* Robert Shapiro, Richard Gilbert Abramson *exec pro* William E McEuen *scr* Phil Hartman, Paul Reubens, Michael Varhol *ph* Victor J Kemper, in Technicolor *ed* Billy Weber *pro des* David L Snyder *mus* Danny Elfman *r time* 90 mins *US opening* Aug 9.
cast Paul Reubens, Elizabeth Daily, Mark Holton, Diane Salinger, Judd Omen, Jon Harris, Carmen Filpi, Tony Bill, James Brolin, Morgan Fairchild.

Brilliant merger of performance art put-on with mass appeal slapstick. Pee-Wee conjures up memories of innumerable comic talents from Langdon and Lloyd to Tati and Lewis, but he is a true original spirit. Abrasive, infantile, spastic and sophisticated, he simultaneously projects a shrewd self-awareness and a sense of coming from another planet. His search for his stolen bike unleashes a series of droll parodies, all flowing out of character. Director Burton creates a childlike environment that perfectly complements his star's rampaging invention.
(See Paul Reubens, Faces of the Year.)

PERVOLA (TRACKS IN THE SNOW)
(Maya/Int'l Home Cinema-Spring Films)
dir-ed Orlow Seunke *pro* Jan Kaandorp *exec pro* Jan Musch, Orlow Seunke, Tys Tinbergen *scr* Orlow Seunke, Dirk Avelt Kooiman *ph* Theo Bierkens, in colour *mus* Dirk Avelt Kooiman *r time* 95 mins *US opening* Apr 12.
cast Gerard Thoolen, Hein van der Vlugt, Melle van Essen, Jan Willem Hees, Thom Hoffman, Jaap Hoogstra, Brigitte Kaandorp, Phons Leussink.

Two feuding middle-aged brothers – one a seedy gay actor, the other a scheming stockbroker – travel to a frozen unnamed country to transport their father's corpse across the icy wasteland for burial. Muddled allegorical drama unredeemed by failed wit comes off as imitation Polanski without his severity, precision, style or passion. Good acting fails to dull the arbitrary events contrived for metaphorical significance or the sanctimonius pretensions that eschew narrative for arty concepts.

POLICE ACADEMY 3: BACK IN TRAINING
(Warner)
dir Jerry Paris *pro* Paul Maslansky *scr* Gene Quintano, based on characters created by Neal Israel and Pat Proft

ph Robert Saad, in Technicolor *ed* Bud Molin *pro des* Trevor Williams *mus* Robert Folk *r time* 82 mins *US opening* Mar 21.
cast Steve Guttenberg, Budda Smith, David Graf, Michael Winslow, Marion Ramsey, Leslie Easterbrook, Art Metrano, Tim Kuzurinsky, Bobcat Goldhwait, George Gaynes, Shawn Weatherly, Scott Thomson, Bruce Mahler, Lance Kinsey, Brian Tochi, Debralee Scott, Ed Nelson.

POLTERGEIST II: THE OTHER SIDE

(MGM-UA)
dir Brian Gibson *pro-scr* Mark Victor, Michael Grais *exec pro* Freddie Fields *ph* Andrew Laszlo, in Panavision, Metrocolor *ed* Thom Noble *pro des* Ted Haworth *mus* Jerry Goldsmith *r time* 90 mins *US opening* May 23.
cast JoBeth Williams, Craig T Nelson, Heather O'Rourke, Oliver Robins, Zelda Rubinstein, Will Sampson, Julian Beck, Geraldine Fitzgerald, John P Whitecloud.

Capably mounted sequel retreads familiar turf as wraiths and demons continue to pursue the hapless family. Julian Beck makes a memorably creepy minister of evil, there are a few scary effects, and the direction and acting are generally adequate. The story, however, has an anticlimactic arc after the more complex undertones of the original, so there's little underlying drive and less reason for anyone to have bothered.

POWER

(Lorimar-Polar/Fox)
dir Sidney Lumet *pro* Reene Schisgal, Mark Tarlov *scr* David Himmelstein *ph* Andrzej Bartkowiak, in Technicolor *ed* Andrew Mondshein *pro des* Peter Larkin *mus* Cy Coleman *r time* 111 mins *US opening* Jan 31.
cast Richard Gere, Julie Christie, Gene Hackman, Kate Capshaw, Denzel Washington, E G Marshall, Beatrice Straight, Fritz Weaver, Michael Learned, J T Walsh, E Katherine Kerr, Polly Rowles, Matt Salinger, Tom Mardirosian, Omar Torres.

A film of deep political seriousness without a thought to communicate. Gere plays a professional political campaign consultant, a marketing specialist who packages dolts for sale to voters on the tube. Lumet must have identified with him as he laboured over this empty-minded exposé, trying to punch it over, and there isn't a moment of personal conviction apparent. The three leads have never been worse.

P.O.W. THE ESCAPE

(Cannon)
dir Gideon Amir *pro* Menahem Golan, Yoram Globus *scr* Jeremy Lipp, James Bruner, Malcolm Barbour, John Langley, from a story by Avi Kleinberger, Gideon Amir *ph* Yechiel Ne'eman, in TVC colour *ed* Roy Watts *pro des* Marcia Hinds *mus* David Storrs *r time* 90 mins *US opening* Apr 4.
cast David Carradine, Charles R Floyd, Mako, Steve James, Phil Brock.

PRETTY IN PINK

(Paramount)
dir Howard Deutch *pro* Lauren Shuler *exec pro* John Hughes, Michael Chinich *scr* John Hughes *ph* Tak Fujimoto, in Technicolor *ed* Richard Marks *pro des* John W Corso *mus* Michael Gore *r time* 96 mins *US opening* Feb 28.
cast Molly Ringwald, Harry Dean Stanton, Jon Cryer, Andrew McCarthy, Annie Potts, James Spader, Jim Haynie, Alexa Kenin, Kate Vernon.

John Hughes takes on the class system in American high schools but let associate Deutsch direct. Molly Ringwald incarnates an idealised breed of teenager with an emotional authenticity that disarms such cavils as posh floral arrangements in the kitchens of the chronically unemployed. The film-makers seem to expect their fantasy concoction to be regarded realistically. As an unconscious reflection of its audience attitudes about itself, an invaluable document.
(See Molly Ringwald, Faces of the Year.)

THE PROTECTOR

(Golden Harvest/Warner)
dir-scr James Glickenhaus *pro* David Chan *exec pro* Raymond Chow *ph* Mark Irwin, in Technicolor *ed* Evan Lottman *art dir* William F De Seta, Oliver Wong *mus* Ken Thorne *r time* 95 mins *US opening* Aug 23.
cast Jackie Chan, Danny Aiello, Roy Chiao, Victor Arnold, Kim Bass, Richard Clarke, Saun Ellis, Rouan O'Casey, Bill Wallace.

QUICKSILVER

(Columbia)
dir-scr Tom Donnelly *pro* Michael Rachmil, Daniel Melnick *ph* Thomas Del Ruth, in Metrocolor *ed* Tom Rolf *pro des* Charles Rosen *mus* Tony Banks *r time* 106 mins *US opening* Feb 7.
cast Kevin Bacon, Jami Gertz, Paul Rodriguez, Rudy Ramose, Andrew Smith, Gerald S O'Loughlin, Larry Fishburne, Louis Anderson, Whitney Kershaw, Charles McCaughan.

RAD

(Tri-Star)
dir Hal Needham *pro* Robert L Levy *exec pro* Jack Schwartzman *scr* Sam Bernard, Geoffrey Edwards *ph* Richard Leiterman, in Technicolor *ed* Carl Kress *art dir* Frank H Griffiths *mus* James Di Pasquale *r time* 91 mins *US opening* Mar 21.
cast Bill Allen, Lori Loughlin, Talia Shire, Ray Walston, Alfie Wise, Jack Weston, Bart Conner, Marta Kober, Jamie Clarke, Laura Jacoby, H B Haggerty, Carey Hayes, Kelly McQuiggin, Beverly Hendry.

RAINBOW BRITE AND THE STAR STEALER

(Warner)
dir Bernard Deyries, Kimio Yabuki *pro* Jean Chalopin, Andy Heyward, Tetsuo Katayama *exec pro* Jean Chalopin, Andy Heyward *scr* Howard R Cohen *ph* Animated, in colour *ed* Yutaka Chikura *art dir* Rich Rudish *mus* Haim Saban, Shuki Levy *r time* 97 mins *US opening* Nov 15.
voices Bettina, Patrick Fraley, Peter Cullen, Robbie Lee, André Stojka, Rhonda Aldrich, Les Tremayne.

RAW DEAL

(Int'l Film Corp/De Laurentiis)
dir John Irvin *pro* Martha Schumacher *scr* Gary M DeVore, Norman Wexler, from a story by Luciano Vincenzoni, Sergio Donati *ph* Alex Thomson, in J D C Widescreen, Technicolor *ed* Anne V Coates *pro des* Giorgio Postiglione *mus* Cinemascore *r time* 106 mins *US opening* Jun 6.
cast Arnold Schwarzenegger, Kathryn Harrold, Sam Wanamaker, Paul Shenar, Robert Davi, Ed Lauter, Darren McGavin, Joe Regalbuto, Mordecai Lawner, Steven Hill, Blanche Baker.

REAL GENIUS

(Tri-Star)
dir Martha Coolidge *pro* Brian Grazer *exec pro* Robert Daley *scr* Neal Israel, Pat Proft, Peter Torokvel *ph* Vilmos Zsigmond, in Metrocolor *ed* Richard Chew *pro des* Josan F Russo *mus* Thomas Newman *r time* 104 mins *US opening* Aug 9.
cast Val Kilmer, Gabe Jarret, Michelle Meyrink, William Atherton, Jonathan Gries, Patti D'Arbanville.

THE ROOMMATE

(American Playhouse/Rubicon)
dir Nell Cox *pro* Neal Miller, Richard Mellman *scr* Neal Miller, based on John Updike's 'Christian Roommates' *pro* Jeff Jur, in colour *ed* Nicolas Smith, Marc Mille *mus* Alan Bacus *r time* 90 mins *US opening* Jan 27.
cast Lance Guest, Berry Miller

A riveting character study of two mismatched college roommates in the early fifties: an uptight minister's son and a nonconforming Jew. The shifts and wrinkles in their relationship are subtly developed as the movie successfully dramatises the virtues of a well-wrought short story, so often elusive on film.

RUNNING SCARED

(MGM-UA)
dir-exec-pro Peter Hyams *pro* David Foster, Lawrence Turman *scr* Gary DeVore, Jimmy Huston, based on a story by Gary DeVore *ph* Peter Hyams, in Panavision, Metrocolour *ed* James Mitchell *pro des* Albert Brenner *mus* Rod Temperton *r time* 106 mins *US opening* Jun 25.
cast Gregory Hines, Billy Crystal, Steven Bauer, Darlanne Fluegel, Joe Pantoliano, Dan Hedaya, Jonathan Gries, Tracy Reed, Jimmy Smits, John DiSanti, Larry Hankin.

Two smart-alec Chicago detectives decide to retire to Florida but must first bust a powerful local druglord. Perhaps the perfect Peter Hyams movie: hyperkinetic, wise-ass, show-offy, snotty, self-absorbed, devoid of values. It also boasts a sustained rhythm and tone, bravura sequences, incessant ersatz wit and genuine excitement, the work of the discernible (if not discerning) artistic personality. Hines and Crystal finally shine through effectively on film as ingratiating star presences, while Hyams brilliantly achieves every intended effect whether obnoxious or exhilarating.

RUTHLESS PEOPLE

(Touchstone/Buena Vista)
dir Jim Abrahams, David Zucker, Jerry Zucker *pro* Michael Peyser *exec pro* Richard Wagner, Joanna Lancaster, Walter Yetnikoff *scr* Dale Launer *ph* Jan DeBont, in DeLuxe colour *ed* Arthur Schmidt *art dir* Donald Woodruff *mus* Michel Colombier *r time* 93 mins *US opening* Jun 20.
cast Danny DeVito, Bette Midler, Judge Reinhold, Helen Slater, Anita Morris, Bill Pullman, William G Schilling, Art Evans, Clarence Felder, J E Freeman.

Upscale 'Ransom of Red Chief' that may be as bold a bit of black humour as today's Hollywood establishment believes its youth audience can tolerate. A venal tycoon plotting to strangle his wife finds her snatched by kidnappers (the nicest people in the film) and encourages them to kill her by refusing to co-operate. Launer's script achieves consistent if never inventive farce, and some of the situations are droll, but there's no vision beyond a superficial playing at cynicism without corrosiveness. Nowhere close to Sturges or Wilder territory, and, for all its determined nastiness, rather tame.

S

SALVADOR

(Hemdale)
dir Oliver Stone *pro* Gerald Green, Oliver Stone *exec pro* John Daly, Derek Gibson *scr* Oliver Stone, Richard Boyle *ph* Robert Richardson, in colour *ed* Claire Simpson *pro des* Bruno Rubeo *mus* Georges Delerue *r time* 123 mins *US opening* Mar 7.
cast James Woods, James Belushi, Michael Murphy, John Savage, Elpedia Carrillo, Tony Plana, Colby Chester, Cynthia Gibb, Will MacMillian, Valerie Wildman, Jose Carlos Ruiz, Jorge Luke, Juan Fernandez.

Searing panorama of El Salvador civil war told from view-point of a misfit freelance reporter embroiled in the tumultuous events. Woods gives his best performance yet as the obnoxious, dissolute, truth-seeking journalist who finds his own redemption amidst the carnage and hypocrisy. Director Stone serves his own vision more acutely than have other helmers of his scripts, creating a hyperkinetic tapestry of political horror. Vaguely left-wing in perspective, sort of right-wing in its swaggering style, the film ends up a vigorously ambiguous entertainment, a Graham Greene plot done with knockabout American moxie.

SESAME STREET PRESENTS: FOLLOW THAT BIRD

(Warner)
dir Ken Kwapis *pro* Tony Garnett *exec pro* Joan Ganz Cooper *scr* Tony Geiss, Judy Freudberg *ph* Curtis Clark, in Technicolor *ed* Evan Landis *art dir* Carol Spier *mus* Van Dyke Parks, Lennie Niehaus *r time* 88 mins *US opening* Aug 2.
cast Caroll Spinney, Jim Henson, Frank Oz, Paul Bartel, Sandra Bernhard, John Candy, Chevy Chase, Joe Flaherty, Waylon Jennings, Dave Thomas.

This children's programme is virtually the only contribution American public television makes to the welfare of the family, and parents are appropriately grateful for its blend of humour, humanistic values and baby-sitting power. The big-screen version preserves the genuine charm of the programme across a longer narrative spectrum, although the characters are more credible on the tube. Debut director Kwapis finds surprising opportunities for visual wit and style that might blossom in a more Tashlinesque setting.

SEVEN MINUTES IN HEAVEN
(Zoetrope/Warner)
dir Linda Feferman *pro* Fred Roos *scr* Jane Bernstein, Linda Feferman *ph* Steven Fierberg, in Technicolor *ed* Marc Laub *pro des* Vaughan Edwards *r time* 90 mins *US opening* Jan 24.
cast Jennifer Connelly, Maddie Corman, Byron Thames, Alan Boyce, Polly Draper, Marshall Bell, Michael Zaslow, Denny Dillon, Margo Skinner, Mathew Lewis, Tim Waldrip, Billy Wirth, Paul Martel, Terry Kinney.

SHORT CIRCUIT
(PSO/Tri Star)
dir John Badham *pro* David Foster, Lawrence Turman *exec pro* Mark Damon *scr* S S Wilson, Brent Maddock *ph* Nick McLean, in Panavision, Metrocolor *ed* Frank Morriss *art dir* Dianne Wager *mus* David Shire *r time* 98 mins *US opening* May 9.
cast Ally Sheedy, Steve Guttenberg, Fisher Stevens, Austin Pendleton G W Bailey, Brian McNamara, Tim Blaney.

A blatantly derivative work that pirates not only 'E.T.' but also Badham's earlier work. A lightning bolt transforms an advanced robot into a demonstrably alive intelligence. The project's built-in sops to the youth audience ennervate a lot of its clever charm, yet the shrewd parallels between the robot's education and human child development are more sentimentally effective than the calculation of the movie deserves.

SIGNAL 7
(Myron-Taylor)
dir-scr Rob Nilsson *pro* Don Taylor, Ben Myron *ph* Geoff Schaaf, Tomas Tucker, in colour *ed* Richard Harkness *art dir* Hildy Burns, Steve Burns *mus* Andy Narrell *r time* 92 mins *US opening* Jul 19.
cast Bill Ackridge, Dan Leegant, John Tidwell, Herb Mills, Don Bajema, Phil Polakoff, Don Defina, Frank Triest, Jack Tucker, David Schickele, Paul Prince, Bob Elross.

Walpurgisnacht *for two cabbies, who must confront the emptiness of their lives and the futility of their dreams despite their desperate attempts at avoidance. Shot in four nights on videotape in conscious imitation of the rougher Cassavetes style, the film flounders continually yet still manages to hit its target insights. The dramatic structure is glib, and the choker close-up style inappropriately oppressive, yet the moments of truth (notably a method-tinged audition where the drivers audition inadequately for Odets roles that could have been modelled on them) register with undeniable force.*

16 DAYS OF GLORY
(Cappy Prods/Paramount)
dir-pro-scr Bud Greenspan *exec pro* Nancy Beffa *ph* Robert E Collins, Gil Hubbs, Michael D Margulies, Robert Primes, in Panavision, colour *ed* Andrew Squicciarini *mus* Lee Holdridge *r time* 145 mins *US opening* Mar 7.
with Joan Benoit, Rowdy Gaines, Michael Gross, Juergen Hingsen, John Moffett, Dave Moorcroft, Edwin Moses, Mary Lou Retton, Ectarina Szabo, Daley Thompson, Yasuhiro Yamashita, Grete Waitz.

SMOOTH TALK
(Goldcrest/Spectrafilm)
dir Joyce Chopra *pro* Martin Rosen *exec pro* Lindsay Law *scr* Tom Cole, based on a short story by Joyce Carol Oates *ph* James Glennon, in colour *ed* Patrick Dodd *pro des* David Wasco *mus* James Taylor, Bill Payne, Russell Kunkel, George Masenburg *r time* 92 mins *US opening* Nov 15.
cast Treat Williams, Laura Dern, Mary Kay Place, Levon Helm, Sara Inglis, Margaret Welch, Elizabeth Berridge.

An adaptation from Joyce Carol Oates that bifurcates into a finely observed absorption into the rhythms of the life of a teenage girl and then a highly theatrical and schematic seductive showdown culminating in rape. Both are unified primarily by Laura Dern's uncanny performance, a rare thesping example of perfect pitch. Chopra's direction tends toward the academically dogged, but the cumulative power of the story and Dern transcend normal formal considerations. (See Laura Dern, Faces of the Year)

SOTTO ... SOTTO
(Intercapital/Columbia-Triumph)
dir Lina Wertmüller *exec pro* Mario and Vittoria Cecchi Gori *ph* Dante Spinotti, in colour *ed* Luigi Zita *mus* Paolo Conte *r time* 98 mins *US opening* Nov 1.
cast Enrico Montesano, Veronica Lario, Luisa de Santis, Massimo Vertmüller.

Clangorous, laboured sex farce of jealous Italian husband who discovers his wife once thought of another woman while they were making love. With an awareness of sexual politics, circa 1963, Wertmüller encourages exaggeration of every aspect of cinema to scream out her obvious points. The three leads are exceptionally attractive, and the music, art direction and lighting superb, but there's naught but noise and chaos onscreen in a new low for this director turned blowhard.

SPACE CAMP
(ABC/Fox)
dir Harry Winer *pro* Patrick Bailey, Walter Coblenz *exec pro* Leonard Goldberg *scr* 'W W Wicket', Casey T Mitchell *ph* William A Fraker, in colour *ed* John W Wheeler, Timothy Board *pro des* Richard MacDonald *mus* John Williams *r time* 107 mins *US opening* Jun 6.
cast Kate Capshaw, Lea Thompson, Kelly Preston, Larry B Scott, Leaf Phoenix, Tate Donovan, Tom Skerritt, Barry Primus, Terry O'Quinn.

STAND ALONE
(Texas Star/New World)
dir Alan Beattie *pro* Leon Williams *exec pro* George Kondos, Daniel P Kondos *scr* Roy Carlson *ph* Tom Richmond, Timothy Suhrstedt, in colour *mus* David Richard Campbell *r time* 90 mins *US opening* Sep 27.
cast Charles Durning, Pam Brier, James Keach, Bert Remsen, Barbara Sammeth, Lu Leonard, Luis Contreras.

A retired man witnesses a crime and refuses to be silenced by hoodlum threats. Durning makes an amusing geriatric Stallone, but his easygoing starpower is the only animus in this predictable movie, uninflected by any theme or viewpoint.

STRIPPER
(Visionaire/Fox)
dir Jerome Gary *pro* Jerome Gary, Geoff Bartz, Melvyn Estrin, *exec pro* Arnon Milchan *ph* Ed Lachman, in colour *ed* Geoff Bartz, Bob Eisenhardt, Lawrence Silk *mus* Jack Nitzsche, Buffy Sainte-Marie *r time* 90 mins *US opening* Jan 31.
with Janette Boyd, Sara Costa, Danyel, Mouse, Gio

A pseudo-documentary comprised mostly of staged footage acted after the event by the real-life participants in an international stripper competition in Las Vegas. The methodology may be highly suspect (it might have been more effective if it had been either fact or fiction), but the doubts it raises are interesting, as are the variety of principals, each one a different psychological case. Even recreated, the emotional charge of many scenes is extraordinary.

SUMMER RENTAL
(Paramount)
dir Carl Reiner *pro* George Shapiro *exec pro* Bernie Brillstein *scr* Jeremy Stevens, Mark Reisman *ph* Ric Waite, in Continental Film Labs Colour *ed* Bud Molin *pro des* Peter Wooley *mus* Alan Silvestri *r time* 88 mins *US opening* Aug 9.
cast John Candy, Karen Austin, Karri Green, Joey Lawrence, Aubrey Jene, Richard Crenna, Rip Torn.

SWEET LIBERTY
(Martin Bregman/Universal)
dir-scr Alan Alda *exec pro* Louis A Stroller *ph* Frank Tidy, in colour *ed* Michael Economou *pro des* Ben Edwards *mus* Bruce Broughton *r time* 107 mins *US opening* May 16.
cast Alan Alda, Michael Caine, Michelle Pfeiffer, Bob Hoskins, Lise Hilboldt, Lillian Gish, Saul Rubinek, Lois Chiles.

T

TARGET
(CBS/Warner)
dir Arthur Penn *pro* Richard D Zanuck, David Brown *scr* Howard Berk, Don Petersen *ph* Jean Tournier, in Technicolor *ed* Stephen A Rutter, Richard P Cirincione *art dir* Willy Holt *mus* Michael Small *r time* 117 mins *US opening* Nov 8.
cast Gene Hackman, Matt Dillon, Gayle Hunnicutt, Victoria Gyodorova, Josef Sommer, Guy Boyd, Herbert Berghof, Ilona Grubel, Richard Munch, Ray Fry, Jean-Pol Dubois.

A boy discovers his milquetoast old man was once a hotshot secret agent when they go to Europe to recapture his kidnapped mother. The themes are closely aligned to director Penn, but the movie merely establishes its points without effectively dramatising them. Penn stages good chase scenes without integrating them into the action. While he does classical thriller shtick better than anyone, this director has usually had far more to offer. The film plays more like an imitation than the genuine article.

TERRORVISION
(Altar Prods/Empire)
dir-scr Ted Nicolaou *pro* Albert Band *exec pro* Charles Band *ph* Romano Albani, in Technicolor *ed* Tom Meshelski *pro des* Giovanni Natalucci *mus* Richard Band *r time* 83 mins *US opening* Feb 14.
cast Diane Franklin, Gerrit Graham, Mary Woronov, Chad Allen, Jonathan Gries, Jennifer Richards, Alejandro Rey, Bert Remsen, Randi Brooks, Ian Patrick Williams, Sonny Carl Davis.

THAT WAS THEN . . . THIS IS NOW
(Media Ventures/Paramount)
dir Christopher Cain *pro* Gary R Lindberg, John M Ondov *exec pro* Alan Belkin, Brandon K Phillips *scr* Emilio Estevez, based on the novel by S E Hinton *ph* Juan Ruiz-Anchia, in TVC colour *ed* Ken Johnson *art dir* Chester Kaczenski *mus* Keith Olsen *r time* 102 mins *US opening* Nov 8.
cast Emilio Estevez, Craig Sheffer, Kim Delaney, Jill Schoelen, Barbara Babcock, Frank Howard, Frank McCarthy, Larry B Scott, Morgan Freeman.

LE THÉ AU HAREM D'ARCHIMEDE (TEA IN THE HAREM)
(K.G.)
dir-scr Mehdi Charef, based on his novel *pro* Michele Ray-Gavras *ph* Dominique Chapuis, Kenout Peltier, in Fujicolor *ed* Jean-Paul Mugel, Claude Villand *art dir* Thierry Flamand *mus* Karim Kacel *r time* 110 mins *US opening* Aug 8.
cast Kader Boukhanef, Remi Martin, Laure Duthilleul, Saida Bekkouche, Nicole Hiss, Sandrine Dumas, Nathalie Jadot, Brahim Ghenaiem, Frederic Ayivi, Pascal Dewaeme, Bouriem Guerdjou, Jean-Pierre Sobeaux, Nicolas Wostrikoff.

Charef uses material from his boyhood in suburban Parisian slums to create a convincing portrait of delinquent teenagers. Though often traversed before, here the subject gains from carefully observed detail that feels immediate and authentic, rather than filtered through memory. This Jean Vigo prize-winner starts slowly with an off-putting indulgence toward its protagonists, until the film-maker's unyielding stare at circumstances and character gradually develops a complex viewpoint.

TOP GUN
(Paramount)
dir Tony Scott *pro* Don Simpson, Jerry Bruckheimer *exec pro* Bill Badalato *scr* Jim Cash, Jack Epps Jr *ph* Jeffrey Kimball, in Metrocolor *ed* Billy Weber, Chris Lebenzon *pro des* John DeCuir Jr *mus* Harold Faltermeyer *r time* 110 mins *US opening* May 16.
cast Tom Cruise, Kelly McGillis, Val Kilmer, Anthony Edwards, Tom Skerritt, Michael Ironside, John Stockwell, Barry Tub, Rick Rossovich, Tim Robbins, Clarence Gilyard Jr, Whip Hubley, James Tolkan, Meg Ryan.

The producers specialise in fashion-plated movies that recycle the essentials of old movie plots as a pretext to strike hip attitudes. They do it well, though greed aside, it may not be worth doing. Cruise is a maverick flyboy who must learn responsibility without losing his independent style. In short, 'Captains of the Clouds' for the Age (and culture) of Reagan, and for all its transparency and slickness, it does make a rousing show. Every cinematic piece is spit polished as if following orders and staying sassy were the bulwarks of a free people.

TORMENT

(New World)
dir-pro-scr Samson Aslanian, John Hopkins *ph* Stephen Carpenter, in Monaco colour *ed* John Penney, Earl Ghaffari, Bret Shelton *art dir* Chris Hopkins *mus* Christopher Young *r time* 85 mins *US opening* Apr 18.
cast Taylor Gilbert, William Witt, Eve Brenner, Warren Lincoln, Najean Cherry, Stan Weston, Doug Leach.

TRANSYLVANIA 6-5000

(New World)
dir-scr Rudy DeLuca *pro* Mace Neufeld *exec pro* Paul Lichtman, Arnie Fishman *ph* Tomislav Pinter, in colour *ed* Harry Keller *pro des* Zaljko Senecic *r time* 94 mins *US opening* Nov 8.
cast Jeff Goldblum, Joseph Bologna, Ed Bedley Jr, Carol Kane, Jeffrey Jones, John Byner, Geena Davis, Michael Richards, Donald Gibb, Norman Fell, Teresa Ganzel, Bozidar Smiljanic, Inge Apelt, Petar Buntic, Rudy DeLuca, Dusko Valentic, Ksenija Prohaska, Sara Grdjan, Robert F Lyons.

TROLL

(Empire Pictures)
dir John Buechler *pro* Albert Band *exec pro* Charles Band *scr* Ed Naha *ph* Romano Albani, in Technicolor *ed* Lee Percy *mus* Richard Band *r time* 86 mins *US opening* Jan 17.
cast Noah Hathaway, Michael Moriarty, Shelley Hack, Jenny Beck, Sonny Bono, Phil Fondacaro, Brad Hall, Anne Lockhart, Julia Louis-Dreyfus, Gary Sandy, June Lockhart.

TROUBLE IN MIND

(Island Alive – Glinwood/Alive)
dir-scr Alan Rudolph *pro* Carolyn Pfeiffer, David Blocker *exec pro* Cary Brokaw *ph* Toyomichi Kurita, in CFI colour *ed* Tom Walls *pro des* Steven Legler *mus* Mark Isham *r time* 111 mins *US opening* Dec 13.
cast Kris Kristofferson, Keith Carradine, Lori Singer, Genevieve Bujold, Joe Morton, Divine, George Kirby, John Considine.

Another phantasmagoria from Alan Rudolph, this time introducing eighties attitudes into traditional film noir *romantic fatalism. The tactile qualities, as usual, are brilliant, and Rudolph's unstinting originality of vision makes for compelling cinema. Kristofferson and Bujold do their best work to date, and everyone else is superb, except for the disastrous Divine (cast straight as a gang boss). Ultimately, Rudolph fails to bring off a slapstick climax that trashes the fundamental seriousness of his film, but until then it had been remarkable.*

TWICE IN A LIFETIME

(Yorkin Co.)
dir-pro Bud Yorkin *exec pro* David Salven *scr* Colin Welland, based on his TV play 'Kisses at 50' *ph* Nick McLean, in colour *ed* Robert Jones *pro des* William Creber *mus* Pat Metheny, Paul McCartney *r time* 117 mins *US opening* Oct 25.
cast Gene Hackman, Ann-Margret, Ellen Burstyn, Amy Madigan, Ally Sheedy, Stephen Lang, Darrell Larson, Brian Dennehy, Chris Parker, Rachel Street, Kevin Bleyer, Nicole Mercurio, Doris Hugo Drewien, Lee Corrigan, Ralph Steadman, Rod Pilloud, Art Cahn, Anne Ludlum.

Transposed by Colin Welland from British coal country to the Pacific Northwest, this story of well-meaning adultery and divorce smacks of wishful thinking. Hackman leaves Burstyn for barmaid Ann-Margret, and while his family and friends disapprove, everything proves to be for the best. The players give the material far more conviction than it really can claim, and Yorkin's direction realises all the pathos and humour in it.

U

UFORIA

(Universal)
dir-scr John Binder *pro* Gordon Wolf *exec pro* Melvin Simon, Barry Krost *ph* David Myers, in DeLuxe Colour *ed* Dennis Hill *mus* Richard Baskin *r time* 100 mins *US opening* Jul 3.
cast Cindy Williams, Harry Dean Stanton, Fred Ward, Robert Gray, Darrell Larson.

'Close Encounters of the Third Kind' reconceived as a cracker comedy, with a sleepily sexy drifter, a scamming preacher and a supermarket checkout girl who believes in flying saucers. Binder shows real feeling for his characters on the fringes of society, and many corners of the story display genuine originality, but overall the realisation is spotty and the development of the ideas routines.

VARIETY

(ZDF-Channel 4/Horizon)
dir Bette Gordon *pro* Renee Shafransky *scr* Gordon and Kathy Acker *ph* Tom Dicillo, John Foster, in colour *ed* Ela von Hasperg *mus* John Lurie *r time* 99 mins *US opening* Mar 8.
cast Sandy McLeod, Will Patton, Richard Davidson, Luiz Guzman, Nan Goldin.

Artsy experimental drama of a woman who becomes a ticket seller at a cheap porno moviehouse and grows fascinated by one patron with mob connections. Gordon achieves a few striking visual effects and a couple of scenes of rare, pungent dialogue between women, but once her heroine starts to follow her quarry, the movie wanders off into protracted nothingness.

VIOLETS ARE BLUE

(Rastar/Columbia)
dir Jack Fisk *pro* Marykay Powell *exec pro* Roger M. Rothstein *scr* Naomi Foner *ph* Ralf Bode, in DeLuxe colour *ed* Edward Warschilke *pro des* Peter Jamison *mus* Patrick Williams *r time* 88 mins *US opening* April 11.
cast Sissy Spacek, Kevin Kline, Bonnie Bedelia, John Kellogg, Jim Standiford, Augusta Dabney, Kate McGregor-Stewart, Adrian Sparks.

Photojournalist returns to her bayside home after many years and rekindles a romance with an old flame, now married. Attempts at sensitivity are muddled by a narrative seemingly determined more by committee then logic, so sympathy tends to flow to Bedelia's wronged wife simply because she's a comprehensible character.

WARNING SIGN

(Fox)
dir Hal Barwood *pro* Jim Bloom *exec pro* Matthew Robbins *scr* Hal Barwood, Matthew Robbins *ph* Dean Cundey, in Deluxe colour *ed* Robert Lawrence *pro des* Henry Bumstead *mus* Craig Safan *r time* 100 mins *US opening* Aug 23.
cast Sam Waterston, Kathleen Quinlan, Yaphet Kotto, Jeffrey De Munn, Richard Dysart, G W Bailey, Jerry Hardin, Rick Rossovich, Cynthia Carle.

WHERE ARE THE CHILDREN?

(Columbia)
dir Bruce Malmuth *pro* Zev Braun *scr* Jack Sholder, based on the novel by Mary Higgins Clark *ph* Larry Pizer, in Metrocolor *ed* Roy Watts *pro des* Robb Wilson King *mus* Sylvester Levay *r time* 92 mins *US opening* Jan 24.
cast Jill Clayburgh, Max Gail, Harley Cross, Elisabeth Harnois, Elizabeth Wilson, Barnard Hughes, Frederick Forrest, James Purcell, Clifton James.

WILDCATS

(Warner)
dir Michael Ritchie *pro* Anthea Sylbert *scr* Ezra Sacks *ph* Donald E Thorn, in Technicolor *ed* Richard A Harris *pro des* Boris Leven *mus* Hawk Wolinski, James Newton Howard *r time* 107 mins *US opening* Feb 14.
cast Goldie Hawn, Swoosie Kurtz, Robyn Lively, Brandy Gold, James Keach, Jan Hooks, Bruce McGill, Nipsey Russell, Mykel T Williamson, Tab Thacker, Wesley Snipes, Nick Corri, Woody Harrelson, M Emmet Walsh.

WISE GUYS

(UA/MGM)
dir Brian DePalma *pro* Aaron Russo *exec pro* Irwin Russo *scr* George Gallo *ph* Fred Schuler, in Technicolor *ed* Jerry Greenberg *pro des* Edward Pisoni *mus* Ira Newborn *r time* 91 mins *US opening* Apr 18.
cast Danny DeVito, Joe Piscopo, Harvey Keitel, Ray Sharkey, Dan Hedaya, Captain Lou Albano, Julie Bovasso, Patti LuPone, Antonia Rey, Mimi Cecchini.

Intermittently interesting attempt to do a Laurel & Hardy movie in 'Godfather' territory stumbles on feeble teamwork between the stars and insufficient inspiration in the gags. Best bit: the boys playing live guinea-pigs to test the boss's new bullet-proof vest and to see if his limo has been boobytrapped. DePalma's penchant for loopy comedy ('Home Movies', 'Get to Know Your Rabbit') adds some class to the antics, but there's no underlying vision or style to invest the show with meaning or value.

YARI NO GONZA (GONZA THE SPEARMAN)

(Schochiko Hyogensha/Japan Society)
dir Masahiro Shinoda *pro* Kiyoshi Iwashita, Tomiyuki Motomochi, Masatake Wakita *scr* Taeko Tomioka, based on a play by Monzaemon Chikamatsu *ph* Kazuo Miyagawa, in Eastman Colour *ed* Sachiko Yamachi *mus* Toru Takemitsu *r time* 121 mins *US opening* May 3.
cast Hiromi Goh, Shima Iwashita, Shohej Hino, Misako Tanaka, Haruko Kalo, Takashi Tsumura, Kaori Mizushima.

Shinoda returns to Chikamatsu twenty years after 'Double Suicide' with a gorgeously mounted, disturbingly ambiguous indictment of Japanese values and celebration of the Japanese heritage. A loyal warrior of great promise is framed as an adulterer by a jilted sweetheart's family; he and the unjustly accused are forced to flee for their lives and become lovers. While some of the motivations may be inescapably obscure to a Western consciousness, Shinoda's stylistic command supplies intuitive guidance through a complex array of large indigenous themes.

YOUNG BLOOD

(Guber-Peters Co/MGM-UA)
dir-scr Peter Markle, from a story by Markle and John Whitman *pro* Peter Bart, Patrick Wells *exec pro* Jon Peters, Peter Guber *ph* Mark Irwin, in colour *ed* Stephen E Rivkin, Jack Hofstra *art dir* Alicia Keywan *mus* William Orbit/Torchsong *r time* 109 mins.
cast Rob Lowe, Cynthia Gibb, Patrick Swayze, Ed Lauter, Jim Youngs, Eric Nesterenko, George Finn, Fionnula Flanagan.

Z

ZONE TROOPERS

(Empire)
dir Danny Bilson *pro* Paul De Meo *exec pro* Charles Band *scr* Danny Bilson, Paul De Meo *ph* Mac Ahlberg *ed* Ted Nicolaou *mus* Richard Band *r time* 88 mins *US opening* Oct 11.
cast Tim Thomerson, Timothy Van Patten, Art La Fleur, Biff Maynard, William Paulson.

ZUCKERBABY (SUGARBABY)

(Pelemele Films/Kino)
dir-scr Percy Adlon *ph* Joanna Heer, in colour *r time* 87 mins *US opening* Dec 13.
cast Marianne Sägebrecht, Eisi Gulp.

Percy Adlon 'Celeste' ventures into eccentric comedy in this tale of the pursuit of an attractive married subway worker by an obese woman who works in a morgue. Adlon and his players reverse the customary ideology of cinematic romance with complete credibility because they work so close to the characters that their emotions seem certifiably real. A style comprised of highly expressionistic lighting and largely single-take scenes creates a visual rhythm that counterpoints the burgeoning obsession and passion, transforming pathology with ecstasy.

THE US YEAR

Movies starring Sylvester Stallone were seen by more Americans this year than the combined output of Robert Redford, Jack Nicholson, Clint Eastwood and any dozen female Oscar winners you can name. Stallone wearing nothing but sweat above the waist in *Rambo: First Blood Part II* and *Rocky IV* and armed to the teeth in *Cobra* defined this year's box office. Proving that nothing beats muscle-flexing in the year of the Libyan raid, Arnold Schwarzenegger (*Commando* and *Raw Deal*) and Mel Gibson (*Mad Max Beyond Thunderdome*) also took off their shirts to good effect.

Pectorals thus replaced spaceships as the major force in American cartoon-action films. There was in fact very little room for any other kind of film besides cartoons. The year's biggest draw was a comic fantasy, *Back to the Future*; the twee *Pee Wee's Big Adventure* was the sleeper hit; *Jewel of the Nile* the most successful copy of *Raiders of the Lost Ark*. In America, screenwriters don't write scripts any more, they fill the dialogue bubbles in comic-book-style storyboards.

Steven Spielberg, the master of cartoon movies, broadened his appeal to include many adults with his virtually all black *The Color Purple*. The virtually all white *Out of Africa* swept the Oscars, including Best Picture, but *Purple* grossed more. Among other popular films for grown-ups, *White Nights* made monkeys out of the Russians and *Jagged Edge* made the law look like a chump.

Comedies for adults made a small comeback. *Hannah and Her Sisters* gave Woody Allen his largest audience. *Down and Out in Beverly Hills* was the first social satire to be a hit in ages. John Huston's droll *Prizzi's Honor* survived a tepid launch until finding its reward nearly a year later at Oscar time. *Compromising Positions* was a return to form for Susan Sarandon.

Younger moviegoers continued to favour wisecrack comedy, turning out in force for three Chevy Chase pictures, *Fletch, National Lampoon's European Vacation* and *Spies Like Us*. Tom Hanks was somewhat less successful with his three, *The Man With One Red Shoe, Volunteers* and *The Money Pit* – probably because they were less silly. *Police Academy 3, Cocoon* and *Short Circuit* showed the unheralded Steve Guttenberg's continuing appeal. Michael Keaton was effective in Ron Howard's dramatic comedy *Gung Ho*. One-time stand-up comics Robin Williams and Richard Pryor probably got too serious in *The Best of Times* and *Jo Jo Dancer, Your Life Is Calling*.

Apart from *Cocoon* and *Back to the Future*, science fiction and fantasy movies did poorly. In the hard sci-fi area, around $100 million was lost on *Lifeforce, Explorers, Invaders from Mars* and *Enemy Mine*. An equivalent sum went down the tubes on *Return to Oz, Santa Claus, One Magic Christmas, Legend* and *The Bride*.

The soundalike *Weird Science, Real Genius, My Science Project, Space Camp* and *The Manhattan Project* were all left sucking canal water. *The Black Cauldron* may be the only Disney animated film to wind up in the red. *Clan of the Cave Bear, Red Sonja* and *Highlander* were ill-advised visits to primitive times. Even Steven Spielberg couldn't make a hit out of *Young Sherlock Holmes*. The movie's relative failure was blamed on the youthful audience's inability to recollect just who that Holmes fellow was. Disney was thereby moved to change the title of an upcoming animated film from *Basil of Baker Street* to *The Great Mouse Detective*.

Americans avoided pictures sold on their female stars' names. Sydney Pollack paid Redford about a million a week so he wouldn't have to hype *Out of Africa* as a Meryl Streep film. Streep's *Plenty* boasted no superstar male and did poorly. Jane Fonda's *Agnes of God* did well enough, though her part was subsidiary to Meg Tilly's. Sally Field was clever enough to let James Garner have the title part in *Murphy's Romance*, giving director Martin Ritt a modest hit.

In the Year of the Muscle, 'women's pictures' were blown out of the water. Kate Nelligan put motherhood back years in *Eleni*. Sissy Spacek played a whistleblower in *Marie* and a home-wrecker in *Violets Are Blue*, but the results were equally bleak. Playing a widow in *Just Between Friends*, Mary Tyler Moore drew few of her fans from TV. Jessica Lange sings! in *Sweet Dreams*, proving again that Stix Nix Hix Pix. Glenn Close sings! in *Maxie*, but audiences preferred her to scream! in *Jagged Edge*.

Women headlining comedies is an American contradiction-in-terms right

'Rambo': pectorals replaced spaceships as the major force in American cartoon-action films.

now. Even Goldie Hawn raised few smiles in *Wildcats*. Comedian Whoopi Goldberg was cast for sobs not laughs in *The Color Purple*. Mariel Hemingway was as funny as a rubber crutch in *Creator*. Lily Tomlin has forsaken movies for Broadway. Lesley Anne Warren and Eileen Brennan were responsible for some of the scattered laughs in *Clue*.

Sex was important, but tender sex, timid sex. "Don't move," says Redford in *Out of Africa*. "But I want to move," says Streep. "Don't move," says Redford. *The Color Purple* virtually omitted the lesbian romance that was at the heart of the book. The erotic high point of *St Elmo's Fire* was Emilio Estevez snatching one quick kiss. Sex as the entire subject of a movie drew few beyond the dirty mac crowd, as the failure of *9½ Weeks* showed.

Speaking of sex, there's the Brat Pack. *St Elmo's Fire* was widely attacked as *Big Chill* for teenagers, but it proved that Brat Pack fans don't just buy posters of their idols. Rob Lowe fooled nobody impersonating a hockey player in *Youngblood*. But *Pretty in Pink* established Molly Ringwald as the Gidget of our age and put her on the cover of *Time*.

Between arguments with photographers, Sean Penn played another bad boy who's really a good boy at heart in *At Close Range*. Emilio Estevez wrote and produced a lightly attended vehicle, *That Was Then, This Is Now*, and one hopes there are no more S E Hinton books with the same two-guys-get-in-trouble plot. Judd Nelson and Ally Sheedy were laughed off the screen in *Blue City* for attempting to play adults. Matt Dillon missed badly in *Target*, a spy movie directed by the once-esteemed Arthur Penn.

Action movies usually require real adult actors, like Michael Douglas, whose *Jewel of the Nile* did better than his musical, *A Chorus Line*. Charles Bronson still chunders on, starring in *Death Wish 3* and *Murphy's Law*, which might almost have been called *Death Wish 4*. Chuck Norris, who entered movies via karate, now uses a machine-gun to better effect, as in *Delta Force* and *Invasion USA*. Lou Gossett uses jet planes. His *Iron Eagles*, otherwise non-noteworthy in the extreme, benefited from its release around the time of the Libyan raid. Residual anti-Libyanism helped make *Top Gun* a hit despite its echoes of *An Officer and a Gentleman*. *F/X* was a pleasant introduction to American movies for Bryan Brown.

This was supposed to be the year that Westerns came back into fashion, except they didn't. More than $20 million couldn't make *Silverado* into anything more than a collection of homages to Larry Kasdan's favourite Westerns, one of which was *Shane*. Clint Eastwood did more than genuflect to that George Stevens classic, he remade it with *Pale Rider*.

Michael Cimino was back in business with the moderately successful *Year of the Dragon*, which put a gun in the hand of gentle Mickey Rourke. Paul Verhoeven's first English-language film, *Flesh and Blood*, received only a negligible release in America, sparing us the sight of Jennifer Jason Leigh being mercy-raped by Rutger Hauer. William Friedkin failed to top *The French Connection* with *To Live and Die in LA*, despite a spectacular wrong-way car chase on the freeway. There are as many as *8 Million Ways to Die* at the box office, as Hal Ashby found out.

Many directors whose careers are the subjects of monographs will rue this year. Walter Hill's *Crossroads*, a tale of the devil and his music, was damned in the casting of Ralph Macchio as a blues guitarist. How about Schwarzenegger as a tap dancer? Sidney Lumet's *Power* was a jumbled exposé of the oft-exposed American election process. It's been a long time since Richard Gere had a hit. Alan Pakula's *Dream Lover* received a minimal release. Hugh Hudson's *Revolution* was withdrawn so quickly the critics' snickers hadn't died down. Richard Brooks is 74, and *Fever Pitch*, an over-documented exposé of compulsive gambling, may be the last film this John Huston contemporary gets to direct.

Martin Scorsese got back in business with *After Hours*, a black comedy that borrowed the trick of encasing humans in plaster-of-Paris statues from Roger Corman's 1959 *A Bucket of Blood*. Scorsese's former scriptwriter Paul Schrader went to Japan to make *Mishima*. Inspired by François Truffaut's *La Nuit Americaine*, Alan Alda wrote and directed *Sweet Liberty*. Russian Andrei Konchalovsky turned an Akira Kurosawa idea into a workmanlike American action movie, *Runaway Train*. Kurosawa remade *King Lear* and called it *Ran*.

Originality was valued spottily. John Boorman's set-in-Brazil *The Emerald Forest* was too novel, perhaps, to be a hit. Hector Babenco's made-in-Brazil *Kiss of the Spider Woman* was the year's most popular art film and won William Hurt the Best Actor Oscar. Terry Gilliam's nothing-to-do-with-Brazil *Brazil* did better in the newspapers than at the box office. Gilliam's successful publicity campaign against Universal's attempt to sweeten his film's ending proved that in Hollywood integrity and failure often go hand in hand. *Absolute Beginners*, while energetically unconventional, wasn't what 1986 kids felt drawn to. *Macaroni* took Jack Lemmon to Italy for the first time since *Avanti!* with no better result.

The year was marked by the number and quality of pictures made and released outside the studio system. Small-scale delights like Henry Jaglom's self-excoriating and self-exculpating *Always* were available at big-city art-houses for months on end. Although such pictures never gross more than Stallone's little finger, there's a large enough audience now for American-made non-mainstream product to support a mini-industry.

Redford's Sundance Institute fostered the talents behind *The Trip to Bountiful* and *Desert Bloom*. John Daly's Hemdale sees commercial prospects even in such flag-stilling fare as Oliver Stone's *Salvador*. Robert Altman has found a late niche making films from plays like Sam Shepard's *Fool For Love*. Altman's prolific former associate Alan Rudolph offered the Schnitzler-meets-Sam-Spade *Trouble in Mind*. Bud Yorkin got Ann-Margret, Gene Hackman and Ellen Burstyn to star in *Twice in a Lifetime*, his film based on Colin Welland's TV drama, *Kisses at Fifty*. Yorkin wound up distributing the film himself and making money.

When all is said and done, Hollywood is a machine for making money. A number of financiers ran the machine up to high revs this year. No one is likely to beat the $500 million profit fat oilman Marvin Davis made owning Fox for four years. The next fatcat to buy Fox with borrowed money ($487 million), Rupert Murdoch, is planning to turn the studio into a TV network.

Kirk Kerkorian and TV magnate Ted Turner tossed MGM back and forth before eviscerating it. No lion was ever dismembered so handily. Lorimar, the company that brought the world *Dallas*, now owns the MGM lot. Turner wound up with the MGM library. Kerkorian is back where he used to be, controlling MGM's picture-making operations. KK also controls UA. UA's troubles two owners ago with Michael Cimino were the subject of a revealing book by former executive Steven Bach: *Final Cut*. A future book on UA might examine Jerry Weintraub's five-month tenure as chairman, during which he cleared $13 million in stock options. KK fired him after he was caught trying to hire Guy McElwaine right after McElwaine was fired by Columbia.

Disney's ownership is now stabilised and its new management of Michael Eisner as chairman and Jeffrey Katzenberg as head of production seems bent on making pictures that any studio could have made. Coca-Cola bought Embassy Pictures and promptly sold it to Dino De Laurentiis. Dino is turning the renamed company (DEG) into a major with a studio in North Carolina, where unions seldom venture.

BART MILLS

THE UK YEAR

The surprise hit of the year: 'My Beautiful Laundrette', a small film about small business.

The British Government's espousal of the maxim that 'small is beautiful', as part of its attempt to build a new entrepreneurial spirit by encouraging small businesses to replace older corporations, could not have found a more pertinent model than the British film industry. It was not a good year for big films or big companies.

The surprise hit of the year was, in fact, a small film about small business. *My Beautiful Laundrette* showed Pakistani entrepreneurs stealing a march on their white-skinned rivals in car-wash services, drug-running and spin-driers. But there were other little films which had the ticket machines buzzing on both sides of the Atlantic. *Dance With a Stranger*, a passionate tale of love and murder, was the second most successful little film in the US during 1985. A later hit was the Merchant Ivory production, *A Room With a View*, which showed English repression in Florence and Surrey.

Four big films, by contrast, swallowed up about $85,000,000 and then hit the flop rocks. The historical fantasy *Highlander* made it big in France but didn't get noticed elsewhere. The musical *Absolute Beginners* couldn't deliver a fraction of the box office that its advance hype had promised. Hugh Hudson's *Revolution* was hissed at the press screening in New York and didn't escape the critical brickbats thereafter. And Rick Herland, who had persuaded some bankers to cough up $18,000,000 for his World War I flying picture *Gunbus*, didn't even steer the film to its first fly-past at the Cannes Film Festival in May.

It wasn't, however, box-office disaster which accounted for the turmoil at Thorn EMI Screen Entertainment that started in the summer. The parent company had its own problems and needed the cash that would come from selling off a not very profitable subsidiary. And chief executive Gary Dartnall thought that he could exploit the fact that management buy-outs were flavour of the month to acquire Britain's only major film company.

But when the competitive bidding got tough, Dartnall found that he couldn't cope and called in Australian Alan Bond to give a helping hand. When Dartnall still couldn't get the money he needed, Bond found himself sole owner of a company that he didn't want.

The hot potato was handed on, at a premium price, to Menahem Golan and Yoram Globus of Cannon Films. When they put in a bid in November, they found themselves assaulted by a flood of nationalist hysteria. Whether they were Israelis or Americans mattered less than the fact that they weren't British. There was real anxiety about the prospect that Cannon, which had already added the Star circuit to its original chain purchased from ACC, would have a dangerous monopoly on British screens. When Cannon did win through, the support they received was due to the recognition that exhibition, like production, needs capital. How Cannon survives may be a mystery to some, but the bankers who turned up in Cannes had big smiles on their faces.

In a better year, Goldcrest might have fronted a bid to take over TESE, but capital was in distinctly short supply at the plush new Wardour Street offices. The company limped and struggled through the year after running out of money in the spring. It had gone out of its league in taking on concurrent production of *Revolution, Absolute Beginners* and *The Mission*. Sandy Lieberson, head of production, was the first to step down. James Lee, chairman and chief executive, followed him some four weeks later, and the company fell back into the hands of its founder, Jake Eberts. The cautious ex-merchant banker seemed the man most likely to ensure Goldcrest's survival.

If national pride peaked at Christmas when the British film industry told Cannon to go away, it was back down to zero by the spring. Just as Margaret Thatcher was begging the tourists to come and visit, overcoming fears of radiation clouds and terrorist bombs, the heads of Britain's studios sought to tap business from Yank producers. Disadvantageous exchange rates and the lack of tax incentives, combined with the rather inward-looking mood of Hollywood, made things look bleak for the service sector. Earlier, customs officials had bent over backwards to allow three American orang-utans to circumvent strict quarantine regulations and appear at Shepperton for Richard Franklin's eccentric horror picture *Link*.

Overall, however, it was a good year for the film industry's foreign policy division. Los Angeles, for example, promised to become a more friendly place for British producers with David Puttnam finally deciding to do what he had always said he wouldn't do and head up a US studio, Columbia Pictures. Also, Clive Parsons remained in charge of the business side of things at King's Road Productions.

The second wave in the growth of American classics distribution is increasingly dependent on English-language imports to feed the sophisticated tastes of the baby-boom generation grown wealthy. The smaller American distributors, therefore, were eager to link with British companies. Hemdale's new distribution company, set up by expatriate John Daly, took US rights in the Greek island romp *High Season* and Peter Greenaway's *Belly of an Architect* tale of Roman architecture, figs and stomach cancer. The same outfit also picked up rights for Jeremy Thomas's mega-budget *The Last Emperor*. Charles Band's Empire Productions picked up *Underword* and *Rawhead Rex*, the first fruits of an attempt by new Alpine Pictures to revive the low-budget horror fantasy genre. And Atlantic Releasing took a stake in Ken Russell's Virgin film *Gothic*.

Also helping to plug the film financing gap was international video company Embassy Home Entertainment, which provided cash for punk rock love story *Sid and Nancy*, as well as for the thrillers *The Whistle Blower* and *Half Moon Street* from Geoff Reeve Productions. The future of that relationship looks dodgy at the time of writing, however, due to André Blay's problems in buying EHE from Coca-Cola. It used to be part of the Embassy group now absorbed into Dino De Laurentiis's DEG.

A handful of British producers overcame the national disinclination for dealing with offshore partners, and became players on the European co-production scene. Simon Perry took two first-time women writer-directors, Conny Templeman and Jana Bokova, to Paris to make, respectively, *Nanou* and *Hotel du Paradis*. After a long hiatus, veteran director Ken Loach was helped back in front of the cameras by producer Irving Teitelbaum and made *Fatherland*, an Anglo-French-German co-production about an East German singer who comes west. Paul Mayersberg's *Captive*, which marked the return to active production of Don Boyd, who had been otherwise quiet this decade, was another Anglo-French co-production. Its cast comprised two French leads, an English actress living in Paris and a London-based Japanese who wants to emigrate – to Paris.

The new Anglo-Norwegian relationship, sparked by the country's access of oil wealth and new tax laws, got off to a rocky start when Viking Films committed rather a lot of resources to *Revolution*. But another Norse entrepreneur, Michael Fant, set up his Major Films just off Soho Square. The company's first film, the dangerously-titled *Turnaround*, was filmed in Florida and Norway. But Fant also has plans to get more actively involved in the British industry.

Abandoning its distaste for pre-selling and pre-packaging proved a good idea for HandMade Films, which got its wheel turning again at the end of the year. The company had run out of money after spending big bucks on two comedies, *Bullshot* and *Water* which turned out flops. But Neil Jordan's *Mona Lisa* picked up a prize for its actor in Cannes and inspired good word-of-mouth prior to its release. And there was tabloid publicity in plenty for *Shanghai Surprise*, which paired newly-weds Sean Penn and Madonna. The latter, who plays a nun in the film, did not get on with the local hacks and press relations sometimes got bloody.

Michael Caine, who appeared in a cameo role for *Mona Lisa*, became a British film star again. He had discovered while making John Frankenheimer's appalling *The Holcroft Covenant* that Langans wasn't the only thing he cherished about London life. Other appearances were in *The Whistle Blower* alongside Sigourney Weaver, *Half Moon Street* and *The Fourth Protocol* which he sponsored along with author Freddie Forsyth.

The new British acting discovery was Daniel Day Lewis, who followed his performance as the reformed fascist in *My Beautiful Laundrette* with an extraordinary performance as Kafka in Richard Eyre's television film *The Insurance Man*. He also made appearances in *A Room With a View* and *Nanou*. Gary Oldman was utterly convincing as Sid Vicious in *Sid and Nancy*. John Cleese furthered his reputation as Britain's best comic actor when he played a time-conscious headmaster losing his mind in *Clockwise*.

The two most talked-about unmade films of the decade finally went before the cameras. Derek Jarman seemed happy to take a budget cut when he got BFI funding for his film on the artist *Caravaggio*. It turned out a visual treat and picked up an accolade at the Berlin festival. Bill Douglas should have made it to Cannes with *Comrades*, his long-gestating film about the Tolpuddle Martyrs, but he was still negotiating with his completion guarantors when the festival came around.

It was *Comrades* producer Simon Relph who finally got the job of heading the British Screen Finance Consortium, after some very public agonising in the local community about whether there was anyone qualified for the post. His first act was to rename the outfit British Screen, but he also moved promptly to allocate some of the £3,000,000 which is to be contributed annually by government and various corporate entities.

Hopes that British Film Year's promotional activities could inject some life into the ever-declining cinema sector seemed, in the end, to be well-founded. Those living in the capital may have wondered what was going on, but that was evidence only that the London-based film industry doesn't know what's going on outside its doorstep. Cynics said that the forty per cent or so increase in admissions had more to do with a wave of good films, the appalling summer weather and the peaking of the video boom, but it was difficult to deny some credit to the year of promotional activity.

In any case, the optimism generated by BFY together with the admissions increase helped to encourage more cinema building. American Multi-Cinema announced great figures for its Milton Keynes multiplex which opened in the autumn with *Rocky IV*. The company is hunting many new sites. CIC Cinemas started building a complex in High Wycombe. Also, Cannon seemed willing to inject some haste into TESE's plans to build new cinemas, which got started with a construction at Salford, near Manchester.

British Film Year didn't formally end its international hustling activities until the Cannes Festival in May when a pavilion was constructed on the beach as a focus for national hustling activities. To no one's surprise, *The Mission* took the big prize. And British films were in favour among buyers. For the first time in years, the sun proved a regular feature. The faces of the British film people who made it down to the Riviera expressed their relief that they had survived this long.

It was, in short, a year of turmoil which left the film industry a little leaner, much wiser and surprisingly confident about its future prospects. JAMES PARK

FILMS OF THE YEAR
HANNAH AND HER SISTERS

After dealing in miniatures and conjuring with the past in his last several films, Woody Allen has returned home in *Hannah and Her Sisters*. In the United States, at least, he has been received like a conquering hero, and the film has been by far his most popular with the public since *Annie Hall* and *Manhattan* for a number of reasons – its warmth, high humour, bounty of attractive characters and, undoubtedly, the overtly happy ending, a distinct rarity in Allen's work. Best of all, however, the film is a sort of modern *La Ronde* which exquisitely delineates so many of the crucial moments in romantic relationships between men and women. *Hannah* is a creation obsessed with the eternal search for *l'amour juste*, and Allen both delights in, and agonises over, every step of the process.

After establishing himself as a world-class director with *Annie Hall* and *Manhattan*, Allen turned away from his on-the-spot examinations of contemporary, upscale New Yorkers and made five films which were, in their own ways, quirky, show business-orientated, technically adventurous, expertly made and, finally, more rewarding thematically than dramatically. Despite many lovely scenes, ingenious inventions and increasingly enchanting performances by Mia Farrow, the string of films including *Stardust Memories*, *A Midsummer Night's Sex Comedy*, *Zelig*, *Broadway Danny Rose* and even the much-liked *The Purple Rose of Cairo* suffered from a uniform conceptual thinness which couldn't fully carry the weight of what their creator was clearly trying to say. Quite quickly, Allen turned from a warm into a cold director, one more concerned with formal and technical exercises than with recognisable characters or emotions.

This is not to dismiss his achievements during this period. Far from it. Indeed, all of these films, with the less prominent exception of *Sex Comedy*, have their impassioned defenders, and the last three are counted by many critics as among his finest films. But the public which was turned off by *Stardust Memories* and not seduced by *Sex Comedy* was slow to return to the others. Even to Allen, who has stated that he becomes worried when one of his pictures is liked too much by audiences, it must have seemed like the right time to return to the real world.

Along with the luminous warmth of Carlo Di Palma's images, what one first notices about *Hannah and Her Sisters* that sets it apart from previous Woody Allen films is that it is centred around a sense of family, instead of a collection of neurotic singles. This beautifully structured piece begins and ends with one of the most cozy, pleasurable occasions in American family life, the Thanksgiving dinner. Food, children, bustling activity and good cheer abound, creating an atmosphere which is only troubled by the wandering eye of host Michael Caine, who has decided that he is hopelessly in love with Barbara Hershey, the invitingly sexy sister of his wife, Mia Farrow.

Although previous Allen films have begun with confessionals to the audience, a distinct difference here is that it is Caine's seemingly well-adjusted, well-married Elliot, rather than Allen's character, who is delivering the guilt-ridden, sexually hung-up monologue. This does not mean that when he finally enters the story, somewhat from left-field, Allen denies himself the opportunity of speaking directly to the viewer; in effect, the picture is told from a double first-person point-of-view.

For much of the running time, Allen's role as Mickey, a hypochondriacal television producer whose health, religious and career vicissitudes constitute a triple-whammy mid-life crisis, seems peripheral and even unrelated to the rest of the characters. Mickey's only connection to the others is that he was once married to Farrow's Hannah, but he is not invited to the Thanksgiving dinner and is evidently out of contact with his ex-wife.

Invited but not present at the dinner is Max Von Sydow, a difficult, demanding, intolerant artist and live-in companion of Hershey's Lee. Committed to his artistic integrity to a demented, self-injurious

degree, Von Sydow's Frederick cannot suffer fools and would rather stay alone in his apartment than endure smalltalk at the family function or expose himself to the unlimited idiocies, outrages and injustices perpetrated by the outside world.

Although nothing is made of it by way of summation, one of the major points of interest in *Hannah* is the composite self-portrait Woody Allen fashions out of the characterisations of the three leading men. Here, Allen endows Mickey with all the paranoia, hypersensitivity and philosophical gloom normally associated with Allen's persona. It is Caine who portrays the nervous, bumbling but persistent romantic suitor, another familiar aspect of Allen's own characters, while Von Sydow expresses the tormented and – need one add – Bergmanesque artist, the absolutist who can't understand how or why normal people cope with the absurdity of the universe. While Allen offers nothing new in what his male characters do or say, it is nevertheless extremely refreshing to see the attitudes expressed and fleshed out by such fine actors with such distinct styles.

And now about these women. If Allen has indeed spread his own personality characteristics among his three main male characters, then perhaps he has distributed what he most likes in women among the three female leads, and cast the roles accordingly. Hannah is referred to as – and really does seem to be – the perfect woman. As beautiful as a carefully crafted miniature, she represents the ideal wife and mother; an actress to boot, she is so successful that she can afford to denigrate her abilities and step quietly out of the Broadway fray, only to return to it every couple of years and undoubtedly pick up a Tony Award for her trouble.

Yet this isn't enough for Elliot. All of Hannah's admirable qualities prove negligible next to the simple, earthy allure of Lee. Even though Allen has enshrouded her statuesque frame with bulky sweaters, coats and scarves, Barbara Hershey has never been sexier or more appealing on the screen, and so effectively does she serve her director's cause that all she need do is walk into a room and smile to make abundantly clear why Elliot is willing to risk everything to get her in bed.

The third sister, Holly, is the eccentric, insecure nut for whom Allen always feels a special fondness, and with whom he certainly most identifies. Frantically active to no measurable effect, either in her assorted careers or with men, Holly is an unintellectual version of Diane Keaton's character in *Manhattan*, an utterly recognisable modern type whose inability to sort out her life results in accumulated but seldom acknowledged desperation. Dianne Wiest practically steals the film with her delightfully batty performance.

With this cast of characters, Allen has orchestrated an extensively elaborate piece in which the emotional currents cross, dovetail, collide and join with great dexterity and resonance. He starts, smartly enough, with the beginnings of attraction – the pure, forbidden, physical lust Elliot feels for Lee. Counterpointed with the complete sexual satisfaction they both feel is the guilty tentativeness with which he treats Hannah, and the more decisive action Lee takes with Frederick. Also seen in parallel to their successful affair is Holly's frustrated lust for the rich and handsome architect played in a cameo by Sam Waterston and, in highly comic flashback, Mickey's deteriorating marriage to Hannah and his hilariously disastrous date with Holly.

As the Elliot-Lee relationship begins to wane, a friendship and, ultimately, romance between Mickey and Holly gets underway, so that the film as a whole constitutes a constantly undulating and overlapping series of emotional rises and declines. A tireless chronicler of privileged, poignant moments between men and women, Allen once again charts the highs and lows and everything in between with these vignettes of love stories, but for the first time has resolved them all on a positive, hopeful note, rather than with resigned melancholy.

The film's few dissenters view the ending as a fairy tale, and some have argued that Allen's character simply retreads old ground in his continued search for meaning and sense. But never before has Allen found solace and satisfaction within the traditional context of marriage, family and children. If, after this apparent long stride, Allen in fact reverts to his familiar comic intellectual groping, a charge of artistic redundancy could plausibly be lodged. The next logical step from the ending of *Hannah* would take Allen into the relatively unfamiliar world of married life, territory in which he has never placed himself on screen and which he has usually portrayed with other characters in broadly comic and/or horrifying terms.

There are many other pleasures offered up by *Hannah*,notably the richly romantic (and artfully selective) display of New York locations and cultural artifacts. Perhaps only Allen among contemporary directors could make an architectural travelogue of the city both edifying and entertaining, and his seemingly casual choices of evocative settings for what is really a rapid-fire succession of dialogue scenes represent one of the factors that has made the film so pleasurable for the vast majority of viewers. After pursuing some tangential ideas and experimenting with diverse styles in his last few films, Allen has once again proven himself as perhaps the prime contemporary master of that perennial genre, the human comedy.

Todd McCarthy

THE COLOR PURPLE

Pleasure in *The Color Purple*, the professional pleasure of a critic, is enhanced for me by a kind of personal satisfaction. I have for some time felt that Steven Spielberg was working beneath his own high standards. Reluctantly, since I respect his achievement, I have felt obliged to condemn. *The Color Purple* restores him to his proper level.

This remarkable director began years ago – in 1971 – with *Duel*: his first feature film, it was made for television. But when it was transferred to the large screen it attracted immediate attention with its handling of speed, of pace, of dramatic edge. You might say it was about two vehicles, a car and a truck. One scarcely saw the truck-driver. But one was increasingly and uncomfortably aware of him. One felt his hostility, a lethal hostility towards the driver of a car which he fancied was challenging his position on the empty highroad. There was a good actor, Dennis Weaver, at the wheel of the car; but there were no big stars; there was just a state of murderous tension. I still think *Duel* was the best thing Spielberg has ever done.

Between that small, constricted action and the long psychological tale of forty years in the life of a black family and their friends, Steven Spielberg has directed or produced or sponsored a long list of movies. They began with more ambitious material: *The Sugarland Express* and *Jaws* – the best of the series, for it was concerned as much with human behaviour as with the appetite of a shark. There was the splendid visionary *Close Encounters of the Third Kind*; there was the endearing fairy tale of *ET*. Then Spielberg went on to the successes with Harrison Ford as star: *Raiders of the Lost Ark* and *Indiana Jones and the Temple of Doom*, adventure in the taste of a young audience longing for extravagant dangers. Then came a series of movies directly aimed at a teenage public: *The Goonies* and *Back to the Future* and *Young Sherlock Holmes*. Spielberg and his fellow executive producers now and then made a hit: *Gremlins* had dazzling ideas. Let's admit it: the screen is in their debt; they were bringing in a new audience. But for the critic, for the enthusiast who for years had followed the development of a creative talent, disappointment was acute. One looked vainly for themes not restricted by the age of an audience. One looked vainly for the unwavering devotion to the possibilities of film which one had seen in *Duel*.

Based on Alice Walker's much-admired, Pulitzer Prize-winning novel, *The Color Purple* is the story of black society in the Georgia of the first half of this century, and it deals with the growth of human character; as such it is remote from the rest of Spielberg's cinema; it is even controversial. And at last he is directing again. There is a beautifully designed opening. In a field of golden flowers two girls run and play; the blossoms yield to let the figures pass, there is the feeling, almost the smell of summer. The girls, laughing, stop to play, clapping hands together; one of them is pregnant. It is a scene of idyllic happiness; then it is interrupted by threat. A man comes to call the two laughing girls – they are sisters – from their careless happiness. And in the next scene the terrors of life press in on the innocent pair. The elder girl is in childbirth; the sister, like her still scarcely more than a child, is at her bedside; and the man we have already seen comes into the room and snatches the twin babies away.

In *Duel* Steven Spielberg had a deserted highway, a truck, and a car driven by an inoffensive traveller – and an idea. In *The Color Purple* he has an actress, the lively and extraordinary Whoopi Goldberg.

Miss Goldberg, one learns, comes from the stage, from one-woman shows; she is new to the cinema. Watching her on the screen, one is convinced that black players have the most expressive faces in the world. She is not beautiful. There are beautiful black faces in the cast of *The Color Purple*; conventionally judged, hers is

not one of them. It never, in the transformation allowed a film star at the end of some ugly-duckling romantic fantasy, takes on the smooth outlines and the graceful proportions of popular charm. But it lives, it speaks; it grieves and jokes; it holds you. It creates its own beauty, the beauty of an emerging human being.

The black girl, carelessly happy in the golden field with her sister, has a dark future; she will become a slave. Not a slave of white society; she is to be the slave of a black. The man who interrupted her happiness with her sister, the man who snatched from her the new-born twins, now summons her to come out of the house. Another man, smiling, masterly, comes riding up. He looks her over. When he rides away she walks behind.

She is far worse than a servant. But for a while the sister she so dearly loves joins her; that is enough. Then the younger girl resists the owner's attempt to molest her. She is forcibly thrown out and for years the submissive servant-slave is left alone with no news. Possibly this is the most subtle part of Miss Goldberg's performance. She is submissive all right. But now something new creeps into that expressive face. It watches; it does more. Observing is different from watching; her face observes; there is irony in her look. Her master still treats her with contempt. He is going out in a hurry, he wants his best clothes. She hands them to him one by one. She stands, she waits, reminding him by producing it that he needs a tie; a look of amusement, almost indulgence, is there. He needs her to see that he is correctly dressed, he can't do without her. She smiles to herself; she is enjoying a moment of power.

Perhaps it is the beginning of her emancipation. She is still the servant, waiting on the blues singer he brings to the house, putting up with the woman's violent insolence, repairing her master's failures to conciliate the visitor. But she is changing. The revelation of his cruel concealment of the letters from her adored sister is the spur to her final rebellion. Not the rebellion of an underling. Now she is anybody's equal.

And that is the point of the film: the birth of a completed human being. Fortune in the end will help her: she will have a bequest, she will have a house. But just as there are no adventitious aids to the change in a face that has learned pride and self-respect, in the same way the transformation of slave into free woman comes of itself; it is in her. We have seen her grow. Fortune is at last on her side; friends help her. But she grows because she is capable of growth.

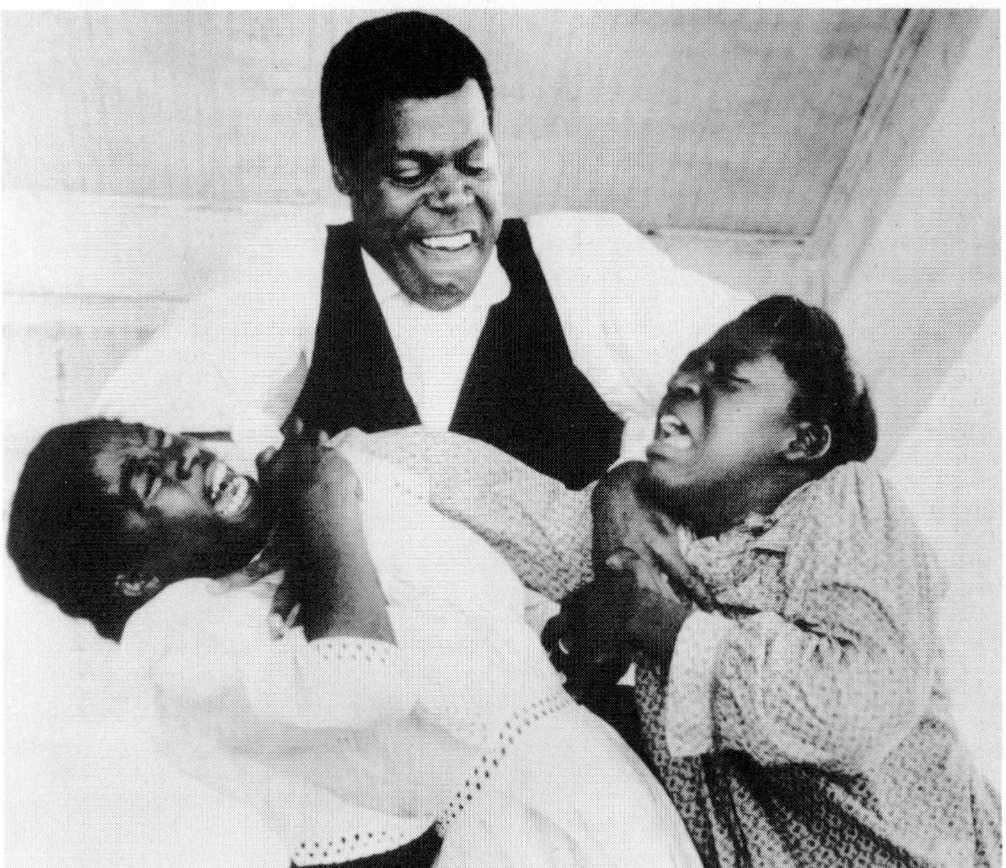

Whoopi Goldberg is a miracle of casting: a delight to meet this uniquely gifted player in a role which so exactly fits her, which like a dress exquisitely worn becomes her own creation. Of course, one must recognise the quality of the rest of the cast. As the enslaver, then, Danny Glover. One marked his performance in *Places in the Heart*, where he played the farm-worker who opportunely appeared to help the bereaved wife. That was a delicate performance of service and victimisation; now he shows his range in a portrait of an oppressor who again and again betrays his own uncertainties; he is the perfect foil to Miss Goldberg's swelling confidence. There is a confident appearance by Margaret Avery as the blues singer who helps in the search for the missing letters from the sister. One notes a strong, clear performance from a newcomer, Oprah Winfrey, who plays the wife of the enslaver's son. It is a well-balanced cast. The director, venturing into unaccustomed emotional country, is effective in control.

The spectator reacts and enjoys. The images of that Georgian society persist; days later one still sees the river and the fields, still recalls the disorder of the blues party or the delighted welcoming at the reunion of the sisters. I am not saying that *The Color Purple* is a masterpiece. One can see its faults. I find it too long. Respect for its original has persuaded Steven Spielberg to reject too little. He uses visions of the Africa where the sister lives as a missionary which may be pleasing and evocative but add little to the reunion. Spielberg has been criticised for cutting short a lesbian passage; at greater length it would surely have weakened the central theme. Even as things are the wealth of incident sometimes makes one lose grip. A novel can support numerous characters; a film doesn't know where to put them. There is occasional overcrowding here. Nevertheless, this is a film which has been honourably felt by its maker; Spielberg is involved in its action. There has been talk of its failure to win an Oscar. One can understand the reasons for the failure. The film hasn't the absolute concentration, the single-mindedness that would win an audience over completely.

However, it is emotionally an extremely warm film. One respects it; there is a mysterious contagion of gentle affection. One finds oneself singling it out from films which are perhaps its superior. Enough; one just likes it.

DILYS POWELL

OUT OF AFRICA

At the foot of the Ngong Hills, they made a $30 million movie. It won eight Academy Awards and, at last glance, was easing itself past the $100 million mark at the US box office. How easy though, in retrospect, to underrate the achievement. Streep-Redford, return to romance, lush colonial settings, skilful director like Pollack – wasn't it always bound to be boffo, certainly critic-proof?

An ace publicist was recently outlining to me the odd breaks in the old film game. Take a film like *Birdy*. Great success at Cannes and much-talked about despite subsequent attempts by the director to scupper all good-will through persistent whingeing. Released in the States pre-Christmas to qualify for Oscars but lost in the general rush. British critics seem to love it but good feelings simply not translated into precious PR column inches. *Birdy* flops.

Out of Africa, based on some obscure historical and literary figures, arrives at release-time with almost no information except annoyance at a closed set, sketchy notes and a dozen production stills. Instant hit in the US followed by clattering cash registers everywhere else. In the absence of stars prepared to do their bit, the few scraps of press material are utilised to bolster screeds on why Redford is miscast as white hunter Finch Hatton or how women will soon be dressing *à la* Baroness Blixen. No hype is more hype.

It appears that *Out of Africa* is that rare Hollywood phenomenon – like *Star Wars*, for example – a success only from the day it actually opened.

Yet, surely, *Out of Africa* seemed pre-packaged for success. The project had, however, eluded Hollywood adaptation for fifteen years. Robert Ardrey wrote a script for Universal in 1969 and around the mid-seventies Columbia tried to crank it up with talk of Nicolas Roeg as director.

The title volume, written by Karen Blixen (Isak Dinesen) in 1937 and described at the time as "a homesick book, the book of one who left her heart in Africa", was, according to Sydney Pollack who finally took on the project near the centenary of Blixen's birth, "never very solvable on a narrative level.

"There was hardly a story. It's a pastorale, a beautifully formed memoir that relied on her prose style, her sense of poetry and her ability to make universal truths out of very specific small things. That's difficult to translate to film."

Screenwriter Kurt Luedtke apparently believed the problem with earlier *Out of Africa* projects was the absence of a strong relationship at the core of the film – in particular the ambiguity of the involvement between Karen and the charismatic, old Etonian white hunter, Denys Finch Hatton. Luedtke, who had always admired Blixen's writing, suddenly one day found a biography of Finch Hatton by Kenyan resident, Errol Trzebinski. Flying to Venice to negotiate the rights, he co-incidentally met Judith Thurman who had just completed what was later generally hailed as the definitive biography of Dinesen.

Columbia still had an option on *Out of Africa* as well as another Dinesen title, *Shadows on the Grass*, from Danish producer Kim Jorgensen. Since Luedtke had written the Oscar-nominated *Absence of Malice* for Pollack and Columbia, he was able to persuade the studio to let him write the screenplay. And now armed with the flesh and blood provided by the biographies he felt he could breathe life into the adaptation.

The film eventually returned to the Universal fold and to Pollack fell the task of casting. In her memoir, Blixen writes of Finch Hatton: "He would have cut a figure in any age, for he was an athlete, a musician, a lover of art and a fine sportsman. . ."

A contemporary, Elspeth Huxley, recalled the duo in her own, rather vivid, way: "I have a picture of her as a witchlike person, small, dark and rather alarming. She was also a monumental snob. Her obsessive horror of the middle

classes led her to refer to the fearful living death of English middle-class mediocrity. Once she wrote it was worth having syphilis in order to become a Baroness. . .

". . . He was tall, very English and, as I discovered to my horror when I first saw him without a hat, bald. An old Etonian, he could quote Greek and Latin poets in the original and once flew to London to hear an opera and back again the next day."

That's life and, of course, the movies are something else.

For Karen, Pollack had toyed with the idea of casting a European actress and indeed has admitted he would have been happy to choose from a number he'd auditioned. Until, that is, he was "besieged" by Meryl Streep's agent "determined that I meet her. I had seen her work, but had no idea who Meryl Streep was. I knew Sophie (from *Sophie's Choice*) or Karen from *Silkwood*, but not the actress."

They met and, apparently, clicked straightaway. Redford, if not immediately identifiable as a tall, bald old-Etonian, made great sense for Pollack – and I think does for us and the film. They'd already made five films together, including *Jeremiah Johnson*, *The Way We Were* and *Three Days of the Condor* and, for Pollack, Redford remains "the most aristocratic of American actors and the most private."

The point being that if you are going to introduce an almost mythical figure as counterpoint to a strong Streep heroine, you're going to need more than just a good actor but also perhaps the most enduring 'presence' on the screen today. That continues to be Redford, though I must add that he also continues to be a mightily underrated actor simply because of that undeniable charisma. Sniping about his accent, or lack of it, is a pointless distraction. For the film, he and it works. Mind you, Pollack's comment on this is relevant: "I couldn't find any way in which an English accent would enhance the depth or profundity of the love story or the tragedy of his death or any of the themes of the story."

Apart from the usual slices of dramatic licence, Pollack has owned up to a couple of other important changes from the original. The 19-year time-span of Karen's struggles to grow coffee on a Kenyan plantation, of her loves and frustrations, has been condensed to just a decade, and ex-husband, the sexually-rampant Baron Bror Blixen (Klaus-Maria Brandauer, in a piece of inspirational casting) is re-introduced to tell her of Finch Hatton's death in a plane crash.

Though Redford hovers over the film like a spectre, from the very first shot of him framed distantly, and romantically, in the sunset, it's Streep and Africa itself that tend to remain long in the memory. Redford, with his megadollar salary, required three separate trips to the location for a total of eight weeks work. She, for marginally less reward, turned up for filming on 99 out of 101 location days already armed with a perfectly-researched accent, and produced a performance that defies you not to accord her the label of finest screen actress of this or any other generation.

Life magazine, earlier this year, indulged itself and us with a scrumptious celebration of the movies which, however, got off to a bad start by draping its cover with what it chose to describe as "Hollywood's Most Powerful Women". Looking curiously like clones were Mesdames Hawn, Lange, Streisand, Fonda and Field. But no Streep. It probably had something to do, mundanely, with agent representation. I prefer to think that the chameleon-like Streep was actually there, probably doubling as the *Life* logo.

Designer Stephen Grimes and cinematographer David Watkin provide the perfect backcloth for Streep's faultless emoting. About seventy per cent of the filming took place within thirty minutes of Nairobi. The Ngong Dairy in Karen, named after her, was used to base a renovated farmhouse duplicating the original which, ironically, stands but a few miles away. Currently a government health training facility, it could not be used for filming. The Muthaiga Club was reconstructed in a field and, in nearby Langata, 1914 Nairobi sprang up.

It's all too easy for critics to dismiss *Out of Africa* as middle-ground and middle-brow, implying it's a kind of glossy pap for the middle-class that Blixen apparently loathed. As with, I suppose, *Passage to India* and, to a lesser extent, *Gandhi*, there is to be had a vicarious feeling of old empire and colonial smugness; but that complacency is each time punctured by events.

The film makes a welcome change from endless reviews of American rites-of-passage and youth culture, British navel exploration, and hybrid special effects fests. It's old-fashioned in the very best sense.

And that opening line of "I had a farm in Africa" – hauntingly recalled throughout the film – now summons the same kind of frisson and heralds the promise of, say, "Last night I dreamed I returned to Mandalay." Except I'd prefer to be at the foot of the Ngong Hills.

QUENTIN FALK

KISS OF THE SPIDER WOMAN

"I wish I could be there ... to feel you all", said William Hurt, thanking the British Film Academy by satellite for his Best Actor award. The line was delivered in almost the identical hesitant, spacy voice – a hushed and hypnotised purr – Hurt uses for *Kiss of the Spider Woman,* the film that won him the coveted gold maskette. It shows that actors can get permanently infected by good roles, just as explorers can get permanently infected by good tsetse flies: the malady lingers on. And in Hurt's case he was at it again a month later, flaky-murmuring his overcome thanks at the Hollywood Oscars.

Now – since Hurt also won Best Actor in Cannes the previous year – there is only knighthood and apotheosis to come.

Hurt's acting as Molina, the gay prisoner sharing a South American slammer with Marxist macho-man Valentin (Raul Julia), may well be the performance of the decade. Straight from scene one, it scoops us into the mood of Hector Babenco's movie and the Manuel Puig novel on which it is based. As the camera glides over the spider's web trappings with which Molina has decked out his side of the cell – the hanging robes, the come-into-my-psyche movie pin-ups – Hurt's voice begins its rapt story-telling purr. Love and intrigue in Occupied France! Tilted angles and sepia shadows! The silent trundle of old Citroëns down cobbled streets! And the *jolie laide* Sonia Braga, who looks like the daughter of Maria Casares out of Charles Bronson, as the slinky cabaret singer who falls for the blond Nazi!

Ah! the stories with which we beguile this brief interregnum between birth and death. For the wonder of Babenco's film, as of Puig's novel, is that a modest tale of two jailbirds, having their paradigmatic punch-up between fantasy and reality, onanistic escapism and political conscience, seems to become an analogue of life itself.

We move through *leitmotifs* of birth (Molina the midwife to new imaginary worlds), of the disenchantments of growing up (Molina revealed as 'plant' to gain information from his cellmate), of love, sex and death: even of toilet training (Valentin's diarrhoea from poisoned beans and Molina's solicitude). And the film's tiny central setting is ventilated not just by this idea of a cradle-to-grave allegory, but by the ease and logic with which the film leaps out into fantasy or flashback; or into the outside scenes in which Molina has his secret trysts with the warden or, later, carries out the resistance mission entrusted to him by Valentin.

All this born out of the claustrophobic circlings of two men: the man of feeling and the man of action, the be-er and the doer, the fantasist and the realist. "Why should I think about reality in a stinkhole like this?" cries Molina, as Raul Julia's Valentin, doggedly macho with his Che Guevara beard and big-lidded, lethargic eyes, rumbles on about the revolution. And the film's artfully developed irony is that *both* men – not just Molina – spend almost every waking and sleeping hour of their cell-lives finding ways to step into other worlds. Valentin does it by mentally blueprinting his revolutionary futures. Molina does it by melting the cell walls with his oxy-acetylene imagination and escaping into orchidaceous B-movies, of the they-don't-make-'em-like-that-any-more variety.

Of course, they never made them like that to begin with. Memory embroiders the past, including old films, and can turn a few threads of tatty melodrama into a spider's web of fatal allurement. As the film progresses it becomes clear that Molina himself is the Spider Woman of the title – and of the climactic movie yarn – and Valentin is his victim.

And the jail cell is the desert island: as blatant an authorial contrivance for marooning two human opposites together as any sun-bleached hump of sand ever was, surrounded by sea and with a palm tree stuck in its midriff.

Indeed the secret joke at the heart of *Kiss of the Spider Woman* is that its main story is as preposterous – as sentimental, as 'arranged', as schematic – as any of the movie-within-a-movie cutaways. It sets up a high-relief antithesis, between the flaky fairy and the macho freedom-fighter (how many real-life Latin American jails would *actually* throw these two together?), and then it guides them towards a mutual transference process. The action man comes to understand the power and beauty of dreams, and the dreamer to understand the need, *in extremis,* for courage and action. The main plot ends by steering Hurt towards a virtual broad-daylight re-enactment of the *film noir* heroics of his French Resistance movie.

Hurt's near-solo as Molina – most of his role is written as a monologue, with laconic interruptions from Valentin – gives the movie all the colour, emotion and lyricism that its setting (necessarily) lacks. First seen with henna-rinsed hair and wrapping a red towel turban-style around his hair, he could be a camped-up, discount-price Scheherezade. He turns his movie stories, delivered in slow-motion, into feats of epic beguilement. And he is just as vivid in reaction as in action. "What kind of a revolution is it that doesn't allow you to eat an avocado?" he querulously asks, munching an avocado, when Valentin is high-horsing his way through a speech about what revolutionaries should and and should not do.

The life-imparting paradox here is that Molina puts a dash of play-acting into even his genuine responses, while Valentin, who seems the more monosyllabically honest of the two, is constantly deceiving himself: about his macho self-discipline, about the subjugation of his feelings to the demands of the revolution. (When he dreams, it is not about his radical girlfriend but about the apolitical Marthe.)

Babenco delightedly exploits not just Hurt's supple delivery of his lines but also his 'takes'. When Molina gives his shopping list to the prison governor (for the hamper of goodies intended to convince Valentin that Molina has had a visit from his mother), the air of 'innocence' with which he reels out ever more outrageous luxuries – wine, cheese, whole roast chickens – is masterfully comic.

Yet in Babenco's hands neither this showpiece performance, nor the runaway visual possibilities of the films-within-a-film, are played up or steered towards a kitsch that might capsize the movie's plausibility of theme and character.

The film's title is straight out of the world of comic strips and cheap movies, as is the 'Two Men Thrown Together!' plotline. But in detail Babenco plays the cell scenes for the dead straight neo-realism of his *Pixote.* He knows there is enough campery in the material without camping up the camera style or performances. So Hurt is no shrieking, wrist-flapping queen but a man of gentle, gawky grace with a soft but still 'masculine' voice and the knack of making his movie memories sound like spoken thoughts. Condemned to solitary refinement, thanks to the grudging responses of Valentin, he paints each detail as if with an artist's pause between each brush-stroke.

And Julia is no biceps-knotted beefcake but a moody self-programmed son of the revolution, who now finds that his programme is being tampered with by new sensibilities.

Both actors are cast against type – song-and-dance man Julia as Mr Macho, *Body Heat* stud Hurt as Mr Gay – but it's exactly this that produces the blends and modulations that create real people. And it's exactly the movie's subtle interweaving of comic strip or B-movie incantations with dead-earnest realism that creates a film with an irresistibly multi-layered power to entrap.

HARLAN KENNEDY

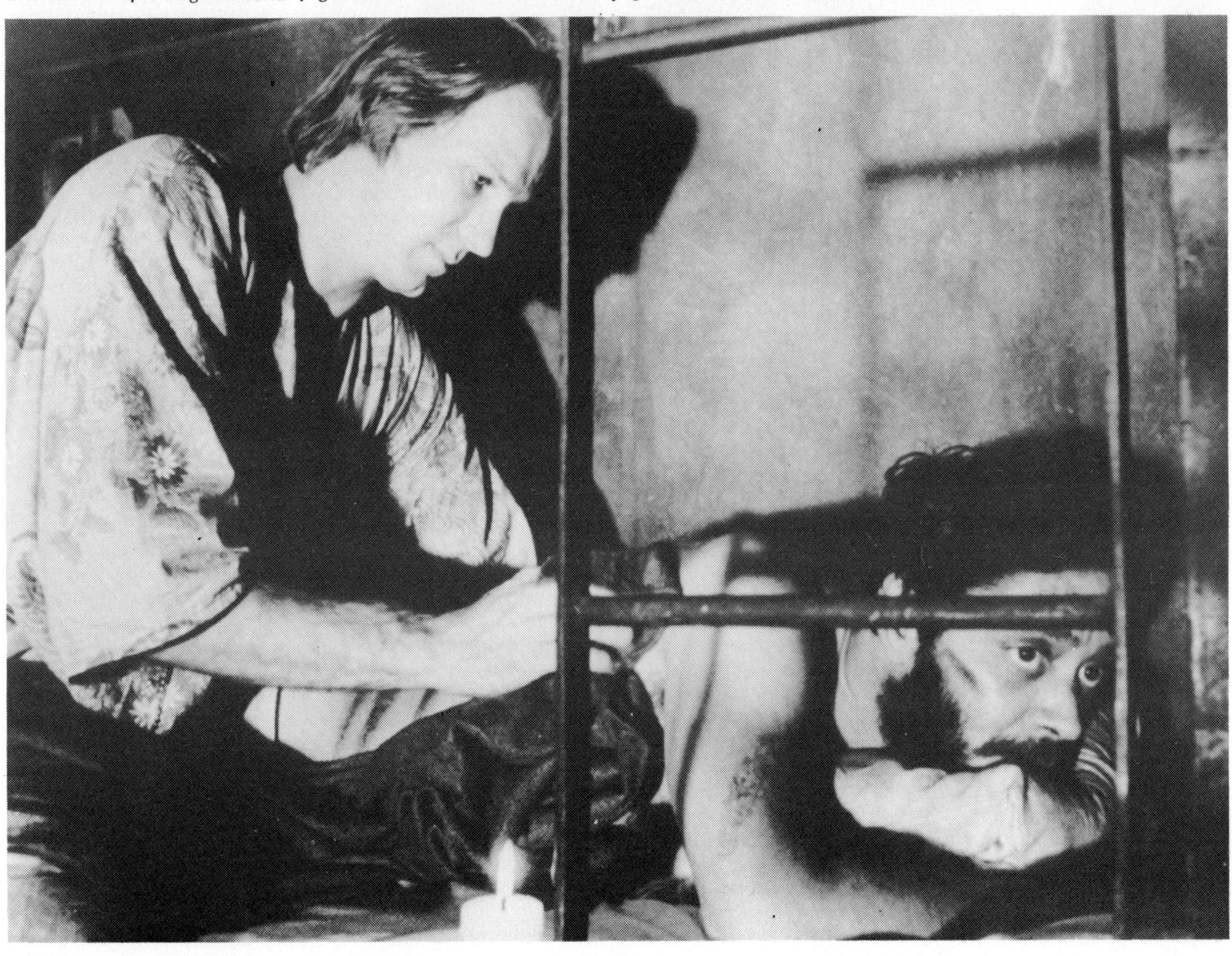

ABSOLUTE BEGINNERS

It's hardly surprising that many British critics sank their teeth into *Absolute Beginners* with such relish. Unlike their American counterparts, who reviewed the film in far more favourable terms, the English press had been subjected to the biggest hype for any movie in years. Advance coverage of its tempestuous progress was enormous; right from the start newspapers, magazines, radio and television were fascinated by the weird phenomenon of a British rock musical about racism. Interviews, location reports, and features on the film's role in the potential demise of the financially stricken co-investor Goldcrest bombarded the public with an insistence akin to that of toothache. Everyone in London knew someone who had something to do with the film; rumours flew. It was impossible to escape the bloody thing.

Director Julien Temple argued that such hype was necessary simply in order to persuade the conservative film-making establishment that such a bizarre project was indeed viable. One is tempted to agree; unfortunately, publicity overkill is almost invariably followed by a critical backlash, and long before the film was finished word was out that Temple's folly was nothing short of a disaster. The story didn't hang together; characterisations were of the cardboard cut-out variety; the musical sequences were inept. Think of a filmic flaw and you can be sure that some hack somewhere *knew* – though just how is unclear – that *Absolute Beginners* suffered from it. Middle-aged and middle-class almost to a man, the British reviewers closed ranks and extended their claws. Dubious about the wisdom of even making such an eccentric film within the beleaguered confines of the British film industry, incensed and bored by the heavy hype, contemptuous of young Temple's success in the pop-video field, they were out for blood.

The carping welcome the film received upon release was thus predictable; the film itself was anything but. It was not a masterpiece, but neither was it the catastrophe long awaited by so many with vengeful glee. It was, however, a film with a difference, and that, though you would never know from the reviews, offered ample cause for celebration.

For the few who may not know, *Absolute Beginners* is a musical adaptation of a cultish but clever novel of the same name by Colin MacInnes about teenage life in the London of the late fifties. Low on plot, the book employs its young photographer's troubled progress through Soho jazz clubs, Notting Hill slums, and various more elegantly exclusive London environs for MacInnes's own somewhat sardonic observations on several facets of post-war Britain: the rise of the rebellious rock'n'roll generation and its inevitable integration into an all-consuming respectable society; the yawning chasms between young and old, black and white, rich and poor; and the seductive trappings of money and fame. The novel is neither profound nor particularly original, let alone logically persuasive, in its analysis of the malaise afflicting Britain in 1958, but it is vivid and colourful, thanks both to the quirky gutter poetry of its language (anticipating to some degree that in Burgess's *A Clockwork Orange*) and to the genuine frustrations of its confused but oddly perspicacious narrator.

Perhaps surprisingly, Temple's musical is largely faithful to MacInnes, in spirit if not in plot details. Its strengths are those of the novel and so are its weaknesses. The story, such as it is, is fragmented and occasionally incoherent as it charts its narrator's path through a series of loosely connected encounters with various symbolic individuals whose function finally becomes clear only during the climactic scenes of the Notting Hill race riots. The characters, including those of the lead couple, the narrator (here named Colin) and his beloved Crepe Suzette, are shallow, rarely engaging the emotions and working for the most part as caricatured stereotypes representing various ages, classes and races. The clash between the disillusioned idealism of flaming youth and the cynical materialism of middle-age is hardly original.

To many, furthermore, the film seems to be a sequence of barely related set-pieces, constructed as baroque stylistic exercises rather than as integral devices advancing the story, and evidence of the saddening influence of the pop-promo medium upon the altogether superior art form of Film. By conventional standards, in fact, *Absolute Beginners* is an artistic mess. We are not, however, dealing with a conventional film. If you want safe, solid, polished entertainment, see *A Room With a View*. If, on the other hand, you want something different, invigorating, adventurous, then *Absolute Beginners* is for you.

Where Temple succeeds in terms of both adapting MacInnes's novel and creating a new and vigorous species of Britfilm is in the relentless energy and the contempt for conventional standards of 'taste' he brings to the screen. After the strangely subdued credits sequence, the movie proper kicks off at a sprint with an outrageously long and complex tracking shot through the teeming alleys of Soho, accompanying Colin's terse introductions of various key characters with the sounds of Gil Evan's thundering, screaming update of Mingus's menacing 'Boogie Stop Shuffle'. Beatniks, pimps, prostitutes, teds, Chinese waiters, beggars: all manner of human life is there in the lurid glare of the neon nightspots, walking, talking, running, dancing, staggering and haggling before Temple's swooping camera. Right at the start of the game, Temple reveals his hand of winning cards: speed, spectacle, sound and brash, brilliant colour, merging to create the most exhilarating opening sequence of any film since Cassavetes's heavenly helicopter shots of New York by night in *Gloria*. Thereafter the pace never lets up; we're swept along with our battered senses until the daring, but delightfully successful, choreographed riot of the Notting Hill finale.

Temple's very evident enthusiasm, however, is not merely for white-hot energy. It is also for the movies themselves. He makes plentiful quotes and gets away with it. The opening rush mentioned above is reminiscent of Welles's *Touch of Evil* in its complexity and its wealth of information; the comic scenes – particularly those featuring Ray Davies as Colin's Dad and Lionel Blair as paedophile pop promoter Harry Charms – include as their inspiration British music hall, the *Carry On* comedies, and the slapstick cartoonish capers of Frank *The Girl Can't Help It* Tashlin; the gaudy primary colours and fantastic compositions of the musical sequences pay homage to talents as diverse as Vincente Minnelli (maestro of the MGM musical) and Michael Powell (daddy of the delirious melodrama in Britain). Temple's influences are manifold and eclectic, but far from purposeless. Firstly, they serve to create an impressionistic, dreamlike portrait of teendream London; secondly, they function as part of Temple's all-out attack on the discreet conventionality of most recent British movies.

Turning his studio-shot never-never London into a dreamy city of the imagination is not only a sensible move, given that the capital is seen through the feverish teenage brain of its narrator-hero Colin. It is also an important part of Temple's stratagem in the stylistic and ideological assault on his peers, obsessed as they are with realism and accuracy. Like Minnelli's St Louis, coloured by Judy Garland's longing, or Powell's Himalayas, imprinted with the nuns' fears in *Black Narcissus*, Temple's Soho and Notting Hill are emotional landscapes rather than precisely recreated realities.

Even more important, however, is the way *Absolute Beginners* makes plain Temple's abhorrence and rejection of the cautious tastefulness that has bedevilled British cinema for so long. He has no truck with sentimental splurges of post-Empire patriotism, recently so fashionable, nor with those dismally duplicitous attempts to assuage middle-class guilt, in which a privileged elite, festooned with glorious traditions, is lovingly established only to be delivered a vicious if ultimately harmless blow beneath the belt. We're far from the muddled moralities that informed the likes of *If. . .*, *Chariots of Fire*, *Gandhi* and *Greystoke*. Instead Temple dazzles us with unadulterated spectacle and speed; brash and often beautifully belligerent, he wheels on disreputable figures as diverse as Blair, Alan Freeman, Eve Ferret, Tenpole Tudor and Irene Handl for crude comic antics and non-stop fireworks action. It's as if he's daring us to accuse him of vulgarity and then taking the wind from our sails by creating something at once vulgar *and* intelligent, crass *and* inventive.

Absolute Beginners is full of such contradictions. It's both cineliterate and populist, glamorous and tacky, thought-provoking and strangely mindless as it insists on itself as a full-blooded sensory experience. It is set in a past which is oddly contemporary. Though packed with moments reminiscent of previous pictures, it is untiringly original. Unafraid of such conflicting forces, Temple miraculously makes them work together to produce a heady cinematic cocktail that defies categorisation as a 'good' or 'bad' film, simply because it is unlike anything else. It is definitely an important film in its proposition of alternatives to the existing aesthetics of commercial movie-making in Britain. Though it occasionally falters and stumbles, it forges a brave new path into unexplored territories. For those few ground-breaking steps, it deserves not only our careful consideration but also our applause and gratitude.

Geoff Andrew

DOWN AND OUT IN BEVERLY HILLS

Beverly Hills is a place where, if money can't buy it, it can't be bought. Happiness . . . what about happiness? Money never bought happiness in the movies. In the movies, a Rolls-Royce cues unhappiness the way a knife in the back cues death.

Thus the Rolls-owning Whitemans, typical Beverly Hills millionaires, are unhappy. Dave and Barbara have everything and spend their time ritually wondering why they're missing something. Dave Whiteman makes coat-hangers but feels guilt at how easily he's amassing a pile. Barbara is oppressed by the necessity to pass her days spending Dave's pile.

All of us have known people like the Whitemans in the movies. They're harmless. We chuckle at them because we know that we ourselves would never be unhappy if only we were rich. But we don't generally give such rich buffoons too much thought because they're minor characters.

The good thing about *Down and Out in Beverly Hills* is that the Whitemans' dilemma is the main story. The movie dares to be a gentle social satire at a time when pie-in-the-face comedy is in vogue. The first product of the newest 'new Disney', the movie is a return to the days when the studio led trends in family entertainment instead of copying them.

Down and Out, a slightly altered remake of Jean Renoir's *Boudu Saved from Drowning* (1932), follows a familiar plotline: a family takes in a mysterious stranger, who somehow offers just what each member of the family needs, thereby upsetting everything. Since *Boudu* the situation has served such diverse films as *Shane*, Pasolini's *Theorem* and Dennis Potter's *Brimstone and Treacle*.

Down and Out opens with a scabrous derelict, Jerry Baskin, and his junk-filled shopping cart and his flea-bitten dog shambling through the scrubbed and manicured streets and lawns of America's richest municipality. Nick Nolte has been playing unshaven low-lifes for so long that it's an obvious casting move to shunt him right down to the very bottom of the social ladder.

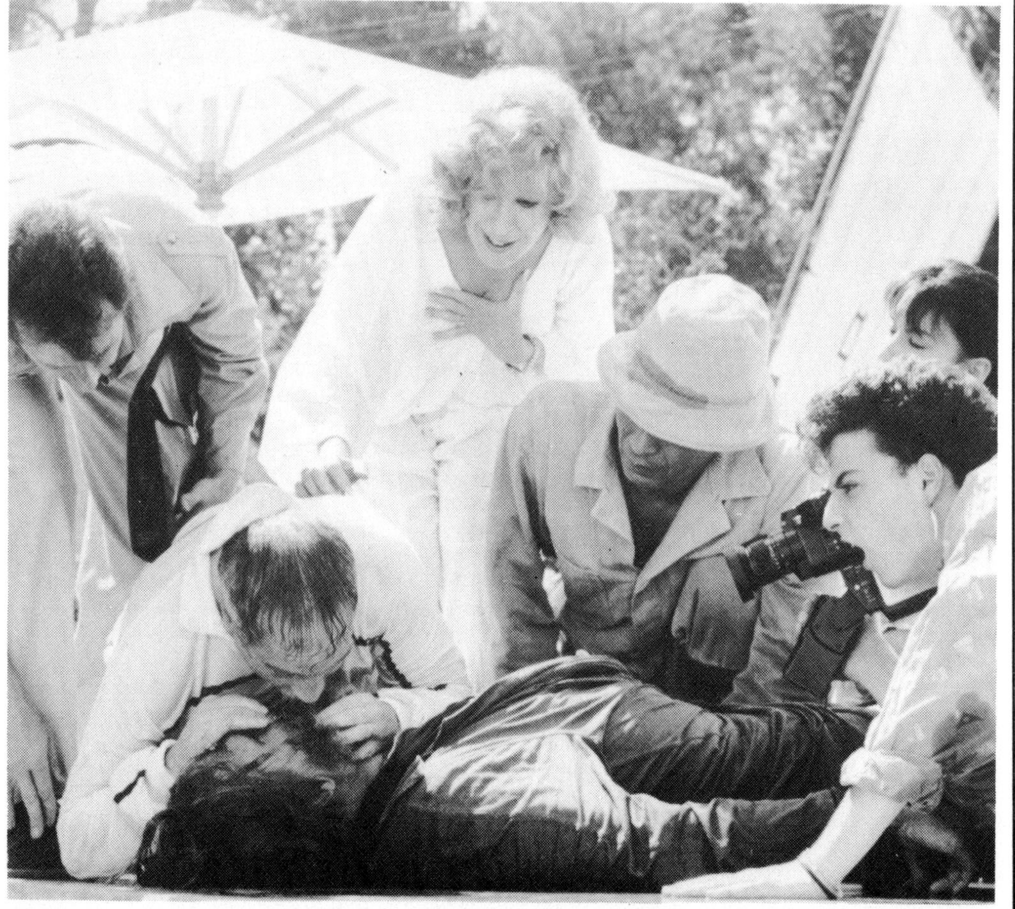

As Jerry, Nolte seems so real from the outset that audiences are tempted to put their handkerchiefs to their noses. The music thundering over Nolte's introductory traipse is the Talking Heads' superbly allusive 'Once In A Lifetime', the best existentialist rock 'n' roll song ever recorded. With lines like *"You might find yourself in a big automobile"* and its refrain of *"Letting the days go by"*, the song might have been written for the film (but wasn't).

As the too-rich Whitemans, Richard Dreyfuss and Bette Midler are made for each other like hell and damnation. Dreyfuss must be on constant call to listen to Midler's latest money-caused problem. Dreyfuss is good at the comedy of desperation and Midler's forte is creating desperation. She minces around the Whiteman mansion like a cat on a hot fudge roof, getting herself and Dreyfuss stuck in largely imaginary dilemmas, such as which guru to follow. Midler used to mock this kind of character in her stage act, and it's a measure of her talent that she can now present the character straight-faced and let the audience find the laughs.

Dreyfuss can't wait to clear out and get to work, even though making millions is so easy he's bored as well as guilty. The only spice in his life is the family's maid, Carmen (Elizabeth Pena), who's also bored enough to accept his nightly thrusts into her bed.

Added irritation is provided

by the Whiteman offspring. Son Max (Evan Richards) suffers from sexual confusion and a bi-gender wardrobe. Anorexia is the curse of daughter Jenny (Tracy Nelson). Alarm-envy plagues neighbour Orvis Goodnight (Little Richard), who sees a racial plot in the Beverly Hills cops' failure to swarm around his house as they do at the Whitemans' whenever their security system gives a false alarm. What could top all this wealth-induced misery? A pet that won't eat, a dog named Matisse (played by an instant star named Mike).

Into this neurotic household splashes Jerry Baskin, whose problem is that he's lost his own dog. In such circumstances, what point is there, really, in going on? Instead of the Seine, Jerry chooses the Whitemans' pool for his rocks-in-his-pockets plunge. For some reason he doesn't understand himself, Dave dives in after Jerry, despite Barbara's objection that the bum probably has AIDS.

Saved, dried off and dried out, Jerry turns out to have a tale to tell – a different tale to every family member. But whatever he says it's just what everyone wants to hear, plus a little something else they needed to experience. Dave needs a pal, so Jerry pals around with him – and then introduces him to the delights of bumdom on Venice Beach. Barbara needs a masseur, so Jerry gives her a rubdown – and then gives her the demon loving that is the real cure for her malaise.

The children also get a hand from Jerry, who blesses Max's coming out and inspires Jenny into eating normally. The maid becomes politicised after a short session with Jerry. Most comically, Jerry succeeds where the canine psychologist failed, turning Matisse on to dog food by getting on the floor and lapping it up himself.

As Jerry forsakes his aimless former existence and adopts the Whitemans' lifestyle, both he and they find a purpose in life – each other. In its denouement, the French original neatly undercut this pat answer to the meaning of life. The Disney version, for the sake of the millions it would not otherwise have earned at the box office, chooses to bring Jerry back into the bosom of the family instead of drowning him for good. Besides pandering to movie audiences' desire to go home with visions of sugarplums dancing in their heads, concluding *Down and Out* on an up-note allowed the studio to sell the movie's 'format' to television for a series that will begin on Rupert Murdoch's new network next year.

Funked finale aside, *Down and Out* offers an antidote to the smugness of this era of getting and spending and laying waste our powers. The fact that producer-director-writer Paul Mazursky has another major hit at last may be a sign of changing tastes. American adults say they want to see films that aren't simple-minded romps starring people whose main talent is looking 17. But when something more thoughtful does somehow come to rest in the local mall, the old folks usually find a reason to stay home. It takes something unique like *Down and Out* to wake these dead.

Since *Bob & Carol & Ted & Alice* in 1969 established Mazursky as American movies' best chronicler of the absurdities of marriage, his box office returns have been diminishing. Despite critical huzzahs for *Blume in Love* (1973) and *An Unmarried Woman* (1978), Mazursky hasn't given equal cheer to Hollywood's money men. The financial failures of *Willie and Phil* and *Tempest* might have put Mazursky out of business if his most recent film,*Moscow on the Hudson*, hadn't proved a moderate grosser in 1984.

Which would have been too bad, because America has no other director who has made a career out of making personal, satirical pictures within the studio system. Perhaps the satire bites less deeply than it might if he made pictures at a tenth of the cost for art houses. Maybe a non-studio *Moscow on the Hudson* would have seen Robin Williams back off to Russia instead of letting him stay ruefully in New York. Maybe a non-Disney *Down and Out* would have had Jerry tasting the paté he finds in the trash at the end of the movie – and deciding against returning to the soft life.

But he's the best Mazursky we've got. Unlike such other major studio contemporary comedy auteurs as John Hughes, Ivan Reitman or even Blake Edwards, Mazursky makes jokes out of real social situations and characters who aren't pre-packaged. There is a real gap between the haves and have-nots, wider perhaps in America than elsewhere, and you don't have to be a 'have' living in Beverly Hills to need reminding of that.

In other countries today, the subject may not seem right for mild satire; revolutionary politics or gloomy alienation may seem more appropriate. In America, we chuckle instead of impeaching Reagan or hanging ourselves. But at least we chuckle, thanks to Mazursky. Though he took his plot from a French movie – a temptation that has buried half a dozen American directors in the last two or three years – Mazursky made a thoroughly American movie.

BART MILLS

RAMBO: FIRST BLOOD, PART II ROCKY IV

RAMBO

1 Physique: The huge appeal of *Rambo* must lie in the area of myth and symbols, for the man himself is no oil painting. His expression, which never alters, is reminiscent of a whipped spaniel. His speech is that adenoidal brand of Bronx dialect which always sounds as if the speaker were about to sneeze. His muscalature has the grotesquely over-inflated look of someone who prefers lifting weights and taking steroids to any natural development through exercise. There is a very curious sinew, most visible on the poster for the film, which connects the bicep of his right arm with the right-hand side of his chest, somewhat below his armpit. One should not mock the afflicted, but it does look very like the kind of control cord seen on film robots that have an anthropomorphic shape. Perhaps Rambo is bionic. The muscles further below his armpits, around his upper ribs, are so overdeveloped they appear to force him to walk with his arms swinging out at forty-five degrees from his body, an effect not unlike that created by Boris Karloff as the Frankenstein monster. When he walks, he walks like a man with a bad case of haemorrhoids.

2 Myth: Rambo's mythological appeal is cleverly crafted to be sufficiently unspecific. Within American mythology, he is one of Fennimore Cooper's leather-stockings, the "stoic American killer of the old great life", as DH Lawrence called the type. He also adopts the headband, bare chest and long bow of the American Indian, although his general stance is more in line with the sixties rediscovery of America's noble

savage than with the cavalry fodder of a thousand old Westerns. In wider terms, he looks very like some of the early, silent film Tarzans, while his long hair and taste for uttering gnomic statements of vaguely Zen import suggests nothing more than a superannuated hippy. "To survive war, you gotta become war" won't win the Lao Tze award for sudden *satori*, but at least it doesn't hold up the action for long. The likeness to a hippy was more apparent in the first Rambo film *First Blood*, in which he ran rings around the National Guard without ever actually killing any of them. In *First Blood Part II* he has no such qualms, presumably because the enemy is now an undifferentiated horde of 'slants' and commies. Writer James Cameron (who directed *The Terminator* and now *Aliens*) claimed that he tried to stick close to the spirit of the first film by having Rambo "not kill anyone that he didn't have to." A dubious precept at best, and not one that wins wars.

3 Symbol: Part of the reason for Rambo's enormous appeal to so many Americans must be his ability to sympathise with both hawks and doves alike. A clever notion: Rambo is allowed the triumph of winning what America failed to, and is also allowed the final message of social reintegration along with a decent amount of expiation. But perhaps what touches the deepest nerve in the American psyche is the fact that Rambo is a brave man betrayed by weak men. Just as he has been set up as a fall guy by the corrupt bureaucrats back home, so too the war must have been lost for the same reasons. This was precisely the tactic employed by Hitler in his rise to power after World War I.

4 Rambo, Queen of the Jungle: While there is no overt homosexual content in the film, nonetheless there is considerable recourse to classic gay iconography. When first captured by the combined Russian and Vietnamese forces, he is strung up by his wrists on a yoke and left immersed up to his neck in a pit full of pig swill. When hoisted out, half conscious, with the slime dripping off his nearly naked torso, he resembles some modern version of Saint Sebastian ready for the ritual piercing by arrows. Similarly, he is later tortured by being spreadeagled on an iron bedstead, and is seen writhing in near orgasmic throes as the Russian torturer passes hundreds of volts through the bed springs. There is, however, little love interest in the film. He does fall for his lithe Vietnamese girl sidekick, but within ten seconds of their first brief kiss she is mown down by a jungle patrol. Kiss of the Spider Man?

5 Spin-offs: Of the many pirate video editions, perhaps the most bizarre is the one circulated throughout the Middle East, with French and Arabic sub-titles. To avoid any potentially embarrassing political repercussions, the story is set in the Philippines in 1943, where Rambo has returned to rescue World War II prisoners still held by the Japanese. The last word of the phrase "You made a hell of a reputation for yourself in 'Nam" is changed on the subtitles to "Guadalcanal". Quite what audiences made of the huge arsenal of modern weaponry, such as rocket-firing helicopters, is not recorded.

It is now possible to have a 'Rambo-gram' delivered to someone whom you wish to frighten. Out-of-work muscular actors will lob a confetti grenade into the birthday party of your choice.

In Lebanon, *Rambo* is cheered to the rafters. The distributor Joseph Vincenti told *Variety* that it was breaking all records "at the worst period in the ten-year events in Lebanon and in the worst period of the year – *the dead season*" (my itals). Best critical aside came from *Village Voice's* Andrew Sarris, who said that the movie did not appeal to him because he had never got used to the idea that it was okay to slaughter people you had not met socially.

6 Action: Vast amounts of verbiage were spilled, especially on this side of the Atlantic, in analysing the film to extinction, and all in the cause of defining what was bad about it. What very few critics remarked on was exactly the thing that surely appealed to audiences worldwide: it is a terrific action movie. In fact it is constructed largely as a series of set pieces, shot and edited with split second precision, each of which manages to outdo the last. Once the afterburners are switched on, then they are kept on. The culmination is when Rambo performs the incredible feat of leaping out of a river like a salmon jumping the falls and, barehanded, hijacks a helicopter which had been passing overhead.

7 Final statement: "I want what every guy who came here to spill his guts wants – for our country to love us as much as we love it." This is one of the few lines in the film which surprisingly did not earn a laugh. In its trembling confusions one can find a tortured message which says more about America than about the film: here is a country still smarting from a war it did not win, a damaged social order that it still does not understand, and a mythology which it simply does not know how to deploy in the movies anymore. To imagine what John Ford would have done with *Rambo* is to see how far Hollywood has fallen from providing America with its own mythology.

ROCKY IV

1 Three act drama: Like all the best punches, *Rocky IV* only travels a very short distance. It is a sucker punch to the emotional breadbasket, structured, like the best amateur boxing contests, in three fast rounds. Round one: Russian bionic mauler Drago arrives in the States and takes a leaf from Mohammed Ali's book by provoking much hissing and booing from the assembled press corps. He takes on Rocky's old chum and mentor Apollo Creed, and

clubs him to extinction. "If he dies, he dies," says Drago; and he does. Round two: the briefest of connecting sequences in which Rocky drives around at night suffering from the dreaded flashback syndrome as he remembers his old sparring partner. This is the cue for a compilation of out-takes from the previous three *Rocky* films. The result affords the same sort of pleasure as watching trailers. Round three: Rocky takes up the challenging glove and departs for Russia. He scorns the Russians high-tech electronic training methods, preferring the good old frontiersman tactics of press-ups in the snow. The appeal here is of much the same values as Rambo embodied; self-reliance and old-fashioned pioneer spirt. Just what Reagan ordered. Rocky then goes the distance with Drago; and if the outcome is exactly as you would predict, that is not to deny the enormous emotional pull of watching an underdog hero slugging his way to victory against superhuman odds.

2 Francis Bacon: Apparently Francis Bacon rates the *Rocky* films among his favourites. It seems that he applied for tickets for the sneak preview at the NFT and for the lecture which Stallone was going to give afterwards (which was in fact cancelled because of Stallone's work on the upcoming *Cobra*). The appeal is not hard to fathom. Most of the killer punches are shown in slow motion, accompanied by a noise rather like a seal being clubbed on the head by a baseball bat. A close-up of the affected area reveals facial muscles being smeared all over the screen, a deluge of sweat spraying from the unaffected side of the face and hair, and a mouthful of blood fountaining out in the same direction as the punch. It is not exactly realistic; just about any of these punches could kill a man. But the likeness to Bacon's distortions and tortured flesh in his portraits is marked. This is the art of the abattoir.

3 The punch: Dolph Lungren, the film's Drago, one time bodyguard to Grace Jones and now her escort, revealed the secrets behind the sound effect of each punch. There are five components. There is the Dry Component, which is the wallop of the glove hitting a punch bag. There is the Wet Component, which is like a slap on the chops from a wet fish put through an amplifier. Then there is the Cannon Component, a crack like a piece of field artillery going off. Finally, there are the two Personal Components: the grunt of effort from the man throwing the punch which is as pronounced as anything heard from the server on the centre court at Wimbledon; and the grunt of pain from the receiver of the punch, which sounds like an ox being stunned.

4 Politics: Unlike Rambo, Rocky is very straightforward in his stance. At heart he is a squishy liberal. The movie is more than fair to the Russian point of view. Drago's first fight with Apollo Creed is staged with all the vulgar razzmatazz that made the opening of the LA Olympics such a camp affair. Drago's silent disapproval merely serves to underline the appalling decadence of Western values. He also receives death threats while in the US, which as a plot point is entirely believable. The Russian bout, on the other hand, is staged with decent restraint. True, the Russians boo Rocky when he first appears, but by the end of the bout they are cheering him to the skies, which proves they are better sports than the Americans. Moreover, Drago finally comes to realise that he is nothing more than an over-trained, steroid-injected stooge for the implacable *Apparatchiks* of the state, who want a killing machine in line with the US Star Wars programme. This is exactly the position in which Rambo found himself, and like Rambo, Drago turns on his rulers, shaking a Gorbachev lookalike until his teeth rattle. It is too late, however, to stop Rocky creaming him in the last round.

5 The last word: Like Rambo, Rocky has a curtain line. This is to effect the lines that it is better for two men to stand up in a ring and batter each other to submission, than for two hundred million to do it to each other over some nuclear ashtray. Is there anyone who would dissent from this view?

CHRIS PEACHMENT

PRIZZI'S HONOR

"The colours are right – that's what counts. Everybody sees shapes differently, but colours are for ever." Telling words on the printed page of Richard Condon's novel, sharply delivered by Anjelica Huston in this film adaptation. But the voice that comes through most strongly in this speech from *Prizzi's Honor* is that of a third party – director John Huston.

For close to half a century Huston has worked at 'getting the colours right' in his films. Sometimes this has been a literal operation. Alternately heightening or muting the colour for such films as *Moulin Rouge*, *Moby Dick*, and *Reflections in a Golden Eye*, Huston created some fascinating visual effects. But for the most part 'colour' with Huston is a figurative term – the tone, the atmosphere, the detail that can bring a story to vivid life. Huston's 'colours' are sometimes garish, sometimes muted, almost always dark, baroque, obsessive, neurotic. Drawn to the margins of culture – its outcasts, its 'failures', its 'freaks' – Huston films like *Treasure of the Sierra Madre*, *The Misfits*, *Fat City*, *Wise Blood* and *Under the Volcano* have offered images from areas of experience few film-makers have ever entered – least of all those in the commercial arena Huston has always called home. Some of his efforts have succeeded, some have failed (most sharply on those occasions when he's entered the 'mainstream' with the likes of *Victory* and *Annie*), but the 'colours' of Huston have almost always been right.

And so we come, with *Prizzi's Honor*, to the great director's 39th film (in all likelihood his last) to find him mixing colour – literal and figurative – in a new way. A comedy of manners set among the denizens of the Mafia, *Prizzi's Honor* clearly carries echoes of other Huston films. Its devious heroine is a direct descendant of Brigid O'Shaughnessy of *The Maltese Falcon*. The plot's twists and turns line up alongside the sinister spy caper doings of *The Kremlin Letter*. And the overall larky spirit of the film bears more than a passing resemblance to that most poised of Huston put-ons *Beat the Devil*. Still there's something different bubbling beneath the surface of this cool, polished, almost serene exercise. It's as if all the confusions and uncertainties of Huston's recent years – quirky, personal *succes d'estimes* mixed with ultra-impersonal commercial failures – had been brushed away and replaced by a clear-eyed sensibility capable of lining up all the elements of film-making in the simplest manner possible and playing them for maximum force. After years of shoe-horning his sensibility to fit the demands of studio style and genre convention, Huston, through Condon's novel, has discovered a way to break free, abandon himself to an act of pure narration.

Huston cues us in from the start that something very special's afoot in *Prizzi's* first major scene. The camera is tracking down the aisle of a church – taking its own slow, sweet time – where a Mafia wedding is in progress. As it does so, Huston resurrects a figure of cinematic rhetoric abandoned for over two decades – the lap dissolve. Gracefully, delicately, the laps take us from an overall view of the church scene to medium-close shots (all slightly off centre) of the key figures in the story that's about to unfold. We see old Don Corrado Prizzi (William Hickey) head of the clan, half-asleep in his pew. Nearby his granddaughter Maerose (Anjelica Huston), alert as an eagle, surveys the scene ruefully. Finally we see Charlie Partanna (Jack Nicholson), our 'hero' – a loyal Mafia hitman of sluggish, if genial appearance. No thoughts of particular import appear to be crossing his dull, creased features. But Charlie, and the story, snap to only a few seconds later when he chances to glance over his shoulder and spy – out of the corner of one eye – a beautiful woman (Kathleen Turner) seated in the balcony. Turning, Charlie catches her eye – and she his in return.

The moment is purest Hollywood – 'love at first sight'. We laugh as Huston knowingly milks it in the wedding reception scene that follows. As the slow-witted Charlie finds himself entranced by this teasing beauty – Irene Walker by name – we in the audience *think* we know what's going on. The film is a satirical comedy, pure and simple. What else could be at play in a story that brings together a knowing sophisticate and a 'Dese Dem Doze' type thug? But nothing is pure or simple in the world of *Prizzi's Honor*. Had we been paying close attention we'd have noticed the deliberate attempt to blur the film's time frame (is it the fifties or is it right now?) Had we been paying attention we'd have been more aware that the dramatic tension in the sub-plot introduced in the same reception scene would pay-off in the main action in a very decisive way. Maerose Prizzi, Charlie's love of years before, whose abandoning of him for another estranged her from her father Dominic (Corrado's son and one of the two sub-heads of the clan), has turned to

Charlie for help in squaring things. But blinded by Irene's beauty Charlie has no time for the Prizzis. Maerose's sharp look at the befuddled Charlie speaks volumes.

But neither we nor Charlie can read them. The action has shifted to California where Charlie and Irene are enjoying a luncheon rendezvous. We don't know whether to laugh at Charlie's prattle about 'hormonal secretions' (something he's read in a magazine about love's physical effect) or give in to the spectacle of full-blown Movie Romance. Either way we won't be prepared for what unfolds shortly thereafter when the rug is pulled out from Charlie – and us – as the truth (some of it; never in Huston's world do we learn all) is revealed about Irene.

It seems that Irene isn't the glamorous bi-coastal tax consultant she claims. Well, she *is* a tax consultant, but mainly she's a hitman – just like Charlie. Born Maida Walchewicz, she began her career as a prostitute. Hooking her fortunes to a small-time hood named Marxie Heller she learned her deadly trade. She taught as much as she learned, however. It was she who prodded Heller and his cohort Louis Palo into setting up a scam to skim off gambling profits from a Vegas casino owned by the Prizzis. On assignment from the Prizzis to 'tap' (kill) Heller, Charlie finds himself face to face with the woman he loves. Irene is Marxie's wife!

"What do I do? Do I ice her? Do I marry her?" Charlie asks a curiously sympathetic Maerose. "Marry her Charlie," Maerose declares. "Just because she's a thief and a hitter doesn't mean she's not a good woman in all the other departments. She's an American. She had a chance to make a buck so she grabbed it!" Precisely.

And so this novel investigation of the American Way of Life continues as Charlie kills Marxie, marries Irene, covers her tracks from the Prizzis' prying eyes and turns his attention to a new job for them. A kidnapping has been contrived to punish a family adversary and solidify Prizzi holdings in an otherwise legal banking operation. Charlie's all-business, no-questions style is just what's needed in this sort of thing. And who better to help him with the strong-arm of the operation than a professional like Irene? But well laid plans go awry when Irene is forced to 'tap' a witness to the kidnapping. Ordinarily this wouldn't be a problem, but in this case the witness turns out be the wife of a high-ranking police official. The killing instantaneously disrupts relations between the police and the Prizzi family. The cops want someone to take the fall. Irene is the guilty party, and in the Prizzis' eyes this guilt is compounded by the fact that by this time they've found out about her involvement in the Vegas scam.

And it's here that the sub-plot mentioned earlier – patiently waiting in the wings all this time – blasts its way through the action, turning itself into the main plot in the process. For rather than a satire about the Mafia, or a film of modern romance, *Prizzi's Honor* reveals itself – at this juncture at least – to be a tale of a woman's vengeance. Maerose, it seems, never got over her loss of Charlie. The affair that disgraced her in Prizzi eyes was done only to get his jealous attention. She encouraged him to marry Irene knowing that it would never work out. Doing some careful legwork on her own she discovered the truth about the Vegas scam. Offering it to Don Corrado in grand operatic style she asks for vengeance.

But while appreciative of the gesture – particularly its drama – the gnarled old tortoise of a mobster isn't ready to act impulsively. He wisely holds this information in abeyance. And a good thing too as the kidnap-killing crisis allows him to play it like the trump card it is. Facing the faithful Charlie, the Don presents him with the painful truth. He – Charlie – will have to 'tap' the woman he loves in order to save the family's fortune and honour. For his efforts he'll be lifted from mere strong-arm status to a major player in the Prizzi game. As the dreaded prospect congeals Charlie's features, comedy, romance, and revenge tragedy evaporate to be replaced by a film of yet another sort – a film about the bottom line. 'Tapping' Irene is the only logical conclusion to the plot's complex machinations.

It was all there from the start. It was there in the way Irene shifted ground from scene to scene – modifying her story, and her own image, as the situation demanded. It was there in the scenes of family meetings – the squabbles between the Prizzi sons (Lee Richardson and Robert Loggia) for their father's affection. It was there in Charlie's scenes with his father (John Randolph), their warmth and familiarity. It was most sharply there in Maerose's scene with the Don – the old rascal peering out at a younger one with a layer of malice that could be cut with a knife. *Prizzi's Honor* is plainly and simply a film about the American family and American business. Not an occulted vision of the Mafia like *The Godfather*, not a piece of magazine-style psychological self-help like *Ordinary People*. Just the truth. Just the fact. Just business.

"It's just business" is a phrase we hear over and over again – always preparatory to a killing. And it is "just business", in Huston's view, that holds society and family together. These 'criminals' aren't psychotics, misfits, outcasts – they're businessmen. It's we in the audience who are out of step. Blinded by genre films and media propaganda about the exploits of the Mafia, we've ignored the extent of corporate complicity in mayhem executed to keep cash flowing. Of course in the real big time you don't need the likes of Charlie. Governments, armies, spy networks are there to do your bidding. Huston's modest proposal is that we simply look at this world for what it really is. "She had a chance to make a buck and she grabbed it." Exactly. "She's an American." And so – very much so – is a film-maker named John Huston.

David Ehrenstein

RAN

Shakespeare, according to some, made his farewell to the stage with a self-portrait as the reluctant mage Prospero in *The Tempest*, an elegiac play about illusion and the power of art to make, break and mend lives. Prospero/Shakespeare, indeed, becomes the first film director, manipulating an unknowing cast as if he were Hitchcock, creating visions of horror and beauty that force onlookers to face the truths about their own lives. (He is also a believer in the auteur theory, creating spirits of air "which by mine art I have from their confines called to enact my present fancies".)

Kurosawa has turned to Shakespeare to make what is likely to be his farewell to the cinema; but he has chosen to go out on a harsher note. Not for him the reconciliations of *The Tempest*. Instead, he conjures a rougher magic, raging against the dying of the light in the magnificent *Ran*, his radical transformation of *King Lear*. In Hidetora, the ageing war-lord who voluntarily puts aside his power and lives to regret it, perhaps there is something of a self-portrait, too.

Ran's final image is of helpless despair: a young, blind man, waiting hopelessly upon a high, ruined tower for the return of his sister. She has gone to find his one comfort, his flute, and will not return, for she has been brutally and needlessly killed, as have thousands of soldiers and the protagonists of the drama – the good, the bad and the unfortunate.

The man strikes out with his staff to find no solid ground, only nothingness. He drops into the abyss a scroll he holds; it unrolls to reveal an image of Buddha's smiling, indifferent face. Light fades and the sun sets upon the desolate landscape.

There is little of comfort in Kurosawa's vision, which is not only more despairing than Shakespeare's, but also subverts the heroic traditions of the samurai film. *Ran* is, in part, an anti-samurai film, in the same way that Sergio Leone's *A Fistful of Dollars* (based on Kurosawa's *Yojimbo*) is an anti-Western. They are at once an anthology of the genre and a criticism of it, taking form and style beyond plausibility into a heightened rhetoric that borders on absurdity.

Kurosawa, like the Shakespeare of *Lear*, is a risk-taking author. *King Lear* is an astonishing play, which after its conventional opening, plunges into another reality. Its setting becomes generalised – a bare heath in a violent storm – and its characters are stripped of all that normally defines a person. There is just thunder, lightning, pelting rain and an old man on the point of madness, accompanied by a fool and an outcast pretending to be mad. It is a world of dread and unspecified fear where misery predominates, and it was not explored again until Samuel Beckett began publishing three hundred and thirty-two years later, in 1938.

Beckett rewrote Descartes' "I think, therefore I am" as "I suffer, therefore I may be". His characters are old, poor and ill, deprived of most that makes life bearable. They assert their humanity at the outer limits, as does Lear, as does Kurosawa's Lear, the "senile old fool" of a samurai Hidetora (Tatsuya Nakadai) – called so by his son at the beginning of the film, and repeating the judgement on himself at the end. They are among that most potent group of artists who offer little of comfort, who – to quote Melville– "say No! in thunder!"

Ran has an unsparing bleakness: Hidetora divides his kingdom between his three sons, an act that brings ruin to himself, and all his family, and the world they inhabit. Hidetora is crueller than Lear – it is he who blinds the young prince and forces his sister into a dynastic marriage. Shakespeare's play has been altered in other ways: Hidetora's youngest son Subaro takes the place of Cordelia in the original – as the one child who does not flatter his father, and whose suffering, exile and death is the pivot of the tragedy. Goneril and Regan, Lear's evil daughters, have been compressed into Lady Kaede (Mieko Harada), the wife of Hidetora's eldest son, lover of his second and orchestrator of the former's murder by the latter. In the tradition of the vendetta that is one of the driving forces of the samurai film, she takes terrible revenge for Hidetora's massacre of her family and, answerable to that tradition, is herself slaughtered.

Kurosawa dispenses with Shakespeare's subplot – of the old man Gloucester and his two sons – but ends the movie in much the same way as the play: a suffering old man acknowledges his own part in the downfall of his house, holding the murdered body of his youngest child as he, too, dies.

Kurosawa uses the conventions of Noh plays, which grew out of the samurai culture of the fourteenth century, and the later Kabuki theatre. It is from these still living traditions that derive the stylised acting and appearance, the transvestite Fool and the elaborate ritual. The battle scenes, a montage of fantastic knights flying coloured banners, of endless slaughter, of muddy death, are superbly controlled epic sequences. Yet they also subvert the usual battles of samurai films, which concentrate on feats of solo swordsmanship, the equivalent of the gunfight in Westerns. Instead, the war is won and the charging warriors slaughtered by riflemen, hidden in a wood. And it is wave upon wave of riflemen who advance up the heights of Hidetora's last refuge, slaughtering as they go (as happened in reality at the battle of Takeda in 1575, thirty-one years before King Lear was written). An old culture goes down before the guns.

At the beginning of the film, there was an old man sleeping in the sun, ruler of all he could see, possessor of three great fortresses. At the end, there is nothing but a universe of ruin inhabited by the trapped and the blind. *Ran* translates as Chaos. Kurosawa's chaos is less an aspect of nature than Shakespeare's. It is an inner condition, a savagery unleashed by human failing. Rarely has any artist raged with such force and energy as Kurosawa does here. In this brilliant mingling of East and West, of Shakespeare and samurai, of tragedy and traditional Japanese drama, Kurosawa says Noh! in thunder.

JOHN WALKER

AFTER HOURS

On the comedy front, this was the year of the black stuff. In Britain, Alan Bleasdale's nightmarish party-piece *No Surrender* joyously and justifiably spat a venomous mixture of Guinness and Mersey effluent over screens otherwise clogged by coyly ingratiating time-warped serio-sitcoms like *Clockwise*, or any number of examples of sub-Forsythian whimsy. Stateside, the undistinguished, indistinguishable ranks of yukky juvenilia and yuppie smirk-fests were finally put into suitably diminished perspective by a welcome quartet of sardonically eccentric visions of absurdist hell-on-earth.

The opulent *Prizzi's Honor* took most of the mainstream plaudits, but several of John Huston's juniors managed equally jaundiced winks at the abyss. Larry Cohen's *The Stuff* toyed cheaply but effectively with the outrageous notion of conspicuously consumerist America literally getting its just dessert(s) through the agency of an organic ice-cream that bites back, and rattled off a damningly ludicrous portrayal of looney right-wing paramilitarism as just one of its sideswipe pleasures. *Static*, a genuine out-of-nowhere original from first-time director Mark Romanek, actually set up – and then with risky abruptness appeared to reverse – a paradisial prospect for its death-obsessed hero, and teased a darkly ironic cross-weave of cosmic gags from its scrutiny of a hi-tech holy fool and his incongruous entourage.

The fourth black-edged American invitation to giggle nervously at the spectre of the New Grotesquerie came from Martin Scorsese. It earned him the Best Director gong at Cannes, but most suggested he'd be just as deserving of an award for valour – not so much for taking a budgetary step-down into the independent ranks after the wondrous but commercially disastrous *The King of Comedy*, but for audaciously extending that movie's grating, fingers-down-a-blackboard ambience in such a risky follow-up.

Shot before, but released after *Desperately Seeking Susan*, Martin Scorsese's *After Hours* might be read as its midnight flipside. The movie turns on notions of control. At this stage in his career, Scorsese's steady guiding hand can be taken on trust, and with *After Hours* he duly delivers a work that, for all its zigzagging paranoia, evidences throughout an elegant formal rigour and relaxed precision. As pertinent, though, is the absolute loss of control experienced by the central character – yuppie-ish computer operator Paul Hackett (played by co-producer Griffin Dunne) – as he steps out of world-of-his-own security for a short walk on New York's wild side and can then find no way back.

First sighted in his office, Paul is distractedly passing on to a new colleague the fundamentals of microchip communication, and drifting dreamily away for a (Mozart-scored) proprietorial scan of his impeccably ordered surroundings, with less than half an ear cocked to his pupil's own self-absorbed riffs on bohemian artistic ambitions. Back in his bachelor apartment, Paul displays a similarly glib, complacent control over his environment as he fiddles capriciously with the remote handset of his TV.

Next, he's head-down in a late-night coffee-shop, cut off behind the cover of a paperback of Henry Miller's *Tropic of Cancer*. A casual conversation with a girl at a nearby table perks his interest; especially when he leaves with her telephone number as a trophy. Having to borrow a pen, though, from a cashier more intent on solo ballroom dancing practice somehow fails to alert him to the soon-to-be-proven contention that Hell might just be Other People....

Anyway, it's his casually libidinous urge to ring that number and rush across town on what promises to be a heavy date which sends him scuttling towards the real rabbit-hole. A manic taxi-driver imperils his life and limbs – and his fare-money flies disastrously out of the cab window on the way into SoHo. A substantial slice of his self-assurance and status is thereby suddenly torn from his grasp, but Paul's not turning back now. After all, he's not privy to the way Scorsese is melodramatically underscoring and magnifying his mishaps, and can't quite see the dread-inducing, loft-to-pavement descent of the keys to the girl's apartment as quite the portents of malign fate they are made to appear to us. When the director then uses a transitional fade to convey Paul from the first to last rungs of the inner stairs, we know instinctively that the latter has made the decisive and almost irreversible move through the looking-glass.

On the other side, initially, is Kiki (Linda Fiorentino), a flaky sculptress who sets Paul to work on her three-dimensional papier-mâché version of Munch's *The Scream*, and drops off to sleep in mid-massage before the original object of Paul's quest, Marcy (Rosanna Arquette), returns. Marcy's initially appealing scattiness soon begins to perturb and then scare Paul, however, as small talk ranges over rape and tales of a husband orgasmically obsessed by *The Wizard of Oz*, as whisperings outside the bedroom door pointedly exclude him, and as a mystery accrues around the possibility that Marcy's body may be disfigured by burn scars. Eventually Paul leaves, frustrated but relieved, and pads through the rain to the subway station – only to find increasingly frantic and futile attempts to fathom the rules lead him into crossed-path confrontations with a good half-dozen more off-centre denizens of the darkness, in various sinister patterns and permutations.

At various stages, he barely escapes a scalping while searching a punk club for Kiki and her bondage-freak boyfriend on Mohawk night, is moody solo drinker in the club in which Paul takes refuge, shares with him a desultory dance to Peggy Lee's 'Is That All There Is?', and then 'saves' him by carrying him off to her basement studio and encasing him in plaster as a living statue. Quite what she is saving him *for* is a question forestalled when he is almost immediately stolen (as a hyper-realist artwork) by the cameraman Michael Ballhaus (*Baby It's You, Old Enough, Heartbreakers*) contributes some idiosyncratically ominous camerawork, but the reckless hallucinatory energy of the movie is mainly Scorsese's. He may be ringing the changes on his earlier epics of street-life, but he's not about to be pinned down by an over-specific set of movie-movie allusions. I for one

that ticket prices have been hiked that very midnight, and his remaining small change will not cover the fare home. He fetches up semi-exhausted at the Terminal Bar. But this apparent end is just the beginning of the rest of his pillar-to-post nocturnal pinballing....

The fact that a bit of low-level lust got him into this mess is mockingly brought home to him by a quick glimpse of some obscene toilet graffiti on the theme of *vagina dentata*, and his rapidly developing fear of the Female is fuelled throughout the night as coincidences and unforeseen connections conspire to feed an all-round paranoia. The plot in which he's the impotent pawn thickens and curdles menacingly, almost defying synopsis yet unravelling with daunting logic. Only Marcy – a guilt-inducing successful suicide – is removed early from the game board, as Paul's pursued relentlessly by a mob of gay vigilantes who believe he's a burglar, witnesses a murder, rambles out his story of this "terrible, terrible night" to an increasingly disinterested gay man who's misread his pleas, and falls prey to the always uncertain intentions of more women.

Waitress Julie (Teri Garr) hands him a note begging for help in escaping the bar tended by disastrously well-meaning Tom (John Heard), and then attempts to seduce him into her sixties time-capsule world (with the Monkees offered as mood-music) before fly-posting his 'wanted' image all over SoHo. Gail (Catherine O'Hara) playfully screws up his attempts to phone for help, and seems oddly keen on the spectacle of burnt flesh herself, before she literally blows the whistle on him and joins the demons on his tail in her Mr Softee ice-cream van. Finally June (Verna Bloom), a two thieves (Cheech & Chong) he's been bumping into all night.

The current dubiously 'happy' ending has Paul falling from his captors' van, and from his cast, immediately in front of his own office building, just in time for work, and some much more comforting communion with his computer terminal. An even darker finale was reputedly tested on some American audiences and was ill-received, but the sense of any real liberation is still precisely what's withheld.

What we've watched is the domino theory of communications breakdown, the death throes of common sociability, and the delirious mutation of the Me Generation into the Fuck You Society. There's no wonder the laughter's nervous.

Film-student author Joseph Minion takes a lot of credit for such a defiantly original and mordant first-time screenplay, and former Fassbinder wouldn't like to guess why both an actor (Will Patton) and a song (the Peggy Lee track) are here shared with Chris Petit's *Chinese Boxes*, or whether the conjunction of Dick Miller's cameo appearance and the image of Paul as a 'live' sculpture constitute any kind of homage to Roger Corman's *Bucket of Blood*. Or whether, indeed, that same image of Paul encased might rhyme crucially with the spectacle of Jerry Lewis similarly immobilised near the end of *The King of Comedy*.

Beyond speculation, though, is the certainty that very few other directors could come up with something this unsettling when their star is in its ascendancy, let alone when they might be excused for running for cover with some cosy, cuddly fantasy. His vision may be coal-black, but Scorsese still mines gold from those old mean streets.

PAUL TAYLOR

BACK TO THE FUTURE

More than any other individual, Steven Spielberg has set the agenda for popular cinema in the 1980s. The lightshow of special effects, the pell-mell adventure *à la* Indiana Jones, the realms where yarn-spinning and magic hold sway – all these bear the Spielberg imprimatur (and no wonder, one may well feel, that he should cherish an ambition to film *Peter Pan*). Spielberg's name has, too, a marquee value that in the movies' past half century has only been anywhere near equalled by Hitchcock and De Mille, or by the rather special case of Walt Disney, whose animated movies Spielberg admits were a key influence.

The fact that Spielberg did not direct or personally produce *Back to the Future*, but as with *Sherlock Holmes* and several other movies is credited as executive producer, merely testifies to the breadth of his dominion; and certainly the creative personality which the film reflects would have to be identified as his. Such a consideration is, however, academic. In practice, and for all that reigning convention decrees the rubric 'a Robert Zemeckis film', *Back to the Future* achieves an exact blend of talent and texture which (and it is in no way exceptional: think for recent instance of *The French Connection* or *The Sting*) renders 'possessive' credit an irrelevance. It may be – who knows? – that in a few years cinemathèques will be mounting Zemeckis retrospectives. What one *does* know is that, as the comedy adventure of *Romancing the Stone* indicated and the trickier comic fantasy of this film confirms, he is a director with an instinct for the indefinable quality of pace who possesses the even less definable capacity to go beyond the illustration of a script to causing it to spring alive on the screen. It is worth insisting, though, that the script (by Bob Gale and Zemeckis himself) has to work before anything else can.

The picture's premise is, in the tradition of the best story-telling, both simple and bizarre. Marty (Michael J Fox) is an amiable 17-year-old, youngest child of an under-achieving suburban family, who speeds to school on a skateboard, has aspirations to local celebrity as a rock guitarist, and dates a pretty girl (Claudia Wells) from a better-off background. He is also, however, amanuensis to the wild-haired, wild-eyed 'Doc' (Christopher Lloyd), a crackpot inventor, who, complete with faithful shaggy dog 'Einstein', resembles a spiritual heir of the absent-minded professor who in the person of Fred MacMurray invented 'flubber' in the Disney comedies of Spielberg's youth. Doc's achievement has been to convert a DeLorean car into a time-machine, and when the terrorists whom Doc has cheated in a deal over the component requirements come gunning for him, Marty's escape in the car inadvertently lands him thirty years before in the same small town where his parents-to-be are now his teenage contemporaries.

It says something for the power of osmosis by which master-showmen like Spielberg tap into popular taste that the film followed closely, though too closely for any question of direct influence, in the wake of *The Terminator*, which in a quite different, luridly violent, manner also scored a big box-office success with the gimmick of time-travel; and perhaps the fact that the terrorist heavies are Libyans might even point, since the film appeared a good few months before the Tripoli bombings, to a prophetic capacity to coincide with a broader popular feeling.

The comedy of culture-shock attendant upon Marty's arrival in 1955 – a period which cunningly coincides with the approximate point at which, for today's youthful cinema audiences, 'history' begins – is confidently boisterous. There is a running joke in which his 'Puffin' jacket is presumed to be a life-preserver; the teenage incarnation of his mother assumes from the inscription on Marty's T-shirt that his name is Calvin Klein; Doc, responding with disbelief to the identity of the 1985 president, counters, "I suppose Jack Benny is the Secretary to the Treasury". And visually, the sequence in which Marty 'invents' skateboarding to turn the tables on a carful of louts is an admirably staged passage of knockabout. But the film also ventures beyond the superficial and farcical. While stopping short of direct realism, the high-school scenes and the encounters with the local bully and his cronies carry a charge of disagreeable conviction. And the byplay between Marty and his 'parents' is invested with a sentimental discretion which is abetted, not smothered, by the surrounding absurdity, with the twin strands woven snugly together in the climactic scene at the dance.

What exerts an additional fascination, however – at least on second viewing, when the initial shock of delight has been absorbed – is the degree to which the film contains a dimension of self-reflectiveness, a commentary on the process of creating fiction. In some respects – for instance, the apparently inconsequential way in which material information, like the bolt of lightning which will eventually provide the conductor for Marty's journey back to 1985, is worked into the exposition – this is no more than a function of well-constructed narrative. But the movie takes the principle considerably further, to the extent that the dramatic motor of the 1955 sequences is driven by the construction of not one 'scenario' but two. The first entails the contriving by Doc and Marty of a means of transporting the latter back to where he started from, a scheme which culminates in a wonderfully edited sequence of mock-suspense which even unblushingly and triumphantly incorporates the venerable chestnut of the car that fails to start at the psychological moment. And the second concerns Marty's ever more desperate manoeuvres to ensure that his parents-to-be are romantically brought together, thus ensuring his own eventual existence, a consummation threatened (and Uncle Walt would surely have drawn the line at this) by his mother's growing infatuation with her own 'son'.

In a refinement of this principle, the dramatisation devolves at several points upon means of photographic reproduction: the videotape which allows the 1955 Doc to foresee his eventual scientific breakthrough; the family snapshots from which Marty and his siblings begin to disappear as their procreation falls into jeopardy. Finally, in a delirium of topsy-turvydom, Marty manages to get back to 1985 a minute before he left it, and for sixty seconds becomes literally a spectator of the wild events in which his 'other' self is participating: life as a movie.

Moreover, if the cinema itself is a kind of time-machine, with Marty's adventures in the past putting a new gloss on the term flashback, it is also traditionally a dream-machine – a means, as the saying used to be, of taking us out of ourselves. And in this sense, too, *Back to the Future* conflates medium and message by making its protagonists' dreams come true. Marty is able during his time-trip to front a successful rock band. Doc gains the priceless encouragement of learning that his experiment will succeed, even though he ruefully concedes that he will have to wait thirty years for it to happen. And more sweepingly, Marty's family, who have been pictured in the early scenes as sufficiently sunk in low-middle-class slovenliness as to resemble a cross between Norman Rockwell and Charles Addams, have been transmogrified by his intervention in their history into *soignés* figures worthy of a glossy magazine ad. (To a British viewer, the contrast may recall that between the real home life of *Billy Liar* and the one he fantasises about.)

But the movie is adroit enough in its sense of proportion to render this paradise gained in terms that are themselves lightly satirical. Nowhere is the sleight-of-hand which wards off sententiousness and the threat of sentimentality more apparent than in the high-speed negotiation of the throwaway conclusion. Doc nips off to the year 2015, only to return forthwith to whisk Marty and his girlfriend off with him to sort out some unspecified dilemma surrounding their 'children', and as they depart in a whirlwind of genial absurdity, the end credits slam on to the screen. Dream-time is over and the audience is back in the present. But as they file out, there can be few among them who do not leave the theatre lighter of step and of heart than when they arrived.

TIM PULLEINE

BRAZIL

Occasionally a film can become so controversial that the furore overshadows the movie itself. That may have happened in the US with Terry Gilliam's *Brazil*. After a mixed Cannes reception to a running time of 142 minutes, Gilliam tightened the work down to 131 minutes. Universal, the American distributor, realising that this was not a goofy fantasy romp like *Time Bandits*, wanted to slice the movie below two hours running time and change the despairing ending to one of upbeat, successful escape, thereby rendering the entire movie essentially meaningless. Gilliam resisted strenuously, publicly waging a guerrilla campaign urging prompt release of his version. As the media picked up the story, the issue became one of power between the company president and the upstart artist. The honchos were quoted that they deemed Gilliam's version "unreleasable", and the film appeared fated to be shelved. (Not since Blake Edwards' *S.O.B.* has a film so presciently illustrated the validity of its satire by the way its philistine targets strike back at it in real life.)

Then the Los Angeles Film Critics Association voted *Brazil* its award for Best Picture, Best Director and Best Screenplay. It was an unprecedented break with convention for a group that traditionally tracks the Oscars closely (ironically, the runner-up in the balloting was Universal's own $30 million *Out of Africa*, which it had pushed mightily with the critics). Instead, they had voted for a film that had never been publicly exhibited (in fact, none of the private screenings were authorised, either), and at the time had no release scheduled. The action prompted the overnight booking of the film intact, and the "unreleasable" *Brazil*, though commercially unsuccessful, did garner two Oscar nominations itself.

Terry Gilliam, the only American collaborator in the popular Monty Python troupe, has developed beyond their inspired silliness to create an intricately mad dystopia that mirrors the absurdities of our contemporary 'civilisation'. Gilliam considers the film an illustration of the French concept of retro-future, "a way of looking at the future through the past, of revealing, so to speak, the other side of now." *Brazil* (which has nothing to do with the country, referring instead to the old popular song) owes an obvious debt to George Orwell: one could fairly call it 1985's version of his *1984*.

Gilliam crams every scene and shot with hilariously inventive satirical details, throwing away more sight gags than most movies ever attempt. The message of *Brazil* may hardly be new, but the gleeful imagination and sustained style on display are so exhilarating that even its most depressing insights evoke thrills and laughter – with the kind of kick that hurts.

Nothing in Gilliam's earlier films (*Time Bandits, Monty Python's Life of Brian*) suggested such vision and skill. Universal notwithstanding, unlike most films that leave you looking at your watch, *Brazil* zips by like a combination of fever, nightmare and wet dream.

Jonathan Pryce plays Sam, a dreamy bureaucrat content to hide in the massive entrails of a government agency, lost in adolescent Wagnerian fantasies of a pure and unattainable love (Kim Griest) earned through mythic combat. But his ambitious mother (a brilliant Katherine Helmond) pulls strings with his late father's cronies to get him promoted, and he ends up embroiled in a confusion of red tape, terrorism, rebellion, betrayal and romantic passion, ultimately becoming a victim of the totalitarian system that seems only a slightly twisted exaggeration of life as we know it.

Brazil renders the most thoroughly realised conception of an extrapolated urban future since *Blade Runner*. The future Gilliam sees doesn't work any better than today: any possibility of progress is strangled by the consumerist conformity of the masses and the ruling class's obsession with social control. It's a cowardly, inefficient world, suffused with the omnipresent banality of evil, clumsily cruel.

Gilliam's political analysis may add little to Orwell's, but it provides ripe satirical opportunities that rarely dip into Pythonesque reflex jokiness. Instead, the gibes resound with melancholy. While Orwell's fable expressed a vision for the age, its story-telling lacked dramatic artistry. Gilliam dares to deliver his narrative impact out of the accumulation of just these farcical details. The absurdity actually enhances emotional credibility, conveying pathos, passion and heroism through a comic dialectic between the individual and society.

On repeated viewings, however, as the bravura grows familiar, the source of *Brazil*'s power becomes more apparently personal rather than satiric. An Oedipal subtext that seems but one of the proliferating strands of whimsy emerges as a unifying principle. Sam's fantasies of omnipotence grow out of his repressed frustrations, yet their quality of arrested adolescence brands them as fundamentally depressing as his waking environment of adult conformity. In a perverted counter-variation on Sam's reveries, his mother and her cronies disfigure themselves through a plethora of faddish cosmetic treatments in a mania to recapture the appearances of their youth.

These dubious, quixotic drives (all of which distract the dreamers from moral and political consciousness) are embodied stylistically by artful recourse to wide-angle lenses even in medium close-ups, not merely to emphasise the grotesqueries and to create a sense of the ubiquitous distortion of appearances, but to establish the fundamental subjectivity of the narrative. Though we are unaware of this implication until Gilliam's indispensable climax, in retrospect the film has plainly been structured throughout to reflect Sam's perceptions and viewpoint. This anchoring within a single, however simple, sensibility enables *Brazil* to achieve resonances beyond mere cleverness.

Gilliam synthesises all these movements in a stunning coup when Sam's mother reveals the end result of her cosmetic surgeries: she has become the identical image of his dream-lover. The purposeful ambiguity – whether Sam has been dreaming all along of his youthful mother, or reacts to his mother's bizarre quest by projecting his dream image onto her – need not be resolved to be joltingly effective. Other, more subtle, Oedipal details abound: for instance, when Sam needs to penetrate a secret high place he is forbidden to enter, his father's name provides the code of entry into where he will make love to his fantasy incarnate, be interrupted, arrested and punished with death.

These themes would mean nothing were there not a significant parallel drawn between the taboos of incest and of political rebellion. Once Sam forsakes his cocoon to pursue his dreamgirl, she naturally proves an object of state suspicion. When he breaks through (literally driving through a barricade), Sam is doomed. There can be no escape, because Gilliam sees the drive for freedom as part of an impulse to self-destruction, since it challenges the nature of society to repress all such drives. Nevertheless, both instincts are ultimately irresistible.

The use of tangled knots of exposed plumbing, then, becomes a peculiarly inspired metaphor for the impenetrable morass of the interior life. The guerrilla tactics of Tuttle, the renegade plumber, consist of bypassing the established ventilation system. Sam commits himself to self-realisation and damn the consequences when he mimics Tuttle by connecting up the vacuum message tubes in his office to make a continuous loop, just as he must bypass his superego to conquer his mother in the guise of his dreamgirl.

Irony, of course, makes a poor harbinger for hope. Tuttle may throw a monkey wrench into the orderly management of chaos (he gets the job done of repairing the air-conditioning, a truly subversive act), but this man who detests the bureaucratic forms that substitute for action is himself smothered to death by a maelstrom of official papers.

For all its apparent absurdity, however, Tuttle's heroism is real and valuable, and so is Sam's. *Brazil* endorses the strategy so common to art under totalitarian regimes of the cryptic symbolic gesture. The film goes beyond Orwell in its understanding of the normalisation of tyranny after forty years of post-war equilibrium. In post-Solidarity Poland, Adam Michnik can exhort his countrymen from prison to concede the power of the state and create meaningful lives of personal and civic virtue in spite of it. The power of the imagination and of the moral impulse are ultimately beyond the control of any centralised authority. Therefore, while Sam's dreams of liberation and escape may only be fantasies, still they are immune to the ministrations of his torturers. Though he fails personally, his bumbling rebellion has significance, indeed, is indispensable.

Thus the bleakness of *Brazil*'s pessimism has a compensating sweetness underscored by the catchy dreaminess of the title tune. Sam, the lovesick rebel without a cause, may go over the brink of the cliff in his hopeless chicken run, yet the idiosyncratic triumph of *Brazil* makes a suitably imperfect antidote for despair about our future: at least it's still possible, no matter how difficult, to make masterful popular art out of the detritus of our culture and civilisation.

MYRON MEISEL

JAGGED EDGE

Jagged Edge is about greed, lust, money, power, corruption and calculated manipulation. It questions the moral validity of the judicial system and exposes the ease with which people can be persuaded to believe anything. It is also a very good thriller.

I suppose the least one should expect from a thriller is that it should *thrill*. Richard Marquand's glossily efficient direction takes care of that right from the opening sequence when a hooded intruder enters a San Francisco mansion, ties the female occupant to a bed and carves her up with a hunting knife. Unlike Brian De Palma, to whom he makes a few visual references, Marquand is not an auteur; he handles the cosmetic and glamorous elements of the story with clinical detachment and the manner in which he can sublimate his ego makes him the perfect choice for the film. For *Jagged Edge* is a well-written film for actors and Marquand is generous enough to let them shine.

With elements of *Witness For the Prosecution* and *Twelve Angry Men*, you might be forgiven for thinking that the film is a courtroom drama. But it is rather more than that. When Jack Forrester's wealthy wife is killed in what amounts to a ritual slaying, suspicion falls on him from the beginning. Forrester is the editor of a city newspaper and the death of his wife elevates him to the president of the board. Tom Krasny, the public prosecutor in the DA's office, wants to nail Forrester for personal reasons and builds a strong case against him, based on character witnesses and the evidence of a hunting knife discovered in Forrester's locker. Forrester hires his family law firm who dig out one of their star lawyers, a former criminal attorney in the DA's office who resigned because she became disillusioned with Krasny's ruthless methods. Teddy Barnes' last case for Krasny resulted in the imprisonment of a black man, Henry Stiles, on circumstantial evidence. Krasny buried evidence that might have freed him and Stiles commits suicide in prison. Teddy's motives are made more complex when she embarks on an affair with Forrester. The great strength of the plot is that each character is given several layers of motivation, not all of which are at first apparent. Dark hints are dropped early on about Krasny's political ambitions and the fact that Forrester exposed them in his newspaper. The subject of Henry Stiles, which seems at first a digression, gradually weighs the evidence against Krasny and accounts for Teddy's distrust of him.

When Forrester persuades her to take his case his motives are clear: a jury will be more sympathetic towards a female defence counsel. As Teddy Barnes, Glenn Close maintains the balance between cool efficiency and emotional involvement with astonishing dexterity. We recognise her professional skill at the same time as her personal fallibility. Here is a woman with a guilt complex who sees a way of absolving herself by beating Krasny in court and then spilling the beans about the Stiles case, effectively destroying Krasny's career. Her motives for defending Forrester are therefore just as suspect as Krasny's are for prosecuting him. Even when she suspects that Forrester is lying to her, she continues to fight for him, the dilemma succinctly pointed in the following exchange: "How can you defend me if you think I'm guilty?" asks Forrester. Teddy replies, "It happens all the time. It's the way our legal system works." The impossibility of pure impartial justice is at the centre of *Jagged Edge*.

Several degrees of manipulation are at work here. Our sympathy is effectively loaded in Teddy's favour. Not only does she detest Krasny (as we do) for all the aforementioned reasons, there is also a hint of sexual jealousy between the two as Krasny has tried unsuccessfully to get her into bed. Divorced from her husband, she maintains a civilised equilibrium with him and her children – a kind of idealised divorce which is guaranteed to appeal. Before long we are in fact acting like a packed jury. The film then forces us to question our responses and explore the difference between our feelings (which are easily manipulated) and the hard evidence presented (ditto).

As Jack Forrester, Jeff Bridges gives his most persuasive performance since *Cutters Way*. He is the bright boy made good, charming, intelligent, sexy and the epitome of the American Success Ethic. Sure, he married the boss's daughter but he has worked his way up to the position of editor through hard graft. A couple of well drafted scenes show him at work; his authority is unquestionable and we feel he deserves his position. He is admirable though not likeable for, like Krasny, Forrester is a user of people. The similarities between the two are crucial to the plot.

Then there is the magnificent and stalwart Robert Loggia as Sam, the has-been-and-may-well-be-again detective. Disillusioned, cynical and world-weary, it is a role that in the hands of a lesser actor would have tipped over into caricature. Loggia cunningly opts for a discreetly clever foul-mouthed performance of abrasive charm. He is Teddy's father figure, conscience and protector all rolled into one. He sees through everybody with a kind of moral X-ray vision but he chooses to believe Teddy is right about Forrester for all the wrong reasons, as we do. It is his love and respect and sympathy for Teddy, his awareness of her vulnerability that blinds him momentarily to the truth.

And the truth is as black as midnight. For beneath the glittering surfaces of the film, beneath its double play of egotistical conflict and revenge, *Jagged Edge* has some pretty devastating things to say about manipulation. Only once or twice does the script, by Joe Eszterhas, falter. In court we are presented with a bright red herring in the shape of a psychotic tennis player who is too obviously a plant. Teddy also destroys the evidence of one or two prosecution witnesses (especially in connection with the knife) with suspicious ease. But these are minor quibbles. In terms of the plotting, most of these formula devices are justified and only noticeable because the rest is so subtle and assured.

The manipulation of the viewer arises from our relationship with the central characters, not from the whims of the director. Having established that Forrester may be guilty, or at least not what he seems, we want him to get off not because we like him (we don't), but because we can't bear the thought that Teddy has been manipulated by Forrester. We have faith in her as a human character and recognise her fallibility even though we do not share her faith in Forrester. Forrester therefore has our support by proxy.

Krasny, as played by Peter Coyote, is reassuringly detestable. His ruthlessness is etched in the opening scenes and he subsequently does nothing to suggest we are wrong in our assumption. In this, Coyote pulls off a magnificent coup of cinema. His relationship to Teddy is the same as it is to us; he is clearly a scheming, conniving son-of-a-bitch who deserves a considerable come-uppance. We share Teddy's delight when his back is against the wall and also her incredulity when he claims, in a scene in the judge's chambers, that Forrester has arranged the whole case and has played Teddy like a puppet throughout. Knowing Krasny, or rather, disliking him, the notion seems so preposterous that neither we nor Teddy entertain it. In a scene of urban Grand Guignol, Krasny hisses: "He's *not* a psychopath. He is an Ice Man. He is a *monster*." How can we possibly believe that?

But Krasny knows his man. A monster himself, Krasny recognises his own deviousness in Forrester. Unpalatable as it is, Krasny has hit the nail on the head. Forrester has done exactly what he has claimed. It is a bleak and bitter indictment of the way evil people can manipulate good people and has nothing to do with intelligence and everything to do with scruples.

As a finale, Marquand once again turns on the traditional theatrics of the thriller and gives us a shock ending as a gloved hand explodes through a pane of glass and a masked and hooded figure enters Teddy's house. Even at the point that the killer is revealed we still pretend we don't know who it really is. But by that time there is no escape, no cavalry charge to rescue us from the truth that subconsciously we have perhaps known all along. We have repressed it because to believe it means believing that the human race is capable of hideous depths of Machiavellian intrigue. How apt that the final words should belong to Sam as he holds the sobbing, mortified but finally absolved Teddy in his arms: "Fuck him. He was trash." Greed, lust, money, power, corruption and calculated manipulation – *Jagged Edge* has its finger on the pulse of it all.

NEIL NORMAN

TURKEYS OF THE YEAR

9½ WEEKS

The problem with *9½ Weeks* is that it's got no balls. Literally and figuratively. Whatever this film – about an intense, vaguely sado-masochistic sexual affair – may once have been in terms of visual explicitness, it was cut down so far as to not come anywhere near an X rating. A successful treatment of this material might have caught viewers' breath up short and caused nervous discomfort at certain moments. Adrian Lyne's predictably slick, self-consciously hip approach dehumanises and desensitises what could have been a film of extreme intimacy, and unsurprisingly fetishises the accoutrements of the characters' lifestyles and sexual preferences.

Style and attitude, of course, are what preoccupy Lyne. In retrospect, *Flashdance* succeeded because of the music, trendy fashions and Jennifer Beals' extraordinary cuteness; but here, the director's shallowness isn't obscured – or compensated for – by any outside elements. Lyne's lack of talent and insight is laid bare for all to see to a much greater degree than are his characters. What is even more lamentable is that, because of this failure, the opportunities to produce American films that frankly address sexual subjects will become fewer still.

In *9½ Weeks,* Mickey Rourke plays a successful, nattily attired Wall Street trader who, it becomes clear, makes a habit out of picking up beautiful young women and mesmerising them sexually for brief, unforgettable periods of time. He pushes the women beyond their normal boundaries, daring, risking all in exchange for heretofore forbidden, unknown pleasures. Anything goes and, once ensnared, the women plunge headlong down a road of no return until it's all played out.

After quietly moving in on his latest prey, Kim Basinger, he begins provocatively by immediately pulling out a blindfold and trying it on her for size; if she protests at this, she just won't be ready for anything else he has in mind. Fortunately for him, she's game, if a little skittish, and it appears that we're in for an evening of fun and games in the deep end.

Disappointingly, however, what follows alternates between the faintly ridiculous and the bafflingly commonplace. Mostly, the pair just gets it on in utterly normal fashion, albeit in somewhat unusual – and threateningly public – locations. A scene in which Rourke force-feeds Basinger some random items from the fridge proves both vaguely repellent and mildly intriguing; Rourke at one point buys a riding crop that we never see again; and a climactic sequence that has him pushing Basinger and a hired prostitute together possesses an uneasy tension and an unresolved intention; otherwise it's mostly posturing and intimidation on his part which she allows herself to fall for.

Lyne forages about in his search for a cinema without need of words, not at all a goal to be scorned in itself; indeed, it would be interesting to see the results if today's feature directors were all required to make one silent film as a test of their story-telling skills. Unfortunately, Lyne seems to feel obliged to make some kind of point with virtually every shot, points which, once made, obviate the need for conventional dramatic and character development. For him, appearances are all; surfaces had better be all-revelatory, or he's sunk. Glances, gestures, hesitations, smiles and (especially) stares are meant to convey more profound depths than dialogue ever could, and this is a safe bet when the dialogue is as inane as it's been in Lyne's three films to date. In any event, we are left with the opportunity to get to know Mickey Rourke through his designer suits, grey-on-grey high-tech apartment and self-satisfied, supposedly devastating little smiles and smirks, and Kim Basinger through the tremulousness of her lips before she capitulates to Rourke's demands, and her admirable choice of lingerie.

Somehow, Basinger, an appealing but limited actress on the basis of all her films to date, manages to survive Rourke and Lyne's combined assaults upon her and emerge with her dignity more or less intact. This impression undoubtedly has something to do with her unflagging sincerity and spirit under adverse circumstances, but also progressively stems from the rooting interest one develops for her to escape the clutches of these slimy characters. Granted, she is there (both as a character and an actress) of her own accord; unlike Samantha Eggar, say, in *The Collector,* she has not been abducted or tied up against her will and, at first, one tends to dismiss her for becoming involved with Rourke at all. But gradually, after her initial total immersion, she conveys a sense of distance from, and superiority to, the nonsense her director and leading man are getting so worked up about. Sex may be important, but it isn't *everything,* and Basinger perhaps unconsciously gets across that she is not as implicated in the overwrought hijinks on view as are her cohorts.

In the current conservative climate of the United States, it unquestionably took a certain degree of courage (and clout) to embark on a project such as *9½ Weeks,* but faintheartedness along the way took its toll – the original distributor, Tri-Star, backed out, an R rating was agreed upon as a commercial necessity, with cuts made accordingly, and Lyne, either to start with, or in the end, didn't go as far as he should have to truly startle the audience. Although very successful in Italy, which is evidently ever-hungry for chic soft porn, *9½ Weeks* flopped in the US, and it wasn't because it was too upsetting or explicit. To the contrary, it wasn't different or provocative enough. As the latest exercise in designer sex, it would have been right at home in the advertising section of any of the fashion magazines, but will never be cited in any discussion of memorable screen erotica.

TODD McCARTHY

LIFEFORCE

Lifeforce's credentials are quite respectable. The source is a novel, with the surely more marketable title of *The Space Vampires*, by Colin Wilson, who thirty years ago became the arch-priest of Hampstead Heath neo-existentialism, even if he has subsequently taken to clothing his philosophical preoccupations in lurid melodrama. The director is Tobe Hooper, whose *Texas Chainsaw Massacre* is highly regarded at least in the more esoteric reaches of cine-academia, even if his subsequent work has on the whole been seen as a letdown. And one of the two screenwriters, Dan O'Bannon, has some kudos within the sci-fi genre on the strength of script credits on *Dark Star* and *Alien*.

Indeed, a précis of *Alien* is rather what the establishing sequences of *Lifeforce* bring to mind, with an Anglo-US space probe into Halley's Comet leading to the sinister discovery first of a mysterious spaceship within the comet's tail and then of some humanoid creatures, who as soon as they are brought aboard the interlopers' vessel waste no time in spreading death and destruction.

So far, so okay, even if the special effects are pretty unimpressive by present-day standards. It is when the picture comes to earth that matters really go awry. The scene shifts to a space research centre in London, whence the humanoids have been taken from the returned spacecraft. Forthwith, the female of the species comes to life and promptly sucks the life out of the commissionaire who is the first person she meets. The hue and cry is raised as she slopes off stark naked into the London night. Meanwhile, the autopsy on the unfortunate factotum is interrupted by the eviscerated corpse suddenly sitting bolt upright and embracing the examining doctor in a shower of sparks, thus regaining his natural form at the expense of the doc's demise. Amid consternation, the crazed fellow is locked up in a cellar, where his frenzied behaviour culminates in his exploding into a heap of ash.

By this time the security forces are on the scene, led by a colonel (Peter Firth) who unaccountably hails not from MI5 but from the SAS. "This is a D-Notice situation," he snaps blithely as members of the press crowd round for some explanation. But then the film's regard for accuracy in its depiction of British life is scant at best, with BBC newsreaders endowed with stentorian American accents. Then again there is the Home Secretary, who may be named Heseltine but who has no further connection with real life; he is, in fact, like nothing so much as a music-hall straight-man, bumbling along in the wake of the police and military as if he were on a par with the tea-boy.

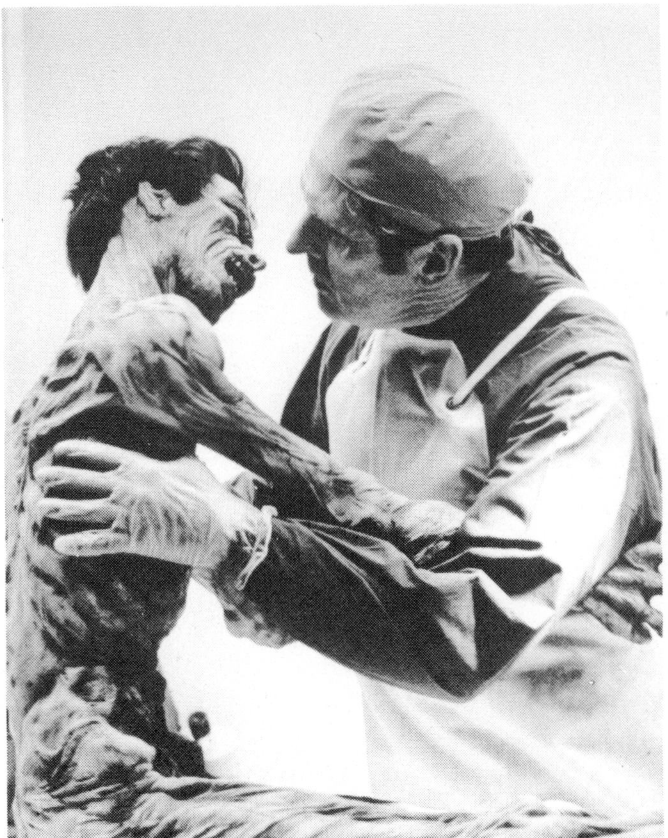

As a trail of corpses is strewn by the space lady (Mathilda May), a lone survivor (Steve Railsback) of the Halley's Comet probe crash-lands in Texas in the ship's escape pod, and is whisked off to London to help with efforts to locate Ms May, by whom he is evidently partly possessed. Enter at this point a further principal character, scientific wizard Frank Finlay; Mr Finlay, who was last seen on the screen besporting himself in ladies' lingerie in *The Key*, is here attired in nothing more unusual than an astrakhan coat of the sort associated with the late Tony Hancock, though in other respects his behaviour is somewhat strange. "Mind if I have a go?" he asks suavely as Railsback is put under hypnosis. As the latter starts to burble about seeing the quarry approach a car, Finlay cuts in, "Can you see the licence number?" Whereupon Railsback facilitates an unparalleled dramatic short-cut by proving able to read off the registration precisely.

Firth, Railsback and others take off in pursuit, to get mixed up in rum goings-on at a mental hospital worthy of *The Cabinet of Dr Caligari*. In their absence, the vampiric plague is spreading like wildfire and London is officially deemed "out of control" – model shot of Big Ben with green streak in the sky above to indicate malign extra-terrestrial influence; modest crowd of extras seen running amok down cursory mock-up of city street. We duly learn that an alien spaceship is hovering – in geo-stationary orbit, no less – roughly above St Paul's and by means of a colossal umbrella (sic) is siphoning off the spiritual energy of the citizenry. Martial law is declared and there is talk of the capital having to be nuked. In a diversionary sequence, Firth is seen confronting the now crazed, presumably infected, Finlay in his lab. "There is life after death," avers the latter. At this, Firth summarily shoots him down, and with a gleeful cry of "Here I go!" Finlay expires in a sheet of lightning.

The movie's concluding stages tend to defy synopsis, or even comprehension, as Firth braves the *cordon sanitaire* that has been thrown round the capital and runs a gauntlet of ravening ghouls who look as if they had been remaindered from one of those bargain basement zombie flicks that the Italians were churning out a few years back. However, there is a happy ending of sorts, or at least a *Liebestod*: Railsback falls into May's fatal embrace, and as the pair are shot by the indefatigable Firth, the crisis and the movie come abruptly to an end.

Shortly after *Lifeforce* opened, Frank Finlay was one of several celebrities officiating at the Critics' Circle film awards ceremony. He genially noted that it had been interesting both to read the reviews of the film and to see that it had achieved notably high placing in the weekly charts of box-office takings. The assembled scribes refrained from exploding or emitting showers of sparks, but their hollow laughter provided clear indication that the critics felt themselves once again out in the cold.

TIM PULLEINE

RETURN TO OZ

Though not financially successful in its original release, the musical *The Wizard of Oz* achieved universal popularity later through television exposure. This belated sequel has no songs and may be far more faithful in its particulars to the Baum originals, yet it is in every way inferior to the 1939 MGM classic. (The film actually resembles *The Dark Crystal* or a Fleischer cartoon more than it does its predecessor.) As the Scarecrow, Tin Man and Cowardly Lion (here reduced to walk-ons) believed about themselves, this movie lacks brains, heart and nerve.

The opening two reels are singularly bleak, as a dejected Dorothy cannot sleep because of her nightmarish Oz memories, while her uncle is too depressed (economically and emotionally) to finish rebuilding the Kansas homestead in time to shelter the family for winter. Auntie Em hauls Dorothy off to a primitive alienist, a threatening quack who is about to administer electroshock therapy with sadistic glee to the terrified girl when lightning strikes, enabling her to flee. Caught in a rampaging river, she nearly drowns before ending up yet again in Oz.

But this Oz is no brighter than the Kansas she has escaped. Lifeless, devastated, festooned with mucky traps for the curious and careless, the landscape seems designed to reflect the traumas within Dorothy's own psyche, a fantastic world of fears and taboos so moulded to her own that she finds she can in fact exert a measure of control over them. By successfully reanimating Oz, Dorothy restores herself to life.

Actually, this rather joyless psychoanalytic component of the movie comprises its most interesting aspect, as Dorothy learns to cope with the deadening situation in Kansas by creating a parallel interior world which she proceeds to conquer and master. In contrast to the Jungian predisposition of *The Company of Wolves*, *Return to Oz* wallows in Freudian orthodoxy.

Sounds unlikely for a children's story? Indeed, *Return to Oz* is children's fantasy decidedly

unsuitable for small youngsters. Some effort has been made to escalate the thrills and chills in order to attract an older audience as well, but the pace is too slow and predictable to satisfy teenagers.

Moreover, the project's air of rectitude concerning its fidelity to Baum, its Yankee-Edwardian design and its therapeutic treatment of the elements of fantasy and myth does nothing to enhance the wonderment of the story. Brandishing concepts in lieu of ideas, calculation instead of imagination, there's precious little magic onscreen.

While the larger clay animation effects are undeniably impressive, they are used too early and often, thus blunting their ultimate impact. The other technical effects are highly variable, sometimes revealing evidence of the major cost-cutting that accompanied the final approval of production. The overall impact is unconvincing, which undermines the spell.

Weakest of all are the new characters: Tic Tok, a mechanical man who feels nothing; Jack Pumpkinhead, a scatterbrained ragdoll type; and a reluctant charger, Gump. These three correspond rather analogously to the Tin Man, Scarecrow and Lion of the 1939 edition, yet none are sufficiently imaginative to overcome their essential lifelessness. They're really little more than prototypes of toy figures to merchandise.

On this proving ground, the crucial failure of the sequel emerges: where the fantasy figures in the earlier film were fully realised characters, each of whom had a distinct relationship with Dorothy that developed dramatically, here they are just concocted concepts that figure arbitrarily in the plotting. Dorothy's love for them isn't earned or real; it's based on nothing more than that they are cute toys. So nothing ever seems at stake in the story, which is essential to effective fantasy.

Fairuza Balk makes a bland, well-mannered moppet, and only Jean Marsh is afforded any opportunity to show some panache as a dashing evil Princess with a fashion gallery of pretty heads for her to wear for all occasions. Nicol Williamson suffers both body and voice submerged in effects.

Director Walter Murch brought a varied and impressive background of editing and sound to his directorial debut, and there are definite indications of intelligence, integrity and talent. But there's no evident desire to delight, no ambition to bewitch. Nor, surprisingly, is there any dramatic dynamism to the way the story unfolds.

The movie's almost puritanical attitude toward giving pleasure undermines the purpose of fairy tales. Bruno Bettelheim analysed the deep psychological import of these stories, a message *Return to Oz* clearly echoes. But Bettelheim also acknowledged that the primary utility of fairy tales came from their ability to entertain and involve a child, encouraging them to identify emotionally with the awesome task of establishing a place in the bewildering world and mastering their sense of self in relation to it. *Return to Oz* fails to accomplish that goal for its audience.

MYRON MEISEL

LEGEND

Told that the great myths of Greece and Rome were translations into narrative terms of natural phenomena, a famous writer treated the idea with agreeable irony. He imagined the creator of some deathless myth saying to his wife: My dear, you and I know that we have sunshine and hailstones and thunderstorms, but we mustn't tell anybody; we must just invent tales about the gods; they have very uncertain tempers and we know they are apt to interfere with the weather and everything else.

Fairy tale and myth are cousins. *Legend* is a fairy tale which reverses the relationship between nature and its translation into narrative. It is a film which starts not with the translation but with the reality, with light and darkness. The cinema, however, still needs what Eliot called an objective correlative. It needs figures to bring the tale alive. *Legend* has to have somebody who is Light and somebody who is Darkness. There we are then, back with myth, back with fairy tale.

The trouble is that to create a new fairy tale is about as easy as finding a new Shakespeare.

The Book of Genesis thought of it first: the blessing of light. We are in one of the sunlit woodlands which in the cinema stand for purity and blamelessness. I am bound to say that on the screen it looks very pretty. At the same time one has to admit that the co-existence of boscage and such elegant illumination is rare in human experience – and is made all the rarer by the presence of a couple of Unicorns, male and female. Apparently they are the symbols of goodness and love; the sanctity of the woodland (in the cinema I feel sure it would be called a glade) depends on them. And they are on good terms with the hero, a youthful rustic type who knows about flora and fauna. He is called Jack O' The Green, and he is of course in love with a Princess.

Time for the intrusion into this rural paradise of the thought of evil. The neighbouring castle, rather poorly lit, is inhabited by the enemy. He is just called Darkness, and it is his aim to extinguish the sunlight in the woodland and presumably everywhere else. The Unicorns are in his way. And you and I are in for a dose of symbolism.

One can't blame anyone for that. Start with the conflict between light and darkness and no matter how many objective correlatives you supply you are pretty well bound to fetch up with moral platitudes. It was Ridley Scott, one is told, the director of *Legend* who had the idea. A film-maker of distinction, he came to prominence with *The Duellists*, a tale which in the obsessiveness of its human motivation – one of the figures persists in fighting needless duels with a reluctant opponent – has an effective element of extravagance. Ridley Scott then moved into the realm of popular fantasy inhabited by so much of contemporary cinema: he made *Alien*, then *Blade Runner*, which was set in a post-holocaust city with dangerous near-human invaders from a slave-planet and a chancy love-story. It may seem a far cry from *Legend*. Nevertheless the link is there, the dependence on fantasy: the area of fantasy has altered, that is all. Instead of a crumbling future Earth and a concern with outer space there is an equally amorphous world of no-time, no-place dominated by abstractions. And this dream-world with its conceptions of good and evil is far more remote from the visual life of the cinema than the fantasies of the future.

The new piece struggles with itself. Burdened with emblems of morality, it fails to capture the simple, practical mood of the traditional fairy tale. The Princess is coveted by the power of Darkness. He wants to possess her. But first he wants to use her. She is tricked into betraying the Unicorns; she leads the stallion to his end. But she isn't merely the beautiful young Princess of the storybook. She is Innocence; one can't get away from the symbols. And the incessant symbolism stands in the way of the drive of the true fairy tale. Nothing new, after all, in the opposition of good and evil. Fairy tales are essentially moral: powers guide the virtuous hero, the disguised godmother looks after the industrious orphan and the cruel giant is defeated.

Perhaps one should be grateful for the lack of heartlessness in *Legend*. Traditional fairy tales are ferocious, sometimes positively vicious; Hans Andersen is full of horrors. Children are brought up on the idea of terrible retribution and no forgiveness. But they aren't bored. Fairy tales aren't boring; myth isn't boring; it depends on dramatic tension. *Legend* builds up to a fight; the young hero faces taunting Darkness. To his credit, he fights for the survival of sunlight. Somehow he would win more applause if he fought, even in these egalitarian days, for the family throne.

Cheated, one looks for performance. Tom Cruise is the hero; Tim Curry plays Darkness. Two agreeable young actors from movies less loaded with message; they do their best, but the direction is short of fervour. Audiences might hope for a new variant on fantasy. Instead there are elaborate visual effects, surprising make-up and the gifts of the Unicorn trainer. Sophistication substitutes for the untutored imagery of myth. *Legend* is the skeleton of fairy tale wrapped up in dead leaves.

DILYS POWELL

THE BRIDE

In the middle of a three-way row between Frankenstein (Sting), his saturnine friend (Anthony Higgins) and the Bride herself (Jennifer Beals), Frankenstein makes an ill-advised allusion to "Keats's *Prometheus*." It was only a matter of seconds before fifteen people sitting around me in the audience all hissed through gritted teeth, "It was Shelley!" And they were just a beat ahead of the Bride, who comes back with this piece of information in order to further her claims to superiority over the man who made her, and indeed over all men in general. Quite where the lady learned all her very modern attitudes is a mystery. No sooner has she got past the first stages of learning to speak, than she is spouting all kinds of cheap feminist nonsense, which is clearly more than the Baron bargained for, in spite of his earlier claims of wanting to make a woman who would be as free and independent and proud as any man. In one particularly fraught exchange she even manages a spirited "You don't own me . . . You didn't create me!" One longs for Sting to develop a mad satanic glint in his eye, throw his head back and scream at the rafters something along the lines of "I made you, and I can break you", which would at least place the film in the camp mode of *The Rocky Horror Show*. Instead there is far too long a pause, followed by a feeble "As a matter of fact . . . I did." Not the sort of stuff which Mary Shelley ever had in mind, nor even the sort of witty and dignified sense of wonder which James Whale created with his two original *Frankenstein* films.

For what Whale realised is that by making his monsters into hideous, alien creatures with little understanding of their own condition, then audiences would inevitably feel sympathy for them simply by way of a kind of paradox. Created to be one man's plaything, and the expression of his wish to play at God, they arrive in the world of men with many of the basic feelings and instincts of humans, but with an animal's inability to express them. The murder and mayhem that they turn to is registered as a form of childish frustration. By giving his 'Bride' not only the perfectly shaped form of Jennifer Beals but also the intelligence of a *Spare Rib* editor, Roddam has fallen into the trap of wishing to recreate all the sympathetic nature of the original, without realising how this came about.

The same applies to the male monster (Clancy Brown), renamed Viktor here for some reason, who is actually allowed to become more handsome as the film progresses. By some curious process, the cranial scars fade away, and his glowering eyebrows become less prominent ridges of bone as his friendship with the midget Rinaldo (David Rappaport) develops. In fact Clancy Brown gives an extraordinarily good performance as the retarded giant, but it is largely thrown away in the witless parallel plot in which he and the midget join the travelling circus and go in search of their dreams. This dream is of Venice, a place known to the midget as pictured on a medallion which he wears around his neck. As the Bride says at one point, "The world is so big. And so full of things!" Well yes, but not here it isn't. When the monster and his bride do finally arrive in Venice for a syrupy finale which has them floating down the Grand Canal in a gondola, one half expects to hear the strains of 'Just One Cornetto'. It certainly would have been preferable to the soupy Maurice Jarre score.

The pity of it all is that here is one of the world's most poignant romantic stories. Of course everybody needs someone to love; but in the case of Frankenstein's creation the need is even more urgent. Created in the 'Romantic' mould as a noble savage, he could only possibly be fulfilled by a woman specifically made for him, much as Eve was created for just the same purpose in the first garden. And this desire to return to the pre-lapsarian state of grace is made plain when the monster tells his bride that he wishes to go far away, "where men don't go". The fact that he is unable to is perhaps his saddest plight, and underlines mankind's similarly fallen state.

But a trip up the Grand Canal will not qualify as a return to primal innocence. For one thing, they couldn't afford the prices, not on what monsters get paid these days.

CHRIS PEACHMENT

PERFECT

With apparently impressive credentials – it's based on real-life articles by *Rolling Stone* writer Aaron Latham, who co-scripted the film with director James Bridges, and features that magazine's editor Jann Wenner, playing *Stone*'s fictional editor Mark Roth – you'd at least expect a certain authenticity in *Perfect*'s portrait of journalistic work. No such luck.

The story, signposted as 'serious', purports to examine the tensions arising from two seemingly contradictory needs: the desire for press freedom and the necessity for press accountability. The script establishes this dilemma by having star reporter John Travolta cover two separate stories for *Rolling Stone*. The first concerns a computer manufacturer on trial and is complicated by the fact that the government – guilty, it seems, of framing the man because of his deals with Iron Curtain countries – intends to subpoena Travolta to obtain the tapes of his inflammatory exclusive interview with the accused. The second, an exposé of the singles bar mentality that leads Californian 'airheads' to join health clubs, is rendered problematic by the fact that Travolta falls in love with Jamie Lee Curtis, the aerobics instructress he decides to exploit as the main source of information for his muck-raking.

If this brief synopsis makes *Perfect* sound simplistic and schematic, it gives no idea of the crass methods employed to deliver the melodrama. The central character of the celebrated *Stone* reporter is rendered almost totally unconvincing both by the script and by Travolta's pathetic performance. The film's authors endow him with what can only be described as acute schizophrenia: protective of his rights and opting for a prison stretch rather than hand over his tapes, he exhibits a moral rectitude akin to that of Henry Fonda's whiter-than-white liberal in *Twelve Angry Men*; but as the vainglorious creep eager to write salacious lies about the health addicts with whom he pretends to make friends, he reveals the cynical, dog-eat-dog instincts of Burt Lancaster's vicious ogre J. J. Hunsecker in *Sweet Smell of Success*. Even an actor as accomplished as, say, Robert De Niro would have a hard time making such a character stick, but the charmless, inarticulate and narcissistic Travolta hasn't a hope in hell of playing a 'serious', respected journalist with any credibility.

Let it be said, however, that the fault lies less with the hapless Travolta than with the ludicrous script, which repeatedly taxes our ability to suspend disbelief. For example, when our hero tries to persuade Jamie Lee Curtis that his intentions in writing about her club are strictly honorable, he strings her the following line: "The Baby Boomers are leading a physical Great Awakening comparable to the spiritual Great Awakenings that have gripped America every hundred years." Would *you* believe this man? *She* does, even when he continues with a risibly untenable thesis that all this prancing around in sweaty leotards signifies a move back to Emersonian values and natural self-reliance. Worse still, when Jamie finally does ditch him and he's forced to rethink his professional ethics, he actually does spew out this Emersonian effluence in print instead of his sensationalist sexual exposé. This is not, you see, a film about journalists; it is about cretinous crackpots with delusions of philosophical grandeur.

The movie as a whole, in fact, resolutely avoids tackling the ethical problems confronting journalists and provides instead a routine love story set against a glossy, glamorously unreal wonderland of jet-set life. Take the scenes with Wenner as *Stone* editor Mark Roth. The first time we meet him, he's in a restaurant giving Travolta a deeply meaningful pep-talk when he suddenly breaks off to proclaim, "Shit! There's Carly!" Sure enough Ms Simon enters to fling her drink in Travolta's face. The next time he appears he's suffering from a hangover: "Mikey Douglas was in town . . . My God, the cocktails flew!" Get the message? This guy is *always* surrounded by the famous. So it's no surprise later when for no apparent reason the frame is suddenly filled with the front-page face of Lauren Hutton. He *must* be around somewhere! Yes, here he comes, sidling into the picture, living it up again. When *does* he ever work?

You can tell, though, that he's really important and busy and famous by the way that, whenever Travolta calls in to report, Roth doesn't actually hold the phone but switches over to broadcast and paces around the room looking anxious. The only time he ever puts the contraption to his ear, in fact, is to underline a particularly vivid if meaningless rhetorical point ("Eat shit and die!" is repeated four times, just in case you missed it). This guy just *lives* headlines.

But all this irrelevance about how the other half lives is secondary to the utterly unmoving tale of John and Jamie's on-off romance. At the beginning his Emersonian chat-up lines bode ill, but hardly prepare us for her seduction technique, typing into his word-processor sweet nothings like "Wanna fuck?" This terse poetry, however, is topped by the morning-after scene. Following what one can only presume to have been a singularly sweaty bout of bed-wrestling, John joins Jamie's aerobics class and the infatuated couple undergo a lengthy, heavy session of leering at each other's genital areas while contorting themselves suggestively to dismal disco sounds. John has what appears to be a pointed cod-piece beneath his tracksuit trousers; Jamie's loin-revealing leotard shows her to be really *into* pelvic thrust. We know this must be love because it sure ain't normal sex.

Later, in a scene of unusual profundity, Jamie confesses, "I'm glad I met you, and I'm sorry I met you," to which John replies, "I'm glad you're glad you met me, and I'm sorry you're sorry you met me." With this communion of great minds firmly established, the scene is set for the implausible finale. John betrays Jamie, letting the world know about her innermost secrets, insulting her friends, ridiculing her work, placing her job in jeopardy. But when he goes to prison after refusing to hand over his tapes to the FBI, she realises he's a grand guy and, upon his release, she's standing there waiting to whisk him off to one more raunchy aerobics session.

It's the most vulgar, absurd, incredible film I've seen in years.

GEOFF ANDREW

THE HOLCROFT COVENANT

"What ever happened to So-and-so?" is a regular cry in and around Hollywood. It usually refers to stars or directors who, famous one decade, drop clean out of sight the next. But there are even sadder cases than this: those directors who are still busy working among us about whom one cries, "Whatever happened to So-and-so?" They are still up there in the public eye, but their talent seems to have dropped clean away like an engine from a plane in mid-flight.

Twenty years after wowing the intelligentsia with *The Manchurian Candidate*, John Frankenheimer comes up with *The Holcroft Covenant*. As if Sam Peckinpah's *The Osterman Weekend* had not already toured the world's cinemas ringing a leper's bell and warning the film industry, "Keep away from Robert Ludlum novels", here is another doomed bid to film a book by that master of formulaic prolixity.

Ludlum's plots usually have three basic ingredients. One is a top secret document and/or a vast cache of money. The second is an assortment of exotic locales. The third is a three-word title which invariably contains a definite article, a predicate and a noun. Anyone can invent his own Ludlum title: 'The Elsinore Escrow', 'The Bognor Identity', 'The Poughkeepsie Palimpsest' . . . The interchangeable mantras hiccup on from one book-jacket to the next.

The reek of formula is all over the movie as over the book. The Holcroft covenant of the title is a $4½ billion bequest left behind by three Nazi officers who shot themselves in a Berlin bunker. We see this in the credits sequence – scarlet Gothic letters over black-and-white action – and then, before you can say "Deutschmarks über alles", we tumble into the present day. Here we meet Michael Caine, all in colour and living as a successful architect in America. Soon banker and 'financial genius' Michael Lonsdale is beckoning Caine to Geneva and saying – or words to this effect – "You are Noel Holcroft, son of Nazi suicide-pact leader Heinrich Clausen, and you claim the four-and-a-half billion smackers."

But wait! Hearken to the labyrinthine ingenuity with which Ludlum and the film wrap up this bequest. Caine-Holcroft will have control of the cache, now stashed in a Swiss bank, only after he has *combed* the world and found the eldest sons of the other two dead Nazis, *proved* that he and they are made of the right stuff (as opposed to the Reich stuff), *convinced* the necessary people that the funds will be channelled in non-Nazi directions, and then co-signed the covenant with the other two Nazi offspring. Comments Lonsdale: "The word 'complicated' does not begin to describe your father." The word 'certifiable' does not begin to describe this film.

Its main narrative strategy is runaway implausibility. We can just about swallow, if we try, this convenant nonsense. And we can just about believe in Michael Caine as "a foreign-born American citizen". We can even accept that there *might* be four-and-a-half billion in Nazi loot swimming around in a Swiss bank.

But not content with these token improbabilities, director John Frankenheimer and his three scriptwriters – George Axelrod (of *The Manchurian Candidate*), Edward Anhalt (*The Young Lions*) and John Hopkins (TV's prize-winning *Talking to a Stranger*) – keep piling on the preposterous.

There is Anthony Andrews, for instance, popping up as Nazi son number two, and behaving as if descended from eight generations of Old Etonians. "He writes brilliant but mysterious articles on international finance for the *Guardian,"* says his sister Victoria Tennant. And there is Miss Tennant herself who becomes Caine's girlfriend ("I love you, Noel, I've never met a man like you before"). The speciality of these two siblings is to keep pointing out to Noel how endangered his (and their) lives are, yet to keep steering themselves into spectacularly exposed places. A Central London all-night riding school. The top of a viewing tower near Berlin's Brandenberg Gate. And, best of all, a midnight orgy in the Berlin streets, where nudes and transexuals cavort around a giant red high-heeled shoe. (I thought I was an expert on Berlin carnivals but this one is new to me.) Here, sure enough, someone tries to assassinate Caine.

Short of standing in the middle of "Checkpoint Charlie" wearing a luminous red tutu and waving a sparkler, it is difficult to see how Noel could more effectively keep putting himself in the firing line than he does in this film.

And so the climax approaches. The following questions require urgent answers. Who is behind all these assassination attempts? Are Andrews and Tennant playing a double game? Is the covenant all that it seems? Or perhaps even less? And what about the epigrammatic, epicene character from 'British Military Intelligence' (Bernard Hepton), is he on our side or theirs?

Goodness knows whose side Frankenheimer is on. He is certainly not on the audience's. The dialogue sustains a level of fatuity that can only be called remarkable. (Who could not cherish Lonsdale's brisk dismissal of a multi-bullet attempt on Caine's life in downtown Geneva? – "The world is full of lunatics shooting each other in the streets.") And Frankenheimer shows a compulsive but completely gratuitous fondness for tilted camera angles. Is he giving us a pastiche of *The Third Man* or did the tripod have one leg shorter than the other two?

With a best-selling novel, a sturdy McGuffin (Nazi millions) and all the high talent on display – top director, top screenwriters, top actors – one would have assumed that a colourful and rattling thriller, if not a deeply intelligent masterpiece, was in the making. But assumption, as Bernard Hepton says in one of the film's pithier moments, is the mother of fuck-up.

HARLAN KENNEDY

CAR TROUBLE

The funniest thing about *Car Trouble*, supposedly an 'outrageous' comedy, turns out to be the graphic used on its press material. This has a 2CV being humped – from the rear, significantly – by an E-type Jaguar. As you may have guessed, *Car Trouble* is all about sex and cars.

Or, perhaps more precisely, sex in cars. Apparently the writers got the idea from a newspaper cutting which detailed a couple who had become locked together while making love in a Mini. Strangely enough, the writers have said, the situation was far more common than most people realise, but it had never before been used as the basis for a piece of entertainment.

And, of course, they are absolutely right. The old vaginal spasm – surely a fun comic device if ever there was one – has been particularly notable by its absence from a whole history of the comic film. Chaplin, Keaton, Tracy & Hepburn, Laurel & Hardy, Mae West, Abbott & Costello and Woody Allen – to name just a neglectful few – seem, almost recklessly, to have ignored the hilarious possibilities of the *pudenda in extremis*.

On the other hand, possibly there are cans full of sparkling spasm sequences lying idly on dusty Hollywood shelves, consigned to oblivion simply because generations of fuddy-duddy executives refused to rip their side as, say, Carole Lombard writhed helplessly beneath Frederic March in *Nothing Sacred* or as Maureen O'Hara attempted to disentangle John Wayne in *The Quiet Man*.

So, after all these years, *Car Trouble* could be deemed a sort of 'first'; almost, in fact, a pioneer for sexual freedom in films.

But, like the mosquito which first introduced malaria or the inventor of napalm, this is another pioneer we would do well without. *Car Trouble* is a thoroughly horrid little film; that is, 'horrid' in its dictionary definition which suggests both 'repulsive' and 'annoying'.

It's said that the project started life as the basis for a half-hour TV sitcom, then mutated into a

possible revue piece for the theatre before evolving, finally, into a feature-length film script.

The real impetus then came as a result of what could be termed the Derek Jarman connection. One of the writers, James Whaley, passed on the script to his friend Howard Malin, with whom he had co-produced Jarman's *Sebastiane* and *Jubilee*, who in turn sent it to his close chum, actor Ian Charleson, another old Jarman alumnus. Charleson, then starring at the National in Sam Shepard's *Fool For Love*, suggested to his co-star, Julie Walters, that *Car Trouble* could be another 'vehicle' for their joint talents. Oddly, Miss Walters agreed.

The pair play a ghastly suburban couple called Gerald and Jacqueline Spong. He's an air-traffic controller and car nut, she's sexually frustrated. Gerald lusts after an E-type glistening in a nearby garage forecourt. Jacqueline, whose vagina remains untrammelled at this juncture, would prefer her husband's lust to be closer to home.

Anyway, Gerald gets his dream motor in part exchange for the tiny Citroën and enlists the help of Kevin, a smarmy, Italianate assistant garagiste to convert the wife to his cause. Which is where the vagina gets trammelled. Attempting a bunk-up, Jacqueline and Kevin's exertions result in the car sliding forward and crashing into a tree, and their being locked together. This pretty little tableau attracts not only casual passers-by but also Kevin's pregnant wife and a network television crew.

The story, "rooted", according to debutant director David Green, "in believability – so much so that it almost hurts", now has Gerald first seeing the newcast then, successively, trying to axe his wife to death, burning his house down and, finally, attempting to cause the mid-air collision of two jumbo jets in order to foil the escape of his spouse to Brazil. Believability?

Made, by today's standards, on a shoestring – that, at least, is in its favour – *Car Trouble* has a slice of American investment presumably to underscore the director's assertion that his models were *Ghostbusters* and *Beverly Hills Cop* rather than the *Carry Ons*. "Pace", and "energy", "a documentary/realistic approach" were Mr Green's tools. The result, I fear, is less *Beverly Hills Cop* and more Wembley Park Plod. In its way it's even more parochial than something like *A Letter to Brezhnev* which, among its many virtues, proudly proclaims its roots.

So what are actors like Walters and Charleson doing in trash like this, apart from doing favours for friends? She might have thought there was some fun to be had out of what she has described as "the Freeman's catalogue version of a character out of *Dynasty* or *Dallas*", and there's no denying she is always good for the odd chuckle. He appears to have no gift whatsoever for comedy and clearly believes that shouting and hysteria equals audience guffaws. His is almost a camped-up version of what constitutes angry, but wimpish, Semi-Detached Suburban British Man.

In fact – and here perhaps the Jarman Connection can be seen coming home to roost – *Car Trouble* could be interpreted as a Gay-eyed version of Straight Life. Certainly the film is deeply misogynistic – the women are fat, stupid or cuckolded, sometimes a mixture of all three – and offensively patronising, with the men merely tiresome stereotypes.

Of course, everything might be forgiven if this unpromising series of incidents yielded anything remotely amusing. What could have developed into something 'black' – by which I don't mean Gerald's proposed jumbo collision, which is unpardonably tasteless – and splendidly surreal remains stultifyingly unfunny and, more often, simply shy-making.

There are no limits to where laughter can be led – in Armageddon, if need be, when the material's as brilliant as *Dr Strangelove*, or even to cannibalism when Monty Python is calling the shots. The film-makers of *Car Trouble* may think the *Carry Ons* beneath them; they'd do well to revisit some of the videos and discover the truth of comic timing and good, clean, smut.

QUENTIN FALK

CREATOR

Is there a bigger ham actor in films today than Peter O'Toole? Leo McKern? Freddie Jones? Laurence Olivier? No. O'Toole it is. He wins not just for his scenery-devouring performance in his latest cinematic flopperoo *Creator* but also for his egotism in shouldering his co-star, poor squeaky Mariel Hemingway, right off the screen.

The movie attempts to pander to today's youthful audience with a *Pygmalion*-style love story. O'Toole plays a Nobel Laureate biologist whose best days in a white coat are behind him. A widower for thirty years now, he has lived in the hope that science would one day advance to the point where his beloved but long-dead wife could be brought back to life with the aid of a few cells from her body that he has kept.

Into this fossil's life bounces *soi-disant* nymphomaniac Mariel. The function of this character, who bears the non-name Meli, is to give the good doctor an egg for his test-tube. Her ovum offered, Meli resolves to stop fuddy-duddy old Prof O'Toole living in the past. She does this by talking dirty, wearing skimpy clothes and scoring a touchdown in a campus touch football game by flashing her scientifically enlarged breasts at her opponents.

The other redemptive force in O'Toole's life is Boris, his adoring assistant, played by Vincent Spano. It's Spano's duty to have a love interest (Virginia Madsen) who dies – Wait! She's still breathing. But she's in a coma, Boris. No, no, don't turn off her life-support system! Give her just forty-eight hours. Something might happen, a miracle maybe. Please, this is the movies, she could come back to life.

Ivan Passer is the unfortunate director of this lifeless romp, written by Jeremy Leven based on his own book. You can't say Passer has had a chequered career. It's been all black for this bounced Czech since he wrote scripts for Milos Forman back in their Prague spring days. *Ace Up My Sleeve, The Silver Bears, Cutter's Way* and now *Creator* – all bear the post-production thumbprint of others.

Completed in early 1984, *Creator*

wasn't released until September 1985, in that no-man's-land between summer comedies and autumn weepies. Whoever recut Passer's version couldn't find a balance between the attempted lightness of Hemingway's scenes and the heavy sexuality and gratuitous tragedy of the Spano-Madsen romance.

O'Toole is supposed to be the bridge between the two halves of the movie. But he's not an actor who you can believe is in love with anyone but the man in the mirror. He was superb in *My Favourite Year* precisely because he was playing a ham actor terminally in love with himself. He's also good as a period-piece TV villain, as in *Masada,* where wine-swilling and toga-swirling came with the territory.

But in *Creator* O'Toole is cast as an eccentric who plays the fool to hide his own deeply hidden hurt, sob. Jagged edges of cardboard backdrops hanging out of both sides of his mouth, O'Toole windmills his arms, angles his chin, pauses wisely and emotes dim witticisms, all but pointing a finger in the air as he does so. Every reel or so he addresses Hemingway as "my child". Put it all together and we're supposed to believe that this crabby old coot is actually a loveable young-at-heart. Mercy!

Like any ham, O'Toole's great talent is for filling vacuums. Business and mannerisms multiply in his scenes with Hemingway because otherwise the screen would be empty. Hemingway is simply unable to play the part of an irrepressible fairy god-daughter. She is not an actress.

This artless granddaughter of the bard of macho is a director's plaything. In *Manhattan, Personal Best* and *Star 80* she has played "herself in situations": underage beloved of Woody Allen, seduced hurdler who goes straight, and nude-posing murder victim. Her strength was her directness and lack of pretence. She was like the subject of documentaries. She was a 'natural'.

In *Creator,* however, she is called on to pretend, and it's painfully clear on the screen that she's play-acting. Not for a second does she believe Meli is real, nor does the audience. Hemingway was equally bad in *The Mean Season,* in a shrieking little one-note role that could only have been played successfully by an actress who could play more than one note.

From a story-analysis point of view, *Creator* is a brave attempt to ring a change on an oft-told situation. Hollywood has seen the declining grosses earned by brat-pack casts in stories you can follow with your eyes closed. A year before, the Vincent Spano part might have been played by Rob Lowe and the O'Toole part would have been a walk-on. Maybe re-orienting the picture towards 16-year-olds would have improved it.

Reincarnation or regeneration or rebirth – whatever it is that Prof O'Toole is trying to accomplish – is a concept people liked to play around with back in the sixties. In the eighties, we're more interested in getting ahead in the world as it is. Sprites like Meli get short shrift now. In the Reagan era, when there's a user-fee for everything, there's no such thing as a free spirit any more.

BART MILLS

SANTA CLAUS – THE MOVIE

Making films for kids has always been a hazardous business. By their very nature, films have to be made by adults, or at least by those who according to the laws of experience, technological skill and management are no longer children. Steven Spielberg might disagree, but as an overgrown kid himself he occupies a unique position in the pantheon of film-makers. The real problem lies in the identification of the needs of the market. Children now, such is the progress of our society, can get as much enjoyment from re-running the nastiest moments of a horror movie on their parents' video as they might have done in the past from watching Dumbo save himself from a squishy death by flapping his ears.

Maybe times change and children have become more cynical over the years, but this possible degeneration is nothing compared with the descending values of film-makers who claim to operate in the long-forgotten land of the Family Film. With the notable exception of Colin Finbow and the Childrens' Film Foundation, who make films for and with children, film-makers have succeeded in cocking up every attempt at inveigling themselves back into the lucrative market of the Kids'/Family Film. Perhaps the last great example was *The Railway Children*, which succeeded in being both entertaining and intelligent, sentimental without being utterly soppy. It appears to have been a one-off for director Lionel Jeffries as he has subsequently failed to come up with anything as influential since. But at least he did it. Most of them never get past the starting gate.

Take *Santa Claus – The Movie*. If ever there was a more cynical exercise in marketing strategy I have yet to see it. One can only rejoice that the whole wretched exercise went so disastrously wrong. Produced by the Salkinds, Alexander and Ilya, who were clever enough to give us *Superman* then stupid enough to give us two sequels and the abysmal *Supergirl*, *Santa Claus* must rank as one of the most ill-conceived

movies of all time. To cast Dudley Moore as a recalcitrant elf may have seemed like a good idea once, but why he agreed to become embroiled in this fiasco remains one of the great unsolved mysteries of our time. He can't have needed the money.

The concept is purest liberal kitsch. Hundreds of years ago, a simple woodcutter (he'd have to be) is magically transported to the North Pole where he becomes Santa Claus. He also becomes immortal so the poor old sod is well and truly lumbered. In modern times one of his toy-making elves, Patch (Moore), makes a mess of his job and heads for New York where he becomes involved in a villain's schemes to produce magical Christmas presents. As the villain, B.Z., is played by the redoubtable John Lithgow we at least get value for money in the corporate evil department, but that's about all. Oh yes, we do get the obligatory special effects from good old Derek Meddings, a Salkind stalwart who worked on the Superperson films, who makes Santa's sleigh fly through the air with the greatest of ease along with Patch's customised contraption – but it's not enough.

What really grates about *Santa Claus* is the way it treats children as imbeciles by attempting to satisfy their cravings for sensation and decimating their brain cells with a witless script that includes a string of 'elf' puns like "elf-conscious" and "elf-portrait". The profoundest irony of all is that the nature of Lithgow's villain is remarkably close to that of the Salkinds themselves. B.Z. wants to institute two Christmases a year so he can sell more toys and make more money. *Santa Claus* was made to capitalise on the Christmas market from now until Doomsday. Well, if you will spend fifty million bucks on a film, I guess you're going to have to go some to see a return. And whatever you may believe about the Salkinds' motivation behind making this film, an act of charity it was not.

It's all so *cute*. *E.T.* looks a real hardnut in comparison, an alien skinhead as opposed to Cuddly Dudley's winsome mischief. And when you consider the really distinctive fantasy childrens' films made in the last few years like *Time Bandits* and *Gremlins*, you can see why *Santa Claus* is such a mess. It tries to please everyone, takes no risks and throws in a completely bogus moral argument to boot. The transparency of the film is one thing, and may escape the youngest of the audience. The lousy direction is another and was duly spotted by just bout everyone. Jeannot Szwarc, who brought us the questionable delights of *Enigma* (which more or less killed Derek Jacobi's film career stone dead) and *Supergirl* (in which he attempted a triple assassination on Helen Slater, Faye Dunaway and Peter Cook), directs *Santa Claus* like a lemming with a limp; he can't wait to end it all but takes a painfully long time getting to his destination.

Distributors and cinema managers who are intending to book this film for the festive season should scrutinise the small print at the bottom of the contract. Be advised: there ain't no sanity clause.

NEIL NORMAN

REVOLUTION

"Dear Member of the Media," ran the Warner Bros press release. "We are sending you these litho prints to give you a better idea of the scope, spirit, and overall magnificence that we believe is inherent in *Revolution.*" Attractively posed portraits of the stars in period dress mixed with similarly striking group scenes (street fighting, marching troops, cast-of-thousands on the battlefields) do create a favourable impression. No question that director Hugh Hudson and his collaborators have something very special in mind.

Or is there something else at play here? Strange how an initially favourable impression suddenly becomes clouded over by an unsettling sense of *déja vu.* Oh yes. Oh *no! Heaven's Gate!*

Industry scribes well remember how months prior to the première of Cimino's Folly a special advertising supplement was inserted in the weekly edition of *Variety.* Ordinarily a glossy extra of this kind would be confected to promote an entire slate of studio products. This time only one film was involved. Featuring portraits of *Heaven's Gate* stars, as well as group action scenes, the insert was designed to give exhibitors a first tantalising peek at a film that up until then had received nothing but negative pre-release publicity. But rather than stave off the doomsayers, the *Heaven's Gate* ad only helped to goad them on. The consensus was that for all the millions spent on the thing it looked . . . well, *dowdy.*

So here we are some five years later looking at another costly graphics snow job designed to disguise a disaster. For off the litho page and up on the silver screen *Revolution* is purely and simply *Heaven's Gate Redux.* Not quite as costly as its predecessor perhaps, but just as tedious, just as pretentious, just as wasteful. What makes *Revolution* worse than *Gate* is the sneaking suspicion that Hudson, rather than cook this turkey of his own accord, used Cimino's fiasco for a recipe. How else to account for an epic historical drama void of character and narrative development but filled to the rafters with meaningless detail (costumes, sets, props, etc) – all dressed up with no place to go?

"Al Pacino is Tom Dobb, the colonialist and widower who is swept into the conflict. Donald Sutherland is Sgt Peasy, the hardened, loyal instrument of the Crown. Nastassja Kinski is Daisy McConnahay, the blue-blooded daughter of a wealthy loyalist who believes fiercely in the cause of independence . . . and Tom Dobb." So reads the film's ad copy. But without this scorecard you'd be hard-pressed to know exactly who's who or what's what as one lifeless shapeless scene follows another. Crowds jeer and bellow as they swarm through city streets. Crowds jeer and bellow as they swarm across battlefields. Pacino, Kinski, and Sutherland are the nominal centres of this jeering, bellowing swarm – but just barely.

We see Pacino "swept into the conflict" but we never discover where he came from, where he wants to go to, or anything that happens to be on his mind along the way. We see Kinski defying her family by leaping from their carriage into a mob of rebel supporters, but we're given no information as to how this "blue-blooded daughter of a loyalist" got radicalised. Clearly such mundane narrative interests are above the likes of Hudson. He wants you to be involved in what's going on all right but not through character and story. The sweep of history itself is what Hudson has in mind and he means to capture it by the literal sweep of his camera.

Every shot in this slightly-over-two-hour production is a moving one. Like a hyperactive adolescent the camera is ceaselessly running across spaces, circling about performers or trundling along after them puppy-dog fashion. *Cinema verité* realism is the desired effect. But motion sickness quickly takes precedence over aesthetics as Hudson's *mise-en-jog* reduces everything in sight to a pile of peripatetic mush. The sole moment of mobile respite comes when the camera pauses to peer at the large hairy wart plastered on Donald Sutherland's face. Underdeveloped as Pacino's and Kinski's parts may be they're virtually multi-layered in comparison to Sutherland's sadistic "instrument of the Crown." Outside of a vague yen for prepubescent drummer boys, only this wart delineates his character.

Okay, okay. Let's be as fair as we possibly can. Perhaps there's something we're missing in all of this. Why should Hudson be held to dealing with conventions of plot and character when the likes of Jean-Luc Godard roam free? Clearly Hudson's people and places aren't being presented simply as dramatic fodder. They're part of a vast tapestry. Why just look at that woman over there! Well, she's gone now, but for the second or two she was on screen she suggested less a character than an ideogrammatic *essence* of the period. No?

No. That's what Hudson's looking to do all right, but that's not what he actually does. Putting conventions on the back burner in order to treat the screen as an audio-visual dynamic can only be done when conventions pertaining to realism are abandoned. Hudson is far too caught up in them. He wants the look and feel of 'the way it was' as much as possible. Throwing plot and character out the window in this context results in all tail and no dog. Like Cimino before him, Hudson has thrown what doubtless started as a perfectly straightforward script to the winds and marched off in search of the images that would somehow galvanise the whole show into life. But as his camera stumbles through smoke, fire, and mobs of expensively costumed extras it's clear he's not going to find them.

What *we* the viewers find is fairly simply stated. Pacino and Kinski cross paths early on, make decorous goo-goo eyes at each other, then get pulled apart by the mob. A few scenes later at a different locale they meet as arbitrarily as before and resume their flirtation. Yes, we know – "heroic individuals torn existentially asunder by the forces of history", right? But all we see on the screen are a pair of international stars trapped in an elaborate, overextended, period-set 'Meet Cute'.

No, this wasn't at all what those prints suggested. But in a way the *Revolution* press kit is the one positive aspect to emerge from the whole affair. After the Sunday supplement callisthenics of *Chariots of Fire,* and the ersatz nineteenth-century landscape painting of *Greystoke,* in *Revolution* Hugh Hudson has discovered his true *métier* – lithography.

DAVID EHRENSTEIN

RED SONJA

I don't know who managed to persuade Dino de Laurentiis that the debased fantasy genre known as Sword and Sorcery would bring big bucks at the box office. Maybe Dino remembered how, in the fifties and sixties, the former Mr Universe Steve Reeves, with muscles where most of us can only manage goose pimples, had posed his way through a succession of silly mythological romps, enriching the Italian film industry and adding to the gaiety of nations.

Thus it was that the great man bought the rights to the ridiculous books of Robert E Howard, realised the grotesque potential of Arnold Schwarzenegger, who makes Reeves look like the 'before' part of a Charles Atlas commercial, and gave *Conan the Barbarian* to an uninterested world.

Whoever the sales genius was, he deserves the death of a thousand cuts, although that might be better inflicted on *Red Sonja,* an attempt at a female, but not a feminist, *Conan,* that can be recommended only as the ultimate soporific. It requires not merely the usual suspension of disbelief, but the narcolepsis of any critical faculty, and a willingness to ignore not only its lack of sense, but the ineptness of its special effects and its not-so-special cast.

Its halting narrative, dire music and dialogue, dramatic bungling and discothèque decor are the more remarkable because they are the work of men of talent. The director was Richard Fleischer, a gentle and eminently civilised man, whose work includes good thrillers *(Compulsion),* swashbuckling adventure *(20,000 Leagues Under the Sea),* and the admirable *10 Rillington Place.* Nothing in his past, not even *Che!,* prepares one for the dullness of *Red Sonja.*

The screenwriters were Clive Exton, one of the great talents of the golden age of British television drama (even though that lasted only a month or two), and the brashly witty George Macdonald Fraser. From the opening lines it is clear that both were out to lunch when the script was written:

"She Lived in a Savage World in an Age of Violence ...
A Fierce Warrior with
Flaming Red Hair.
In the Hyborian Kingdom
Her Quest for Justice and
Vengeance Became a Legend
This is How the Legend Began"

The plot is the usual nonsense. Sonja's family is slaughtered by the army of a wicked queen who then tries to seduce her. Whereupon a shimmering shape materialises in mid-air, gives her the strength that will defeat all comers and provides a summary of the plot for late-comers. Who this fairy godmother is, is never explained. Sonja's idea of justice turns out to be slaughtering those who don't agree with her, which is a novel notion. Meanwhile at a nearby temple, the priestesses – who look as if they've been recruited from a Las Vegas floor show – are burying a talisman used to create the world because light has made it too powerful. Don't ask why. If you want logic, go watch James Bond.

Enter the baddies who kill the chorus girls and grab the crystal, which they take back to the queen's castle, where they keep it in a room full of candles. Most of the movie's budget seems to have been spent on the candles, though (presumably as an economy measure, or maybe becuase it was a windy studio) they are never all alight at the same time.

Sonja's sister escapes from the temple and, making her getaway, is shot by a wicked archer. I say shot, but the arrow clearly sticks in a large square object that, for some reason, she wears on her back under her skimpy costume. Maybe it was the fashion among priestesses. Grieving over her punctured box, she finds Sonja and expires.

Watching is Schwarzenegger, as a Conan look-alike called Kalidor. His brow furrows slowly and you can almost see the synapses closing as a message struggles along the difficult journey from brain to lips and tongue. There is a pause long enough for even the slowest members of the audience to buy an ice-cream or some popcorn and settle back in their seats. Finally, the revelation comes. "She's dead," he says.

Kalidor is also aggrieved with the queen, who "slaughtered my parents like caddle." (All the dialogue tends to tarnish upon contact with the air, especially when delivered by actors with wooden tongues.) "You're a brave girl," mouths Schwarzenegger at one point, in that curious voice which sounds as if he's been dubbed by Henry Kissinger, "but danger is my trade." Says Sonja, "Then I'll learn it by myself," a reply which increases his ever-present bafflement, as well it might. Learn what?

Brigitte Nielsen as the long-legged Sonja matches his monotone (though as with Victor Mature and Hedy Lamarr in *Samson and Delilah,* he is the one with the bigger breasts). But the performance that must rank (and that's definitely the right word) among the worst not merely of this film, but of any movie ever made is that of Sandahl Bergman as the evil queen. She can't even laugh convincingly.

Face to face with the talisman, she remarks in the voice of a provincial housewife confronted by a new miracle cleaner, giving each word the same emphasis: "So. This. Can. Make. Worlds. Or. Shatter. Them. By. Storm. And Earthquake."

What intrigues is Miss Bergman's cheek, clawed open by Sonja at the beginning of the film. The scars are still there in close-up in the final confrontation. But in long shot and during the screaming struggle between them, they have disappeared. Maybe the make-up man went home early that day.

The movie is not so much about a legendary female warrior as something closer to the tastes of the suburban male. Whenever Sonja faces trouble, there is Kalidor to save her. It's the story of the helpless little woman who can't manage without a man – needing him to perform the equivalent, in a savage world and a violent time, of mending fuses and putting up bookshelves. It is, as all Robert E Howard's stories are, a fantasy fuelled by the wish-fulfilment of an unattractive, mother-dominated braggart. Howard shot himself. Maybe the film's makers could do likewise.

John Walker

FACES OF THE YEAR
DANIEL DAY LEWIS

Meet four men. The first has the swagger of a street-smart Cockney, the cocky strut of a man looking for trouble. From his short hair with its bleached fringe to his heavy boots, made for kicking, he is a would-be thug playing at fascism. He slouches threateningly, seeking some provocative act to enrage passers-by, hoping to find a Paki to bash. His wiry body suggests a tensile strength. His voice has the aggressive whine of Sarf London, know what I mean . . ?

The second is an etiolated aristocratic aesthete, who has a pale passion for art, preferring it to the headier excesses of life. From his long, wavy hair and precisely placed pince-nez, he is a man who might form one angle of a platonic triangle in some Bloomsbury square. He holds himself carefully erect, as if contact with anything might prove too much for his fastidious sensibilities. He speaks in the precise and strangulated tones of Edwardian England . . .

The third is an impassioned poet, violently opinionated. With his cropped hair and charismatic gifts as a performer, he is a sort of intellectual skinhead, putting the poetic boot in all who oppose revolution, scarifying smug bureaucrats and complacent philistines. Arms flapping as he reads his verse, dark eyes staring from a gaunt profile, he resembles a fierce bird of prey . . .

The fourth is Daniel Day Lewis, an actor who has brilliantly succeeded in the above three widely different roles in the past year. Two were in excellent low-budget British films – as a Cockney in *My Beautiful Laundrette* (cost £600,000) and as the ascetic Cecil Wyse in *A Room With a View*, which was made for £2.4 million. The third was as the hectic, suicidal Russian poet, playwright and film star Vladimir Mayakovsky in Dusty Hughes' play *The Futurists*, first performed at the National Theatre although it was originally commissioned as a television drama.

What was astonishing was not only the range Day Lewis displayed, but the depth of characterisation that he brought to each role. There is a great deal of wit in his acting, which is especially evident in *A Room With a View*, in his cruelly exact portrayal of the sadly insufferable Cecil Wyse, the languid, ideal bachelor who becomes Lucy Honeychurch's unloved fiancé. There was the delicately-timed comedy of Cecil attempting to kiss Lucy for the first time. His self-conscious, tentative approach, as if advancing over a mine-field, his bungling while trying to keep his pince-nez in place was a superbly judged moment. So was the later scene, as Cecil slashed at the undergrowth with his cane to lead a party of ladies away from the unseemly sight of men bathing naked in a woodland pond. The abrupt movements of the man captured Cecil's character of rigid refinement.

Johnny, the Cockney of *My Beautiful Laundrette*, evaded stereotype. He was convincingly tough, but also surprisingly tender, particularly in gently passionate love scenes with Pakistani Omar (Gordon Warneke), an old schoolfriend who involves him in his get-rich-quick plans to revive a dilapidated launderette. Johnny, a former fascist who eschews violence, becomes with Omar's father the moral centre of the movie. Indeed the confrontation between him and Omar's father (the brilliant Roshan Seth), Johnny's former mentor and an alcoholic left-wing journalist, carries a powerful emotional charge not so much because of what is said – virtually nothing is said – but in the interaction of the two: the old man and the young remembering the past, with its betrayal when Johnny marched with the racist National Front, and the present, with both joined in their love for Omar.

That same feeling of truth, of a relationship that extends in time beyond the limits of the movie, comes through in the love that exists between Omar and Johnny, which must be one of the most natural homosexual relationships to find its way on to film. In the final scene, as Johnny washes away the blood from the beating he has received from his fascist friends, little again is said. But as the two boys stand stripped to the waist, splashing each other with water, the audience is left with a feeling of a sustaining tenderness.

Day Lewis bears a famous name. His father was Cecil Day Lewis, publisher, detective-story writer and poet of the thirties, though presumably his talent derives more from his mother, the actress Jill Balcon. He began as a stage actor, playing at the Bristol Old Vic, which also nurtured the mercurial Peter O'Toole, although his performances there were not particularly memorable. He first came to notice in *Another Country*, Julian Mitchell's play of the public-school betrayals that underlay the Burgess-Maclean affair.

His acting has that sense of danger that marks the best performances, although his screen roles have not yet displayed all his talents. He can also manage the style of a romantic hero, if anyone still makes films that require such, and has done so on television in superior soap opera. He is not only an actor to watch with pleasure, a character actor of rare accomplishment. Given the right role, he could prove an enduring star.

John Walker

AIDAN QUINN

I had never heard of Aidan Quinn, let alone seen him, before *Desperately Seeking Susan*. Quinn plays Dez, a projectionist, who, via the plot's intricate web of mistaken identity, is lucky enough to snare an affair with Rosanna Arquette.

Arquette is rather lucky, too. She might, after all, have been lumbered with grotesque Sean Penn or mannered Nicolas Cage from the same generation of young actors as Quinn and to whom he is a glowing exception. His Dez was a performance of such effortless charm and his screen presence so easy on the eye that I remember actually jotting down in my 'Film Critic's Notebook' that he was an actor to watch.

Born in Chicago of Irish immigrant parents – second of five children – he moved back to Ireland with his family first when he was tiny and again when he was 13. After high school, he returned yet again to Dublin where he would attend lunchtime shows at a local college because soup and a sandwich came with the ticket price.

It was while he was, at the age of 19, toiling as a roofer atop a 30-story Chicago skyscraper that Quinn first seemed to have pangs about the Meaning of Life, and his own in particular.

"I was freezing to death, pouring boiling tar and surrounded by alcoholics, ex-convicts and street hoods. It was 7.30 in the morning and we were washing down our breakfast of greasy doughnuts with half pints of whisky. Suddenly I thought, 'What the hell am I doing here? Is this where my life is going?'" The answer appears to have been 'nowhere', so he took acting classes instead.

So impressed were they with his natural acting ability that Quinn was awarded a scholarship. He scored enough of a hit in his very first role, in the play *The Man in 605* by Alan Gross, that choice parts in Chicago productions of Chekhov, Brecht and Faulkner followed. This led to a casting agent showing director James Foley a Polaroid of Quinn which, in turn, led to the lead in a film called *Reckless*, co-starring with Daryl Hannah. Before the film opened there was talk of the newcomer as "the next James Dean". Quinn was sent out on a promotional tour where interviewers asked him how he liked the movie. "Not much", came the indiscreet answer. He said he tried avoiding the question but it kept coming up, "and I can't lie."

Quinn took his $20,000 fee from *Reckless* and blew it on another trip back to Ireland before returning to Chicago, this time as a cocktail waiter and, in his own opinion, an extremely inept one at that.

Having got *Reckless* out of his system, he went back to the stage, first in Marisha Chamberlain's award-winning *Scheherazade*, followed by Sam Shepard's *Fool for Love*. Despite his own feelings about his movie debut, it did lead to a lot of offers of work, most of which he turned down. Until *Desperately Seeking Susan*, and "I wouldn't have taken Dez if I didn't like the character, the director or the project." Quinn says he is very choosy about roles.

"I know most guys would jump at things I've said no to. I can understand why when I turned down roles a lot of people are infuriated. I just have very strong principles." Such introspection is rumoured to make him difficult to work with. According to Seidelman: "I won't say we had an easy working relationship but what I got on film is worth it. He's a thinker and it shows."

She also pinpointed another aspect of his personality: "He's enormously appealing on screen – sexy, warm and very vulnerable. He's the kind of guy women want to take care of them." For his part, he said he liked "the sense of humour and the wackiness" of her film.

His next assignment couldn't have been much more different – a modern-dress *Hamlet* in Chicago, complete with video cameras, tape recorders, and Talking Heads' 'Burning Down The House'. His soliloquy opened with him can-spraying a wall "To be or not to be," before whirling round to the audience with, "that is the question". Madness was feigned with the help of a Slinky – one of those yo-yo like, extending wire tube affairs. The production appears to have been a huge success.

If he has, from time to time, frustrated film-makers with his choosiness, then he must have endured a considerable slice himself when he found himself tapped for a major role in a movie that was cancelled less than a month before filming. He was to have been the lead in Martin Scorsese's *The Last Temptation of Christ*, adapted from Kazantzakis's work.

When the project collapsed, the director turned round swiftly into *After Hours* while Quinn took what, frankly, amounts to little more than a spit and cough in Roland Joffé's *The Mission*. He plays Robert De Niro's younger brother in the epic tale of slave traders versus Jesuits in mid-eighteenth century South America. Barely surviving the first reel before being dispatched by his jealous sibling, Quinn has, apart from a continuingly handsome presence, no real chance to impress with his acting.

The balance is redressed by his fine work in one of American television's most impressive 'issue' movies to date, *An Early Frost* in which he co-stars with Ben Gazzara and Gena Rowlands. Quinn plays Michael Pearson, a successful young lawyer and erstwhile yuppie who also happens to be a homosexual and AIDS victim. The tale traces his decline, set against his conservative family's initial horror and eventual sympathy. While not managing totally to eliminate elements of a liberal public service announcement, it works very well as drama and Quinn quite simply confirms that he is "the next James Dean" but very much his own man. His future, straddling stage and screen, seems bright indeed.

Quentin Falk

MOLLY RINGWALD

A few good things had to come out of the teen-pic movement of the last few years, and one of them is definitely Molly Ringwald. A fashionable ugly duckling, to whom the lips are what the nose is to Streisand, an idol within the reach of any awkward, real-life high-school girl, a young lady of "charismatic normality", in Pauline Kael's phrase, an actress who celebrated stardom at 16 and a multi-pic development deal at 18, she and her former boyfriend Anthony Michael Hall are easily the most likeable and accessible of the new crop of kid stars, as well as the ones with the most visible potential.

She is best known for her John Hughes 'teen princess trilogy' of 1983-1986 – *Sixteen Candles, The Breakfast Club* and *Pretty in Pink*. In the surprising and engaging first entry, Hughes made splendid use of her talent for expressing exasperation, pique and gaping incredulity at the imbecility of her family and the outrageous antics of the pixie-ish suitor so forwardly played by Hall. Caught at the difficult, transitional age of 15, she was unafraid of displaying her adolescent flaws and even of complaining about them, but was convincingly attractive enough to flower at the end as the object of her dream boy's attention.

Although she had proved in one outing that she could carry a film, she merged with the ensemble in *The Breakfast Club,* Hughes' half-successful attempt at a serious think-piece. Ringwald has said she didn't identify with her character of a stuck-up rich girl forced to spend a detention day with low-life classmates and finally stripped of her pretensions by them, and rather responded to the eccentric loner portrayed by Ally Sheedy. It's easy to see why, since Sheedy's character, like Ringwald herself, emerges as a winner in spite of apparent initial handicaps; her innate sense of style makes her hip, whereas everything Ringwald's condescending goody-goody thinks she is has to be destroyed before she can emerge with some dignity. Once again, and in a more dramatic context, Ringwald displayed impressive vulnerability, notably when being grilled about the true (and nonexistent) extent of her sexual life.

Hughes wrote *Pretty in Pink* expressly for her, and Ringwald and those around her allowed that in it she basically played herself. Her penchant for imaginative wardrobe creations was indulged extravagantly, and even though Howard Deutch, not Hughes, directed this time, Ringwald embellished and expanded upon her humorous repertoire of expressions for boredom and the patience necessary to endure the fools life often puts one up against. Even better, she had a quiet, tearful, devastated scene with Andrew McCarthy in a car in the rain that, for the first time, indicated what she might achieve as a mature actress. It's a brief scene, almost a throwaway, but it showed something brand new and extremely promising from her.

Born in 1968 in Roseville, California, she has been an irrepressible performer all her life. At four she began singing with the Great Pacific Jazz Band, of which her father, blind Dixieland jazz musician Bob Ringwald, was a prominent member. Two years later, she cut an LP called *Molly Sings,* and at about the same time began appearing in school and community theatre productions, including Truman Capote's *The Grass Harp* and *Through the Looking Glass* (as the Dormouse).

Her big break came at nine, when she won the role of Kate, one of the orphans, in the West Coast production of the hit musical *Annie*. This relocated the family to Los Angeles (the San Fernando Valley, to be specific), and at 11 she became a semi-regular on the television show, *The Facts of Life*.

Crushed when cut from the series after one year, she quickly recouped by snaring the part of John Cassavetes' pubescent daughter in Paul Mazursky's *Tempest*. It was a bit of a stretch for this girl, who had never been outside California, to become such a thoroughgoing New York kid, but Mazursky put the family up in an apartment in Greenwich Village for a few months and Ringwald responded with a lively, watchful performance which served as an admirable counterpoint to the louder histrionics of others in the cast.

From there, it was on to play a superbrat in the already forgotten 3-D sci-fi epic, *Spacehunter: Adventures in the Forbidden Zone,* as well as leads in the TV movies *Packin' It In* and *Surviving,* in the latter as a suicidal teen.

The John Hughes films made her a star, and up until now it has been well worth seeing anything she's done simply to observe her work (it is difficult to think of many other performers of her generation for whom this is the case). But a key connection had been made as early as *Tempest,* for, after seeing it, Warren Beatty called her at her parents' home to say how much he'd liked her in it. Beatty soon became friendly, not only with Ringwald, but with her family and other young actors in her group. The story is told of Beatty's taking her to dinner with Democratic Presidential hopeful Gary Hart, and of how she related the experience to her disbelieving high-school history class the next day.

Ringwald dismisses rumours of romance, but, whatever the case, she and Beatty appear to have quite a present and future together. She most recently starred in Beatty's production of *The Pick-Up Artist* for writer-director James Toback, who can't help but take the actress into rawer, more adult territory. Directly thereafter comes *To Gillian on Her 37th Birthday,* from the Off-Broadway play, for Peter Bogdanovich. Cooking slowly with Beatty, though, waiting for her to grow old enough, is the life story of Warhol superstar Edie Sedgwick. Beatty bought the book about Edie with Ringwald in mind but, strangely, the actress was obsessed with playing Edie even before, at 15. A poster of the doomed, upper-class drug addict adorned her wall at home, and she has professed a willingness to play nude scenes if necessary in order to get the story on the screen. A dark subject for a well-adjusted kid to tackle, but it seems that it is the very unfamiliarity, the complete differentness of Edie, that attracts Ringwald, that drives this California girl East, underground and back in time to a scene that was playing itself out when she was a baby. From the looks of things, it won't take long for Molly Ringwald to leave the Brat Packers in her dust.

TODD McCARTHY

MICHAEL J FOX

The fact that the past action of *Back to the Future* – the film which at a stroke made Michael J Fox a bankable name – is set in 1955 has a certain appropriateness. For this was the year which witnessed not only the effective inauguration of youth culture but also the death and apotheosis of James Dean; and for all that the social pendulum has in the intervening decades swung toward permissiveness and back to conservatism, Dean remains the figure against whom youth heroes in the movies tend to be measured. But while such present-day performers as Emilio Estevez or (particularly) Matt Dillon are in some ways cast in the Dean mould, Fox is not, in terms of either appearance or aura (though he bears a passing likeness to the Martin Sheen of a dozen years ago, when the latter attracted attention in a Dean-like role in *Badlands*).

There is, however, one intriguing parallel: Dean's most celebrated screen manifestation, in *Rebel Without a Cause*, saw him at the age of 23 incarnating a high school student of 17; and precisely the same discrepancy applies to the casting of Fox (born 9 June 1961) in *Back to the Future*. And if Dean was slight in stature, Fox at 5ft 4in is slighter still, and this ability to pass for younger than his years proves to have been his stock-in-trade as a performer.

Fox's professional beginnings came when in his early teens and at the instigation of his drama teacher he successfully auditioned for the part of a 10-year-old in a TV series, *Leo and Me*, then being prepared in his native Canada, where he had spent a contented if peripatetic childhood as one of the five offspring of a professional soldier. From this encouraging start, Fox hardly looked back. In 1978 he was cast as Art Carney's grandson in an American TV movie shot in Vancouver, and the following year he decamped for Hollywood and an intensive grounding in television soaps and sitcoms. He also played minor roles in a couple of less than minor theatrical movies: *Midnight Madness*, a Disney farce, and *Class of '84*, a rabble-rousing

exploitationer ("It achieves a degree of awfulness that, though rare, isn't funny" – *New York Times*).

These undertakings seem to have been of little more than alimentary use, but a breakthrough came when he landed a key role in the NBC comedy series *Family Ties*, which (though it has kept a low profile in Britain) recovered in the US from a slow start to gain a consistent place near the top of the ratings – an achievement resting substantially, it would appear, on the basis of Fox's appeal in the role of a boy five years his junior. It is interesting, moreover, that the role which set the seal on Fox's TV reputation should have been that of the arch-conservative son who in an ingenious twist on the generation gap is forever at odds with his ex-hippie parents – a buttoned-down comic hero for the Reaganite times.

Fox was apparently the original choice of Steven Spielberg and Robert Zemeckis for *Back to the Future*, but was ruled out because of a contractual commitment to *Family Ties*. But after the picture was closed down when producer and director became dissatisfied with Eric Stoltz's performance, a deal was struck whereby Fox could work on the TV show by day and on the movie at night. This regimen unsurprisingly left Fox with a minimum of spare energy, but the strain fails to show on the screen.

The part of Marty in *Future* gives Fox a star 'entrance' – removal of sunglasses in close-up – and he proceeds to live up to it. Fox's capacity to hijack the viewer's attention comes partly from technique, both physical, in the matter of taking pratfalls, and verbal, too: note the exact timing and intonation of his one-word reply, "Nothing", to Doc's inquiry about what his parents enjoy doing together. But he reveals also the movie actor's capacity for stillness, for not seeming to be acting at all (cleverly played off by the director against the manic demeanour of Doc and the exaggerated clumsiness of Marty's father). But of course Fox is not really doing nothing: watch, for instance, the discreet play of hand gestures during the long, dinner-table scene where he first meets his familial antecedents. There is a delicacy, here and elsewhere, which is a reassuringly far cry from Stallone-style machismo; it might even be claimed that Fox, with his slightly high voice and occasionally fluttering eyelashes, possesses an undertow of the androgynous, a sort of male equivalent of the young Audrey Hepburn.

Pauline Kael in the *New Yorker* aptly termed Fox's playing "a form of aerobics – he's poised, he's nimble and proficient," but rather spoiled things by adding that "he delivers a processed TV actor's charm." Such responses are necessarily subjective, but Fox's charm to this writer looks processed only in the sense of being photographed. Perhaps, though, his quality of spontaneity emerges more demonstrably in *Teen Wolf* (a quickie made before *Future*, but cannily released after it to enormous box-office success, seemingly predicated to a high degree on Fox's presence in it). For just because this witless comedy provides so undistracting a frame for its central performer, one can perceive the more clearly the natural ease and loose-limbed conviction which Fox can bring to inconsequential scenes such as that in which he walks home from school with his girlfriend.

Fox understandably hankers after escaping from teenage parts, and has said that "I always envisaged myself as a character actor"; the middle 'J' in his name proves to have been an invention in homage to Michael J Pollard, the diminutive side-shot player who gained fame as 'C.W.' in *Bonnie and Clyde*. Somehow, though, with the central role in Paul Schrader's *Light of Day* ("Maybe I'll even be allowed to shave in this one") already lined up, one would risk a modest wager that his name will remain safely above the title for some little time to come.

TIM PULLEINE

KIM BASINGER

"You have to be a little unreal to be in this business," Kim Basinger remarked – almost matter-of-factly – in a recent interview. No argument there. Unreality has always been Hollywood's stock-in-trade – particularly when it comes to feminine beauty. With her too-full Bardot lips, smooth creamy features, and elegant high-fashion bearing, Basinger more than fits this bill. Moreover, it's the 'little' aspect of her 'unreality' that's most apparent. For beneath the deluxe surface trappings this Georgia-born beauty has always managed to let a solid bedrock of the 'real' show through. She's a stunner, but *sane*. You can sit down and *talk* with Kim Basinger. Well, you can't talk for long of course – she's got a career to take care of. But you can talk.

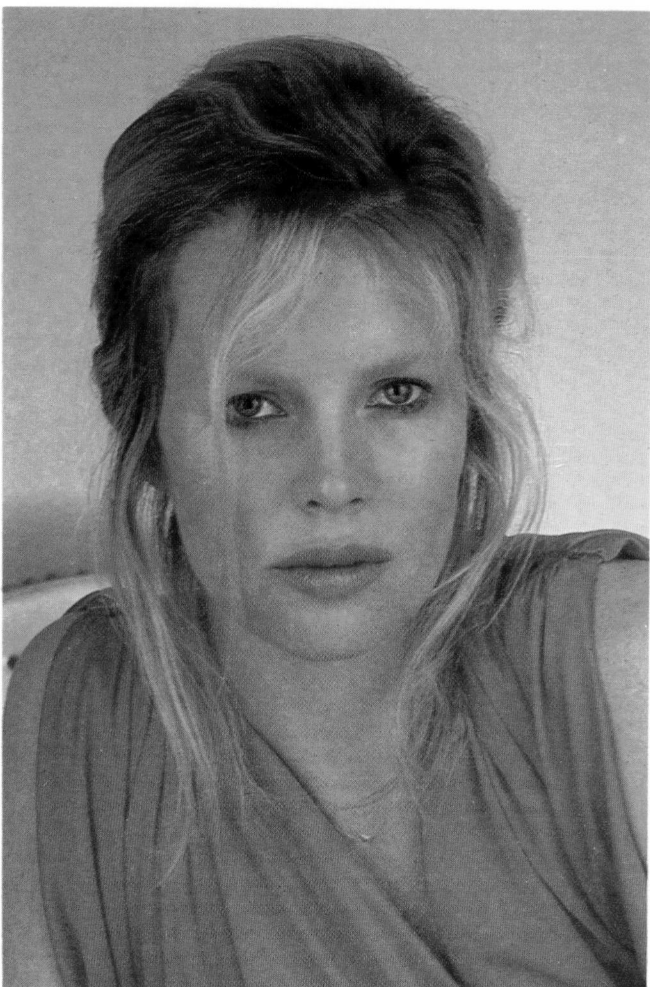

All the more disappointing, then, that despite her pleasant manner, epidermal appeal and technical skill (as an actress) Hollywood has found so little to do with Kim Basinger. Make no mistake, her career is in full working order. It's simply that on an artistic level she's being wasted. To date Basinger's most complete performance remains one of her very first – *Hard Country*. This 1981 release was little more than an *Urban Cowboy* knock-off. But as knock-offs go it had many qualities to recommend it – most preferable to the original. Chief among them was Basinger who made an excellent impression as a sweet-spirited Texas girl trying to make the most of a bad marriage to a shiftless (the film would have one believe 'alienated') contemporary lumpencowpoke (Jan-Michael Vincent). A minor movie all things considered, but it soon led to major ones for Basinger.

In *The Man Who Loved Women* she was sexy and funny as a bored Dallas matron prone to perilous dalliances with the film's hero. In *Never Say Never Again* she was similarly fetching as James Bond's love interest. Unfortunately the film was stolen right from under her by Bond's *hate* interest – the tempestuous Barbara Carrera. *The Natural* found Basinger in another all-dressed-up-with-no-place-to-go role as a baseball-team owner's sexually reckless daughter. The part was barely sketched out, but Basinger managed to make the most of her scenes – generally pitting her opposite the film's star Robert Redford. Hard to say whether Basinger's air of frustrated dissatisfaction proceeded from the script or was merely a side effect brought on by being forced to play with this most unresponsive of leading men.

This year Basinger's fortunes would seem to have risen sharply. She was cast in the lead of two high-profile productions – *Fool for Love*, and *9½ Weeks*. Yet just as before, Basinger's fires were unaccountably banked on both occasions, *Fool* being the more frustrating. She would appear to be ideally cast in this Robert Altman adaptation of Sam Shepard's play about an incestuous, all-consuming love-hate relationship. Instead she was cast adrift in it. For rather than stoke the hothouse intensity of this claustrophobic bit of neo-Strindberg, Altman chose to flatten it out.

The play's single room setting was traded in for a sprawling, detailed motel/gas station/ restaurant locale. Instead of the play's pell-mell all-of-a-piece monologues and dialogues, pauses, flashbacks and other digressions were inserted, with sudden shifts in camera placement, undercutting whatever dramatic tension was left over. As for Basinger, rather than front and centre, she was most often found crumpled up at the margins of the frame, brooding and pouting. She was clearly in character, yet one couldn't help but wonder if her depressed demeanour didn't proceed from the little Altman was allowing her to do.

Still, lamentable as the failure of *Fool for Love* may be, it's an artistic one. With a film like *9½ Weeks*, cosmetics – not aesthetics – were involved. As directed by Adrian Lyne, this exceedingly timid adaptation of the anonymously written best-seller about a sado-masochistic love affair, comes to the screen with all the dramatic force of a new soft drink campaign. Just as in *Flashdance*, Lyne proves himself more a confectioner than a director. We get plenty of high contrast back-lighting, steam, dry ice, and fancy cutting, but no images or sounds of any consequence (you can forget about characters in a bit of sub-Leloucherie like this.)

Mickey Rourke seems oddly cast, at first, as a well-heeled stockbroker with a taste for kink – until you listen closely to his voice. Its fuzzy purr proves an appropriate 'come hither' for the sort of 'sensuous woman' Basinger is playing – an upper-crust SoHo art dealer. Basinger goes well above and beyond the general call of thespic duties throughout the film. Writhing as Rourke drips melted ice cubes over her tummy, exhorting as he spoon feeds her cherries and whipped cream while blindfolded, she wins 1985's 'Game Girl' award in a walk.

Still Basinger manages to salvage from this wreckage one genuinely sexy moment. She does a delightful strip-tease to the strains of Randy Newman's 'You Can Leave Your Hat On'. Clearly enjoying every minute of this, Basinger is a sight for sore eyes. Now if she could only get a film to showcase her acting talents as well as her natural physical attributes. But as she would be the first to admit, in this business such demands are more than "a little unreal."

DAVID EHRENSTEIN

HELENA BONHAM CARTER

They are a triumvirate of discoverers. James Ivory, Ismail Merchant and their distinguished writer Ruth Prawer Jhabvala have an eye for the unfamiliar; again and again they have discovered players. Now their observant eyes have lighted on the young actress who is at the heart of *A Room With a View*. It is not her first film, though it was the first to be shown to an English audience. Helena Bonham Carter played the title part in *Lady Jane* before she appeared in *A Room With a View*; the credit for finding her should be given to Trevor Nunn, the director of the first piece. But it is to the Ivory-Merchant-Jhabvala version of EM Forster's novel that she seems to belong. She lives, one would say, in that distant society.

Not an easy role, not a great deal to hold on to. From the start she looks spirited, but that again is not much of a foothold for a performer. But she makes an immediate impression of English upper-class manners – the manners, that is, of the past. She has the air of that indefinable and today almost extinct species, a lady. This Lady, one feels, has been brought up to know her class; even as a girl she expects deference. It is something natural to her. Miss Bonham Carter is a great-grandchild of a Prime Minister, Asquith. Perhaps that has something to do with it all. Anyway, on the screen she seems to need no underlining of her social background. That, one feels, is the way she is.

But she develops the character. She develops it in the style and within the limitations which, no matter how much her circumstances alter, her background has imposed on her. One sees her at the start as a girl taken by a chaperoning cousin to the Florence of the beginning of this century. And Italy, at any rate as shown by the writers of the period, exercises romantic influences. The cousin, older, shrinks with virginal English dismay from a male fellow-guest's offer of a room instead of the one with no view in which the two women have been installed; Lucy recognises that the offer is kindly meant. She even ventures to walk about the city by herself. But inborn habits cling. An English lady does not – or did not – engage in conversation with a young man to whom she has scarcely been introduced; if the young man takes liberties that must be the end of the acquaintance. Writing his romantic novel, EM Forster enjoyed ironic reflections on the reactions of English visitors to the perils of the Europe of the early nineteen-hundreds. Lucy obeys the basic rules of behaviour. Nevertheless, in the actress's performance there is a suggestion of enquiry. No rebellion, of course; just a questioning in the eyes.

The first point about Miss Bonham Carter's playing is its capture from the start of the style of class; she doesn't perform the style, it exists in her presence. The second point is the skill with which she modifies the conventional style. She never becomes a girl of today. In tussles with her brother, in family games of tennis she may fall and roll on the lawn. She has the physical freedom of youth; but it is the freedom of three-quarters of a century ago, it is not today's sexual liberty. She moves without the constraint sometimes employed to suggest the manners of a past age, but the walk is correct. It has none of the surrender to carelessness which one might see today.

There are no scenes of the violent surrender to emotion which help a player to capture an audience's attention. Once there is a moment of exasperation with the pedantic figure to whom she has allowed herself, free from the unbalancing atmosphere of Florence, to become engaged. Once she gives way to tears; Lucy confronts the fond plain-speaking father of the young man she met in Italy, and, faced with his blunt but gentle statement of her hidden feelings, she dissolves. Her submission to the truth is all the more effective for being unspectacular. Extravagant emotional display is not in her nature. One recognises the accuracy of her reaction, one accepts the scene as an admission to her state of tension.

Looking back, then, at *A Room With a View* – and it exercises the fascination of a memorable conversation piece – one begins to recognise the essential quality of the playing of the heroine. Helena Bonham Carter, almost a beginner, is surrounded by experienced performers. Maggie Smith as the chaperoning cousin brilliantly suggests a life of emotions dutifully supressed and frozen into prejudice. There is a lively sketch by Judi Dench of the tourist one always meets. Denholm Elliott as the anxious father of the true lover breathes a natural warmth in contrast with the thoughtless insolence of some of the visitors. Everything challenges the new actress; but this Lucy is unobtrusively at one with her companions in the conversation piece. Unobtrusively, for there is no emphasising isolation of the central figure; she begins as the object of shelter, she looks about her, and in the renewed shelter of an English country house she realises the pressures of tradition; but she recognises her proper path. The essence of the performance is its modest self-assertion. As I say, a difficult role to play, a difficult place to fill; but nature and background have fitted her for it.

Somebody I met who had watched during the filming of *Lady Jane* spoke of questioning: we have been wondering, he said, if she is an actress. At this stage uncertainty is natural. Good fortune may have cast a young player in a situation which completely suits her. Yet, the image of the face persists. There is promise. Fulfilment must wait.

DILYS POWELL

ALEXANDRA PIGG MARGI CLARKE

Two working-class girls from Kirkby, a not altogether exotic Merseyside town, take a bus into Liverpool one night in search of fun and excitement. Elaine, unemployed but overflowing with dreams of romance, is tired of the boorish ways of the local men and longs for an adventurous life in Casablanca. Teresa, on the other hand, manages momentarily to forget her dull, dirty job – removing the intestines of chickens, wrapping them in plastic bags, and restuffing them – by "drinking vodka and getting fucked". After lifting a wallet from a drunken lout in a wine bar, they escape to a disco where they methodically pick up a couple of Russian sailors, Peter and Sergei. After spending the night with them in a hotel, however, the girls lose their dream lovers the next day when the men are required to return to their ship, which sets sail for home. But Elaine is madly, passionately in love, and determined to be with Peter once more she writes to Soviet premier Brezhnev, who somewhat miraculously responds with an invitation for her to go and live in his country. Family and friends, contemptuous in their ideas of what life in Russia entails, try to dissuade her from taking such a drastic step, while a Foreign Office official gently suggests that Peter is already married. Finally, Teresa persuades her friend to go and find out for herself, while she remains behind with her vodka and chickens.

Not, I'm sure you'll agree, a particularly original story, even though the idea of Russians and Westerners fraternising so successfully may come as something of a surprise in these days of *Rambo* and *Rocky*. Nor is it entirely plausible, since for all its working-class awareness of unemployment, urban decline and suburban tedium, it is essentially, a True Romance for our times. And yet *A Letter to Brezhnev* garnered praise galore upon release. Its critical success may have something to do with the fact that such a positive and romantic movie had been made in beleaguered Liverpool; or with the fact that it was made by newcomers to the film industry, on a minute budget (around £250,000) while rarely revealing its financial limitations. Its widespread success with the public, however, may be firmly attributed to its two central performances: as Teresa and Elaine, Margi Clarke and Alexandra Pigg won the hearts of audiences everywhere the film played.

It's easy, in fact, to see why filmgoers in Britain should take to these two relatively inexperienced actresses with such fervour. In the film, both girls – young, lively, and attractive – seem simultaneously 'ordinary' and 'different': ordinary in that they're patently working-class lasses, brimming with that thick-accented Northern naturalism so beloved by the British; different in that they're the sort of girls you don't often see on screen: foul-mouthed, fun-loving, strong-willed and voraciously sexual. Girls with spunk and spine. Girls intelligent enough to know what they want. Girls at home in the mean streets of the city.

In this sense the film both has its cake and eats it. Teresa and Elaine are at the same time ordinary and extraordinary, and the fact that they are played by comparative unknowns is essential. No star, no esteemed actress could ever imbue either of these characters with that quality of being just like you and me. But Pigg – a former night-club dancer with a modicum of respectable theatrical training, known mainly for a year-long stint as the suicidal housewife Petra in the TV soaper *Brookside* – and Clarke – previously involved (with her brother Frank, who wrote *Brezhnev*) in punk, TV comedy and Liverpool theatre – were perfect for their parts and, seemingly effortlessly, give it all they've got. Though roles like Teresa and Elaine are rare, they are also gifts to any aspiring young actress: larger than life, calculated to appeal to popcorn-munching masses and good liberal critics alike, endowed with plentiful colourful one-liners, the characters may seem radical but are in fact thoroughly unremarkable creations in themselves.

Take, for example, Elaine. The dreamily romantic stereotype is merely made palatable for present-day audiences by the injection of a certain vulgarity.

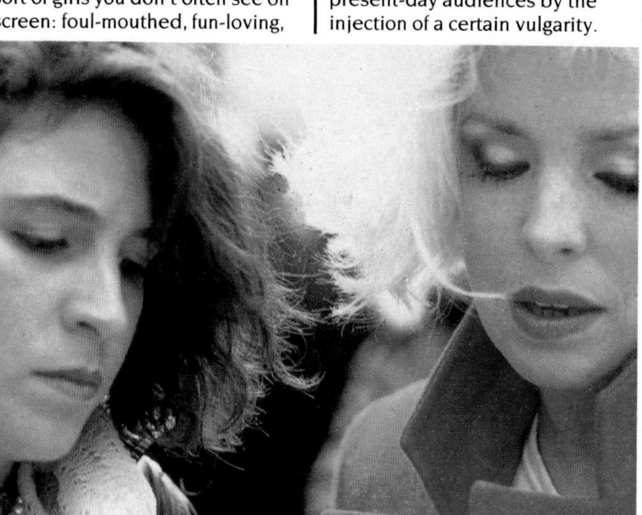

Given to genuinely witty coarseness when aroused (one spitefully meddling girl is informed by Elaine that she has slept with the former's ex-boyfriend – but would still "rather sit on me finger"), Elaine is nevertheless *nice* enough to complain of horrible, pushy men and to fall for the gently angelic Peter (who, as played by Peter Firth – Angel Clare in Polanski's *Tess* – is too good to be true). Pigg makes these apparent contradictions in character cohere by performing a clever balancing act between acidic energy and dewy-eyed romanticism. But what really impresses is the way in which she handles the more introspective elements of her role: passive, timid, but gently determined as she sits before the bureaucrat who's intent on destroying her dreams of life in Russia, Pigg simply sits there, barely reacting to the slurs being made both on Peter and his country.

In some ways Margi Clarke's task is easier, in others harder. Hers is the more attention-grabbing role: blonde, brassy, impetuous, good-time and strangely glamorous. Clarke grabs the part as effectively as she grabs Sergei. As a girl unashamedly on the make, Teresa is a winning stereotype, assured of public approval but difficult to dignify with depth of feelings. And yet, for all her delightful delivery of some of the most deliriously vulgar lines written for a woman in years, Clarke's finest moments come when she is called upon to suggest an inner vulnerability, a rarely seen but barely concealed desperation in this Harlowesque hot-shot who dreams of one day exchanging chickens' arses for a secretary's desk. We're not talking here of that rather oversentimental admission of her love for Igor (her pet name for Sergei) in the final cloying shot, but of the moment in the hotel room when Teresa's courage fails her, when she wants to abandon the sailors because paying for the hotel bills herself makes her feel cheap; or of those strange and saddening moments when the fixed lipsticked smile briefly cracks to reveal self-doubt and terror.

If Pigg and Clarke can avoid the typecasting that might follow their success as these two irrepressibly lively Liverpool lasses, they should be assured of fine, fulfillng futures in the film industry. They have intelligence, 'presence', and, most importantly, an apparent willingness to commit themselves to a character's feelings. And that, in a country where emotional restraint has too long been applauded as an actorly virtue, should be both nurtured and cherished.

GEOFF ANDREW

KEVIN COSTNER

To be cut from one movie, Mr Costner, may be regarded as a misfortune; to be cut from two looks like carelessness (with apologies to Oscar Wilde). Until *Silverado* proved his debut in a leading role, Kevin Costner was living on the dubious reputation of being an actor whom many admired within the business, while being largely unseen by the public. He had a small role in the Jessica Lange vehicle *Frances*, which ended up on the cutting-room floor. Then he was offered a larger one in John Badham's *WarGames*, but backed out some weeks after shooting had begun in order to take a part in Lawrence Kasdan's *The Big Chill*. People warned him that it was a risky move, but apparently Costner was adamant about wanting to work with Kasdan, whom he rates very highly. Unfortunately, he played Alex, the lynchpin of the movie and the *raison d'etre* for the reunion of sixties survivors that is at its core: he had already committed suicide before the film's opening, and it was at his funeral that all the ex-hippies, radicals and Vietnam vets were arriving during the credit sequence. He was allowed some ten minutes of flashback in the movie proper; but if there was ever a role ripe for the knife in the editing room, then it was that one. Sure enough, he was lopped.

He has, however, defended his decision to swap films as "the biggest single move of my career" and since Kasdan went on to make amends by casting him as Jake in *Silverado* (after Costner had appeared in Badham's *American Flyers!*), there is some truth in this. A large part of that movie's charm was that it included all the classic setpiece scenes from every Western that audiences could remember. Gambling saloons, corrupt sheriffs, fist-fights, stampedes, they were all cleverly dove-tailed into a large and sprawling plot line, with only the Indians missing (they, too, ended up on the cutting-room floor).

Jake is first encountered in the local slammer, waiting for the noose at dawn. It thus becomes Scott Glenn's duty, as Jake's elder brother, to spring him from the jail, although Jake himself seems in no doubt that he will somehow live to see another day. This incorrigible optimism is perhaps the one trait which continues throughout the film, and softens Costner's physical excess. His boundless energy would be in danger of turning him into nothing more than a human squash-ball, bouncing off the scenery, were it not for the likeable cheeriness with which he carries it all off.

There comes a moment towards the end of the film when a tearful child is relating to Glenn that his brother is almost certainly dead. While captured by outlaws, the child had seen him ride his horse over the edge of a precipice, which, the boy confirms, would unseat anyone. At the mention of the likelihood that Jake has fallen off his horse, Scott Glenn gives a knowing smile: the prospect of Jake doing anything like that is indeed remote. As if to prove the point, Jake is riding to the rescue within minutes, and performing the extremely tricky manoeuvre of jumping his horse onto the house veranda without benefit of the reins (both hands being full of six-gun). Clearly, the only problem with Jake is in holding him back.

The other tricky piece of business which seems to stick in audiences' minds is his backward exit from a saloon followed by a twin-handed gunfight with two villains, each of whom is disappearing down separate alleys which are at right angles to each other. Costner just stands on the corner and, with a cheery "Hey!", gets the drop on both of them simultaneously.

If one is forced to describe the actor as a sum of the action setpieces in which he is the mainspring, that is because there is little else to hold onto in Costner's performance. In fact, he is never given a scene of dialogue with either the beaming villain Brian Dennehy, or with the diminutive saloon-bar queen Linda Hunt.

Of course, he is a character who defines himself through action, but one hopes that the reasons for his isolation had more to do with giving him a lot of room than with the possiblity of his not coming off too well opposite another actor. Or, indeed, because it would make his role easier to cut. One had suspicions that the child's story was a setpiece that might have been seen in the original.

He is on record as saying that his favourite actor is Steve McQueen; one can certainly see the parallels. The same boyish charm, the same small, taut physique, the same taste for expression through action. Costner's horse could easily give way to a McQueen motorcycle. One hopes that Costner is also aware of the pitfalls into which McQueen occasionally dropped. A misplaced taste for the meretricious facility of a *Thomas Crown Affair;* the reliance on fast machinery to stand in for exciting acting; indeed the increasing resemblance of the man to a piece of machinery. McQueen gave his best performances when clearly troubled; by failing love in Peckinpah's *The Getaway*, by failing professionalism in the same director's *Junior Bonner*, and by his own failing body in the elegiac *Tom Horn*. It's a lesson that Costner might take to heart: get in harm's way.

CHRIS PEACHMENT

KEITH GORDON

Keith Gordon – co-writer as well as star of *Static* – seems to upset orthodoxies everywhere. How many other 25-year-old American actors can claim viable screen careers without either a bratpack coming-of-age comedy or an art'n'soul rumble-flick to their credit? How many would admit in these cool-conscious days to having come across *2001* as a key inspirational experience? How many would now be pouring their energies into an attempt to mount an off-Broadway production of Barrie Keeffe's *Barbarians?*

New York-born Gordon decided early that he wanted to be a film-maker, helping out around the Musuem of Modern Art's film set-up when barely into his teens. Acting just seemed the most likely way in. A slimline supporting role to the shark in *Jaws 2* represented a first, very minor, splash. The lead in Brian DePalma's misfired madcap comedy, *Home Movies,* proved more valuable in terms of initiating relationships than in establishing a profile. Gordon auditioned by reading a love scene with one of the writers – a lady with whom he has been living ever since. He befriended on set the assistant director Mark Romanek – now his collaborator on *Static.* And DePalma himself was impressed enough by Gordon's performance, as the nerdy object of Kirk Douglas's experimental 'Star Therapy', to cast him again as Angie Dickinson's son in *Dressed to Kill.*

Here, as the young electronics whiz sleuthing after his mother's slasher-killer, he again got to cuddle Mrs DePalma – Nancy Allen – and also again got to play the camera-wielding voyeur-surrogate for his rather obsessive director. Bob Fosse's flashy ego-bleed, *All That Jazz,* at least brought some variation to the Gordon gallery at this period, with the actor 'begging for' and receiving the role of Joe Gideon/Roy Scheider's younger self, despite looking little like Scheider, being unable to dance, and being committed to a concurrent stage run in Barrie Keeffe's *Gimme Shelter.* Hectic chases from set to theatre, a double for the hoofing sequences,

and a daily hair-spray saw him through.

More stage experience and a couple of upper-case telemovies followed. Parts in *Studs Lonegan* and – as one of the murdered students – in *Kent State* bracketed a seven-month stint in *Richard III,* opposite Al Pacino. Then John Carpenter hit on Gordon as the perfect human foil to the eponymous automotive Fury in *Christine.*

Shading the character of Arnie from the dim to the demonic (and from the pimply to the Presleyesque) was a challenge Gordon and Carpenter met between them by a unique form of acting-by-numbers. "Before we started shooting, we came up with Arnies 1, 2, and 3: the nerdy, pathetic Arnie, the cool and only slightly crazy Arnie, and the full-tilt case. Then on set, for every different take of each scene, we'd scale the performance, with John just shouting out 'one-point-eight' or 'two-point-six', or whatever."

A little worried that Carpenter's customised satire on the American male – "relating more easily to a piece of machinery than to a woman" – might get him typecast as a weirdo, Gordon was glad to take on two straighter roles: in the telefeature *Singles Bar, Single Woman,* and in Matthew Robbins' unfortunately muddled mutation of the Joan of Arc story into folksy female outlaw pic, *The Legend of Billie Jean.* The script for which Gordon signed aboard initially boasted the name of veteran writer Walter Bernstein, but subsequent tinkerings by other hands dissipated its impact: "It was fun to do, though, if only as the first time I'd got to play the guy who's only there to get kissed a lot."

It was during this period, too, that Gordon and Mark Romanek began the long process of bringing a more personal project to the screen. Romanek contributed the germ of an idea for *Static* with three barely-linked elements: a crucifix factory, a desert setting, and an inventor. The pair then worked in parallel, with sheaves of script passing back and forth between the on-location actor and New York. The story that emerged – of a small-town teenaged orphan who believes he's tuned his TV into live pictures of heaven, and will go to some lengths to convince others of his discovery – came from contradictory impulses. "Mark would be stressing the spirituality, and I'd be working on its negative aspects. He'd be asking how you can live without faith, and I'd be working on the fact that too much faith is clearly dangerous. Then Mark's strengths are visual and thematic, where I'm more interested in character and story."

Static, though, is anything but schematic in its darkly absurdist configurations. It's set one Black Christmas in an Arizona Anyplace that's base for an assembly-line of religious accessories (Gordon's Ernie is fired from here for adding to his collection of deformed crucifixes), home for a model post-nuclear family commanded by a survivalist dingbat ("Have a painless death, now, y'all) and bolt-hole for a dropped-back-in rock musician, Julia (Amanda Plummer). It features pensioners, a patents lawyer, a SWAT team and a lot of laughs, pain and torment, and juggles them into ambivalent coherence witnout resort to second-hand surrealist sleights-of-hand. (Though Gordon smilingly accepts that a double-bill of *Static* and Buñuel's *Simon of the Desert* will probably become a provocative rep-house staple before long.)

For all its peripheral joys, though, the movie's prime focus is on Gordon's Ernie Blick: a disconcerting tunnel-visionary of charismatically blank conviction, all the more effectively ambiguous for the actor's refusal to play tic-for-tat with any sort of sub-Anthony Perkins role model.

The controversially jarring, tragi-happy ending of *Static* has already upset both Cannes selectors and potential US distributors. Gordon's response is warming: "We made the movie we wanted to; there was really no point listening to the guys in polyester suits who thought a few glimpses of a heaven packed with naked women would give us a hit. There was equally no way we'd let this questionable character off scot-free, or become just a martyr. Look, we're two guys in our twenties, we've not got answers, we just thought the questions worth asking...". In my book, such indulgences are distinctly allowable.

PAUL TAYLOR

DIANNE WIEST

She has large lips and a delicate Roman nose. She has strong but not indomitable cheekbones. Her hair may be frazzled brown (*Hannah and Her Sisters*) or sleeked-down black (*Independence Day*) according to movie. But the eyes are the knock-out factor. You have heard of bee-stung lips? Dianne Wiest has bee-stung eyes. They have a permanent pixillated squint, as if she is fending off the glare of sunlight or the approach of a thousand hornets or the latest insult hurled her way by Hollywood, which continues to treat a major actress with minor roles.

However, Miss Wiest need fear no longer. Looking into my crystal ball, I see superstardom just ahead. Already she has stolen two movies from their respective starry casts – Robert Mandel's *Independence Day* and Woody Allen's *Hannah and Her Sisters* – and the only way the film industry can respond to such burglarious feats is to banish her back to the live theatre whence she came or to make her a star herself.

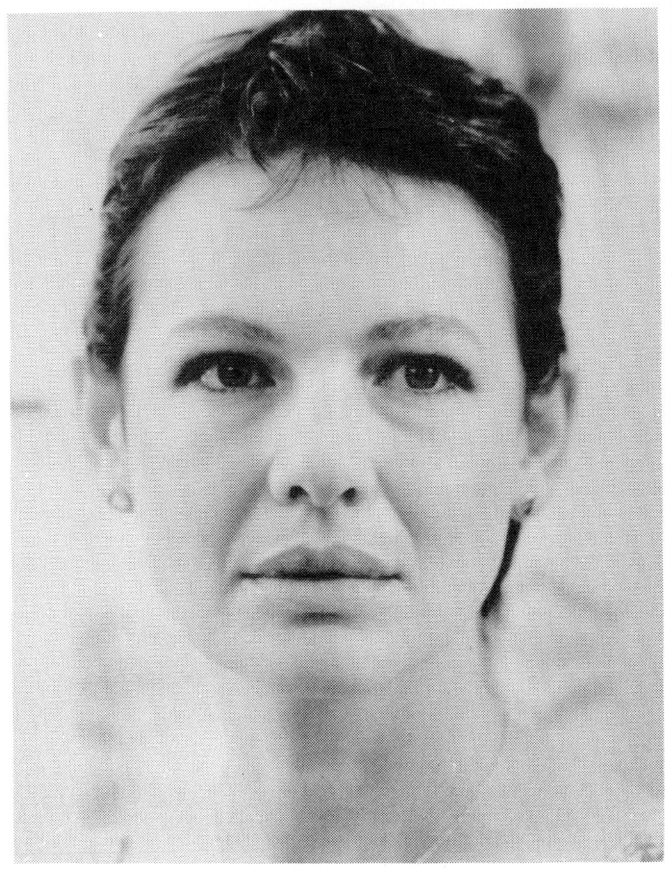

In the new Allen movie, Wiest is the sister with the crazy Bohemian bent who talks nineteen-to-the-dozen, runs the Stanislavski Catering Company with Carrie Fisher and drives men mad with desire: the desire, in most cases, to get as far away as possible. "I've had a great time tonight," says Woody Allen as the film's hero after his first date with her. "It was like the Nuremberg trials". She made the error of taking this mild-mannered jazz and Bach fancier to a heavy rock gig ("My ears are in *melt*down," complains Allen), and she also treated him to an overdose of screwball-intellectual conversation with mannerisms resembling a highly-strung female Afghan on benzedrines.

However – and this is the point to remember – Wiest ends up with Allen at the fade-out. The girl with the bee-stung eyes and the bee-stung brain gets her man.

In *Independence Day* Wiest doesn't steal the hero, she steals the whole damn movie. Here we are in the Deep South small-town of Mercury, where a cast of neo-Chekhovian no-hopers flutter away their days and nights in bits of romance, bits of vain ambition, bits of domestic warfare. Weist plays hero David Keith's sister, who is nutty as a piece of nougat. Or is she? The poor woman, a pretty, hunched young thing with slicked-down black hair, whose nervous smiles do not conceal an expression of permanent terror, is married to wife-beater Cliff De Young. De Young abuses, throws lighted matches at her in the presence of guests, and beats her up when the guests have left.

Wiest's role is almost purely reactive. But with a superpowered sensitivity, she makes her ripples of mute emotion – facial tics, or absent nods or turns of the head, or sudden smiles that stretch wide with panic – tell far more than cascades of dialogue. An actress like Gena Rowlands might have gone way over the top with this role, chewing up the carpet and climbing up the walls. (Or, failing that, she would have beaten up Cliff De Young.) But Wiest keeps the emotions terrifyingly pent in, even when struggling with a mixture of tears, laughter and incomprehension in the mental ward she's been carted off to after a suicide attempt.

Here as ever with Wiest, the eyes have it. One moment they are bit with a bland, faraway dreamer's look. The next they take on that shuttered, fluttering vulnerability, as if bright lights are being shone on them or water splashed at them.

In the age of the Streep-Fonda-Lange movie heroine, when superstars walk the globe flexing their virtuoso foreign accents or holier-than-thou ideologies or operatic country gal performances, it's no surprise that Wiest's homegrown miniaturism and superfine detailing have been overlooked. She gets lumbered with 'heroine's best friend' roles, in *It's My Turn* or *Falling in Love* or *The Purple Rose of Cairo*. And between-whiles she beetles back to the theatre to pick up awards and applause in plays like *Heartbreak House, Othello* and *Hedda Gabler*.

Hedda Gabler? Now there's a symbiotic role for Wiest. Wasn't Ibsen's heroine the daughter of an army officer: Correct. Likewise Wiest, born to a Colonel and following Dad as a child all over America and Germany. Wasn't Hedda a self-willed woman capable of burning her ex-lover's manuscripts and destroying life-styles or relationships at the drop of a between-acts curtain? Correct. Likewise Wiest, who burned her academic bridges in her teens by quitting the University of Maryland and going on tour with the American Shakespeare Company.

Since then she has kept on going. This brave Ibsenite flame was soon burning large holes in theatregoer's emotions by performances of what one critic called "vulnerability raised to an art form". She won an Obie, the top US theatre award, for her role in *The Art of Dining* at the New York Shakespeare Festival. She was strangled nightly by James Earl Jones when playing Desdemona to his Othello on Broadway. And after multiple baptisms in the classics of world theatre – Shaw, Gorky, Ibsen, Aeschylus – she wowed audiences on TV as well: notably as a crippled Jewish girl opposite Tom Conti and Lisa Eichhorn in a drama of the Warsaw Ghetto uprising, *The Wall*.

Hannah and Her Sisters now proves that Wiest can play winners as well as losers, high comedy as well as heartbreak. The actress's name tells us everything about her versatility. 'Wiest'. It isn't West and it isn't East: it is both at the same time. Dianne Wiest can face in both directions, and in her best performances she does so, combining wit and pain, vulnerability and toughness, laughter and tragedy. She is stardom-due and Oscar-due.

HARLAN KENNEDY

PAUL REUBENS (PEE-WEE HERMAN)

When a character can conjure up memories of an entire wing of the Comedy Hall of Fame, he must be stunningly original. Paul Reubens' incarnation as Pee-Wee Herman has been variously (and aptly) compared to Buster Keaton, Harry Langdon, "a new wave Stan Laurel", Marcel Marceau, Eddie Cantor, Andy Kaufman, Steve Martin, Peter Lorre, Pinky Lee, Peter Pan, Dennis the Menace, Mr Rogers and "Soupy Sales on speed".

Set amok in a universe of toy-store surrealism for his first star vehicle, *Pee-Wee's Big Adventure*, Pee-Wee effortlessly accomplishes much of what Jerry Lewis has so fascinatingly failed at over the last two decades: simultaneously to review and embody the infantilism of contemporary culture, to play the hipster while putting on a grotesquely square act, and to create a universal identification figure who is nevertheless unique and personal. (It helps perhaps that first-time director Tim Burton has absorbed so much Tati and so little Tashlin: the formal aspirations of the movie are far less ambitious and varied than in, for example, Lewis' *Smorgasbord* [aka *Cracking Up*], and as a result are far more consistently realised).

At first blush, Pee-Wee appears to be conceived as a thoroughly obnoxious creation. With his creepy crewcut, outsized red bow-tie, too-small polyester jacket, tight pants, heavy white make-up, rouged cheeks, lipsticked smackers and his shrieking, whiny voice (punctuated by smug cackles), he seems an insulting burlesque of both adults and children. Pee-Wee has the independence and sophistication of a grown-up and the petulance and fixations of a bratty five-year-old. In the context of the movie, this is not a liability; in fact, Pee-Wee is rather a leader of his pack, all of whom resemble members of Hal Roach's *Our Gang* series incarnated by overripe actors. While Pee-Wee exhibits a childlike fascination for mechanical devices, he also invents elaborate Rube Goldberg toys. He has absorbed all the elements of American series television of the fifties, yet he can also jive in eighties argot. Despite a prepubescent disinterest in sex (the "mushy stuff"), he is capable of seductive manipulation to get his way. Pee-Wee appeals directly to toddlers like a cartoon-show host, anchored by a ruthless deadpan irony that is in the vanguard of hip. Reubens has married conceptual comedy and performance art to the slapstick tradition, not so much finding the common denominator between the mass audience and the cognoscenti as straddling the barrier between them, never pandering to either.

Pee-Wee may be hard to take on initial impression, but his abrasive confidence becomes hilariously compelling: he's so deep into his own offbeat persona that he can launch into paroxysms of parody *in character*. Self-aware without being self- conscious, frighteningly inventive and daring us to dislike him, he has something of the nasty relish of the smarmy Tramp character of the early Keystone period, the blithe malice of Langdon's baby-faced innocent, and the preening bravado of Lewis being sucked into one of his runaway routines.

It's all fascinating and appalling, and the movie built around him is shrewd and ingenious, too. The plot elements are actually little more than a series of parodies, yet the interaction of the character Pee-Wee with these fondly kidded and meticulously echoed clichés gives them freshness and keeps the film from sagging into mere pastiche. The main hook is a take-off of *Bicycle Thieves*, wherein Pee-Wee's prized possession, his bike, is stolen. He takes off cross-country in search of it, and on the way encounters Hell's Angels, escaped convicts, a phantom lady trucker, a dreaming waitress out of *The Petrified Forest*, an Alamo tour group, etc, until he finally filches it off a movie set where it's being used as a prop. This sets up the culminating parody: Pee-Wee's own saga is bowdlerized into a glamorous Hollywood adventure, starring James Brolin as Pee-Wee.

Despite a few lapses in invention (notably the extraneous dream sequences and a tired climactic chase through the Warner lot), the movie lurches from one inspiration to another. Reubens uses Pee-Wee's eccentricities as unpredictable accents, creating a comic commentary that freshens golden oldie gags. Pee-Wee is like a splayed cubist rendering of our mishmashed collective sensibilities: nostalgic and contemporary, regressive and expressive, conformist and rebellious, brash and insecure.

Director Burton's visual style isn't complex, but it's perfectly calibrated to interact with Pee-Wee's oddball perspective. The physical comedy is greatly enhanced by the film's playroom design, and the ear for American dialogue is keen enough to make all the intentional dissonances pitch perfectly.

Reubens created the character while working with the Los Angeles improvisational troupe, The Groundlings, expanding the sketches into a local nightclub revue before achieving cult status on late-night television. While taking co-screenplay credit under his real name (ensuring his residual checks can be cashed), Reubens has otherwise adopted the corny pretence that Pee-Wee Herman is an actual person, doing interviews in character and providing facetious fictional biographical information on Pee-Wee. This noxious silliness cheapens the Pee-Wee character, turning him into a phoney publicity clown that detracts from the powerful originality of his creation.

Onscreen Pee-Wee is resolutely unphoney, manically upbeat and uncompromised by any drive to please. This freakish figure is funny primarily because his gravity and integrity (however grotesque) command attention, respect and unaccountable affection. Pee-Wee takes himself seriously, so we do, too. He's never the butt of the jokes but always in cahoots with them, drawing us into his comic conspiracy practically against our wills. He can even brush up against the comedian's bane, sentimentally, because he so resolutely eschews pathos. Pee-Wee the unregenerate spastic, the defiantly proud nerd, brandishes an infant's power to make himself the centre of his universe. The audience is invited to play with his toys, by his rules, and to our dismay and glee, we find ourselves having an uproarious time.

MYRON MEISEL

IRINA BROOK

Much has been written about Irina Brook which, at best, seems unjustified and, at worst, plain bloody silly. In this respect she is at a distinct disadvantage in having a famous father. It is virtually impossible to discuss the qualities of the one without reference to the other, especially when they work in the same field. Accusations of nepotism subsequently fly across newspaper pages or the smoke-filled rooms of actors' parties where the less fortunate or the downright jealous gather to tear each other to pieces.

Irina Brook is not yet a great actress and has had scant opportunity to prove that she is even a good actress. But at 22 she has made four films in the space of a year and currently presents a very enticing prospect for the future. Her qualities owe nothing to anyone beyond herself. If one had to pin it down, I suppose the phrase that best describes her onscreen charisma is cultivated liberation. Her wit and intelligence are married to an unconventional attractiveness which makes her good magazine fare. But in addition there is an elusiveness about her that forces you to watch her on the screen. This self-assurance and detachment is most in evidence in her latest film, *Captive*, in which she plays a lonely little rich girl who is kidnapped by 'emotional terrorists'. It is, arguably, the first film that has stretched her talent as her character has to show some development during the course of the plot. She has to go, in her own words, "from glamorous to gaunt; from rebellious to serene." Brook's performance is remarkably mature for one so young and relatively inexperienced. Subjected to a series of sensory deprivation tests she moves from the frustrated boredom of the opening scenes to a woman of substance, cool and in control, by the end. The outcome for her is consequently more rewarding than it is for her captors.

Psychologically, the role must have been hard enough; physically, it was surely punitive. Brook is kept in a box, made to wear goggles much of the time, hung upside down semi-naked and generally subjected to a bewildering and disorienting array of treatments that would be enough to give anyone the screaming abdabs. Whatever the response to the film, Brook's performance will be remembered as never less than watchable, and often remarkable in that she maintains a dignity and self-affirmation right through to the end.

Before *Captive*, Brook had appeared in various guises. A nurse in *The Last Days of General Patton*, a futuristic dolly bird in *Underworld* and as a wimpy girlfriend in *The Girl in the Picture*. Despite the varying quality of these films, Brook's resonance lingers long after the vehicles themselves have been forgotten. That seems to me to be the mark of a true star.

Brook's globetrotting, freewheeling lifestyle may account for her quality of luminous detachment. She spent much of her childhood flitting between London and Paris where her parents, theatre director Peter Brook and actress Natasha Parry, had their home. Despite making her stage debut at the age of six, saying three lines in ancient Greek, she was not to pursue her acting ambitions until after she left her hated school with the headmistress' oft-quoted report ringing in her ears: "At this rate Irina's future looks decidedly bleak." Having been turned down by her own father for the part of Anya in his celebrated production of *The Cherry Orchard* in Paris, Brook ran off to New York to live with a rock musician and work as a waitress. She studied at Stella Adler's acting studio and wound up in a handful of fringe productions off-off-Broadway. Two years later, Daddy called in to see her and offered her the part of Anya. Since then she has moved swiftly.

Whether she cares to admit it or not, Brook seems ultimately to be a cinema actress more than a stage actress. The qualities she possesses are those that are best explored by the camera. There is a feeling, a sensation that the screen needs her more than she needs the screen. There is something diabolically attractive about that. She has the propensity for intelligent rebellion and while she has yet to deserve the indiscriminate plaudits of the press I detect that she has the potential for being a truly great screen actress. At this rate Irina's future looks decidedly rosy.

NEIL NORMAN

LAURA DERN

It's not true that most young American actresses are showroom dummies. They just seem that way because of the airheaded roles they're forced to play. Junior bimbos, screaming mimis, plucky tag-alongs, adored-from-afars, irritating siblings – these are the only roles available to most of the best products of American drama schools and soda fountains.

Laura Dern is the exception. She doesn't look plastic enough to get the career-killing roles that most women think are the first steps to stardom. Instead, Dern has taken what Hollywood calls 'meaningful' roles – character leads that allow the expression of talent rather than the display of beauty. Dern has been seen in just three movies, *Teachers, Mask* and *Smooth Talk*. In *Teachers* she had a walk-on part as a girl who gets pregnant by her gym teacher. On the strength of her performances in *Mask* and *Smooth Talk*, though, many are 'talking her up' for this year's 'next Meryl Streep' award.

Dern came into *Mask* halfway through to give the horribly disfigured hero somebody to love. The gimmick was that Dern was blind and could only see the hero's beautiful soul. It was an ick-making situation and it could have been the occasion for a stumbling, glassy-eyed performance. Instead, Dern impressed audiences with her depth of feeling and her realistic portrayal of blindness (for one scene, she practised horse-riding blindfold for two weeks). Cher got the Academy Award nomination, but Dern got everyone's attention.

In *Smooth Talk*, this year's one movie about teenagers for adults, Dern excelled as a shopping-mall tease who unfortunately caught the eye of a psychotic sharpie. At home, Dern's character suffered the restricting love of her mother, but at the mall and at a nearby burger stand, she was free to practise growing up. Again, the situation (taken from a Joyce Carol Oates short story) was a movieland cliché, but Dern transcended it. Her performance reminded grown-ups in the audience how our own adolescent longings and inexperience sometimes collided tragically.

Dern, blonde and statuesque, is the daughter of actors Bruce Dern and Diane Ladd. They divorced when Laura was two, and she was raised by her mother. When she was nine she went along when her mother made *Alice Doesn't Live Here Anymore* for Martin Scorsese. She was given a role eating an ice-cream cone in one scene and on the basis of this experience announced that she wanted to become an actress.

Both parents pooh-poohed the idea. Dern recalls, "I went and got an agent on my own. I used to have to ride my bike to the agent's office because my mother wouldn't drive me." When she was 11, she was up for one of the leads in Adrian Lyne's *Foxes*. "I told Adrian I was 14 and could play 17. He decided to go with a girl in her twenties but he gave me a little part in the movie because he liked me. I got back to school after working with Scott Baio, who all the seventh graders had crushes on, and my best friend was so jealous she never spoke to me again. Here I thought I was so great, and instead I got denounced as a bitch."

Such pubescent upheavals are money in the sense-memory bank for an actor. Despite her exposure to the movies from an early age, she says she grew up something of a sheltered momma's girl. When she was the age of her character in *Smooth Talk*, 16, she was "more introverted," she says. "I told mom everything, and we've always been best friends. I used to write poetry and actually do my homework and things like that of a nerdish consistency. I was never into 'scenes'. I've never even been to a rock club. I wouldn't have enjoyed it and besides my mom wouldn't let me.

"That's why acting is so neat. My mom would never allow me near boys like the character Treat Williams plays in *Smooth Talk*. But boys like that are very attractive. You can play with fire in the movies where you wouldn't in life. You can have a love affair with the camera. I'm afraid of it. I'll do things I'd be embarrassed to do otherwise. I see myself in a film and I have a hard time connecting that person with me. I don't even know what I look like sometimes. Sometimes I'll look in a mirror and think, 'You're lovely.' Other times I'll look at myself and think how homely I am."

Maybe Meryl Streep has outgrown such musings, but she and Dern share that quality of being both plain and beautiful. There have been times, as Dern says, when "It was me or Molly Ringwald." If it turned out to be Ringwald or Phoebe Cates or Ally Sheedy, it was because what Dern has to offer doesn't include the ability to pose well. And she can't play dumb.

In choosing jobs, Dern says, "I look for a character who is intelligent. I'm sick of seeing girls in movies who have no mind. I look for a script that deals with something important. Who needs more dumb exploitation movies? I'm definitely a dreamer. People tell me, 'You should be more of a game-player. Don't tell people you love them. They'll manipulate you.' Maybe so, but I won't give up. Being pessimistic is so boring. It just isn't as much fun as idealism."

For the future Dern aspires "to play young women, women you'll fall in love with even when they're obnoxious, because they're so real. I have a lot of time. I might as well play teenagers now, since that's what I am. But I won't do any part that I can't make real."

Dern's next leap is into *Blue Velvet*, from *Dune* director David Lynch. "It will be very strange," she promises of the Lynch film, to be released in America this autumn. "Some people advised me not to take the job, saying Lynch's script was fascinating but dangerous. Well, God forbid the movie might not make scads of money!"

BART MILLS

QUOTES OF THE YEAR

Compiled by Tony Crawley

"Steven [Spielberg] *must* be making a movie, physically shooting something at some point during the course of the year – or he'd go mad." *Producer Kathleen Kennedy*

"I'd rather direct. Any day. And twice on Sunday." *Steven Spielberg on producing*

"They held up *The Outlaw* for five years. And Howard Hughes had me doing publicity for it every day, five days a week for five years." *Jane Russell*

"I don't need final cut. I only cut the thing once. If they're dumb enough to fool around with it, let 'em do it." *Martin Ritt*

"Being in the movie business is rather like being a tennis player. You have to keep your total concentration and mind on the ball. The minute you fall in love with Tatum O'Neal or get flabby, you've had it." *Michael Winner*

"When I showed 20th Century Fox the finished movie of *Romancing the Stone*, they fired me from *Cocoon*. And I don't know why. It's the great mystery of my career." *Robert Zemeckis*

"I'm in so many Charles Bronson films because no other actress will work with him." *Jill Ireland, Mrs Bronson*

"I'd hope that anyone who's sentimental and human and has got a bit of room in their heart for people who are a bit fucked up will see it and like it."
Alex Cox on 'Sid and Nancy'

"I've never felt so brilliant and intelligent as I feel now." *Franco Zeffirelli*

"I love Reagan. I think he's a wonderful man and he represents all the good qualities of American and Irish people." *Paul Morrissey*

"According to the doctors, I'm only suffering from a light form of premature baldness." *Federico Fellini, after four days in a Rome clinic*

"I don't think I'm, like, really handsome in the classical sense. The eyes droop, the mouth is crooked, the teeth aren't straight, the voice, I've been told, sounds like a Mafioso pallbearer, but somehow it all works." *Sylvester Stallone*

"I'd like to sink their boat. I'd like to pull out the goddamn plug and drain them. I think they're totally disrespectful people, they have absolutely no concern for the law, they have no concern for this country, they have no concern for anything except themselves." *John Derek on Golan and Globus*

"He's the jerk of all jerks." *Menahem Golan on John Derek*

"When I started in films they used to sign on girls for a seven-year contract at the age of 17 or so, because studio doctors and people who were supposed to be in the know thought women had passed their peak by the age of 26." *Joan Collins, 53*

"Aggressive feminists scare me." *Omar Sharif*

"The more I go to the movies, the more I like French movies." *Claude Lelouch*

"Raising pre-sales money in France is a slow process. You have to have three lunches in Paris, where it's one telephone call in London." *Producer Simon Perry*

"Filming is like a long air journey – there's so much hanging around and boredom that they keep giving you food. Food is very important. The other actors don't really matter."
John Cleese

"Of course, the last thing my parents wanted to see was a son who wears a cocktail dress that glitters, but they've come around to it."
Divine

"It can be pretty tough saving the world sometimes. It's a special branch of work, isn't it?"
Mel Gibson, 'Mad Max'

"There are people in the industry who *cannot* imagine a woman director being in charge of the crew. There is a certain Boys' Club reality to *all* business, not just film. It's breaking down now."
Director Martha Coolidge

"I'm glad to be part of the family. I've always thought the English aristocracy needed a good injection of convict blood."
Bryan Brown to Rachel Ward's father

"I wouldn't have made the picture – is it *Rainbow? Rambo* ... whatever its name is – I wouldn't have made it even if I'd known it was going to reap so many millions of dollars."
One-time Stallone director, John Huston

"Anybody who can get any movie made, whether it's any good or not, is doing pretty well. Because they really make it hard for you in Hollywood." *Joe Dante*

"My kids were off from school and I figured out I could direct just as badly as the film-makers who keep screwing up my books."
Stephen King on directing 'Overdrive'

"Do you believe that *Love Streams* by John Cassavetes played in Taiwan? It did – only because the Taiwanese wanted a Bronson picture from us."
Menahem Golan

"My mother was against me being an actress ... until I introduced her to Frank Sinatra." *Angie Dickinson*

"The nice thing about the future is that you don't know what it is. At various points in my career, if I could have seen what was going to be ahead, I probably would've left town." *Joe Dante*

"As an actress I didn't have young handsome men for admirers. I had unhappy creatures from loony-bins. Crackpots who whispered they would pray for me, who sent me long poems about God, about reincarnation. These chosen few with the mark on their foreheads have always been drawn to me and I to them."
Mai Zetterling

"You are not a star until they can spell your name in Karachi." *Roger Moore*

"I think I'm the first person to say 'fuck' in a Disney movie." *Actor Fisher Stevens on 'My Science Project'*

"I'll never get used to paparazzi. Despising that kind of work makes it hard for me in my photography class." ***Jennifer Beals***

"The only person I know that fights violently to pay the bill is Marlon Brando. I once managed to get the plate away from him and he's very strong and he said: 'If you won't give me that bill, Michael, you're going to leave this restaurant naked.' And he meant it."
Michael Winner

"It's very hard to find anyone with any decency in the business. They all hide behind the corporate structure. They're like landlords who kick people out of tenement buildings. There's no compassion, and there's certainly no interest in the arts."
Robert Altman

"As far as A Martin Ritt Film is concerned, I wouldn't embarrass myself to take the credit. What about the Ravetches [writers Irving Ravetch and Harriet Frank]? They wrote it. What about the actors who are in it? How can it be a Marty Ritt Film? It's not. If I ever write one, direct one and star in it, then you can call it a Marty Ritt Film."
Martin Ritt

"All these guys are around 21 to 23. I feel like a grandma around here."
Kelly McGillis on the 'Top Gun' set

"I've met those who I thought were – perhaps – connected with the Mafia and they weren't all that dreadful." *John Huston*

"I've always had the ability to say to the audience: Watch this if you like; and if you don't, take a hike."
Clint Eastwood

"*Dynasty* was the opportunity to take charge of my career rather than walking around like a library book to be loaned out." ***Joan Collins***

"I have one question. By *Star of Tomorrow*, do you mean Friday? Because if it's just tomorrow, Friday's not a good day for me. I have all these appointments. Could we change it to Saturday?"
Actress Christine Lahti, on receiving a Motion Picture Books Club award

"There hasn't been that much of a market for what I can do. I'm not able to do outer-space epics or youth pictures." *Arthur Penn*

"For a few moments there, I thought I'd died and you were reading my obituary."
Producer Joe Levine, on receipt of a lifetime achievement award

"I don't consider *Crimes of Passion* a mistake. Part of why I took the role was to work with Ken Russell ... It was fabulous and very frightening. I learned a lot about myself."
Kathleen Turner

"The nice thing about egoists is that at least they don't talk about *other* people." ***Roger Moore***

"One of the other problems for black writers is that you are often measured on a black rage scale. You've got to be angry. James Baldwin was always seen as being furious or angry; Saul Bellow didn't *have* to be angry." *Hanif Kureishi, writer of 'My Beautiful Laundrette'*

"It was very contagious, this feeling that in order to be a true, honest, heroic artist you had to do yourself in or go bananas, so that your insanity became a badge of honour. I knew guys who walked off roofs. I was determined not to go under." *Sam Shepard*

"When I first spoke to Mel Gibson, I told him what the film's story really was: Listen mate, it's Jesus in black leather."
Terry Hayes, writer of 'Mad Max Beyond Thunderdome'

"I love *Rambo*. But I think it's potentially a very dangerous movie. It changes history in a frightening way."
Steven Spielberg

"I'd say between three pm and eight, I look great. After that, it's all downhill. Don't photograph me in the morning or you're gonna get Walter Brennan."
Sylvester Stallone

"I think I'm finally growing up – and about time."
Elizabeth Taylor at 53

"The film business? I enjoy film – but the business is shit." *Writer-director Oliver Stone*

"I grew up on a bizarre mixture of fantasy comics, spaghetti Westerns and Fellini and Antonioni films."
Producer Charles Band on his youth in Italy

"I'd never be a pimp or a drug-runner. I wouldn't do anything I wouldn't want my guru to see."
Rock saxophonist turned film-TV actor Clarence Clemons

"Make a comedy? Sure. I'd love to. But I think this *is* a comedy." ***Mel Gibson on 'Mad Max Beyond Thunderdome'***

"I think that people assume I'm some primordial being, wallowing in a morass of mud and carrying a club on my shoulders. I don't think people understand that my life is much more cerebral than physical."
Sylvester Stallone

"I'm like a wild animal who is behind bars. I need air. I need space." *Klaus Kinski*

"I really don't remember much about *Cleopatra*. There were a lot of other things going on..."
Elizabeth Taylor

"I don't have a lot of problems in my life that take a psychiatrist and a lot of couch time to solve. I've never been through psychotherapy or psychoanalysis. I solve my problems with the movies I make. When there's a character in conflict in a movie, some part of that character is part of me that needs to be straightened out." *Steven Spielberg*

"I was always fascinated by size and bigness."
Arnold Schwarzenegger

"I'm no alcoholic. I'm a drunkard. There's a difference. A drunkard doesn't like to go to meetings."
Jackie Gleason

"I'm an absolute hermit. If I'm asked to dinner, I ask who's coming. I have to know exactly who's coming and where I'm sitting. I say, 'These people sound absolutely dreadful' and she says they're all her best friends. I stay at home. I don't get asked out much now, of course."
Michael Winner

"Basically, I'm a blue-collar redneck who loves his tequila." ***Eric Roberts***

"I've no idea what I'll do next. I'm not anxious to write for a while. I'm not anxious to work in television. I'm not anxious to work." *Lawrence Kasdan*

"I'm a great gossip. Don't pay any attention to what I'm saying."
Alec Guinness

"I didn't go out of my way to get into this movie stuff. I essentially think of myself as a writer." *Sam Shepard*

"I'm not afraid to fail, providing I fail honourably. The only thing I don't want to do is to end up being an irrelevant 70-year-old egomaniac."
David Puttnam

"I'm not an old-fashioned romantic. I believe in love and marriage, but not necessarily with the same person." *John Travolta*

"I'm still a very romantic person. I always have been. I find I function better with a mate. I simply hate the transient life of dating."
Joan Collins

"My mother said it was simple to keep a man, you must be a maid in the living-room, a cook in the kitchen and a whore in the bedroom. I said I'd hire the other two and take care of the bedroom bit."
Jerry Hall

"Reclusive? I'm not reclusive. I'm a guy that dances on tables, puts lampshades on his head, sticks his dick out in crowds. But I'm married now, got kids. I figure, stay healthy, live longer." *Mel Gibson*

"I suppose I'm the boy who stood on the burning deck whilst all about had fled. The trouble is, I still don't know if the boy was a hero or a bloody idiot."
Lindsay Anderson

"I'm 23. We hip girls don't lie about our age. We don't do anything. We just say: We're here!" *Tahnee Welch*

"Our standard joke was that if the film ever got made, no one would be left to see it because everyone had read the screenplay." *Midge Sanford, producer of 'Desperately Seeking Susan'*

"I don't remember a film I enjoyed making. It's damned hard work." *Sydney Pollack*

"The producer who believes he's an artist but doesn't do anything terrifies me." *Arthur Penn*

"There's not a stand-up comic in the world who could hold the floor the way he did. When you can get my son and me to shut up for three-and-a-half hours, it's extraordinary." *Jack Lemmon on dining with Fidel Castro*

"The more and more terrified people get of making Westerns, the more I want to do one." *Steven Spielberg*

"I love Westerns. I always have. I'd make another in a minute. You can tell any kind of story in a Western. How can you not be fascinated by them?" *Lawrence Kasdan*

"It'll be a wonderful movie – a family sex'n'violence film. I don't want to give too much away. But I do save the world." *Barry Humphries on 'Les Patterson Saves the World'*

"I've yet to be convinced that the film business is a profession for adults." *New producer Frederick Forsyth*

"You can't eat food on aeroplanes – instant death. There's more illness caused on planes than going to gay bars. I just take the tray and take everything off – never eat the meal – and put it in my case. I've a complete set of Concorde cutlery." ***Michael Winner***

"Every part is hard. And if it's not hard – then you have to make it hard!" *Klaus Maria Brandauer*

"In my naiveté, I handed in a screenplay for *Sparkle* that was over 300 pages long. When I asked: Howda like the story?, the answer was – which one?" *Writer-director Joel Schumacher*

"Thrift and industry – I'm the Mrs Thatcher of British film." *Stephen Frears*

"Acting is the easiest thing I've ever done. I guess that's why I stick with it." *Charles Bronson*

"I hate two towns; Edmonton and Aswan. I've enjoyed all the rest. Even New Zealand." *John Cleese*

"Nobody makes a profit on a Jean-Luc Godard picture. As from today we have more than a million dollar profit on the Godard *King Lear* project." *Menahem Golan*

"There's nothing original in British cinema today. It's the bastardisation of any other cinema you like to name. Instead of speaking English, it speaks American." *Hugh Hudson*

"Norman Mailer will play King Lear. He's a natural. He has five daughters and a crazy life." *Menahem Golan*

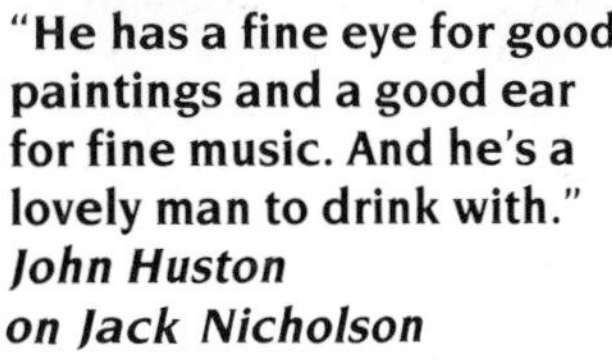

"He has a fine eye for good paintings and a good ear for fine music. And he's a lovely man to drink with." ***John Huston on Jack Nicholson***

"One only has to look at that media non-event, British Film Year, to understand that the modern perception of British cinema has nothing to do with British *films* – merely with the business of getting more money through the box-office." *Lindsay Anderson*

"When John Huston dies, I'll cry for the rest of my life." ***Jack Nicholson***

"I feel I'm working with the best film-maker that's come along in many years – a sort of David Lean figure." *David Puttman on Roland Joffé*

"I'm fully equipped with male plumbing and very happy that way – why shouldn't I play men?" *Divine*

"Terry Jones had to play a woman's part. He said if he didn't it would be the only film which he didn't direct in women's clothes or in the nude." *David Leland, 'Personal Services' scenarist.*

"Eddie Murphy makes more money than Mrs Marcos spends in an afternoon." *Robin Williams*

"I could declare bankruptcy and make a lot of people happy. But I would have to deny it the next day. I have no losses to report." *Arnon Milchan, producer of 'Once Upon a Time in America', 'Brazil', 'Legend'*

"In some ways, you see yourself as a hitman. You go in, do the job, pick up the cheque and leave." *Ian McShane on Hollywood acting*

"We have some good news. We didn't buy anything today." *Menahem Golan opening Cannon's Cannes Press conference*

"Bob Altman is a great guy. For him, life comes first, movies second." *Kim Basinger*

"I'm so naive about finances. Once when my mother mentioned an amount and realised I didn't understand, she had to explain: That's like three Mercedes." *Brooke Shields*

"I've always had a good head for deals. Not for handling money. Until he died, my father used to send me my allowance, which was how I preferred it." *Katharine Hepburn*

"There are three things I never saw Elizabeth [Taylor] do: be on time ... tell a lie ... be unkind to anyone at all." *Mike Nichols*

"Michael Frayn was so flattered to have a film made of his own script that if we'd done it in Swahili he'd have been perfectly happy. The thrill of having us mangle his script was all he asked for." *John Cleese on 'Clockwise'*

"I think marriage is a great institution." *Elizabeth Taylor*

"There's no moralistic side to *Death Wish* – it's a pleasant romp." *Michael Winner*

"France has tax-shelters. And where there is tax-shelter, we are there." *Cannon's co-chief, Yoram Globus*

"Film directors don't understand acting. Film directors are visual artists, they're perceiving the exteriors of things. They don't give a shit about the interior. So the actor has to go off and work that out by himself." *Sam Shepard*

"I've never worked with an eight-year-old director before. It's wonderful fun." *David Bowie on Jim Henson's 'Labyrinth'*

"Mia's mother [Maureen O'Sullivan] is in this picture. We also shot a large section of the picture in her apartment, which is perfect for me because I always go over there anyhow." ***Woody Allen on 'Hannah and Her Sisters'***

"There's no question that the Woody Allen character that appears up on the screen is a Greek god version of what he's like in real life. I met him once, and he tried to hide behind Mia Farrow." ***John Cleese***

"An actor called Patrick Magee died a few years back. I was in Australia at the time. They announced on US TV that Patrick Magee, star of *The Avengers*, had died. So they rang up my daughter in Palm Springs: 'Sorry to hear that your father's dead.' She said: 'But I was talking to him 12 minutes ago in Australia.' They said: 'No, he's dead – it's just the time difference'." *Patrick MacNee*

"Umberto Eco's attitude is that of many Italian novelists. He considers his work finished and doesn't feel like making a statue or an opera out of it." *Italian producer Franco Cristaldi, on why Eco didn't script 'The Name of the Rose'*

"I still get letters from Michael Jackson, regularly. We're pen pals and pen pals have no excuse *not* to write." *Katharine Hepburn*

"You really have to pull your socks up to stay in the same game with her." *Sting on Meryl Streep*

"Directors, in general, understand shit. Herzog is a less big asshole than the others." *Klaus Kinski*

"You have to throw a little cold water on him every once in a while." ***Meryl Streep on Dustin Hoffman's acting***

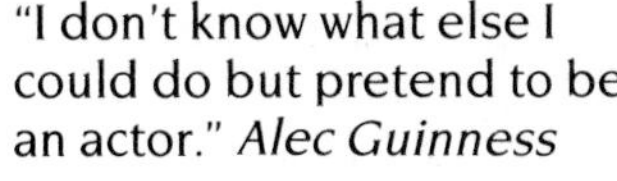

"I don't know what else I could do but pretend to be an actor." *Alec Guinness*

"I pounded on her door, and when it opened I saw this wonderful vision. She had the flaming red hair from *Red Sonja*, and she looked extraordinary. I said, 'Well, I'm only going to stay fifteen minutes, but maybe I can stretch it into four hours'." *Sylvester Stallone, on meeting Brigitte Neilsen*

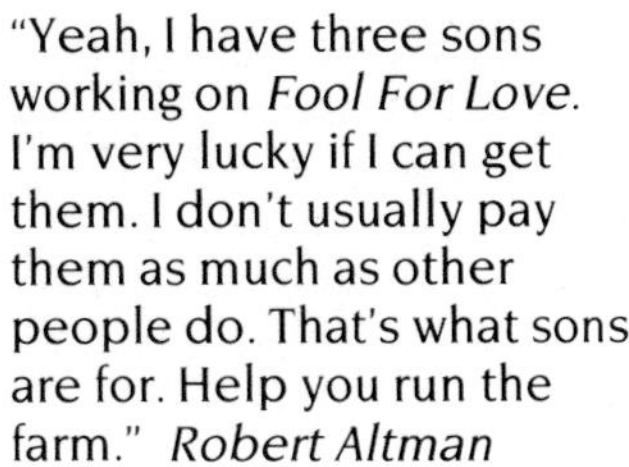

"Yeah, I have three sons working on *Fool For Love*. I'm very lucky if I can get them. I don't usually pay them as much as other people do. That's what sons are for. Help you run the farm." *Robert Altman*

"Hollywood is the Mecca of the film industry. We will stay in Mecca." *Menahem Golan on Cannon's HQ*

"Okay, I'm not Doris Day yet. But I'm getting there." *Divine*

"Every asshole has a script in his back pocket." *Larry Cohen*

"I'm not bitter about Hollywood's treatment of me – but of its treatment of Griffith, von Sternberg, von Stroheim, Buster Keaton and a hundred others." *Orson Welles*

"To get her into the gym, I have to use a John Deere tractor. We've had some major Vesuvian clashes in the gym." *Sylvester Stallone, on Brigitte Neilsen*

"I think I get sent the roles that Meryl's not doing." ***Sigourney Weaver***

"Naming a national forest after Ronald Reagan is like naming a day-care centre after W C Fields." *Bob Hope*

"To me she is Marilyn Monroe, Brigitte Bardot and Judy Holliday in one girl – with the talent of Julie Christie. She is the most talented girl I've seen in my life. Just looking at her makes me want to screw her." ***Menahem Golan on Kim Basinger***

"I know a producer in Hollywood who always throws a party when his film is a flop on the theory that people are happy with someone else's failure. *Producer Arnon Milchan*

"There are only three things you need to do if you want to make it in Hollywood. Learn how to make your own salad. Learn how to fall in slow motion. And learn how to cry." *Gary Busey*

"It was always harder to make films for their own sake in Britain than it was in France or Germany. Now it's almost impossible. That radical enthusiasm has given way to a need for conformity and materialism. We are not encouraged to be political any more." *Lindsay Anderson*

"Believe me. If all the majors were still run by movie directors or cameramen instead of bankers and agents, the face of Hollywood might be very different." *Menahem Golan*

"The danger in talking about her is that she tends to sound boring because she is so perfect." *Sydney Pollack on Meryl Streep*

"We don't know how to lose money." *Menahem Golan*

"I've come to terms with the fact that I've almost acted my way out of this business because the business doesn't know what the fuck to do with me." *Eric Roberts*

"Films are home movies of your past." *Michael Cimino*

"There's nudity in the film but it's not me. I'm just *not* comfortable with my body yet." *Jennifer Beals on 'The Bride'*

"It makes you wish there was a retroactive birth control pill."
Katharine Hepburn, on the book by Bette Davis' daughter

"In all my films there is three or maybe four minutes of real cinema."
Akira Kurosawa

"I've never kissed a girl yet without kidnapping her first." *Hollywood actor Don Stroud on his roles*

"I was always a director and I just produce for myself as it gets rid of the producer who is usually an unpleasant person."
Michael Winner

"It's some sort of tribute, I suppose, that *Cathy Come Home* and *Up the Junction* were among the first things that Mary Whitehouse ever complained about."
Ken Loach

"Cannon didn't care about my screenplay or that I had no Hollywood experience. Frankly, they didn't even want to talk to me. They wanted a package. They wanted a low-budget film. They wanted Nastassja Kinski."
Andrei Konchalovsky on 'Maria's Lovers'

"This is the best possible movie I could've done. I'm not *terrific*, but I'm good enough for this part."
Tina Turner on 'Mad Max Beyond Thunderdome'

"Ten years ago my ambition was to be one of the world's top models; now I've achieved that, my goal is to be one of the world's great actresses." *Jerry Hall*

"I didn't really want to come to Cannes with *Max Mon Amour*. I've gone through enough exams in my life."
Producer Serge Silberman

"Movie acting is all about narcissism. Terry Malick called it: sanctioned vanity. Everything is attended to. Would you like some Perrier? Anything we can do? May we throw ourselves on the ground in front of you?
Sam Shepard

"Yes, he invented a bra for me. Or he tried to. And one of the seamless ones like they have now. He was way ahead of his time. But I never wore it. And he never knew. He wasn't going to take my clothes off to check if I had it on. I just told him I did."
Jane Russell on Howard Hughes and 'The Outlaw'

"I'm open to anything. But I'm not a director for hire and I don't read scripts. Mostly I like inventing my own movies."
Steven Spielberg

"Making movies is better than cleaning toilets."
Klaus Kinski

"He and my daughter have lived together for 12 years. That's longer than any of my marriages lasted."
John Huston on Jack Nicholson

"The second was clearly a Western. The third is an odyssey, a fable." *Director George Miller on 'Mad Max'*

"If there was ever going to be a *Mad Max IV*, we'd have to take into account what occurred to Max in *III*. You couldn't suddenly revert to having him as a closet human being." *Terry Hayes, writer of 'Mad Max Beyond Thunderdome'*

"I'm a Democrat with Republican underpinnings. I'm liberal about a lot of things, but I'm bullish about America." *Steven Spielberg*

"I don't know anything about French movies – I don't go to pornographic films." *Catholic anti-Godard 'Hail Mary' protestor in New York*

"It's the same in Russia and America. You pitch the story and try to sell it. In Hollywood, you have to convince them it's commercial. In Russia, you have to convince them it's ideological." ***Andrei Konchalovsky***

"David Lean and François Truffaut are my gods, but I consider Henry King and Henry Hathaway two of the most underrated directors there are." *George Pan Cosmatos, director of 'Rambo II'*

"After this film, there's not a part in hell that I couldn't do. I was really proud of everything I did – although it'll never be shown. I have eight hours of film. Not just out-takes but the actual movie." *Kim Basinger after '9½ Weeks'*

"I made *Ran* as if it was my last film." *Akira Kurosawa*

"People in the street still call me Popeye and *The French Connection* was 15 years ago. I wish I could have another hit – and a new nickname." ***Gene Hackman***

"See, one of the troubles with people who make prison movies is that they tend to base their stories on the first prison movie they saw. It's understandable. There aren't too many ex-cons around to correct them." *Edward Bunker, one ex-con who is co-scripter of 'Runaway Train'*

"I don't think there's anything you *can't* be light-hearted about. In the kind of world we live in, one's either light-hearted about everything or very down-hearted about everything. I prefer to be light-hearted." *John Huston on 'Prizzi's Honor'*

"He was a very sweet guy saddled with the job of being Sid Vicious. He was naive, not very sensible, with an enormous desire to be loved, famous and approved of. But he wasn't the monster that he effectively portrayed – no more than was Boris Karloff." *Alex Cox, 'Sid and Nancy' director*

"If you make an American film with a beginning, middle and end, with a budget of less than $5 million – you must be an idiot to lose money." *Menahem Golan*

"I make movies for money. Exclusively for money. So, I sell myself for the highest price. Exactly like a prostitute. There is no difference." *Klaus Kinski*

"I asked one studio executive if he'd ever seen any Russian films. Sure, he said, I've seen *Dr Zhivago* and *Nicholas and Alexandra*." *Andrei Konchalovsky*

"I think the intelligentsia should understand that this country now is functioning on emotional energy more than intellectual energy." *Sylvester Stallone*

"When I heard who my predecessors were, I thought I had better send them a retrospective of my reviews ... they've made a mistake." *Elizabeth Taylor at her Lincoln Center's Film Society tribute (after Fellini, Wilder, Newman, Woodward, Hitchcock)*

"I'm always under budget by the time we get to the music, so the composers love me, 'cos I say: If you want a 95-piece orchestra – have it." *Michael Winner*

FEATURES

THE BRAT PACK

By Simon Banner

If Hollywood these days reflects the moods and fashions of America at large, rather than in any way defining them, then one of the more significant developments of the eighties has been the emergence of a wave of actors, and an accompanying flood of films, which seem to be expressly designed for the neo-conservative Reagan generation. The movie capital's response to the Yuppies has been the Yactors, young upwardly mobile thespians whose screentime is divided, as often as not, between primevally unintelligent teenage fantasy and a kind of cosy encounter therapy, and who, off-screen, have proved themselves, if the popular press is to be believed, to be spoiled, self-conscious, and self-dramatising, with nothing more on their minds than leisure, romance, and having a Porsche before turning 30.

Not, of course, that you will know them as Yactors, which was what somebody attempted to christen them, because, to describe the mid-eighties wave of young American film stars, somebody else came up with the Brat Pack, and that's the name which has stuck.

It's certainly a good name, not only for its punning reference to the famous Rat Pack of Sinatra, Martin, Davis, Lawford and friends, or even for the hint it gives of their cinematic precocity, but also, and most of all, as an indicator of their brattish attitudes and standards of behaviour off-screen. For the Brat Pack have largely been defined by the press in terms of what, in the 1980s, goes unselfconsciously by the name of style: what they wear, what and where they eat, what cars they drive (apart from Porsches) etc.

Sean Penn

According to the publicity, Brat Packers dress in a uniform of sunglasses, designer T-shirts, jeans and sports jackets. Notoriously rowdy, they haunt LA's smartest restaurants and hotels, such as the Century Plaza (the place Ron and Nancy stay when they're in town), noisily acknowledging each other and yelling "Havin' a good time?" to startled guests as they race off to their cars. They eat at Spago's or Ma Maison, escorting one or other of the beautiful young actresses with whom they work, drinking such favourite drinks as Corona Beers from Mexico and Stolichnaya Vodka from Russia.

It's a silly game, yet to define the Brat Pack in any other way – by their style of acting, the types of film they make, and so forth – is harder to do, and even to say just who they are is not easy. Some young actors, like Vincent Spano (*Baby, It's You*), Michael Paré (*Eddie and the Cruisers*), or Kevin Bacon (*Footloose*), sometimes referred to as Brat Packers, seem to have had brief moments of prominence, while names like Aidan Quinn or Michael J Fox, which could credibly be included in the list, usually aren't, and two that are, Matthew Broderick and Timothy Hutton, are perhaps misrepresented, both in respect of their careers and their characters, by association with the movie tearaways.

The essential Brat Pack list, however, would certainly have to include Tom Cruise, Matt Dillon, pretty Rob Lowe, and Martin Sheen's son Emilio Estevez, as well as Judd Nelson, the one who looks more like a Republican senator than a film star, and Andrew McCarthy, the one who looks more like a frightened sheep. Matthew Modine and Nicolas Cage (seen together in Alan Parker's *Birdy*) might also now warrant inclusion. All have made hit movies of one sort or another and continue to be in demand in Hollywood.

Probably heading the list, though, should be Sean Penn, the 26-year-old husband of singing superstar and aspiring actress Madonna, who has latterly established himself as the undisputed Leader of the Pack, and who could be said to typify the group in the course his brief and brilliant career has taken.

With a mean and moody image obliquely descended from James Dean via Robert De Niro, with a hint of Jack Nicholson thrown in, Penn first commanded attention with a starring role in *Taps* alongside Timothy Hutton and Tom Cruise back in 1981. His performance as a doped-out surfer in *Fast Times at Ridgemont High* earned further praise and sowed the seeds of Penn's reputation, one he shares with most of the other Brats, as a self-taught 'method' man who assiduously stays in character after the cameras have stopped rolling.

Once losing his character off-screen while filming *Fast Times*, Penn's dramatic solution to getting back in touch with the basket-case surfer he was playing was to stub a cigarette out on the palm of his hand. Preparing to play a teenage hoodlum in *Bad Boys*, Penn grew his hair shoulder-length and insisted on a real tattoo of a wolf's head rather than a make-up department's simulation; and it was, apparently, only his mother's protestations which stopped him having his teeth filed down as well.

In an age where having the

odd tooth or two pulled, silicon implanted left and right, if not centre, and gaining or losing considerable amounts of weight have all become commonplace matters for movie stars, the Brat Packers remain notable for their pre-eminent devotion to such tactics. Nicolas Cage surrendered several teeth for *Birdy*; Matt Dillon, like Penn, apparently 'is' his character for the course of filming; Rob Lowe became a hockey player of international standard before portraying one in *Young Blood*; and for *Iceman*, Timothy Hutton immersed himself in anthropology, *and* learned to speak the Eskimo dialect of Inuktituk.

Sean Penn could also be regarded as typical of the Brat Pack in his, to say the least, ambivalent attitude toward the press. His stance on publicity is obviously duplicitous – he claims to avoid it, yet still deems it worthwhile to retain an expensive public relations man – though what began as shrewd promotion of a certain self-consciously starry image looks now to be doing more harm than good. The hostility that Penn engenders, and which rose to spectacular levels when he accompanied Madonna to England to work on *Shanghai Surprise*, has certainly tended to cloud judgement of his work – one West Coast press agent famously referred to him as a "no-talent slob" (although Richard Rosenthal, his director on *Bad Boys*, called him "the most talented actor of his generation"). More significantly, his habit of throwing tantrums on and off set is said to have lost him work, including a role in the top-grossing *Top Gun* to the calmer Tom Cruise.

Kevin Bacon

The slob, in truth, is really a rather talented one – his work in Louis Malle's *Crackers* and in John Schlesinger's *The Falcon and the Snowman* is enough to prove that – but like the majority of his fellow Brat Packers, with as yet no really discernible pulling power at the domestic box office, let alone in the rest of the world, positive publicity is not to be scorned.

The very notion of the Brat Pack itself has, after all, been as much as anything a conspiracy between Hollywood publicity departments and the press. The press likes nothing better than some phenomenon – such as a supposedly homogeneous group of rising young stars – endlessly to analyse, parade and investigate, while the studios still hanker after a fixed stable of stars around whom films could be produced. Interestingly though, the audiences of the eighties have so far proved themselves much more likely to associate with such directorial brats as Steven Spielberg than with Brat Pack actors.

Aside from the Rat and the Brat Packs, there have been other such groups before. In the late fifties Robert Wagner was part of a group of young contract actors nicknamed "the bobby-sox idols" and was one of the few to survive the experience. Similarly, the clutch of young actors who shot to fame at the start of the seventies in such films as *The Last Picture Show* and *American Graffiti* only yielded a few adult stars with real staying power: Jeff Bridges, Harrison Ford, and Richard Dreyfuss amongst them.

Matt Dillon

The Brat Pack remain notable, however, for their extreme youth. Matt Dillon, star of Coppola's *The Outsiders* and *Rumble Fish*, had made ten movies before reaching the age of 20 (and he's only 22 now). Matthew Broderick had made the successful *WarGames*, and was reputedly earning more than $1m a movie, before he was 21, and seemingly before he'd started shaving as well. Sean Penn and Timothy Hutton, both 26, are about the oldest of the bunch.

It has been suggested that the emergence of such youthful stars represents some sort of shifting attitude towards cinematic verisimilitude. When, for example, back in 1967 Dustin Hoffman played the lead in *The Graduate*, his character had just graduated from college but the actor himself was 30. If today's audience, as it is said to be, is less accepting of older actors playing young people, the reason for that is not so much a scrupulous regard for realism as the simple fact that the audience itself is getting younger and younger.

More than half the US movie audience is now in the 12-to-24 age group, a fact which is apparent enough from the tailor-made product Hollywood has been busily churning out for the last decade, though at the *Porky's Revenge* end of the scale, many of the films suggest not so much an audience which is young as an audience which is brain-dead. The return of science fiction as the most bankable genre of all is itself a reflection of the dominance of a younger audience, but that audience's increasing

Judd Nelson

Anthony Michael Hall

Emilio Estevez

innurement to any but the most innovative, and hence most expensive, special effects, has left science fiction a risky prospect. A far better bet, at least in terms of guaranteeing a decent return on a modest financial investment, and usually an even more modest creative one, has been the straightforward teen movie.

It was *National Lampoon's Animal House* which set the pace back in 1978 – snapping towels in the locker room and dancing senselessly in the streets, ogling the girls in the shower and getting crazy drunk, tearing up the strip in a 'borrowed' Porsche and generally grossing out Mum and Dad. This proved a hugely profitable recipe, a configuration that has been shamelessly repeated in films which perhaps now total almost half of any year's output, though it is worth gratefully remembering that relatively few have done well outside the US and only a small proportion are released in Europe at all.

The rise of the Brat Pack, then, could be said to be quite simply a result of the dominance of teen movies, and the preponderance of young audiences. Admittedly at the comparatively high-brow end of the market, the sudden rush, for example, to produce films from the novels of S E Hinton alone brought a whole crop of young actors to attention. Matt Dillon pre-eminently, but Emilio Estevez, Rob Lowe, Tom Cruise and Vincent Spano have also featured in screen versions of Hinton's tales of rebellious and misunderstood youth: *Tex, Rumble Fish, The Outsiders,* and, more recently, *That Was Then, This Is Now.*

On the subject of the quality of movies, it is clear that the relative status of the Brat Pack actors has a lot to do with the quality of the movies in which they appear as well as their ability to rise above ordinary material. If Matt Dillon is one of the few with a fairly unimpeachable record to set beside his unquestionably charismatic screen presence, others have often struggled to turn performances in lamentably bad films to some sort of advantage.

The remorselessly silly *Fast Times at Ridgemont High* was clearly most notable for Sean Penn's persuasive cigarette-stubbing performance. Matthew Modine (something of a Brat Pack dark horse with nice performances in *Birdy* and Gillian Armstrong's unjustly neglected *Mrs Soffel*) almost single-handedly redeemed the appalling *Vision Quest,* though it was left to Madonna's title song to redeem the film at the box office (for video release the film was even renamed after it: *Crazy For You*).

Anthony Michael Hall, a sort of Brat Pack nerd, even emerged critically unscathed from Robert Hughes' dreadful *Weird Science*, though some, like Andrew McCarthy and Rob Lowe, look lucky to have careers at all after indifferent performances in films as bad as *Class.* Judd Nelson, apart from being the least pretty Brat Packer, has the added disadvantage of being almost brutally untalented on the strength of his performances in *The Breakfast Club* and *St Elmo's Fire*, both films in which he failed to act beyond tilting his chin at the camera.

Those two films, however, could be said to be quintessential Brat Pack movies, films where the very concept of a Brat Pack is most meaningful and which usefully demonstrate the strengths and weaknesses of the actors involved (aside from Judd Nelson himself, Emilio Estevez was in both films, while in one or the other there are appearances from Rob Lowe, Andrew McCarthy and Anthony Michael Hall). Judgement of the films would probably depend on one's initial perspective on them. Judged as a teen movie which rather cleverly breaks some of the rules, *The Breakfast Club* might represent the best of all possible teen worlds, though ultimately it has the throwaway look of an extended pop video, a cliché of whine and poses.

A Chorus Line without the dancing, *The Breakfast Club* flattered its young audience with a detention-class-as-

Tom Cruise

Rob Lowe

Matthew Broderick

encounter-group scenario in which five high-school students swap stories of how rotten their parents are. Half-sarcastically referred to as John Hughes' "Bergman film" – lots of deep talk and salt in psychic wounds – it worked to define its characters as much as anything by their hairstyles, make-up, props, even by their lunches, but was saved from confusion and one-dimensionality by some creditable performances from its Brat Pack cast (as well as by Ally Sheedy, who, with Molly Ringwald, could be said to be a leading member of the closest thing Hollywood's young actresses get to a Brat Pack).

Emilio Estevez especially manages a limited role well, but then Estevez has already proved himself capable of much more than Hughes required of him anyway. He was the delightfully punk hero of *Repo Man*, and looks to be a writer and producer of some talent too, having worked in both capacities on *That Was Then, This Is Now*. His career didn't need *The Breakfast Club*, and it can also survive *St Elmo's Fire* as well, albeit that the *New York Times* called it "a graveyard for the acting ambitions of its hot young cast."

St Elmo's, aka 'The Little Chill', was variously regarded as either the acceptable face of Hollywood's teen sycophancy or its depressing outer limit. At any rate it did little for the actors involved, none of whom had time to develop their characters even where characters could be supposed to have existed, though again it was probably Estevez who came out best. Interestingly, it also failed to find a very large audience, because, as its studio, Columbia, had rather late in the day suspected, it proved to be too old for teens, too young for adults, and too American for Europeans. Paramount have played much safer with this year's hit, *Pretty in Pink*, firmly set back in high school with a cast obviously too old to be there.

The irony of *St Elmo's* failure to catch the imagination of America's youth also points to the limited viability of several of the Brat Packers themselves who could soon be caught in a limbo between teen movies for which they are too old and movies aimed at older audiences for which they are either too young or, more importantly, for which they lack the necessary range of acting abilities.

As a Brat Packer destined for oblivion before the end of the decade, Rob Lowe must be a prime candidate. He may be breath-stoppingly good-looking, but he has a dead voice and very little real screen presence – "the charisma of a doorknob" as one critic candidly put it. He looked his best in one of last year's superior flops, *The Hotel New Hampshire*, though his role was hardly demanding. This year's *Young Blood*, designed to show off his body as well as his face, has failed to make much of an impression either in the US or elsewhere. The Warren Beatty of the eighties, as he has been called, has a long way to go to prove himself worthy of the title.

Andrew McCarthy has at least the hit movie *Pretty in Pink* in his favour for the time being, yet he might still prove to be the "no name nerd" *The New York Times* long ago suspected him of being. Judd Nelson could go the same way as some, like Kevin Bacon, already seem to have gone. Film stars at the age of 20 and past it at 25.

Matt Dillon is clearly a much more serious contender as a Hollywood survivor. Since making his first movie in 1978, Dillon has cleverly managed to carve out a career in films which look to have had fairly serious intentions (even the recent *Flamingo Kid* was a cut above the average), and has also worked to compensate for his initial lack of technical experience with stints at the Actor's Studio. A thing of beauty he may be, but he can't be a boy for ever: perhaps Dillon's largest problem will be making the transition to playing non-teenage parts.

Tom Cruise is another Brat Packer who seems sure to stay the course, already starring in one of the year's most successful films, *Top Gun*, and set to appear in *The Color of Money*, the prestigious, much belated sequel to *The Hustler*. Emilio Estevez, as shrewd as he is talented, is sure to be a survivor too, though it may well turn out to be as a producer, or even as a director, rather than as an actor.

Similarly, Matthew Broderick may show himself to be more comfortable as a stage actor than a screen star. Rave reviews for performances in *A Torch Song Trilogy* off-Broadway, as well as for Broadway performances in Neil Simon's *Brighton Beach Memoirs* (for which he was awarded a Tony) and *Biloxi Blues*, suggest a depth which hasn't been evinced on screen as yet (he looked merely awkward in last year's *Ladyhawke*). Said to dislike Hollywood anyway, and to be wary of mixing with other stars, Broderick is the young actor who least fits the Brat Pack stereotype.

Timothy Hutton doesn't seem to fit the stereotype too well either in that, though still only 26, he has been at the top of his profession for longer than most of the Pack, having won an Oscar as far back as 1980 as Conrad in *Ordinary People*, and has a more considerable body of work behind him than most, including an excellent performance in Sidney Lumet's underrated *Daniel*. He arrived before the Brat Pack was invented and will be around when the name itself is all but forgotten, like the Rat Pack and the Bobby Sox Idols in past decades.

By that time 'brat' will simply be a word for describing Sean Penn's behaviour, and even he might yet grow up.

HITS AND MYTHS

Taking the pulse of American popular cinema in the mid-1980s

By Harlan Kennedy

"The blood-dimmed tide is loosed, and everywhere
The ceremony of innocence is drowned;
The best lack all conviction, while the worst
Are full of passionate intensity."

W. B. Yeats, *The Second Coming*

In 1985 and 1986 one-man-army heroes have been coming at us with a vengeance. *Rambo, Missing in Action, Invasion USA, Commando, The Delta Force* ... In the last twenty months you've hardly been able to enter a cinema without having missiles or hand-grenades hurled at you by Arnold Schwarzenegger, Chuck Norris or Sylvester Stallone. And if the film didn't get you, in many instances the audience would. Whoopin' and hollerin', they are the first generation in movie history to flourish a tub of popcorn as if it were an MX missile. And the movies have kept goading them on. With their evangelistic machismo, these celluloid saviours and superheroes have been all but saying, "I want you to get up now out of your seats and come and give yourselves to America."

This gung-ho sub-genre is but the hard edge of an inspirationalist, pop-mythic tendency running all through popular cinema today. From the first stirrings of the Lucas/Salkind variety of mythic battlings back in the late seventies – *Star Wars* and *Superman* – we've moved in the mid-eighties to a new wish-fulfilment evil-whacking that defies gravity and probability and stretches all the way from the Stallone-Norris-Schwarzenegger axis to the scarcely less prolific 'power of innocence' pics *(The Black Cauldron, Legend* and co) in which beautiful wonderboys use their moral radiance to blind wickedness into oblivion.

What has helped to breed these movies is in part a kind of failure: the fertile disproportion between political posture and accomplishment in modern America in particular, the Western world in general. If the Reaganite up-and-at-'em credo worked in action as effectively as in words, there would be no need for the *superman* and *wonderkid* fantasies we're being regaled with.

But in a West assailed by nuclear tension and epidemic terrorism, total conquest and retaliation can only exist in the mind, or in the thirst-slaking dreams and fantasies we enact on the screen. Thus in America a President hitherto largely powerless (Grenada and Libya apart) to turn defiant rhetoric into military action presides over a nation whose cinema regularly conquers evil on a global scale: and a former film star whose most famous screen role was as a legless cripple (in *King's Row)* becomes the national leader in a movie era where "You'll believe a man can fly."

Not only fly but also flex Herculean muscles, become a walking one-man arsenal and completely rewrite the statistics of (even Hollywood) plausibility in one-against-many movie battles. Even the Errol Flynn of *Operation Burma* would blench at the action hyperboles in *Rambo, Commando* or *Invasion USA.*

Schwarzenegger: cleaning up America

But the wonder of the new gung-ho school of movie is that its mythic strivings, and many of its story-telling strategies, are shared by other movies today which are quite *un*-gung-ho in style. Fantasy and evangelism can be found even in films where there's not a flak-jacket in sight. An increasing number of mid-eighties popular movies use today's state-of-emergency climate (the Western world under siege) to shoot stories out of the barrel of probability into a new dimension of dream satisfaction.

The *locus classicus* for this stunt is the scene in *Back to the Future* where our hero revs out of the 1980s and heads for the 1950s. In a film that has built up a credible, 'realistic' (if folksy) small-town setting, there is arguably no grown audience that would accept this fantasy time-jump without extraordinary plot circumstances as an ignition. Writer-director Robert Zemeckis cannily provides them. Our hero's life is in danger! Our adrenal glands are flooding our powers of reason! Rain, night, fire, light! And the emergency that finally kick-starts us into accepting the impossible is – what but the supreme mid-eighties phobia? – an armed terrorist attack.

From this nightmare we roar through time to a securer, sweeter decade. Here the fate of the family (microcosm for the state of the nation) can be sorted out with lofty hindsight, bullies are put down with a little stand-and-fight determination, and Ronald Reagan still presides over the landscape, albeit on a movie marquee rather than in top billing at the White House.

You'll believe a boy can time-travel! And you'll believe a nation can stand still while hopping three decades. For how Reaganite is hero Marty's visit to the fifties! It is not an impotent spree of gosh-golly amazement in which the hero is more acted upon than acting (as it might have been in an early *Twilight Zone* episode). It is a policing mission. Just as Rambo charges off to South-East Asia to sort out the Vietnamese, so Marty in *Back to the Future* zooms back to police the pieces and players of the past so that they will cohere for a happy, all-American future.

This image of the American hero as an ambassadorial-action-man – to a different country or different time – runs through virtually all of today's hit action movies. It unites *Rambo* and *Rocky IV*, in both of which our adenoidal wonder-hulk barges off to the other side of the world to demonstrate US guts and gung-ho to the underprivileged foreigner. (In *Rocky IV* he even dons a giant Stars and Stripes as an ambassadorial cloak.) It unites the *Indiana Jones* and *Romancing the Stone/Jewel of the Nile* sagas, freely flirting with xenophobia as brave-if-screwball Yank adventurists go to sort out the scheming foreigners. And it even unites USA-set pictures like *Code of Silence*, *Commando* and *Death Wish 3*, where an American hero is mobilised to go and clean up parts of America that have fallen into UnAmerican hands: whether delinquents, muggers, crime syndicates or mini-Mafias. (*Beverly Hills Cop* is a comic variant on this – California the foreign land where a Detroit Galahad comes to sort out the corrupt Gucci-clads.)

Stallone: demonstrating US gung-ho to the underpriveleged foreigner

In all these movies the ambassador-hero, suiting the frontier ideas of Reaganite America, is no grey eminence from the corridors of institutionalised power but a semi-vigilante firebrand doing his own unorthodox thing for the Land of the Free in the land of the Chained or Corrupt.

Even in a relatively non-gung-ho film like *Witness*, a similar equation is being subtly and reciprocally worked out. The Amish community to which Harrison Ford is an involuntary ambassador of big-city American values is shackled and weakened by its refusal to come to terms with the reality of violent provocation, and of the violent response needed to counter it. So the hero-as-ambassador comes, blesses the community with action-man Americanism and leaves, taking in return a token lesson himself in the peace-loving life.

And in even less likely mid-eighties movies the ambassadorial theme pops up. *Amadeus* triumphed in part – or even primarily – because Mozart was presented as Vienna's answer to John McEnroe: a Messianic music brat cleansing the Austrian court of cant and mediocrity much as J M goes about today cleaning up the tennis courts of the world. The hellraiser kissed with genius fights for freedom and self-expression against the mediocrity (Salieri) cursed with envy.

Norris: a walking one-man arsenal

What steers all these films towards the mythic is the emphasis on an increasingly high-contrast world view. Shades of grey are separated out into archetypal blacks and whites: good and evil, genius and mediocrity, heroism and cowardice, patriotism and treachery, honour and dishonour.

In the dream-world of today's popular action cinema, the good guys with a mission fight the foreign or UnAmerican bad guys, and (usually) win. And with this moral polarisation go other components of classic myth structures: the narrative as obstacle-riddled quest or 'trial' (through the jungles of Vietnam in *Rambo*, the mazes of intrigue and protocol in *Amadeus*) and the buying of victory or self-knowledge through struggle and adversity.

This increasing mytho-centrism – the fad for colourful and emblematic stories in which human beings are replaced by archetypes and plausibility by wish-fulfilment or moral paradigm – mirrors the mood of an America in which politics as the "art of the possible" is being upstaged by politics as the appeal of the inspirational: the appeal of the heroic, the patriotic, even the religious.

On the Presidential speech platform it is the age of the tall story as political heart-stirrer. Commentators have already pointed out how many of Reagan's 'true-life' inspirational anecdotes of US courage, circa World War II, are actually taken straight from old movies.

And in the pulpit and on the TV God-slots, the Moral Majority and the media gospellers are also born up on the wings of the Reaganite appeal to 'higher values' and conviction morality. The religious revival, just like the new movie mood, rises on stepping stones of mythic self-endorsement to higher – or at least louder – things. In this instance, of course, the myth invoked is the most durable Western myth of all: the Biblical God, with a clear preference for Old Testament morality over New.

The God of the Moral Majority is a no-nonsense lawmaker who metes out censure and punishment to those who deserve them. And cinematic, kind of revenge at work in these movies. It's hard not to see the Rambo era as representing a vengeful backlash against the movie-making of the sixties and early seventies, when the cinema psychologised or politicised all its myths off the screen, influenced by the siren songs Kate Millett championing women. Take the good-guy-bad-guy opposition up and out into the galaxies. Find a whole new landscape for myth-making.

Star Wars, closely followed by *Superman*, set the style for the hyperbolic heroism and improbable, even magical, American flag, Chuck, Arnold and Sylvester perform feats of strength, mobility and derring-do that few heroes in the previous history of the cinema (outside of animated films) could equal. And their wish-fulfilment triumphs are fuelled by America's real-life failures and frustrations in the field,

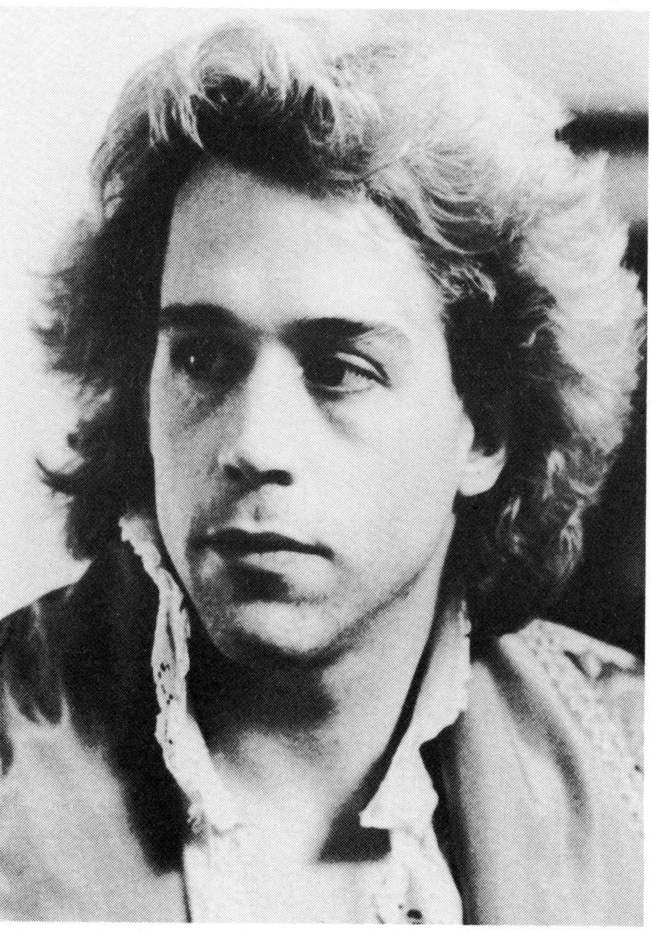
'Amadeus': Mozart as Vienna's answer to John McEnroe

'Back to the Future': policing an all-American future

the God who rules destiny in most modern action movies is also, Old Testament-style, a God of retribution, revenge and even blood sacrifice. The motto is not so much "Heal our bleeding land" – the cry of the hippies and student protesters in the sixties – as "Bleed our healing land". According to the Book of Rambo, only the unstaunched flow of blood can wash away a nation's humiliations. However heavily disguised as morality dramas they may be, films like *Rambo* and *Commando* are powered as much by vengeance, anger and primal mythic ideas of atonement as by any recognisably twentieth century notion of justice.

There is another, more

of liberalism and radicalism. The Western, especially, was shot down in a Custer's Last Stand by liberal attacks on racial stereotyping (the Red Indian could no longer be a villain), the rise of the anti-hero (*Easy Rider* and co) and the parlaying of Western tropes into modern settings (*Lonely Are the Brave, Hud, Junior Bonner*).

The first major riposte to the myth-endangering liberalism and ideologising of those years came with *Star Wars* (1977). George Lucas had found the answer. The hell with trying to stage myths on Planet Earth where you're going to run into Jane Fonda championing the Indians or Eldridge Cleaver championing the blacks or

feats of survival that have now been taken up again on Planet Earth by Stallone, Norris and Schwarzenegger. Behind all these quasi-medieval hero yarns, in which knights are called to arms by the far summons of patriotic (or astriotic) duty, lies the notion of destiny taking a hand, of physical odds being transcended and of the ethical power of Right coming in to compensate for the good guy's disadvantages in numbers or weaponry.

We've moved into a cinematic age that believes – if not on the street, then on the screen – in a kind of miraculous intervention. Spurred on by righteous anger, Messianic machismo and the

both under Carter (who offered little compensatory sabre-rattling rhetoric) and Reagan (who offers plenty). In these movie tales of fantasy conquest and one-man rescue missions, no helicopters collide humiliatingly in the Iranian desert, no Sixth Fleet hovers impotently offshore in the Mediterranean, no prisoner tradings are done under the guise of non-negotiation.

The one moral motif drawing together most of popular cinema today is that of the 'crusade'. Compared to sixties/seventies cinema, in which the dominant themes were of tormented introspection or impotence (*The Manchurian Candidate*), the existential virtues of going nowhere *(Easy Rider)* or the convoluted ambivalence of good and evil *(The Godfather)*, every hero worth his salt in modern cinema is ready to answer the "scramble scramble" call to heroic action.

And this climate of apocalyptic swashbuckle is even entering TV soap opera. Who could have predicted in the early years of *Dynasty* that a family saga lathering through the usual local crises of adultery, birth, love, jealousy and breakfast would, in 1985-86, have changed into a tale of Moldavian monarchies, heroines hurled into dungeons, eyepatched villains, mass assassinations at weddings (yes, all right, they all get up again, but it's the thought that counts) and even freelance commando heroes (Dex Dexter or, as Latinists might render him, Right Righter)?

'Witness': the hero as ambassador of big-city values

'Gandhi': a moral sermon for simpletons

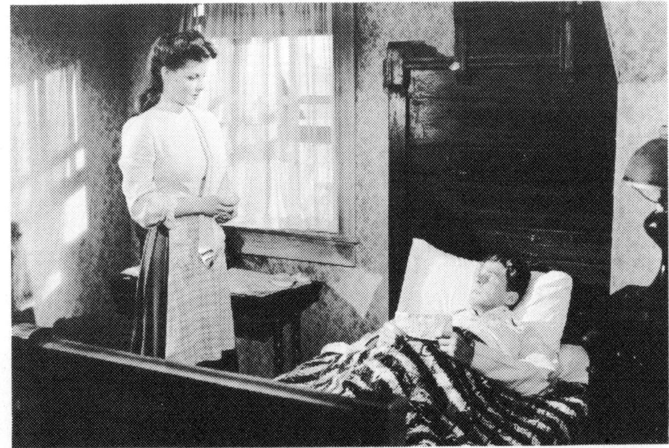

'King's Row': Reagan's most famous screen role was as a legless cripple

In this era, the enemies of popular entertainment are psychological ambivalence and aesthetic backsliding. The richly labyrinthine ambiguities of *The Godfather* (1970), where you never quite knew who or what you were rooting for as family homilies jostled with family homicides, marriages with massacres and whose characters were made up of good and evil in almost equal measure, would be almost inconceivable as a popular hit in the age of *Rambo* and *Commando*. And as for backsliding, many movies that get the popular thumbs-down today are those that hark back to the pacifist-liberal-dropout days *(Birdy, Fandango)* when love, peace and radicalism set America up for the well-meaning impotence of the Carter era. *The Right Stuff* similarly failed at the box office, because our great space heroes were being paraded before us as human beings rather than as mighty, macho icons (at a time, even, when one of them was running as a Presidential nominee).

Today's preference for a child's-eye picture of Total Goodness battling with Total Evil means that as well as spurning good films not made in the absolutist-inspirational mould, audiences (and sometimes critics) can be suckered into a false respect for bad movies that *are* made in that mould. *Gandhi*, for instance, is a moral sermon for simpletons; but it is writ so large and across such a sweep of story and landscape that it wins filmgoers and scoops Oscars, convincing everyone of its mature and majestic sensibility. And *Gremlins* and *Ghostbusters* are camped-up fairy tales for ten-year-olds, in which the moral universe – of heroic youngsters versus nasty ghoulies – is choreographed for us with all the subtlety of pantomime (which is myth for kiddywinks) and all the big-screen fireworks of the Special FX men.

But good things can yet come out of the new hyperbolised action movies and pop-mythic screenbusters. In the right hands – and devoid of crude sermonising or nationalistic baloney – popular cinema can profit immeasurably from strong stories and strongly sculpted heroes and villains. Certainly the non-mythic cinematic interregnum of the Johnson-Nixon years often seemed like a bread-and-water diet. Reaganite cinema is busy restoring the hero to the screen, plus fresh versions of the American frontier vision. When this restoration has been assimilated, it will surely lose its imperialist and crudely xenophobic aspects and give us an America for which the frontier spirit is measured not in baddies felled or countries overrun, but in the push of the mind and imagination towards unknown times and uncharted space(s).

A frontier spirit, what's more, that rejoices not in propaganda or bullhorning exaggeration, but in truth imaginatively heightened by art. We should have – we surely deserve – a popular action cinema in which stories can walk tall without being tall stories.

WOMEN DIRECTING IN HOLLYWOOD

By Nancy Mills

"I knew I wanted to be a director." Martha Coolidge recalls about her early days in the film business, "but I also knew I couldn't go to Hollywood because no woman was directing except Elaine May. That wasn't enough to make me feel I could go out there and make a career for myself. If I were graduating today, I would come to Hollywood because the doors are open at least partially to women."

Circumstances have greatly improved for women in Hollywood in recent years. Although no woman yet heads a studio, many have risen to key executive positions in the film world. Only one, Dawn Steel, president of production at Paramount, is said to have the power at a major studio to say "yes" to a project, but other women are quietly gathering experience. And many are producing.

Meanwhile, more than a dozen women have directed at least one studio-financed film in the past five years. This may not sound like a golden age, but the contrast between the eighties and earlier eras is startling. An investigation of Directors Guild of America records in 1980 showed that out of 7,332 feature films released by major distributors during the previous thirty years, only fourteen had been directed by women. The statistics for television over the same period were equally one-sided: out of 65,500 hours of national network, prime-time dramatic television, only 115 hours had been directed by women.

The history of women directing in Hollywood, like American social history in general, is uneven. Twice in this century – the film century – American women have made gender an issue: the Women's Suffrage Movement in the early 1900s and the Feminist Movement in the late sixties and early seventies. The fall-out from both battles led to more women directing in Hollywood. The two peaks of women directing, in the 1910s-1920s and the present, coincide with times when Suffragism and Feminism flourished. In the off years, between 1930 and 1970, only two women – Dorothy Arzner and Ida Lupino – developed a body of work. In 1974, the American Film Institute (AFI) became so concerned about the lack of directing opportunities for women that it started a special Directing Workshop for them. At the same time, more young women began enrolling in film school programmes. Today, every Hollywood studio is developing projects with woman directors attached.

During 1986, at least ten films directed by American women will have a major release: Joyce Chopra's *Smooth Talk*, Donna Deitch's *Desert Hearts*, Linda Feferman's *Seven Minutes in Heaven*, Randa Haines' *Children of a Lesser God*, Sondra Locke's *Ratboy*, Michelle Manning's *Blue City*, Penny Marshall's *Jumping Jack Flash*, Elaine May's *Ishtar*, Evelyn Purcell's *Nobody's Fool*, and Penelope Spheeris' *Hollywood Vice Squad*.

Another ten will be booked into at least a few cinemas: A K Allen's *The Ladies Club*, Laurie Anderson's *Home of the Brave*, Ronnee Blakely's *I Played It For You*, Lizzie Borden's *Working Girls*, Zane Buzby's *Last Resort*, Joan Darling's *The Check Is in the Mail*, Carol Frank's *Sorority House Massacre*, Yvonne Mackay's *The Silent One*, Gaylene Preston's *Dark of the Night* and Susan Shadburne's *Shadow Play*.

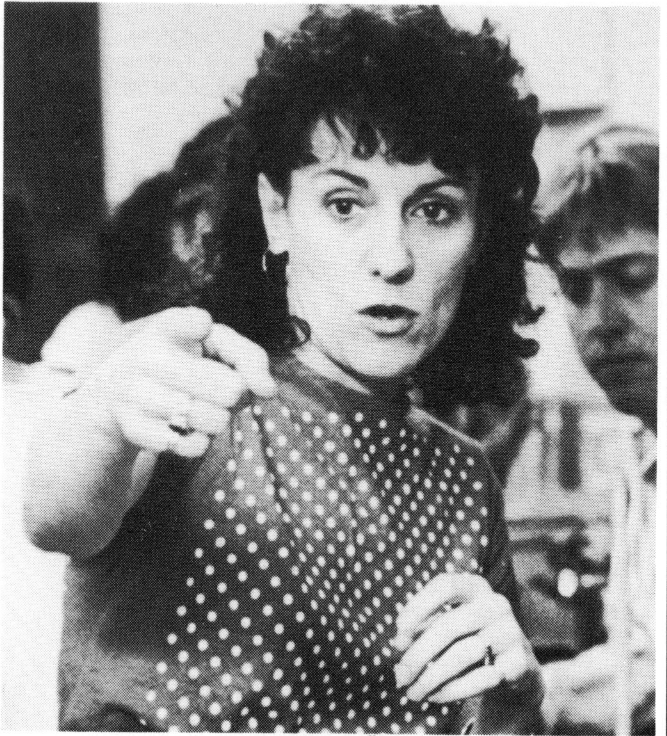

Martha Coolidge

A further eleven are either currently filming or close to it: Karen Arthur's *Lady Beware*, Leslie Glatter's *Leaving Cheyenne*, Jill Godmillow's *On the Trail of the Lonesome Pine*, Jackson Hunsicker's *The Frog Prince*, Amy Jones' *Maid to Order*, Mary Lambert's *Siesta*, Lynne Littman's *The Measuring Wall*, Penelope Spheeris' *Dudes*, Susan Seidelman's *Making Mr Right*, Coline Serreau's remake of *Three Men and a Cradle* and Linda Yellin's *Almost Everybody Wins*.

These do not include television films, an area where women have made equally impressive gains. Women directors may still be in the minority in Hollywood, but their presence hasn't been this strong since the days of silent film.

Although complete statistics aren't available, film historians believe that there were fewer bars to women directors working in Hollywood during the first two decades of the century than in any period since. It was a time before the studio system solidified. Eventually, however, smaller companies consolidated or went out of business, and today only a few of the women from that era are remembered.

Alice Guy-Blaché, born in Paris in 1873, was the first woman director. She joined the Gaumont film company as a secretary, and when it began to produce films instead of cameras, she became a director. In 1907 she moved to America and three years later formed her own production company, for which she directed. When it went out of business, she directed for other studios. After her divorce in 1922, she returned to France but found no directing work.

Lois Weber, who began directing in 1913 after being a concert pianist and an actress, is considered to be the most outstanding woman director of the silent era. In 1918, she was described by a *Photoplay* columnist as "the highest paid director in the world." At the time she was earning more than $5,000 per week. Her career came to an abrupt halt when 'talkies' arrived in 1927. She directed only one more film – *White Heat*, in 1934.

Lillian Gish directed her sister Dorothy in one film, *Remodeling Her Husband*, in 1920, but she said she preferred to do her work in front of the camera. Frances Marion, a highly regarded screenwriter, directed several films in the early twenties, including Mary Pickford's *The Love Light* (1921). Actress Dorothy Davenport directed a handful of films in the late twenties and early thirties after the death of her actor/husband Wallace Reid. She continued to write screenplays until 1955 but left directing to others.

Dorothy Arzner, thought to be the only woman staff director for a major American studio, has a star on Hollywood Boulevard. Between 1927 and 1943, Arzner directed almost two dozen pictures for Famous Players-Lasky/Paramount, RKO, MGM and Columbia. She directed Claudette Colbert and Frederic March in *Wild Party* (1929), Ginger Rogers in *Honor Among Lovers* (1931), Katharine Hepburn in *Christopher Strong* (1933), Rosalind Russell in *Craig's Wife* (1936), Joan Crawford in *The Bride Wore Red* (1937), Lucille Ball, Ralph Bellamy and Maureen O'Hara in *Dance, Girl, Dance* (1940) and Merle Oberon in *First Comes Courage* (1943).

The next woman to direct regularly was Ida Lupino. An English actress who moved to Hollywood in 1933, Lupino began writing, directing and producing movies in 1950. She formed her own production company and directed five films, including *The Hitch-Hiker* and *The Bigamist*, both

Lynne Littman

with Edmond O'Brien. She then began directing episodic television but returned to film briefly with *The Trouble with Angels* (1966) with Rosalind Russell and Hayley Mills. Lupino hasn't been seen since the mid-seventies and her affairs are now managed by a conservator.

Lupino was unique in her time. Almost thirty years separate her predecessor, Arzner, and the next woman to direct a studio picture – Elaine May. A few women did achieve directing credits in the fifties and sixties, but not in Hollywood. Shirley Clarke, a one-time dancer and choreographer, made several highly regarded independent films in New York, including *The Connection* (1962), *The Cool World* (1963) and *A Portrait of Jason* (1967). New York writer Susan Sontag directed three artistic films, two in Sweden – *Duet for Cannibals* (1969), *Brother Carl* (1971) – and one – *Promised Lands* (1974) – in France. Since a successful battle with cancer, she has returned to writing full-time.

Elaine May was the first of her generation to direct in Hollywood, basing her career in movies on her success directing and writing for the stage. *A New Leaf*, starring Walter Matthau and May, opened in 1971 and reminded everyone that women hadn't directed for a very long time. May immediately wrote and directed *The Heartbreak Kid* in 1972. But then came a glitch in her career called *Mikey and Nicky*, a film notorious in its time for missed deadlines. Starring John Cassavetes and Peter Falk, it has recently been re-released to some acclaim, but its reception was poor when it finally came out in 1976. May had spent years shooting and editing the reported 1.4 million feet of film. Considerably over-budget, *Mikey and Nicky* did little to encourage studios to put projects in the hands of women.

After *Mikey and Nicky* appeared, May beat a tactical retreat to her typewriter. She developed a reputation as Hollywood's most accomplished comedy script doctor, although she always insisted on anonymity when the credits rolled. Only this year has she ventured behind the camera again, in Columbia's big-budget *Ishtar*, starring Warren Beatty and Dustin Hoffman.

When May began *A New Leaf*, she had no real film directing experience and no way to get any except on the job. In order to help women already established in the industry in other capacities learn how to direct, the AFI started its Directing Workshop for Women. Successful applicants would receive a minuscule budget, use of the Institute's video equipment and the help and encouragement of their peers to direct a short film. Actress Dyan Cannon received an Academy Award nomination for her film *Number One* (1977). A number of graduates, including Karen Arthur, Anne Bancroft, Lee Grant, Randa Haines and Lynne Littman, went on to direct feature films.

Karen Arthur, one of the first to be accepted in the programme, observes, "The workshop let women cut their teeth in private. It shot down a lot of myths about directing. Some of the women discovered they didn't want that enormous responsibility. A lot saw that in order to be a director you have to have a very good business head or you get fucked over."

A dancer, actress and choreographer before she got interested in directing in 1971, Arthur made two independent films – *Legacy* (1975) and *The Mafu Cage* (1978) – before tackling the studio system head-on. On the basis of her two films, she got a three-picture deal at Universal in 1978, but nothing came of it. *Lady Beware*, which she announced then, was finally set to go into production this summer. "It's had 100 homes, seventeen drafts and eight writers," she says. Had Arthur chosen to make a teen sex comedy, she undoubtedly would have completed it long ago. However, she wanted to make a movie about psychological rape. And that – in her experience – is a subject male studio executives don't understand.

"The purseholders are men," Arthur observes, "and they attempted to make *Lady Beware* a violent picture. I'm not interested in making a picture where a woman gets beat up. I want to show how a woman deals with this kind of insidious violence where a policeman can't help." A new American production company, Scotti Brothers Entertainment, finally agreed to finance and distribute *Lady Beware*. "This is the first time people have said, 'Make your movie.' No one is asking for blood, tits and gore."

While she waited, Arthur solidified her reputation by directing numerous award-winning television films and episodes of *Cagney & Lacey*.

This year she became the first woman to direct an American mini-series (*Crossroads*).

Randa Haines had been a script supervisor for nine years before she enrolled in the Directing Workshop for Women. "The program was very helpful in that I came away with a piece of film I could show," Haines says. She hustled up her first directing assignment – an historical epic for America's Public Broadcasting System (PBS). Its success led to another PBS film and then a few episodes of *Hill Street Blues*. Haines' reputation was made with *Something About Amelia*, an Emmy-Award-winning TV film about incest, which resulted in an offer to direct Paramount's autumn release *Children of a Lesser God*.

Another workshop graduate, Lynne Littman got her first crack at directing a feature by bringing her project (*Testament*) to the attention of PBS' American Playhouse. A drama about the effects of a nuclear holocaust, *Testament* turned out to be so powerful that a cinema release was arranged in 1983, prior to the television airing.

A one-time producer and award-winning documentary film-maker, Littman was suddenly 'hot'. "Until I make my next film and fall on my face, I'm being beautifully treated by executives," she says. "men are beginning to look at us as exotic and something to pay attention to. They're curious and will give it a shot." Littman's next film, *The Measuring Wall*, for Tri-Star was scheduled to start in the summer of 1986.

Penelope Spheeris

Amy Heckerling

Susan Seidelman

Amy Jones

The AFI Women's Directing Workshop was the impetus for some women. Others advanced without it. Joan Micklin Silver directed her first feature, *Hester Street*, in 1975 after making three short educational films. "It was a period of high sexism in the industry," she recalls. "I remember being told by a male executive, 'Feature films are expensive to make and release. A woman director is one more problem we don't need.'

"In those days it took a bolt of lightning for women to make the jump to directing. Now I don't think it's so hard." Silver has since directed *Between the Lines* (1977) and *Chilly Scenes of Winter* (1979). Now she has moved into television. She is currently writing and will direct a six-hour NBC mini-series, *Glory Days*, about the Vietnam era.

Actress Joan Darling's directing experience with the soap opera comedy *Mary Hartman, Mary Hartman* led to other episodic directing assignments and then a feature film *First Love* (1977). Her 1986 independent feature *The Check Is in the Mail* was barely noticed. Documentarist Claudia Weill made *Girlfriends* (1978) independently. After Warner Bros distributed it, Weill got $7 million from Columbia to make *It's My Turn* (1980). Joan Tewkesbury supervised scripts for Robert Altman, and wrote two movies for him (*Thieves Like Us*, 1974, *Nashville*, 1975). Then, with the encouragement of Paul Schrader, she took the reins herself on his script *Old Boyfriends* (1979). All three have had difficulty getting studio backing for further films and have directed mostly for television.

After the Directors Guild published its discouraging statistics on women directors in 1980, no directing doors were suddenly thrown open for them. Some men in authority did send down word that women should be looked upon favourably. Chevy Chase was quoted as saying, "I wanted a woman director for *National Lampoon's European Vacation*, and I was very happy to approve Amy Heckerling." But progress came primarily because young, ambitious, hard-working women gnawed away at Hollywood. One by one they created spaces they could slip into.

"I think it's easier now than ever before for women to direct," observes Amy Jones, who has directed two films – *Sorority House Massacre* (1982) and *Love Letters* (1983). "Ten years ago it was virtually impossible."

Jones got her film training at Massachusetts Institute of Technology (MIT), a university more noted for its engineering graduates than its film-makers. But she won a prize at the American Film Institute Student Film Festival in 1973 and attracted the attention of Martin Scorsese. He hired her as his assistant on *Taxi Driver*. She then worked for Roger Corman as an editor. Eager to get out of the role of editor, she invested $1,000 of her own money into making a seven-minute section of *Slumber Party Massacre*. "Roger loved it and came up with a tiny amount of money to finish the movie," she says. "After that, Roger said he wanted an art picture, so I went off to write and direct one." The resulting *Love Letters* starred Jamie Lee Curtis, and helped end her image as the Queen of Scream.

Three American film schools, New York University (NYU), University of California at Los Angeles (UCLA) and University of Southern California (USC), have trained a high proportion of today's working women directors.

Martha Coolidge (NYU)

Sondra Locke

Barbra Streisand

chose initially to make documentaries because the opportunities for women to direct studio-financed projects appeared almost non-existent. Then in 1978 Francis Coppola invited her to develop projects at his Zoetrope Studios. She spent more than two years working on a rock and roll movie, and then Coppola ran out of money. "It was a learning experience at a very expensive school," she says.

Eventually Coolidge got a job directing the $350,000 *Valley Girl*. When the film grossed more than $17 million for Atlantic Releasing in 1983, Coolidge moved on to Paramount (*The Joy of Sex*, 1984) and Tri-Star (*Real Genius*, 1985), both teen comedies.

Work breeds work, but now Coolidge is tired of directing teen comedies. "A large portion of the feature industry is still completely closed to women," she complains. "However, it's harder for men to admit it [their bias]. A lot of men can't imagine women doing action pictures. Certain genres are still sexually typecast and closed to us."

And yet, 25-year-old Michelle Manning (USC) just directed *Blue City*, a tough action picture, for Paramount. It was Manning's first job as a director after working as associate producer on two popular John Hughes films, *Sixteen Candles* (1984) and *The Breakfast Club* (1985).

Like Coolidge, Manning got her first break from Francis Coppola, who hired her to help supervise Zoetrope's apprentice programme for high school students. She then worked on *The Outsiders* (1983). When Zoetrope fell apart, Manning moved on to a new mentor, Ned Tanen. Tanen's two Hughes pictures gave Manning her producer credits. When Tanen became president of Paramount, he hired her to direct *Blue City*.

The example of Susan Seidelman (NYU), whose first studio film, *Desperately Seeking Susan* (1985), was a hit, may have led studios to hire what became a flock of woman directors in 1986. After *Susan*, Seidelman signed a three-picture deal with the same studio, Orion. Her *Making Mr Right* went into production in mid-year. Seidelman started by creating her own opportunities. In 1980, she wrote, produced and directed an $80,000 feature, *Smithereens*, which became an official American entry at the Cannes Film Festival.

Penelope Spheeris (UCLA) finally attracted Hollywood's attention with her punk rock documentary *Decline of Western Civilization* (1981) eight years after she graduated. *Decline* was made on a $10,000 investment from two insurance salesmen. Spheeris' first feature film, *Suburbia* (1984) was also about the punk scene. This time a furniture chainstore owner helped with finance; Roger Corman distributed. Spheeris has since made two more films, *The Boys Next Door* (1985) and *Hollywood Vice Squad* (1986).

Amy Heckerling (NYU) got a studio directing assignment on the basis of her student film. *Fast Times at Ridgemont High* (1982), a low-expectations teen comedy, was a surprise success for Universal and helped launch the career of Sean Penn. *Johnny Dangerously* (1984) followed for 20th Century-Fox, and then the high-grossing *National Lampoon's European Vacation* (1985) for Warners. This past year she helped produce a CBS TV series based on *Fast Times*.

Joyce Chopra's *Smooth Talk* (1986), which also started as an American Playhouse project starring Laura Dern and Treat Williams, received excellent notices. Now, James Bridges (*Terms of Endearment*) has hired her to direct a film he is producing for 20th Century-Fox. Chopra made highly regarded documentaries for more than twenty years before Hollywood adopted her.

A woman associated with a project deemed to have been a failure may have difficulty continuing to direct in Hollywood. Jane Wagner directed Lily Tomlin and John Travolta in *Moment by Moment* (1978). The film was laughed off the screen. Wagner has since spent her time writing material for Tomlin, including Tomlin's hugely successful Broadway one-woman show *The Search for Signs of Intelligent Life in the Universe*. Actress Nancy Walker directed *Can't Stop the Music* for Allan Carr (1980). Choreographer Pat Birch directed *Grease II* (1982). Neither film was successful. Neither lady has directed since. Joan Rivers directed *Rabbit Test* (1978). She is now a Las Vegas peformer and a talk-show host. Anne Bancroft wrote and directed *Fatso* (1980). She then returned to acting. Barbra Streisand directed *Yentl* (1983). Streisand is powerful enough to direct again if she so chooses, but for now she will simply star in the upcoming Warner Bros film *Nuts*.

Three more first-time directors got their chance this year. Actress Sondra Locke, a close friend of Clint Eastwood, has directed *Ratboy* for Warner Bros. A comedy/suspense/ science fiction film, it stars Locke and Sharon Baird, one of the original Mouseketeers, as the ratboy. Because Eastwood was busy running for Mayor of Carmel, California, and wasn't using his crew, Locke was able to hire them for her project. *Ratboy* opens in October 1986, as does *Jumping Jack Flash*, a 20th Century-Fox feature starring Whoopi Goldberg. Howard Zieff began directing *Jumping* but was then replaced by Penny Marshall. An actress with a few episodic TV directing credits, Marshall has been talking about directing a film for years. Meanwhile, Mary Lambert, the American video director whom Prince hired to direct him in *Under the Cherry Moon* and then fired when filming started, is now directing *Siesta* for Palace Pictures.

With so many women directing, perhaps the novelty will finally wear off. Observes French director Coline Serreau, who is working at Disney Studios in Hollywood on the remake of her popular French film *Three Men and a Cradle*: "In France, there are many women directors. It's not anything we speak about. It's just normal. If you know your work, you work. You make good films, bad films. It doesn't matter if you're a woman or a man."

THE AWARDS

THE ACADEMY OF MOTION PICTURE ARTS AND SCIENCES 'OSCARS'

BEST PICTURE
Out of Africa

BEST DIRECTOR
Sydney Pollack
Out of Africa

BEST ACTOR
William Hurt
Kiss of the Spider Woman

BEST ACTRESS
Geraldine Page
The Trip to Bountiful

BEST SUPPORTING ACTOR
Don Ameche
Cocoon

BEST SUPPORTING ACTRESS
Anjelica Huston
Prizzi's Honor

BEST ORIGINAL SCREENPLAY
William Kelley
Pamela Wallace
Earl W Wallace
Witness

BEST SCREENPLAY BASED ON MATERIAL FROM ANOTHER MEDIUM
Kurt Luedtke
Out of Africa

BEST CINEMATOGRAPHY
David Watkin
Out of Africa

BEST FOREIGN FILM
The Official Story
(Argentina)

BEST ORIGINAL SCORE
John Barry
Out of Africa

BEST ORIGINAL SONG
Say You, Say Me
White Nights

BEST COSTUME DESIGN
Emi Wada
Ran

BEST FILM EDITING
Thom Noble
Witness

BEST SOUND
Chris Jenkins
Gary Alexander
Larry Stensvold
Peter Handford
Out of Africa

BEST VISUAL EFFECTS
Ken Ralston
Ralph McQuarrie
Scott Farrar
David Barry
Cocoon

BEST MAKE-UP
Michael Westmore
Zoltan
Mask

THE BRITISH ACADEMY OF FILM AND TELEVISION ARTS FILM AWARDS

BEST FILM
The Purple Rose of Cairo

BEST ACTOR
William Hurt
Kiss of the Spider Woman

BEST ACTRESS
Peggy Ashcroft
A Passage to India

BEST SUPPORTING ACTOR
Denholm Elliott
Defence of the Realm

BEST SUPPORTING ACTRESS
Rosanna Arquette
Desperately Seeking Susan

BEST ORIGINAL SCREENPLAY
Woody Allen
The Purple Rose of Cairo

BEST ADAPTED SCREENPLAY
Richard Condon, Janet Roach
Prizzi's Honor

BEST CINEMATOGRAPHY
Miroslav Ondricek
Amadeus

BEST SCORE
Maurice Jarre
Witness

BEST PRODUCTION DESIGN
Norman Garwood
Brazil

BEST COSTUME DESIGN
Milena Canonero
The Cotton Club

BEST EDITING
Nena Danevic, Michael Chandler
Amadeus

BEST FOREIGN FILM
Manfred Durniok, Istvan Szabo
Colonel Redl (*Yugoslavia*)

BEST SOUND
John Nutt
Chris Newman
Mark Berger
Amadeus

BEST SPECIAL EFFECTS
George Gibbs
Richard Conway
Brazil

BEST MAKE-UP
Paul Leblanc
Dick Smith
Amadeus

CANNES FILM FESTIVAL

PALME D'OR
The Mission
(UK)

GRAND PRIX DU JURY
The Sacrifice
(Sweden)

BEST ACTOR
Bob Hoskins
Mona Lisa
Michel Blanc
Tenue de Soirée

BEST ACTRESS
Barbara Sukowa
Rosa Luxembourg
Fernanda Torres
Speak to Me of Love

BEST DIRECTOR
Martin Scorsese
After Hours

BEST ARTISTIC CONTRIBUTION
Sven Nykvist (Cinematographer)
The Sacrifice

INTERNATIONAL CRITICS PRIZE
The Sacrifice

GOLDEN PALM FOR SHORT FILMS
Jane Campion
Peel

STANDARD BRITISH FILM AWARDS

BEST FILM
Stephen Frears
My Beautiful Laundrette

BEST ACTOR
Victor Banerjee
A Passage to India

BEST ACTRESS
Miranda Richardson
Dance With a Stranger

THE PETER SELLERS AWARD
Michael Palin
A Private Function

BEST SCREENPLAY
Malcolm Mowbray, Alan Bennett
A Private Function

MOST PROMISING NEWCOMERS
Alexandra Pigg, Margi Clarke
A Letter to Brezhnev

BEST TECHNICAL ACHIEVEMENT
Norman Garwood
Brazil

SPECIAL AWARD FOR OUTSTANDING CONTRIBUTION TO BRITISH FILMS
George Harrison & Denis O'Brien
of HandMade Films

CRITICS CIRCLE AWARDS

BEST FILM
The Purple Rose of Cairo
(US)

BEST FOREIGN LANGUAGE FILM
Heimat
(W Germany)

BEST DIRECTOR
Roland Joffé
The Killing Fields

BEST SCREENPLAY
Alan Bennett
A Private Function

BEST ACTING PERFORMANCE
Richard Farnsworth
The Grey Fox
James Mason
The Shooting Party

FILM DISTRIBUTOR'S AWARD
Palace Pictures

SPECIAL AWARDS
Michael Powell &
Emeric Pressburger
Kevin Brownlow & David Gill
Donald Murrey

DAVID DI DONATELLO AWARDS

BEST FILM
Let's Hope It's a Girl

BEST DIRECTOR
Mario Monicelli
Let's Hope It's a Girl

BEST PRODUCER
Giovanni Di Clemente
Let's Hope It's a Girl

BEST ACTRESS
Angela Milina
Camorra

BEST ACTOR
Marcello Mastroianni
Ginger and Fred

BEST SUPPORTING ACTOR
Bernard Blier
Let's Hope It's a Girl

BEST SUPPORTING ACTRESS
Atheni Cenci
Let's Hope It's a Girl

BEST FIRST FILM
Enrico Montesano
I Like Myself

BEST CINEMATOGRAPHY
Giuseppe Lanci
Camorra

BEST COSTUME
Damilo Donati
Ginger and Fred

BEST SCREENPLAY
Mario Monicelli
Tullio Pinelli
Suso Cecchi d'Amici
Leonardo Benvenuti
Piero De Bernardi
Let's Hope It's a Girl

BEST SET DESIGN
Enrico Job
Camorra

BEST SCORE
Nicola Piovani
Ginger and Fred
Riz Ortolani
Graduation Party

BEST FILM – FOREIGN
Out of Africa

BEST DIRECTOR – FOREIGN
Akira Kurosawa
Ran

BEST PRODUCER – FOREIGN
Steven Spielberg
Frank Marshall
Kathleen Kennedy
Back to the Future

BEST ACTOR – FOREIGN
William Hurt
Kiss of the Spider Woman

BEST ACTRESS – FOREIGN
Meryl Streep
Out of Africa

BEST SCREENPLAY – FOREIGN
Robert Zemeckis/Bob Gale
Back to the Future

RENE CLAIR AWARD
Federico Fellini

LUCHINO VISCONTI AWARD
Ingmar Bergman

GOLDEN GLOBE AWARDS – US

BEST MOTION PICTURE (DRAMA)
Out of Africa

BEST DIRECTOR
John Huston
Prizzi's Honor

BEST ACTOR (DRAMA)
Jon Voight
Runaway Train

BEST ACTRESS (DRAMA)
Whoopi Goldberg
The Color Purple

BEST MOTION PICTURE (MUSICAL OR COMEDY)
Prizzi's Honor

BEST ACTOR (MUSICAL OR COMEDY)
Jack Nicholson
Prizzi's Honor

BEST ACTRESS (MUSICAL OR COMEDY)
Kathleen Turner
Prizzi's Honor

BEST FOREIGN FILM
The Official Story
(Argentina)
When Father Was Away on Business
(Yugoslavia)
Year of the Quiet Sun
(Poland)

BEST SCREENPLAY
Woody Allen
The Purple Rose of Cairo

BEST SUPPORTING ACTOR
Klaus Maria Brandauer
Out of Africa

BEST SUPPORTING ACTRESS
Meg Tilly
Agnes of God

BEST ORIGINAL SCORE
John Barry
Out of Africa

BEST ORIGINAL SONG
Say You, Say Me (Lionel Richie)
White Nights

VENICE FILM FESTIVAL AWARDS

GOLDEN LION
Sans Toit Ni Loi
Agnes Varda

FIPRESCHI INTERNATIONAL CRITICS PRIZE
Sans Toit Ni Loi

FIPRESCHI INTERNATIONAL CRITICS PRIZE (FOREIGN)
Yesterday
(Poland)

GRAN PREMIO SPECIAL JURY PRIZE
Tangos El Exilo De Gardel
Fernando Solanas

JURY SECOND PRIZE
The Lightship
Jerzy Skolimowski

SILVER LION
Marion Hansel
Dust

BEST ACTOR
Gerard Depardieu
Police

SPECIAL GOLDEN LION
Manoel De Oliveiro
Le Soulier de Satin

SPECIAL GOLDEN LION
Federico Fellini
Ginger and Fred

SPECIAL GOLDEN LION
John Huston
Prizzi's Honor

OCIC AWARD
Sans Toit Ni Loi

PASINETTI AWARD – BEST ACTOR
Robert Duvall
The Lightship

SPECIAL EFFECTS
The Lightship

NO BEST ACTRESS AWARD GIVEN IN 1985 BUT SPECIAL MENTIONS GIVEN TO:
Sandrine Bonnaire
Sans Toit Ni Loi
Jane Birkin
Dust
Themis Bazata
Year of Stone
Galja Noverts
Tango of Our Childhood
Sonja Savic
Life Is Beautiful

DIRECTORS GUILD OF AMERICA AWARD

BEST DIRECTOR
Steven Spielberg
The Color Purple

AUSTRALIAN FILM INSTITUTE AWARDS

BEST FILM
Bliss

BEST DIRECTOR
Ray Lawrence
Bliss

BEST ACTOR
Chris Haywood
A Street to Die

BEST ACTRESS
Noni Hazlehurst
Fran

BEST SUPPORTING ACTOR
Nique Needles
The Boy Who Had Everything

BEST SUPPORTING ACTRESS
Annie Byron
Fran

BEST ORIGINAL SCREENPLAY
Glenda Hambly
Fran

BEST ADAPTED SCREENPLAY
Peter Carey, Ray Lawrence
Bliss

BEST CINEMATOGRAPHY
Peter James
Rebel

BEST PRODUCTION DESIGN
Brian Thomson
Rebel

BEST SOUND
Mark Lewis, Penn Robinson
Julian Ellingworth, Jim Taig
Rebel

BEST EDITING
Brian Kavanagh
Frog Dreaming

BEST COSTUME DESIGN
Roger Kirk
Rebel

BEST ORIGINAL MUSIC SCORE
Ray Cook, Chris Neal
Peter Best, Billy Byers
Bruce Rowland
Rebel

SAN SEBASTIAN FILM FESTIVAL

GOLDEN SHELL
Yesterday
(Poland)

SILVER SHELL
Les Motives De Luzlight
(Mexico)

FRENCH CESAR AWARDS

BEST FILM
Coline Serreau
Trois Hommes et un Couffin
(Three Men and a Cradle)

BEST DIRECTOR
Michel Deville
Peril en la Demeure
(Death in a French Garden)

BEST ACTOR
Christopher Lambert
Subway

BEST ACTRESS
Sandrine Bonnaire
Sans Toit Ni Loi
(Vagabonde)

BEST FOREIGN FILM
The Purple Rose of Cairo (US)

BEST CINEMATOGRAPHY
Jean Penzer
On Ne Meurt Que Deux Fois

BEST SCREENPLAY
Coline Serreau
Trois Hommes et un Couffin
(Three Men and a Cradle)

BEST ART DIRECTION
Alexandre Tranner
Subway

BEST SUPPORTING ACTOR
Michael Boujenahn
Trois Hommes et un Couffin
(Three Men and a Cradle)

BEST SUPPORTING ACTRESS
Bernadette Lafont
L'Effrontée

SPECIAL CESARS
Bette Davis
Jean Delannoy
Maurice Jarre
Claude Lanzmann

TAORMINA FILM FESTIVAL

GOLDEN CHARYBDIS (GRAND PRIX)
Man of Ashes
(Tunisia)
Nouri Bouzid

SILVER CHARYBDIS
Malajunta (Bad Company)
(Argentina)
Jose Santiso

BRONZE CHARYBDIS
Eat the Peach
(Eire)
Peter Ormrod

GOLDEN MASK FOR ACTING ACHIEVEMENT
Tom Conti
Heavenly Pursuits

SILVER MASK FOR ACTING ACHIEVEMENT
Micheline Presle
Beau Temps Mais Orageux En Fin De Journée

BRONZE MASK FOR ACTING ACHIEVEMENT
Marian Rolle
Almacita Di Desolato

ITALIAN CRITICS PRIZE
Desert Bloom (US)
Eugene Corr
Le Declin de L'Empire Americain
(Canada)
Denys Arcand

BERLIN FILM FESTIVAL

GOLDEN BEAR (GRAND PRIX)
Stammhein
(W Germany)
Reinhard Hauff

SILVER BEAR (SPECIAL JURY PRIZE)
The Mass Ended (La Messa E Finita (Italy)
Nanni Moretti

SILVER BEAR (BEST DIRECTOR)
Georgi Shengelaya
A Young Composer's Journey
(USSR)

SILVER BEAR (OUTSTANDING STYLE)
Gonza, The Spearman
(Yari No Gonza) (Japan)
Masahiro Shinoda

SILVER BEAR (BEST ACTRESS)
Marcelia Cartaxo
The Hour of the Star
(Brazil)
Charlotte Valandrey
Red Kiss (France)

SILVER BEAR (BEST ACTOR)
Tuncel Kurtiz
The Smile of the Lamb
(Israel)

SILVER BEAR (OUTSTANDING SINGLE ACHIEVEMENT)
Gabriel Beristain (for photography)
Caravaggio (UK)

SPECIAL MENTION
Paso Doble
(Romania)
Dan Pita

BEST FILM IN FORUM
Shoah (France)
Claude Lanzmann

CANADIAN GENIE AWARDS

BEST PICTURE
My American Cousin

BEST ACTOR
John Wildman
My American Cousin

BEST ACTRESS
Margaret Langrick
My American Cousin

BEST DIRECTOR
Sandy Wilson
My American Cousin

BEST SUPPORTING ACTOR
Alan Arkin
Joshua Then and Now

BEST SUPPORTING ACTRESS
Linda Sorensen
Joshua Then and Now

BEST SCREENPLAY
Sandy Wilson
My American Cousin

BEST CINEMATOGRAPHY
François Protat
Joshua Then and Now

BEST ART DIRECTION
Anne Pritchard
Joshua Then and Now

BEST COSTUME DESIGN
Louise Jobin
Joshua Then and Now

BEST MUSIC SCORE
François Dompierre
Le Matou

BEST ORIGINAL SONG
Lewis Furey
Leonard Cohen
Angel Eyes – Night Magic

VARIETY CLUB OF GREAT BRITAIN AWARDS

BEST ACTOR
Bob Hoskins
The Cotton Club

BEST ACTRESS
Dame Peggy Ashcroft
A Passage to India

MOST PROMISING ARTISTE
Miranda Richardson
Dance With a Stranger

BOOKS

Reviewed by Al Clark, John Walker and Nicholas Pole

ALEC GUINNESS: A CELEBRATION
John Russell Taylor
(Little, Brown & Co/Pavilion)
A useful companion to Guinness's witty autobiography, with some excellent pictures – notably, a sequence of Guinness as spymaster Smiley, anonymous yet immediately recognisable in a wooded landscape. He is, decides Russell Taylor, an unknowable actor whose strength is that he does not care who he is.

ALFRED HITCHCOCK
Gene D Phillips
(G K Hall/Columbus)
A select bibliography rubbishes just about every other book on Hitchcock so far written, but offers little of substance itself. Father Phillips, a Jesuit from Chicago, provides a detailed plot summary of each film rather than indicating why they, and their director, are worth writing about. (Our review copy was also flawed, full of blank pages.)

ALL-TIME BOX-OFFICE HITS
Joel Finler/Neil Sinyard
(Columbus)

DIRECTORS: THE ALL-TIME GREATS
Neil Sinyard
(Columbus)

THE MOVIE DIRECTOR'S STORY
Joel Finler
(Octopus)
Books with 'all-time' in their titles are usually brief in text, generous in illustration and more concerned with broad stokes than detailed analysis. Neither of these 'all-timers' deflate the notion of the cine-literate coffee-table book (and some of the pictures are superb), but one longs for a bit more. The hits book is self-defining, the director's one so subjective and restricted as to be meaningless beyond its entertainment value. (Nicolas Roeg is rightly featured, but Ken Russell isn't even mentioned; Oshima and Herzog are featured as 'New Voices', but Bertolucci and Forman hardly get a look in). Finler's director's book is a companion volume to last year's *The Movie Stars Story* and shares its assets and liabilities: part picture book, part directory, with career biographies of 140 directors split into three twenty-year chapters each prefaced by a summary. The quality of analysis varies, although much of it is interesting. What's inexplicable, though, is the presence of directors like Robert Aldrich, Stanley Kramer and John Sturges – all of whom were at their most influential in the fifites – in the 1960-85 chapter.

ANTONIONI: OR, THE SURFACE OF THE WORLD
Seymour Chatman
(University of California Press)
The extended title, from a quote by Rudolf Arnheim which prefaces the book, prepares you for what's to follow: an absorbing, if occasionally impenetrable, analysis of pretty much everything Antonioni has done (there's little attempt at a personal biography), from his early documentaries and features to a lengthy critique of his most recent, and largely disappointing film, *Identification of a Woman*.

ARROWS OF DESIRE
Ian Christie
(Waterstone)
Soundly written, handsomely presented career biography of Powell and Pressburger, together and apart, with an affectionate foreword by Martin Scorsese. A little starchy and over-reverential at times, as most appraisals of P and P have tended to be since their rediscovery, it still makes absorbing reading; and the colour illustrations – given how much of the legend focuses on their use of it – are beautifully reproduced.

ART POLITICS CINEMA: THE CINEASTE INTERVIEWS
Edited by Dan Georgakas & Lenny Rubenstein
(Lake View Press/Pluto Press)
It's politics rather than art that dominates these reprints of thirty-six earnest question-and-answer sessions with leading film-makers, reprinted from *Cinéaste*. Costa-Gavras, represented by three interviews, is its favourite director. Others include a fascinating memoir from John Howard Lawson, one of the 'Hollywood Ten', to Fassbinder, Wajda and Wertmuller. John Berger is the sole British representative and European names outnumber American.

AS TIME GOES BY – THE LIFE OF INGRID BERGMAN
Laurence Leamer

(Harper & Row/Hamish Hamilton)
Bergman's tears at the end of *Casablanca* were pure glycerine – "It's not whether you really cry, it's whether the audience thinks you are crying," was her credo. The gap between reality and illusion is explored here in an engrossing biography, the result of detailed, well-documented research. She was both ambitious and insecure, promiscuous, conducting as many as three simultaneous affairs, and boring in bed, superb in films and unconvincing on stage. An exemplary biography of a remarkable actress and woman.

BARDOT, DENEUVE & FONDA – THE MEMOIRS OF ROGER VADIM
Roger Vadim

(Simon & Schuster/Weidenfeld & Nicolson)
Only the biggest stars get their names above the title. For there's also his second wife Annette Stroyberg; and Catherine Schneider, another wife who gets just a brief mention because she's not an actress; and Francesa and Maria, passing fancies; and Ursula Andress, with whom he only, innocently, slept. He's a tease, is M Vadim, determined to turn his readers into voyeurs, just as he did the audience for the films in which he exhibited his sexual conquests. With becoming modesty, he records his infatuation with young girls, and ends on a gentlemanly note: "Brigitte Bardot is fifty years old. I wonder what she thinks of it?" M Vadim is 58.

THE BEGINNERS' GUIDE TO ABSOLUTE BEGINNERS – THE MUSICAL

(Corgi Books)
A stylish souvenir of the movie, all flash and dazzle and designer's tricks, which means that the words are treated as part of the decor. It mixes film stills and song lyrics with documentation of fifties pop culture and an occasional nod in the direction of Colin MacInnes, who preferred the music of Rodgers and Hart and recorded the coming of the teenager from the distant observation-post of middle age.

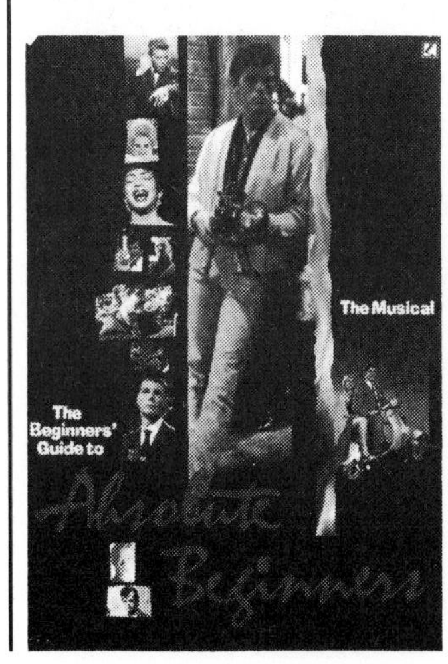

BETTE DAVIS
Christopher Nickens

(Doubleday/Columbus)
Another biography in pictures from the unflagging Nickens, devoted to an overexposed (in print, anyway) actress. The pictures are good.

BETTE DAVIS
Alexander Walker

(Little, Brown & Co/Pavilion)
Another slim celebration of a great star, packaging illustrations with an elegant, biographical essay that skates over awkward facts, such as her daughter's bitter book, to hail her as Hollywood's 'Mother Courage'.

BLESSINGS IN DISGUISE
Alec Guinness

(Knopf/Hamish Hamilton)
One of the best of actor's autobiographies by one of the best actors. His work takes second place here to a celebration, with witty and telling anecdotes, of such friends as the two grand Ediths (Sitwell and Evans), the exotic Martita Hunt, who taught him about acting and elegance, and Gielgud who once said, "I can't think why you want to play big parts. Why don't you stick to the little people you do so well?"

BURTON – THE MAN BEHIND THE MYTH
Penny Junor

(St Martin's Press/Sidgwick & Jackson)
Is there anything that we don't already know about Burton? The familiar story of talent and fame and waste is well told here, with saddening anecdotes of his last self-destructive, mainly alcoholic years. But there's little attempt to assess his achievements as an actor on stage or film.

CANNED GOODS AS CAVIAR
Gerald Weales

(University of Chicago Press)
This is the goods: twelve intelligent, informative and rambling essays on American film comedies of the thirties from *City Lights* to *Destry Rides Again*, taking in W C Fields and the Marx Brothers on the way. The style is discursive, stopping off to discuss the careers of minor character actors, or the importance of corsets in the creation of Mae West, but always stimulating and full of unexpected asides that illuminate the social realities, as well as the films, of the period.

CAUGHT IN THE ACT
David Shipman

(Elm Tree)
Although Shipman is responsible for some superior reference books, this briskly superficial analysis of sex in the cinema amounts to little more than an extended magazine article. *Last Tango in Paris*, the film which redefined how far you could go, merits only six lines of attention.

A CERTAIN TENDENCY OF THE HOLLYWOOD CINEMA 1930-1980
Robert B Ray

(Princeton University Press)
In accordance with its publishing source, a scholarly study of the ideology of Hollywood movies, with particular attention, for reasons which become apparent when parallels are drawn, to *Casablanca, It's a Wonderful Life, The Man Who Shot Liberty Valance, The Godfather* and *Taxi Driver*. An absorbing read, but hard to follow at times.

CHAPLIN
Julian Smith

(G K Hall/Columbus)
Is there room for yet another book about Charlie? This monograph justifies itself by its deft combination of fact and criticism and its unusual approach, arguing that his greatest achievement lies in his talking pictures *The Great Dictator, Monsieur Verdoux* and *Limelight*.

CHARLIE CHAPLIN
Maurice Bessy

(Harper & Row/Thames & Hudson)
The former director of the Cannes Film Festival writes a few words, which are printed in very large type, as if for the purblind old. But what makes the book is its photographs – 1090 of them, covering all of the subject's major, and many of his minor, films. There are pictures, too, of Chaplin at play and of lost films such as Josef von Sternberg's *The Seagull*, which Chaplin produced but refused to distribute.

CHARLTON HESTON
Michael Munn

(St Martin's Press/Robson)
Heston himself has told us most of what we want to know about him in his excellent journals. This dutiful and admiring account details his life from his beginnings in *Dark City* to his agreeing to star in *The Colbys*, the geriatric variation on *Dynasty*. It includes a filmography and some familiar photographs.

CHARLTON HESTON – THE EPIC PRESENCE
Bruce Crowther

(Columbus)
A dull and sometimes inaccurate (*The Prince and the Pauper* was shot in Budapest, not England, for example) trudge through a long career, of interest only to those who want detailed plot summaries of his films. The best book on Heston remains his own journals, *The Actor's Life*.

DAVID O SELZNICK'S HOLLYWOOD
Ronald Haver

(Secker & Warburg)
Reprint of Haver's superb epic-scale biography of Selznick, doubling as a history of the changing ways of Hollywood during his forty-year connection with the film world. One of the most extravagantly illustrated cinema books ever, with an exhaustive chapter on *Gone With the Wind* as its centrepiece.

THE DEATH OF JAMES DEAN
Warren Newton Beath

(Sidgwick & Jackson)
Is there room for another book about James Dean? Not when it is as pointless as this leaden recreation of the last day of Dean's life, padded out with detailed accounts of the boring lives of anonymous people who have no bearing on the events. (One chapter begins: "Stan Pierce (not his real name) was three years old when James Dean died . . .") For necrophiliacs only.

DEREK JARMAN'S CARAVAGGIO
Derek Jarman
(Thames & Hudson)
A scrapbook of an obsession, combining Jarman's script with his ruminations on the difficulty of making the film and Gerald Incandela's photographs. Less effective than the movie and coming no closer to bridging the gap between Jarman's Caravaggio and others' conception of the artist.

THE DISNEY VERSION
Richard Schickel
(Simon & Schuster/Pavilion)
When Uncle Walt died in 1966, the Disney corporation was one of the 500 largest in America. Schickel argues that Disney saw himself not as an artist but as a great inventor-entrepreneur, with Disneyland as his supreme achievement. He could never draw Mickey Mouse – a character designed by a friend – nor, to the disappointment of autograph hunters, could he duplicate the familiar 'Walt Disney' trademark. "I've always had a nightmare," he said, "I dream that one of my pictures has ended up in an art theatre, and I wake up shaking." In the often tedious details of this book's 400 pages it is easy to agree with Schickel that Disney, though obsessive about business, was pretty dull as a man.

DUKE – THE LIFE AND TIMES OF JOHN WAYNE
Donald Shepherd and Robert Slatzer with Dave Grayson
(Doubleday/Weidenfield & Nicolson)
The most detailed account of Wayne's life so far, using the reminiscences of the man who fixed his toupee for the last fifteen years. Admiring for the most part, it cheats by dealing with his rabid side – what he called, during the time of HUAC, "running a lot of people out of the business" – in one short chapter, as if his failings could be so easily separated from his virtues.

ELIZABETH TAYLOR
Christopher Nickens
(Doubleday/Hutchinson)
Subtitled "a biography in pictures", this is a work in the James Spada style, which means instantly forgettable, anodyne prose trickling through pages of sumptuous photographs, ideal reading for illiterate fans. The pictures are remarkable for the star's quality of self-absorption, the way she looks through, or beyond, her husbands and other partners.

EXPORTING ENTERTAINMENT: AMERICA IN THE WORLD FILM MARKET 1907-1934
Kristin Thompson
(BFI)
Fascinating account, despite the author's turgid style, of America's movie imperialism. It concentrates on the means US distributors used to dominate the world market for film, but does not attempt to explain why foreign audiences preferred Hollywood movies to their own.

FAYE DUNAWAY
Allen Hunter
(St Martin's Press/W H Allen)
Along with Fonda, Streisand and Streep, she is one of the four "bankable" actresses of our time, it says here. Certainly, she is the only one whose bad films far outnumber her good. The mystery is not explained; but nothing much is. The facts are here, though if anyone's interested in them.

FILM MAKING IN 1930s BRITAIN
Rachel Low
(Allen & Unwin)
The seventh, and last, volume in Rachel Low's indispensable history of the British film, covering one of its brief moments of creativity, with Korda and Balcon producing, Hitchcock directing, and Charles Laughton, Leslie Howard, Robert Donat, Jessie Matthews and Gracie Fields among the stars.

FINAL CUT
Steven Bach
(William Morrow/Jonathan Cape)
The story of how a new administration at United Artists tried to establish itself with a prestigious film, and of how the film – *Heaven's Gate*, budgeted at $7.5m and written off a $44m – pretty much finished off the company. It's really about decent-minded dithering in the face of a director's monstrous egomania, about a failure to challenge tyranny and about the stages in the film-making process at which you have a choice only between putting in more money, establishing control or closing down. Bach is a perceptive chronicler and this is one of the most revealing (and subtly self-critical) books ever about the way a Hollywood studio works.

FIVE SCREENPLAYS
Preston Sturges

(University of California Press)
A welcome, and long overdue, anthology of Sturges screenplays, collecting (of the twelve films he made as a writer-director) his shooting scripts for *The Great McGinty* (1940), *Christmas in July* (1940), *The Lady Eve* (1941), *Sullivan's Travels* (1942) – his first four, made for Paramount – and *Hail the Conquering Hero* (1944), the last of his pictures for that studio before his decline began. Each screenplay is prefaced by an introductory chapter and the whole thing is a delight to read, confirming Andrew Sarris' view of Sturges as "by far the wittiest scriptwriter the English-speaking cinema has known."

FONDA: HER LIFE IN PICTURES
James Spada

(Doubleday/Sidgwick & Jackson)
If it's pictures of Fonda you want, this has more than 200. There's Fonda at four-and-a-half; as Vadim's sexpot; as 'Hanoi Jane'; and as today's all-American capitalist, selling *Workout* to housewives. If it's intelligent commentary on her life and work you require, look elsewhere.

FRANK SINATRA, MY FATHER
Nancy Sinatra

(Doubleday/Hodder & Stoughton)

FRANK SINATRA
Derek Jewell

(Little, Brown & Co/Pavilion)
Take your choice – an extravagantly admiring filial biography (a real Dearest Daddy, unusual enough in itself) or a less gushing, less lavish essay-with-pictures that at least mentions the singer's darker side, his paranoia and aggression and his less-than-lovely acquaintances. Nancy's book has the better photographs, Jewell's the better prose.

GENTLEMAN: THE WILLIAM POWELL STORY
Charles Francisco

(St Martin's Press)
Little of Powell's slender wit and elegance survive in a plodding account of the life of one of the few actors to have made the transition from silent movies to talkies with ease. He married Carole Lombard, had a long affair with Jean Harlow, survived cancer and quit acting while he was still ahead, at the age of 63 in 1955, living happily for another twenty-nine years.

GIRLS ON FILM
Julie Burchill

(Virgin)
A fashionable commentator on pop culture – crowing as the thinking man's Jean Rook – gives a once-over-brightly, pun-packed, full of fun and fact, to the screen goddesses. She laments the way girls have been bred out of films by modern, macho movie brats or by the likes of the *Psycho*-pathetic Hitchcock ("Hell hath no fury like a physically repellent reject with a director's chair").

GODDESS – THE SECRET LIVES OF MARILYN MONROE
Anthony Summers
(Macmillan/Victor Gollancz)
The definitive biography, based on exhaustive interviews from everyone who knew her, from Mafia villains and the police to her many lovers, including the obscure and famous. Raising many questions about her death and her relationship with US President John Kennedy and his brother Robert, it exposes the dark side of Hollywood. Required reading for anyone who wants to understand the signficance of stardom in America.

HOLLYWOOD ENGLAND
Alexander Walker
(Harrap)

NATIONAL HEROES
Alexander Walker
(Harrap)
The best account of the last twenty years or so of the British film industry, reissued in paperback. *Hollywood England,* on the sixties, is more detailed and engrossing than the later book, which takes the story up-to-date, providing 493 pages on the decade to *National Heroes'* 296 on the next twenty years. But maybe this discrepancy is more the fault of British movie-makers.

HOLLYWOOD: THE YEARS OF INNOCENCE
John Kobal
(Abbeville/Thames & Hudson)
The years were the early ones, the decade that began in 1911, when no one was quite sure what a movie producer or director was, and stars were only just being created. The fascinating photographs, which have not appeared in book form before, were taken by a Los Angeles photographer, Nelson H Evans, who had a studio on Hollywood Boulevard. With a introduction by Kevin Brownlow, it captures the film capital in its brief and carefree youth.

THE GOLDWYN TOUCH
Michael Freedland
(Harrap)
A mostly affectionate portrait of an American primitive. Sam "and how did you love my picture?" Goldwyn, mangler of the English language, producer of polished middlebrow entertainment, was a sprat who emerged as a shark in the goldfish bowl that was Hollywood in its big studio heyday. Goldwyn believed small was beautiful – until it came to his ego – keeping few stars under contract, producing only a couple of films a year and raking in the *largesse.*

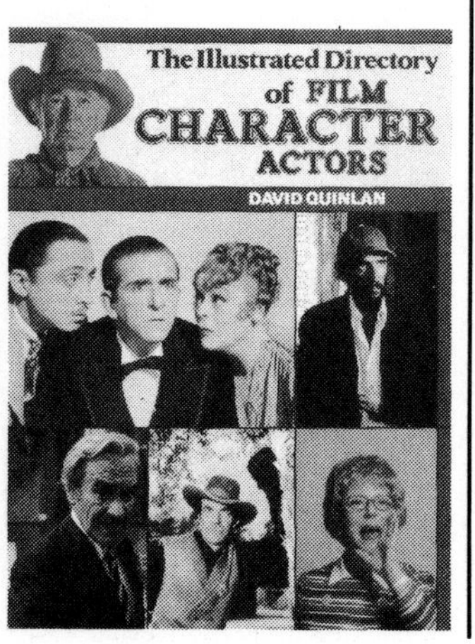

HALLIWELL'S FILM GUIDE
(Granada)
The fifth edition of Halliwell's resilient chronicle, covering most, but certainly not all, feature films up to the end of 1984 and adding the name of the British video distributor where applicable. Ever-improving in information, and always fascinating to flick through, one still senses a basic contempt for the bold or experimental.

HITCHCOCK
François Truffaut
(Simon & Schuster/Secker & Warburg)
Revised and updated edition of Truffaut's celebrated book of conversations with Hitchcock, originally published in 1967. The additional chapter is on the thin side, but the rest remains as absorbing as ever.

JOHN HURT
David Nathan
(W H Allen)
Slim, engagingly anecdotal account of the slim, sensitive, sleaze-loving, hard-drinking art student turned actor which concludes, reasonably enough, that "he is a greatly admired actor who has occasionally touched greatness and will not be satisfied until he has done so again." It also explains what has happened to his fascinating early film *Little Malcolm and His Struggles Against the Eunuchs,* which has hardly been seen since its first three-week showing – George Harrison, who financed it, screens it after dinner at his home.

THE ILLUSTRATED DIRECTORY OF FILM CHARACTER ACTORS
David Quinlan
(Batsford)
A commendable companion volume to Quinlan's directories on stars and directors, featuring mini-biographies, photographs and filmographies of 850 or so supporting actors and actresses. Possibly the only book in the world to reveal that Jay C Flippen lost a leg in her later years.

INSIDE OSCAR
Mason Wiley and Damien Bona
(Valentine/Columbus)
Subtitled 'The Unofficial History of the Academy Awards' (with a registered trademark, no less) and proudly emphasising that the book "is neither authorised nor endorsed" by the academy, an entertaining and exhaustive behind-the-scenes account of Oscar history, subdivided by year – between the background stories and the presentation night events. Particularly revealing on string-pulling, in-fighting, outfits, hairdos and the other things people really want to know about, it also has the benefit of being wittily written and endlessly anecdotal. The perfect bedtime browser, with plenty of lists at the back for readers who can't stand the pace of the events themselves.

INSIDE WARNER BROS
Rudy Behlmer
(Viking/Weidenfeld & Nicolson)
Subtitled, with an appropriate sense of melodrama, "The battles, the brainstorms and the bickering", this collection of the studio's tetchier letters and memos – covering films and individuals from *Rin Tin Tin* (1929) to *A Streetcar Named Desire* (1951), and including a whole chapter devoted to *Casablanca* – provides as revealing a backdrop to Warner history, and the ways of the film world generally, as any number of erudite-outsider analyses. A fascinating read, satisfying every curiosity from the budget breakdown of *Casablanca* to what Jack Warner thought of Errol Flynn's drinking habits.

THE INTERNATIONAL FILM POSTER
Gregory J Edwards
(Columbus)
An erudite and entertaining visual history of poster design – as art, as commerce, as propaganda – intelligently subdivided and beautifully illustrated.

JAMES CAGNEY
Richard Schickel
(Little, Brown & Co/Pavilion)
Schickel believes that the image a popular star presents is a greater work of art than the individual movies in which he or she appears, a dubious proposition which he fails to substantiate in his celebration of tough-guy Cagney. Movies that don't fit his thesis are underplayed. His other view, that a desire to penetrate actors' private lives is both feckless and socially undesirable, is to be applauded: it would put an immediate end to all the dreary showbiz biographies, fan mags and gossip columns. The book itself is pretty good, too, if wrong-headed, and is based on interviews with the man.

JANE RUSSELL
Jane Russell
(Franklin Watts/Sidgwick & Jackson)
A story of Hollywood and bust. How could she fail to be a star and a survivor when God is on her side, communicating with her in some of the most tortuous English this side of Paradise? Praying when she tires of her marriage, the message comes, "You two have not grown forward but, yea, backward and are destroying each other. So know this separation is of Me. And see, through all thy troubled, yea, grievous path, have I not thrown rose petals, yea, strewn them on every side?" Along with the Biblical excursions, there's gossip and the sort of drama soap operas are made of, yea, verily.

JOHN BOORMAN
Michel Ciment
(Faber)
One of the most lavish books ever published about the work of a director, particularly one who's still alive and has only made nine films. Ciment interviews Boorman about each of them, prefaced by his own analysis, and adds the recollections of former colleagues, some of them, like Lee Marvin, quite revealing. As befits someone identified by Ciment as "essentially a visual director", the illustrations are abundant and superbly reproduced.

KATHARINE HEPBURN
Anne Edwards
(William Morrow/Hodder & Stoughton)
HEPBURN: HER LIFE IN PICTURES
James Spada
(Doubleday/Columbus)
Read Edwards' book – the best biography of Hepburn so far – for the facts and insight into perhaps the most remarkable of American actresses, one with the strength to turn her limitations (including her fondness for Spencer Tracy) to advantage. And look at Spada's for its remarkable collection of photographs from her gilded youth to the palsied present day.

THE KILLJOY'S BOOK OF THE CINEMA
John H Irving
(Virgin)
Why do Julie Andrews' gloves change from white to black to white again when she is reading a letter in *Mary Poppins*? Why does someone call out "Hi, Judy" as Garland sings 'The Trolley Song' in *Meet Me in St Louis*? Why is one of the starving poor wearing a wristwatch in *El Cid*? The answers to these, and hundreds of other mis-takes in movies, are lovingly brought together in an indispensable Schmoviegoer's Companion.

MARILYN, MON AMOUR
André de Dienes
(St Martin's Press/Sidgwick & Jackson)
De Dienes was a famous fashion photographer in Paris who went to Hollywood to seek his fortune. One day a schoolgirlish 19-year-old with a dazzling smile walked into his studio, calling herself Norma Jean Baker. Soon besotted, he took her on a long car trip, planning a joint photographic and romantic adventure, but their brief affair was forgotten by Norma as soon as she got back to Hollywood, and he had to make do with being her favourite photographer.

This collection of sex-kitten poses catches almost nothing genuine except her exuberant love of posing, save for four harrowing shots of her in the pits of tranquillised despair taken at the height of her fame.

KINO-EYE
Dziga Vertov
(University of California/Pluto Press)
A neglected Russian theoretician of the cinema lives again, in a collection of his essays detailing his struggles with the form of film, seeing it as a means of the transformation of human consciousness. In 1922 he wrote the manifesto of the kinoks, who were opposed to the cinematographers, which he defined as "a herd of junkment doing rather well peddling their rags". Why don't directors think like that anymore?

LEGENDS
Terry O'Neill
(Viking/Jonathan Cape)
One of the most sheerly *enjoyable* books of celebrity photographs ever, all of them distinctive, some of them – like a stony-faced Glenda Jackson holding a pint of bitter in her *Mary Queen of Scots* outfit, or Albert Finney working out in the St Tropez dawn – extraordinary.

THE MAKING OF CITIZEN KANE
Robert L Carringer
(University of California Press/John Murray)
In a counterblast to Pauline Kael's book and to the *auteur* theory, Carringer argues that *Kane* was a collaborative masterpiece and discusses the particular contributions of the screenwriter, art director and cinematographer. As interesting as his detailed research into the genesis of *Kane* is his account of Welles's planned treatment of Conrad's *Heart of Darkness*, which was to have been his first film.

MARLON BRANDO: THE ONLY CONTENDER
Gary Carey
(St Martin's Press/Robson)
America's greatest actor is the just verdict in a dull book that never captures the spark and excitment of the man, nor digs deeper than what can be found in piles of yellowing press cuttings.

MARY TYLER MOORE
Jason Bonderoff
(St Martin's Press)
Gossip column stuff on the private life of the resilient star who began as a Hotpoint Pixie, dancing on a stove, and survived appearing as a nun in love with Elvis Presley in *Change of Habit*. It details her two failed marriages, the death of her son in a shotgun accident, her problem with social drinking, her diabetes and her need for weekly visits to her psychoanalyst – and concludes that she has shown "what femininity is all about."

MEL GIBSON
Keith McKay
(Doubleday/Sidgwick & Jackson)
A picture book containing dull photgraphs – hardly any sex or violence – and a depressingly overwritten text in celebration of Australia's first international star (not counting Rolf Harris and Dame Edna Everage).

THE MGM GIRLS: BEHIND THE VELVET CURTAIN
Peter Harry Brown and Pamela Ann Brown
(St Martin's Press/Harrap)
The curtain concealed the iron fist of Louis B Mayer who, in the subtext of a lively, gossipy account of the lives of some durable, and some fragile, actresses, emerges as a power-crazed, petty, lecherous, unforgiving, vindictive villain. He ran what the authors call "a throwaway organisation", forever building up, and then ruthlessly discarding, stars. Among the victims chronicled here are Barbara LaMarr, Hedy LaMarr, Mae Murray, Alma Rubens, Jean Harlow and Judy Garland. There were survivors, too, notably Garbo, Ann Miller, Debbie Reynolds and Margaret O'Brien, who could outwit him at the age of ten.

MONEY INTO LIGHT
John Boorman
(Farrar Straus & Giroux/ Faber & Faber)
One of the few essential books about movie-making, a diary kept by the director while setting up and making *The Emerald Forest*, a process that occupied three years of his life and took him from London and Hollywood to the rain forests of Brazil. His tales range from the horrendous and scandalous to the marvellous, revealing the unnecessary horrors and the unexpected joys of the movie industry.

THE MOVIE BUSINESS BOOK
Edited by Jason E Squire
(Prentis Hall/Columbus)
INDEPENDENT FEATURE FILM PRODUCTION
Gregory Goodell
(St Martin's Press)
DIRECTING FOR FILM AND TELEVISION
Christopher Lucas
(Doubleday/Columbus)
Three books about the process of making films, which the unlikely-named Mr Squire extends into distribution and exhibition, with essays by numerous industry notables about the area in which they specialise. Published in the US in 1983, some of it is inevitably already out of date. Goodell's book also covers distribution as part of the independent producer's armoury of knowledge, which he outlines with great clarity and precision. With regular updating, this could easily become the standard text on the subject. Lucas's book on directing is inevitably more subjective and is written somewhat in the style of a self-improvement manual. But there's plenty of useful advice, and it takes the trouble to define its terms and a crew's job definitions.

MOVIES AND METHODS
Bill Nichols
(University of California Press)
With two thousand PhDs in film studies being awarded each year in the USA, it's a relief to see that not all film academics insist on addressing their readers through mouthfuls of broken 'poststructuralist' teeth. Nichols treads a diplomatic path between the practitioners of feminist, structuralist and psychoanalytic semiotics on one hand and the humbler followers of old-fashioned 'applied criticism' on the other in this collection of writings from the film journals of the late seventies.

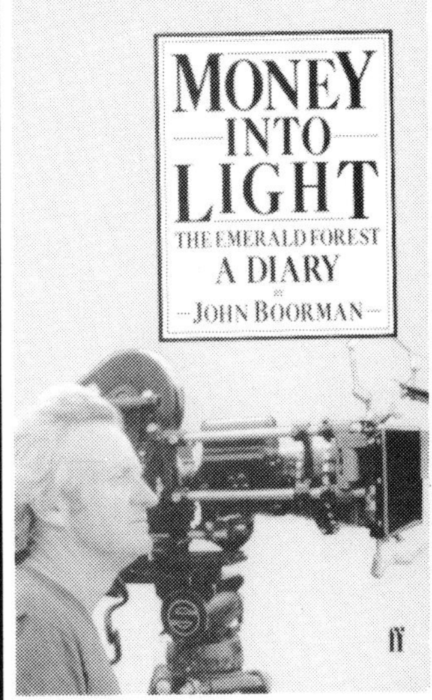

Some of the most readable pieces come – amazingly – under the Structuralist Semiotics heading, and some of the films discussed are *The Searchers, Jaws, Vent d'est* and Chantal Akerman's *Jeanne Dielman*.

MY LIFE IN THE SILVER SCREEN
Gerald Kaufman
(Faber & Faber)
As good a reason as any for voting SDP at the next election is this fustian reminiscence by Labour's Shadow Home Secretary, who is claimed to be the House of Commons' foremost film buff. One of yesterday's men in his appreciation of movies, his views are even more reactionary than Halliwell's and less interesting. "Monty Python is not fit to wipe Hellzapoppin's boots," he raves in his sentimental socialist lament for the death of cinema, complaining, too, that the standards of criticism have fallen to match the levels of cinematic achievement.

NOTES ON THE CINEMATOGRAPHER
Robert Bresson
(Quartet)
J M G Le Clezio claims, in his introduction to a collection of memos Bresson made to himself, that they are gems, shining like stars "showing us the simple, troublesome way to perfection". Maybe remarks such as "retouch some real with some real" or "neither beautify nor uglify. Do not denature" sound better in French. His laundry lists would make more interesting reading.

OLIVIER: THE COMPLETE CAREER
Robert Tanitch
(Abbeville/Thames & Hudson)
A full, sympathetic pictorial record and chronology of the stage, film, television and radio career of this century's greatest bravura actor.

ON ACTING
Laurence Olivier
(Simon & Schuster/Weidenfeld & Nicolson)
"This is not a book for the gossips," begins Olivier. He then proceeds to gossip for 200 or more pages, clumsily edited from his tape-recorded reminiscences. There are some splendid stories on Ralph Richardson, who once nearly dropped him from a high balcony, a few cool words about Gielgud, and chatty stuff about his career. It's good quality dinner-table conversation, but don't expect any great insights into his art.

ORSON WELLES: A BIOGRAPHY
Barbara Leaming
(Viking/Weidenfeld & Nicolson)

ORSON WELLES: THE RISE AND FALL OF AN AMERICAN GENIUS
Charles Higham
(St Martin's Press/New English Library)
There are many obvious differences between a largely authorised biography (as Leaming's is, its acquiescent tone reflecting "the privileged relationship" with her subject) and one involving no co-operation (Welles never forgave Higham for his first book on him in 1971). Higham has made effective use of the filing cabinet and revised his homework. Leaming has accepted Welles' charming and persuasive myth-reinforcing line, to the extent that she has him saying, eighteen months old and looking out of his crib at the Russian-Jewish orthopedist who was to become his mother's lover: "The desire to take medicine is one of the greatest features which distinguishes men from animals." No biography, however, can diminish Welles' wit and wisdom, a tireless subversive who always aspired to, and often achieved, the extraordinary. But the definitive account is still to be written.

THE OTHER SIDE OF THE MOON
Sheridan Morley
(Harper & Row/Weidenfeld & Nicolson)
More accurate than Niven's own accounts of his life, but less fun, this is, nevertheless, a cut above the average showbiz biography. Morley explores the contradictions in Niven's character: as the devoted but adulterous husband, the patriotic expatriate, the diffident professional, the wealthy miser, the unbankable star. He also pays due tribute to his debonair charm, unforced gaiety and talent to amuse.

THE PARAMOUNT STORY
John Douglas Eames
(Crown Outlet/Octopus)
Another exemplary studio history in the now regular Octopus series which has covered, with similar thoroughness, the films of MGM, Warner Bros, RKO and Universal. Impeccably researched, beautifully illustrated, it covers Paramount's 2805 films to the end of 1984, and suffers only from the extreme eccentricity of some of the opinions expressed.

PAULETTE
Joe Morella and Edward Epstein
(St Martin's Press)
Subtitled "the adventurous life of Paulette Godard", it leaves few turns unstoned, no trick treated well. Chaplin, who taught her to act in *Modern Times* and married her, is characterised as a chaser after underage girls. Gershwin, who wanted to marry her, is said to have hesitated because it would have meant him giving up his call girls. Erich Maria Remarque, her fourth husband, was not much of a lover. Godard herself is treated as harshly. Acquisitive – "I never give anything back," she said – relentlessly charming, a Ziegfeld girl at 15, she married a rich, older man, received $100,000 dollars at the divorce two years later, and went to Hollywood. The rest is a little bit of cinema history, here amplified by gossip and once confidential FBI files.

PETER CUSHING
Peter Cushing
(Weidenfeld & Nicolson)
A story that comes to a sad, premature conclusion, finishing on January 14, 1971 – the day his wife, Helen, died and his life, he says, ended. Fifty years an actor, with a career that encompassed American and British theatre, television (a memorable award-winning performance in *1984*), and film, from *Hamlet* to Hammer horrors, he emerges as a modest, witty, likeable professional.

PLAYBACK
Raymond Chandler
(The Mysterious Press/Harrap)
"Raymond Chandler's Unknown Thriller" turns out to be the second draft of the screenplay he wrote for Universal in 1947 – never produced and later revived as the basic thread of his last novel eleven years later. It isn't a patch on *Double Indemnity*, his collaboration with Billy Wilder, or even on *The Blue Dahlia*, which he wrote himself. Lacking in pace, narrative subtlety and a strong central character, it rarely rises above its rather schematic form, and the half-hearted hard-boiled dialogue that keeps it ticking along. An interesting read, but mainly for Chandler students.

PORTRAITS OF THE BRITISH CINEMA
John Russell Taylor and John Kobal

(Aurum)
Although subtitled '60 Glorious Years' and spanning Ivor Novello (1925) to Rupert Everett (1984), the portaits pretty much dry up at the end of the sixties, which is to say that the last sixteen of those years have been far from glorious as far as the nostalgic authors are concerned – "It's not the screens that have got bigger, it's the people that have got smaller."

RAISING HELL – THE REBEL IN THE MOVIES
Terence Pettigrew

(Columbus)
A 'so what?' book, in which a pointless theme is explored in a series of disconnected essays. A definition of rebel that can encompass Bogart's Duke Mantee and Bronson's vigilante gunman is so loose as to be meaningless. You could as easily take the same stars – Cagney, Brando, Dean, Newman and Eastwood – and demonstrate their importance as upholders of the status quo.

RED – THE TEMPESTUOUS LIFE OF SUSAN HAYWARD
Robert Laguardia and Gene Arceri

(Robson)
The blurb promises "the unexpurgated story", but there's nothing particularly sensational here, just the usual round of ruthless ambition, broken marriages, disastrous love-affairs, alcoholism, an appalling death – and all to be picked over by insensitive biographers. She first came to attention hitting Ronald Reagan over the head in a variety act, but after vented her violence on the talented and, very occasionally, turned in a blazing screen performance.

REX HARRISON
Allen Eyles

(W H Allen)
Harrison, who dislikes books about actors, will hate this slight account that concentrates on his stage and film career, mingling quotes from old newspaper and magazine interviews with comments on his performances. It quite lacks Harrison's own elegance and gift for light comedy.

RICHARD ATTENBOROUGH'S CHORUS LINE
Diana Carter, Josh Weiner, Alan Pappe

(The Bodley Head)
A riveting read for the Mums and Dads, boy and girl friends of the cast, wth its chatty outlines of the aspirations of the principal dancers, interspersed with little asides from Sir Richard, telling them all that they were super. Otherwise, it's only for uncomplaining fans of the film.

ROBERT DE NIRO
Keith McKay

(St Martin's Press)
Subtitled "The Hero Behind the Mask", this windy, wordy book ("The labyrinthine city streets form a well-known breeding ground for artist, poet, cabbie, comedian, actor, dreamer and overachiever alike," it rambles at one point) does not even penetrate the mask, if there is one. Why is it that biographies of actors never discuss acting?

ROBERT DUVALL: HOLLYWOOD MAVERICK
Judith Slawson

(St Martin's Press)
From his theatrical beginnings in *Call Me By My Rightful Name* in 1961 and his first film *To Kill a Mockingbird* in 1963, Robert Duvall's career is carefully chronicled in a chatty biography that celebrates his originality. It's short on insight, but admirably fills in the background to his unobtrusive brilliance.

ROCK HUDSON: HIS STORY
Rock Hudson and Sara Davidson

(William Morrow/Weidenfield & Nicolson)
Would this have been written, and become a best-seller, had not Hudson succumbed so publicly to AIDS? Probably not, as his life and his interests – gardening and needlepoint – are not riveting. But that bland onscreen personality hid a complex man with overwhelming charm and, understandably as it turned out, an obsession with privacy. Hudson supplied information and access to friends as he was dying and Davidson tells it well, always giving him the benefit of any doubts. She talks of his "being romantically involved" with men when it's clear that his involvement was predominantly sexual – although he did inspire lasting love in some and faced his final disintegration with dignity.

SCREEN DECO
Harold Mandelbaum and Eric Myers
(St Martin's Press/Columbus)
A luscious, marvellously illustrated celebration of High Style in Hollywood, when Art Deco interiors in the movies set nationwide fashions in decor and Cedric Gibons was the arbiter of taste. Then, even the savage kingdom of *She*, or the lamasery of *Lost Horizon*, or the future landscapes of *Buck Rogers* and *Things to Come* displayed Deco's curvilinear style.

SCREEN WORLD
John Willis
(Crown/Muller)

FILM REVIEW 1985-86
F Maurice Speed
(Columbus)

INTERNATIONAL FILM GUIDE 1986
Peter Cowie
(Tantivy)
The senior statesmen of annuals take their 36th, 41st and 23rd bows respectively. Willis's, as ever, is the model chronicle of the American film year. Beautifully compiled and presented, its usefulness continues to be limited by the absence of a proper overview, and as usual there's no explaining why barely releasable failures like *Hard to Hold* and *Tank* should have so much prominence and runaway successes like *Police Academy* and *Nightmare on Elm Street* so little. Speed's annual is now comfortably settled into its larger format and remains a thorough and reliable summary of the year, undermined only by the author's tetchily avuncular introduction (this year films are too long and language is still bad), and by the unfortunate bit of crystal ball gazing which led to *Revolution* providing the cover still. Cowie's book is solid and informative, but one longs for a little liveliness in the various contributors' country-by-country accounts.

THE SECRET LIFE OF DANNY KAYE
Michael Freedland
(St Martin's Press)
A meaningless title, since this well-researched biography is concerned with the man as the public know him. He's described here as "something of a Pinocchio who became a real boy, a Peter Pan boy who didn't want to grow up." It raises the question, which it fails to answer, of why Kaye abandoned what he did best – live entertainment – and made so many movies that did little more than limit his talents.

SEX SYMBOLS
David Malcolm
HEART THROBS
Tim Pulleine
(Octopus)
Twenty-two stars per book – from Clara Bow to Brooke Shields, and from Rudolph Valentino to Richard Gere – shown in photographs of varying familiarity accompanied by brief biographical information.

SHIRLEY MACLAINE
Michael Freedland
(Salem House/W H Allen)
Lively, well-researched look at the increasingly odd Miss Maclaine, in which the identity of her British lover, the MP who was the star of one of her autobiographical volumes, is revealed. He doesn't exist, insists Freedland who, for the first time in seventeen showbiz biographies, writes with a welcome touch of asperity – maybe because Miss Maclaine's agent told him that she earns $900,000 for each *book* she writes.

STAR BILLING
David Brown
(Weidenfeld & Nicolson)
Subtitled "Tell-Tale Trivia from Hollywood", a slim volume of quotes, lists and funny stories, entertainingly written and presented, and particularly useful if you want to know things like how many Mai Tais Robert Mitchum drank every evening before dinner while filming *Rampage* (1962).

SUCH DEVOTED SISTERS: THOSE FABULOUS GABORS
Peter H Brown
(St Martin's Press/Robson)
Written in suitably breathless prose, and with the co-operation of the quick-witted Zsa Zsa, this is a celebration of the seduction of American innocence by European sophistication. Led by the formidable Jolie, the archetypical stage mother who has had more facelifts than daughters, Eva, Magda and Zsa Zsa acquired between them nineteen marriages and eighteen husbands – two of them married George Sanders, though not at the same time – and innumerable lovers, not to mention several fortunes, most of them originally belonging to other people. A fable for our time.

2000 MOVIES: THE 1940s
Robin Cross
(Charles Herridge)
A record of 200 films for each year, divided into categories, and each one identified by a photograph, the names of its director and its stars, with a brief synopsis. For *Casablanca*, the comment goes: "Time may go by, but it only serves to enhance this seamless example of the Hollywood machine at its smoothest". There are 1,999 others of similar insight.

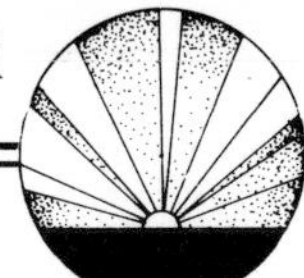

OBITUARIES

1 JULY 1985–30 JUNE 1986

Compiled by Tim Pulleine

BRIAN AHERNE

A child actor in England, Aherne achieved popularity in British silents such as *Shooting Stars* (1928) and was in Hollywood from 1933 on the strength of having starred in the Broadway production of *The Barretts of Wimpole Street*. He played romantic leads in such films as *Songs of Songs* (1933) and *Sylvia Scarlett* (1935) and subsequently gave a strong performance as the Emperor Maximilian in *Juarez* (1939). Later he played secondary roles, often as Hollywood's notion of an English or crypto-English gent, one of his best later performances being as the prosecutor in Hitchcock's *I Confess* (1953). He was briefly (1939-45) married to Joan Fontaine. Died in Florida on 10 February 1986, aged 83.

ROBERT ALDA (Alphonso Guiseppe D'Abruzzo)

An actor whose one well-remembered screen role was his first, as George Gershwin in the biopic *Rhapsody in Blue* (1945), Alda periodically played subsidiary roles in Hollywood films over the next several years, such as *Nora Prentiss* and *The Man I Love* (both 1947). More recently he settled in Rome, and appeared sporadically in Italian and other European pictures of little or no distinction. However, his stage career was happily more noteworthy, achieving its high point when he starred in the Broadway production of *Guys and Dolls*. He was the father of actor Alan Alda. Died in Los Angeles on 3 May 1986, aged 72.

EVELYN ANKERS

This blonde leading lady of an assortment of Hollywood programmers of the forties carved a minor niche as the 'scream queen' of low-budget horror movies of the period, among them *Son of Dracula* (1943), *The Mad Ghoul* (1943), and *The Frozen Ghost* (1945). Born to British parents in Chile, she went to RADA and played small parts in several British films, including *Rembrandt* (1936) and *Wings of the Morning* (1937), before moving to Broadway and then Hollywood, making her first American film in 1941. Non-horror movies in which she had roles ranged from *Hold That Ghost* (1941), with Abbott and Costello, to *His Butler's Sister* (1943) and *Last of the Redmen* (1947). Married to actor Richard Denning, she retired from films after *The Texan Meets Calamity Jane* (1950) to live in Hawaii. Died of cancer in Maui, Hawaii, on 28 August 1985, aged 67.

HYLDA BAKER

A veteran North Country comedienne, who made her stage debut at the age of 10 and went on to become a stalwart of the music hall and variety stage, as writer and director as well as performer, Baker also made several screen appearances. The best remembered of these was in the non-comic role of Albert Finney's down-to-earth aunt in *Saturday Night and Sunday Morning* (1960). Others were in *Up the Junction* (1968) and *Oliver!* (1968). Her most recent film was *Nearest and Dearest* (1972), a feature spin-off from the TV sitcom in which she co-starred with Jimmy Jewell. Died in her native Lancashire on 3 May 1986, aged 78.

PATRICK BARR

A stalwart British actor who made his debut on the West End stage in 1936, Barr encompassed stage, film and TV in a long and busy career. His greatest popularity came on television in the early fifties, the period when the medium became fully established in Britain, when his roles ranged from thriller serials to playing the lead in John Whiting's *Marching Song*. Although he occasionally played leads in second-feature films at this time, he more usually took supporting parts, appearing in, among many other movies, *Robin Hood* (1951), *Singlehanded* (1953) and *St Joan* (1957). His last film appearance was in the horror movie *House of Whipcord* (1974). Died in London on 29 August 1985, aged 77.

ANNE BAXTER

The granddaughter of architect Frank Lloyd Wright, Baxter was something of an infant prodigy, making her Broadway acting debut at 13 and her first film four years later. When still only 19 she played the ingenue in *The Magnificent Ambersons* (1942) and after some less distinctive roles gave an Oscar-winning performance in *The Razor's Edge* (1946). Her most famous role was as the duplicitous understudy in *All About Eve* (1950), but though she made films for Hitchcock (*I Confess*, 1952) and Lang (*The Blue Gardenia*, 1953), she mainly failed to find rewarding roles and spent most of the sixties in semi-retirement in Australia. In 1971 she took over from Lauren Bacall in *Applause*, a Broadway musical adaptation of *All About Eve*, playing the equivalent role to that taken by Bette Davis in the original. More recently she had been in several TV movies and in the series *Hotel*. Her final big-screen movie was *Jane Austen in Manhattan* (1980). Died following a stroke, in New York on 12 December 1985, aged 62.

HERSCHEL BERNARDI

A distinctly burly and bald-headed actor, pehaps best known in the US for a long stint on Broadway in *Fiddler on the Roof*, Bernardi also had a regular role in the popular TV series *Peter Gunn* (1958-60). Born into an acting family, he learned his trade in New York's Yiddish theatres. He played character roles in a number of films, among them several offbeat independent productions such as *Stakeout on Dope Street* (1958) and *A Cold Wind in August* (1961). Other films include *Irma la Douce* (1963) and *Love With the Proper Stranger* (1964). Died of a heart attack in Los Angeles on 9 May 1986, aged 62.

ALVAH BESSIE

Journalist, novelist, and briefly a screenwriter, Bessie achieved most lasting fame as one of the 'Hollywood Ten' who were jailed in 1950 for contempt of Congress after refusing to affirm or deny Communist Party membership when summoned before the House UnAmerican Activities Committee. He had served with the International Brigade in Spain, and subsequently wrote a number of not particularly distinguished screenplays for Warners, among them *Northern Pursuit* (1943) and *Hotel Berlin* (1945); he also provided the original story for *Objective Burma* (1945). After his release from jail, he worked for a time as a nightclub manager, but later published several novels, as well as a book, *Inquisition in Eden* (1965), about the studio blacklisting of which he was one of the victims. Died of a heart attack in Terra Linda, California, on 21 July 1985, aged 81.

GUNNAR BJORNSTRAND

One of the most distinctive and distinguished members of the informal repertory company of performers in Ingmar Bergman's films, Bjornstrand was the son of an actor, and made his first screen appearance in a bit part in *The False Millionaire* (1931). He later made regular appearances in prominent roles, the squire in *The Seventh Seal* (1957) and the despairing pastor of *Winter Light* being two of the most memorable (1963). Other films by Bergman in which he acted include *Wild Strawberries* (1958), *Persona* (1966) and *Autumn Sonata* (1978). Among significant films by other directors for which he will be recalled are *Loving Couples* (1964) and *My Sister, My Love* (1965). Died in Stockholm on 24 May 1986, aged 76.

LOUISE BROOKS

A sex symbol before the event, but assuredly in the true sense, Louise Brooks gave extraordinary performances in two German-made classics of the late silent period, *Pandora's Box* and *Diary of a Lost Girl* (both 1929). With her bobbed hair and deceptively impassive features, she had already achieved some small success on the American screen, notably in *A Girl in Every Port* and *Beggars of Life* (both 1928); the fact that for much of the latter she was disguised as a boy gave a suitably

perverse twist to her distinctive brand of sexuality. After she returned from Germany to Hollywood, she proved too much of an individualist to fit easily into the studio system and was virtually reduced to a bit player before she returned to being a chorine. She made a brief Hollywood comeback in the mid-thirties but retired from acting altogether shortly afterwards: her final film role was the somewhat improbable one of female lead in a B-feature Western starring the then little-known John Wayne, *Overland Stage Raiders* (1938). She subsequently lived in poverty-stricken obscurity, but in her later years won renewed acclaim as the writer of some witty and perceptive memoirs of both her own and others' experiences in the cinema. Died of a heart attack in Rochester, NY, on 8 August 1985, aged 78.

YUL BRYNNER

Of cosmopolitan background, and a one-time circus aerialist, Brynner will essentially be remembered for

a single role, that of the Siamese monarch in *The King and I*. He created the role in the Rodgers and Hammerstein musical on Broadway in 1951, staying with it for over 1,200 performances, then repeated it in the 1956 film version. This launched him onto movie stardom, initially in blockbusters like *Solomon and Sheba* (1959), later in a polyglot succession of mainly indifferent pictures. His one indisputable success away from the King of Siam was in the somewhat improbable guise of the gunslinger of *The Magnificient Seven* (1960), which with cruel irony he was to reprise in *Westworld* (1973), this time as a robot. In 1972 he played the King in a non-musical TV series based on *The King and I*, and in 1977 starred in a Broadway revival of the musical show, continuing to appear in touring productions of it almost until his death. Died of cancer in New York on 10 October 1985, aged 70.

ADOLPH CAESAR

Born in Harlem, Caesar established himself by acting with black theatre groups before moving on to play supporting roles in a number of films, starting with *Che!* (1969). His performance as the driven black sergeant and murder victim in the stage production *A Soldier's Play* won widespread notice, and he reprised the role to savagely telling effect in Norman Jewison's film version (1984). Subsequently he gave another notable performance in *The Color Purple* (1986), but his career was cut short by early death. Died in Los Angeles on 6 March 1986, aged 52.

JAMES CAGNEY

The most celebrated movie gangster of them all, and a perennial subject for impersonators – though he claimed never to have spoken on screen the phrase 'You dirty rat' which the latter invariably attributed to him – Cagney began in revue as, of all things, a female impersonator, then became a Broadway chorus boy and was a stage star by the time Warners signed him up in 1930. Within a year, the role of the hoodlum in *Public Enemy* (1931) – cocksure and aggressive, ready to silence his moll's breakfast-table complaints by pushing half a grapefruit in her face – made him into one of the most distinctive screen presences of the thirties. He moved to the other side of the law in *G-Men* (1935), and played in various genres, even in Shakespeare – a sprightly Bottom in *A Midsummer's Night's Dream* (1935). He returned to song and dance in *Yankee Doodle Dandy* (1942), winning an Oscar in the process. But it was in gangster parts that his dynamism won its greatest public response: *Angels With Dirty Faces* (1938), with its endlessly anthologised finale of Cagney's feigned cowardice as he is dragged to the electric chair; *The Roaring Twenties* (1939); and later *White Heat* (1949), with his powerhouse portrayal of a murderous, mother-fixated psychotic. On the whole, his fifties films furnished him with less rewarding roles, and he retired to a quiet life on his farm after giving a definitively energetic comedy performance in *One Two Three* (1961). He made a comeback with a cameo role as the moustachioed police commissioner in *Ragtime* (1981): the frame was bulkier now and the movements slower, but the precision was intact and the voice had lost nothing of its quietly ironic relish; Cagney proved once and for all that however much he was impersonated, he remained in the end inimitable. Died at his farm in Duchess County, New York, on 30 March 1986, aged 87.

YAKIMA CANUTT (Enos Edward Candutt)

Beginning as a ranch-hand and then joining a Wild West show, Canutt became a rodeo champion and then entered films as a stuntman and bit-part actor in Westerns, graduating to leads in the mid-twenties. With the coming of sound, he reverted to minor parts. But his stunt reputation grew, and by the late-thirties he was setting up stunt sequences and functioning as a second unit director, notably on *Stagecoach* (1939). He was second-unit director on many of the spectaculars of the late fifties and the sixties and was responsible for the chariot race in *Ben-Hur* (1959), which involved him in teaching eighty Yugoslav horses to pull chariots as well as in instructing Charlton Heston how to drive one. In 1966 he received a special Oscar "for creating the profession of stuntman as it exists today." Died in North Hollywood, California, on 24 May 1986, aged 90.

JAMES CRAIG

A reliable but never very memorable performer, Craig made his Hollywood debut in 1937 and appeared in a run of assorted movies until the early seventies, generally as the second lead or 'other man'. His most considerable role came comparatively early, as the Faust figure in *All That Money Can Buy* (GB: *The Devil and Daniel Webster*, (1941)). Among his other movies were *Kitty Foyle* (1941), *Kismet* (1944), *Side Street* (1950), *Drums in the Deep South* (1951) and Lang's *While the City Sleeps* (1956), which gave him his best later role, putting his moustachioed air of latent caddishness to sardonic effect. Died of cancer in Santa Ana, California, 28 June 1985, aged 73.

BRODERICK CRAWFORD

The son of vaudeville star Lester Crawford and comedy actress Helen Broderick, began in vaudeville, then made a 'legitimate' stage debut in London in 1932, subsequently appearing on Broadway and achieving particular success as Lennie in the 1937 stage production of *Of Mice and Men*. His first film role was in *Woman Chases Man* (1937), but the first dozen years of his movie career were mainly spent in routine minor roles as a heavy or comic stooge. He suddenly came into his own when cast as the southern demagogue (modelled on Huey Long) in *All the King's*

Men (1949), a performance which won him the Best Actor Oscar. He had another big success as the vulgarian businessman in the comedy *Born Yesterday* (1950), but subsequently was seldom offered rewarding roles. An exception was the con-man in Fellini's *Il Bidone* (1955), and near the end of his career he gave a notable performance as the elderly Hoover in *The Private Files of J Edgar Hoover* (1977). In the meantime, he had been a TV stalwart, particularly in the series *Highway Patrol* (1955-58). Died in Palm Springs, California, on 26 April 1986, aged 74.

FLOYD CROSBY

A former stills photographer, Crosby first established a reputation as cinematographer of several notable documentaries of the thirties, working with Flaherty, Ivens and Lorentz, and winning an Academy Award for *Tabu* (1931). From 1950, he worked on Hollywood features, *High Noon*

Left: James Cagney

(1952) being a particularly striking early example of his flair with high-contrast monochrome. Later, however, he worked almost entirely within the low-budget/second-feature area, and throughout the late fifties and early sixties was a frequent collaborator of Roger Corman, providing crisply functional monochrome for movies like *Rock All Night* (1957) and colour of a sumptuousness that belied the low budgets in several of Corman's Poe adaptations, starting with *The Fall of the House of Usher* (1960). He appears to have been in retirement since 1973. David Crosby, the rock musician, is one of his two sons. Died in Ojai, California, on 30 September 1985, aged 85.

Howard Da Sylva
(Harold Silverblatt)

A character actor of considerable versatility, Da Sylva was on the stage from 1929, and played the role of Jud in the Broadway production of *Oklahoma!* in 1943. He appeared in films from 1940, often as a heavy, such as the sadistic skipper of *Two Years Before the Mast* (1946), but one of his most memorable parts was that of the sympathetic barman in *The Lost Weekend* (1945). He was blacklisted in Hollywood following the HUAC hearings, and during the fifties was active in the theàtre. He subsequently returned to movies, in the role of the psychiatrist in *David and Lisa* (1963), and appeared in several further films, most prominently as Benjamin Franklin in the musical *1776* (1972). Died of cancer in Ossining, NY, on 11 February 1986, aged 76.

Leif Erickson
(William Anderson)

Erickson appeared in dozens of films from 1935 onwards, after an earlier career as a trombonist and band singer. Most of his roles were routine and minor, however. His more worthwhile appearances included *Sorry Wrong Number* (1948), *Show Boat* (1951) and *On the Waterfront* (1954). His most substantial screen role was probably in *Tea and Sympathy* (1956). He also appeared on Broadway and on television, notably in the series *The High Chaparral*. He was married from 1934 to 1942 to actress Frances Farmer. Died of cancer in Pensacola, Florida, on 29 January 1986, aged 74.

Chester Erskine

Starting off as an actor, Erskine achieved success as a director and producer on Broadway, and in 1932 went to Hollywood, where he was assistant to Lewis Milestone on *Rain* (1932), later directing a few nondescript pictures like *Frankie and Johnnie* (1935). He returned to the theatre but had a further stint in Hollywood in the post-war years, from which his best remembered film is the comedy *The Egg and I* (1946). He produced *All My Sons* (1947) and directed a rather odd Shaw adaptation, *Androcles and the Lion* (1952). His final film credit was as producer of a quite impressive Western, *The Wonderful Country* (1959). Died in Beverly Hills, California, on 7 April 1986, aged 80.

Derek Farr

A dependable second lead and occasional star of British comedies and thrillers in the post-war decade, Farr was a former schoolmaster who embarked on an acting career in 1937. His first film was *The Outsider* (1939), and after war service he returned to a run of pictures, such as *Quiet Wedding* (1945), *Bond Street* (1948), *Reluctant Heroes* (1951). By the time of *Town on Trial* (1957) and *The Truth About Women* (1958), he was playing smaller roles but still to incisive effect. Later he appeared on the stage and on TV but made only occasional film appearances, the last being *Pope Joan* (1972). Died in London on 24 March 1986, aged 74.

Frank Faylen

A reliable character player for over thirty years, from *Bullets or Ballots* (1936) to *Funny Girl* (1968), Faylen was the son of vaudeville performers and was himself a song-and-dance man before embarking on a screen career. Lacking any particular physical distinctiveness, he still brought a sharp edge of observation to a variety of roles, of which the most memorable was probably the sadistic male nurse who torments Ray Milland in *The Lost Weekend* (1945). Somewhat later he was particularly effective as the pusillanimous politican in *Riot in Cell Block 11* (1954). Other appearances included *The Grapes of Wrath* (1940), *It's a Wonderful Life* (1946), *14 Hours* (1951), and *Gunfight at the OK Corral* (1957). From 1959 to 1962 he was in the US TV series *Dobie Gillis*. Died in Burbank, California, on 2 August 1985, aged 79.

Stepin Fetchit
(Lincoln Theodore Perry)

The first black actor to receive featured billing in American movies, Fetchit made his first Hollywood film in 1927 after an earlier career in vaudeville, taking his stage name from that of a racehorse which he had successfully backed. He appeared, though inevitably in stereotyped roles, in numerous films throughout the thirties, most memorably for John Ford in *Judge Priest* (1934) and *Steamboat Round the Bend* (1935), living lavishly and reputedly becoming the first black millionaire; however, in 1947 he was declared bankrupt. Later movie appearances were less frequent, though they included Ford's *The Sun Shines Bright* (1953). Fetchit retired from acting and converted to the black Muslim faith in the sixties, but subsequently made a short-lived comeback, his final film being *Won Ton Ton, the Dog Who Saved Hollywood* (1976). Died in Woodland Hill, California, on 19 November 1985, aged 83.

Martin Gabel

An actor on Broadway from 1933, Gabel played in several hit plays, among them *Dead End*, later joining Orson Welles' Mercury Theatre company, for whom among other roles he played Cassius in the 1937 modern-dress production of *Julius Caesar*. He subsequently directed numerous stage productions, and in 1947 directed his only film, *The Lost Moment*, a stylish adaptation of Henry James' *The Aspern Papers*. He was seen in character roles in many films, including *14 Hours* (1951), *Deadline USA* (1952), and *Tip on a Dead Jockey* (1957). Probably his most memorable screen role was as the unsympathetic robbery victim in *Marnie* (1964). Later film appearances include *There Was a Crooked Man* (1970) and *The Front Page* (1974). Died in New York on 22 May 1986, aged 73.

Ruth Gordon

Gordon had a multifarious film career as both actress and writer, though until her later years her fame was more closely linked to the theatre. She acted in two silent movies (*Camille*, 1915; *Wheel of Life*, 1916) while seeking to break into the Broadway theatre. She subsequently achieved wide-reaching fame as a stage actress, and also acted in several movies in the early forties, including *Dr Ehrlich's Magic Bullet* (1940) and *Edge of Darkness* (1943). She also wrote several plays and screenplays, frequently in collaboration with her second husband Garson Kanin; the screenplays notably included *A Double Life* (1948), *Adam's Rib* (1949) and *Pat and Mike* (1952). In the mid-sixties she launched upon a new phase of her career, as a movie character actress, perhaps most memorably in *Rosemary's Baby* (1968), for which she won an Oscar as best supporting actress. Other appearances included *Inside Daisy Clover* (1966), *Harold and Maude* (1971) and *Every Which Way But Loose* (1978). Died of a stroke in Edgartown, Massachusetts, on 28 August 1985, aged 88.

Sterling Hayden
(John Hamilton)

Tall (6ft 5in) and handsome (he was dubbed 'the most beautiful man in the movies' by publicists when he entered films in 1940), Hayden had been a sailor in early life and became an actor by chance after being spotted as a male model, work he had undertaken to finance buying his own ship. He made his debut in *Bahama Passage* (1941), co-starring with his first wife, actress Madeleine Carroll, and saw active service with the Marines before returning to films after the war. Mainly in routine action roles, he rose to the occasion with the few movies that

offered him a challenge, notably as the criminal heroes of *The Asphalt Jungle* (1950) and *The Killing* (1956) and as the enigmatic loner of *Johnny Guitar* (1954). The fact that he had been a friendly witness before HUAC apparently caused him considerable soul-searching, and he was increasingly drawn back to the sea, taking occasional acting jobs in character parts to pay the bills. However, he was highly effective as the mad general in *Dr Strangelove* (1963) and as the self-destructive novelist of *The Long Goodbye* (1973). Died of cancer in Sausalito, California, on 24 May 1986, aged 70.

Rock Hudson
(Roy Scherer)

Belonging to the last generation of contract players, Hudson appeared in numerous supporting roles in Universal programmers and was promoted as a 'beefcake' pin-up, subsequently graduating to leads in action pictures like *Sea Devils* (1953). A little later, his

Right: Rock Hudson

range was extended in matinée melodramas like *Magnificent Obsession* (1954), and on loan-out to Warners he gave probably his best performance as the Texan land-baron of *Giant* (1956), which brought him an Oscar nomination. In the early sixties his popularity reached new heights when he starred in a run of glossy comedies, frequently opposite Doris Day. Thereafter his career declined sharply, his last worthwhile movie being *Seconds* (1966), though he enjoyed some success in the long-running TV series *MacMillan and Wife*. His last big-screen role was in *The Ambassador* (1984), in which he resembled a ravaged shadow of his former self. His last days were spent in a glare of publicity after it became known that he was terminally ill with AIDS. Died in Beverly Hills, California, on 2 October 1985, aged 59.

ISABEL JEANS

An actress of high style, Jeans had a career which began on the London stage in 1909 and spanned more than sixty years. Her fame was essentially achieved in the theatre, but she also appeared in numerous films, of which the most memorable was *Gigi* (1958). Her screen career began in 1917 and she acted in several British silents, among them *Tilly of Bloomsbury* (1921) and *Downhill* (1927), and a few early sound features. Her first Hollywood picture was *Tovarich* (1937) and though most of her American roles were in mediocre films, she had a good part in *Suspicion* (1941). After *Gigi*, she appeared to elegant and incisive effect in *A Breath of Scandal* (1960) and the British-made *Heavens Above* (1963). Her last film role was in *The Magic Christian* (1969). Died in London on 4 September 1985, aged 93.

PHIL KARLSON
(Philip Karlstein)

Karlson began as a propman and worked up by way of being assistant director and editor to making B-pictures at the lowly Monogram studio. In the fifties he progressed to medium-budget programmers and made several taut crime pictures, such as *Scandal Sheet* (1952), *Five Against the House* (1955), and *The Phenix City Story* (1955), the last being filmed on location in Alabama only a few months after the violent events it described had taken place. On the whole, his later films were less effective, but his penultimate picture, *Walking Tall* (1973), was a big box-office hit; its hard-nosed approach to civic corruption and law enforcement had all the vigour of his best work of the fifties. His last film was *Framed* (1975). It seems appropriate to the functional asperity of his best work that he should have asked for his death not to be marked by either services or publicity; as a result it was not reported until several weeks later. Died of cancer in Los Angeles on 12 December 1985, aged 77.

BESSIE LOVE
(Juanita Horton)

An actress who spanned seven decades, Love entered movies straight from high school in 1916, and the same year played a minor role in *Intolerance*. Very soon she was playing leads opposite Douglas Fairbanks Sr and William S Hart. She adapted to sound with aplomb, in musicals like *Broadway Melody* (1929), but in the mid-thirties decided to move to England. After the war, in which she was an entertainer with the American Red Cross, she continued in films but was more prominent in the theatre, and latterly on TV. More recent movies in which she was featured include *The Barefoot Contessa* (1954), *The Story of Esther Costello* (1957), and, as Isadora Duncan's mother, *Isadora* (1969). In 1972 she played Aunt Pittypat in a West End musical version of *Gone With the Wind*. One of her last appearances was in the TV series *Edward and Mrs Simpson* (1978). Died in London on 26 April 1986, aged 87.

GORDON MacRAE

A former radio vocalist and Broadway musical lead, MacRae was signed up by Warners in 1948 and over the next several years was the pleasant if not very distinctive lead in various musicals, often with Doris Day (*Tea for Two*, 1950; *On Moonlight Bay*, 1951). He was also in a couple of non-musicals (*Backfire*, 1950; *Return of the Frontiersman*, 1950) without making much impact. His most notable roles came a little later, as the leading men of *Oklahoma!* (1955) and *Carousel* (1956). But after a subsequent, lesser film, *The Best Things in Life are Free* (1956), he disappeared from movies, a casualty of the decline of the musical. He continued with a recording and TV career, and successfully recovered from a bout of alcoholism. He made one further film, *The Pilot* (1979), and continued with live appearances until the end of his life. Died in Lincoln, Nebraska, on 24 January 1985, aged 64.

UNA MERKEL

Merkel began as a stand-in for Lillian Gish in *Way Down East* (1920) and other films, before spending several years on Broadway. She returned to the cinema as Ann Rutledge in Griffith's *Abraham Lincoln* (1930), and went on to become a prolific screen performer of that decade. She played in sundry styles but will be remembered best as a wisecracking second lead in comedies and musicals like *42nd Street* (1933). Her most famous appearance was probably as Marlene Dietrich's opponent in the saloon brawl of *Destry Rides Again* (1939). During the forties she devoted more of her energies to the theatre, but continued to make frequent film appearances, her most striking later role being as Geraldine Page's mother in *Summer and Smoke* (1961). Her final movie was *Spinout* (1966). Died in Los Angeles on 2 January 1986, aged 82.

RAY MILLAND
(Reginald Truscott-Jones)

As a guardsman and man-about-town, Milland drifted into acting through a chance meeting, to have some success in early British talkies and to be taken up by Hollywood a few years later. From featured billing in mainly light comedy roles, he progressed to stardom in films like *Easy Living* (1937) and *Beau Geste* (1939), establishing a reputation as a dependable, debonair presence, able to lend substance and wit to frequently mediocre material. With *The Ministry of Fear* (1944) and especially *The Lost Weekend* (1945) – in which his playing of an alcoholic brought him an Oscar – he moved with impressive ease into darker roles. In the subsequent decade, he moved into directing, though not before he had given as the would-be wife murderer in Hitchcock's *Dial M For Murder* (1953) a brilliantly modulated performance in the black comedy register. The five films he directed were variable, but included an effective Western, *A Man Alone* (1955), and a tense

post-nuclear bomb thriller, *Panic in Year Zero* (1962). Later he ventured with aplomb as an actor into some offbeat and mildly disreputable movies, like Corman's *The Premature Burial* (1962). He returned to big-budget films as a character actor (minus toupée) as the father in *Love Story* (1970) and continued gamely to enhance mainly mediocre pictures over the next dozen years. Died of cancer in Torrance, California, on 10 March 1986, aged 81.

DAME ANNA NEAGLE
(Marjorie Robertson)

Something of an institution of the British stage and screen, Neagle began as a chorine in revue in the mid-twenties, and by the end of the decade was a star performer. She made her first film in 1930, and with *Goodnight Vienna* (1932) became established as a film star. While she continued to appear in the theatre, venturing into straight acting and even Shakespeare, she made a steady run of films, achieving great popular success as Queen Victoria in *Victoria the Great* (1937) and its follow-up *Sixty Glorious Years* (1938); these were directed, as were almost all her films, by Herbert Wilcox, whom she married in 1943, and with whom she made four Hollywood movies in the early years of the war. Back in Britain she played her sole unsympathetic role, a spy in *The*

Yellow Canary (1943), and later co-starred with Michael Wilding in such curious, but at the time hugely popular, comedies as *Spring in Park Lane* (1948) and *Maytime in Mayfair* (1949). Her screen popularity waned somewhat during the fifties, and *The Lady Is a Square* (1959) was her last film. But she carried on resiliently in the theatre, in both plays and musicals, surmounting the vicissitudes of illness and her husband's bankruptcy. Only a few months before her death, she had been appearing twice nightly in the London Palladium pantomime. Died at a nursing home in Surrey on 3 June 1986, aged 81.

RICKY NELSON
(Eric Nelson)

It is as a pop singer of considerable skill and vitality that Nelson will be remembered, but he also had a varied show business career. He was the elder son of Ozzie and Harriet Nelson, popular radio stars of the forties and TV personalities of the fifties, and Ricky and his brother David both performed with their parents in these shows. Ricky was a child actor in *The Story of Three Loves* (1953), and a few years later his fame as a singer led to several movie appearances, notably in *Rio Bravo* (1959). His popularity faded during the sixties, but he made a strong comeback in the subsequent decade; it was a sign of passing times that in the TV movie *High School USA* (1983) he played the role of the school principal. Died in a plane crash in Texas on 31 December 1985, aged 45.

DANDY NICHOLS

Although she will be indelibly associated with the put-upon wife of Alf Garnett in the TV series *Till Death Us Do Part*, in which she appeared from 1966 until 1974, Dandy Nichols had begun on the stage and in films in 1947. Her many small roles in films included *Hue and Cry* (1947), *The Deep Blue Sea* (1954), and *Georgy Girl* (1966). Her last film part was in *Britannia Hospital* (1982), though subsequently she returned to the television role of Ma Garnett in the 1985 sequel series *In Sickness and in Health*. Died in London on 6 February 1986, aged 78.

LLOYD NOLAN

A stalwart Hollywood actor for half a century, Nolan began as a stage actor in 1927, made his broadway debut in 1933 and his first film two years later. Minor roles in such movies as *G-Men* (1935) and *The Texas Rangers* (1936) led to his playing leads in a string of B-picture crime yarns, notably those featuring him as private detective Michael Shayne. By the mid-forties he had graduated to character roles in A-pictures, and proved himself able to adapt to every conceivable genre of material. To name but a few of his best roles, he was the kindly cop in *A Tree Grows in Brooklyn* (1945), the hard-nosed FBI man in *The House on 92nd Street* (1945), a grizzled old westerner in *The Last Hunt* (1956), the weakling big-city father in *A Hatful of Rain* (1957), the avuncular small-town editor in *Peyton Place* (1958). Meanwhile, he had attracted considerable admiration for his playing of Captain Queeg in the Broadway production of *The Caine Mutiny Court-Martial*. More recent movie roles included *Earthquake* (1974), *The Private Files of J Edgar Hoover* (1977), and the posthumously released *Hannah and Her Sisters* (1986). Died of cancer in Los Angeles on 27 September 1985, aged 83.

GEORGE O'BRIEN

The son of a San Francisco police chief, O'Brien was a naval boxing champion in World War I and started in films in 1922 as an assistant cameraman. He soon gravitated to being a stuntman and supporting actor and sprang to fame when he was chosen by John Ford to play the lead in *The Iron Horse* (1924). He subsequently starred to notable effect in Murnau's *Sunrise* (1927); but in the thirties his career continued on a lower plane, though still profitably, as a leading man in Westerns, few of which have retained any reputation. In later years he made sporadic appearances in supporting roles, notably for Ford in *Fort Apache* (1948), *She Wore a Yellow Ribbon* (1949), and – his last role – *Cheyenne Autumn* (1964). He was married from 1933 to 1948 to the actress Marguerite Churchill. Died in Broken Arrow, Oklahoma, on 4 September 1985, aged 85.

ARTHUR J ORNITZ

A New York-based cameraman, who had also photographed many TV commercials and some films for TV, Ornitz broke into the cinema as cinematographer of some of the 'off-Hollywood' movies of the late fifties and early sixties. Among these were *The Goddess* (1958) and *The Connection* (1961), both distinctly shot in harsh black and white. The same style recurred in *Requiem for a Heavyweight* (GB: *Blood Money*, 1963), but Ornitz also revealed a gift for lyrical colour cinematography with the comedy *The World of Henry Orient* (1964). Among his later films, the most striking were *The Anderson Tapes* (1971) and *Minnie and Moskowitz* (1971). Died in Manhattan, NY, of cancer on 10 July 1985, aged 68.

LILLI PALMER
(Lillie Marie Peiser)

An actress of quiet versatility, Palmer had a cosmopolitan career; she began on the stage in Berlin, but left Germany after the Nazi takeover, and settled in England. She rose to star status in the British cinema, notably in *The Rake's Progress* (1945), subsequently going to Hollywood with Rex Harrison, to whom she was married from 1943 to 1958. Her films of this period, including *Body and Soul* (1947) and *The Fourposter* (1952, in which she and Harrison were the only players), did not achieve great impact, and later she alternated between American and European films. Only once in a while, as in *The Counterfeit Traitor* (1962), did she find roles which brought out her distinctive combination of the grave and sympathetic. In her later years she turned to writing, producing both an autobiography and a novel. Died in Los Angeles on 27 January 1986, aged 71.

JERRY PARIS

Best known to the public as the actor who played Dick Van Dyke's neighbour in the long-running TV show, Paris also directed many episodes of that show and of *Happy Days*. He had previously been a supporting player in many movies, of which the last was *The Great Imposter* (1961). He was associate producer of *The Caretakers* (1963), and later directed several features, mainly routine comedies like *Viva Max!* (1969). His final two pictures were the pre-sold successes *Police Academy 2* (1985) and *Police Academy 3* (1986). Died in Los Angeles on 31 March 1986, aged 60.

OTTO PREMINGER

Viennese-born Preminger was the son of a prominent lawyer and was himself destined for the law, before opting for the theatre. He became an assistant to Max Reinhardt and under the latter's aegis progressed to Broadway. From there he moved to Hollywood, directing several minor pictures before establishing himself with *Laura* (1944), an elegant murder mystery which he apparently came to direct almost by accident. After several efficient melodramas as a producer-director at Fox, he turned independent in the early fifties, blazing a trail many others would follow. His first film in this guise was *The Moon Is Blue* (1954), a lightweight comedy, but one

whose 'outrageous' dialogue caused it to be denied Production Code approval. The film was released without it and its success represented an undeniable triumph over industry censorship as well as a demonstration of the box-office value of notoriety. Preminger continued to exploit controversy with the drug addiction picture *Man With the Golden Arm* (1955); took a flyer into culture with *St Joan* (1957), featuring his discovery Jean Seberg; then embarked on a series of large-scale adaptations of bestseller novels on controversial themes – *Anatomy of a Murder* (1959), *Exodus* (1960), *Advise and Consent* (1962), *The Cardinal* (1963), of which all are impressive in certain respects, despite some superficiality, and the first is a brilliant dissection of the ambiguities of the law. On the whole, Preminger's instincts, commercial and artistic, faltered in later years, but his final movie, the Graham Greene adaptation *The Human Factor* (1980), happily showed some recovery of his earlier acumen. Reputedly not an endearing figure to professional associates, he was at his best a film-maker of very considerable skill. Died of cancer in New York on 23 April 1986, aged 79.

DONNA REED
(Donna Belle Mullenger)

A high-school beauty queen in her Iowa home town, and later Campus Queen of Los Angeles City College, Reed was signed up by MGM and played a succession of minor roles before appearing in several notable films of the mid-forties. She was the ingenue in *The Picture of Dorian Gray* (1945), a naval nurse in *They Were Expendable* (1945), and James Stewart's wife in *It's a Wonderful Life* (1946). She played leading roles in several mainly routine films after moving to Columbia, where her one really worthwhile role was that of the prostitute in *From Here to Eternity* (1953), which won her an Oscar as best supporting actress. In 1958 she started a long run in the TV series *The Donna Reed Show*. In 1984 she emerged from effective retirement to take over the role of Miss Ellie in *Dallas*. Died of cancer in Los Angeles on 14 January 1986, aged 64.

HELEN ROSE

One of the most celebrated costume designers of Hollywood's heyday, Rose had designed for the Ice Follies during the thirties before joining Fox in 1941. She went to MGM two years later and remained there until 1966. She was said to be the favourite designer of

both Grace Kelly and Elizabeth Taylor, and during her time at MGM won two Oscars – for *The Bad and the Beautiful* (1953) and *I'll Cry Tomorrow* (1956) – and received a further eight nominations.
A frequent collaborator of Vincente Minelli, she received a dual credit on his comedy *Designing Woman* (1957), for both the gowns and the story idea. Died in Palm Springs, California, on 9 November 1985, aged 81.

KATHLEEN RYAN

An Irish actress of striking dark-haired good looks, Ryan made her stage debut in Dublin in 1940 and her first – and most memorable – screen appearance in *Odd Man Out* (1947). She later played leading roles in several British films, including *Christopher Columbus* (1949) and *The Yellow Balloon* (1952), and also made a brief foray to Hollywood for *The Sound of Fury* (1951). She played a secondary role in the Irish-made *Captain Lightfoot* (1955), but her screen career came to an end shortly afterwards. Died in Dublin on 11 November 1985, aged 63.

MICKEY SHAUGHNESSY

A veteran American character actor, Shaughnessy played supporting roles in a total of forty-nine films between 1952, when he made his debut in *The Marrying Kind*, and 1970. His burly features and rumpled mug made him a natural for comic heavies or dumb toughs, as in such movies as *Designing Woman* (1957) and *The Sheepman* (1958), though he was occasionally in more sympathetic straight roles, as in *Gunman's Walk* (1958). Other appearances included *North to Alaska* (1960), *Adventures of Huckleberry Finn* (1960) and *A Pocketful of Miracles* (1961), a Damon Runyon adaptation in which his eccentric features and halting vocal delivery found a perfect home. Subsequent roles, in such pictures as *A House Is Not a Home* (1964), were on the whole less distinctive. Died of a heart attack in New Jersey on 23 July 1985, aged 64.

SIMONE SIGNORET
(Simone Kaminker)

Simone Signoret began in films as an extra during the Occupation, when she had to support her mother and two brothers, and moved into leading roles soon after the war. Her most famous performances came a few years later, in *La Rode* (1950) and *Casque d'Or* (1952); especially in the latter she projected a resonant, down-to-earth sensuality which has seldom been rivalled on the screen. Another good part was as the scheming villainess of *Les Diaboliques* (1955), but she achieved her greatest renown in the British-made *Room at the Top* (1958), winning an Oscar for her unforgettable portrait of sensual, love-lorn middle age. Although she made several other English-language movies, receiving an Oscar nomination for *Ship of Fools* (1965), in the main her roles both in France and abroad in later years were less rewarding. Her last film was *L'Etoile du Nord* (1981), and despite failing health and eyesight, she published a novel shortly before her death, having previously authored two volumes of memoirs. She had been married for many years to actor Yves Montand. Died of cancer in Normandy, France, on 30 September 1985, aged 64.

PHIL SILVERS
(Philip Silver)

After starting as a vaudeville singer at the age of 13, Silvers became a successful burlesque comedian and gravitated to Hollywood movies appearing in secondary roles in a string of musicals and comedies of the war years, most memorably in *Cover Girl* (1944). His real fame, however, was achieved elsewhere, first when he starred in the Broadway musical *Top Banana* in the early fifties, but essentially through his playing of the balding, bespectacled and incorrigible Sergeant Bilko in the long-running TV series launched as *You'll Never Get Rich* but rapidly retitled *The Phil Silvers Show*. On the strength of his fame in this role he appeared in a number of movies during the sixties and seventies, among them *It's a Mad Mad Mad Mad World* (1963), *A Funny Thing Happened on the Way to the Forum* (1966) and *The Cheap Detective* (1978). Died in Century City, California, on 1 November 1985, aged 73.

GALE SONDERGAARD
(Edith Holm Sondergaard)

The daughter of a professor, Sondergaard embarked on a stage career which took her to Broadway by the mid-twenties. A few years later she made the move to Hollywood in the wake of her husband, the director Herbert Biberman, to whom she was married from 1930 until his death in 1971. Her first screen role, in *Anthony Adverse* (1936) won her an Oscar as best supporting actress and led to a succession of often meaty secondary roles, notably as the Empress Eugenie in *Juarez* (1939). Her rather severe appearance proved effective when she played villainesses in comedy-thrillers like *The Cat and the Canary* (1939) and *My Favourite Blonde* (1942), as well as in dramatic films like *Christmas Holiday* (1944). But her career in Hollywood was terminated by her being blacklisted after the House UnAmerican Activities Committee hearings, in the wake of which Biberman was jailed as one of the 'Hollywood Ten'. In 1965, she appeared in a one-woman show off-Broadway, and returned to the cinema in *Slaves* (1969), directed by Biberman, and subsequently in *Return of a Man Called Horse* (1976). Died in Woodland Hills, California, after a long illness on 14 August 1985, aged 86.

SAM SPIEGEL

One of the most creatively successful producers, Spiegel was born in Austria and entered the cinema as a producer of French and German versions of films made by Universal. He went to the US in 1935 as a refugee from the Nazis and some years later emerged as an independent producer of considerable artistic ambition. His early productions included Welles' *The Stranger* (1946) and Huston's *We Were Strangers* (1949), and it was with Huston that he achieved his first big commercial hit, *The African Queen* (1951). The range of his work was uncommonly wide, encompassing *On the Waterfront* (1954) and *The Bridge on the River Kwai* (1957), both of which won 'best picture' Oscars, as did *Lawrence of Arabia* (1962). Nor did he neglect more intimate and controversial material, as *The Strange One* (GB: *End as a Man*, 1957) and *Suddenly Last Summer* (1959) demonstrated. His later films, such as *Nicholas and Alexandra* (1971), were more anonymous, and *The Last Tycoon* (1976) was generally rated a considerable disappointment. His last production was the modestly scaled *Betrayal* (1982). Died on the Caribbean island of St Martin on 31 December 1985, aged 82.

ROBERT STEVENSON

Stevenson's lasting niche in movie history will be as a Walt Disney 'house' director: working for that studio from 1956 until his retirement at the end of the seventies, he was responsible for such pictures as *The Absent-Minded Professor* (1961), *The Love Bug* (1969) and the phenomenally popular *Mary Poppins* (1964). But his career was considerably more extensive. British-born, he took an engineering degree at Cambridge, where he also edited *Granta*, and entered films as a writer in 1930, translating to directing only two years later. His best known British films are *Tudor Rose* (1936) and *King Solomon's Mines* (1937). With actress Anna Lee, who was one of his several wives, he went to Hollywood in 1939 and directed a run of polished, if not particularly personal, movies, of which probably the most striking was *Jane Eyre* (1944). Other pre-Disney pictures included efficient thrillers like *To the Ends of the Earth* (1948) and *Walk Softly Stranger* (1950). Died in Santa Barbara, California, on 30 April 1986, aged 81.

PAUL STEWART

A member of Orson Welles' Mercury Theatre in both its stage and radio manifestations, Stewart made an unforgettable film debut as the sinister valet in *Citizen Kane* (1941). For the next dozen years he was a perennial movie character actor, usually as a menacing heavy or unsympathetic presence, but always providing strongly individual performances. Among his more memorable appearances were *Champion* (1946), *The Window* (1946), *Deadline USA* (1952) and *Hell on Frisco Bay* (1955). For several years he was mainly active as a director of TV series, but subsequently returned to acting, notably as the journalist in *In Cold Blood* (1967); one of his last screen roles was as Florenz Ziegfeld in *W C Fields and Me* (1976). Died in Los Angeles on 17 February 1986, aged 77.

NIGEL STOCK

A dependable character actor, probably best remembered as an ideal Dr Watson to Peter Cushing's Sherlock Holmes in the 1967 TV series, Stock began his stage career at the age of 12, and ranged

Left: Simone Signoret

in the theatre from the classics to farce. He appeared in numerous films, usually a somewhat self-effacing presence in subsidiary roles, such as the pilot in *The Night My Number Came Up* (1955). Other appearances include *The Lady with the Lamp* (1951), *The Battle of the River Plate* (1956), and *Cromwell* (1970). More recently he was in the TV serial *Tinker, Tailor, Soldier, Spy* (1979). Died in London on 22 June 1986, aged 66.

Victor Vicas

Moscow-born Vicas grew up in France and became an assistant cameraman in the late thirties. He served with the French army and was taken prisoner by the Germans, but managed to escape to the US. There he worked on documentaries, a vein in which he continued after returning to Paris. He began to direct features in the early fifties, initially in Germany, also in France. In Hollywood he directed *The Wayward Bus* (1957), a Steinbeck adaptation which included Joan Collins and Jayne Mansfield in its cast, then went to Britain to make *Count Five and Die* (1958), a wartime espionage story in which the protagonists operated under cover of being documentary film-makers. He subsequently made films in various European countries, and latterly had been active in French television productions. Died in Paris on 9 December 1985, aged 67.

Joseph Walker

An eminent cinematographer who entered films in 1919 and was under contract to Columbia from 1927 until 1952, Walker provided a key element in that studio's 'look', most especially through the films that he shot for Frank Capra, ranging from *Platinum Blonde* (1931) and *The Bitter Tea of General Yen* (1933) to *Mr Deeds Goes to Town* (1936) and *Mr Smith Goes to Washington* (1939). Trained as an electrical engineer, he began by working in a film laboratory and made the jump to cinematographer with *The Girl From God's Country* (1921). His last movie was *Affair in Trinidad* (1952) and perhaps oddly he only once ventured into colour, with *The Jolson Story* (1946). He retired from films to engage in research and was responsible for developing a zoom lens for TV cameras. Died in Las Vegas on 1 August 1985, aged 92.

Orson Welles

In the polls of international critics run by *Sight and Sound* in 1962, 1972 and 1982, the same film held the number one place: *Citizen Kane* (1941), the first screen work of its then 26-year-old creator, albeit that he was already a legendary figure in the American theatre and on radio. (Parenthetically, Welles' second film, *The Magnificent Ambersons* (1942), was also voted into the top ten in the two later polls; and the fact that neither it nor *Kane* was placed in 1952 testifies not just to the critical conservatism of the day but to just how far ahead of his time Welles was.) 'This is the greatest train set a boy ever had', Welles reputedly said on first setting foot on a sound stage; it is no overstatement to propose that with *Kane*, Welles reinvented the cinema. And in a sense he remade it in his own image. There is inescapably some truth in the facile belief that the apotheosis and dying fall of Kane himself (the man who 'never finished anything') presaged the chequered career of his creator. From *Ambersons* onwards, Welles' work was dogged by misunderstanding and misfortune, and by his own over-reaching stubbornness and egotism. Yet the achievements remain extraordinary, flawed though they may be by the exigencies of haphazard production – *Macbeth* (1948) dashed off in three weeks at Republic; *Othello* (1952) made piecemeal over years and continents – or of ostensibly uncongenial material. *The Lady From Shanghai* (1948), *Mr Arkadin* (1955) and above all *Touch of Evil* (1958) elevate melodrama to sublime heights; and with *Chimes at Midnight* (1966), evidently his own preferred film, he created a 'lament for merrie England' in which the recurrent Wellesian themes of power, trust, betrayal and their reciprocal relationships, are woven together in a work not only of virtuosity (the unforgettable battle sequence) but of true elegiac grandeur. Since then there has been the 'miniaturist' *The Immortal Story* (1968), the enigmatic *F for Fake* (1975), and there have been shelved, though apparently completed, projects like *The Deep* and *The Other Side of the Wind* which may now, it must be hoped, become visible. Of course, Welles the actor has been ubiquitous: in early days there was a fine Rochester in *Jane Eyre* (1944), and there was the marvellously sardonic Harry Lime (the one part he played with absolutely no make-up) in *The Third Man* (1950); a little later, strong performances in *Man in the Shadow* (1957, GB: *Pay the Devil*) and *Compulsion* (1959), with its virtuoso courtroom address. But in more recent years, Welles the actor seemed to gravitate to almost perversely unworthy material. Welles was always a showman, and had in his time been a magician in the literal as well as the aesthetic sense. This most mysterious of creators lived in the milieu of TV talk shows and commercials, not in an ivory tower. 'What does it matter what you say about people?' asked Marlene Dietrich's gypsy fortune-teller at the end of *Touch of Evil*. But whatever they are saying, people will be talking about Welles' work for a long time to come. He died in Hollywood on 10 October 1985, aged 70.

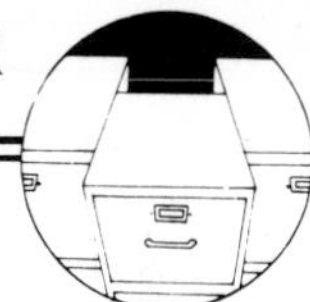

REFERENCE

US PRODUCTION COMPANIES

ABC Motion Pictures
1330 Avenue of the Americas,
New York NY 10019
Tel: (212) 581 7777

and

2040 Avenue of the Stars,
Century City, CA 90067
Tel: (213) 553 2000

The Aldrich Company
606 North Larchmont Blvd,
Los Angeles, CA 90004
Tel: (213) 462 6511

Irwin Allen Productions
Columbia Plaza,
Burbank, CA 91505
Tel: (818) 954 3601

The Almi Group
1585 Broadway,
New York, NY 10036
Tel: (212) 975 8300

Amblin Entertainment
100 Universal Plaza, Bld 477,
Universal City, CA 91608
Tel: (818) 508 4600

Arkoff International Pictures
9200 Sunset Blvd,
Penthouse 3,
Los Angeles, CA 90069
Tel: (213) 278 7600

Bakshi Productions
8132 Sunland Blvd,
Sun Valley, CA 91352
Tel: (213) 768 4000

Batjac Productions
9570 Wilshire Blvd,
Suite 400,
Beverly Hills, CA 90212
Tel: (213) 278 9870

Warren Beatty Productions
5555 Melrose Avenue,
Los Angeles, CA 90038
Tel: (213) 468 5000

Brooksfilms
PO Box 900,
Beverly Hills, CA 90213
Tel: (213) 203 1375

Buena Vista International
350 South Buena Vista Street,
Burbank, CA 91521
Tel: (818) 840 5414

The Cannon Group
6464 Sunset Blvd,
Suite 1150,
Los Angeles, CA 90028
Tel: (213) 469 8124

CBS Theatrical Films
4024 Radford Avenue,
Studio City, CA 91604
Tel: (213) 760 6134

Chartoff-Winkler Productions
10125 West Washington Blvd,
Culver City, CA 90230
Tel: (213) 204 0474

Cine Media International
1 Transglobal Sq.,
PO Box 7005,
Long Beach, CA 90807
Tel: (213) 426 3622

Dick Clark Cinema Productions
3003 West Olive Avenue,
Burbank, CA 91505
Tel: (213) 841 3003

Columbia Pictures
Columbia Plaza,
Burbank, CA 91505
Tel: (818) 954 6000

and

711 Fifth Avenue,
New York, NY 10022
Tel: (212) 751 4400

Dino De Laurentiis Corporation
1 Gulf & Western Plaza,
New York, NY 10023
Tel: (212) 399 0101

Walt Disney Productions
500 South Buena Vista Street,
Burbank, CA 91521
Tel: (818) 840 1000

Blake Edwards Productions
1888 Century Park East,
Suite 1616,
Los Angeles, CA 90067
Tel: (213) 553 6741

Embassy Communications
Suite 666,
1901 Avenue of the Stars,
Los Angeles, CA 90067
Tel: (213) 553 3600

First Artists Production Company
150 El Camino, Suite 110,
Beverly Hills, CA 90212
Tel: (213) 274 0200

Samuel Goldwyn Productions
10203 Santa Monica Blvd,
Los Angeles, CA 90067
Tel: (213) 552 2255

Group 1 Films
9200 Sunset Blvd,
Los Angeles, CA 90069
Tel: (213) 550 8767

Hanna-Barbera Productions
3400 Cahuenga Blvd West,
Los Angeles, CA 90068
Tel: (213) 851 5000

Larry Harmon Pictures Corporation
650 North Bronson Avenue
Los Angeles, CA 90004
Tel: (213) 463 2331

Home Box Office
2049 Century Park East
Los Angeles, CA 90067
Tel: (213) 557 9400

and

1100 Avenue of the Americas,
New York, NY 10020
Tel: (212) 484 1100

Horizon Pictures
745 Fifth Avenue,
New York, NY 10151
Tel: (212) 421 6810

ITC Productions
12711 Ventura Blvd,
Studio City, CA 91604
Tel: (213) 760 2100

115 East 57th Street,
New York, NY 10022
Tel: (212) 371 6660

Jalem Productions
141 El Camino, Suite 210,
Beverly Hills, CA 90212
Tel: (213) 278 7750

Norman Jewison Productions
9336 W Washington Blvd,
Culver City, CA 90230
Tel: (213) 202 3402

Howard Koch Productions
5555 Melrose Avenue,
Los Angeles, CA 90038
Tel: (213) 468 5996

Kurtz and Friends
2312 W Olive Avenue,
Burbank, CA 91506
Tel: (818) 841 8188

Edy and Ely Landau
2029 Century Park East,
Los Angeles, CA 90067
Tel: (213) 553 5010

Alan Landsbury Productions
11811 West Olympic Blvd,
Los Angeles, CA 90064
Tel: (213) 208 2111

Walter Lantz Productions
6311 Romaine Street,
Hollywood, CA 90038
Tel: (213) 469 2907

Glen A Larson Prods
10201 West Pic Blvd,
Los Angeles, CA 90035
Tel: (213) 203 1076

Jerry Leider Productions
12711 Ventura Blvd,
Studio City, CA 91604
Tel: (818) 760 2110

Joseph E. Levine Presents
767 Third Avenue,
New York, NY 10017
Tel: (212) 826 0370

Lion's Gate Films
1861 South Bundy Drive,
Los Angeles, CA 90025
Tel: (213) 820 7751

Lorimar Productions
3970 Overland Avenue,
Culver City, CA 90230
Tel: (213) 202 2000

Lucasfilm
PO Box 2009,
San Rafael, CA 94912
Tel: (415) 457 5282

The Malpaso Company
4000 Warner Blvd,
Burbank, CA 91522
Tel: (818) 954 6000

Manson International
9145 Sunset Blvd,
Los Angeles, CA 90069
Tel: (213) 273 8640

MCA
100 Universal City Plaza,
Universal City, CA 91608
Tel: (818) 985 4321

and

445 Park Avenue,
New York, NY 10022
Tel: (212) 759 7500

Bill Melendez Productions
439 North Larchmont Blvd,
Los Angeles, CA 90004
Tel: (213) 463 4101

Metromedia Producers Corporation
5746 Sunset Blvd,
Hollywood, CA 90028
Tel: (213) 462 7111

MGM/UA
10202 West Washington Blvd,
Culver City, CA 90230
Tel: (213) 558 5000

and

1350 Avenue of the Americas,
New York, NY 10019
Tel: (212) 708 0300

Mirisch Corporation of California
100 Universal City Plaza,
Universal City, CA 91608
Tel: (818) 508 1271

MTM Enterprises
4024 Radford Ave,
Studio City, CA 91604
Tel: (818) 760 4000

NBC Film Productions
9336 West Washington Blvd,
Culver City, CA 90230
Tel: (213) 836 5537

New Horizons Picture Corporation
11600 San Vicente Blvd,
Brentwood, CA 90049
Tel: (213) 820 6733

New World Pictures
1888 Century Park East,
Los Angeles, CA 90067
Tel: (213) 551 1444

Orion Picture Corporation
(incorporating Filmways)
1875 Century Park East,
Los Angeles, CA 90067
Tel: (213) 557 8700
and
711 Fifth Avenue,
New York, NY 10022
Tel: (212) 758 5100

The Pakula Company
330 West 58th Street,
New York, NY 10019
Tel: (212) 664 0640

Paramount Pictures Corporation
1 Gulf & Western Plaza,
New York, NY 10023
Tel: (212) 333 7000
and
5555 Melrose Avenue,
Los Angeles, CA 90038
Tel: (213) 463 0100

Persky-Bright Organisation
485 Madison Avenue,
New York, NY 10022
Tel: (212) 421 4141

Polygram Pictures
3940 Overland Avenue,
Culver City, CA 90230
Tel: (213) 202 4400

Rastar Films
Columbia Plaza West,
Burbank, CA 91505
Tel: (818) 954 2899

The Walter Reade Organisation
241 East 34th Street,
New York, NY 10016
Tel: (212) 683 6300

Republic Pictures Corporation
12636 Beatrice Street,
Los Angeles, CA 90066
Tel: (213) 306 4040

RKO Pictures
129 North Vermont Avenue,
Los Angeles, CA 90004
Tel: (213) 383 5525
and
1440 Broadway,
New York, NY 10018
Tel: (212) 764 7000

Rollins/Joffe Productions
5555 Melrose Avenue,
Los Angeles, CA 90038
Tel: (213) 468 5000

Rosemont Productions
1990 Westwood Blvd, Suite 200,
Los Angeles, CA 90025
Tel: (213) 474 4700

Mark Rydell
100 Universal City Plaza,
Universal City, CA 91608
Tel: (818) 508 1078

Screen Entertainment Films
9489 Dayton Way,
Beverly Hills, CA 90210
Tel: (213) 278 4770

The Richard Shepherd Company
10202 West Washington Blvd,
Culver City, CA 90230
Tel: (213) 836 3000

Showtime Entertainment
10900 Wilshire Blvd, 4th Floor,
Los Angeles, CA 90024
Tel: (213) 208 2340

Simon/Reeves/Landsburg Productions
260 South Beverly Drive,
Beverly Hills, CA 90212
Tel: (213) 273 5450

Aaron Spelling Productions
132 South Rodeo Drive,
Beverly Hills, CA 90212
Tel: (213) 858 2000

Spiegel-Bergman Productions
2029 Century Park East,
Suite 1850,
Los Angeles, CA 90067
Tel: (213) 552 0577

Robert Stigwood Productions
5451 Marathon Street,
Los Angeles, CA 90038
Tel: (213) 468 5000

David Susskind Productions
10202 West Washington Blvd,
Culver City, CA 90230
Tel: (213) 558 5000

Taft International Pictures
10960 Wilshire Blvd, 10th Floor,
Los Angeles, CA 90024
Tel: (213) 208 2000

Tri-Star
711 Fifth Avenue,
New York, NY 10022
Tel: (212) 265 6130

and
1875 Century Park East,
Los Angeles, CA 90067
Tel: (213) 277 9434

Twentieth Century-Fox Film Corporation
Box 900,
Beverly Hills, CA 90213
Tel: (213) 277 2211
and
40 West 57th Street,
New York, NY 10019
Tel: (212) 977 5500

Universal Pictures
Universal City Studios,
Universal City, CA 91608
Tel: (213) 985 4321
and
445 Park Avenue,
New York, NY 10022
Tel: (212) 759 7500

Viacom Enterprises
10900 Wilshire Blvd,
Los Angeles, CA 90024
Tel: (213) 208 2700

Warner Bros
75 Rockefeller Plaza,
New York, NY 10019
Tel: (212) 484 8000
and
4000 Warner Blvd,
Burbank, CA 91522
Tel: (213) 954 6000

Witzend Productions
5555 Melrose Avenue,
Hollywood, CA 90038
Tel: (213) 468 4882

World Wide Pictures
2520 West Olive Avenue,
Burbank, CA 91505
Tel: (818) 843 1300

Wrather Corporation
270 North Cannon Drive,
Beverly Hills, CA 90210
Tel: (213) 278 8521

Saul Zaentz Company Film Center
2600 10th Street,
Berkeley, CA 94710
Tel: (415) 549 1528

Zanuck-Brown Company
202 North Canon Drive,
Beverly Hills, CA 90210
Tel: (213) 274 0261

UK PRODUCTION COMPANIES

Acorn Pictures
49 Old Bond Street,
London W1X 3AF
Tel: (01) 493 1420

Allegro Films
27b Elsworthy Road,
London NW3 3BT
Tel: (01) 586 1443

Allied Stars
Cannon Elstree Studios,
Borehamwood, Herts WD6 1JG
Tel: (01) 953 1600
and
60 Park Lane,
London W1
Tel: (01) 439 5379

Ariel Productions
162-170 Wardour Street,
London W1
Tel: (01) 437 7700

Arts International
32 Eccleston Square,
London SW1 1PB
Tel: (01) 834 6811

Astramead Ltd
38 Gloucester Mews,
London W2 3HE
Tel: (01) 723 4678

Peter Batty Productions
Claremont House,
Renfrew Road,
Kingston,
Surrey KT2 7NT
Tel: (01) 942 6304

Boyd's Company
9 Great Newport Street,
London WC2H 7JA
Tel: (01) 836 5601
Tx: 27107 PETERS G

Brent Walker
Knightsbridge House,
197 Knightsbridge,
London SW7 1RB
Tel: (01) 225 1941.
Tx: 23639

British Film Institute Production Board
29 Rathbone Street,
London W1P 1AG
Tel: (01) 636 5587

British Lion Films
Pinewood Studios,
Iver Heath,
Iver, Bucks SL0 0NT
Tel: (0753) 651700
Tx: 847505

Brooksfilms
PO Box 472,
London SW7 2QB
Tel: (01) 373 3269

Burrill Productions
51 Lansdowne Road,
Lodon W11 2LG
Tel: (01) 727 1442
Tx: 896691 TLXIR G

The Callender Company
38 Long Acre,
London WC2 9JT
Tel: (01) 240 8644
Tx: 25166

Cannon International
167-169 Wardour Street,
London W1V 3TA
Tel: (01) 437 9844

Charisma Films
Russell Chambers,
London WC2E 8AA
Tel: (01) 240 9891

Children's Film and Television Foundation
Cannon Elstree Studios,
Borehamwood,
Herts WDG 1JG
Tel: (01) 953 1600

Chrysalis Visual Programming
12 Stratford Place
London W1N 9AF
Tel: (01) 408 2355

Columbia (British) Productions
19-23 Wells Street,
London W1P 3FP
Tel: (01) 580 2090

Consolidated Productions
56 Ennismore Gardens,
London SW7
Tel: (01) 589 2262

Cosgrove Hall
Albany House
2 Albany Road,
Chorlton-cum-Hardy
Manchester M21 1BL
Tel: (061) 881 2305

Courier Films
Shepperton Studios,
Studio Road,
Shepperton TW17 0QD
Tel: (09328) 62611

Walt Disney Productions
31 Soho Square,
London W1V 6AP
Tel: (01) 734 8111

Diverse Productions
6-12 Gorleston Street,
London W14 8XS
Tel: (01) 603 4567

Dumbarton Films
Dumbarton House,
68 Oxford Street,
London W1N 9LA
Tel: (01) 631 4926

Embassy Pictures
3 Audley Street,
London W1Y 5LR
Tel: (01) 409 1925

Ian Emes Animation/Timeless Films
132 Royal College Street,
London NW1
Tel: (01) 267 7625

EMI: see Cannon

Enigma Productions
15 Queensgate Place Mews,
London SW7 5BG
Tel: (01) 581 0238

Eon Productions
2 South Audley Street,
London W1Y 5DQ
Tel: (01) 493 7953

Euston Films
365 Euston Road,
London NW1 3AR
Tel: (01) 387 0911

Film Contracts
2 Lower James Street,
London W1R 3PN
Tel: (01) 437 7015

Film Four International
60 Charlotte Street,
London W1P 2AX
Tel: (01) 631 4444
Tx: 892355

Filmscreen International
37 Bedford Square,
London WC1B 3HW
Tel: (01) 631 0800

S Benjamin Fisz Productions
51 South Audley Street,
London W1
Tel: (01) 493 7428

Flamingo Productions
47 Lonsdale Square,
London N1 1EW
Tel: (01) 607 9958

Forever Films
82 Warwick Avenue,
London W2
Tel: (01) 286 1948

Mark Forstater Film Productions
42a Devonshire Close,
Portland Place,
London W1N 1LL
Tel: (01) 631 0611

Bob Godfrey Films
55 Neal Street,
London WC2
Tel: (01) 240 1889

Goldcrest Films and Television
180 Wardour Street,
London W1V 3AA
Tel: (01) 437 8696
Tx: 267458 GOLDCR

Golden Communications
(Golden Harvest)
47 Greek Street,
London W1V 5LQ
Tel: (01) 439 1431

GPA Films
22 Romilly Street,
London W1
Tel: (01) 734 6994

The Grade Company
3 Audley Square,
London W1
Tel: (01) 409 1925

Grand Slamm Animation
100 St Martin's Lane
London WC2N 4AZ
Tel: (01) 240 2273

Greenpoint Films
5a Noel Street,
London W1V 3RB
Tel: (01) 437 6492

Colin Gregg Film Productions
Floor 2, 1-6 Falconberg Court,
London W1
Tel: (01) 439 0257

Grenadier Films
Crown House,
High Road,
Loughton, Essex
IG10 4LG
Tel: (01) 500 0936

Halas and Batchelor Animation
3-7 Kean Street,
London WC2
Tel: (01) 836 5108
Tx: 269496

Hammer Film Productions
Cannon Elstree Studios,
Borehamwood
Herts WD6 1JG
Tel: (01) 953 1600

HandMade Films
26 Cadogan Square,
London SW1X 0JP
Tel: (01) 584 8345
Tx: 8951338 EURODOG

Hanstoll Films
4 New Burlington Place,
London W1
Tel: (01) 734 3864

Hartswood Films
56 Ennismore Gardens,
Knightsbridge,
London SW7
Tel: (01) 589 2262

Hemdale
21 Albion St.,
London W2 2AS
Tel: (01) 724 1010
Tx: 25528

Henson International Television
2 Old Brewery Mews,
Hampstead High Street,
London NW3 1PZ
Tel: (01) 435 7121

Island Pictures
22 Saint Peter's Square,
London W6 9NW
Tel: (01) 741 1511

ITC Entertainments
ACC House,
17 Great Cumberland Place,
London W1 1AG
Tel: (01) 262 8040
Tx: 261807 EYETEECEE LONDON

Kestrel Films
45 Walham Grove,
London SW6 1QR
Tel: (01) 385 5577

Kestrel II
23 Hamilton Gardens,
London NW8 9PU
Tel: (01) 286 8602

Ladbroke Films
4 Kensington Park Gardens,
London W11 3HB
Tel: (01) 727 3541

Limehouse Productions
Limehouse Studios,
Canary Wharf,
West India Docks,
London E14 9SJ
Tel: (01) 987 2090
Tx: 296149 LIMHSE G

Euan Lloyd Productions
Pinewood Studios,
Iver Heath, Iver,
Bucks SL0 0NH
Tel: (0753) 651700

London Film Productions
44a Floral Street,
London WC2E 9DA
Tel: (01) 379 3366
Tx: 896805

Lorimar Telepictures
49 Berkeley Street,
London W1X 5AE
Tel: (01) 409 1190

MCA Television
170 Picadilly,
London W1
Tel: (01) 400 0188

Bill Melendez Productions
32-34 Gt Marlborough Street,
London W1
Tel: (01) 439 4411

Memorial Films
6e Ladbroke Square,
London W11
Tel: (01) 727 7107

Merchant Ivory Productions
34 South Molton Street,
London W1
Tel: (01) 387 6778

Mersham Productions
41 Montpelier Walk,
London SW7 1JH
Tel: (01) 589 8829

Metropolis Pictures
8-10 Neal's Yard,
London WC2
Tel: (01) 836 1056

MGM-UA
UIP House, Beadon Road,
London W6
Tel: (01) 741 9041

Moving Picture Company
25 Noel Street,
London W1
Tel: (01) 734 9151

MPL Communications
1 Soho Square,
London W1V 6BQ
Tel: (01) 439 6621

Norfolk International Pictures
107 Long Acre,
London WC2E 9NT
Tel: (01) 240 0863

Orion Pictures Company
31 Soho Square,
London W1V 4AP
Tel: (01) 437 7766
Tx: 894030

Palace Productions
16/17 Wardour Mews,
London W1V 3DG
Tel: (01) 734 2575

Paramount Pictures (UK)
162 Wardour Street,
London W1V 4AB
Tel: (01) 437 7700

Pennies From Heaven
83 Eastbourne Mews
London W2
Tel: (01) 723 7326

Picture Partnership Productions
73 Newman Street,
London W1P 3LA
Tel: (01) 637 8056

Portman Productions
Tennyson House,
159 Great Portland Street,
London W1N 6NR
Tel: (01) 637 2692

Poseidon Films
113 Wardour Street,
London W1V 3TD
Tel: (01) 734 4441

Primetime Television
Seymour Mews House,
Seymour Mews,
Wigmore Street,
London W1H 9DE
Tel: (01) 486 9425

Python (Monty) Pictures
25 Newman Street,
London W1P 3HA
Tel: (01) 935 0307

Quintet Films
Station House, Harrow Road
Wembley, Middx HA9 6EH
Tel: (01) 903 5111

The Rank Organisation
6 Connaught Place,
London W2 2EZ
Tel: (01) 629 7454

Recorded Picture Company
8-12 Broadwick Street,
London W1
Tel: (01) 439 0607

Rediffusion Films
Carlton House,
Lower Regent Street,
London SW1Y 4LS
Tel: (01) 930 0221

Red Rooster Films
11-13 Macklin Street,
London WC2B 5NH
Tel: (01) 405 8147

Geoff Reeve Associates
45 St James's Place,
London SW1A 1PG
Tel: (01) 499 0662
Tx: 295574

RKO Productions
33 Dover Street,
London W1X 3RA
Tel: (01) 629 4799

RM Productions
1 Rockley Road,
London W14
Tel: (01) 734 3474

Sydney Rose Productions
9 Clifford Street,
London W1
Tel: (01) 439 7321

Rosemont Productions
Pinewood Studios,
Iver Heath,
Iver, Bucks SL0 0NH
Tel: (0753) 651700

Salon Productions
13-14 Archer Street,
London W1V 7HG
Tel: (01) 734 9472

Sandfire Productions
Pinewood Studios,
Iver Heath,
Iver, Bucks SL0 0NH
Tel: (0753) 651700

Sands Films
119 Rotherhithe Street,
London SE16 4NF
Tel: (01) 231 2209

Satellite Television
Craven House,
25 Marshall Street,
London W1
Tel: (01) 439 0491

Scimitar Films
6-8 Sackville Street,
London W1X 1DD
Tel: (01) 734 8385

Silver Chalice Productions
10 Dover Street,
London W1
Tel: (01) 629 0500

Skreba Productions
5a Noel Street,
London W1V 3RB
Tel: (01) 437 6492

Robert Stigwood Group
118 Wardour Street,
London W1V 4BT
Tel: (01) 437 2512

Sword and Sorcery Productions
20 Stradella Road,
London SE24 9HA
Tel: (01) 274 3215

Tempest Films
4 New Burlington Place,
London W1
Tel: (01) 734 3864

Third Eye Productions
82 Wardour Street,
London W1V 3LF
Tel: (01) 437 7687

Twentieth Century-Fox Film Company
31 Soho Square,
London W1V 6AP
Tel: (01) 437 7766
Tx: 27869

Umbrella Films
31 Percy Street,
London W1P 9FG
Tel: (01) 637 1169

United British Artists
73 St James's Street,
London W1
Tel: (01) 629 5276

Universal Pictures
139 Piccadilly,
London W1V 9FH
Tel: (01) 629 7211

Video Arts
Dumbarton House,
68 Oxford Street,
London W1N 9LA
Tel: (01) 636 9421

Virtue Consolidated
56 Ennismore Gardens,
Knightsbridge,
London SW7 1AJ
Tel: (01) 589 2262

Virgin Vision
328 Kensal Road,
London W10 5XJ
Tel: (01) 968 8888
Tx: 892890

Warner Bros Productions
135 Wardour Street,
London W1V 4AP
Tel: (01) 437 5600
Tx: 22653

Michael White
13 Duke Street
London SW1 6DB
Tel: (01) 839 3971

David Wickes Television
169 Queen's Gate,
London SW7 5HE
Tel: (01) 224 1382
Tx: 262284

Richard Williams Animation
13 Soho Square,
London W1V 5FB
Tel: (01) 437 4455

Winkast Programming
Pinewood Studios,
Iver Heath,
Iver, Bucks, SL0 0NH
Tel: (0753) 651700

Witzend Productions
4 Queenborough Studios,
London W2 3SQ
Tel: (01) 402 2238

World Film Services
10 Mount Row,
London W1Y 5DA
Tel: (01) 493 3045
Tx: 23328 HAYMAN G

Yellowbill Prods
11 Cross Keys Close,
London W1M 5FY
Tel: (01) 486 9721

Zenith Productions
8 Great Titchfield Street,
London W1P 7AA
Tel: (01) 637 7941

UK FILM DISTRIBUTORS

Alpha Films
Unit 1,
McKay Trading Estate,
Kensal Road,
London W10 5BX
Tel: (01) 960 8211

Anglo-American Distributors
68 Wardour Street,
London W1V 3HP
Tel: (01) 437 1563

Apollo Film Distributors
303 Wimbourne Road,
Bournemouth BH9 2AA
Tel: (0202) 533577

Artificial Eye Film Company
211 Camden High Street,
London NW1 7BT
Tel: (01) 267 6036

Avatar Communications
Unit 5, Imperial Studios,
Imperial Road,
London SW6
Tel: (01) 736 6304

Barber International Films
43 Great Windmill Street,
London W1V 7PA
Tel: (01) 434 4411

Black Cat Films
12 D'Arblay Street,
London W1V 3FP
Tel: (01) 437 8968

Blue Dolphin Films
15/17 Old Compton Street,
London W1V 6JR
Tel: (01) 439 9511

Bordeaux Films International
92 Wardour Street,
London W1
Tel: (01) 434 3459

Brent Walker Film Distributors
Knightsbridge House,
197 Knightsbridge,
London SW7 1RB
Tel: (01) 225 1941

British Film Institute Film and Video Library
81 Dean Street,
London W1V 6AA
Tel: (01) 734 6451

Butcher's Film Distributors
1st Floor, Townsend House,
22 Dean Street,
London W1V 5AL
Tel: (01) 437 7282
Tx: 892604

Cannon Distributors
167/169 Wardour Street,
London W1
Tel: (01) 437 9844
Tx: 268840

Cinegate
Gate Cinema
87 Notting Hill Gate,
London W11
Tel: (01) 727 2651

Columbia-Cannon-Warner
135 Wardour Street,
London W1V 4AP
Tel: (01) 734 8400
Tx: 8955617

Connoisseur Films
167 Oxford Stret,
London W1R 2DX
Tel: (01) 734 6555

Contemporary Film
55 Greek Street,
London W1V 6DB
Tel: (01) 434 2623

Crawford Films
15/17 Old Compton Street,
London W1V 6JR
Tel: (01) 734 5298

Curzon Film Distributors
38 Curzon Street,
London W1Y 1EY
Tel: (01) 626 8961
Tx: 21612

Walt Disney:
see UK Production Companies

Eagle Films
15/17 Old Compton Street,
London W1V 6JR
Tel: (01) 437 9541
Tx: 928152 GALAFI G

Enterprise Pictures
113 Wardour Street,
London W1V 3TO
Tel: (01) 734 3372

Entertainment Film Distributors
60/66 Wardour Street,
London W1V 3HP
Tel: (01) 734 4678
Tx: 27950

Essential Cinema
122 Wardour Street,
London W1
Tel: (01) 437 8127

Facelift Film Distributors
Suite 4,
60/62 Old Compton Street,
London W1
Tel: (01) 439 2047

Gala: see Cannon

Golden Communications
47 Greek Street,
London W1
Tel: (01) 439 1431

Grand National Film Distributors
26 Oak Grove,
Ruislip,
Middx HAA 8UF
Tel: (01) 866 9757

GTO Films
36 Soho Square
London W1V 5DG
Tel: (01) 734 4334
Tx: 297648 GTO ARC

HandMade Films (Distributors)
26 Cadogan Square,
London SW1X 0JP
Tel: (01) 584 8345
Tx: 8951338 EURODOG

Hemdale Leisure
21 Albion Street,
London W2
Tel: (01) 724 1010
Tx: 25558

ICA Projects
12 Carlton House Terrace,
London SW1H 5AH
Tel: (01) 943 0493

ITC Film Distributors
5/7 Carnaby Street,
London W1V 1PG
Tel: (01) 439 6611

London Films
44A Floral Street,
London WC2E 9DA
Tel: (01) 379 3366
Tx: 896805

Mainline Pictures
37 Museum Street,
London WC1A 1LP
Tel: (01) 242 5523

MGM: see UIP

Miracle International Films
22 Soho Square,
London W1V 5FJ
Tel: (01) 437 0507
Tx: 21879 MIRICFILMS

New Realm Film Distributors
Townsend House,
22 Dean Street,
London W1V 5AL
Tel: (01) 437 9143
Tx: 892604 NRDLON G

Osprey Film Distributors
328 Kensal Road
London W10 5XJ
Tel: (01) 968 8888
Tx: 892890

The Other Cinema
79 Wardour Street,
London W1V 3TH
Tel: (01) 734 8508
Tx: 20604

Palace Pictures
16/17 Wardour Mews
London W1V 3DG
Tel: (01) 734 7060

Paramount: see UIP

Premier Releasing
93 Wardour Street,
London W1V 9TE
Tel: (01) 437 6516

Rank Film Distributors
127 Wardour Street,
London W1V 4AD
Tel: (01) 437 9020
Tx: 262556

Supreme Film Distributors
Suite 6,
60/62 Old Compton Street,
London W1
Tel: (01) 437 4415

Target International
22 Romilly Street,
London W1V 5TG
Tel: (01) 734 8809

TCB Releasing
Stone House, Rudge,
Frome, Somerset
Tel: (0373) 830769

Tigon Film Distributors
5/7 Carnaby Street,
London W1V 1PG
Tel: (01) 439 6611
Tx: 291004 ITCFD G

Twentieth Century Fox: see UK Production Companies

UIP (United International Pictures)
Mortimer House,
37/41 Mortimer Street,
London W1A 2LJ
Tel: (01) 636 1655

UK Film Distributors
31/33 Soho Square,
London W1V 6AP
Tel: (01) 437 7766
Tx: LONDON 21532

United Artists: see UIP

Universal: see UIP

Virgin Vision
328 Kensal Road,
London W10 5XJ
Tel: (01) 968 8888
Tx: 892890

Watchgrove
6 New Road,
Ham,
Richmond, Surrey TW10 7HY
Tel: (01) 948 5839

FILM STUDIOS

AUSTRIA

Schönbrunn Film
Neubaugasse 1,
1070 Vienna
Tel: (0222) 932265

WDS Film
Göllnergasse 8-10,
1030 Vienna
Tel: (0222) 735436

Wien Film
Engelshofengasse 2,
1238 Vienna
Tel: (0222) 882541

BELGIUM

Studio L'Equipe
92 rue Colonel Bourg,
1040 Brussels
Tel: (02) 736 38 46

CANADA

David Bier Studios
1085 St Alexander Street,
Montreal, Quebec H2Z 1P4
Tel: (514) 861 3469

Magder Studios
793 Pharmacy Avenue,
Toronto, Ontario M1L 3K3
Tel: (416) 752 8850

Studio Centre
2264 Lakeshore Blvd. West,
Toronto, Ontario M8V 1A9
Tel: (416) 255 7976

Studio 523
523 Richmond St East,
Toronto, Ontario M5A 1R4
Tel: (416) 862 0523

Toronto International Film Studios
11030 Highway 27, Box 430,
Kleinburg, Ontario L0J 1C0
Tel: (416) 857 3090

Yorkville Studio
47 Scollard Street,
Toronto, Ontario M5R 1G1
Tel: (416) 968 1822

FEDERAL REPUBLIC OF GERMANY

Arnold & Richter Cine Technik
Turkenstrasse 89,
8000 Munich 40
Tel: (089) 38 09 240
Tx: 524317 ARRI D

Aventin Film Studio
Aventinstrasse 4-6,
Munich 5
Tel: (0811) 22 55 05

Bavaria Atelier Gesellschaft
Bavariafilmplatz 7,
8022 Geiselgasteig
Tel: (089) 649 91
Tx: (05) 23 254 bavat

Berliner Unon Film
Oberlandstrasse 26-35,
1000 Berlin 42
Tel: (030) 75 94 1
Tx: 184233

Deutschlandhalle
Messedamm 26,
1 Berlin 19
Tel: (030) 20 13 1

Internationale Film Union
Haus Calmuth, Postfach 150,
54 Remagen-Calmuth
Tel: (02642) 24051
Tx: 863812

Studio Hamburg
Tonndorfer Haupstrasse 90,
2000 Hamburg 70,
Tel: (040) 6688 2222
Tx: 0214218

FRANCE

Eclair
10 rue du Mont,
93800 Epinay
Tel: (01) 821 63 03

Images de France
29 rue Vernet,
75008 Paris
Tel: (01) 720 53 17

Paris Studio Cinema
50 quai du Point du Jour,
92100 Boulogne-Billancourt
Tel: (01) 609 93 24

Studios de Boulogne
137 av. Jean Baptiste Clement,
92100 Boulogne-Billancourt
Tel: (01) 605 65 69

Studios Francoeur
6 rue Francoeur,
75882 Paris Cedex 18
Tel: (01) 257 12 10

Victorine Studios
16 avenue Edouard Grinda,
06200 Nice
Tel: (93) 72 54 54
Tx: 970 056F

IRELAND

National Film Studios of Ireland
Ardmore, Bray,
Co Wicklow
Tel: Bray 862971
Tx: 30418

ITALY

Cinecitta
Via Tuscolana 1055,
00173 Italy
Tel: (06) 74 641
Tx: 620478 CINCIT I

Dear International
Via Nomentana 833,
00137 Rome
Tel: (06) 826 801

De Paolis – I.N.C.I.R.
Via Tiburtina 521,
00159 Rome
Tel: (06) 43 85 341

Filmauro
Via della Vasca Navale 58,
00173 Rome
Tel: (06) 55 84 875

ICET De Paolis
Via Cinelandia 5,
20093 Cologno Monzese,
Milan
Tel: (02) 25 43 184

RAP – Elios
Via Tiburtina Km 13, 600,
00131 Rome
Tel: (06) 61 90 424

Vides Cinematografica
Via Concesio Km 1,800,
Prima Porta,
00188 Rome
Tel: (06) 69 10 891

MEXICO

Estudios America
Calzada de Tlalpan 2818,
04620 Mexico DF
Tel: (05) 677 6011

Estudios Churubusco
Atletas 2,
Country Club
04220 Mexico DF
Tel: (05) 549 3060
Tx: 1760298

NETHERLANDS

Cinetone Studios
Duivendrechtsekade 83-85,
1096 AJ Amsterdam
Tel: (020) 93 09 60
Tx: 13186

Cinevideo Studios
Ambachtsmark 3,
1355 EA Almere-Haven
Tel: (03240) 12324

SPAIN

Estudios Apolo
Carretera de la Coruna Km 41,8000,
Los Negrales-Alpedrete,
Madrid
Tel: (01) 850 1268

Estudios Cinematograficos Roma
Carretera de Irun Km 11,700,
Madrid 34
Tel: (01) 734 2050

Estudios Isasi
Esplugas de Llobregat,
Barcelona
Tel: (03) 271 1404

Vallehermoso
Vallehermoso 59,
Madrid 15
Tel: (01) 446 1450

SWEDEN

AB Europa – Film
Box 20065
S-161 20 Bromma
Tel: (08) 98 77 00

Accord Film
Fiskhamnsgatan 10,
S414 55 Götenborg
Tel: (031) 12 12 11

Svenska Filminstitutet
Filmhuset,
Borgvagen,
Box 27 126,
S-120 52 Stockholm
Tel: (08) 63 05 10

UK

Bray Studios
Down Place, Windsor Road,
Water Oakley, Windsor,
Berks SL4 5VG
Tel: (0628) 22111
Tx: 24130

Bushey Film Studios
Melbourne Road,
Bushey, Herts.
Tel: (01) 950 1621

Cannon Elstree Studios
Borehamwood,
Herts WD6 1JG
Tel: (01) 953 1600
Tx: 922436 E FILMS G

Edinburgh Film and TV Studios
Nine Mile Burn, Penicuik,
Midlothian EH26 9LT
Tel: (0968) 72131

Halliford Studios
Manygate Lane,
Shepperton, Middx
Tel: Walton 26341

Isleworth Studios
Studio Parade,
484 London Road,
Isleworth, Middx TW7 4DE
Tel: (01) 568 3511

Lee International Film Studios
Wembley Park Drive,
Wembley, Middx
Tel: (01) 902 1262

Jacob Street Studios
Mill Street,
London SE1
Tel: (01) 232 1100

Limehouse Studios
Canary Wharf,
West India Docks,
London E14 9SJ
Tel: (01) 897 2090

Marylebone Studios
245 Old Marylebone Road,
London NW1 5QT
Tel: (01) 402 8385

Pinewood Studios
Iver Heath, Iver
Bucks SL0 0NH
Tel: (0753) 651700
Tx: 847505

The Production Village
100 Cricklewood Lane,
London NW2
Tel: (01) 450 8969

St John's Wood Studios
87a St John's Wood Terrace,
London NW8 6PY
Tel: (01) 722 9255

Shepperton Studio Centre
Studios Road, Shepperton,
Middx TW17 0QD
Tel: (09328) 62611
Tx: 929416

Twickenham Film Studios
St Margaret's,
Twickenham, Middx
Tel: (01) 892 4477
Tx: 8814497

US

ABC Television Center
4151 Prospect Avenue,
Los Angeles, CA 90027
Tel: (213) 557 7777

Burbank Studios
4000 Warner Blvd,
Burbank CA 91522
Tel: (818) 954 6000

CBS/Fox Studios
4024 Radford,
Studio City, CA 91604
Tel: (818) 760 5000

Columbia Pictures
Columbia Plaza,
Burbank CA 91505
Tel: (213) 954 6000

Walt Disney Productions
500 South Buena Vista Street,
Burbank, CA 91521
Tel: (818) 840 1000

Falcon Studios
5526 Hollywood Blvd,
Los Angeles, CA 90028
Tel:.(213) 462 9356

Samuel Goldwyn Studios
10203 Santa Monica Blvd,
Suite 500, Los Angeles, CA
90067
Tel: (213) 552 2255

Hollywood Center Studios
1040 North Las Palmas Avenue,
Hollywood, CA 90038
Tel: (213) 469 9011

Le Brea Studios
1028 North La Brea Avenue,
Hollywood, CA 90038
Tel: (213) 462 7216

Laird International Studios
9336 West Washington Blvd,
Culver City, CA 90230
Tel: (213) 836 5537

MGM/UA Studios
10202 West Washington Blvd,
Culver City, CA 90230
Tel: (213) 558 5000

NBC Television
3000 West Alameda Avenue,
Burbank, CA 91503
Tel: (213) 845 7000

Paramount Studios
5555 Marathon St,
Los Angeles, CA 90038
Tel: (213) 468 5000

The Production Group
1330 North Vine Street,
Hollywood, CA 90028
Tel: (213) 469 8111

Raleigh Studio
650 North Bronson Avenue,
Los Angeles, CA 90004
Tel: (213) 384 2331

Ren-Mar Studios
846 North Cahuenga Blvd,
Los Angeles, CA 90038
Tel: (213) 463 0808

Twentieth Century-Fox Film Corporation
10201 West Pico Blvd,
Los Angeles, CA 90035
Tel: (213) 277 2211

Universal City Studios/MCA
100 Universal City Plaza,
Universal City, CA 91608
Tel: (818) 985 4321

Valley Production Center
6633 Van Nuys Blvd,
Van Nuys, CA 91405
Tel: (818) 988 6601

Warner Bros
4000 Warner Blvd,
Burbank, CA 91522
Tel: (818) 954 6000

MAGAZINES

AFTERIMAGE
1 Birnham Road,
London N4
Ed: Simon Field, Guy L'Eclair
Irregular

American Cinematographer
ASC Holding Corporation,
1782 North Orange Drive,,
Hollywood, CA 90028
Ed: George Turner
Monthly

American Film
30 East 60th Street,
New York, NY 10022
Ed: Peter Biskind
Ten issues p.a.

American Premiere
8421 Wilshire Blvd,
Penthouse,
Beverly Hills, CA 90211
Ed: Susan Royal
Ten issues p.a.

L'Avant-Scène (Cinema)
1 rue Lord Byron,
75008 Paris
Ed: Claude Beylie
Monthly

Bianco e Nero
Via Tuscolana 1524,
00173 Rome
Ed: Giovanni Grazzini
Quarterly

Cahiers du Cinema
9 Passage de la Boule-Blanche,
75012 Paris
Ed: Serge Toubiana
Monthly

Chaplin
Filmhuset,
Box 27 126,
102 52 Stockholm
Ed: Lars Ahlander
Bi-monthly

China Screen
25 Xin Wai Street,
Beijing, China,
Editorial Board
Irregular

Cineaste
200 Park Avenue South,
New York, NY 10003
Editorial Board
Quarterly

Cine Cubano
Calle 23 no 1155,
Habana, Cuba
Ed: Julio Garcia Espinosa
Irregular

Cinefantastique
PO Box 270, Oak Park, IL 60303
Ed: Frederick S. Clarke
Five issues p.a.

Cinema 86
14 rue de Provence
75009 Paris
Ed: Jacques Guenee
Monthly

Cinema
Milchstrasse 1,
2000 Hamburg 13
Ed: Jörg Altendorf, Willi Bär
Monthly

Cinema Canada
834 Bloomfield Avenue,
Montreal, Quebec H2V 3S6
Ed: Connie Tadros,
Jean-Pierre Tadros
Monthly

Cinema Journal
Department of English,
Box 4348,
University of Illinois at Chicago,
Chicago, IL 60680
Ed: Virginia Wright Wexman
Bi-annual

Cinema Nuovo
Edizioni Dedalo,
Casella Postale 362,
70100 Bari
Ed: Guido Aristarco
Bi-monthly

Cinema Papers
644 Victoria Street,
North Melbourne,
Victoria 3051
Ed: Nick Roddick
Quarterly

Cinema Sessanta
Piazza dei Caprettari 70,
00186 Rome
Ed: Mino Argentieri
Bi-monthly

Dirigido Por
Rbla de Catalunya,
108 3° 1°,
Barcelona
Ed: Edmundo Orts Climent
Monthly

Film
British Federation of Film Societies,
Film Society Unit,
British Film Institute,
81 Dean Street,
London W1V 6AA
Ed: Peter Cargin
Monthly

Film Comment
140 West 65th Street,
New York, NY 10023
Ed: Richard Corliss,
Harlan Jacobson
Bi-monthly

Film Criticism
Allegheny College,
Meadville, PA 16335,
Ed: Lloyd Michaels
Three issues p.a.

Film Dope
45 Lupton Street,
London NW5 2HS
Ed: David Badder, Bob Baker
Irregular

Film Echange
50 avenue Marceau,
75008 Paris
Ed: Rene Thevenet
Three issues p.a.

Filmkritik
Filmkritiker-Kooperative,
Kreittmaystrasse 3,
8000 Munich 2
Editorial Board
Monthly

Film Quarterly
University of California,
Berkeley, CA 94720,
Ed: Ernest Callenbach
Quarterly

Film Reader
Film Division,
Northwestern University,
1905 Sheridan Road,
Evanston, IL 60201
Editorial Board
Irregular

Film Review
30-31 Golden Square,
London W1A 4QX
Ed: John George
Monthly

Films and Filming
Alan Wells International,
Competition House,
Farndon Road,
Market Harborough, Leics
Ed: John Russell Taylor
Monthly

Films in Review
PO Box 589,
Lennox Hill Station,
New York, NY 10021,
Ed: Robin Little
Ten issues p.a.

Framework
40a Topsfield Parade,
Lodon N8 8QA
Ed: Paul Willemen
Irregular

Interview
19 East 32nd Street,
New York, NY 10016
Ed: Frederick W Hughes,
Gael Love
Monthly

Jump Cut
PO Box 865,
Berkeley, CA 94701
Ed: John Hess, Chuck
Kleinhans, Julia Lesage
Two issues p.a.

Literature/Film Quarterly
Salisbury State College,
Salisbury, MD 21801
Ed: Thomas L Erskine,
James M Welsh
Quarterly

Making Better Movies
Henry Greenwood,
28 Great James Street,
London WC1N 3HL
Ed: Tony Rose
Monthly

Media, Culture and Society
28 Banner Street,
London EC1Y 8QE
Editorial Board
Quarterly

Monthly Film Bulletin
British Film Institute,
81 Dean Street,
London W1V 6AA
Ed: Richard Combs
Monthly

Movie
25 Lloyd Baker Street,
London WC1 9AT
Editorial Board
Irregular

Photoplay/Movies and Video
1 Golden Square,
London W1R 3AB
Ed: Lisa Dewson
Monthly

Positif
Nouvelles Éditions Opta,
1 quai Conti,
75006 Paris
Editorial Board
Monthly

Prevue Magazine
Box 974, Reading, PA 19603
Ed: Steranko
Five issues p.a.

Primetime
c/o Illuminations
16 Newman Passage,
London W1
Editorial Board
Irregular

La Revue du Cinema
3 rue Recamier,
75341 Paris 07
Ed: Jacques Zimmer
Monthly

Screen
29 Old Compton Street,
London W1V 5PL
Ed: Mandy Merck
Five issues p.a.

Screen International
King Publications,
6-7 Great Chapel Street,
London W1
Ed: Peter Noble
Weekly

Sight and Sound
British Film Institute,
81 Dean Street,
London W1V 6AA
Ed: Penelope Houston
Quarterly

Stills
10 Museum Street,,
London WC1
Ed: Nicolas Kent
Six issues p.a.

Variety
154 West 46th Street,
New York, NY 10036
Ed: Syd Silverman
Weekly

Undercut
London Filmmakers Co-op,
42 Gloucester Avenue,
London NW1
Editorial Board
Irregular

Wide Angle
Ohio University Press,
Box 388, Athens, OH 45701
Ed: Peter Lehman,
Donald Kinhara
Irregular

US FILM SCHOOLS

ALABAMA

University of Alabama
Department of Broadcast and Film Communication,
PO Box D, University,
AL 35486
Tel: (205) 348 6350

ARIZONA

University of Arizona
Department of Radio and Television,
221 Modern Languages Building,
Tuscon, AZ 85721
Tel: (602) 626 4731

ARKANSAS

University of Arkansas, Fayetteville
The Film Program,
417 Communication Center,
Fayetteville, AR 72701
Tel: (501) 575 2953

CALIFORNIA

American Film Institute Center for Advanced Film Studies
501 Doheny Road,
Beverly Hills,
CA 90210
Tel: (213) 278 8777

Art Center College of Design
Film Department,
1700 Lida Street,
Pasadena, CA 91103
Tel: (213) 577 1700

Brooks Institute
Cinema/TV Department
School of Photographic Art and Science,
2190 Alston Road,
Santa Barbara, CA 93108
Tel: (805) 969 2291

California College of Arts and Crafts,
Film/Video Department,
5212 Broadway,
Oakland, CA 94618
Tel: (415) 653 8118

California Institute of the Arts,
School of Film and Video,
24700 McBean Parkway,
Valencia, CA 91355
Tel: (805) 255 1050

California State University, Fresno
Department of Radio-TV-Cinema,
Cedar and Shaw Avenues,
Fresno, CA 93740
Tel: (209) 487 2627

California State University, Humboldt
Theatre Arts/Film Department,
Arcata, CA 95521
Tel: (707) 826 3566

California State University, Northridge
Radio-TV-Film Department,
18111 Nordhoff Street,
Northridge, CA 91330
Tel: (213) 885 3192

Columbia College, Hollywood
Department of Cinema,
925 North La Brea Avenue,
Hollywood, CA 90038
Tel: (213) 851 0550

Loyola Marymount University
7101 West 80th Street,
Los Angeles, CA 90045
Tel: (213) 642 3033

New College of California
777 Valencia Street,
San Francisco, CA 94110
Tel: (415) 626 1694

San Diego State University
Telecommunications and Film Department,
College Avenue,
San Diego, CA 92182
Tel: (714) 286 6575

San Francisco Art Institute
Filmmaking Department,
800 Chestnut Street,
San Francisco, CA 94133
Tel: (415) 771 7020

San Francisco State University
Film and Creative Arts Interdisciplinary Department,
1600 Holloway Avenue,
San Francisco, CA 94132
Tel: (415) 469 1629

Stanford University
Communication Department,
Cypress Hall,
Stanford, CA 94305
Tel: (415) 497 4621

University of California, Los Angeles
Theatre Arts Department,
405 Hilgard Avenue,
Los Angeles, CA 90024
Tel: (213) 825 7891

University of California, Santa Barbara
Film Studies Program,
Santa Barbara, CA 93106
Tel: (805) 961 2347

University of California, Santa Cruz
Theater Arts Board,
Santa Cruz, CA 95064
Tel: (408) 429 2974

University of Southern California
Division of Cinema/Television,
School of Performing Arts,
University Park,
Los Angeles, CA 90007
Tel: (213) 2235

CONNECTICUT

University of Bridgeport
Cinema Department,
84 Iranistan Avenue,
Bridgeport, CT 06602
Tel: (203) 576 4430

Western Connecticut State College
Photography, Film and TV Department,
181 White Street,
Danbury CT 06001
Tel: (203) 797 4047

DISTRICT OF COLUMBIA

American University
School of Communication,
Washington, DC 20016
Tel: (202) 686 2055

University of the District of Columbia, Mount Vernon Square Campus
Communicative Arts Department,
916 G Street NW,
Building T-10,
Washington, DC 20001
Tel: (202) 727 2717

FLORIDA

Florida State University
Department of Communication,
Diffenbaugh Building,
Room 356,
Tallahassee, FL 32306
Tel: (904) 644 5034

University of Florida
Film Studies Program,
408 GPA Building,
Gainesville, FL 32601
Tel: (904) 392 0777

University of Miami
Communications Department,
PO Box 248127,
Coral Gables, FL 33124
Tel: (305) 284 2265

GEORGIA

University of Georgia
Radio-TV-Film Department,
School of Journalism,
Athens, GA 30602
Tel: (404) 542 3785

ILLINOIS

Columbia College
Film Department,
600 South Michigan Avenue,
Chicago, IL 60605
Tel: (312) 663 1600

Northwestern University
Radio, Television and Film Department,
School of Speech,
Evanston, IL 60201,
Tel: (312) 492 7315

School of the Art Institute of Chicago
Filmmaking Department,
Columbus Drive and Jackson Blvd,
Chicago, IL 60603
Tel: (312) 443 3700

Southern Illinois University at Carbondale
Department of Cinema and Photography,
Carbondale IL 62901
Tel: (618) 453 2365

University of Illinois, Urbana-Champaign
Cinematography Program,
Department of Art and Design,
129 Fine Arts Building,
Champaign, IL 61820
Tel: (217) 333 0855

INDIANA

Indiana University, Purdue University at Fort Wayne,
Communications Department,
2101 Coliseum Blvd East,
Fort Wayne, IN 46805
Tel: (219) 482 5348

KANSAS

University of Kansas
Radio-Television-Film Department,
217 Flint Hall,
Lawrence, KS 66045
Tel: (913) 864 3991

KENTUCKY

Northern Kentucky University
Department of Communications,
Highland Heights, KY 41076
Tel: (606) 292 5435

LOUISIANA

University of New Orleans
Drama and Communications Department,
Lakefront,
New Orleans, LA 70122
Tel: (504) 283 0317

MARYLAND

John Hopkins University
The Humanities Center,
Baltimore, MD 21218
Tel: (301) 338 7616

University of Maryland at College Park
Radio-Television-Film Division,
College Park, MD 20742
Tel: (301) 454 2541

University of Maryland, Baltimore County
Visual Arts Department,
5401 Wilkens Avenue,
Catonsville, MD 21228
Tel: (301) 455 2150

MASSACHUSETTS

Boston University
Department of Broadcasting and Film,
School of Public Communication,
640 Commonwealth Avenue,
Boston, MA 02215
Tel: (617) 353 3483

Emerson College
Department of Mass Communication,
148 Beacon Street,
Boston, MA 02116
Tel: (617) 353 3483

Hampshire College
Film and Photography Department,
Route 116, Amherst, MA 01002
Tel: (413) 549 4600

MICHIGAN

Central Michigan University
Broadcast and Cinematic Arts Department,
340 Moore Hall,
Mount Pleasant, MI 48858
Tel: (517) 774 3852

University of Michigan
Program in Film and Video Studies,
131 Old A & D Building,
Ann Arbor, MI 48109
Tel: (313) 764 0147

MINNESOTA

Minneapolis College of Art and Design
Design Division,
133 East 25th Street,
Minneapolis, MN 55404
Tel: (612) 870 3161

MISSOURI

University of Missouri – Columbia
Area of Radio-Television-Film,
Speech and Dramatic Art Department,
200 Swallow Hall,
Columbia, MO 65201
Tel: (314) 882 3046

MONTANA

Montana State University
Department of Film and Television Production,
Bozeman, MT 59717
Tel: (406) 994 2484

NEVADA

University of Nevada, Las Vegas
Department of Film Studies,
4505 Maryland Parkway,
Las Vegas, NV 89154
Tel: (702) 739 3325

NEW JERSEY

Jersey City State College
Media Arts Department,
2039 Kennedy Blvd,
Jersey City, NJ 07305
Tel: (201) 547 3207

NEW YORK

Adelphi University
Department of Communications,
South Avenue,
Garden City, NY 11530
Tel: (516) 294 8700

Bard College,
Film Department,
Annandale-on-Hudson,
New York, NY 12504
Tel: (914) 758 6822

City University of New York, Brooklyn College
Film Department,
Bedford Avenue and Avenue H,
Brooklyn NY 11210
Tel: (718) 780 5136

City University of New York, City College
Leonard Davis Center for the Performing Arts,
138th Street and Convent Avenue,
New York, NY 10033
Tel: (212) 690 8173

City University of New York, Hunter College
Department of Theater and Film,
695 Park Avenue,
New York, NY 10021
Tel: (212) 570 5747

Columbia University
School of the Arts
513 Dodge Hall,
116 Street and Broadway,
New York, NY 10027
Tel: (212) 280 2875

Cornell University
Theater Arts Department,
College of Arts and Sciences,
Lincoln Hall, Ithaca, NY 14853
Tel: (607) 256 3533

Ithaca College
Department of Cinema Studies and Photography,
School of Communications,
Danby Road, Ithaca, NY 14850
Tel: (607) 274 3242

New York University
Undergraduate Institute of Film and Television,
65 South Building,
Washington Square,
New York, NY 10003
Tel: (212) 598 3702

Pratt Institute
Film Department,
215 Ryerson Street,
Brooklyn, NY 11205
Tel: (718) 636 3766

Sarah Lawrence College
Film Department,
Bronxville, NY 10708
Tel: (914) 337 0700

School of Visual Arts
Film Department,
209 East 23rd Street,
New York, NY 10010
Tel: (212) 679 7350

State University of New York at Binghamton
Cinema Department,
Vestal Parkway,
Binghamton, NY 13901
Tel: (607) 798 4998

State University of New York at Buffalo
Center for Media Study,
310 Hochstetter,
Buffalo, NY 17222
Tel: (716) 831 2426

State University of New York at Purchase
Film Program,
Lincoln Avenue,
Purchase, NY 10577
Tel: (914) 253 5000

Syracuse University
College of Visual and Performing Arts,
Syracuse, NY 13210
Tel: (315) 423 2214

University of Rochester
Film Studies Program,
Rush Rhees Library,
River Station, NY 14627
Tel: (716) 275 2121

Vassar College
Drama Department,
Poughkeepsie, NY 12601
Tel: (914) 452 7000

NORTH CAROLINA

University of North Carolina at Chapel Hill
Department of Radio, Television and Motion Pictures,
College of Arts and Sciences,
Swain Hill 044A,
Chapel Hill, NC 27514
Tel: (919) 933 2313

Wake Forest University
Speech, Communication and Theater Arts Department,
PO Box 7347,
Winston-Salem, NC 27109,
Tel: (919) 761 5406

OHIO

Bowling Green State University, Bowling Green
Radio-Television-Film Area,
School of Speech and Communication,
413 South Hall,
Bowling Green, OH 43403
Tel: (419) 372 2138

Cleveland Institute of Art
Photography Department,
11141 East Blvd,
Cleveland, OH 44106
Tel: (216) 421 4322

Denison University
Department of Theatre and Cinema,
Granville OH 43023
Tel: (614) 587 0801

Ohio State University
Department of Photography and Cinema,
Columbus, OH 43210
Tel: (614) 422 1766

Ohio University, Athens
Film Department,
Lindley Hall 378,
Athens, OH 45701
Tel: (614) 594 5138

University of Cincinnati
Film and Media Program,
Mail Location 184,
Cincinnati, OH 45221
Tel: (513) 475 2551

Wright State University
Department of Theater Arts,
Dayton, OH 45435
Tel: (513) 873 3072

OKLAHOMA

Oklahoma State University
Radio-Television-Film Department,
Stillwater, OK 74078
Tel: (405) 624 6354

University of Oklahoma
Video-Film Program,
520 Parrington Oval,
Norman, OK 73019
Tel: (405) 325 2691

OREGON

University of Oregon
Film Studies Area,
Department of Speech,
Villard Hall, Eugene, OR 97403
Tel: (503) 686 4228

PENNSYLVANIA

Pennsylvania State University
Department of Theater and Film,
University Park, PA 16802
Tel: (814) 865 7586

Philadelphia College of Art
Photo-Film Department,
Broad and Spruce Streets,
Philadelphia, PA 19102
Tel: (215) 893 3140

Temple University
Department of Radio-Television-Film,
Philadelphia, PA 19122
Tel: (215) 787 8423

RHODE ISLAND

Rhode Island College
Film Studies Program,
600 Mount Pleasant Avenue,
Providence
RI 02908
Tel: (401) 274 4900

SOUTH CAROLINA

Bob Jones University
Unusual Films,
Division of Cinema,
1700 Wade Hampton Blvd,
Greenville,
SC 29614
Tel: (803) 242 5100

TEXAS

Baylor University
Division of Radio-Television,
Waco, TX 76706
Tel: (817) 755 1511

North Texas State University
Radio-Film-Television
Division,
Denton, TX 76203
Tel: (817) 788 2537

Southern Methodist University
Broadcast-Film Arts
Department,
Binkley and Bishop Streets
Dallas, TX 75275
Tel: (214) 692 3090

Stephen F Austin State University
Communication Department,
PO Box 13048, SFA Station,
Nacogdoches, TX 75962
Tel: (713) 569 4001

UTAH

Brigham Young University
Theater and Cinematic Arts
Department,
D-581 HFAC, Provo, UT 84602
Tel: (801) 378 4574

University of Utah
Film Studies Program,
205 Pioneer Memorial Theater,
Salt Lake City, UT 84112
Tel: (801) 581 6356

WISCONSIN

University of Wisconsin – Milwaukee
BA/BFA in Film, Curtin Hall,
685 and Mitchell Hall B-69,
PO Box 413,
Milwaukee, WI 53201
Tel: (414) 963 5970

University of Wisconsin – Oshkosh
Radio-Television-Film
Division,
Speech Department,
Arts and Communication
Center,
Oshkosh, WI 54901
Tel: (414) 424 3131

UK FILM SCHOOLS

Bournemouth and Poole College of Art and Design
Department of Photography,
Film and Television,
Wallisdown Road,
Poole, Dorset BH12 5HH
Tel: (0202) 533011

University of Bristol
Department of Drama,
29 Park Row,
Bristol BS1 5LT
Tel: (0272) 24161

Croydon College
School of Art and Design,
Barclay Road,
Croydon CR9 1DX
Tel: (01) 688 9271

Derby College of Higher Education
School of Art and Design,
Kedleston Road,
Derby DE3 1GB
Tel: (0332) 47181

Dewsbury and Batley Technical and Art College
School of Art and Design,
Cambridge Street,
Batley,
West Yorkshire WF17 5JB
Tel: (0924) 474401

Gwent College of Higher Education
Faculty of Art and Design,
Clarence Place, Newport,
Gwent NP9 0UW
Tel: (0633) 59984

Harrow College of Higher Education
Faculty of Art and Photography,
Northwick Park, Harrow,
Middlesex
HA1 3TP
Tel: (01) 864 5422

Humberside College of Higher Education
Schools of Visual
Communication,
Design and Fine Art,
Queens Gardens,
Hull HU1 3DH
Tel: (0482) 224121

Lanchester Polytechnic
Faculty of Art and Design,
Gosford Street
Coventry CV1 5RZ
Tel: (0203) 24166

Leeds Polytechnic
School of Creative Arts
and Design,
Calverly Street, Leeds LS1 3HE
Tel: (0532) 462439

Liverpool Polytechnic
Faculty of Art and Design,
Department of Graphic Design,
2a Myrtle Street
Liverpool L7 7DN
Tel: (051) 709 9711

London College of Printing
Department of Photography,
Film and Television,
Elephant and Castle,
London SE1 6SB
Tel: (01) 735 8484

London International Film School
24 Shelton Street
London WC2H 9HP
Tel: (01) 240 0168

Maidstone College of Art
Oakwood Park, Oakwood Road,
Maidstone, Kent ME16 8AG
Tel: (0622) 57286

Manchester Polytechnic
Faculty of Art and Design,
Capitol Building, School Lane,
Didsbury,
Manchester M20 OHT
Tel: (061) 434 3331

Medway College of Design
Fort Pitt, Rochester
Kent ME1 1DZ
Tel: (0634) 44815

Middlesex Polytechnic
Faculty of Art and Design,
Cat Hill, Barnet,
Herts, EN4 8HU
Tel: (01) 440 5181

National Film School
Beaconsfield Film Studios,
Station Road, Beaconsfield,
Bucks HP9 1LE
Tel: (04946) 71234

Newcastle-upon-Tyne Polytechnic
Faculty of Art and Design,
Squires Building,
Sandyford Road,
Newcastle-upon-Tyne NE1 8ST
Tel: (0632) 326002

North East London Polytechnic
School of Art and Design,
Greengate Street, London E13
Tel: (01) 590 7722

North Staffordshire Polytechnic
Department of Design,
College Road, Stoke-on-Trent
ST4 2DE
Tel: (0782) 45531

Polytechnic of Central London
School of Communication,
18-22 Riding House Street
London W1P 7DP
Tel: (01) 486 5811

Portsmouth Polytechnic
Department of Fine Art,
Lion Terrace,
Portsmouth PO1 3HF
Tel: (0705) 827681

Ravensbourne College of Art and Design
Department of Television,
Wharton Road, Bromley,
Kent BR1 3LE
Tel: (01) 464 3090

Royal College of Art
School of Film and Television,
Kensington Gore,
London SW7 2EU
Tel: (01) 584 5020

St Martin's School of Art
Film and Video Unit,
27-29 Long Acre,
London WC2E 9LA
Tel: (01) 437 0611

Sheffield City Polytechnic
Faculty of Art and Design,
Brincliffe, Psalter Lane,
Sheffield S11 8UZ
Tel: (0742) 556101

Trent Polytechnic
School of Art and Design,
Department of Fine Art,
Burton Street,
Nottingham NG1 4BU
Tel: (0602) 418248

University of Ulster
Coleraine,
County Londonderry,
Northern Ireland BT52 1SA
Tel: (0265) 4141

West Surrey College of Art and Design
Department of Audio-Visual
Studies,
Falkner Road, The Hart,
Farnham,
Surrey GU9 7DS
Tel: (9252) 722441

FESTIVALS

ANNECY

Annecy International Festival of Animation
BP 399, 74013 Annecy Cedex,
Tel: (50) 51 78 14
Tx: 310503 I FOLSAVH/JICA
Held: June

ADELAIDE

Adelaide International Film Festival
GPO Box 354, Adelaide,
South Australia 5001,
Tel: (08) 278 6330
Held: June

ANN ARBOR

Ann Arbor Film Festival
PO Box 7283,
Ann Arbor, MI 48107
Tel: (313) 663 6494
Held: March

AVORIAZ

Avoriaz International Fantasy Film Festival
Promo 2000,
33 avenue MacMahon,
Paris 75017
Tel: (755) 71 40
Held: January

BERLIN

International Film Festival
Budapester Strasse 50,
D-1000 Berlin 30,
Tel: (030) 263 41
Tx: 185 255 FEST D
Held: February

Berlin International Radio and Television Competition
Prix Futura Berlin,
Sender Freies Berlin,
Masurenallee 8-14
D 1000 Berlin 19
Tel: (030) 308 2302
Tx: 1 82813
Held: April

BRIGHTON

British Film and Video Festival
c/o British Industrial and
Scientific Film Association,
102 Great Russell Street
London WC1E 3LN
Tel: (01) 580 0962
Held: June

BRISTOL

The Animation Festival at Bristol
(formerly the Cambridge
Animation Festival)
41b Hornsey Lane Gardens,
London N6 5NY
Tel: (01) 341 5015
Held: Bi-annual, October

BRUSSELS

Brussels International Film Festival
32 avenue de l'Astronomie,
1030 Brussels,
Tel: (02) 218 12 67
Held: January

CAIRO

Cairo International Film Festival
9 Oraby Street
PO Box 2060, Cairo
Tel: (02) 741 112
Tx: 92041 SHERA UN
Held: November

CAMBRIDGE

Cambridge Film Festival
Arts Cinema,
Market Passage,
Cambridge CB2 3PF
Tel: (0223) 316914
Tx: 81574 CAMARTS
Held: July

CANNES

Cannes International Film Festival
71 rue du Faubourg St Honore,
75008 Paris
Tel: (01) 266 92 20
Tx: FESTIFI 650 765 F
Held: May

MIP-TV
179 avenue Victor Hugo
75116 Paris
Tel: (02) 505 14 03
Held: April

CARTHAGE

Carthage International Film Festival
Journées Cinematographiques
de Carthage,
BP 1029, 1045 Tunis RP,
Tunisia
Tel: (01) 242 189
Tx: 12032 TN
Held: October

CHICAGO

Chicago International Film Festival
415 North Dearborn Street
Chicago, IL 60610
Tel: (312) 644 3400
Tx: 253655
Held: November

CORK

Cork International Film Festival
38 MacCurtain Street,
Cork, Eire
Tel: (021) 502221
Held: October

EDINBURGH

Edinburgh International Film Festival
Film House,
88 Lothian Road,
Edinburgh EH3 9BZ
Tel: (031) 228 6382
Tx: 72165
Held: August

FLORENCE

Festival dei Popoli
Via Fiume 14,
50123 Florence,
Italy
Tel: (055) 294 353
Tx: Festivalpopoli 570093-570215
Held: December

HONG KONG

Hong Kong International Film Festival
Room 807,
New World Office Building,
Tsim Sha Tsui,
Kowloon, Hong Kong
Tel: (03) 678873
Tx: 38484 USDHK
Held: March/April

KARLOVY VARY

Karlovy Vary International Film Festival
c/o Ceskovensky Filmexport,
Jindrisska 34,
11206 Prague 1
Tel: (02) 22 37 51
Tx: 122059 Film Praha
Held: July

LOCARNO

Locarno Film Festival
Via F Balli 2,
PO Box 186,
CH-6600 Locarno,
Switzerland
Tel: (093) 31 82 66
Tx: 846147
Held: August

LONDON

London International Film Festival
National Film Theatre,
South Bank,
London SE1 8XT
Tel: (01) 928 3842
Tx: 929220
Held: November

London Market
C/o Chris Snowdon,
Dennis Davidson Associates,
57 Beak Street,
London W1R 3LF
Tel: (01) 439 6391
Held: October

LOS ANGELES

Los Angeles International Film Exposition (Filmex)
Berwin Entertainment
Complex,
6525 Sunset Blvd,
Hollywood, CA 90028
Tel: (213) 469 9400
Tx: 194 728
Held: March

MELBOURNE

Melbourne Film Festival
21 Victoria Street,
Fitzroy, Melbourne,
Australia 3065
Tel: (03) 417 3111
Tx: AA 31624
Held: June/July

MILAN

MIFED – International Film, TV Film & Documentary Market
Largo Domodossola 1,
20145 Milan
Tel: (02) 4997 267
Tx: 331360 EAFM I
Held: April/October

MONTREAL

World Film Festival
1455 blvd de Maisonneuve est,
Montreal, Quebec H3G IM8
Tel: (514) 879 4057
Tx: 05 25472 WOFILMFEST
Held: August

MONTREUX

Montreux TV Festival
Direction du Concours de la Rose d'Or de Montreux,
PO Box 97, 1820 Montreux, Switzerland
Tel: (021) 63 12 12
Tx: 453 222
Held: May

MOSCOW

Moscow International Film Festival
Sovinterfest,
10 Kokhlovsky per,
Moscow 109028
Tel: (095) 297 76 45
Tx: 411263 Fest Su
Held: July

MUNICH

Munich International Film Festival
Turkenstrasse 93,
8000 Munich 40,
Tel: (089) 393011
Tx: 5 214 674 IMFD
Held: June

NEWCASTLE UPON TYNE

Tyneside Film Festival
Tyneside Cinema,
10-12 Pilgrim Street,
Newcastle upon Tyne
Tel: (0632) 321507
Held: October

NEW DELHI

International Film Festival
National Film Development Corporation,
13-16 Regent Chambers,
208 Nariman Point,
Bombay 400021
Tel: (224924
Tx: 011 5700 NFDC
Held: January

NEW YORK

International Film and TV Festival of New York
246 West 38th Street,
New York, NY 10018
Tel: (914) 238 4481
Held: November

New York Film Festival
The Film Society of the Lincoln Centre,
140 West 65th Street,
New York, NY 10023
Tel: (212) 765 5100
Held: September-October

American Independent Feature Film Market
21 West 86th Street,
New York, NY 10024
Tel: (212) 496 0909
Held: October

OBERHAUSEN

Oberhausen International Festival of Short Films
Westdeutsche Kurzfilm Tage,
Grillostrasse 34,
4200 Oberhausen 1,
Federal Republic of Germany
Tel: (0208) 825 2652
Tx: 856414
Held: March

ROME

Prix Italia
c/o RAI, Viale Mazzini 14,
00195 Rome
Tel: (06) 3878 4118
Tx: 614432
Held: September/October

ROTTERDAM

Rotterdam Film International
Westersingel 20,
3014 GP Rotterdam,
Holland
Tel: (010) 363111
Tx: 21378 FINTR NI
Held: February

SAN SEBASTIAN

San Sebastian International Film Festival
Apartado Correos,
397 Reina Regente s/n,
San Sebastian, Spain
Tel: (43) 424 106
Tx: 36228
Held: September

SAN FRANCISCO

San Francisco International Film Festival
3051 California Street,
Suite 201,
San Francisco, CA 94118
Tel: (415) 221 9055
Tx: 356414 Cunwest
Held: April

SYDNEY

Sydney Film Festival
Box 25, PO Glebe, NSW 2037
Tel: (02) 660 3844
Tx: AA 75111
Held: June

TAORMINA

Taormina International Film Festival
c/o Ente Provinciale Turismo,
Via Calabria, isol 346,
98100 Messina
Tel: (090) 360 84 30
Held: July

THESSALONIKI

Thessaloniki International Film Festival
Thessaloniki 36,
Greece
Tel: (031) 220 440
Held: September/October

TORONTO

Canadian International Animation Festival
Box 5009, Station F,
Toronto, Ontario, M4Y 2TI
Tel: (416) 364 5924
Tx: 0623 499 ANIFEST TOR
Held: August

Festival of Festivals
Suite 205,
69 Yorkville Avenue,
Toronto, Ontario M5R 1B8
Tel: (416) 967 7371
Tx: 06 219724
Held: September

VARNA

World Animated Film Festival
Organising Committee,
96 Rakovsky Street
1000 Sofia, Bulgaria
Tel: 595061
Tx: 22447 FILMEX BG
Held: October

VENICE

La Biennale di Venezia
Ca' Giustinian,
San Marco, 30100 Venice
Tel: (041) 700 311
Tx: 410685 BLE VE I
Held: August/September

VIENNA

Viennale
Künstlerhaus, Karlsplatz 5,
1010 Vienna
Tel: (0222) 56 98 23
Tx: 113985
Held: April

ZAGREB

World Festival of Animated Films
c/o Zagreb Film, Nova Ves 18,
41000 Zagreb, Yugoslavia
Tel: (041) 276 636
Tx: 21790
Held: June

GOVERNMENT ORGANISATIONS

ALGERIA

Office National pour le Commerce et l'Industrie Cinematographique (National Office for Commerce and the Film Industry)
Immeuble les Asphodeles,
Ben-Aknoun, Algiers
Tel: (213) 782255

ARGENTINA

National Institute of Cinematography
Lima 319,
1073
Buenos Aires
Tel: (01) 378429
Tx: 21104

AUSTRALIA

Australian Film Commission
8 West Street,
North Sydney,
New South Wales
2060
Tel: (02) 922 6855
Tx: 25157

AUSTRIA

Bundesministerium für Handel, Gewerbe und Industrie (Ministry for Trade and Industry)
Sektion I,
Abt. Filmwirtschaft,
Stubenring 1,
1010 Vienna
Tel: (0222) 7500

Bundesministerium für Unterricht und Kunst
(Ministry for Art and Education)
Sektion IV,
Film, Video und Fotoangelegenheiten,
Freyung 1,
1010 Vienna
Tel: (0222) 66200

BELGIUM

Ministry of Education and Culture (Cinema Department)
7 quai du Commerce,
1000 Brussels
Tel: (02) 217 4190

BRAZIL

Consuelho Nacional do Cinema
(National Cinema Council)
Rua Visconde de Inhauma 58,
Rio de Janeiro
Tel: (021) 233 8329

CANADA

Telefilm Canada
Banque Nationale Tower,
600 de la Gaucheliere Street W,
25th Floor,
Montreal, Quebec H3B 4L2
Tel: (514) 283 6363

and

130 Bloor Street W, Ste 901,
Toronto, Ontario M5S 1N5
Tel: (416) 966 6436

CHINA

China Film Corporation
25 Xin Wai Street,
Beijing
Tel: 667831

CUBA

Cuban Institute of Arts and the Film Industry
Calle 23, no 1155,
Entre 10 y 12,
Vedado, Havana 4,
Tel: (07) 305041

CZECHOSLOVAKIA

Central Management of the Czechoslavak Film
Jindrisska 34,
112 06 Prague 1
Tel: (02) 223751

DENMARK

Danish Government Film Office
Vestergade 27,
1419 Copenhagen K
Tel: (01) 1 32 686

FRANCE

Centre National de la Cinematographie
12 rue de Lubeck,
75784 Paris
Tel: (01) 505 1440
Tx: 750784

GERMANY, DEMOCRATIC REPUBLIC OF

DEFA
c/o DEFA Aussenhandel,
Milastrasse 2,
Berlin 1058
Tel: (02) 440 0801
Tx: 114511

GERMANY, FEDERAL REPUBLIC OF

Bundesministerium für Wirtschaft
(Federal Ministry for Economic Affairs)
Villemombler Strasse 76,
Bonn-Duisdorf
Tel: (0228) 6151
Tx: 886747

Filmförderungsanstalt des Offentlichenrechts
(Office for the Administration of Film Aid)
Budapester Strasse 41,
PO Box 30 18 08
1000 Berlin 31
Tel: (030) 261 6006

HUNGARY

Central Board of Hungarian Cinematography
Szalai u. 10,
1054 Budapest
Tel: (01) 126417

Mafilm
Lumumba u. 174
1145 Budapest
Tel: (01) 631473

INDIA

National Film Development Corporation
1st Floor,
13-16 Regent Chambers,
208 Nariman Point,
Bombay 400021
Tel: (022) 231832

IRELAND

Department of Industry, Commerce and Tourism
Kildare Street
Dublin 2
Tel: (01) 789411
Tx: 4651

Irish Film Board
65 Pembroke Lane,
Dublin 2
Tel: (01) 607544
Tx: 90242

ITALY

Ministry of Tourism and Entertainment
Via della Ferratella 51,
Rome
Tel: (06) 7732

JAMAICA

Jamaica National Investment Promotion
Film Office,
15 Oxford Road,
Kingston S
Tel: (809) 926 4613

JAPAN

Agency for Cultural Affairs
3-2-2 Kasumigaseki,
Chiyoda-ku, Tokyo 100
Tel: (03) 581 4211

MEXICO

Direccion General de Radio, Television y Cinematografica
Guanajuato 125,
Col.Roma, Mexico DF
Tel: 584 5077

NETHERLANDS

Ministry of Cultural Affairs, Recreation and Social Welfare,
Steenvoordelaan 370,
PB 5406, HK Rijswijk
Tel: (070) 949233
Tx: 31680

Netherlands Information Service
Communication Techniques Department,
Anna Paulownastraat 76,
2518 BJ The Hague
Tel: (070) 614181
Tx: 33159

NEW ZEALAND

New Zealand Film Commission
PO Box 11-546,
Wellington
Tel: (04) 859754
Tx: 30386

POLAND

Ministry of Culture and Art
Central Board of Cinematography,
Warsaw
Tel: (022) 267489

SPAIN

Direccion General del Libro y de la Cinematografia
Ministerio de Cultura,
San Marcos 40,
Madrid
Tel: (01) 429 2444

SWEDEN

Svenska Filminstitutet
Filmhuset, Borgvagen,
Box 27126,
S-102 52 Stockholm 27
Tel: (08) 651100
Tx: 13326

SWITZERLAND

Federal Office of Cultural Affairs
Film Section,
Thunstrasse 20,
Postfach 3000, Bern 6
Tel: (031) 619262

UK

Arts Council of Great Britain
105 Piccadilly,
London W1V 0AU
Tel: (01) 629 9495
Tx: 8952022

Arts Council of Northern Ireland
181a Stanmillis Road,
Belfast BT9 5DU
Tel: (0232) 44222

British Screen Finance
22 Southampton Place,
London WC1 2BP
Tel: (01) 831 7561

Department of Education and Science
Office of Arts and Libraries,
Elizabeth House,
York Road,
London SE1 7PH
Tel: (01) 928 9222

Department of Trade – Films Branch
16-20 Great Smith Street,
London SW1P 3DB
Tel: (01) 215 7877

Scottish Film Council
Dowanhill,
74 Victoria Crescent Road,
Glasgow G12 9JN
Tel: (01) 334 9314

Welsh Arts Council
9 Museum Place,
Cardiff CF1 3NX
Tel: (0222) 394711

USA

International Communications Agency
1776 Pennsylvania Avenue NW,
Washington, DC 20546
Tel: (202) 376 7806

US Department of Commerce
Bureau of Industrial Economics,
14th and Constitution,
Washington, DC 20230
Tel: (202) 377 0136

USSR

State Committee of Cinematography of the USSR Council of Ministers
7 Maly Gnesdnikovsky Pereulok,
Moscow
Tel: (095) 229 9912